THE **LIVES** OF **ERICH FROMM**

LOVE'S PROPHET

Lawrence J. Friedman

with assistance from Anke M. Schreiber

COLUMBIA UNIVERSITY PRESS

NEW YORK

Columbia University Press
Publishers Since 1893
New York   Chichester, West Sussex
cup.columbia.edu
Copyright © 2013 Columbia University Press

Library of Congress Cataloging-in-Publication Data
Friedman, Lawrence Jacob, 1940–
  The lives of Erich Fromm: love's prophet/Lawrence J. Friedman with assistance
from Anke M. Schreiber.
     p. cm.
  Includes bibliographical references and index.
  ISBN 978-0-231-16258-6 (cloth : alk. paper)—ISBN 978-0-231-53106-1
(e-book)
  1. Fromm, Erich, 1900–1980.   2. Psychoanalysts—Germany—Biography.
3. Psychoanalysts—United States—Biography.   I. Schreiber, Anke M.   II. Title.

BF109. F76F75, 2013
150.19'57092—dc23
[B]
                                                              2012024631

Columbia University Press books are printed on permanent and durable acid-free paper.
This book is printed on paper with recycled content.
Printed in the United States of America

c 10 9 8 7 6 5 4 3 2 1

COVER PHOTO: Photo by Liss Goldring, 1970, © Erich Fromm Estate
COVER DESIGN: Milenda Nan Ok Lee

In memory of Ronald Takaki and Adam Sarnecki

Love is the only sane and satisfactory answer to
the problem of human existence.

—ERICH FROMM

The alternatives he [man] is confronted with are either to escape the
burden of freedom into new dependencies and submission, or to advance
to full realization of positive freedom which is based upon the
uniqueness and individuality of man.

—ERICH FROMM

Contents

Illustrations follow page 211.

Foreword

Gerald N. Grob

HENRY SIGERIST PROFESSOR OF HISTORY EMERITUS,
RUTGERS UNIVERSITY

As a student at the City College of New York in the late 1940s, I enrolled in an honors program in the social sciences. We were required to read about forty or fifty books that had shaped society since the Greeks. Among these books was Erich Fromm's *Escape from Freedom*. I was so taken with this book that I followed up by reading *The Sane Society*, and in subsequent decades I remained an avid reader of his writings. What I found especially impressive was Fromm's ability to write in a way that avoided jargon while presenting important and complex ideas in a clear and coherent manner. Lawrence Friedman has that gift, as this very important and eminently scholarly biography attests. It is one of the most exciting books I have read in years.

My attraction to Fromm's writings grew out of my background. As a child of parents who came from Eastern Europe, I attended Hebrew school for a number of years, where I was exposed to the Talmud and especially the prophetic tradition within Judaism. Friedman's volume shows us with clarity and an eye for nuance how Fromm exemplified this tradition; he was a critic of society while at the same holding out the hope that a better future was possible. Living at a time when the world seemed threatened by nuclear annihilation, Fromm was unable to limit himself to a life of scholarly writing and contemplation or psychoanalytic practice. During the height of the Cold War, Friedman has discovered that Fromm had caught the attention of President John F. Kennedy and may have helped modify the president's belligerent rhetoric. Indeed, Kennedy subsequently began to call for coexistence and nuclear disarmament with words, phrases, and logic that resembled Fromm's. During these dangerous years, Fromm maintained regular contact with important policy makers such as Adlai Stevenson and William Fulbright and often testified before congressional committees on developments in postwar Germany, his specialty in international relations. As well,

Fromm enjoyed contacts with heads of state in several countries. All of this was part of an effort to bridge the gap between high government officials and human rights and peace activists. Indeed, he was a founder and major funder of the National Committee for a Sane Nuclear Policy and then Amnesty International. Based upon the remarkably thorough research for which he is known, Friedman's biography is the first to reveal these important personal and institutional connections.

Fromm's early life shaped much of his subsequent thinking. We have a richly textured and closely documented analysis of that early life in all of its complexities—another first for this remarkable volume. His anxiety-ridden father and sometimes depressed mother provoked him to attempt to break free of a dysfunctional household. These experiences ultimately shaped his adult focus on "social character." Unlike Freud, who emphasized the role of libidinal energy in shaping individual personality, Fromm increasingly stressed that humans are social beings whose lives are also shaped by social structure and culture. Such views were regarded in orthodox psychoanalytic circles as a form of heresy, even as Freud sometimes found them worth considering—and said as much. Nevertheless, by the mid-to-late 1930s, after Fromm had done much to move his endangered colleagues in the Frankfurt Institute for Social Research out of Nazi Germany and to the safety of the Columbia University campus, Freud and Fromm seemed to part increasingly (never totally) intellectual company. Fromm was moving too fast and too far from the perspectives of Freud's psychoanalytically orthodox associates. During the mid-1950s, he was accused by Herbert Marcuse—a friend from his years at the Frankfurt Institute—of having purportedly emasculated psychoanalysis by abandoning Freud's essential insights. Friedman explains why Marcuse's critique was off the mark. More generally, he portrays the Fromm-Freud relationship in more complex terms than any other scholar, showing important areas of accord at times even as, over the long haul, the theoretical differences grew. It was more a changing conceptual "dance" than a mutually dismissive relationship. Indeed, the two may have made direct contact in Baden Baden to discuss their theoretical perspectives. Once again, we see the remarkable depth and sophistication of this biography. Coupled with much new evidence, exciting new interpretations abound.

Throughout his career, Fromm's appeal was not—with the exception of a few figures like David Riesman, Arthur Schlesinger Jr., and Robert Lynd—to academics. Although Fromm rarely alluded to his exclusion from the American academic community, he felt that its narrow focus, confined and specialized fields of interest, and even vocabulary were too far removed from the enormous problems that confronted humanity. Consequently, he directed his books toward a broad public, and, as Friedman demonstrates, the way they were received was nothing short of spectacular. Their sales were not in the thousands but in the millions. Indeed, only one of his books sold fewer than a million copies. The record was set by *The Art of Loving*, which since its publication more than half a century ago has sold more than twenty-five million copies and still sells well today. His emphasis on the importance of love, his hatred of war, his commitment to democratic socialist values, his searching critique of consumerism and materialism, and his overarching humanism has made him one of the most read and admired figures of the twentieth century. It is a remarkable story, and Friedman tells it with artistic prose coupled with a sharp eye for an array of interpretive possibilities. This is scholarly biography at its best.

Despite his remarkable popularity in the public arena and his decided influence over important elected officials, including three presidential candidates, Fromm's writings never resonated with the American professoriate. His books, which continue to sell in almost every corner of the world, draw praise from heads of state and even the papacy, and remain a favorite of students everywhere, nonetheless seem to arouse little interest among American professors. Why this is so remains somewhat of a mystery, for he has been lauded by academics in Germany, Italy, Switzerland, Mexico, and much of Eastern Europe.

Professor Friedman's magnificent volume, beautifully written and with an eye for nuance and complexity, is so interesting and thoughtful that it is bound to awaken interest in Fromm's career. Based on remarkably extensive research into a myriad of primary manuscript and printed sources in several countries and languages, it traces Fromm's life from his early childhood in an observant Jewish household. His religious training in some ways foreshadowed the direction that his later life would take. Friedman demonstrates how culture and environment shaped his thinking and personality and subsequently led him in a direction reminiscent of the prophets in the Hebrew Bible. This study is so interesting, so artfully composed, and so eminently fair and balanced that it will find a broad readership willing to grapple with the problems that Fromm dealt with in his life. It is clear to me that Fromm has a great deal to say to modern society, and Professor Friedman's book will contribute heavily to a renewed interest in the life of this fascinating figure. Fromm would have been pleased that his life story has been told so proficiently and fairly. Once again, Friedman has written a book that shows us why he is regarded as a remarkable biographer and eminent, prize-winning historian.

Acknowledgments

This book took much longer and was much more difficult than any other I have written. Therefore, I have a great many people to thank along the way, beginning with Rainer Funk, the director of the Fromm Archive in Tubingen, Germany, where I spent many years examining Fromm's voluminous correspondence.

Anke Schreiber, perhaps the most brilliant student with whom I have worked in the past forty-four years, stands out from all contributors. Initially, I put her on a grant to correct my problematic German translations. Within a few years, the two of us were having daily discussions about the basic conceptual structure of the biography and the nuances of Fromm's life. I looked forward to those always exciting conversations. Anke has become much more than a student; she has evolved into a trusted colleague. Indeed, I have come to consider Anke almost a coauthor. It was a remarkable collaboration.

I called on a substantial number of critics over the course of the four drafts of this manuscript. At the onset, Stephen Whitfield, my friend of forty years, asked a key question: What, after his classic *Escape from Freedom* (1941), did Fromm do that commands our attention? Richard King, who introduced me to Steve, raised an equally telling and related question: What new conceptual insights would this biography bring to the reader? Steve and Richard critiqued draft after draft with cogency, encouraging me as I got closer to answering their questions. They were soon joined by Jack Fitzpatrick, a friend since graduate school and a clinician, who reviewed two drafts of the manuscript and helped me to provide a balanced psychological profile of Fromm. Four other clinician friends, James Clark, Lynne Layton, David Lotto, and Peter Lawner augmented this profile. Anne-Louise Strong helped me to understand the dynamics of Fromm's marriage to Frieda Fromm-Reichmann. Eliane Silverman, who long ago taught me the significance of gender in the historical process, marked every passage in the manuscript where I was not sufficiently sensitive to the ways Fromm needed and treated the women in his life. In her meticulous reading of my chapters, Susannah Heschel was especially helpful in allowing me to understand the complex and changing ways in which Fromm thought of himself as a Jew. Here in Cambridge, sessions with my colleague Howard Gardner were stimulating beyond belief. Howard insisted that I must never lose sight of the basic storyline, or I would lose the book. Long after he supervised my dissertation and taught me to ask the big questions, Donald Meyer helped again—this time with my more problematic chapters. Don remains the same tough but fair and deeply insightful critic that he was forty-five years ago. Some of my own former dissertation students, now accomplished scholars, helped me with the manuscript as I had once helped them. Indeed, Scott Eberle, Mark McGarvie, David Andersen, Milton Bentley, Adrea Lawrence, Joseph Gerson, and Damon Freeman seemed more demanding of this manuscript than I was of theirs.

There were some very special moments over the past nine years as I tried to understand Fromm. I had wonderful days and nights with Bertram and Anne Wyatt-Brown on their porch in Booth Bay Harbor, where we discussed the chapters of this book substantively and stylistically. Discussions with Robert Jay Lifton in Wellfleet and Cambridge as I sought to conceptualize and reconceptualize the biography were remarkably exciting and help to explain why I have come to call him "coach." In the case of Neil McLaughlin, a Fromm scholar himself, the "magic moments" came while fishing for documentation and ideas within the mounds of photocopies and notations that filled his entire living-room floor. Daniel Burston wrote one of the stronger books on Fromm some decades back and shared his probing and often unique ideas with me in exciting conversations. Martin Jay, the author of a classic volume on the Frankfurt Institute, gave his predictably tough yet convivial critique of my chapters on the Institute and on the context for *Escape from Freedom*. There was a tradeoff with my longtime friend Robert Abzug. He went over my chapters on Fromm as I went over his on Rollo May, Fromm's analysand. I had a different type of exchange with Kenneth Friedberg, a semiretired New York doctor who explained to me a great deal about Fromm's persisting health problems. Stephen Berger reviewed problematic chapters to see if they passed muster. Alan Petigny shared his understanding of the 1950s with me in some very exciting conversations. Bonnie Sturner, a specialist on personality theory, mixed wonderful humor with cogent insights on the structure of Fromm's thought. And for all who know Charles Rosenberg, it is no surprise that he invariably knew what it would take to clarify an argument, usually at our lunch place off Harvard Square.

With many of Fromm's personal letters destroyed by his third wife, discussions with his friends and colleagues became mandatory. Michael Maccoby, who worked closely with Fromm in Mexico and cooperated with him in campaigns against nuclear weapons, tops this list. Since I started this project, I enjoyed a great many free-ranging discussions with Michael about Fromm. He also shared with me his correspondence with Fromm and helped me to contextualize each letter. Early in the project, Sandy Lee Maccoby made me attentive to aspects of Fromm's private life that I would otherwise have missed. Salvador and Sonya Millan put me up when I did research in Mexico City and explained a great deal about Fromm's twenty-three years in their country. Salvador threw in some excellent photographs he had taken—and an array of jokes, for good measure. I visited Zurich at least once a year to spend time with Gertrud Hunziker Fromm, Erich's much-loved cousin. More than anyone else, she explained the particulars of Fromm's early family life and shared with me letters and books that Fromm had sent to her over the years. Moshe Budmore, Fromm's executor and friend, was also excellent in helping me understand nuances of Fromm's life, especially his last decades. Marianne Horney Eckardt, the daughter of Karen Horney and Fromm's analysand, told me a good deal about Fromm's clinical techniques and his affair with her mother. I met with Fromm's analysand, Gerard Khoury, in Paris and the south of France to contextualize the remarkable tape-recorded interview he conducted with Fromm as death approached.

Ellen Meyer, who decades ago taught me how to write for a general readership, provided new lessons as I completed the final draft. Diane Bingham also helped me make important decisions as the manuscript moved toward completion. My editor at Columbia University Press, Jennifer Perillo, was everything a writer could conceivably want: kindness, proficiency, learnedness, and a capacity to "look out" for her authors. Together, Ellen, Diane, and Jennifer convinced me the manuscript was as strong as I could make it and that I needed to move on to another book project. Three others at Columbia who skillfully kept the production of the book on track, Robert Fellman, Michael Haskell, and especially Stephen Wesley, explain as well why it is a press of choice. Columbia might have had little to produce if not for Jayson Walker, my "computer guy," who repeatedly rescued parts of the manuscript. Nor would the book have had many of its wonderful photographs if not for the generosity of Nita Hagan, Fromm's sister-in-law.

Although I received a great deal of help from a good many friends and colleagues over the past decade, Ronald Takaki was not around to guide me in closing out this project. Ron had been my closest friend since 1966. We wrote all of our books together. Indeed, I would probably have finished this one sooner, and with perhaps a stronger manuscript to show for it, had Ron been around during the final years. Ron and I sometimes joked that each of us wrote the other's books. It often felt that way. "It was a beautiful process. May we have many more," Ron had inscribed in his first book, fresh off the press. I am fortunate to have had many decades participating in this "beautiful process" with Ron.

Prologue
Writing Lives

It was late summer of 1958, and I was preparing to leave the Los Angeles home of my parents and grandparents. Within days, I would be a freshman at the new Riverside campus of the University of California. The one television program my Eastern European émigré grandfather and I watched together was *The Mike Wallace Show*, a forerunner of *Sixty Minutes*. Wallace conducted an hour-long interview of Erich Fromm, introducing him as a man with essentially two "lives"—the most important psychoanalyst since Freud and a major champion of peaceful coexistence with the Russians. Over the course of the interview, Fromm tastefully expanded on Wallace's descriptions of his two apparent lives, defining himself, first, as a psychoanalytically informed clinician; second, as a political activist; third, as a social critic; and, fourth, as a writer committed to instructing society. Fromm underscored that these roles were neither exclusionary nor disparate but tied together by his vision of himself as a prophet for the love of life in the face of man's seeming inability to move beyond hatreds, violence, and war.

For the next fifty-two years of my life, and, since 2008, with the appreciable assistance of Anke Schreiber, I have pursued my own conceptual and sometimes personal dialogue with Fromm, the Renaissance man—his ideas, his "lives," and his inner conflicts. The conflicts occurred in part because he was a sensitive humanitarian who needed to range over life's possibilities, spiritually and aesthetic in one broad sweep, yet still place aspects of his existence into defined components (his "lives") so as to deal with the necessities in everyday experiences. In turn, these two aspects of the man clashed, personally and conceptually.

An example is illustrative. I have come to regard Fromm's conceptual sparring with Freud not so much as a rebellious rejection of Freud's psychoanalytic formulations but as a free-ranging dance of civility in the life of the mind and spirit of two cultivated Europeans uprooted by Hitler's crude and violent authoritarianism. Each had been forced to leave his homeland and to redefine the varied roles and requirements of everyday existence abroad. Moreover, both had searched in similar and in different ways to understand broadly the razor's edge that can separate the proprieties of civil society from barbarism and mass murder. In some sense, Freud's *Civilization and Its Discontents* and Fromm's *Escape from Freedom* were representations of that conceptual and spiritual search. It was a dance of mind and emotion involving two practicing psychoanalysts, each seeking in his own ways and specific circumstances to explain the destructive currents of the twentieth century. Fromm concluded that love was the antidote. Freud was less hopeful.

In his life as a political activist, Fromm never realized his primary political goal of lasting international peace and justice sealed by love, though there were some magic moments when his prophetic vision for a world without war was taken seriously by very high officials. A prime example was his influence on President John F. Kennedy during the most dangerous years of the Cold War.

In the fall of 1960, an article Fromm had published in the journal *Daedalus* on arms control and disarmament commanded presidential candidate Kennedy's attention. In the article, Fromm advised that the United States pepper the Soviets with a stream of sequential weapons-reduction proposals, culminating in the elimination of all nuclear weapons. He also called for a strong federal disarmament agency. Ten months into his presidency, Kennedy prompted Congress to create the Arms Control and Disarmament Agency. He also instructed his advisors to consider Fromm's proposal for sequentially pressuring the Soviets. In response, Kennedy's national security advisor, McGeorge Bundy, incorporated several of Fromm's writings on Soviet and German politics in his Oval Office briefing materials. This pattern of indirect contact continued into the fall of 1962, when the Cuban Missile Crisis nearly led to nuclear war. There is reason to believe that Kennedy made a telephone call to Fromm soon after the crisis. Then, in June 1963, in a major address at American University, the president departed markedly from his often hawkish Cold War rhetoric and emphasized the need for peaceful coexistence with the Soviets, along with nuclear disarmament, as a means to avert global extinction. Many briefing documents and private conversations with "insiders" obviously had shaped the address. But Kennedy's reasoning, the ethical values he presented, and even some of the specific language of the speech approximated parts of Fromm's own writings, especially the *Daedalus* article.

During the most dangerous days of the Cold War, when global nuclear annihilation was a real possibility, including the disastrous American presence in Vietnam, and amid the civil rights movement and global cries for human dignity, Fromm's public lectures and books, coupled with his exceedingly generous donations, helped to mobilize peace and human rights activists to speak out for a world without war. Here, as in the other, less political of Fromm's lives, he often spoke in prophetic language—a man with a global mission for humanity. To that end, he helped to found and fund the National Committee for a Sane Nuclear Policy and Amnesty International and was active in the leadership of both groups.

Fromm counted among his friends influential elected officials. Adlai Stevenson, William Fulbright, Philip Hart, and Eugene McCarthy sought his advice on world affairs. He spoke to senior members of Congress, to officials at the United Nations, and to several figures in the Kennedy administration. While he coupled new information on global issues with cogent analysis, his prophetic disposition sometimes limited the effectiveness of his communication with politicians, who were accustomed to the compromises and evasions endemic to the political process. Still, in the contacts he established, Fromm helped to build a sometimes-traveled bridge between peace and human rights activists and their allies, on the one hand, and the deliberations of high government officials, on the other.

I came to identify with Fromm the activist and theoretician during the 1960s. To be sure, I took issue with some of his perspectives on Freud and Marx. But his work in the American peace movement and his refusal during the most perilous years of the Cold War to castigate the purportedly "demonic" Russians heavily affected both my scholarship and my activism. Indeed, it sparked my involvement in the bloody Mississippi Freedom Summer of 1964 and the struggle to reverse the American military involvement in Vietnam. This stretch of activism helped to facilitate the thematic structures of all the books I have written since and to prompt political ventures that seem to know no end. The spirit of political activism, mine and Fromm's, is quite evident in *The Lives of Erich Fromm: Love's Prophet.*

Fromm's "life" as a social critic and "public intellectual" was facilitated by his remarkable capacity to convey complex thoughts in psychoanalysis, ethics, theology, political theory, social philosophy, cultural creations, and much more in simple, direct prose that appealed to the latent ideals and fears of his time. Readers who had never heard of Aristotle, Goethe, Schiller, Tolstoy, Hesse, Einstein, Bertrand Russell, and other intellectual giants were exposed to their ideas in Fromm's clear, crisp writing, which contextualized them in terms of specific issues and concerns of the contemporary world. He used these formidable thinkers, for example, to facilitate a scathing criticism of consumer culture, corporate capitalism, militarism, and authoritarianism. Alternatively, he became something of a prophet of biophilia—the love of life and the life of love.

Fromm's 1956 volume, *The Art of Loving*, has sold more than twenty-five million copies globally and is a favorite of my Harvard undergraduates today as it was with my classmates at the University of California half a century ago. For generations, it has been a volume with remarkable ties to its readers' personal and social lives. The deepest and most important of Fromm's books, *Escape from Freedom* (1941), which excavated the social psychology of authoritarianism during the age of Stalin and Hitler, has sold more than five million copies in twenty-eight languages. Since the Hungarian revolt of 1956, it has seen surprisingly good sales wherever dictatorial regimes have been challenged. The Arab Spring of 2011 is the most current example. Whatever the topic, most of Fromm's books have sold in excess of a million copies.

Fromm was a remarkably effective global educator—a substantial accomplishment that few intellectuals and scholars of any generation can claim. That fact contributes significantly to the thematic structure of this biography, for in Fromm's life one finds a decided link between his experiences and the fears and hopes of the society around him. This was particularly so in the late 1960s, when student protest movements in Europe and Latin America converged with those in the United States. Fromm's books and public addresses, reflecting the issues of that day, provided basic guidance on a global level. He advocated a democratic socialist "Third Way" alternative to both the Western capitalist marketplace and the bureaucratic Stalinist state, insisting that both corporate capitalist society and bureaucratized state socialism had much to do with the alienation of modern man.

Fromm initially envisioned his Third Way as a "humanist" society that would value the well-being and happiness of the individual in a democratic polity where elected officials became directly accessible. But by the early 1970s, he had come to regard war, aggression, and humiliation of others as inherent in the very nature of many countries, whether capitalist, socialist, or another social and economic orientation, and the Third Way became

Fromm's somewhat vague metaphor for an alternative to the nation-state itself. After the Holocaust, the Stalinist executions, Hiroshima, and Vietnam, there was a small number of social commentators, scholars, and public officials who, like Fromm, announced in public forums that nations and nationalism had caused more harm than good. They called for "One World" and a "Family of Man." But few of them advanced this message as clearly and as plausibly as Fromm or were capable of persuading an audience of millions to rethink their national allegiances.

Fromm's significance in the public realm, nationally and internationally, brought him a measure of disfavor among a number of American academics. To some degree, this was a function of his proclivity to distance himself from the professorate, from specialized libraries and databases, and from the ways in which scholarly research and writing had been conducted in the United States. He was on the outside, looking into what Fromm's friend, the prominent sociologist David Riesman, would come to call the "academic revolution," where units in the social sciences became highly particularized, each with their own "languages" and professional fields and subfields and exacting standards of research and writing.

Other factors contributed to Fromm's difficulty in gaining recognition as a formidable scholar. In 1955, he ran up against Herbert Marcuse, a friend from his years in the Frankfurt Institute. Marcuse, a philosopher and academic in good standing, became familiar with psychoanalysis by reading Freud's more abstract theoretical work, but he lacked clinical experience or much understanding of the therapeutic encounter. The two exchanged barbs in a few issues of *Dissent*, an important New York journal for postwar intellectual and cultural discourse. Echoing attacks on Fromm by his Frankfurt Institute colleagues Theodor Adorno and Max Horkheimer eighteen years earlier, Marcuse charged that Fromm had emptied psychoanalysis of its revolutionary content by abandoning Freud's essential premise that libidinal drives are deeply embedded biological entities that energize human personality. Put somewhat differently, Marcuse accused Fromm of bypassing what some scholars have come to call a "modernist" agenda—a "Freudian" quest to liberate the interiority of a human being from societal manipulations and repressions (i.e., superego constraints). A number of influential American thinkers on the Left (some of whom came to be called "the New York intellectuals") repeated Marcuse's charge. It stuck for a time among some scholars and persists among diehards.

But Marcuse's charge did not preclude overwhelming support from other quarters for Fromm's capacities as a political activist and global educator. Nor did Marcuse's charge persuade Riesman to renounce Fromm's theoretical alternative to Freud—a vaguely outlined concept of "social character" where external social structures recast inner impulses and provided a person his orientation in life. In fact, Riesman credited social character for much of the thematic structure of his classic and widely instructive book, *The Lonely Crowd*. From the early 1940s on, Benjamin Spock drew heavily on Fromm's view of the "authoritarian character" in teaching parents to avoid imposing excessive control over their children. Pope John Paul II spoke of Fromm as a great teacher to humankind, characterized his *To Have or to Be?* as a remarkable spiritual volume, and invited Fromm to the Vatican to discuss aspects of spiritual instruction. Examples such as these underscore Fromm's substantial and continuing influence beyond academe. If he encountered difficulty in his ventures as a scholar, his other lives remained intact.

In another of his lives, that of a social commentator and intellectual, Fromm played a conspicuous role in the comings and goings of a generation that included figures such as Karen Horney, Paul Lazarsfeld, and Paul Tillich. Their writings and general discourse were products of that interval between the rise of authoritarian European governments in the 1930s, on the one hand, and the prospect of nuclear war in the Cold War years, on the other. Like Fromm, many in this generation were secular Jews who had experienced gruesome encounters with fascism, and they addressed a number of difficult topics, including raw bigotry, mass alienation, crude nationalism, and the human potential to exterminate others by the millions. Most of these thinkers slowly shifted from a universalist perspective that spoke to all of humanity toward a pluralism that by the 1960s recognized people's commonalities but also the import of their differences.

Currently, these thinkers have come to be called "public intellectuals." However, because the term "public intellectual" did not gain currency until the late 1980s, there may be utility in choosing a term they would have recognized and sometimes invoked—"social commentators" or even "social philosophers." While several were in academe, they wrote for wider audiences than their specialized colleagues. They looked askance at the requirements of academic specialty fields, peer reviews, and conferences restricted to "experts." Instead, they examined crucial issues that crossed disciplines and addressed pervasive human concerns. Like Fromm, many wrote quickly and engagingly while eschewing systematic research and jumping over connecting specialty scholarship and primary sources. Often, they recycled their arguments, sometimes restating them with interesting twists over the decades.

The vision holding Fromm's generation of "public intellectuals" together was that of a peaceful, tolerant, and increasingly global civil society. To the extent that the brutal wars of the past and the potential outbreak of nuclear war were anathema to that vision, Fromm allied himself with many celebrated intellectuals and activists. He cooperated with Hannah Arendt in taking a measure of the new Israeli nation and its reticence to embrace its Arab neighbors. Fromm also established direct contact with Albert Einstein in campaigns for peace and disarmament, especially those dedicated to reducing tensions in the Middle East. He worked with Margaret Mead and her interdisciplinary circle in applying new cultural theories to global trouble spots. While at Columbia University, Fromm fostered scholarly collaboration between the highly regarded sociology department and the transplanted Frankfurt Institute when the two addressed broad public issues. At one point, he persuaded Theodor Adorno, the historian Richard Hofstadter, and the sociologists Robert Lynd and C. Wright Mills to meet and share their thoughts regarding the fears, bigotries, and paranoid politics of the postwar world.

Taking the full measure of Fromm, with all of his "lives," is difficult but not impossible. The focus of scholars—the ideas that emerge from his published texts—have been exercises in intellectual biography. Some of their work has been quite good. Yet they do not factor in the way Fromm's personal life shaped and was shaped by his intellectual contributions. One can understand why. Fromm instructed his third wife to destroy all of his personal letters when he died. Fortunately, there are ways to navigate this problem.

Consider one example—what we know about Fromm's signal concept of "social character," which shows up in most of his publications. The three clearest explanations are a 1932 article, "Psychoanalytic Characterology and Its Relevance for Social Psychology," *Escape from Freedom* (1941), and *Man for Himself* (1947). In one of his more elucidating formulations on the nature of social character, Fromm wrote: "Character can be defined as the form in which human energy is canalized in the process of assimilation and socialization. . . . The character system can be considered the human substitute for the instinctive apparatus of the animal." To clarify the nature of social character as it contrasted with the Freudian or modernist paradigm of instincts and restraints, Fromm wrote: "Socially produced drives are specifically human and have to be explained as reactions toward a particular fit of social conditions and not as 'sublimations' of instincts." This was Fromm's clearest explanation of social character. What is the background of this concept?

In the late 1930s—his final years at the Frankfurt Institute—Fromm explained in letters to colleagues that he was disposed to drop Freud's premise that libidinal energy was at the core of individual personality. His important study of the social and economic worlds of German workers earlier in the decade, before Hitler rose to power as chancellor, had contributed to these reservations. While giving Freud his due, Fromm found in the course of this study that it was mandatory to pursue an alternative to libidinal theory. Fromm's colleagues at the Frankfurt Institute, clinging to the literal wording of Freud's early texts even as Freud departed from them, felt betrayed and called for Fromm's termination.

After Horkheimer let him go in 1939, Fromm supported himself by developing a lucrative private psychoanalytic practice, which left him free to flesh out what was becoming his notion of the social character. He again questioned Freud on the centrality of libidinal impulses while writing *Escape from Freedom*. He concluded at first that the self was not born as a Lockean tabula rasa—a blank slate that lacked unique experiential qualities. Fromm observed that at birth and immediately after, one had already become a socialized individual. From that point on, the self was shaped and reshaped by interactions between one's unique personality and feelings, on the one hand, and the surrounding social circumstances, on the other. Fromm was shaping his social character concept, but still not definitively.

He continued to modify the concept for the rest of his life, sometimes making it more obtuse, other times clearer. The crucial issue all along was the degree to which Fromm was willing to acknowledge the import of libidinal drives (central to the modernist agenda of Freud's followers) in his concept of social character. At times, he assigned libidinal drives only a minor role in social character formation, especially in a number of his early formulations, developed when he worked at the Frankfurt Institute. But at other times, he argued that libidinal drives and, more generally, human energy was absolutely central to the process of socialization. That is, beginning with his writings in the 1940s, he still often (but not always) accorded considerable importance to the libidinal drives. Why did he soon shift, and quite decidedly and consistently, on this signal issue? When asked, he maintained that changes in his therapeutic techniques and his patient clientele had much to do with his revised formulations and that his patients were often his teachers as he considered and reconsidered the elements of social character. As his clinical experiences changed, the concept did as well. In brief, Fromm underscored how his life as a practicing psychoanalyst was not to be separated from his life as a personality theorist. The two lives were always interconnected.

The inability to understand how Fromm arrived at the social character formulation without biographical information is but one case in point. The motives and actions in all of Fromm's lives and contributions require some understanding of his private and personal existence. His massive correspondence is central to understanding his personal life. But at the time of his death, he wanted his wife to destroy all of his letters. When Rainer Funk, his literary executor, argued against destruction of his correspondence, Fromm relented, allowing Funk to archive his professional letters; all others were to be destroyed. What Fromm did not account for was that many of his professional letters housed personal information and that all of his letters, personal and professional, such as those to Fulbright and Riesman, would eventually be deposited in various university archives. Furthermore, and despite his instructions, his wife failed to destroy a good many of the entirely personal letters.

Despite the recovered letters, there is no getting around the fact that Fromm's correspondence before 1934 is unavailable, necessitating alternative approaches to his early years. Late in life, Fromm consented to several tape-recorded interviews. These were complemented by an essay in his book *Beyond the Chains of Illusion* (1962). Together, they reveal much about the younger Fromm. He described his upbringing "as an only child, with an anxious father and a depression-prone mother." His parents depended on him, sometimes in less than conscious ways, to hold the family together. Fromm felt marginalized and estranged by this household arrangement and needed to break away. He explained how he found comfort by studying Old Testament passages with calm and friendly mentors, which afforded him an entryway into the life of a scholar. Essentially, he was characterizing estrangement—a social and emotional quality that revealed much about his own social character. Indeed, estrangement illustrated how social circumstances shaped his emotions and his entire interiority. His feelings of estrangement prompted Fromm to move on to happier situations, a pattern repeated, if in different circumstances, for the rest of his life.

Fromm's twenty-three years in Mexico (1950–1973) began with the suicide of his second wife, Henny Gurland. His recovery from the tragedy was rapid, for he fell deeply in love with Annis Freeman, who became his third wife. Short notes and more extended epistles between them flowed daily with exuberance and joy, and Fromm drew on them to frame *The Art of Loving*. His narrative for the volume was rooted in an exciting, credible, and tangible personal love story that has appealed to the dreams, hopes, and aspirations of millions of readers. The fervor and joy of a compelling writer in love—a prophet of love—became infectious.

While Fromm and Annis enjoyed a loving marriage in Mexico City and nearby Cuernavaca, Fromm essentially introduced psychoanalysis to the country, constructing a psychoanalytic culture rooted in his neo-Freudian premises and preparing a substantial number of Mexicans from diverse backgrounds to become psychoanalysts. All of his trainees enrolled in the Mexican Psychoanalytic Institute, where he presided. At the same time, he launched a massive research project concerning an impoverished Mexican village. In both ventures, he sometimes displayed a compulsion to control others. It resembled Freud's narcissism during the first decades of psychoanalysis. Both regarded themselves as founders of unique psychoanalytic ideas, institutions, and traditions.

In the formative years of Mexican psychoanalysis, Fromm did not always use his power and influence sparingly. He capitalized on the deference many Mexicans showed to a strong and determined male leader. Fromm was often disposed to make his ideas on social character almost a baseline for much of the Mexican Psychoanalytic Institute's dialogue, teaching, and administrative practices. He was at times distressed with students who did not subscribe to the concept or make it central in their own clinical work. Several who tended to be loyal to him were awarded with important positions in the Institute. Those who did not might find themselves limited in influence and power. In the abstract, Fromm was one of the most distinguished and determined foes of anything approximating authoritarianism. It is therefore striking that he sometimes tended to impose his perspectives and values on the Institute, gradually relinquishing his control as he mellowed in temperament and as his health deteriorated and because he wanted to embrace more fully his life as a writer.

Fromm behaved similarly in a second venture in Mexico: a project to study an impoverished Mexican village. Initially, he hired two cultural anthropologists, Theodore and Lola Schwartz, to gather background data about the village while they helped Fromm launch a larger research project. His intent was to measure villager attitudes on a diversity of topics through lengthy, psychoanalytically informed questionnaires that all of the villagers were to complete. The questionnaires essentially replicated those that Fromm had helped design in late Weimar Germany to measure the authoritarian attitudes of workers. The Schwartzes told Fromm the obvious: a detailed questionnaire would not work because he was dealing with semiliterate and poor peasants, whereas the German project had dealt with more educated and worldly laborers. What was needed, they noted, were direct field observations of the villagers by anthropologists like themselves. Fromm was not persuaded, but the Schwartzes held their ground until they saw no point in continuing the dispute and left. It was Fromm's project, they saw in the end, and he would take no advice on how to conduct it.

Fromm replaced them with Michael Maccoby, a talented young social science researcher determined to accommodate Fromm in any way possible. He exercised further control over Maccoby by agreeing to psychoanalyze him, which gave Fromm a certain power through his knowledge of the interiority of Maccoby's life. The double role as Maccoby's professional supervisor and psychoanalyst violated or, at the very least, bent the code of ethics of the psychoanalytic profession. Unlike the Schwartzes, however, Maccoby concluded that he still learned much by working with Fromm and, in time, they became coauthors of a book on the village project.

This is not to say that Fromm embraced the authoritarianism or "totalism" that he had written about and abhorred. Through much of his life, he held intense, indeed prophetic, visions of a good society and pushed hard to have those visions realized. Sometimes he saw the "good society" embodying what he called "socialist humanism." At other times, he invoked the term "sane society"—a polity that eschewed consumerism and militarism. But whatever his prophetic visions and goals in Mexico were, Fromm expected others to cooperate and help him so that he could institute them.

Albert Camus's 1951 classic *The Rebel* is instructive here. For much of his life, Fromm played the part of what Camus termed the "rebel"—an outsider and a gadfly who critiqued existing social and political arrangements and called for expanding the realm of freedom. For Camus, an individual and a society should not follow traditions that restricted human freedom—a persistent theme in Fromm's writing. But during times of trouble at the Mexican Psychoanalytic Institute and in the village project, Fromm sometimes tended to emulate aspects of Camus's "revolutionary"—one who pursued substantial control over the people and organizations around him. We would do well to keep in mind that the author of *Escape from Freedom*, while usually Camus's "rebel," could sometimes share a modest resemblance to the "revolutionary." He was a complex man of varied visions, temperaments, and "lives."

For much of his life, Fromm responded to disappointments and adversities with strong reactions, jumping from one location to another, quitting one professional association and joining or creating another, altering his conceptual and clinical approaches, and switching from one intimate friendship or bed partner to another. There was a pertinacity here. Fromm would rarely allow a difficult situation to immobilize him. He usually ended up establishing a more functional, productive, and congenial set of circumstances for himself, even as he could be imprudent, narcissistic, and erratic. This duality was a central theme in his life. David Riesman, for one, spoke of Fromm's gumption despite serious illnesses, always taking on difficult challenges "in order to keep going if there was a speech to be made or an article to be written which might in some small way serve the cause of peace realistically." He could always be depended upon, however difficult the mission, Riesman emphasized, even if his manner was sometimes curt and unpleasant.

Fromm's changing dispositions and behaviors can be explained as changing elements in what might be described metaphorically and nondiagnostically as an emotional triangle. The three corners represent exuberance, depression, and marginality. The three were crucial in accounting for much about Fromm's childhood struggle, which recurred in different ways and contexts for the rest of his life. Resembling the triangular structure that some clinicians have found in families and other groups, where two join up against the third, this was a triangulation within the self.

It was difficult for Fromm and for those close to him to predict which two of the three corners might dominate a given situation and which might ally with a second corner to establish hegemony over the third. The first corner, exuberance, consisted of what clinicians too readily label "hypomania"—a state of boundless energy, reduced self-governance, and socially inappropriate words and deeds. This diagnosis falls short in understanding Fromm. His exuberance reflected an exceedingly joyous but hardly a precarious temperament. Boundless happiness and delight was evident at many of his parties, which revolved around stimulating discussions, gourmet food, and a limitless supply of jokes and good wine. Fromm's intense, frequent, spontaneous, and loving letters to his third wife, Annis, were also expressions of this strong exuberance but hardly cause for clinical concern. The same deep happiness and contentment ensued when Fromm listened to his favorite classical records with brandy and a cigar. In one of his letters, Fromm told Annis that a life well lived was an exuberant state of existence where prudence sometimes had to be cast aside.

The danger was that his exuberance occasionally pushed beyond safe limits. Though he suffered from major coronary-artery disease, for example, Fromm ignored the advice of his cardiologists and gorged on high-cholesterol food. Consider, too, that his outbursts against orthodox Freudian psychoanalytic societies exceeded the bounds of prudence. He seemed, as well, to harbor excessive furor against the Frankfurt Institute after Horkheimer refused to publish the findings of Fromm's study of German workers. While it is not helpful to tag Fromm's feelings and behaviors in these instances as hypomanic, he certainly seemed at times to show a vaguely manic disposition.

The second corner of Fromm's emotional triangle was represented by a depressive mood that was also characteristic of his mother's. The suicides that punctuated his life weighed heavily on Fromm, from the early death of a promising young woman painter through the self-inflicted deaths of several of his patients to the ultimate personal pain of his second wife's passing. Major illnesses throughout his life were also dispiriting, and by the early 1960s, Fromm's certainty that there would be a global nuclear war caused him tremendous despair.

A sense of marginality occupied the third corner of the internal triangle. Whereas extreme exuberance and depression are often unique to an individual and carry a heavy genetic component, marginality and estrangement derive to a large extent from social situations. Fromm felt estranged from his family as his parents clung emotionally to him to mitigate a miserable marriage. In the late 1930s, Fromm felt rejected and bitter when he was fired from the Frankfurt Institute. The feeling recurred when he was ousted not only from orthodox psychoanalytic societies but from societies run by neo-Freudians. In these situations, Fromm saw himself on the sidelines in a world where consumerism and warrior virtues were in vogue.

This triangular emotional life might not have generated significant distress if the three corners had been relatively stable and predictable in their trajectories. In Fromm's case, they were not. On a given day, he could feel depressed and marginalized. On another day, a sense of exuberance might be reduced by the feelings of estrangement. Once in a while, however, these unpredictable interactions worked out well—and always when he dined with Riesman or Fulbright or spent time with Annis.

In addition, when Fromm felt distressed or downcast, he could rely on a number of "stabilizers" he had built along the outskirts of the emotional triangle. There were at least four interrelated long-term stabilizers. First, he maintained a regular, predictable daily schedule. As he wrote to Lewis Mumford, "I actually live pretty much the same way I used to live." He started every day by walking for thirty minutes, writing for four hours, then meditating for an hour. He had a quick lunch and spent afternoons in a varied allotment of tasks—clinical work with his patients, reviewing materials relevant to his writing projects, and dictating letters.

Second, but also illustrative of his effort to retain equanimity, Fromm progressed energetically on each of his writing projects once he decided his approach to the topic. He began each new book or article by locating what Freud and, to a lesser degree, Marx had written about the topic. Next, he reviewed and incorporated what he had already written about the topic. Fromm was often self-referential. Drawing more from his earlier formulations than from the feedback of thoughtful critics or new evidence, he could write quickly but was necessarily limited in depth and nuance. Fortunately, Fromm's early formulations were among his most profound. These were the brilliant and probing articles he had prepared at the Frankfurt Institute that prompted his concept of social character and the core perspectives for *Escape from Freedom*.

Fromm usually structured his writing around binaries—freedom and authoritarianism, love and hate, biophilia and necrophilia, "having" consumer items or "being" a productive self. These binaries stabilized and organized his writing. In some measure, he was pursuing the teaching of D. T. Suzuki, his sometime mentor. In his variation of Zen Buddhism, Suzuki postulated that thinking was dualistic—dividing all phenomena into opposites. Fromm thought of them as binaries and deployed them in a way that simplified complex materials. Binaries discouraged the examination of points along a continuum and limited the focus to progress through a dialectic. Whether binaries were or were not congruent with Suzuki, they simplified the content of Fromm's books even as they helped to make them accessible to millions. Thus a weakness in Fromm's life as a scholar contributed to his strength in his life as a global teacher of serious subjects.

Third, Fromm would always seek out convivial groups of intellectuals and artists that in some ways resembled Mable Dodge Luhan's assemblage in Taos. These, too, were stabilizers, providing him with comfort and perhaps a bit of humor, a lively and supportive social life, and a helpful forum in which to test out new concepts, intuitions, and clinical perspectives. He referred to these groups as "humanistic" collectivities. Between 1916 and 1921, Fromm actively studied topics linked to the Hebrew Bible in a small group, led by Rabbi Nehemia Nobel in Frankfurt, that included Martin Buber, Leo Baeck, and Gershom Scholem. In the 1930s, Fromm was a central presence in gatherings of the neo-Freudians—Karen Horney, Harry Stack Sullivan, and Clara Thompson. During Fromm's years in Locarno he participated in a group that included the social critic Ivan Illich; the retired director of the Leo Baeck Institute, Max Kreutzberger; and the Italian psychoanalyst Boris Luban-Plozza. The group discussed Buddhism, the problems of Israel as a Jewish state, and Fromm's latest binaries—Having and Being. Fromm recognized that the underlying theme of these discussions was usually the nature of a "humanistic" society. He thrived in these groups of convivial and thoughtful colleagues.

In the most general sense, what Fromm meant by "humanism" was a kind and caring connectedness that extended to his work with his patients. He considered the therapeutic relationship to be salutary if it promoted a deep rapport and affinity between the clinician and patient. Initially, he referred to this rapport as "central relatedness"—a state of affairs where clinician and patient "flowed" emotionally into the "cores" of the other. In time, Fromm characterized this relationship as a form of "dancing" with his patients. Both terms spoke to a kind and humanistic clinical relationship. Fromm found that with obvious exceptions his clinical work afforded him the same sort of stability and energy that he experienced with his writing.

Spirituality, the fourth stabilizer, was perhaps the most important. Fromm's embrace of spirituality derived from his exposure to prophetic Judaism, Christian mysticism, and Zen Buddhism. He considered spirituality to be something within the self but also beyond both the self and the society. Yet it did not require the premise that a God existed. For Fromm, the nature and depth of one's spirituality governed one's entire orientation toward the world, shaping personal conduct and relationships. Fromm's spirituality affixed itself to his prophetic disposition, energizing his prophetic call for freedom, justice, and the love of life. Most important, it was a plea from the heart. Fromm found the most intense and fundamental form of spirituality in the unconditional love of a mother for her newborn. The task at hand was to extend that spirituality to all human relationships. The spirituality Fromm had in mind was beyond man and at the same time within man—an integration of elements in one's inner being. Most essentially, an earnest spiritual pursuit encased, protected, and grounded the self, stabilizing one's life and confirming one's orientation and values.

Fromm once acknowledged that through stabilizers, "I've done what I could to repair that damage" of his parental household. If not for these grounding elements, his creative and scholarly productivity and his political activity would have been negligible. We might never have heard of Erich Fromm. Fromm was his own best clinician.

The deployment of stabilizing or coping social strategies to check inner turmoil was hardly unique to Fromm. Some who have been diagnosed with acute depression, sundry forms of psychosis, excessive narcissism, or other psychological maladies have tried to structure their lives around stabilizing strategies to make their existence more functional. Fromm's strategies worked well for him, accounting in part for a remarkably accomplished and productive career attended by joy and exuberance.

The stabilizers or social strategies were more than a match for the apprehensions and uncertainties that could torment Fromm. When, by the mid- to late 1950s, they were firmly in place, friends and colleagues observed a difference in his temperament. He had mellowed and was less abrasive, less narcissistic, more content, and easier to get along with. And after two difficult marriages, he had found one that worked. But there may have been a price to be paid for this inner calm and contentment. Fromm's toughness and pertinacity had been connected to his willingness to take on difficult and consequential issues—authoritarianism, psychoanalytic orthodoxies, the potential for war, and the demonic in the human condition. His energy supply had, in part, been grounded in his discontent. Now that he was less agitated and more at one with himself, he seemed at times more willing to take chances. He was able to break out of the constricted life of the psychoanalyst and the scholar, for example, in order to write bestsellers that educated millions. He uncovered the leadership skills to shape a global movement for a "Third Way." And he found that he could be taken seriously by the president of the United States on an issue of human survival. At base, Fromm experienced an array of complex tradeoffs as he conquered the demons of his past. Although he remained successful—perhaps becoming even more so—something of the earlier and more conceptually profound intellectual was lost in the exchange. One could not expect otherwise from a man of so many "lives."

On balance, Fromm preferred the more relaxed, contented, and loving self that emerged after he had built his stabilizing techniques. Most of us would want this outcome, as well. If there is a lesson here, it is that mental "abnormalities" and "pathologies" can sometimes be reduced and occasionally even canceled out if supportive social factors are constructed around inner emotional disorders.

In sum, Fromm was a flawed man who devised coping mechanisms and diverse "lives" to rise more often than not above difficult familial circumstances and to contribute substantially to his day—and to ours. During the middle decades of the twentieth century, he explained passionately and to vast numbers that war resolves nothing and that nuclear war would kill us all. The problem persists. War is still a primary vehicle used to deal with conflict. Nuclear weapons still proliferate. Established superpowers as well as rogue states and terrorist groups are all too ready to live by the sword.

Fromm helped to pave an alternative path for his day and for ours, one contoured by love and what he called humanism. The goal was to promote a joyous and caring community where the love of life and the realization of everybody's creative potentialities held hegemony over the forces of repression, conformity, and destructiveness. Fromm described it best:

> It is a system of thought and feeling cultured upon man—his growth, integrity, dignity and freedom—as an end in himself and not as a means towards anything—upon his capacity to be active not as an individual but as a participant in history and the fact that every man carries within himself all of humanity.

PART I

GERMANY

When Erich Fromm was born at the turn of the century, many Germans were experiencing upheaval in their lives. As a student in a Frankfurt gymnasium, he witnessed the last months of the German empire and the outbreak of the "Great War." He was still a student when the Weimar Republic emerged from the war's rubble. Experiments in democratic socialism pervaded Weimar, especially in new social services such as free medical clinics and psychological counseling agencies. But there was also an ideological and political struggle being waged between communists and fascists, which deepened as inflation crippled the national economy. This was a time of great creativity in German art, theater, architecture, and film. A 1930 film, *The Blue Angel*, starring Marlene Dietrich, reflected the uncertainties of the time. In the film, Immanuel Rath, an eminent professor at a distinguished gymnasium, falls in love with Lola Lola, a beautiful if deceptive cabaret dancer. The film ends with Rath, disgraced and humiliated in front of his former colleagues, clinging to a desk that had once represented his eminence and learnedness. In brief, *The Blue Angel* registered a clash in German culture—old traditions and values facing off against the more liberated spirit of Weimar. When Hitler took power, the world of Lola Lola was pushed aside, and the cultural and social institutions of Weimar were upended. What had been the world's center of scientific innovation, research, and scholarship when Fromm was born became a crude and bellicose nation—a development that prompted his classic, *Escape from Freedom*.

1

The Unsteady Apprentice

Erich Fromm was born in Frankfurt at the start of the twentieth century. At the time, Frankfurt was the financial capital of Germany. Situated on the Main River near its juncture with the Rhine, it was one of Europe's major transportation and commercial centers and a historical magnet for Jewish business and intellectual ventures. Goethe had been born in Frankfurt, and idealistic liberals had gathered there in 1848 to try to create a democratic and united nation. In brief, major German economic, political, and intellectual changes often registered themselves first in Frankfurt.

The city resonated deeply with Fromm for much of his life. It was there that he first became acquainted with the Talmud, with Jewish ethical traditions, and with new socialist ideas. As a student in a local gymnasium (an advanced secondary school) during World War I, he became disillusioned with jingoistic nationalism, sought world peace, and became what he would eventually call a "humanist." A young man after the war, Fromm was seduced by an older woman, Frieda Reichmann, while he was her analysand. To Fromm, Reichmann seemed brilliant, exciting, even angelic. He married her, and she helped him to become acquainted with the clinical and theoretical dimensions of Freud's new "science of the psyche." Joining the esteemed Frankfurt Institute for Social Research and becoming a significant contributor to its work in Critical Theory, Fromm proposed new ways of discussing the findings of Freud through the aid of Marx. This became the basis for his work as a social commentator, what we have come to call a "public intellectual." Although young Fromm sometimes lived outside Frankfurt—in Heidelberg, Munich, and Berlin—"home" remained the city of his birth. Whenever he considered what it meant to be a German Jew— psychologically, intellectually, and historically—he thought of Frankfurt. Indeed, Fromm's enduring classic on authoritarianism, *Escape from Freedom*, was written with Frankfurt in mind.

When Fromm was born in 1900, Frankfurt Jews had yet to be fully assimilated into middle-class culture. Some clung to rituals of the past even as they embraced the modernizing presence of money and the marketplace. Fromm experienced this dual pull as discomforting: "I felt quite at home neither in the world I lived in, nor in the old world of traditions." But if he was to choose between modern capitalism and traditional Jewish orthodoxy, he preferred the latter. He described his earliest years in Frankfurt's Jewish community as having a reclusive, "medieval atmosphere, in which everything is dedicated to traditional learning." Fromm would seek out or promote this kind of community for the rest of his life.[1]

Consistent with his embrace of a "medieval" tradition of Talmudic study over the marketplace, Fromm offered an admittedly "idealized" portrayal of his great-grandfather on his father's side, Seligmann Bär Bamberger, who had been one of the most prominent and learned German rabbis during the middle decades of the nineteenth century. Indeed, Bamberger had founded a center of Torah study and was regarded as a preeminent authority on a variety of Hebrew Bible topics. He wanted his writings to be studied by women and was known for his books that dealt with Halacha, focusing on ethics in matters of daily life. Bamberger urged Jews to cling to Orthodoxy by resisting Reform-dominated congregations. Above all, he appealed to the more traditionally minded to resist modernizing trends in German Jewish life and doctrine. So fundamental was Rabbi Bamberger to Fromm's vision of this "medieval" past that he minimized the elements of nineteenth-century biological racism in Bamberger's publications.[2]

Bamberger's daughter, Rahel, married Rabbi Seligmann Pinchas Fromm, who became a leader of the Frankfurt Jewish community. They had ten children. Five of the six girls married professionals—primarily teachers. The sons were ambitious, one becoming a successful merchant, one a doctor, and one a distinguished lawyer and ethicist. Naphtali, Fromm's father, considered himself the most marginal son in the family—an undistinguished wine merchant who regretted that he had not become a rabbi. Like their parents, the children were Orthodox Jews and attended synagogue regularly. Intelligent, humorous, and interested in the arts, Rahel was close to all of her children and did much to hold the family together; her husband devoted most of his time to Talmudic study.[3]

The Krause family—Erich's maternal relations—was less distinguished. Initially, the Krauses had migrated from Russia to Finland, where they had been converted to Judaism. We do not know the reasons for the conversion.

From Finland, the Krauses moved to Posen, part of the German empire at the time (though it became Polish after 1918), where they lived under difficult economic conditions. Moritz Krause, Erich's maternal grandfather, had started a cigar factory but died early, leaving his wife Anna without funds but with six children to feed. Moritz's brother Ludwig tried to assist Anna on the meager earnings of a Talmudic scholar. One of Moritz and Anna's sons tried desperately but without success to keep the cigar factory going, but there is little information on most of his siblings. One of the sons remained in Posen and died in World War I. A daughter, Sophie, married David Englander, a high-school English teacher, and resided in Berlin. Another daughter, Martha, also married a professional, Bernhard Stein. They too took up residence in Berlin. Rosa Krause, affectionately called Rosita, was fair, blue eyed, and blond as a child (revealing the family's Finnish roots). She had a pleasant disposition and was a source of good cheer to her mother and her siblings. Not wanting to be a financial burden to her struggling mother, she sought a husband for sustenance and security more than for love. Rosa settled for a successful local wine merchant, Naphtali Fromm, whom the larger Krause family did not regard highly, and the marriage seemed to cost her much of her good cheer.[4]

Rosa and Naphtali had a strained relationship, and Erich sometimes speculated that his presence may have held a bad marriage together. He was born scarcely nine months after the wedding, on March 23, 1900, and no siblings followed. Rosa clung to Erich as the pride and joy of her life, projecting onto him an idealized vision of herself. She began struggling with depression, gained a good deal of weight, and cried frequently. "I always felt that I was the defender of my mother, who used to cry a lot," Erich recalled, "and I felt I had to defend her against my father." Often, Rosa sought relief by taking Erich to visit with her sisters and their families; in their company, her lighter and happier self seemed to reawaken. She held Erich up during these visits as a Krause more than a Fromm and often spoke ill of Naphtali's family. This made Erich uncomfortable and may have cultivated a lifelong unease with most of his Krause relatives. Regarding her son as inseparable from herself and betraying a preference for a daughter, Rosa kept him in long hair and girl's clothing well beyond the age where boys began to wear masculine attire. Rosa also insisted that Erich excel at the piano despite his strong preference for the violin, hoping that he might become another Paderewski, the celebrated Polish pianist and statesman. Through much of his childhood, Erich recalled that Rosa embraced him more as a prize possession than as a person. He felt a mildly depressive sort of bondage to Rosa, a sense that would be rekindled in his subsequent relationships to considerably older lovers.[5]

Young Erich felt somewhat closer to his father, Naphtali. A thriving peddler of fruit wine but embarrassed by the calling, he frequently traveled to sell his wares within a 124-mile radius of Frankfurt and sent postcards to Rosa and Erich even when he was away for only a night. All his business transactions were pursued in accord with the Shulhan Arukh, the guidelines to ethical conduct. Naphtali became active in the local synagogue and served as cantor, observing all of the Jewish holidays and customs meticulously. He met all of the formal imperatives of Orthodox Judaism, even as his son considered him short on inner spirituality and ethical introspection. Indeed, Erich characterized his father as "very neurotic, obsessive, anxious," reflecting deep personal insecurities that he projected upon Erich: "I suffered under the influence of a pathologically anxious father who overwhelmed me with anxiety, at the same time not giving me any guidelines and having no positive influence on my education." At some times he spoke of Naphtali as "a sick man" and "a very odd man" and even "a [mental] case." Naphtali worried constantly about Erich but never quite moved beyond viewing him as a young child. Thus he decreasingly served his son's need for a father. As Erich matured, Naphtali insisted that during inclement weather he remain at home, for fear that Erich might catch a cold. He regularly tried to isolate Erich from others his age and rejected the youngster's dream of pursuing Talmudic studies abroad. Erich sometimes interpreted Naphtali's obsessive and nervous energy as indifference—that his father "was not interested in my personal development." But there was another, more endearing side to this father-son relationship. When Erich sat on Naphtali's lap—though well beyond his toddler years—the rapport between father and son temporarily seemed to rekindle. Erich also attempted to emulate Naphtali's mannerisms and speaking style, trying desperately to look to his father as a role model.[6]

To be sure, Rosa and Naphtali cared deeply for Erich even as their marriage remained troubled. But the absence of consistent love and good cheer in the household set Erich in search of alternatives. Retrospectively, he characterized his life caught between Naphtali's neurotic unevenness and Rosa's smothering possessiveness as one of much "suffering" that was producing an "unbearable, neurotic child." For relief from such troubled and unempathic parenting, Erich became a frequent visitor at the house of his uncle, Emmanuel Fromm, where he confided to his cousin, Gertrud, that he preferred her father to his own. (She remained his lifelong confidante and something like a sister. In time, she became a prominent psychoanalyst.) Emmanuel represented what might be characterized as a stabilizer in the boy's life; he was gentler and far more easy going than Naphtali. Emmanuel was also an eminent lawyer and ethicist known for taking on only clients whose causes he deemed principled and righteous. He had a special talent for connecting law and ethics, which Fromm admired. Little is known about his wife, Clara, but Emmanuel often seemed to be both father and mother to Gertrud and Erich. Whereas Rosa and Naphtali raised their son in the sparse cultural world of the petty bourgeoisie, Uncle Emmanuel introduced Erich to Goethe, Schiller, Beethoven, and other luminaries of German and European high culture. He recognized that the boy had a special ear for complex music, which his parents lacked, and he encouraged Erich to cultivate that capacity. For the rest of his life, Erich would cross and recross the divide between middlebrow and high culture, perhaps feeling more comfortable emotionally with the former but sensing that it was more appropriate to embrace the cultural riches that Uncle Emmanuel brought into his life.[7]

Another influence during Erich's childhood—one helping to account for his strong, if nostalgic, embrace of a "medieval milieu"—was his great-uncle, Ludwig Krause, a prominent Talmudic scholar from Posen. Calm and convivial, Ludwig preferred a kosher household but accepted his wife Sophie's dietary departures. He frequently visited members of the Krause family in Germany, eventually taking up residence near Frankfurt when after World War I Posen ceased to be German and its residents were required to become Polish citizens. Far more than Erich's parents and Uncle Emmanuel, Uncle Ludwig acquainted the young boy with the world of Talmudic study and deepened his appreciation of the contribution of his great-grandfather Bamberger. Erich became fascinated with the Hebrew Bible, especially with the prophetic writings of Isaiah, Amos, and Hosea and their visions of peace and harmony among nations. During Ludwig's visits, he and Erich spent whole days studying Talmudic passages together. Erich soon came to regard the world of biblical study, free of marketplace concerns, as a desirable alternative to the modern world of commerce and profits that seemed increasingly to pervade life in Frankfurt. Indeed, Uncle Ludwig had such a transformative effect upon the young boy that he gave Erich a sense of what he might want his future to be. Following in

Ludwig's footsteps, Erich might end up "an old Jew," generous, pious, and an expert in Hebrew Bible passages. While Erich attended a local school (the Wohlerschule) and experienced the more secular marketplace trends of middle-class Frankfurt society, Uncle Ludwig exemplified a comforting alternative: a world of study and contemplation that was in eclipse.[8]

As Erich matured, he noticed that his mother focused increasingly on Krause family affairs, a habit that augmented her happiness and distanced her from her husband and many others in the extended Fromm family. Rosa became especially close to her older sisters, Martha and Sophie, who lived in Berlin, planning family gatherings with them and sometimes inviting Naphtali's spinster sister, Zerline. At these gatherings, Erich became especially close with Martha's daughter, Charlotte, regarding her as an older sister and a companion in a world of adults. The two liked to spend their summers together. When Rosa was not with her family, she arranged excursions with Naphtali and Erich to popular resorts such as Baden Baden, Davos, and Montreux, hoping that travel could kindle greater happiness in their dour family life. Whether at home or on vacation, however, photographs of the three together are rare and hardly depict joyous relationships. Pictures of Rosa and Naphtali alone are almost nonexistent. Decades later, Erich wrote to a niece, Annelie Brandt, recalling "a good deal of the suffering when we were children."[9]

World War I and Talmudic Studies

When Erich was twelve, his father hired Oswald Sussman, a young Galacian Jew, to help with the wine business. Sussman lived in the Fromm household for two years, and Erich found him a wonderful companion with a direct personal interest in his well-being. Sussman took Erich to the Frankfurt Museum for the first time, introduced him to the works of Marx and other socialist classics, and engaged him in serious political discussions. Erich now realized quite clearly what his discussions with Uncle Emmanuel had vaguely suggested—that there was a world out there with pressing contemporary issues that required bold solutions: Sussman "was an extremely honest man, courageous, a man of great integrity. I owe a great deal to him." If Sussman did much to cultivate in Fromm an interest in the public sphere and the works of Karl Marx, the fate of a family friend prodded the twelve-year-old to ponder the nature of private emotional experience, and that would eventually lead him to Freud. A beautiful twenty-five-year-old painter and family friend broke off an engagement to give more time to her widowed father. When he died, she committed suicide, stating in her will that she wanted to be buried with her father. "How is it possible," Erich wondered, "that a beautiful woman prefers to be buried with him to being alive to the pleasures of life and of painting?" Erich would eventually find answers in Freud's concept of the Oedipus complex and incestuous father-daughter relationships and later in his own revisionist Freudian concept of necrophilia. Indeed, suicide would be the antithesis of his notion of a life-affirming "productive social character." But for now, the news of a youthful suicide in a familial context was more than striking to this rather unhappy adolescent.[10]

Erich later labeled World War I "the most crucial experience in my life," an event that accelerated his personal maturity as much as it ushered in a bloody and traumatic interval in human experience. When war broke out, he was fourteen and a student at Frankfurt's Wohler Gymnasium. His Latin teacher, who had previously argued that the German arms buildup would keep the peace, was jubilant: "From then on, I found it difficult to believe in the principle that armament preserved peace." Even though the Wohlerschule purported to emphasize the humanism of the classics, with the onset of war almost all the students and their teachers lost any belief in the dignity of the individual and the unity of humankind. Most became "fanatical nationalists and reactionaries," attributing the war to British duplicity and German innocence. Only in Fromm's English class did he encounter a more sober perspective. There, his deeply respected teacher cautioned students who expected an instant German military triumph, in a historical overstatement: "Don't kid yourselves; so far England has never lost a war!"[11]

As the war progressed and the prognostication proved increasingly correct, Erich came to herald those words as a "voice of sanity and realism in the midst of insane hatred." Following the example of his English teacher, he came to resist the simplistic portrayal of innocent Germany attacked by bellicose Britain. He understood that Germany and the Austrian-Hungarian government had contributed substantially to the outbreak of hostilities. Several antiwar socialist deputies in the Reichstag voted against the war and offered what Fromm considered persuasive reasoning. So did a number of publications from France. As soon as Fromm "saw the wounded and the reports of the battles, the war became the center of my thinking and feeling. How was it possible that people went on killing each other and being killed?" Some of his uncles, cousins, and older schoolmates were among the dead—and to what end? Hereafter, he would strive to avoid "partisanship and non-objectivity" and never again "fall under the spell of emotional slogans" as he had in 1914. He would forever distrust official dogma offered by the "establishment" and become a reflective dissident against all such orthodoxies. When the war ended in 1918, Fromm saw himself as "a deeply troubled young man who was obsessed by the question of how war was possible, by the wish to understand the irrationality of human mass behavior, by a passionate desire for peace and international understanding." With this new, more critical, and antiwar perspective, Fromm sensed that he was shedding adolescence and becoming a reflecting, serious, and independent young man. A lifelong interest in politics and public affairs was emerging. Sussman, who apparently died in the war, would have been proud.[12]

Midway through the war, Fromm came under the influence of Rabbi Nehemiah Nobel of the Borneplatz synagogue, the leader of Frankfurt's Orthodox Jewish community. Nobel had taken his rabbinical training in Berlin's Hildesheimerschen Seminar and studied in Marburg with the renowned neo-Kantian and socialist Hermann Cohen, who taught him that ethics was not a matter of consensual validation within prevailing norms and traditions. Rather, while they were discovered through reason, ethical laws applied to all of humanity, irrespective of time and place. Early in their relationship, after a service at the Borneplatz synagogue, Nobel reviewed Cohen's works with Fromm and introduced the young man to his intellectual mentor. Cohen's view of a universal code of ethics became the bedrock of Fromm's thought, especially after he read Cohen's *Religion of Reason out of the Sources of Judaism*.[13]

Soon Fromm discovered that Nobel had "a strong Hasidic bent" and embraced Jewish mysticism as well as propagating the philosophy of Cohen. Fromm was attracted to Nobel's simple, humble, but exciting and intellectually penetrating sermons, which often took off on themes of the German Enlightenment. He began taking walks with Nobel on the outskirts of Frankfurt, where they discussed the rabbi's sermons. Indeed, Erich could not get enough of Nobel, often visiting his apartment for additional conversation. Through Nobel, Fromm's knowledge of the messianic ideas of the prophets deepened. In time, he was able to offer a coherent synthesis of the ethical code Nobel embraced, summed up in three major points. For one, it was imperative for those who stood for ideals of progressive change to practice them in their daily lives. For another, one had to take seriously the questions and needs of others and to help them find answers for their queries and the satisfaction of their needs. Finally, no ideal could be reached through raw power. Rather, love, humility, and the embrace of justice marked out the proper path. Through Nobel, Fromm also became a Zionist and helped form the Kartel Jüdischer Verbindungen of Frankfurt, a league of Jewish organizations that embraced Zionist ideals. However, his Zionism was tempered by Cohen's insistence that the universalism and humanism of the prophets precluded loyalty even to a Jewish state. Fromm resigned from the Kartel in 1923. By then he openly took issue with Nobel's premise that religion and nationalism were organically connected to Judaism.[14]

When Fromm introduced two of his closest Frankfurt friends, Leo Löwenthal and Ernst Simon, to Rabbi Nobel, they too found a Judaism mixing mysticism and the Enlightenment in a way that seemed exceedingly relevant to their lives. Soon a small Nobel circle of young enthusiasts gathered, including Franz Rosenzweig, an emerging young philosopher of religion. Periodically, Georg Salzberger, a young liberal rabbi from Frankfurt, made contact with the circle, and he cultivated a special friendship with Fromm. In a sense, this circle represented Fromm's first experience with a small group of convivial colleagues, the type of collectivity that would promote stability and comfort in his life for decades to come.[15]

Salzberger's particular concern was to remedy the widespread ignorance of local Frankfurt Jews about their religion and its history. Fromm strongly concurred in this goal. Late in 1919, he and Fromm formed a local Association for Jewish People's Education, and Nobel read a chapter from the Kabbala to inaugurate the lecture program. The Association was instrumental in creating the Free Jewish Teaching Institute, which was directed by Rosenzweig, and it became the Association's main focus.[16]

The Free Jewish Teaching Institute quickly evolved into a pioneer secular center for adult Jewish education in Germany. Martin Buber, a major Jewish philosopher and theologian celebrated for his long essay I and Thou; Gershom Scholem, a philosopher and historian who pioneered the modern interpretation of the Kabbala; and Leo Baeck, an important philosopher and rabbi, joined. Indeed, the Nobel circle, the Association, and the Institute combined to become a formidable hub of Jewish intellectual discourse. For the first time in his life, Fromm was in regular contact with an array of creative minds sharing his enthusiasm for religion and the life of the mind. Baeck became a close friend and supporter for the next fifty years.

When Nobel died suddenly in 1922 at the age of fifty-one, Rosenzweig wrote to Buber that their circle had suffered a formidable blow and that "a fundamental part of life has been pulled from under my feet." Fromm wrote the obituary in Frankfurt's *New Jewish Press*, stressing that Nobel "lived what he said and only said what he lived. He taught that love bound people together and [his students] understood because he loved [them]."[17]

Alfred Weber and Salman Rabinkow

Fromm completed his final examination at the Wohlerschule in 1918. Influenced by his Uncle Emmanuel, he considered becoming a lawyer and consequently studied jurisprudence for two semesters at Frankfurt University. Fromm soon realized that his deeper love lay in the close study of the Hebrew Bible. To break from his stifling family and enhance his training, Fromm sought additional study in Lithuania, an innovative center for Talmudic scholarship and training. His parents (especially his mother), however, would let him study no further away than nearby Heidelberg. Consequently, in May 1919, he entered the University of Heidelberg, for one semester on a trial basis. Since there was no specialty in Hebrew Bible studies, he listed jurisprudence as his focus. However, he discovered that his academic interests were eclectic, and he took courses in medieval German history, the theory of Marxism, social movements, and the history of psychology. He also had a strong interest in Buddhist thought and began privately practicing Tai Chi and meditation. The experimental semester extended into a year, at which point Fromm switched into Heidelberg's department of national economy, with a specialty under Alfred Weber in sociology.[18]

Alfred, Max Weber's brother, was his first and only Gentile mentor. Attending Alfred Weber's lectures and seminars, Fromm was impressed by the courage and integrity with which the professor expressed his thoughts and commitment to universal humanism over the rigid nationalism that Fromm ascribed to his brother. However, a certain shyness—perhaps even a sense of awkwardness at relating closely for the first time to a non-Jew—set limits on Fromm's rapport with Weber: "I avoided as much as I could to see him alone." Yet Fromm wrote to Weber decades later that "studies with you were one of the most fertile experiences [of] my life; not only in what I learned but also through your personality as a model." As Fromm profited from his association with Ludwig Krause and Rabbi Nobel, his relationship with Weber seemed as important as the content of his ideas. Weber taught Fromm that while it was essential for the sociologist to be attentive to the individual, it was imperative to recognize that an individual was inescapably rooted in collective life. This vaguely presaged what Fromm came to call social character. While Weber rejected Gustave Le Bon's notion of a collective or crowd psychology, he impressed Fromm with the idea that culture was a product of concerted and interlinked individual agencies spread over historical time and space. Moreover, any belief system was rational if it adapted to the exigencies of a particular time and place, however irrational it might later be regarded. For Weber, linguistic and juridical norms as well as aesthetic and musical forms were phenomena that helped the sociologist to discern the nature of collective life. He represented an important tradition in German social thought, one congruent with Wilhelm Dilthey and Georg Simmel.[19]

Although Weber was no expert on Jewish law, theology, or history, he knew that the young Fromm was hardly disposed to write a dissertation on any other topic. To be sure, Weber insisted that Fromm master his own writings as well as those of Dilthey and Simmel. He recognized, however, that Fromm also wanted to draw on key Jewish theologians and philosophers. They agreed that Fromm would write his dissertation ("Jewish Law: A Contribution to the Study of Diaspora Judaism") on the function of Jewish law in maintaining social cohesion and continuity in three Diaspora communities—the Karaites, the Reform Jews, and the Hasidim. Without a state, a common secular language, or even the opportunity to build a place of worship, Fromm argued, a Jewish social body bound by a law-abiding ethos was able to endure and to perpetuate both a belief system and a unique culture. By "law," Fromm meant the applied religious and moral code of a people. Indeed, there was a "soul" within Jewish law, which established the moral-ethical unity of the people. The collective content within the law was sufficiently flexible to allow individuals to interpret and implement its requirement; freedom of interpretation was embedded in the ethos of the community.[20]

To be sure, the Karaites had formed during the economic dislocations the Jews had experienced in eighth-century Babylon. They came to pursue trade in the nascent Arab empire and adjusted their sense of law to make it congruent with their ethical needs in this pursuit. European Jewish emancipation commenced in the eighteenth century, and as it progressed in the nineteenth century, Jews also experienced the "victory of the civil-capitalistic culture" that afforded increasing opportunities to amass private wealth. At this point, another transformation occurred. European Reform Judaism shaped law to become a much-needed spiritual and ethical anchor that served as a counterpoint to marketplace culture; law was also invoked as a source of an increasingly endangered social cohesion. For Fromm, however, Hasidism represented the ideal adherence to law broadly construed.[21]

Of the three Diaspora communities, Hasidism afforded the ideal "social cement" to bind together the essentials of Jewish tradition. Fromm was taken by the Hasidism because they emphasized feeling over erudition and contemplation over economic activity. Indeed, they promoted an inner sense of wholeness, integrity, joy, and sincerity that resisted the amassing of wealth. In the next few years and informed by Marx, Fromm would characterize this as a sense of "being" over "having," and for the rest of his life, the joyous and celebratory spirit stressed in Hasidism would dispose him to lead a life of exuberance and the pursuit of joy, even in the face of totalitarianism, bureaucratization, and threats of nuclear war. To be sure, the Orthodox Jewish community where Fromm grew up in Frankfurt looked down on the Hasidim as undisciplined and erratic. Perhaps because of his mother's Eastern roots, Fromm admired the "extravagant" qualities inherent in the Hasidic experience—reverent, joyous, and full of gratitude for the "good life." In addition, Salman Baruch Rabinkow, a Talmudic scholar whom Fromm met in 1912, was now helping him with his dissertation. Rabinkow reinforced this disposition toward Hasidism. Through Hasidism and its tie to Jewish law, Fromm stated in his dissertation, "the Jewish historical body had really preserved its own life so well" and became "the full issue of the cultural and social cosmos of Judaism."[22]

Fromm's dissertation was a remarkable essay in social psychology. With its focus on Jewish law most richly exemplified by the Hasidic tradition, he was seeking out a conceptual unit connecting the morality of the individual "soul" and especially the collective "soul" with larger social processes. Fromm was trying to determine how to integrate morality (both individual and group) with the collective lifestyle. Within a decade, as he became thoroughly grounded in Freud on the unconscious and Marx on economic and class structures, he would equate this soul with the "libido structure or organization of social entities" before settling on his signature term: social character.

Weber was impressed with Fromm's work. In contrast, Naphtali appeared in Heidelberg the day of Erich's defense of his dissertation before a faculty committee. He feared that Erich would not pass the defense and would subsequently commit suicide. Fromm was awarded the second-best grade ("very good") after defending the dissertation, and he realized that Naphtali had simply "transferred his strong inferiority feeling about himself" to his son. He was learning to distance himself from his father's neuroses. Not privy to this familial baggage, Weber suggested proudly that Fromm might want to pursue an academic career. But Fromm felt "that such a career would restrain me," given his emerging interests. He had little sense that a university base could position him in the decades ahead to research and write in a community of scholars with specialties and library resources.[23]

In addition to his feeling that academia would restrain him, Fromm's decision not to remain in the university was attributable to Salman Rabinkow's influence. A devout socialist from Russia, where he had studied at a yeshiva as an adherent of Habad Hasidism and been ordained as a rabbi (but never practiced), Rabinkow had been a tutor to Jizchok Steinberg, an activist in both the 1905 and 1917 Russian revolutions. He sympathized with Steinberg's revolutionary Marxist socialism, and he actively raised funds for poor Jewish students from Eastern Europe.[24]

Fromm visited Rabinkow's austere apartment almost daily, sometimes finding others that Rabinkow mentored there. He instructed Fromm in the Talmud through the Lithuanian emphasis on the deeper psychological and spiritual truths inherent within its unifying themes (in contrast to the Hungarian approach, involving the formal mastery of specific Talmudic texts and the delineation of the internal contradictions within that text). With Rabinkow, Fromm also studied the philosophical writings of Moses Maimonides, the great medieval philosopher and Torah scholar, and the *Tanya*, a central text of Habad Hasidism written in the early nineteenth century. Fromm became expert in the *Likutej Amarim*—the collected sayings of Schneur Zalman, the eighteenth-century founder of Habad Hasidism. Guided by Rabinkow, Fromm learned that Habad Hasidism was a populist reaction against the legalism and rationalism of the rabbinic orthodoxy.[25]

Rabinkow had a knack for synthesizing Marxism and socialist protest politics with traditional Jewish pietism. It is likely that Rabinkow introduced Marx to Fromm. He taught Fromm to interpret Jewish tradition in the spirit of "radical humanism" (the individual and his society cultivating their full revolutionary potential) even as he himself remained a scholar and politically inactive. Fromm also regarded himself unfit for political activism during his student days. Soon, however, Rabinkow's notion of radical humanism would become the basis for Fromm's notion of a productive social character and would spark his interest in psychoanalytically informed Marxism. Fromm identified himself not only intellectually with Rabinkow but held him up as an ego ideal; Rabinkow displayed most of the qualities Erich hoped to find in himself.[26]

The degree to which Fromm patterned his life on the teacher "who influenced my life more than any other man" is striking. Rabinkow impressed on Fromm the idea that professional or political positions, wealth, and power were not a valuable measure of man but rather his endearing qualities and the depth of his thought. Rabinkow seemed to subsist on herring and tea. Creature comforts were secondary. If Fromm's own diet during his student days was not as sparse, he professed to place little stock in consumption. Fromm remembered how fastidious Rabinkow was in his hygiene and general appearance and emulated him. An early riser, Rabinkow disciplined himself to put in long days of study. For the rest of his life, Fromm devoted the early morning hours to sustained reading and writing. When he was not studying, Rabinkow welcomed students to join him in warm and open-ended discussions, offering questions but rarely answers and seldom charging even minimal tutorial fees. Fromm particularly enjoyed singing Hasidic songs with Rabinkow and would sing or hum them for the rest of his life. He noted that Rabinkow had "an inexhaustible sense of humor" that seemed to be rooted in the commonalities of Jewish life; this became one of Fromm's most marked personal characteristics. Stressing the universalistic humanism of Hebrew Bible prophets, Rabinkow (like Hermann Cohen before him) made it clear to Fromm that wisdom did not lie in loyalty even to a Jewish state. Though he started as an ardent Zionist, Rabinkow was reexamining Zionist premises at the time he met Fromm. By 1923, Fromm also revised his views on the subject and became a lifelong critic of Zionism and nationalism generally.[27]

As much as he sought to emulate Rabinkow, Fromm departed from him in two essentials. First, Fromm was less reclusive and more attentive to his place in society. He agreed with Rabinkow that rank and title were less important than a life-loving and caring personality and intellectual profundity. He admired Rabinkow's humility, diffidence, and devotion to his Yiddish roots over the assimilatory tendencies of middle-class and university-educated German Jews. Yet Fromm was also keenly ambitious. He determined to distinguish himself within the Heidelberg and Frankfurt professional and academic communities and in prominent Jewish intellectual circles.

Second, Fromm connected Rabinkow's diffidence and reclusive existence to writer's block and saw it as a tragedy. Fromm felt Rabinkow was rarely able to transform his enormous store of knowledge into text for the sake of posterity, which kept him from being recognized as the great man that he was. By the time he completed his dissertation, Fromm knew he did not share Rabinkow's literary shortcoming. Writing was easy for him.

Over the course of his life, Rabinkow published only one article, "The Individual and Society in Jewish Life and Lore" (1929). His style was awkward, the essay was poorly organized and often redundant, and the content was sometimes less than clear. During the years he was meeting with Fromm, Rabinkow had been struggling with this essay, which was intended to systematize the basic philosophic, historical, and theological perspectives he presented to his students. The parallels between this essay and Fromm's 1922 dissertation on Jewish law are striking. They show how profoundly Rabinkow influenced Fromm. And by comparing the dissertation to the article, it seems likely that in return Fromm's chapter drafts helped Rabinkow find the proper words and phrases, even its organizational framework, so that he could complete his only publication.[28]

In the article, Rabinkow explained that the organizing principle in Jewish life and the core of Jewish law was the covenant with God. That covenant determined "the ethical maximum" of the community as well as its cultural and religious life and became the basis for its political institutions. "From the living covenant with God," Rabinkow postulated that there "grew not immovable formulations but cultural tasks in continued change," as conditions in the community required. Similar to Fromm's dissertation, Rabinkow's article argued that Jewish law and ethics adapted to evolving human needs. Whereas the dissertation (perhaps reflecting Weber's emphasis on social structure and collective life) merged the needs of the individual soul with the soul of the community, Rabinkow elevated the individual: "the moral autonomy of the individual is basic." Indeed, "everyone is entitled and obliged to say: 'The world has been created for me.'" While the dignity of the individual derived from the community, Rabinkow insisted, far more forcefully than Fromm, that the perfection of the community required the complete autonomy of every person. Religious and ethical duties could only be performed properly and life's joys fully experienced through the "autonomous individual." Finally, Rabinkow argued that the ethical-legal core of Jewish life, while based on a covenant with God, was valid in the "special community of Judaism" but did not apply to other groups. In his dissertation, Fromm differed. He presented his discussion of Jewish law and ethics as an illustration of universal human needs and experiences.[29]

When Fromm's commitment to Judaism began to ebb during the mid- and late 1920s, he moved beyond the limits set by Rabinkow. That is, he applied Rabinkow's vision of Jewish life to humanity at large but focused more on the needs of the individual. For Fromm, as he ceased to be an observant Jew, humanity became a unified moral community rooted in individuals with moral autonomy and the freedom to fulfill individual needs for productiveness and happiness within a humane society. Rabinkow voiced no disappointment at Fromm's drift from Judaism. Indeed, he understood that when Fromm spoke of a life-affirming human character structure, the young man was very close to his own Jewish humanism: "the world has been created for me." Writing in 1964, Fromm asserted that "Rabinkow influenced my life more than any other man perhaps, and . . . his ideas . . . remained alive in me."[30]

Frieda Reichmann

While studying in Heidelberg, Fromm sparked amorous interest in several young women. He became engaged to a Königsberg woman, Golde Ginsburg, until his friend Leo Löwenthal won her heart and married her. Ginsburg was a close friend of Frieda Reichmann, who was almost eleven years Fromm's senior and whose adopted daughter was also attracted to Fromm.[31]

Reichmann was born in Karlsruhe to a middle-class Orthodox Jewish household with politically progressive values. The oldest of three daughters, her mother was trained as a teacher but never labored outside the household, in which she was domineering and possessive. Reichmann's mother had no respect for her husband, who, like Naphtali, had failed to train as a rabbi and instead became a leader of the local Jewish community with a rather lackluster business career in banking. When he suggested, against her mother's objections, that she might pursue medicine, Frieda was intrigued by the idea and commenced her medical studies at the University of Königsberg when she was only seventeen. She chose a psychiatric specialty and spent a semester in Munich studying with Emil Kraepelin, a professor of clinical psychology. Graduating from Königsberg's medical school in 1912, she published her dissertation on pupillary changes in schizophrenics. At this point, Reichmann had spent several years in both Königsberg and Frankfurt working in the psychiatrist Kurt Goldstein's pioneering clinics for the treatment of brain-injured soldiers. Just as the war affected Fromm, World War I had a transformational effect on Reichmann, as she witnessed the effects of combat quite vividly in her patients. She treated brain-injured soldiers at the university hospital in Königsberg and coauthored papers on neurotraumatology with Goldstein based on her clinical observations. Reichmann first met Fromm in Frankfurt toward the end of the war, but both were exceedingly shy, and nothing initially came of the acquaintance. From Frankfurt she went to Dresden, where she became an assistant physician-psychiatrist at the Weisser Hirsch Sanatorium from 1920 to 1923. There she determined to become a psychotherapist. At the time, Weisser Hirsch was the only facility in Germany with a structured psychotherapy program. When Fromm visited her there, the relationship became more serious.[32]

At some point during her medical studies, Reichmann had been brutally raped, which dimmed her marriage prospects and possibly her childbearing interests or capabilities. During her last two years at Weisser Hirsch, doubtless sparked by the rape, a growing interest in psychoanalysis, and perhaps Fromm's visits, Reichmann traveled regularly to Munich. She had arranged to be analyzed by Wilhelm Wittenberg, a convivial fellow and a less-than-orthodox Freudian. Wittenberg belonged to the German Psychoanalytic Society. He did not make much of an impression on Reichmann. She then had a training analysis with Hanns Sachs, a member of Freud's inner circle, in Berlin and became a practicing psychoanalyst as well as a psychiatrist. All the while, the attraction between Frieda and Erich grew stronger. An important commonality was that both were strict practitioners of Orthodoxy and were apprehensive that German Jews generally were assimilating too rapidly and losing their unique identity.

Reichmann appreciated Fromm's interest in grand theory and his passionate engagement in broad questions about human existence, even if he did not seem terribly talented in navigating life's day-to-day requirements. Fromm was taken by her excitement over intellectual topics and by her more practical side, sensing that like his mother, Reichmann might take care of him. She began a therapeutic analysis of Fromm, which, as Reichmann acknowledged, was probably professionally inappropriate: "and then we fell in love, so we stopped. That much sense we had." A sexual relationship ensued—probably Reichmann's first intimate contact with a man since the rape. This may or may not have been Fromm's first sexual encounter, but it is clear that Reichmann's proficient biographer Gail Hornstein was off the mark in characterizing him as a "ladies' man" at this precise point in time.[33]

In 1923, Reichmann and Fromm decided to open a therapeutic facility (a therapeuticum) for Jewish patients in Heidelberg. Their mission was utopian: to create what, years later, would be called a therapeutic community. Reichmann based the idea on the sense that psychotherapy was *tzedakah*, a Jewish religious commitment to social justice. The goal was to nurture simultaneously Jewish identity and psychic health along quasi-socialist lines. As Reichmann put it, "we first analyze the people and second make them aware of their tradition and live in this tradition." In the midst of horrendous German inflation, she managed to borrow twenty-five thousand marks from friends and family to purchase a large house and furnish it properly. The facility integrated the basics of Jewish life—celebration of the Sabbath and other holidays and rituals, kosher food, a steady diet of traditional Jewish literature, common prayers, and Fromm's lectures on theology. Ten to fifteen patients lived in the house and paid what they could afford or donated their labor in exchange. Others came for scheduled meals and treatment, also based on what they could afford. Like several other analysts with socialist allegiances in Germany and Vienna, they "didn't want to go on only treating wealthy people." Each patient received psychoanalysis or psychoanalytically informed therapy. Initially, Reichmann was the sole therapist, but as his psychoanalytic training advanced, Fromm joined her. Both were friends with Martin Buber, and, as did Buber, they conceived of therapy as a close interpersonal "I-Thou" relationship as well as a method to alleviate deep psychic repression. Less than informed about transference problems (i.e., the interpersonal perils involved in projecting imagined persona onto a "neutral" clinician), they undertook analyses of friends such as Leo Löwenthal, Ernst Simon, Rabinkow, and even household staff. In the evening, they conducted an early form of group therapy—open-ended community discussions of personal conflict. "It was a wild affair" of enthusiasm and good cheer, Reichmann recalled, going on while "Erich and [she] had an affair. [They] weren't married and nobody was supposed to know about that."[34]

As this therapeutic community developed, Reichmann and Fromm grew closer, even as she continued to regard him as "spoiled." Middle-class sexual propriety and the presumption within Orthodox Judaism that a woman like Frieda, who at thirty-six was well into middle age, should marry was relevant to their decision. She had to prod the twenty-six-year-old Erich, however, to agree to a firm wedding date: his parents' wedding anniversary, in June 1926. "I got what I wanted," Reichmann recalled, "a very intelligent, very warm, very well-educated man who knew lots of things in another field from mine." She made little of the age gap between them, perhaps because she felt that her rape had seriously reduced her marriage prospects. The wedding was held at her mother's house, and Reichmann recalled almost missing it because she had tonsillitis. At the conclusion of the ceremony, Naphtali felt relieved, telling Reichmann, "Now, you can take care of him." He knew that she would attend to Erich's domestic needs and perhaps his parental needs as well. As she later wrote, Naphtali was "so glad because I could take care so well of his only son and by golly wasn't he right!"[35]

Even before the marriage, Fromm moved to Munich in 1925 to complete an analysis with Wilhelm Wittenberg and to attend Emil Kraepelin's lectures, much as Reichmann had done earlier. From Kraepelin, he learned elements of what came to be called psychopharmacology, and this put him in good stead as he advised colleagues and patients concerning their medications. Kraepelin also increased his interest in the neurosciences generally, and that interest never flagged. Fromm's analysis with Wittenberg turned out to be less eventful. Although Fromm found him a great conversationalist, he considered Wittenberg an ineffective psychoanalyst. That said, Wittenberg died within a year of the analysis. Reichmann paid Fromm's expenses of six hundred marks a month.

By then it was clear to both of them that their newly launched therapeuticum was failing for two reasons: First, the utopian therapeutic goal had not been reached. Many of the patients craved the kosher food and Jewish social life but dismissed the efficacy of psychoanalysis within a therapeutic community and were reticent to pursue it. This was especially true of the rabbis and rabbinical students. And second, as their analytic training deepened, Fromm and Reichmann found that their commitment to Orthodoxy and its rituals had slackened. As she noted, "After four years, we decided we couldn't keep the sanatorium any longer because our conscience and hearts were no longer in it." One Passover, they went into a park and ate leavened bread—a grave sin professedly resulting in *korvat*, childlessness. But they "were a little surprised that nothing happened actually," Reichmann recalled, and they proceeded to eat food that was especially forbidden, including ham, lobster, and oysters. This break from Orthodox dietary laws was a first step for Fromm in living a life, if not wholly of material extravagance, then certainly wary of social norms. Although the deliberate dietary departures were kept secret from patients and staff at the therapeuticum, they both essentially publicized their break from Orthodoxy in articles published in the psychoanalytic journal *Imago* in 1927. The contents of the articles became common gossip among their patients. The therapeuticum was at an end, and so were Fromm's plans for becoming a Talmudic scholar. Once more he seemed to be on uncertain footing, and so did she.[36]

A certain sadness or lack of zest began to appear in the marriage as they wound down the work of the therapeuticum; the initial spontaneity and rebellious experimentalism in the relationship was ebbing along with the dissolution of their joint venture. The substantial age disparity probably contributed to this malaise. By now Frieda was having a number of affairs, one of which may well have been with Rabinkow. Erich took an interest in other women, especially Karen Horney. But although affairs and flirtations were not uncommon in European psychoanalytic circles in the 1920s, there was something deeper at work. The marriage was childless—*korvat*. Although Erich sometimes told others that Frieda could have no children, the evidence indicates otherwise. Nearing menopause, Frieda craved a child and confessed as much to Erich early in their marriage. He responded mockingly, betraying a certain arrogance and insensitivity: "Having a child is nothing; even a cow can do it." Erich also felt that the presence of children would reduce his professional productivity while increasing pressure on him to adapt to prevailing social values, a not uncommon perspective in Weimar intellectual and cultural circles. Memories of his own unhappy and troubled childhood may also have contributed to his unwillingness to father a child. In mid-July 1932, Frieda had a surgical procedure in a Basel hospital. Two days later, her doctor brought her the body of what appeared to be a stillborn child. It had a large head, torso, and limbs and looked like a dead fetus. However, in her correspondence with Georg Groddeck, Frieda claimed that it was not a dead fetus but a myoma (a benign tumor) that looked like a developed fetus. In that event, she had not been pregnant, whether by Erich or another man. A third possibility is that there was both a fetus and a tumor, and that the tumor undermined the viability of the fetus, resulting in a stillbirth. Whatever occurred, it contributed to an already deeply strained marriage. Rainer Funk, Fromm's research assistant, once asked Fromm late in his life if he regretted having no children—by Frieda or by his subsequent wives. For the only time Funk can recall, Fromm's face showed deep emotional pain, and he was unable to reply. The issue resonated deeply through much of his life. There would be no successor generation.[37]

As their marriage became increasingly difficult, Frieda urged Erich to accompany her on her visits to Groddeck for potential assistance. Born in 1866, Groddeck was a psychoanalyst and directed the Marienhohe Sanitarium near the spas of Baden Baden. He administered therapeutic massage as a part of analytic therapy, and Freud was supportive of his insights. Indeed, Freud delighted in his irreverent 1921 novel, *Der Seelensucher* (*The Soul Seeker*) about a retired bachelor who went mad and then became capable of extraordinary psychological interpretations of special human situations, sometimes explaining his perspectives with very humorous if embarrassing sex-charged observations. Groddeck's more substantial *The Book of It* (1923) laid out his essential thoughts through a series of letters. His concept of the "it" (*das Es*) overlapped with Freud's concept of the id, which Freud openly acknowledged. However, Groddeck was more intent than Freud on preserving a unity between psyche and soma. His "it" drew heavily from German romantic tradition and stood for the unconscious, broadly construed, as well as for the ego—the totality of human potentiality (organic and spiritual). In contrast, in *The Ego and the Id* (1923), Freud differentiated between ego, id, and superego as separate forces in forging his structural theory. In brief, for Groddeck, the "it" symbolized the inner wish to become sick and to become well. This "it" manifested itself in specific illnesses, and the psychoanalyst responded to the illness by assuming a maternal kindness and concern that enjoined the patient to fathom the underlying repressed sources of the malady through a childlike trust and innocence. The "it," which had brought on the physical illness, would thereby be undermined and disappear. Groddeck had thus fashioned an early psychosomatic perspective. With Groddeck's help, for example, the Berlin psychoanalyst Ernst Simmel, who could only see with glasses, was suddenly able to read a very distant clock without them. But when Simmel returned to his old lifestyle habits in Berlin, his improved distance vision ceased.[38]

It was Groddeck's therapeutic and personal manner—warm, open, humble, and direct—that impressed Sandor Ferenczi, Karen Horney, and other less-than-orthodox psychoanalysts who came to Baden Baden. Their visits often coincided with Erich's and Frieda's, which gave the couple a sense of joining a Groddeck-led psychoanalytic community of sorts just as their therapeuticum collapsed. While the evidence is inconclusive, there is a good possibility that Fromm met Freud at one of these convivial gatherings in Baden Baden, and if he did, the conversation almost certainly involved Freud's "science of the psyche." After a few such trips with Frieda, Erich became captivated by Groddeck's very presence, despite the man's contempt for rigorous science and his reactionary positions on social issues. Given Groddeck's theoretical flexibility, his nonjudgmental sincerity, his appreciation of matriarchy, and his remarkable psychological intuitions, Erich felt freer to ponder his emerging reservations mixed with affirmations concerning orthodox Freudianism. With Groddeck and his circle, he felt that he could speak openly and independently and express growing skepticism about Freud's mechanistic theory of libido, the universality of the Oedipus complex, and Freud's strong patriarchic premises, even as he never entirely dismissed any of them. Without Groddeck's psychosomatic emphasis, Erich would not have given his first public lecture on "The Healing of a Case of Lung Tuberculosis During Psychoanalytical Treatment." With Erich and Frieda feeling increasingly comfortable in the Groddeck circle, they found that they could better articulate the strengths and weaknesses of their precipitous marriage and whether it was meant to be.[39]

Groddeck was no intellectual, Fromm concluded, but he had an engaging personality, a quality in people that always attracted Fromm. Now in training to become a psychoanalyst, he needed an instructor with a therapeutic personality who integrated the life of the mind with other personal qualities. Fromm could have found no better clinician to emulate than Groddeck—a consummate therapist and kindly human being who made the patient's inner subjective world his own and learned from the patient.

The nature of the interpersonal relationship between clinician and patient was the key. Groddeck taught Fromm to feel the patient's emotions within himself and to work through the patient's problems until the outward symptoms of the inner emotional illness subsided. As such, the clinician was to discover the unfolding of the totality of the patient's qualities, what Fromm would later call the "total man." Of all the German psychoanalysts that Fromm encountered, he concluded that Groddeck was the least comfortable with clinical abstractions or theory and the first in "truth, originality, courage, and extraordinary kindness. He penetrated the unconscious of his patient, and yet he never hurt." Indeed, it was largely Groddeck's presence and skill, Fromm recalled, that drew him and Reichmann into a study group of southwestern German psychoanalysts, which established the Frankfurt Psychoanalytic Institute in 1929.[40]

The couple likely joined the Southwest German Psychoanalytic Study Group in Frankfurt in 1927. The Vienna-trained psychoanalyst Heinrich Meng, a staunch socialist with a psychosomatic approach and a desire to present psychoanalytic ideas to the public in an accessible form, had elicited Groddeck's help in establishing the group. Also trained in Vienna and specializing in the treatment of narcissistic disorders and the way inhibitions of the ego contoured feeling and thinking, Karl Landauer soon became a central presence in the group as well. Erich and Frieda participated in the group, and Erich had some therapeutic contact (and perhaps some supervision) with Landauer in Frankfurt, even though Wittenberg analyzed him in Munich.[41]

With the demise of the therapeuticum in 1927–1928 and with Erich requiring additional psychoanalytic training unavailable in southwestern Germany, the couple moved to Berlin. There Frieda set up a private psychoanalytic practice and continued as the principal breadwinner, while Erich continued to be the less-than-practical student.

At the Berlin Psychoanalytic Institute, Erich took his training analysis with Hanns Sachs, of Freud's inner circle, as well as with Theodor Reik. Fromm regarded Sachs as unquestioningly loyal to Freud—an accurate appraisal. Indeed, Sachs was the least controversial and inquisitive of Freud's closest colleagues, echoing Freud's positions on all but his one interest outside the clinical setting: the psychoanalytic interpretation of art. Sachs insisted that Fromm had experienced a "positive transference" toward him because he always hung his coat beside Sachs's in a little vestibule before each session. Fromm considered this utter nonsense. Reik shared Fromm's interest in the psychology of religion and had a more active and exploratory mind than Sachs, but he, too, seemed excessively orthodox to the rather arrogant young Fromm.

While still unsteady in his temperament and disappointed with his training analysts, Fromm nonetheless seemed to thrive in Berlin's psychoanalytic climate, which was more innovative than Vienna's. Indeed, it was not uncommon for senior analysts to sit in cafes with their candidates until the early morning hours discussing not only Freud but also philosophy, politics, and art. The richness of Weimar culture was on conspicuous display in Berlin. Fromm met Otto Fenichel, who had begun his Kinderseminar for young left-leaning analysts, working on Marxist-Freudian theoretical integrations as well as progressive social and economic reforms. Karen Horney, whom Fromm had first met in Baden Baden, was a founder and central figure at the Berlin Institute and was already building her case against the Freudian premises on women. Erich found her interesting and exciting. The creative and eclectic Marxist-Freudian Wilhelm Reich expanded Erich's interest in character patterns and in the ways social and political conditions affected analytic therapy. As a Freudian with reservations often mixed haphazardly with confirmations about orthodox psychoanalytic theory, Erich found that he was also evolving into a Marxist. Indeed, he offered a lecture in 1928 on "The Psychoanalysis of the Petty Bourgeoisie." At this early date, he already suspected some dangerous authoritarian proclivities in the German lower middle class, and he would soon transform his interests into an active research project.[42]

By 1929, Fromm had completed his training analysis and started a psychoanalytic practice in Berlin. It is more appropriate, however, to regard him at this point as a social psychologist who was beginning to focus on the concept of a social unconscious—the underlying drives that bind people together and promote a sense of collectivity. Having been credentialed in both disciplines, he offered a paper to the Frankfurt psychoanalytic community in 1929 on "Psychoanalysis and Sociology." The thrust of the paper was to encourage analysts to avoid giving psychoanalytic answers to questions that could be sufficiently dealt with through economic, political, or sociological explanations. But Fromm also urged sociologists and other social scientists to recognize that "society" was an abstraction and that the underlying unit was the specific individual. Ultimately, both the psychoanalytic and the social scientific communities had to recognize the socialized human being as the central concern, both a product of society and a unique personage.[43]

That same year, the Southwest German Psychoanalytic Study Group transformed into the Frankfurt Psychoanalytic Institute, and Fromm was regarded as one of its founders. The group shared a building with the Marxist-oriented Institute for Social Research, of which Max Horkheimer was the director. Karl Landauer conducted an analysis of Horkheimer, which stimulated Horkheimer's interest in bringing psychoanalytic perspectives into Institute deliberations. Landauer suggested the very ambitious Fromm for this task. Consequently, in addition to his psychoanalytic practice in Berlin and his work in the Berlin and Frankfurt psychoanalytic institutes, Fromm was invited to be a visitor and part-time investigator at the Institute for Social Research during its formative years. His unsteady career was taking another turn, and he entered the life of a research scholar.

A turning point was also occurring in his marriage to Frieda. In 1931, Erich fell ill with tuberculosis, moved out of his home, and sought treatment in Davos, Switzerland. Groddeck explained to the couple that the illness was a psychosomatic compromise of sorts—Erich's way of denying the fact that it was best for him to separate from Frieda. The tuberculosis was symptomatic of their very troubled relationship. Although Frieda visited him during his convalescence, and they wrote frequent letters, they never again lived under one roof. Erich had to learn to cook and clean on his own and to support himself with a small psychoanalytic practice. With neither his mother nor Frieda attending to his practical needs, he felt that he was finally ready to assume significant personal autonomy—until he came under the wings of another woman much his senior, Karen Horney.[44]

2

Frankfurt Scholar

By 1929, Erich Fromm's experiment with the therapeuticum had ended, his marriage to Frieda was deeply troubled, and his analysis with Hanns Sachs seemed to be going nowhere. Generally dejected, Fromm arrived at the Frankfurt Institute of Social Research, a group of eclectic but skeptical Marxist scholars, many of whom doubled as social critics and tended to be philosophical in their approach. At the Institute, Fromm became reacquainted with Leo Löwenthal, his childhood friend, and he enjoyed working with Max Horkheimer, the central intellectual presence.

Within a few years, Fromm came to regard his calling not so much as a sociologist, a social psychologist, or a psychoanalyst but as a social critic—what we have since come to call a public intellectual. Like most colleagues at the Frankfurt Institute, he looked askance at the rigid, dogmatic characterization of Marx's writings—the "official" interpretation promoted in the Soviet Union and Eastern Europe. The preference of those at the Institute was the more flexible and psychologically sensitive interpretation of Marx that was evident in much of Western Europe and parts of Germany. Fromm linked psychoanalysis to Marxism and began to move the topic toward what became his trademark concept of social character. He also headed a major Institute survey research project on the surprisingly authoritarian propensities of a number of German workers, conducted as the German Right was enhancing its power base. By the mid-1930s, Fromm had come to articulate the theoretical contours of *Escape from Freedom* (1941), his most enduring work of social criticism.

Fromm continued to suffer from tuberculosis, which depleted his energy and sent him searching for ocean breezes and invigorating climates quite distant from the offices and responsibilities of the Frankfurt Institute. Predictably, his influence there became increasingly marginal over the course of the 1930s. An intellectual émigré from the Nazi social experiment, Fromm, like many other Institute scholars and social critics, would find refuge at Columbia University and the neighborhoods of New York City around Morningside Heights. Unlike his colleagues, however, he was hardly reclusive. Indeed, he delighted in the diverse aspects of American culture and popular customs, especially in New York City.

The Frankfurt Institute: A Circle of Skeptics

The Frankfurt Institute came into being in 1923 through an endowment from a prosperous, German-born grain merchant in Argentina who wanted to support the intellectual endeavors of his son, Felix Weil. The Institute's first active director, Carl Grünberg, was close to members of the German Communist Party and accepted their Soviet-centered, mechanistic, Marxist-Leninist perspectives. Grünberg and his colleagues focused their investigations on the German labor movement. According to Marx's "scientific" laws of historical development, German workers should have displayed considerably more revolutionary fervor than they actually did in the face of the country's defeat in World War I and the massive inflation that followed. According to Max Horkheimer and other young members of the Institute, something was lacking in Grünberg's mechanistic-deterministic reading of Marx, which highlighted impersonal economic forces and deemphasized subjective individuality.

Horkheimer and his colleagues, on the other hand, were attracted to a new "Marxist humanism," elaborated by Georg Lukács and Karl Korsch during the early 1920s, that emphasized the element of consciousness in the dialectic process and the role of working-class alienation from labor in explaining the dearth of revolutionary fervor. Rejecting a monistic materialism focused on the economic substructure of a society, younger members of the Institute turned toward an interdisciplinary Marxism. Their version concerned itself with a broader social, psychological, and cultural totality. When Grünberg had a stroke in 1927, Friedrich Pollock, a member of this younger circle, became interim director until 1930, when Horkheimer, who was much more attuned to Marxist humanism, became the Institute's long-term head.[1]

The rediscovery of Marx's *Economic and Philosophic Manuscripts* (i.e., the *Paris Manuscripts*) in the late 1920s was exceedingly important to Horkheimer and many of his colleagues at the Institute. In the manuscripts, a younger and more flexible Marx addressed the topic of worker alienation and suggested the importance of social psychology. Because exploitation was antithetical to man's natural needs, it could produce a revolutionary sense of class consciousness, Marx had noted. But exploitation could also yield to worker disenchantment and resignation, Marx warned, by creating an excessive gap between the human potential for growth and happiness on the one hand and increasingly constrictive conditions on the other. For Horkheimer, this "new" and more flexible and "humanistic" Marx was consistent with the revisionist directions of Lukács and Korsch. The individual consciousness and need for gratification would not be explained away by "structures" or external "forces." Horkheimer found this slant particularly appealing, as he had become quite interested in Freud and psychoanalysis over the course of his personal analysis with Karl Landauer. With personal analytic experience and a deepening interest in human subjectivity, Horkheimer hoped to bring Freudian insights to bear on Marx. With a fusion of the ideas of these two German Jewish intellectual giants in mind, Horkheimer searched for someone who might lead the Institute in this direction.[2]

At this point, Landauer told Horkheimer about Erich Fromm, a founding member of his Southwest German Study Group and the Frankfurt Psychoanalytic Institute. Fromm was then completing his psychoanalytic training in Berlin. According to Landauer, the young man might be an appropriate colleague to help introduce psychoanalysis and, more generally, research on social psychology to Horkheimer and his colleagues. After all, as Landauer explained to Horkheimer, Fromm understood Freud's "modernist" agenda and its call for a freer flow of instinctual life in the face of social constraints. But Fromm was also heavily disposed toward viewing the individual in a social context. In 1929, Leo Löwenthal introduced Fromm to Horkheimer, who was familiar with "Psychoanalysis and Sociology," a paper Fromm had delivered to the Frankfurt Psychoanalytic Institute at its opening meeting and that had been published in its journal. In the essay, Fromm had followed the lead of Wilhelm Reich and Siegfried Bernfeld by proposing a unified social theory that accommodated Freud's structures of psychosexual development and Marx's sociological concern with economic and technological developments shaping the individual. Fromm's very preliminary take on Marx and Freud was that both men recognized that Marx's emphasis on social-economic conditions and

Freud's focus on the inner psyche had to be fused. Effective fusion would require modifying both rigidly materialistic Marxism (with its diminishment of the individual) and the rigid Freudian focus on the archaic psychic inheritance of the individual (devoid of the collective social context). In the end, Fromm argued that collective social attitudes, aesthetic sensibilities, cognitive styles, and the psychic needs of individual actors all had to be considered simultaneously if there was to be a common theoretical and empirical concern. Although Fromm might have found Marx's *Paris Manuscripts* helpful in making this argument for holism, he did not make systematic use of them until the early 1960s.[3]

In exploratory negotiations, Horkheimer invited Fromm to join in some of the Institute's gatherings and offered to pay his travel expenses from Berlin to Frankfurt. As Fromm participated in Institute discussions, Horkheimer came to appreciate Fromm's interpretation of Marxist humanism, especially when Fromm underscored the importance of transforming social relations so that a person's latent sociability and full productive powers might gain expression. As the first major research project under his directorship, Horkheimer proposed a comprehensive study that involved systematic survey research of the attitudes of the German working class. He suspected that with Fromm's doctoral training in sociology, he might help to launch the endeavor. If this transpired, and if Fromm helped introduce psychoanalytic and therapeutic perspectives to the Institute's colleagues, Horkheimer intended to place him on a regular salary as a full-time member. For his part, Fromm was impressed by Horkheimer's captivating personality and his wide-ranging interdisciplinary interests. As Fromm did not seek a full-time academic professorship and was not interested in making his living entirely as a practicing psychoanalyst, Fromm found employment at the Institute for Social Research useful for economic security. His work introduced him to an intellectual support network not unlike those he had enjoyed as a student. It did not preclude a modest private psychoanalytic practice. In fact, he was thrilled at the prospect of working for the Institute and sensed that he had found his proper calling as a social researcher and critic as well as a psychoanalyst. Here was his opportunity for financial security, which would free him to develop his own unique perspectives on social psychology. To be sure, he would participate in the Institute's cooperative projects. But Fromm also assumed from the start that he would shape his own theories distinct from those of the group.[4]

Early Writings

At the Institute, Fromm discovered that he could write with ease and facility. He launched the Institute's massive social science survey of German working-class attitudes and the underlying psychological dispositions. As well, he wrote a substantial number of articles that Horkheimer, Pollock, and other Institute colleagues found extraordinarily important in their effort to develop a quasi-Marxist Critical Theory that exposed the contradictions of capitalist society and accessed the potential for a humanistic, socialist alternative. Exploratory in tone and occasionally housing contradictions, the articles seemed to be Fromm's way of fusing Marx and Freud by gradually modifying both. Through this fusion, Fromm moved increasingly close to what would soon become his most important theoretical construct: the concept of social character. As this concept slowly solidified in his mind, it in turn brought greater coherence and meaning to the German workers survey project. This new concept also helped Fromm establish his own distinctive place among a number of formidable and pioneering Freudian Marxists—left-wing activist psychoanalysts such as Wilhelm Reich, Paul Federn, Siegfried Bernfeld, and Otto Fenichel, who made Freud uneasy with their psychoanalytic revisionism and likewise distressed orthodox Soviet-oriented Marxists by their openness to the "subjective factor" in the human condition. Fromm had met all of them over the course of his psychoanalytic training and regarded them as his intellectual superiors. But as his articles followed one another in rapid succession and his concept of social character began to cohere, Fromm felt increasingly confident of his own unique fusion of Freud and Marx.

The clearest indication that Fromm was aiming to promote a common ground of his own between Marx and Freud was the article "The Dogma of Christ," published in 1930, which he had worked on for almost a year. Theodore Reik, one of Fromm's teachers at the Berlin Psychoanalytic Institute, had published a fairly orthodox Freudian account of how the dogma of the crucified son of God was rooted in the Oedipal hatred of a son for his father. While giving Reik's perspective some credence, Fromm focused on the social and economic conditions of the first generations of Christian believers, the poor and downtrodden who initially invoked the dogma of the suffering Jesus to reveal their hatred of their rulers and of paternal authority (God the father). For Fromm, the Oedipal drama was undergirded by the material deprivation of the lower classes. These early Christians pursued a community that would enhance the social and economic well-being of the masses by turning Jesus into a revolutionary God of justice whose vision would be made manifest on Judgment Day. Gradually, however, Fromm noted that the educated and well-to-do began to infiltrate Christian communities and change the dogma, curbing the demand of the masses for social change. For the affluent, a new day of justice (Judgment Day) ceased to be close at hand, the appearance of Jesus became a miracle that had already occurred, and, consequently, society's social structures no longer had to change. Fromm argued that the idea of salvation had become transformed into a spiritual belief guaranteed by faith in Jesus. In sum: "The change in the economic situation and in the social composition of the Christian community altered the psychic attitude of the believers." Owing to ruling-class hegemony within Christianity, the downtrodden lost hope. There was no longer a possibility for the dogma of Christ to be invoked for the purpose of class warfare and social transformation in the here and now. By changing the dogma, the affluent class prompted the dispossessed to lose hope for social change and to turn their emotional aggression against themselves. Outward class structures (Marx) interacted with inner emotional drives (Freud).[5]

Fromm was comfortable with his grasp of Marx as he formulated "The Dogma of Christ," and he shared his findings with his colleagues. By the time the essay was published in 1930, Horkheimer had promoted Fromm to a full-time tenured and salaried member of the Institute. (Fromm earned a substantial monthly wage and expenses, which were supplemented by his private income as a practicing analyst.) Whereas Horkheimer chaired the board of directors and set basic policies, the economist Friedrich Pollock was second in command, managing financial and administrative matters. Leo Löwenthal edited the Institute's journal, *Zeitschrift für Sozialforschung*. Eminent young scholars such as Herbert Marcuse and eventually Franz Neumann were hired as collaborators, and Walter Benjamin, the eminent literary critic and philosopher; Alfred Sohn-Rethel, a Marxist economist and philosopher; and others were designated as part-time salaried or "freelance" researchers. Fromm was positioned somewhere between Löwenthal and the younger scholars and was assigned to cover social psychology. Despite Fromm's long absences when convalescing from episodes of tuberculosis, Horkheimer and Pollock still regarded him as a colleague, continued his salary, and kept him informed of major changes at the Institute. One such change came in 1932, when the administrative offices and funds were moved to Geneva. Fromm had warned his colleagues that their assets would be confiscated if Hitler came to power and that the move from Germany was essential.

In the early 1930s, nearly all of the Institute participants were Jews, but only Fromm and Benjamin remained preoccupied with religion or anti-Semitism. Despite the quest to become "modern," they refused to curtail their interests in Jewish thought and culture. However, Fromm and Benjamin shared their colleagues' focus on monopoly capitalism and class conflict. Led by Horkheimer, they hoped their studies would attract the attention of Weimar politicians and help promote progressive social change. Unlike Fromm, however, they shared a personal aversion to political participation themselves.

Early in 1932, Horkheimer wrote a letter to Freud, the first of Horkheimer's efforts to forge an informal affiliation between the Institute and mainstream psychoanalysis. He outlined the various research projects of the Institute and emphasized how, with the addition of Fromm as its first trained analyst, psychoanalytic premises were being integrated into all of its research projects. What Horkheimer did not admit was that there were signs even during Fromm's first years at the Institute that he was not entirely comfortable with Freud's modernist conceptual itinerary.[6]

Two articles on the criminal justice system, "The State as Educator" (1930) and "On the Psychology of the Criminal" (1931), illustrated this discomfort and suggested that Fromm was evolving into a rather independent social critic—a free spirit fusing Marxism with psychoanalysis in his own unique way. These articles suggested that, unlike most of his colleagues, he had few qualms about addressing pressing topics about which he had little expertise. Professedly, Fromm argued, the state created its criminal justice system not only to transform human behavior and encourage people to be upright citizens but also to deter the upright from criminal behaviors. On a more basic and psychological level, however, the state was referring to crime and deterrence in order to present itself on a subconscious level as a father image. The child knew that he was defenseless against the power of the father, particularly the capacity of the father to castrate the child. By drawing upon this subconscious fear of paternal punishment, Fromm noted, the state sought to promote obedience to its dictates.[7]

The state also used the criminal justice system to enhance itself, Fromm claimed, by treating the criminal as a scapegoat instead of confronting society's deep social problems. In dwelling on crime and punishment, the state manipulated society into becoming less attentive to the social and economic inadequacies and oppressions in daily life. That is, a punitive criminal justice system was employed to divert the anger of the masses from the oppressive social conditions that required governmental remedies. In brief, the criminal rather than state policy became the scapegoat for social ills, economic inequality, and governmental corruption and callousness.[8]

Did the criminal justice system at least deter crime? Fromm answered in the negative. Reliable evidence consistently demonstrated that imprisonment, harsh sanctions, and even capital punishment had no salutary effect on the crime rate and thus did not protect the public.[9]

Fromm's final point linked to the others—that the criminal justice system had a decided class bias. Whereas the propertied classes had opportunities to sublimate their aggressive propensities into socially acceptable channels, the disadvantaged lacked these channels and were consequently more likely to commit crimes. Therefore, the reform of social inequities through the redistribution of wealth constituted a more effective plan for combating crime than a harsh system of incarceration and punishment that offered little protection to the public. In essence, these papers reflected Fromm's own rather eclectic fusion of psychoanalytic commentary and Marxian analysis to promote a view of criminal justice that was ahead of his time.[10]

"Politics and Psychoanalysis" (1931) was the first essay Fromm published as a regular member of the Institute. The essay illustrated how Fromm's writing was becoming more precise, if still decidedly exploratory, as he worked to delineate further his own theoretical positions. Although an individual's neurosis was rooted in a fixation at an early point in life where one's drives did not adapt to new life conditions, Fromm maintained that this was not true of society as a whole. By helping the individual to deal with illusions rendered at the point of fixation, psychoanalytic therapy could help cure neurotic conditions. But society, with its sundry political, economic, ideological, and social structures, was more than a mass of neurotic patients with shared emotional problems. After all, wars, revolts, and other signs of social discontent were not rooted in infantile fixations but in external economic structures, concrete social conditions, and shared ideologies and emotions. Social cures or at least reforms could be implemented only by changing these collective structures through political actions. To be sure,

Fromm conceded, after social, economic, and ideological structures were changed, a number of individuals might still retain illusions based on prior social conditions. Only at this point could psychoanalysis come into play as a collective form of therapy, a therapy that could help to dissolve common illusions so that people would adapt better to new structural realities.[11]

Less than a year after Fromm published "Politics and Psychoanalysis," with its sharp dichotomy between social structure and individual psyche, he wrote an article for *Zeitschrift für Sozialforschung* modifying that position. The young man's mind was working overtime to link as persuasively as possible the Marxist analysis of social structures with a psychoanalytic excavation of the individual psyche. In his new article, "The Method and Function of an Analytic Social Psychology," Fromm insisted that Marxism and psychoanalysis were both materialist sciences that focused not on abstract ideas but on concrete, earthbound life conditions and needs. Psychoanalysis was attentive to the instinctual biological apparatus of the individual—specifically the libidinal structure. Marxism focused on the economic and social structures that sustained the instinctual structures. Yet the human instinctual apparatus was "to a high degree modifiable; the economic conditions are the primary modifying factors." As fundamental socioeconomic structures in a society were altered by collective action, instinctual needs became inadequately satisfied by the old channels for release: "Libidinal forces become free for new forms of utilization and thus change their social function. Now they no longer contribute to the preservation of society but lead to the building of new social formations; they cease, as it were, to be cement and instead become dynamite." Thus, much as new societal structures mandated new instinctual needs, the new instinctual needs further modified the social structures. Fromm was close, here, to fashioning a complex theory of historical continuity and change. He postulated that the entire interaction between changing instincts and changing social forms took place most conspicuously within the family, the primary mediating agency between the individual psyche and broad social structures. For Fromm, an "analytic social psychology" based on these Freudian and Marxian premises supplied the means to excavate the fundamental instinctual and social processes within family life. Within a few years, this idea would become the conceptual basis for the Institute's important *Authority and the Family* research project.[12]

Fromm concluded this string of exploratory articles with "Psychoanalytic Characterology and Its Relevance for Social Psychology." In this essay, he very nearly arrived at the concept of social character, which would unite his social and psychoanalytic thought and become the signature theoretical contribution of his career. From the way Fromm began this article, there was no telling what a revealing essay it would be. He dryly recapitulated Freudian orthodoxy: "the general basis of psychoanalytic characterology is to view certain character traits as sublimations or reaction formations of certain instinctual drives that are sexual in nature—'sexual' being used in the extended sense that Freud gave it." Next, he tediously glossed Freud's developmental theory, which posits that the individual experiences three progressive stages in his or her libidinal organization—oral, anal, and finally genital. Often, an individual remained fixated on one of the three stages, and this became a "character trait"; the fixation constricted one's development and general productivity as it shaped one's character.[13]

At this point, Fromm's "Psychoanalytic Characterology" essay took an important turn away from Freudian orthodoxy. According to Fromm, one had to consider more than the "libidinal basis of character traits," for characterological qualities were also "conditioned by the distinctive nature of that society" in which the individual lived. Fromm invoked social psychology as the discipline to understand how society shaped "the character traits common to most members." By tracing how individual libidinal character structure is modified first in the family and then in the larger society, social psychology could produce an understanding of one's broader social character. But, Fromm cautioned, "the libidinal structure from which these character traits develops, has a certain inertia; a long period of adaptation to new economic conditions is required before we get a corresponding change in the libidinal structure and its consequent character traits." Fromm was not yet ready to assert that specific social-economic structures produced and rewarded certain character traits while eliminating others. Rather, he postulated that a person's character began with libidinal qualities and then gradually assumed social qualities as he or she adjusted to the surrounding society. With the publication of this article, the day was not far off when Fromm would eschew Freud on libidinal development as the necessary predecessor of what he now explicitly referenced as "social character."[14]

The final section of "Psychoanalytic Characterology" indicated that Fromm was now as engaged by his own if still somewhat vague concept of social character ("the psychic traits of individuals in a given class or society") as he was in rehashing Freud on individual, libidinally produced

"character traits." Indeed, Fromm came close to asserting that the socialization of character began at infancy and was rooted not so much in instincts as in interpersonal relationships. Citing passages from Daniel De-
foe's *Giving Alms No Charity* and Benjamin Franklin's *Autobiography* as
examples of an emerging bourgeois mentality, Fromm discussed how
bourgeois capitalist society came into being by promoting a structure for
social character through which discipline, thrift, deferred gratification,
and duty became dominant traits while sensuality, pleasure, enjoyment,
kindness, empathy, sharing, and love came to be devalued. Max Weber had
characterized this as the emergence of the "iron cage" of early capitalism.
Fromm agreed.[15]

In these final pages of his article, Fromm set forth a historical perspective of changing social character that, by 1941, would frame his classic *Escape from Freedom*. In characterizing medieval society, he invoked a problematic view of the Catholic Church and the papacy that was more serviceable
to a broadly ranging social philosopher than to a historian dedicated to
historical exactitude. Medieval people purportedly sought to *be* happy
above all else and to enjoy all that life had to offer. They took joy in the
"blessedness" promised by the Church and the worldly pleasures derived
from feast days, costumes, festivals, beautiful paintings, ornate buildings,
and similar phenomena. However, through Calvinism and emerging capitalism, self-regulation and single-minded devotion to one's work duties
replaced enjoyment in the here and now. Arduous labor and disciplined
thrift were essential to maximize one's wealth and possessions (i.e., acquiring or having). Even more deleterious, under emerging bourgeois capitalism a sense of community declined; "there was no trace of individual responsibility for the lot of others, no hint of love for one's fellow men as
such without any conditions being attached."[16]

Early capitalism, under which one owned and managed one's own business, came to be replaced toward the end of the nineteenth century, Fromm
noted, by monopoly capitalism. The social character of most classes of society changed in response to this new state of affairs, yet, especially in
Germany, the social character of the lower middle class persisted, almost
as an anachronism. Although its members had become "economically and
politically powerless," and though their parsimonious duty-bound character traits were incompatible with modern forms of corporate capitalist
production, they demonstrated a rebellious authoritarian quality that worried Fromm: "The desire for authority is channeled toward the strong

leader, while other specific father figures become the objects of the rebel-lion." Of course, Fromm was referring to the rise of Hitler and those of the petit bourgeoisie that he postulated had found the Nazi movement so appealing.[17]

When studying with Alfred Weber, Fromm had not been terribly atten-tive to his brother Max Weber's *The Protestant Ethic and the Spirit of Capi-talism*. By 1932, however, the study was forming a substantial, if largely unacknowledged, part of Fromm's historical perspective. Indeed, *The Prot-estant Ethic* structured Fromm's view of the emergence of "bourgeois-capi-talist character traits." However, Marx was also shaping Fromm's view of the emotionally barren and distressingly alienating aspects of the capital-ist marketplace. Finally, Fromm still invoked Freudian libidinal baggage, seeing remarkable compatibility between Freud on the fixations of the anal character and the early capitalist's single-minded sense of duty and acquisition. In fact, Fromm still had to determine the extent to which the "anal" capitalist social character represented "an adaptation to the require-ments of the capitalist economic structure and to what extent, on the other hand, the underlying anal eroticism itself served as a productive force in the development of the capitalist economy." The young man's mind was deeply engaged, the more so as he tried to understand twentieth-century monopoly capitalism and the authoritarian qualities of the petit bourgeoi-sie. By connecting Max Weber, Marx, Freud, and other intellectual giants, he was moving away from drive theory and offering his own synthesis through a concept of social character. What Fromm meant by social char-acter at this point, in his early thirties, was still vague. It had much to do with the way instincts were shaped less by sublimations than by concrete social conditions. His mind was working at a remarkably rapid and cre-ative pace between 1929 and 1932, by which time he had written articles that previewed some of the major intellectual contributions of his career. One of the most productive—if iconoclastic and independent—scholars in the Frankfurt Institute, Fromm was flourishing intellectually despite a failing marriage and an intermittent battle with tuberculosis.

The German Worker Study

Even before Horkheimer officially became the director of the Frankfurt Institute, he hoped that Critical Theory would be its unique marker. What he intended by this was a shift from a perpetually upbeat and dogmatic Marxism focused on impersonal economic forces to a relentlessly critical negation of the culture of modern capitalism. In part, this approach, echoing Hegel's dialectic materialism, though without its mysticism, theological content, or its progressive developmental logic, would take the shape of constant criticisms of major works in social theory. Essentially, Horkheimer saw Critical Theory as an unending series of hard-boiled intellectual crossfires that continually if unevenly exposed the fault lines of capitalist society. Psychoanalytic thought was to help sharpen and perhaps preserve the critical and patently Marxist edge.[18]

Horkheimer also felt that it was important in the development of Critical Theory to test and retest premises through empirical data. In 1929, his colleague Felix Weil had written to the German Ministry of Science, Art, and Education that the Frankfurt Institute sought to launch an empirical investigation of the thoughts and material conditions of German workers. Commuting from Berlin during his early months at the Institute, Fromm helped to outline the scope of this project. By 1930, Horkheimer had instructed him to make the project his principal responsibility. At this point in time, most Institute participants politically allied with the Social Democrats and the Communists were apprehensive of the increasing National Socialist electoral strength in Germany. They assigned much of the blame to the industrialists and bankers who were funding Hitler. If the tide of National Socialism was to be turned back, Horkheimer and his colleagues fantasized that heroic German workers would join the resistance. The hope was that the workers might have the determination and the courage to fight against Hitler. But hope was not empirical evidence. Indeed, few German workers had embraced progressive social programs after the country's humiliating World War I defeat and peace settlement. Nor had workers been mobilized in the face of the ruinous inflationary pressures of the 1920s. Given this evidence of despondency and his own unfounded hope, Horkheimer charged Fromm with the task of systematically investigating the attitudes of German workers since 1918 in order to determine what one could expect from them as the Nazis increased in visibility and power.

Because this German worker study was to be the Institute's first exhaustive empirical undertaking, as well as being a test of whether he could really fit into the Institute's agenda, Fromm felt it imperative to embrace survey research even though this had not been central to his doctoral training in sociology. He realized that he had to "retool" himself—to become more than a social theorist. He relied on Paul Lazarsfeld as a statistical advisor and Ernst Schachtel, Herta Herzog, and Anna Hartoch as research associates. Hilde Weiss turned out to be the most valued associate in the undertaking; she was charged with the distribution of the questionnaire and taking the measures necessary to guarantee a high return rate from the respondents. Weiss had studied earlier German survey research ventures, especially Max Weber's pioneering protocols to solicit data about the social psychology and feelings of German workers. She familiarized Fromm with Weberian survey research approaches. Probably at her suggestion, Fromm reacquainted himself with the six volumes his mentor Alfred Weber had published between 1910 and 1915 on the attitudes of German workers in heavy industries.[19]

Probably through Weiss, Fromm discovered that in 1912 the sociologist Adolf Levenstein had been inspired by Max Weber to conduct the first explicit and comprehensive social-psychological interpretive survey of German industrial workers. Levenstein had focused on the connection between industrial technology and the "inner life" of the worker. Formerly an industrial worker himself, Levenstein had suspected that the routine and monotony of industrial labor increased the spiritual and psychological impoverishment of the worker. Although the Levenstein survey had not been replicated, Fromm and Weiss were deeply impressed and considered it a central reference for their own survey. Fromm was especially influenced by Levenstein's three "psychological types" of workers (revolutionary, ambivalent, and conservative-deferential). He also appreciated the Levensteinian protocol that correlated a worker's answer to his political orientation and economic status. What, Fromm wondered, was the correlation between class orientation, party affinity, and "psychological type"? Levenstein's protocol had to be adjusted, Fromm felt, to make the questions psychoanalytically informed so that they might more closely differentiate superficial from more deeply rooted worker attitudes. In the end, Fromm hoped that his reformulation of the Levenstein survey would offer considerable "insight into the psychic structure of manual and white-collar workers." By conducting a similar survey, he might be able to respond to the basic question Horkheimer had asked him to answer: could German workers be counted upon to resist the threatening Nazi movement of the late Weimar period?[20]

In an unusually exhaustive document, Fromm's research team decided upon 271 open-ended questions. The low 33 percent completion rate, compared with Levenstein's 63 percent, was indicative of the complexity of the questionnaires; even among the 33 percent who responded, there was a high number of nonreplies to certain questions. One hundred and fifty-six of the questions, the core of the study for which Fromm wanted oral answers, dealt explicitly with worker attitudes and had no predetermined answers. He hoped that the respondents would provide answers to his interviewers as if they were talking to a psychoanalyst; their responses would be interpreted as if they were participating in a psychoanalytic therapy session. Because the cost of oral interviews was prohibitive, as Weiss made clear, Fromm had to settle for written responses. Still, in keeping with the spirit of open-ended psychological inquiry, Fromm insisted that all responses be preserved in their totality and not summarized by categories. He hoped that each completed survey might at least convey something of the flavor of a psychoanalytic session. Nuances and signs of impulsivity in each written response were to be "heard," much as a psychoanalyst listens to the associations of his patient. Key words and recurrent expressions were to be interpreted as clues to the latent content of the respondent's underlying personality disposition.[21]

With this distinctively therapeutic perspective, Fromm did not regard statistical exactitude in scoring and tabulating responses as the basic goal. Besides registering the unique and deep-seated psychological qualities of each respondent, he sought to uncover more general tendencies in workers' thoughts and feelings. Most importantly, he wanted to make general statements about the personality structures of these workers. When the questionnaire was designed and distributed, neither Fromm nor his project staff recognized they were involved in an investigation of authoritarianism. Consequently, they asked no questions about Nazi philosophy or practice—that concern would come later. The questions also failed to register anti-Semitism or ethnocentrism; the staff did not yet appreciate how important these sentiments were to Hitler's appeal.[22]

In all, 3,300 questionnaires were distributed, but the sampling was not very representative. Most respondents came from the urban centers between Frankfurt and Berlin, and most were socialists. Factory workers represented 64 percent of the sample and white-collar workers 29 percent. Of all respondents, 53 percent belonged to the Social Democratic Party and 29 percent to the Communist Party. Members of the Nazi Party made up an "insignificantly small" percentage of the total sample. Ninety-three percent of trade unionists in the sample attended union meetings, while 71 percent of them assumed formal union responsibilities. Fewer than 9 percent of the respondents were women, only 3 percent were older than sixty, and only 6 percent were below the age of twenty-one. In terms of religious disposition, 57 percent of the respondents were avowed atheists, 25 percent were Protestant, 11 percent Catholic, and 7 percent "other."[23]

By the end of 1931, roughly 1,100 questionnaires had been completed and returned by the field staff. Of these, some may later have been lost or misplaced. Nevertheless, Fromm, Weiss, and the staff plodded on, year after year, in New York as they had in Germany, committed to completing the project. Each questionnaire was perused for a sense of the respondent's personality. Even as the vast majority of German workers showed up as anti-Nazi in 1929–1930, Fromm queried whether their underlying character structures or "psychological types" revealed that they would be sufficiently antiauthoritarian to oppose the National Socialists in a showdown and to mobilize more recalcitrant workers.[24]

In some measure, the mode of framing the questionnaire to look for correlations among the established Weimar political parties, the economic status of the respondents, and Levenstein's three "psychological types" may have reflected the perspective of the Weimar Left—that they and their socialist parties were supported by revolutionary working-class personality types. But that bias opened the door to "falsification"—for detecting potential disparities between professed political allegiances and underlying personality types (what Fromm called "manifest" and "latent" beliefs).

This is just what happened when the responses were tabulated. The big shock for Fromm's research team was that while 82 percent of the respondents associated themselves with the parties on the Left (the Social Democrats and Communists) and their socialist slogans and ideals of government, few could be characterized by the devoutly nonauthoritarian revolutionary character that the leftist parties professed. Only 15 percent were consistently antiauthoritarian in their underlying character structure (psychological type) and deepest feelings. On the other hand, 25 percent of supporters of the socialist parties displayed either ambiguously authoritarian (20 percent) or consistently authoritarian (5 percent) dispositions, favoring, for instance, punitive policies such as corporal punishment. Most Communist and Social Democrat workers surveyed were somewhere in between. As Fromm summed up the results retrospectively and perhaps too simplistically, there was a marked "discrepancy between [the workers'] leftist conscious political opinions and the underlying personality structure;

a discrepancy which may [have been] responsible for the [subsequent] collapse of the German workers' parties." Fromm never explained why his research team did not take the logical next step of trying to explain how the discrepancy originated.[25]

Despite this shortcoming and the tendency of the minute detail of the survey to obfuscate broad conclusions, the German worker study was unprecedented for its breadth and significance. Although Fromm reported the preliminary results in *Studies on Authority and the Family* (1936), it was at this point that he decided to turn the project materials into a book. Now the importance of understanding the psychology behind worker responses to the Nazi movement was much more transparent than it had been at the outset. Nevertheless, even as recent scholarship has underscored how Weimar workers had not been able to halt Hitler's rise to power, the conclusions of Fromm's project were less than compelling. Moreover, a curious dispute arose between Fromm and colleagues closer to Horkheimer over the number of questionnaires that had been lost when the Institute vacated its European offices in 1934. Horkheimer asserted but did not demonstrate that nearly half were missing. He questioned the efficacy of continuing the project.

Fromm and his team persisted. He claimed that purported shortage of completed questionnaires was a cover that Horkheimer had manufactured. Horkheimer purportedly wanted to conceal his real concern: that the project's negative characterization of many German workers was a potential "danger for the Institute." Some of the Institute's supporters on the Left might not be happy. At any rate, team members insisted that they had devoted enormous time and effort to the project, and the process of tabulating and interpreting the responses continued until 1938. In summing up the entire undertaking, Fromm noted that "the most important result is the small proportion of left-wingers who were in agreement in both thought and feeling with the socialist line." Only 15 percent had "the courage, readiness for sacrifice, and spontaneity needed to rouse the less active and to overcome the enemy." Thus, the actual strength of leftist anti-Nazi parties was much less than met the eye. Still, this 15 percent represented "a hard core" of "reliable fighters." With more decisive leadership and "correct evaluation" of the political situation, they might have inspired another quarter of Social Democrats and Communists (who were less decidedly antiauthoritarian in their underlying personalities) to present a united front and stronger resistance to Hitler. Reflecting his impatience with notions of historical inevitability and perhaps a bit of discomfort with the qualifications that nuanced empirical research required, Fromm was given to prophecy. He claimed that the antiauthoritarian parties on the Left could have been decidedly more effective.[26]

The import of the German worker study is amplified if we compare Fromm to Wilhelm Reich. Both were original and profound interpreters of the Nazi and other authoritarian movements threatening to dominate Europe. Both Fromm's German worker study and Reich's *The Mass Psychology of Fascism* (1933) emerged from the ideological and intellectual concerns of the Weimar psychoanalytic Left. Reich formulated his themes while Fromm was proceeding with the worker project. And, at the time, both were marginal figures in the Berlin psychoanalytic community. Both assumed that party loyalties of the German masses manifested inner character structures, and both sought to give Marxism a social psychology that embraced Freud without invoking Freud's concept of a death wish or an aggressive instinct. To be sure, Reich felt Fromm was inattentive to sexual repressions in German life, and Fromm thought Reich overemphasized genital sexuality and was short on empirical research, but these were the only substantial differences between them. By June 1932, Reich had characterized Fromm as an ally in the Marxian approach to Freudian psychoanalysis and wished him well: "We need you urgently." Together, *The Mass Psychology of Fascism* and *The Working Class in Weimar Germany* launched a remarkable tradition in the study of authoritarianism.[27]

Building Theoretical Foundations

When Fromm and Karen Horney traveled to America in the fall of 1933 to give several lectures at Franz Alexander's Chicago Psychoanalytic Institute, Horkheimer entrusted Fromm with exploring where and how the Frankfurt Institute might establish an American branch or even move to the United States. Consequently, Fromm (more fluent in English than most of his Institute colleagues) made contact with numerous scholars and psychoanalysts in America, including John Dollard, Harold Laswell, and Sandor Rado. Fromm recommended that the Institute move from Geneva to Philadelphia, a move that did not materialize. The heavily quantitative and empirical sociology department at Columbia University sought to hire Fromm because a respected senior colleague, Robert Lynd, held out

Fromm's survey of German workers as a pioneering empirical social science undertaking. Lynd did not reveal that Fromm was the project theoretician and that research associates had attended to the empirical research that specifically interested his department colleagues. When Fromm explained that he would not abandon his Institute colleagues, the sociology department acquiesced, and the normally frugal president, Nicholas Murray Butler, made a generous offer. This offer was made to a group of German Jewish émigrés in an era where anti-Semitism was increasing everywhere, including the Ivy League. Horkheimer traveled to New York to sign the contract and found the Morningside Heights offices, salaries, and support services that Butler would provide, effective immediately, almost too good to be true.[28]

Despite his bouts with tuberculosis, therefore, Fromm's contribution to the Frankfurt Institute was substantial. He played a central role in its move to Columbia, assuring its survival as conditions in Europe deteriorated. And as his theories developed, he was taking a lead that his Institute colleagues often failed to acknowledge. He was fusing Marx and Freud around his developing concept of social character, in which outer social structures shaped instinctive life. Instincts existed, but they were socially grounded. As such, he was distancing himself from the orthodox Freudian or "modernist" agenda, which held that instincts were endemic to the inner self, even as sublimations, and were determinative of human personality.

Fromm had also come to feel that he needed a fresh perspective about gender. At some point in the 1920s, he had begun to question Freud's premise of an Oedipus complex and the underlying assumption that a patriarchal society had always existed—that it was endemic to the human condition. Indeed, he had been taken by Groddeck's idea of male envy of the female capacity to give birth. Groddeck's corollary was that a global order based on matriarchy had existed in early prehistory but was not mentioned in the Old Testament. To sustain his perspective, Groddeck had elaborated on *Mother Right and the Origins of Religion* (1861), by the eminent Swiss Lutheran jurist, Johann Jakob Bachofen, who almost certainly had been an acquaintance of Carl Jung. Bachofen had been a professor of Roman law in Basel, an avid classicist, a philologist, and a mythologist who cited folk customs, sculpture, and myth to support his theories. A revival of interest in Bachofen took place after World War I, and this may have been when Groddeck gained familiarity with *Mother Right*.

When Groddeck first spoke to Fromm of Bachofen at his spa in Baden Baden, Fromm had been preoccupied with his psychoanalytic training, but Groddeck persisted. When tuberculosis substantially sidelined Fromm in the early 1930s, *Mother Right* was part of his reading program. He was deeply affected by the book and read other works of Bachofen to discuss with Karen Horney, who was also rethinking her own perspectives on issues that later scholars would analyze under the heading "gender." Bachofen provided Fromm the first substantial challenge to the premise that patriarchal society represented a natural state of affairs and thereby validated capitalism, oppression, and male hegemony. He soon became an expert on Bachofen's ideas, including the notions that social life was rooted in a powerful mother-child bond and a tie to nature and instinct—and also that a sense of divine presence was inherent in the "feminine nature." In a matriarchal order, Bachofen taught him, there was no strife, conflict, or even private property. Bachofen also provided Fromm with the first clear vision of what he would later call "socialist humanism," prodding him to consider the relationship between socialism and "gender." Bachofen's writings made Fromm even more skeptical than Groddeck of the Freudian embrace of patriarchy. He became respectful of societies in which women held leadership roles. Echoing Bachofen's utopian prehistory, Fromm discerned traces of a matriarchal order in the European Middle Ages. Horney recognized that Fromm was beginning to advocate a more expansive female influence and power in society than she had come across. He elaborated the vision that Bachofen presented within his developing notion of social character. Essentially, Bachofen allowed him to integrate his psychoanalytic and Marxist concepts (which yielded to his social character construct) with a basic historical orientation.

In Bachofen's portrait of matriarchy, people were optimistic and happy. Goods were shared within what Fromm characterized as a "primitive socialist democracy" with group marriage. However, retributional justice was practiced, and special culpability was attached to the physical injury of another. A spirit of sociability, religiosity, tenderness, egalitarianism, and kinship prevailed. There was an instinctual democratic tenderness and an ego ideal of motherly compassion for the weak and helpless. Superego pressures balancing guilt against atonement were less intense. The mysteries of birth, death, and regeneration were celebrated with pious devotedness.[29]

Only after a considerable period of "prehistoric" time, Fromm stated in his elaboration of Bachofen, did women invent monogamous marriage to free themselves of multiple sexual partners and unbridled sensuality. Soon, a hierarchically based patriarchy emerged; society became stratified, with men struggling for wealth and domination over women and the needy. With patriarchy, the Oedipal struggle between father and son emerged. Whereas maternal love for the newborn had been free and unconditional, enhancing the child's self-confidence, the patriarchic system made fatherly love contingent on fulfillment of duties. Since the child inevitably fell short, he became psychically insecure. Patriarchy elevated rationality and abstract juridical concepts, private property, and the power of the state, replacing the priorities of sensuality, emotion, pleasure, and happiness. Thought became more refined and nuanced under patriarchy, replacing the intuitive aspect of matriarchy. Finally, new technologies that alienated the worker from nature were designed to maximize productivity and subjugate the weak. Society became plagued by conflict and notions of guilt and atonement, and emotional life was constricted. Protestantism and capitalism, the twin evils of the Reformation in Fromm's emerging historical perspective, helped to promote this unhappy new order that replaced matriarchy and democratic socialism, through their stress on patriarchy and competition.[30]

As Fromm studied Bachofen's works and life, he learned that despite Bachofen's favorable portrayal of matriarchy, he was an aristocrat with limited views of democracy and a sternly patriarchal proponent of bourgeois Protestant morality. The fact that Bachofen embodied such contradictions made him human, Fromm perhaps rationalized—a creature of time and place. Far more important was the fact that Bachofen filled gaps in his understanding of ancient history and sharpened his view of the entire historical process. Fromm was taken, above all, by Bachofen's emphasis that religious sentiment was most deeply rooted in women and their propensity for egalitarianism and sharing. Thus, it was folly to equate human nature with patriarchal institutions, capitalism, authoritarianism, and exploitation.[31]

Clearly, allegiance to Bachofen's perspectives loosened Fromm's ties to Freudian orthodoxy, especially the premise of an Oedipal struggle, among other patriarchal premises. For Fromm, Freud explained patriarchal society quite profoundly but did not account for the earlier matriarchal society. Following the Old Testament, Freud's view of history began and ended with patriarchy. The child's earlier attachment to the mother, the security she afforded, and the trauma of separation from her became more important developments in the child's life, Fromm was beginning to sense. While Bachofen encouraged Fromm's resistance to Freudian patriarchy, *Mother Right* also made him a more committed Marxist socialist. Fromm learned that Friedrich Engels had been impressed by the theory of matriarchy when he was writing on the origins and nature of the family and that Marx and a number of other socialists had also been influenced by matriarchal theory. For instance, matriarchy could sanction revolutionary change. Fromm was convinced that "under different social conditions, quite different drive structures have been and can be operative as productive forces." By expanding possibilities for individual gratification and happiness and the productive development of the personality rather than "domination of the masses," a socialist order of economic plenty and equality could exist as it had in matriarchal prehistory.[32]

Through Bachofen, Fromm was integrating Marx and Freud in his own unique way, with a decidedly feminist perspective and a unified view of historical change from matriarchal prehistory to patriarchal and exploitive capitalism. In his reading of Old Testament prophets, Fromm had developed a loose identification with utopianism, which was deepened by Bachofen's vision of matriarchy. By the late 1930s, utopianism became one of several factors that set Fromm at odds with Horkheimer and a new Institute colleague, Theodor Adorno.

It is unlikely that Bachofen would have had such a decided influence on Fromm's thought if the theory of *Mother Right* had not found elaboration and confirmation in more contemporary scholarship. Even though Bachofen was well read, he was not a meticulous scholar. Indeed, he cited myths and folk customs to sustain his perspective. Moreover, Fromm suspected that Bachofen's view of matriarchy had been shaped in part by adoration of his own mother.

Importantly, Fromm found in Robert Briffault's 1928 book, *The Mothers: A Study of the Origins of Sentiments and Institutions*, the meticulous and persuasive scholarship that enhanced his comfort with Bachofen's characterizations. For Fromm, Briffault's was a monumental research work based not only on comparative ethnology but also social psychology and economics. Covering the earliest matriarchal societies, the institution of marriage, and the shift into patriarchy, Briffault showed how changes in human sentiments and institutions were rooted in changes in everyday social life, especially concrete economic changes. That is, biologically shaped instincts were gradually transformed by socioeconomic influences.

Consequently, what was psychologically "masculine" and "feminine" at a given point in time did not derive from "human nature" but from the different ways in which the two sexes were allowed to function in their social lives. For example, maternal love was rooted in the mother's long-term care of the needy. Eventually, matriarchy expanded into a mother's altruistic social feeling. All social evolution in the form of caring relations derived from mother love, especially the matriarchal family and "all lasting social groupings." Fromm found Briffault's delineation convincing not only because he provided a substantial evidential base for Bachofen but because the evidence Briffault invoked was compatible with Marx and Engels on the "social determination of sentiments." It is interesting that Fromm was hardly the only personality theorist with Freudian training to branch out from Freud's patriarchal premise through Bachofen and Briffault and to explore possibilities more congruent with notions of woman's nurturing and creative propensities and the trauma of separation from her. While he was still alive, this would become central to what came to be called attachment theory. A generation of feminist clinicians and scholars, such as Mary Jane Sherfrey, Elaine Showalter, and Carol Gilligan, moved in that post-Freudian direction.[33]

"Social-Psychological Aspects"

Fromm discovered that within the Frankfurt Institute only Walter Benjamin and (to a more limited degree) Horkheimer shared his interest in Bachofen. As Fromm began to find himself less comfortable with Freud's libido theory, moreover, Horkheimer began to embrace it. Although Fromm's German worker study was hardly a finished piece of work until late in the decade, some Institute colleagues were concerned by the loss of half the questionnaire responses during the Institute's relocation, which they felt made its conclusions methodologically suspect.

Nonetheless, Fromm presented the findings of his German worker study in an appendix to a major integrative research undertaking by the entire Frankfurt Institute—*Studies on Authority and the Family* (1936). *Studies* was a massive, thousand-page, two-volume research report addressing relationships between family and authority, in response to the emergence of Hitler's totalitarian rule. Publication coincided with the 1934–1935 move to the Morningside Heights area of the Columbia campus, which therefore made the project a work of intellectual émigrés. Premised on the assumption that the family transmitted to the individual the values of the larger society, Institute researchers pursued the social and psychological factors in German family life that had rendered authoritarian rule. The study addressed "the psychological impulses which cause people to submit to authority, and which make this submission pleasurable without regard to the nature of the commands." Horkheimer edited the first section of the study, which consisted of long theoretical essays that he, Fromm, and Marcuse had written. Fromm edited the second section, which contained studies of socialization of different classes, of youth, and of unemployed families. Löwenthal edited the third section, essays that addressed topics of family and authority within different countries. To be sure, the three parts were poorly integrated, and while all of the contributors connected the rise of authoritarianism to a crisis of capitalism, none addressed German anti-Semitism.[34]

Fromm's long essay in the theoretical section, "Social-Psychological Aspects,"—gave some degree of coherence to the entire project by providing a clear, logical, and sophisticated explanation of the psychological appeal of authoritarianism. Rolf Wiggershaus, the historian of the Frankfurt Institute, calls the essay "the best he ever wrote"; in it, Fromm crystallized and synthesized much of his work since joining the Frankfurt group. (As a cohesive and developed essay, it probably surpassed his 1932 piece, "Psychoanalytic Characterology," where the most innovative insights emerged almost as afterthoughts.) Fromm's cardinal concept of character structure (which he formerly called "libido structure") was more fully developed, and he enumerated several varieties: the anal character, the patricentric character, the matricentric character, and the revolutionary character. The essay concentrated on the authoritarian character in a way that foreshadowed the basic theoretical conceptualization for the most important publication of Fromm's life, *Escape from Freedom* (1941), and was of incalculable importance.[35]

Fromm began "Social-Psychological Aspects" by underscoring the major contributor to authoritarian character—the decline of ego strength in modern man as it manifested itself in the patriarchal family within contemporary capitalist society. With a strong ego, Fromm emphasized, one had abundant psychic energy and sought to shape one's life and society according to personal desires for harmony and contentment. Consequently, one thought logically and made decisions actively and energetically.

Departing from Bachofen, Fromm emphasized that this capacity for choice and autonomy augmented itself when society promoted "rational, active, and systematic rules" for the individual and the collective well-being. The rules were intended to promote joy and hopefulness, to enhance individual choice and autonomy, and to foster a caring communal spirit. As the ego strengthened, it was "more in a position to avert instinctual drives without the help of emotional connections to the superego or authority, and it can thus establish itself independently."[36]

Fromm postulated that monopoly capitalist society run by elite groups endangered healthy, strong, self-directive egos, in part because "the ruling class has far greater opportunities to satisfy desires than the scant opportunities of the oppressed classes." Especially among the lower classes, feelings of powerlessness and inconsequentiality prompted ego disorganization and depletion. As the individual and his family ceased to feel autonomous, members were increasingly disposed to identify with and follow the dictates of a "superior power." The ruling class contributed to this dynamic, by promulgating constrictive social rules that reduced choice, and the lower class, bound by the superego, sustained those rules.[37]

The primary agency for this internalization of the superego—the ego-depletion process—was the patriarchic authority structure of the family, Fromm maintained. Under an increasingly authoritarian social order echoed by both rigid patriarchy and superego constraints, the individual felt lacking in internal psychic resources; he felt increasingly isolated and estranged. As the ego disintegrated through repression of desire and the taboos of the superego strengthened, masochism became a conspicuous personality trait. One relinquished personal happiness, felt increasingly guilt ridden, and turned the self over to the dictates of external social and internal psychic authorities: "This wish, to receive commands and behave accordingly, to submit oneself in obedience to a higher power, indeed, to lose oneself in it, allows the authoritarian to enjoy punishment and abuse from the stronger power." For Fromm, masochistic thought was authoritarian thought, satisfying the need of the individual to remedy the sense of helplessness, guilt, and a depleting sense of agency. Masochism filled this void by prompting identification with a higher power that provided rules and direction and punishing any recalcitrance on the part of the self. Over time, one lost one's sense of self entirely. Individual love and choice were supplanted by fear and blind obedience: "whoever punishes him, he will love." Security against anxiety and participation in the glory of power were at the core of masochism, Fromm insisted. The revolutionary character was the only viable alternative.[38]

Fromm's "Social-Psychological Aspects" essay borrowed from his German worker study by invoking this "revolutionary" character structure. A person with abundant ego strength and who sought to change his destiny was "revolutionary." The "revolutionary" was antithetical to the masochist, who submitted to his fate: "The helplessness of the person is the basic theme of this masochistic philosophy." Unlike the revolutionary, the masochist reverently submitted to seemingly historical and providential decrees—to fate as defined by the leader. In this way, the masochist could participate in the glory of the ruler, his nation, and his race.[39]

Fromm postulated, as Freud had insisted before him, that sadistic aggression against the weak represented the flip side of masochism. The masochist turned the weakened self over to the dictates of a higher power. The sadist turned the insecure self against others who showed signs of weakness or were lower in the social hierarchy. With the desire to submit came the urge to dominate in a hierarchic and paternalistic family and society. Consequently, sadomasochism was at the core of authoritarianism— love and deference to those above and contempt for and assault against those below. Fromm also postulated that the sadomasochist had a weak heterosexual genital identification and corresponding anal (pregenital) strivings for order, punctuality, and frugality. Because women seemed strange and uncanny, the sadomasochist degraded them to preserve his own sense of superiority over the weak.[40]

If sadomasochism was at the core of the authoritarian social character, Fromm identified patriarchy as a central ingredient. In this context, he was never clear on whether patriarchy was the cause or effect of sadomasochism. One always had to satisfy the demands of fatherly authority for obedience and duty, in both the family and the larger society. Only in this way could one be loved by the leader, who demanded "self-sacrifice"—the renunciation of one's own happiness and the fulfillment of one's duty. While promising protection and security, the authoritarian leader also maintained his following by traumatizing society through unpredictable terror. Always fearing random punishment, a follower had to submit unconditionally. This perpetuated the distance between leader and followers and erased hope of eventually bridging the gap.[41]

What Fromm had brilliantly delineated in "Social-Psychological Aspects" was one of the first psychologically informed explanations of authoritarian character. Locating the roots of this sadomasochism and strong attendant guilt in the social and emotional fabric of the patriarchal family and monopoly capitalism (i.e., social-structural factors), Fromm rejected Freud's notion of an "archaic inheritance" of guilt feelings. For support, Fromm cited Wilhelm Reich's *Character Analysis* (1933) and a 1935 article by Karen Horney—both of whom placed the masochistic character in the foreground of social pathology.[42]

Throughout "Social-Psychological Aspects," Fromm held that under monopoly capitalism, it was less taxing and in some ways more satisfying emotionally to submit to authority than to struggle to enhance one's ego strength and regain one's autonomy. While most of his colleagues despaired of the possibility of human ebullience and inner psychic strength in a corporate marketplace society, Fromm remained hopeful. Even in dealing with monopoly capitalism, the rigidly patriarchal family, and the increasing ascendance of authoritarian political structures, Fromm believed that all was not lost. Diverse social circumstances rooted in a spirituality and spontaneity were still evident in Western capitalist culture and might coalesce to reduce the gap between leader and follower, renew ego strength and ebullience in the citizenry, enhance the more joyous values of matriarchy, and reverse the descent toward sadomasochism. Even as he delineated the psychological advent of authoritarianism in a clear and compelling manner, Fromm did not rule out the possibility that this evil might be mitigated and eventually confronted. In the face of authoritarianism, he settled for less-than-revolutionary social transformation. Certain forms of capitalism crushed the ego more decidedly than other forms, Fromm concluded. Just as the Weimar worker who supported the parties on the Left revealed an underlying authoritarian disposition, some seeming authoritarians under the Third Reich might eventually pursue greater freedom, autonomy, and happiness. In his diverse essays of the 1930s, Fromm had essentially conceptualized *Escape from Freedom*.[43]

Termination

In terms of research and writing, Fromm was more productive than a good many scholars associated with the Frankfurt Institute in this decade. His "Social-Psychological Aspects" essay may have been the most creative and compelling, if largely unacknowledged, contribution to *Studies on Au-*

thority and the Family. That and other articles marked him out as a social psychologist distancing him from the Freudian orthodoxy predicated on the primacy of instinctual life that Horkheimer and Löwenthal embraced. He replaced it with his concept of social character through which "a particular fit of social conditions" shaped our inner psyches, instincts and all.

After Fromm migrated to the new Institute headquarters at Columbia in May 1934, his tuberculosis, which had gone into remission in the summer of 1932, recurred. He spent three months at a New Mexico sanitarium and found, on his return to New York, that he was able to visit the Institute offices only for very short periods. During the winter of 1934, he took a sea cruise to help restore his lungs. This was followed by trips to mountains near Alberta and to three coastal cities—San Francisco, Santa Barbara, and Los Angeles. Following trips to Bermuda and Taxco, Mexico, in mid-1936, Fromm went into remission again and rejoined his colleagues. In September 1938, he was forced to return to Davos after a second relapse and persistent kidney problems. It was not until new antituberculosis drugs were prescribed in February 1939 that his doctors pronounced him cured. In fact, these drugs likely helped him simply go into another, if longer, remission. A drug that permanently eradicated the malady (the antibiotic streptomycin) was unavailable before 1946.[44]

Horkheimer sympathized with Fromm and his struggle to regain his health even as his rapport with Institute colleagues became problematic. As long as he was a productive and creative member of the Institute, Horkheimer was willing to continue Fromm on full salary and cover many of Fromm's medical expenses. Late in 1935, for example, he assured Fromm of Institute support and urged him to conserve his energy. In 1936, Horkheimer had a special contract drafted to assure Fromm of his full salary of four hundred dollars a month until the age of sixty-five (with a reduced salary thereafter). A year later, the contract offered even more generous provisions, allowing Fromm to conduct non-Institute research with the director's consent at no loss of compensation. Fromm also provided regular statements of expenses to the Institute, including a wide variety of costs: substantial doctor bills, apartment rental expenses, maid service, book and newspaper purchases, and hotel bills during travel. Fromm wrote to Horkheimer expressing gratitude for the strong financial support and regretting that his medical bills were straining the Institute's resources. He promised Horkheimer a major new book on the "bourgeois character" (i.e., *Escape from Freedom*), noting that without it his own life as well as

Horkheimer's generous investment in him would be wasted. Fromm summarized matters in a memorandum to his friend Kurt Rosenfeld: "The
relationship was a very close one, theoretically, personally and as far as the
affairs of the Institute were concerned, which Dr. Horkheimer used to
discuss with me . . . in full confidence."[45]

Late in 1938, however, the first overt sign of difficulties between Fromm
and the Institute emerged. After Kristallnacht, his mother, Rosa, finally
recognized the Nazi danger and became willing to leave Germany. By this
point, German authorities demanded considerable money to authorize
departures, and Fromm asked Horkheimer to bear the preponderance of
the cost. Horkheimer replied that the Institute could not afford that expense. Although Fromm was able to procure funds from other sources,
especially from Horney, it was the first time Horkheimer had rejected a
financial request. The refusal underscored the major financial problems
that were emerging at the Institute. It cost a good deal more to publish
Zeitschrift für Sozialforschung in America than it had in Frankfurt and Geneva. In addition, the Institute's endowment had suffered major setbacks
because of the bear stock market and a disastrous upstate New York real
estate investment. Staff labor costs were also going up significantly; Horkheimer and Pollock, who managed the Institute's finances, were spending
considerable money to provide work for European émigré scholars. Fromm
recognized the emerging crisis in the Institute's balance sheet, which included over two thousand dollars of his medical expenses, which had covered the cost of his convalescence in Switzerland. He offered to pay back
half that sum to help ease the Institute's financial burdens. Pollock noted
that this would not be necessary; the larger issue was whether the Institute
could continue to make good on Fromm's salary.[46]

In May 1939, Pollock and Horkheimer breached Fromm's lifetime contract and declined to pay his salary. Institute funds had reached very low
levels. Beginning in October, they asked him to voluntarily agree to go off
salary, noting that he could support himself by expanding his psychoanalytic practice, whereas others on the payroll could not. Emphasizing that
they had always supported Fromm during his illness, they asked him to
continue to participate in the Institute without pay. Fromm protested
loudly at what he called a blatant contractual breach, arguing that he had
declined other job offers to remain at the Institute and had limited his
psychoanalytic practice to fulfill Institute duties. He suggested that he had
essentially been fired, which underscored his sense of personal estrange-

ment from his colleagues. Pollock tried to resolve matters by offering to pay Fromm's mother or widow a pension in the event of his death. Fromm refused. When he did not receive a salary check on October 1, Fromm approached Horkheimer privately. Horkheimer reaffirmed that he valued Fromm as a colleague. Purportedly, there had been a misunderstanding, and Fromm had not been terminated. Indeed, Horkheimer provided salary checks for October and November. Fromm did not deposit these checks for fear that he might undercut his legal claim of contractual breach. He also advised Horkheimer and Pollock that because they had disregarded his contract, he could no longer work at the Institute, and he requested a severance settlement. Pollock offered a year of salary, but Fromm insisted on more, noting that he still had a legal cause of action against the Institute. In the end, Fromm waived his contract for a twenty-thousand-dollar settlement. He had driven a hard bargain—the equivalent of roughly four years of salary—and still had a clinical practice to fall back upon.[47]

The dispute over Fromm's salary was obviously very central to his leaving. It involved money, to be sure, but it may also have tapped a sense of estrangement that extended back to his childhood years. Yet there were other important factors that reinforced Fromm's feeling that he had been terminated. He had assumed that the Institute would subsidize the publication of the German worker study at a cost of $750, but Horkheimer had refused, citing insufficient financial resources. Fromm was furious, pointing out that money had been found to subsidize less important Institute publications. There was no mention, at this point, of the missing worker questionnaires, which undermined the quantitative validity of the study, but it was not irrelevant. Since *Studies in Authority and the Family* (1936), moreover, Fromm had published only one article in *Zeitschrift für Sozialforschung* and was seeking other venues for his work. Comporting with his longstanding social role of marginality, his writing had become less central to the Institute after the move to Morningside Heights.[48]

In part, Fromm's increasing loss of standing at the Institute was rooted in growing personal differences with other participants. Horkheimer and most of his colleagues resisted hasty Americanization. When they arrived in New York, they continued to perceive themselves as European intellectuals, persisted in writing for a specialized scholarly audience, and preferred to communicate in German. In contrast, Fromm moved from a familiarity to a mastery of English, making it his primary language. He developed a capacity to write graceful English prose and worked at becoming more accessible to the general American reading public. He studied and became conversant in the works of major American thinkers, especially the transcendentalist poets and essayists Ralph Waldo Emerson and Henry David Thoreau, the psychologist and philosopher William James, and the philosopher and education reformer John Dewey, and he participated in the American Culture and Personality movement with new friends such as the linguist Edward Sapir and the prominent anthropologists Ruth Benedict and Margaret Mead. He cultivated friendships with Harry Stack Sullivan and other American clinicians interested in interpersonal social psychiatry. He also was interested in popular culture and began to write for American audiences who were concerned generally with politics and social psychology. (Fromm was also pleased that American intellectuals and scholars seemed more interested in religion than his Frankfurt Institute colleagues.) Although the Institute was located in a corner of Columbia University, only Fromm sought to cultivate connections and rapport with faculty elsewhere on the campus, especially the sociologists and political scientists.[49]

As early as June 1934, Horkheimer wrote to Pollock privately of his discomfort with Fromm on these counts, fearing that Fromm's interests were moving beyond traditional European scholarly concerns. Writing from Oxford in the mid-1930s, Theodor Adorno, who lived in Britain, augmented Horkheimer's discomfort with Fromm. A music critic during the Weimar period, Adorno was from a wealthy family and did not require an Institute salary. He positioned himself not only to be brought into the Institute "in the manner of a girlfriend intent on marriage" but to become Horkheimer's second in command. Based on his letters to Horkheimer, Adorno disliked Fromm instinctively, reinforcing the sense of Institute researchers that Fromm lacked refined aesthetic sensibilities, was going too far astray in his publications, and seemed too comfortable with popular culture.[50]

Adorno's suggestion of intellectual heresy was substantially reinforced when Fromm submitted what he characterized as a "seminal essay" for Institute publication: "A Contribution to the Method and Purpose of an Analytical Social Psychology." Late in 1936, Fromm described to his friend Karl Wittfogel the central theme of the emerging essay. It would contrast quite explicitly Freud's tenet of the primacy of instinctive life with Fromm's concept of social character as the shaping force: "I try to show that drives which motivate social behavior are not, as Freud assumes, sublimations of sexual instincts. Rather, they are the products of social processes, or, more precisely, reactions to certain [social] constellations under which the individual has to satisfy his/her instincts." The article found no favor at the Institute when it was submitted for publication in 1937, and Horkheimer wrote a harsh critique, one based upon his increasing embrace of Freudian orthodoxy. Fromm replied that "the basic point of principle I am driving at is correct, but I do see that I did not manage to formulate it adequately." He revised the essay substantially, enlarging it from fifty-eight to eighty-three pages, but the Institute again refused to publish it. If there was any doubt that he had become a peripheral figure in Frankfurt Institute affairs by the late 1930s, these two rejections made it clear.[51]

Basically, "A Contribution to the Method and Purpose of an Analytical Social Psychology" showed unmistakably what had become increasingly apparent over the course of the decade: Fromm disagreed fundamentally with his colleagues' stance on Freud as he sought to forge a divergent psychoanalytic perspective, which he would call "socially typical character." Ironically, by this point in time, Freud, unlike his more orthodox followers, had become modestly receptive to such formulations. However, Fromm's critique of Freud in this essay was explicit and unsparing but based on a flattened version of Freud's actual text. Freud's delineation of the psychic apparatus endemic to "human nature," centering on the Oedipus complex, was, Fromm thought, not universal but rooted in the peculiarities of the patriarchal middle-class society in which Freud lived. For example, Freud had described women as bound by their anatomy and envious of the male phallus. Drawing on Bachofen, Horney, and others, Fromm insisted that women had had very different self-images in different times and places. Fromm also chastised Freud for regarding "the estranged person that he finds in our society as the necessary product of human nature." There was no corresponding evidence that such primary narcissism and social isolation were endemic to humanity in all times and circumstances. Freud was also mistaken in disconnecting the death drive from social conditions; the death drive had to be amalgamated with erotic drives to neutralize them. Otherwise, Fromm noted, they would be turned destructively against the self or against society. Finally, he accused Freud of mistakenly reducing much spiritual and psychic phenomena to sexual drives and their release or repression. In sum, Fromm charged that the preponderance of Freud's so-called universals were derivative of the evolution of the structures and values of the middle-class family.[52]

Detailing how Freud's so-called psychic universals were really characteristics of the late nineteenth- and early twentieth-century middle class,

Fromm focused much of his 1937 "Contribution to the Method and Purpose" essay on his alternative to Freudian orthodoxy. He intended to replace libido theory—the underpinning of orthodoxy—with his concept of historically and socially grounded "social character structure." Physiological impulses represented only one of several energizing forces in a person's "social character structure," he insisted. One could also be energized by specific historically grounded social forces: "Character is the form in which a large portion of human energy finds its expression, the tools of the individual so to speak, loaded with impulse energy with which he carries out his needs under the given life conditions and protects himself against dangers." Essentially, "character structure" was "the adjustment of the person within the given natural social conditions with the goal of satisfying his physiological and historically created needs." Character structure was the interplay of impulsive energy, religion, political ideologies, and, most basically, the economic organization of society upon an individual as he sought to satisfy his psychological, historical, and social needs. Citing a young and nondogmatic humanist, Karl Marx, who was deeply attuned to social psychology, Fromm stated that his own concept of character structure "stands closer to the viewpoints of historical materialism than the Freudian ones, insofar as the psychic structure of man is regarded as the product of his activity and his manner of life and not as a reflex thrown up by his physical organization (i.e., the libido). The life practice determines the socially typical character." With his focus on inner subjectivity, Freud would have disagreed, though not entirely, with this formulation.[53]

Horkheimer seems to have sent a copy of Fromm's "A Contribution to the Method and Purpose" essay to Adorno after he, Löwenthal, and Marcuse had rejected it for publication. A year earlier, Adorno had written to Horkheimer of his extreme suspicion of Fromm's perspective on psychotherapy, even though at that point Fromm had scarcely written about the topic and had not yet given it a great deal of conceptual thought. Adorno charged that Fromm's therapeutic perspective was entirely rooted in the approaches of Georg Groddeck and Sandor Ferenczi, which emphasized using kindness and empathy and which gently encouraged the patient to experience how emotionally pleasurable life could be. In contrast, deriving in part from his interest in the theory of aesthetics, Adorno promoted a very different approach. The clinician should compel the patient, through the reality principle, to enter life's emotional darkness, so that he could begin to see the light of hope. Adorno had also described Fromm as too much of a "professional Jew," owing to his longstanding interest in Jewish prophetic traditions and his love of Hasidic culture. Finally, Adorno labeled Fromm a "sentimental" social democrat who had been unable to wrestle with Marx very profoundly and had developed far too loose a synthesis of Marx and Freud. Still insecure at this point, Fromm broke with his traditional etiquette and called Adorno "a puffed up phrase-maker with no conviction and nothing to say." Adorno had the last word. He characterized Fromm as a threat to both his and Horkheimer's theoretical agenda.[54]

That agenda was rooted in a deepening embrace of Freudian orthodoxy to the near exclusion of Marxist humanism. Like Löwenthal, Marcuse, and others closest to Horkheimer, Adorno doubted that a democratic revolution among the working class would erupt to replace the alienating capitalist conditions of labor with socialist freedom and a happy and productive work force. The failure of Weimar democracy and the triumph of Nazi and Stalinist totalitarianism were hardly testimony to the viability of humane democratic socialism. Consequently, the Horkheimer inner circle looked with acute skepticism at Fromm's almost ebullient vision of the evolution of social character. Whatever hopes for humankind remained, Horkheimer and his associates proclaimed, was in the biological instinctual structure of human personality described by Freud.[55]

By 1938, when Adorno arrived at the offices in Morningside Heights, Horkheimer relied upon him to help define the organization's conceptual and research agenda. Wielding a heavily philosophical and aesthetic perspective on just what Critical Theory should mean, Adorno emphasized Freudian metapsychology, especially Freud's biologically rooted instinct theory. Whereas Fromm had insisted that man derived his energy and resources from the specific socioeconomic character of his society, Adorno proclaimed that Fromm's social character construct was simply a program for social adjustment or conformity of the self to the dominant values of society. Underscoring Freud's focus on biological instincts, Adorno insisted that man was inherently asocial and antagonistic to the society around him. That is, man's instinctual essence made him nonidentical with all aspects of his socialized self. Therefore, contrary to Fromm's beliefs, man could never acquire a unified social character. A disconnect would always exist between subject and object, essence and appearance, particular and universal. Quite unlike Fromm, Adorno was postulating a "negative dialectic" in which the freedom of the individual resided in instinctual resistance "outside" the existing social and political order. Horkheimer,

Löwenthal, Pollock, Marcuse, and others at the Institute were increasingly sympathetic with Adorno's adamant defense of Freudian orthodoxy. Adorno wrote to his parents that Fromm was on the periphery because of his "grave scientific differences, first with myself, then also between him and Marx, which made further collaboration impossible."[56]

Certainly by 1938, when it became clear that *Zeitschrift für Sozialforschung* would not publish even a revised version of "A Contribution to the Method and Purpose," Fromm realized that he would have to find his own way as an independent thinker. The intellectual underpinnings of this debate would resurface in 1956, when Herbert Marcuse reiterated Adorno's positions in an acerbic exchange with Fromm.

Fromm turned increasingly to unorthodox psychoanalysts such as Harry Stack Sullivan and Karen Horney because they found his orientation compatible with their own. They encouraged him to expand his clinical practice, learn from his patients, help them reform the American psychoanalytic profession, and communicate in a powerful and compelling way to the general public about the fate of humankind in an increasingly precarious world. *Escape from Freedom* was the result. It was narrated with such a strong and engaging voice that it quickly became one of the most profound and captivating books ever written on the conflict between freedom and authoritarianism. Triggered in part by personal experiences at the onset of the Nazi terrors, the process of drafting *Escape* also helped Fromm reach inward and discover personal resources, including the potential for deep and enduring joy, that he never quite knew existed. A new Erich Fromm emerged as he gifted humankind with an enduring classic on freedom and its discontents.

PART II

THE AMERICAS

If less volatile than Nazi Germany, Franklin Roosevelt's America was suffering from a severe economic depression when Fromm arrived in 1934. Whereas most dislocated Jewish scholars sought positions in American universities or in other professional agencies, sometimes unsuccessfully, Fromm had an advantage. He had been a central figure in transplanting the Frankfurt Institute to Columbia University and simply continued as a senior Institute researcher. Like many émigré scholars, he discerned increasing anti-Semitism in both academe and the larger society. Yet it was clear to him and other scholars who fled Hitler (most of whom lived at least temporarily in New York) that despite its pockets of provincialism and bigotry, the home of Broadway, Greenwich Village, and the Museum of Modern Art surpassed war-torn Berlin, bombed-out London, and once-glittering Paris in literary, cultural, and intellectual excitement.

Nevertheless, when American fighter planes ushered in the Nuclear Age by dropping the atomic bombs that incinerated Hiroshima and Nagasaki in August 1945, it became clear that the postwar world would remain a troubled one. The bombs did double duty, underscoring American military superiority to the Russians while pressuring Japanese warlords to surrender. The Cold War began under these auspicious circumstances, though its hazards did not deter consumer culture or the flight to bucolic suburbs. McCarthyism ran roughshod over Bill of Rights freedoms. Some blacklisted writers and artists sought refuge in Mexico City and Cuernavaca. A few became Fromm's friends after he moved south in 1950. But most remained focused on the United States. They garnered new hope when movements for civil rights and peace emerged north of the border. A number of these exiles returned. A few, including Fromm, became political activists in America and assumed leadership positions in progressive causes.

3

The Americanization
of a European Intellectual

In 1935, Fromm told Max Horkheimer that he wanted to write a book examining the dangers of authoritarianism generally and the Nazi threat in particular. Wilhelm Reich was also attentive to the extreme danger posed by Hitler, and several years earlier, in 1932, Fromm had been in the audience when Reich had presented a paper on the subject to the Berlin Psychoanalytic Institute. Reich's *The Mass Psychology of Fascism* was an elaboration of that presentation and preceded *Escape from Freedom* by eight years. To some extent, *Escape* elaborated on the argument of Reich's book. Reich maintained, as Fromm would later, that strong patriarchic traditions made the German father into a crude ruler of his home and family but a follower of the authoritarian leader in the public realm. These traditions were central, Reich insisted, to the Nazi appeal to the German middle class. In brief, patriarchy turned men of this class into sadomasochists. On the one hand, they treated the weak, the disabled, and the Jews sadistically. On the other, they masochistically submitted to the authority of the dictator as he promoted the concept of master race. With a greater (if hardly overwhelming) stock of evidence and a fuller command of pertinent scholarship than Reich, Fromm would broaden the scope of Reich's analysis, pointing out that authoritarianism was not exclusively a German problem. In the twentieth century, it was the essential problem of humankind.[1]

What became *Escape from Freedom* was initially titled "The Individual in the Authoritarian State." Yet in searching for the book's focus, he also planned it to be a more general study of "character and culture." Late in 1936, he wrote to Margaret Mead that he intended his book to replace explanations of human motivation lodged in Freudian drive theory by invoking the premise that "socially produced drives are specifically human and have to be explained as reactions toward a particular fit of social conditions" and "not as 'sublimations' of instincts." Articles written at the

Frankfurt Institute on his emerging concept of social character required elaboration, he told Mead: "I feel I would have to write a whole manuscript to make my point sufficiently clear." In addition to the very influential exchanges with Mead and others in the culture and personality movement, Fromm sought out rich intellectual dialogue with colleagues in the psychoanalytic community. In October 1936, Fromm started an extensive correspondence with his Zurich friend and confidant, the psychoanalyst Gustav Bally, on the shape of his book. As a post-Freudian study of social character, he told Bally, it would focus on the social psychology of authoritarianism.[2]

Fromm's 1937 "A Contribution to the Method and Purpose of an Analytic Social Psychology" represented a first installment toward a complete manuscript. The paper was uncharacteristically harsh toward Freud, postulating without qualification that "social character" was less reductionist and more illuminating than Freud's drive theory. A more theoretical essay or two on ethics and social character might follow. Over the next several years, Fromm's distress over authoritarianism was solidified by continuing news of Stalin's Moscow show trials and increasingly brutal Nazi atrocities. He was determined to complete a book that would balance the theoretical with an analysis of emergent totalitarianism.[3]

In early March 1939, the focus of *Escape from Freedom* shifted again, toward a greater level of abstraction. Fromm's first cousin, Gertrud Hunziker-Fromm (with whom he had always been very close) reminded him of the canary in a cage he had given her for her seventh birthday and that she had opened the cage door to give the bird the option of freedom. That memory now provided new importance to the nature of freedom. Fromm wrote to Robert Lynd that he intended to refocus the manuscript from contemporary Nazi and Stalinist varieties of authoritarianism to "the problem of freedom and anxiety or the fear of freedom or the escape from freedom." Individual freedoms and opportunities to live rich, loving, spontaneous, and productive lives had multiplied significantly since the Renaissance, Fromm asserted. Yet enhanced freedom often promoted overwhelming anxiety and uncertainty about how one was to shape one's fate. It was less burdensome to delegate newfound freedoms to authority figures and to embrace the false securities they promised (i.e., simply to conform to external social pressures) than to trust one's own powers of rational decision making. Although Fromm had not studied Alexis de Tocqueville's *Democracy in America*, the Frenchman's warning on how people "dread their own free agency [and] fear themselves" approximated Fromm's correspondence with Lynd. An emerging world of freedom and its discontents became the book he was committed to writing. Lynd provided concrete and systematic suggestions on Fromm's evolving text and suggested *Escape from Freedom* as the title. Of course, 1939 was the year that World War II erupted in Europe. It was also the year that newly developed drugs seem to have put Fromm in long-term remission in his struggle with tuberculosis, enabling him to write with considerably more energy. He completed the book in under two years, and it quickly became a classic in Western thought. Despite some significant flaws in both data and argument, the volume struck a chord with a substantial readership. There were five different printings during the war. Between 1941 and 1964, the hardcover edition went through twenty-four printings, multiple translations, and sold millions of copies.[4]

As the totalitarian threat spread throughout Europe and the pressures of social conformity threatened Western democracies, what, in addition to his poor health, made it so difficult for Fromm to find the final focus of *Escape from Freedom*? Why did he decide, after wavering between a focus on authoritarianism and one on freedom, to address both? How did relationships with professional and intellectual colleagues come into play? What factors in Fromm's direct personal experience help to explain the remarkable strength and clarity of his voice and the vigor of his prose when he finally penned the book? How salient were the particulars of his own life at the time of the construction of *Escape from Freedom*?

These questions speak to the complex and changing context of a volume with an enduring message. Because the pressures of conformity that Fromm elaborated so cogently still predominate in the twenty-first century and because authoritarian and semiauthoritarian governments still clearly enjoy power, *Escape from Freedom* remains critical to our lives nearly seven decades after publication. Given Fromm's own emphasis on social influences, it is instructive to fathom the biographical particulars that helped produce this result.

Emigration

Although *Escape from Freedom* focused more on the social psychology of freedom and the threats of conformity and authoritarianism than on the particulars of the Hitler regime, Fromm was deeply apprehensive about the state of German politics. For a decade, he had been preoccupied with the Nazi menace. To appease the Nazi regime, Jewish members of the German Psychoanalytic Society in Berlin had been pressured to resign. As a member of the German society, Fromm protested angrily without effect to Karl Müller-Braunschweig, one of two Gentiles who had been left in charge. Once he moved to New York, Fromm could scarcely let a social gathering go by without discussing the terror of Nazism. When he met Gertrud Hunziker-Fromm in Davos in 1938, he tried to calm her fears over the potential threat to their German relatives. It is generally unknown that Erich Fromm expended a great deal of time and money to help German Jews, especially friends and family, escape from the oncoming Holocaust. He did not conceive of *Escape* as the venue to discuss this personal aspect openly. However, that dimension contributed to the vibrancy and urgency of his authorial voice and probably to the book's appeal. Indeed, *Escape* gathers strength in the later chapters, as Fromm underscores the dangers of delegating the freedom of individual selfhood to authoritarian regimes such as Hitler's or even of giving in to the conformist pressures of political democracies.[5]

When Fromm decided to emigrate in May 1934—after the rise of Hitler but before it became difficult and prohibitively costly to leave—he lived for a time in Switzerland. From there, he traveled through Paris to Southampton and from there to New York. Fromm had spent several weeks in America the previous year, was familiar with the urban northeast and Chicago, and had made many contacts in the New York psychoanalytic and scholarly communities. American citizenship was awarded as a matter of course in 1940. Perhaps because his migration had not been particularly onerous, Fromm never elected to characterize himself as a refugee from Hitler's Germany, even though his return was precluded at least until the end of Nazi rule. Even so, and despite having to leave behind many of his books and possessions, Fromm considered his move to America his own choice rather than the result of an immediate threat to his survival.[6]

His father, Naphtali, had died unexpectedly, apparently of a heart attack, late in 1933, leaving Rosa alone in the family's house in Frankfurt. Erich urged her to emigrate with him, but she preferred to remain in Frankfurt, where she had friends, in addition to her family in Berlin and elsewhere in the country. Like many German Jews, she could not be persuaded of the grave threat of Nazism. In May 1936, Fromm cashed in his savings account at a Frankfurt bank, and the funds were transferred to Rosa; her own money was quickly being depleted, and she had no husband to bring in income. In the summer, he transferred additional funds so that Rosa could visit him that fall in his New York apartment. Fromm hoped to persuade her not to return to Germany, but after two months in New York, she returned to Frankfurt in November.[7]

According to his U.S. federal tax returns for the late 1930s, Fromm was earning a respectable middle-class income. He still received an annual salary between five thousand and six thousand dollars from the Frankfurt Institute, plus two thousand more from his small psychoanalytic practice, for a total of approximately $125,000 in 2012 dollars. He listed his mother on tax forms as his dependent and regularly sent her hundred-dollar payments through money orders to a Frankfurt bank. To assure no disruptions, he also opened an account late in 1936 with Charles Somlo & Company, a New York financial firm with good connections in Germany. He instructed Somlo to transfer the equivalent of another seventy-five dollars a month from his account to his mother, and he had increased that sum to $105 by the end of 1937. At this point, therefore, Rosa received $205 monthly. By 1930s standards, this was a good deal of money.[8]

Despite his occasionally disparaging references to Rosa as a mother, Fromm certainly sent her ample funds, which represented a significant incursion on his own assets. At this point in Fromm's life, he managed his money closely, wanting enough funds to live comfortably and to be able to help not only his mother but others as well, as the German situation deteriorated.

Even though Rosa was receiving the maximum amount that was legally permissible, Fromm became increasingly apprehensive about her safety. In March 1938, German troops invaded Austria, and through the Munich accord in September, Hitler forced Czechoslovakia to cede the Sudetenland. At this point, Fromm became very vocal in urging his mother to join him in America and prepared an affidavit promising to support her if she migrated. Still, Rosa refused to leave—until Kristallnacht. Kristallnacht marked two days in early November 1938 when violent attacks were organized against Jews in Germany and sections of Austria, including Vienna. Jewish villages, homes, businesses, and synagogues were destroyed. By this time, the Nazi regime had imposed very high fees and other requirements for the right to migrate, and the American policy for admitting German Jews had also toughened. England would host Rosa for eighteen months before she could migrate to the United States. For permission to do this, however, she would have to post a surety of one thousand American dollars. Early in December and despite his tepid relationship with the Frankfurt Institute, Fromm asked Horkheimer for a five-hundred-dollar cash loan. Karen Horney had already pledged five hundred, he told Horkheimer, and though Fromm remained on good terms with his estranged wife, Frieda, she had paid five thousand dollars to rescue her own siblings and was financially strapped. "In case it's not possible" to come up with the needed five hundred, Fromm wrote Horkheimer, "please send me a cable, so I do not raise false hopes in my mother." Horkheimer immediately replied that the Institute had its own financial crisis and could not arrange the loan. Although the details are unclear, Fromm somehow raised the money—perhaps from his own funds and those of friends, and probably from the assistance of a relative at the National Coordinating Committee for Aid to Refugees and Emigrants Coming from Germany. He had his mother transported to England, where he kept her well funded until she was legally permitted to immigrate to America in 1941.[9]

Pathos and Exuberance: Aunt Sophie's Choice

As Hitler expanded his control over much of Europe, Fromm pondered the troublesome future of humanity under these terrible circumstances. And though he was able to get his mother out of Germany, he had to reckon with requests for help from other distressed family members and friends.

Heinz Brandt was Fromm's second cousin on his mother's side. His grandfather, Ludwig Krause, played a very important role in Fromm's childhood and encouraged his scholarly inclinations. Fromm promised Uncle Ludwig before he died "that I would always do my best to help his grandchildren whenever they were in need." By the mid- and late 1930s, Ludwig Krause's oldest grandson, Heinz, was certainly in need.[10]

When Hitler came to power, Heinz Brandt was a student of sociology and economics and something of an intellectual. As a member of the German Communist Party, he joined the anti-Nazi underground. Because of his opposition to the Nazi regime, Heinz, along with several communist colleagues, was arrested in December 1934, convicted of high treason, and sentenced to six years in Prussian prisons. After having served their full sentence in December 1940, Heinz's non-Jewish accomplices were released, but he remained in prison. In 1941, he was transferred to Sachsenhausen, an early concentration camp in Oranienburg, a town on the outskirts of Berlin. The camp had initially been established to deal with political prisoners. In October 1942, he was deported again—this time to Auschwitz. After over two years in Auschwitz, Brandt was required to participate in the notorious death march from Auschwitz to Buchenwald, which he miraculously survived.[11]

Fromm learned of Heinz Brandt's initial imprisonment in the mid-1930s and began corresponding with Heinz's mother (Gertrud), sending her considerable amounts of money. When the Germans occupied Posen, she, her husband, and their youngest child, Wolfgang, were deported to a Jewish resettlement area at Ostrow-Lubelski, near Lublin. With economic survival even more difficult in the new location, she became active in a mutual support organization of fellow deportees. When her husband died in 1940, Fromm offered to do anything for Gertrud that he possibly could, but his options were limited.[12]

He used some of the channels he had relied on to support and rescue his mother, including the Somlo financial firm, and forwarded the equivalent of seventy-five dollars monthly to Posen to help the Brandts. By 1938, Gertrud informed Fromm that Heinz's life hung in the balance and urged him to pursue a pardon from German authorities and a visa out of Germany. Fromm wrote to Horkheimer, asking whether, through the Frankfurt Institute affiliation with Columbia University, he might secure a student visa for Heinz. When that option failed, Fromm contacted Hermia Neild of the German Emergency Committee of the Society of Friends in London and worked with her on strategies to have Heinz released and gain entry to England. Although Heinz was a late registrant for the limited quota of Polish migrants to England, Fromm secured the appropriate visa. But when war broke out between Germany and England, the Nazi regime refused to honor a British visa for a Jewish communist, and Heinz remained in prison.[13]

Early in 1940, Fromm contacted Madame Favez of the Frankfurt Institute office in Geneva and sent her money to keep track of Heinz and to make sure Gertrud and her family had sufficient food. Favez and Fromm then tried to secure a visa for Heinz to a Latin American country. When Gertrud discovered that Heinz might be released if he migrated to Shanghai, Fromm immediately contacted the Jüdische Hilfsverein (an organization established in 1841 to give financial assistance to Jewish students) in

Berlin, donated $280, and had Brandt relatives in Seattle and Boston contribute the three hundred dollars more he had been told would be needed for transport. After German authorities rejected transport to China, Fromm filed several affidavits asking the American consul to issue Heinz a visa for the United States: "Since this young man has lost his father and since his mother is unable to assist him, I am the only one who is in a position to help him and therefore feel a strong moral obligation to do so."[14]

The Nazis repeatedly refused to free Heinz. When he was sent to Auschwitz in the fall of 1942, Fromm understandably predicted that he would be executed. Despite this, Fromm continued to explore his options. Heinz survived the death march to Buchenwald, which was later liberated by the American army. It was "luck, luck, and luck again," Heinz stated to explain his survival, and he gave Fromm the credit for facilitating that "luck."[15]

Fromm and Brandt remained lifelong friends. Fromm never ceased to encourage him in his political activism and in his scholarly interests and supported him financially. Whenever Fromm wrote of freedom as a responsibility to behave ethically, his reflections on Heinz Brandt helped shape his words. Thoughts of his cousin were important in almost all of Fromm's future formulations on authoritarianism.[16]

In addition to helping Gertrud and Heinz, Fromm was involved in a web of correspondence among members of the Krause family during the years when he formulated and completed *Escape from Freedom*. This correspondence is of incalculable importance in comprehending the book. More generally, it is a treasure trove in understanding one of the options German Jews had in responding to the Nazis.

The correspondence among Sophie Krause Engländer; her daughter, Eva Krakauer; and the rest of the Krause family reveals how a German Jewish family frantically worked to stay together emotionally as they were forced to separate in a world less than welcoming to Jewish émigrés. Having escaped to but feeling isolated in La Paz, Bolivia, Eva wrote to all of her immediate Krause relatives, providing long accounts of the information she received in Sophie's detailed letters (periodically enclosing an original letter itself). Family members, including Rosa in London and Erich in New York, were instructed to add to the pool of family information and to urge the recipients to do the same, especially when they received a direct letter from Sophie, creating in effect a chain letter. When Sophie and her husband, David, were ultimately executed in the Theresienstadt concentration camp, she left behind a very extensive correspondence that revealed quite concretely Fromm's place in the family's relief and rescue effort. More than any other source, this correspondence reveals the strong personal dimension in *Escape from Freedom*. Indeed, it is inconceivable that Fromm could have written with such a deep, passionate, and compelling voice if the Krause family tragedy had not been a central experience in his life. Nevertheless, though Fromm played a significant role, letters hint repeatedly that given his resources and connections, he could have done considerably more for family members in distress. It was this fact that caused Fromm not only to break with much of his extended family but also ultimately with the Jewish religion.[17]

In March 1939, when Sophie Krause Engländer's weekly letters to Eva's family in La Paz began, she was sixty-five, and her husband was seventy-six. Not unlike many other German Jews, Sophie and David found themselves trapped in post-Kristallnacht Germany. In addition to employment restrictions and its curbs on earning power, the Nazi regime started charging very high fees for emigration. The Jüdische Hilfsverein prioritized the departure of younger generations of Jews, and Sophie and David gave what money they had to help Eva and her husband, Bernhard, move to La Paz. From La Paz, Eva and Bernhard attempted to raise a considerable amount of money to get her parents out of Germany and counted heavily on a contribution from Fromm. However, the outbreak of war late in 1939 meant that it was unlikely Sophie and David would ever leave Germany, for now there were even more stringent limitations on visas and passage by ship.[18]

Notwithstanding, Sophie and David Engländer were determined to escape, but this required even more money than they anticipated. They had to pay special fees, to be sure, along with very substantial bribes to Nazi officials. The couple appealed to the larger Krause family, though they expected that much of the money would come from the New York relative who had mastered some of the procedures involved in post-Kristallnacht rescue operations and was already quite prominent.[19]

"Unfortunately, we haven't been careful when choosing our American relatives," Sophie wrote to Eva in January 1940, obliquely referring to Fromm. He chipped in some funds, but Sophie knew that the money he had sent was nowhere near the sum he had sent to the Brandt family. In his efforts for the Brandt family, Fromm had cooperated modestly with Lisa Jacob, a veteran of Jewish rescue efforts, but he did not approach her to help free Sophie and David Engländer. Eva implied that because Fromm was childless, he lacked a sense of family responsibility. Sophie was trying to prod her sister, Rosa, to persuade her son to do more.[20]

In addition to documenting their own efforts of escape, Sophie's letters to Eva and her family described the escapes and locations of family around the world. Besides accounting for Rosa, Sophie reported on Anna Ruth, her oldest sister, who managed to escape from Germany. She and her husband, the foreign correspondent Wilhelm Breslauer, had been able to immigrate to Chile in 1939 (one of the last countries to issue visas to German Jews). Erich's cousin, Charlotte, left for São Paulo, Brazil, with her husband, Leo Hirschfeld, a once prominent Berlin judge, in 1937. Charlotte's brother, the architect Fritz Stein, and his wife, Lotte Munthe, followed to São Paulo. Charlotte and Fritz rescued their parents, Martha and Bernhard Stein, getting them to São Paulo as well.[21]

Hasty references indicate that others ended up in Palestine, while some Jewish friends of the family went to Cuba and from there to other locations. Fromm supported these various efforts in what ways he could; for instance, he swore an affidavit promising to support his uncle and aunt, Martin and Johanna Krause, in New York as late as May 1941, though their ultimate fate is unclear.[22]

Sophie's letters were always upbeat. Circulating from Eva to the larger Krause family, they were life-affirming emotional glue that held the wider family together and kept news circulating among its members in Bolivia, Chile, Brazil, England, North America, and other locations. Sophie described how she put photographs of family members on her desk or her walls, as if she was conversing with them: "your faces are smiling at me. Don't complain that we couldn't come to you any more. . . . Regards to the Steins, all Hirschfelds, Aunt Rosinchen (Rosa), Erich, Altmanns, Meta, Ita, Aunt Irma, (and) Greti when you are writing to them." On the verge of departing with her husband for Theresienstadt, Sophie remained positive: "We have had a good and beautiful life because we have good children and grandchildren that we can be proud of. We had brothers and sisters with whom we lived in great harmony. How beautiful it was in our beloved Hohenberge when we were all together." On another occasion, Sophie broadcast to the family through Eva "all the joy that one has had and one is grateful for everything that made one's life so rich." "How nice it was that we were so lucky to know so many good people and dear people in our life." Sophie concluded her final epistle: "I have to tell you again and again what these letters mean to us." Warm and hopeful correspondence maintained a sense of family despite the Nazi rampage. If one wonders why Erich's personal life was often joyous despite the destruction of his family and other serious troubles, the letters from Sophie were hardly extraneous.[23]

Because Rosa also maintained an extensive, if less detailed and hardly as revealing, correspondence with the entire Krause family, Erich became drawn even more into the web of Krause family communication. Because German authorities censored the length and content of Rosa's letters as well as Sophie's, both used subtle hints in code to describe the precarious situation of German Jews. For example, "Mr. H" or "Number 1" referenced Hitler, "Mr. M" was Mussolini, and a "traveling" person signified someone who had recently been executed.

In addition to engineering this code and supervising most family communication, when Sophie suspected that her own letters to a particular family member had not arrived, she wrote to Fromm for help. When her cherished communication with Eva seemed to get "lost" in the mail, Sophie relayed to Fromm the information that he must somehow convey to her. Sophie and Eva also counted on Fromm to keep them posted on Heinz Brandt's difficult situation. Perhaps most concretely, and despite intimations that Fromm was not doing enough financially for them, family members acknowledged that he embodied the Jewish sense of "God," essentially representing ethical conduct. They mentioned the many books and articles he mailed to them. The concreteness of these gifts provoked Sophie to characterize Fromm as the most "secure" source of assistance that the larger family had.[24]

Despite his activity on behalf of his relatives, his generally limited role in assisting Sophie and David Engländer signaled an emerging family rift between Erich and the larger Krause family. Fromm felt that whereas Heinz Brandt and his mother and siblings had actively pursued their freedom, Sophie and David's efforts were lacking. Even as late as Kristallnacht, the Engländers continued to hope that Hitler would fall from power, which Erich considered absurd. He failed to recognize that the Engländers were considerably older than Heinz Brandt and that conditions for escape were increasingly constricted for Jews in Berlin as Hitler pondered the "final solution."[25]

If Sophie was displeased that Fromm did not make sufficient efforts on her behalf, she did not understand that the lives and welfare of a good many other German Jews had commanded his attention, including his mentor Salman Rabinkow and Peter Glück, a brilliant German economic and political critic. Indeed, he came to the assistance of quite a few Jewish intellectuals, religious leaders, and political activists. The point is that as Fromm was writing *Escape from Freedom*, he was actively working to help émigrés escape the Hitler regime so that they could enjoy their freedom. The force and clarity of the book was surely influenced by his almost daily interventions for émigré assistance.[26]

The Culture and Personality Movement

After Fromm's Frankfurt colleagues relocated to New York City, most continued to speak and write in German and confined their activities to the Institute's building in Morningside Heights. In contrast, Fromm mixed enthusiastically with the Columbia faculty and made contact with New York psychoanalysts. In these and other activities, he made a concerted effort to speak and write proficient English. The process of mastering the language began with his American patients at the Berlin Institute for Psychoanalysis. Fromm's first English-language papers appeared in 1937 and 1938. When the Frankfurt Institute refused to publish "A Contribution to the Method and Purpose of an Analytic Social Psychology," he translated it himself into respectable English so that it could reach an American audience. As Fromm drafted early chapters of *Escape from Freedom*, he asked Yale's prominent social psychologist, John Dollard, to go over his text to be sure that it could be readily understood by an American audience. Aside from a few grammatical errors and infelicities, Dollard assured Fromm that his English prose was clear and compelling. Indeed, the manuscript approached literary elegance. Nonetheless, Fromm worked very hard at streamlining his narrative in his redrafts. He also tried, at least modestly, to increase his command of American scholarship, especially the latest material in psychological and philosophical journals. Fromm also felt that it was very important to gain familiarity with the popular culture of his new country so that *Escape from Freedom* would be effective in warning American readers about the pressures to conform inherent even in democratic societies purporting to be free.[27]

As Fromm slowly disengaged from the Frankfurt Institute, he found a new social and intellectual home with a group of neo-Freudians, notably Harry Stack Sullivan, Clara Thompson, and Karen Horney, who were forging connections with a group of "culturist" anthropologists (including

Margaret Mead, Ruth Benedict, and Edward Sapir); they initiated the exciting and creative "Culture and Personality" movement. Fromm's interest stretched beyond the Monday-evening meetings with the Zodiac group, an informal neo-Freudian discussion group led by Sullivan and frequently joined by others such as Abram Kardiner and Fromm's estranged wife, Frieda. He also attended the exciting and joyous weekly gathering at Horney's apartment, which focused on culture and personality and which, by the late 1930s, had replaced the Zodiac meeting, and he shared with the group a reverence for the humanistic therapeutic approaches of Groddeck and Ferenczi and the promise of the Washington (D.C.) School of Psychiatry. Although the group shared a resistance to Freudian orthodoxy and rejected (in varying degrees) the concept of libidinal drives, they could not all be persuaded to accept the premise that society decidedly influenced a person's psyche.

Fromm's new "home" essentially represented the "culturist" psychoanalytic pioneers at the high point of their creative powers. John Dollard and Edward Sapir invited the analysts to their homes and to their Rockefeller Foundation–funded "Culture and Personality" seminar at Yale. Brilliant and exuberant as a facilitator of interdisciplinary movements, Mead invited them to a wide variety of professional and informal gatherings. As officers of the Washington-Baltimore Psychoanalytic Institute, Thompson and Sullivan invited the anthropologists to their gatherings, and Horney tried unsuccessfully to draw them into forums of the orthodox New York Psychoanalytic Society.

The Culture and Personality movement provided an important backdrop for Fromm while he was writing *Escape from Freedom.* His interaction with this group of eclectic, liberal-minded anthropologists and neo-Freudian psychologists placed him among scholars who fully and productively embraced their personal and intellectual freedom. They countered the orthodox establishment and mainstream norms, especially in their claim that culture trumped biology in explaining human behavior.[28]

The group was hardly an orthodox representation of academia at the time; members represented a diverse array of ethnicities, genders, and sexual orientations. In an attempt to explain the influence of culture on individuals, they melded psychology and anthropology. Rather than explaining differences among individuals by way of biology, they believed that individual differences could be accounted for by cultural conditioning, especially during early childhood. Though the influence of social-constructionist thinkers is doubtless of critical importance when considering the conceptualization of *Escape from Freedom*, their lifestyles are also important. Fromm found himself among scholars who exemplified an autonomous exercise of freedom, principally in terms of sexuality. It was a variant of what some scholars have described as the broadly "modernist" turn in intellectual and social life sanctioned by Freudian formulations—a break from libidinal repressions. Affairs among members of the group were numerous, including homosexual liaisons, notably between Mead and Benedict but also involving Harry Stack Sullivan and his diverse male housemates. Fromm may have speculated that this group exemplified the productive freedom from authority he outlined in his book. Among these scholars, several stand out as particularly influential to Fromm: Horney, Sullivan, and Mead.[29]

Karen Horney

Fromm's long friendship with Karen Horney contributed to his effort to understand and reach out to Americans and to familiarize himself with his new country and colleagues. He had taken an interest in Horney when he and Frieda visited Georg Groddeck in Baden Baden. Horney was fifteen years his senior, a physician, and the first female member of the Berlin Psychoanalytic Institute, where she was a senior training analyst. By the early 1930s, the friendship with Horney had deepened. She helped guide Fromm through the politics of the Berlin Institute, which was free from Freud's overwhelming dominance. Fromm found that it was possible there for Otto Fenichel, Wilhelm Reich, Franz Alexander, and others to innovate in theory and technique and to draw inspiration from the political and cultural atmosphere of Weimar.[30]

In his years at the Institute, Fromm had frequently visited Horney's home in Berlin, where her three teenage daughters regarded him as part of their family. To some degree, he seemed to replace their father, Oskar Horney, who had separated from Karen in 1926. Although it does not appear that Fromm was sexually involved with Karen Horney until 1934, his marriage to Frieda had effectively ended when he moved to the sanitarium in 1931, though the divorce would not be finalized until the 1940s. Through Groddeck, their common reading of Bachofen, and the comparatively flexible psychoanalytic atmosphere of Berlin, both Fromm and Horney began to entertain doubts about what they somewhat simplistically perceived as Freud's emphasis on patriarchy, the Oedipus complex, and a female sense of genital inferiority. Helene Deutsch, Freud's close disciple, recognized that Freud had become less dogmatic and more qualified on matters of gender, but she rarely conveyed this observation beyond an inner circle of loyalists. Never privy to discussions in that circle, Horney took direct issue with her perceptions of Freudian orthodoxy in her early work. She insisted that female psychology had little to do with envy of the male penis; rather, it was based on lack of self-confidence and overemphasis on the love relationship. Fromm agreed with Horney that Freud had made short shrift of traditions of matriarchy and male insecurities over women's capacity to create and sustain life. More generally, the two were beginning to examine culture and society as well as intrapsychic explanations of human motivation.[31]

In 1932, Horney migrated to America to become associate director of Franz Alexander's newly established Chicago Psychoanalytic Institute. It was an uneasy relationship, for he had been her junior in Berlin. The more Horney experienced the marked distinctions between German and American culture and language, the further she strayed from Freudian orthodoxy and lent credence to the idea that cultural specifics reinforced parentally influenced character traits. Knowing that Fromm shared her culturist perspective and could speak and read English, she invited him to become a lecturer at the Chicago Psychoanalytic Institute in 1933, while he was visiting the United States and soon to be charged with the responsibility of finding a home for the Frankfurt Institute. When Naphtali died in Frankfurt while Fromm was in Chicago, Erich did not return to Germany for a funeral or memorial. Time, distance, and the cost of a ship voyage aside, his absence underscores his effort to avoid rekindling painful childhood memories. Instead, he remained in the United States and followed Horney the following year to New York. Horney left Chicago for a position with more independence and responsibility, though she had run-ins with the orthodox Freudians at the New York Psychoanalytic Institute; Fromm settled with his colleagues of the Frankfurt Institute at Morningside Heights.[32]

Fromm and Horney became intimate even as he remained legally married to Frieda, helped her to leave Europe, and assisted her in establishing herself professionally in America. To be sure, Fromm was aware of the string of affairs Horney had with younger men; she had been a supervisor or training analyst for many of them. Apparently these men made her feel rejuvenated. A negative self-image and sense of homeliness had plagued Horney since childhood. Sexual conquests reassured her that she remained young and desirable, while young psychoanalytic trainees often saw career advantages in sleeping with a prominent senior analyst. An abundance of professionally questionable affairs in Chicago had contributed to Alexander's sense of relief when Horney left his institute and moved to New York. Fromm appreciated Horney's blunt, earthy manner and her passion. She seemed to "burn" with an inner energy and directness that overshadowed her less-than-spectacular physical appearance and her bedtime proclivities with multiple partners. He also considered Horney "a rather courageous person who said what she thought." Despite their substantial age difference, Horney regarded the younger Fromm as somewhat of an idealized father figure, perhaps replacing her suboptimal relationship with her own father. Obviously, this complicated and perhaps compromised the sexual liaison between the two. Fromm was her "magic helper" who approved her challenges to psychoanalytic orthodoxy during the day and slept with her at night. From Fromm's perspective, the relationship with Horney may have fulfilled a stabilizing need for female companionship that was evident throughout his life in his steady string of serious and sometimes casual relationships.[33]

Horney's attack on the orthodox Freudians went well beyond Freud's misunderstanding of female psychology. By 1935, Horney began to advance arguments on the roots of neurosis that shaped her exceedingly popular classic, *The Neurotic Personality of Our Time* (1937). Differing explicitly with Freud's *Civilization and Its Discontents* (1930), which argued that neurosis was rooted in the need for institutional stability through instinctual repression, Horney's retort was culture bound. If parents were empathetic toward their child and enhanced the child's sense of security, fostered the child's unique life-affirming individuality, and reduced the competitive, unsettling qualities in the environment, the child could escape neuroses and live a happy and productive life. However, Horney missed what Fromm and Freud periodically emphasized: civilization could be a force of repression, but it could also be a force of social solidarity.[34]

Horney's next two books, *New Ways in Psychoanalysis* (1939) and *Self-Analysis* (1942), were more upbeat. Indeed, they underscored a "life-affirming" perspective not unlike what Fromm was soon to call a "productive character." Even if one was not necessarily good, one was able to overcome imperfections as one grew older, owing to an innately constructive and malleable "constitution." In addition to life-affirming parenting, a "constructively friendly" analyst and a supportive and relatively noncompetitive environment could (at any age) free up a person's repressed neurotic character defenses (usually rooted in alienation) and allow for full self-realization.[35]

Horney and Fromm were intensely curious about America and thrived on constant discussions of subjects both personal and social. Knowing that they would not be able to return to Germany for some time to come, they were determined to make themselves at home in America. She enhanced his knowledge of psychoanalytic theory and the politics of the profession in America much as she had in Berlin. They discovered that they were better able to amplify a "culturist" alternative to Freudian orthodoxy in their new surroundings. Horney increased his awareness of mothering and the psychological issues of girls and women, the importance of warmth and empathy in the therapeutic process, and the great potential and elasticity of human personality. As Fromm came to understand Horney's concept of neurosis rooted in basic anxiety, he equated it to the inner sense of powerlessness and distress that he increasingly referred to as alienation. Her "life-affirming" goal closely approximated his goal of a "productive social character." He in turn taught Horney about socioeconomic structures and social class, acquainted her with classical social theory, and enabled her to understand more clearly competitive capitalist society's deleterious effects on its citizens.

Horney also helped to acquaint Fromm with a cluster of revisionist psychoanalysts who sympathized with his often exaggerated differences with Freud and were influenced by his evolving notion of social character—Harry Stack Sullivan, Clara Thompson, and William Silverberg among them. They called themselves the Zodiac circle. From time to time, Horney also invited others from the overlapping culture and personality movement to her apartment, and there Fromm met John Dollard, Ruth Benedict, Margaret Mead, Harold Laswell, and Abram Kardiner. They played roulette together and raised one another's spirits, and Fromm sometimes entertained the group by singing Hasidic songs. As Fromm struggled to establish the focus of *Escape from Freedom*, it was these friends who became his chief intellectual support group. They provided an element of joy and conviviality in his life as he analyzed the pathos of contemporary authoritarianism and found clarity in expounding on the psychological basis of the Nazi appeal to the German public.[36]

Although the rapport between Fromm and Horney was very close, it also had its limitations. Horney's autobiographic *Self-Analysis* clearly alluded to these friends in her semifictional account of the relationship between Clare and Peter. Like Horney, Clare was troubled by a plethora of insecurities and compulsions and depended on Peter's (i.e., Fromm's) strength as her "magic helper." Horney had written generally of the neurotic need for a "partner" who guides one's life and will not leave one deserted or alone; Clare had precisely these needs. Although Peter was kind and cared deeply for Clare, avowed his "deep and everlasting love," and often presented her with gifts, she realized in the course of her self-analysis that he was excessively detached, wrapped up in himself, and remote. He resented excessive demands on his time and energies and wanted to remain free from demanding long-term personal commitment. Peter also had a self-righteous messianic or prophetic quality that limited the degree of emotional sharing with Clare.[37]

Just as Peter would not marry Clare, it became increasingly clear to Horney that although Fromm might be an exacting intellectual colleague and exciting lover, he would not consent to marrying her. He did not want to be her "magic helper" and feared that Horney's dependence on him threatened his autonomy. He told her that he needed to concentrate his energy on completing his book on authority and freedom. Horney was resentful; Fromm's rebuff rekindled her sense of inadequacy.[38]

One factor that undermined their relationship was that in 1937 Fromm had taken on Karen Horney's middle daughter, Marianne, who was in a psychiatric residency at New York's Payne-Whitney Clinic, for a three-year training analysis. Karen had recommended Fromm to Marianne despite the emotional risks of having her companion and lover act as her daughter's analyst. Fromm lacked the professionalism and understanding to refuse to analyze Marianne. Marianne told him, during the analysis, of Karen's parental deficiencies, which he took as fact, and Fromm's rapport with Karen deteriorated.[39]

By 1940, the relationship between Fromm and Horney was ending. Fromm experienced this as liberating; he could focus his energies on completing *Escape from Freedom*. Indeed, he augmented his emotional distance from Horney by becoming sexually involved with the young black dancer and choreographer Katherine Dunham. Though this quick transition to a new relationship seemed at odds with his self-proclaimed need for time to work on the book, it underscored Fromm's narcissistic need for female companionship to help stabilize a hectic life. Over the next few years, Horney, her sense of inferiority having resurfaced, found solace by sleeping with Paul Tillich, Erich Maria Remarque, and others, sometimes revealing her pain and anger toward Fromm.[40]

In April 1941, the New York Psychoanalytic Society charged Horney with "disturbing the students" in analytic training, disqualified her as a training analyst, and demoted her from instructor to lecturer. Horney's blatant critique of Freudian orthodoxy and her outspoken manner largely contributed to this outcome. It is unclear whether her sexual habits did as well. She resigned and founded the Association for the Advancement of Psychoanalysis. The AAP reflected Fromm's, Sullivan's, and, above all, her own "culturist" or neo-Freudian psychoanalytic perspectives and especially Horney's desire to lead an institution and movement of her own. Fromm and Horney retained a professional relationship for a few more years and occasionally traveled together until 1943. That year, she stripped him of the right to supervise AAP students in clinical work and relegated him to teaching a seminar on psychoanalytic technique (much as the New York Psychoanalytic Society had deprived her of such responsibilities). Horney claimed that because Fromm was not a medically trained analyst, his presence on the AAP faculty would jeopardize the affiliation it sought with the New York Medical College. As Fromm's analysand and friend, Clara Thompson insisted that the issue of lay analysis was a false one; the medical college would likely have made an exception in Fromm's case. By reducing his responsibilities, Horney had bested Fromm in the internal politics of psychoanalysis, demonstrating that the AAP needed only one distinguished and uncontested leader. This effectively ended their relationship.[41]

Fromm's tumultuous relationship with Horney affected the thematic direction for *Escape from Freedom*. Freedom required that the individual summon the energy and courage to make spontaneous, productive, reasoned, and life-affirming use of his autonomy, Fromm argued. One must not delegate choices to authority figures that offered sadomasochistic appeals and demanded social conformity. This theme of his first book crystallized when Fromm was with Horney. She defended his theoretical position and helped him to augment it, emphasizing that her concept of basic anxiety dovetailed with his on alienation and stressing that Fromm's notion of sadomasochism was a neurotic strategy for coping. Essentially, Horney helped Fromm to free himself from the straitjacket of intellectual orthodoxy at the Frankfurt Institute and within the psychoanalytic community. But as their amorous relationship faltered, he felt that this was for the best—that the relationship was circumscribing his own freedom.[42]

Harry Stack Sullivan

Next to Horney, no one was more important to Fromm in the years that he conceived, reconceived, and completed *Escape from Freedom* than Harry Stack Sullivan. Fromm discussed its contents at length with Sullivan and borrowed from Sullivan's conceptualizations. As he concluded *Escape*, Fromm emphasized that his and Sullivan's approach to the human condition were congruent. In the process, Fromm overemphasized his disagreement with Freud:

> We believe that man is primarily a social being, and not, as Freud assumed, primarily self-sufficient and only secondarily in need of others in order to satisfy his instinctual needs. In this sense, we believe that individual psychology is fundamentally social psychology or, in Sullivan's terms, the psychology of interpersonal relationships; the key problem of psychology is that of the particular kind of relatedness of the individual toward the world, not that of satisfaction or frustration of single instinctual desires.

Sullivan thought very highly of the book and, as editor of the journal *Psychiatry*, he was glad to publish Fromm. Indeed, Sullivan treated *Escape* very specially in his journal, arranging eight lengthy reviews of Fromm's book in a single issue, involving interdisciplinary scholars such as Ruth Benedict and Ashley Montagu and leading thinkers in the culture and personality movement.[43]

In all probability, Fromm first met Sullivan through Clara Thompson, whom Fromm later analyzed, shortly after he arrived in New York. Trained as a psychiatrist largely by William Alanson White at St. Elizabeth's Hospital in Washington, D.C., and taking his first job at Sheppard and Enoch Pratt Hospital near Baltimore, Sullivan became a pioneer during the 1920s in work with schizophrenics who had been characterized as narcissistic and incapable of emotional attachments. Sullivan discovered that the young male schizophrenics on his ward at Sheppard-Pratt were unapproachable using the traditional Freudian technique of probing their inner lives to reconstruct depleted egos. Instead, the patients became communicative when he treated them with warmth and empathy. For Sullivan, the personality of the therapist became the key to cultivating or failing to cultivate attachments to the patient. While Freudian excavation of a patient's inner drives was unproductive, the quality of social life and relationships in the present helped the schizophrenic find a path toward self-understanding. Sullivan found that schizophrenics, approached with kindness and patience, could discuss the patterns of their relationships, past and present. Initially, the transference between patient and therapist was rather intermittent, touching erratically upon relationships in his distant past. As the patient found favor and trust in the therapist, however, he revealed and came to understand paralyzing discontinuities and anxieties in the total field of his relationships. [44]

This experience with schizophrenics influenced Sullivan's general approach to human personality. In 1930, he left for New York to open a private psychiatric practice on Park Avenue and to organize the Washington-Baltimore Psychoanalytic Society. By 1933, he was president of the William Alanson White Psychoanalytic Foundation and split his time between his New York practice and the foundation offices in Washington, D.C. As he finished his work at Sheppard-Pratt and refocused his professional life in psychoanalytic directions, Sullivan formulated and fleshed out what he called "interpersonal theory."

The social psychologist George Herbert Mead's remark that the self was formed by "the reflected appraisals of others" acted as a catalyst, and by the early to mid-1930s Sullivan was able to formulate a comprehensive theory based on the premise that one's personality did not reside within an inner self but in the interpersonal field—in a social environment with other people. Individual personality was the pattern of recurrent interpersonal encounters, real and imagined, which characterized one's life. In some encounters, one pursued biological needs and satisfactions such as food and sex, but in others, one pursued personal security within society. For Sullivan, an effective psychoanalyst was a "participant-observer" who eschewed Freudian neutrality and faced the patient warmly but directly. (Although Sullivan held that the therapist, as "participant-observer," had to be empathetically interactive with the patient, the therapist must eschew deep personal involvement.) He encouraged the patient to present the patterns of his social interactions, actual and fantasized, focusing on present relationships but using them as a tunnel into the past. As the patient described those patterns, Sullivan probed for the conflicts and dissatisfactions inherent within them and the defense machinery the patient deployed at those contested points to satisfy biological needs in order to restore a sense of interpersonal security. But "security" or "defense operations" perpetuated troublesome interactive patterns because they promoted intense and unfocused anxiety akin to what Horney described as "basic anxiety." Such anxiety interfered with thinking, communicating, learning, emotional intimacy, and sexual performance. The analyst as a supportive participant-observer relived those troubling experiences with the patient and helped him dissolve the anxiety that propped up the defenses. At that point, the patient understood that his defenses or security operations interfered with effective living and could cease depending on them. The personality field would be free of obstructions and insecurities.[45]

When Fromm heard Sullivan elaborate his interpersonal theory, he sensed their affinity. Fromm had serious misgivings about Freud's libidinal theory, and Sullivan likewise had no place for it. Fromm felt that Freud was insufficiently attentive to the influence of external social forces, and Sullivan held that personality was wholly a social construct. Fromm was struggling to articulate what was to become his concept of social character, where the self was grounded in the cognitive and emotional field of a specific group or culture. Sullivan's defining of the self in a field of real and fantasized social interactions guided Fromm as he worked on his social character formulation, which became a crucial theoretical essay at the end of *Escape from Freedom*. Fromm also realized that Sullivan's clinical approach as a participant-observer echoed Sandor Ferenczi, Georg Groddeck, and, above all, his beloved mentor Salman Rabinkow.[46]

Nevertheless, in their early discussions Fromm insisted that personhood reflected more than the interpersonal aspect of social relationships. There was also an internal depth, spirituality, and uniqueness to each human being. Moreover, although interpersonal theory was compatible with Marxism, Sullivan had not drawn on what Fromm called "Marxist humanism" or emphasized economic and class forces. Above all, for Sullivan, the therapist was an expert in personal relations. Fromm preferred the term "observant participant," as he felt that effective therapy required the analyst to establish a deep relationship between the inner essence of his very being and the inner essence of the patient.[47]

In the decade ahead, Fromm would offer a rather substantial critique of interpersonal theory as he developed his concept of the "marketing character." But for the time being, Fromm was overjoyed with his new friend. Sullivan, for his part, was attracted to the creative spark and strength in Fromm that allowed him, like Horney, to break from their orthodox Freudian training and embrace socially grounded psychoanalysis. Although Sullivan did not read German, he became familiar with Fromm's German worker study and the contents of several of Fromm's articles in *Zeitschrift für Sozialforschung*. More importantly, Sullivan soothed Fromm's insecurities by assuring Fromm that he was learning from him. Interpersonal theory required constant revision and fine tuning, he insisted, and Fromm was helping him in that process.[48]

Indeed, as a distinguished psychiatrist and psychoanalyst, Sullivan served as perhaps Fromm's most important patron and advocate from the mid-1930s through the publication of *Escape from Freedom* in 1941. As president of the William Alanson White Psychoanalytic Foundation, Sullivan wrote Fromm a letter in October 1936 that assured him a future as a psychoanalyst outside the Frankfurt Institute. Sullivan's psychoanalytic foundation planned to establish the Washington School of Psychiatry for interdisciplinary graduate training in "the investigation of human personality," and it would focus on "man as a psychobiological organism social in orientation within a world of cultural emigrants." Psychoanalysts and psychiatrists would become social-cultural theorists as well as clinical instructors. Fromm was invited to be a professor of social psychology at the Washington school, to offer eight lectures each school year, and to participate in advanced seminars whenever he was in New York. Fromm immediately and happily accepted the appointment, viewing it as a mark of his legitimacy in prestigious clinical circles where his Freudian revisionism would be taken seriously. "The new school," he wrote, "promises to become a new beginning and a center of psychiatry and of psychoanalytic theory, freed from the shackles of sterile dogmatism and fertile through being rooted in the soil of an understanding of culture and social dynamics." Before he joined the Washington school, Fromm had no institutional source for psychoanalytic patients, so his practice was limited to a few academics in areas like sociology and anthropology who wanted to become acquainted with or sought emotional relief through psychoanalysis. With the affiliation came the opportunity for patient referrals, and Fromm's psychoanalytic practice grew to the point where he became less dependent on other sources of income. By the end of the decade, he was earning a comfortable five thousand dollars a year from his various income sources. Additionally, in 1939 the Frankfurt Institute paid him a very substantial severance settlement of twenty thousand dollars.[49]

Sullivan nominated Fromm for inclusion in the *Biographical Directory of American Men of Science*. Also, he was asked to critique early drafts of Fromm's papers as well as crucial sections of *Escape from Freedom*. Fromm was deeply grateful and acknowledged that Sullivan's interpersonal approach helped him to frame issues that Freudian metapsychology could not accommodate. He came to see "love," for example, as "one of these readinesses stimulated to active expression by a certain object" (i.e., person). Fromm sent Sullivan a case of Alsatian wine for all his help. Sullivan enhanced Fromm's writing style as he navigated the transition from German to English and clarified his theory of social character. Sullivan also helped Fromm frame the argumentative structure for *Escape from Freedom*. All the while, Fromm knew Sullivan's support would withstand even his conceptual deviations from interpersonal theory; Sullivan took pleasure in seeing Fromm develop his own metapsychological framework. There was an element of exuberance in the Fromm-Sullivan relationship, thanks to their mutually supportive and productive rapport both intellectually and personally.[50]

Having introduced Fromm to Sullivan, Clara Thompson played a substantial role in enhancing that rapport and articulating how their ideas overlapped and diverged. Over time, she came to regard the two men as her joint mentors. Sullivan met Thompson in the Baltimore area in 1922 when she began a three-year residency at Adolf Meyer's Phipps Clinic. Sullivan worked nearby at Sheppard-Pratt. After spending her childhood in Rhode Island, Thompson pursued a career in medicine, completing her undergraduate studies at Pembroke (the women's college at Brown University). In 1916, she entered medical school at Johns Hopkins. Her psychiatric residency with Meyer brought her into contact with Sullivan, whom she helped to grasp the thinking and techniques of Meyer's "psychobiology," which connected a patient's life experiences with his physiological and biological particulars.

Sullivan, for his part, enhanced Thompson's understanding of his mentor, William Alanson White, who had tried to develop a socially grounded psychoanalysis that traditional psychiatrists might find acceptable. The intellectual rapport between Thompson and Sullivan had shades of romance, even as both prized their autonomy and separate households and despite Sullivan's less-than-secret bisexuality. Like others in Fromm's intellectual circle, especially Mead, Benedict, and Horney in the Culture and Personality movement, Sullivan hardly conformed to the gender norms of the times. In 1927, when James Inscoe (Jimmy) moved into Sullivan's house to serve as his cook, secretary, and "foster son" companion, Sullivan persuaded Thompson to travel to Budapest to be analyzed by Ferenczi, who died before his analysis of Thompson was complete. With Thompson in Budapest, Sullivan and Jimmy almost certainly had an affair. She left Budapest after Ferenczi died unexpectedly, her analysis incomplete, returned to New York, and resumed her increasingly troubled friendship with Sullivan. Thompson conveyed to him elements of Ferenczi's therapeutic approach, which were quite compatible with his interpersonal theory. While she was analyzing Sullivan (and doubtless learning of Jimmy's importance in his life), Thompson asked Fromm to complete her own analysis. Fromm unwisely took on the task, just as he had similarly defied accepted professional standards in analyzing Horney's daughter. The analytic process seemed to make Thompson an important, if unstable, connecting link, emotionally as well as intellectually, between Sullivan and Fromm.[51]

As the "middle person" in this triad, Thompson began a lifelong process of working out fusions between the theories of both, yielding what she called an interpersonal theory of psychoanalysis. She tried to integrate Fromm with Sullivan in the mid- to late 1930s and summarized years of reflection in 1956 with her penetrating essay "Sullivan and Fromm," in which she concluded that the "work of each supplements the other, and their basic assumptions about human beings are similar." Both were decidedly influenced by exchanges with others in the Culture and Personality movement, facilitating a fusion of cultural anthropology with psychoanalysis. Sullivan, however, moved decidedly away from Freudian premises after he concluded that orthodox psychoanalysis did not work on schizophrenics. In contrast, Thompson noted that Fromm had been trained as a classical, if somewhat eclectic, Freudian. By the time she met Fromm, he was gradually moving away from psychoanalytic orthodoxy, although that was not in all respects a distancing from Freud.[52]

Fromm realized, Thompson stated, that contrary to Freud, man was the least instinct ridden of all animals and literally had to be taught by society how to live. Unlike Sullivan, to be sure, Thompson understood that Fromm believed (with Freud) that each individual had a unique and distinctive inner core, but Fromm also believed that core was modified significantly by society. Thompson pointed out that unlike Sullivan, Fromm expounded a developmental process that was not anchored in chronological stages such as Sullivan's (i.e., infancy, juvenile life, preadolescence, early adolescence, late adolescence, and adulthood). As man recognized his freedom to develop his intellectual and technical powers, he gained mastery over nature and felt increasing distance from his neighbors. "According to Fromm," Thompson underscored, "man is constantly tempted, therefore, to go back to some form of relatedness to his fellows, even at the price of giving up some of his individuality." What Thompson came to realize, as she tried to make sense of over two decades of living within her emotional and intellectual "triangle" connected to Sullivan and Fromm, was that Fromm was working on the conceptual structure for *Escape from Freedom*. Thompson felt, however, that Fromm would not have been moving so firmly toward that structure without Sullivan's notion that the self was the product of an emotional field of interpersonal social relationships and Sullivan's premise that social isolation was the dilemma of modern man. But Thompson recognized in her 1956 essay that what was most striking was the interpenetration of the ideas of Fromm, her second analyst, with those of Sullivan, her colleague, analysand—and someone with whom she had once contemplated marriage.[53]

Margaret Mead

While Fromm's relationship with the neo-Freudians certainly influenced both his life and ideas, he also formed significant connections with the anthropologists Ruth Benedict, Margaret Mead, and Edward Sapir. Their ideas had considerable weight and influence on his work. Fromm's extensive correspondence with Margaret Mead, in particular, illustrated not only the fusion of these two "communities" of New York–based friends but also that he was afforded a professional and social "center" substantially more convivial, upbeat, and supportive than the Frankfurt Institute. He once wrote to Mead, for example, that he had read her book *Sex and Temperament in Three Primitive Societies* (1935) and was immensely impressed with her demonstration that different cultures yielded different "underlying psychic types," which seemed to resonate with the concept of character structures he was pursuing. Through Mead's discussion of how specific cultures created specific "configurations" of self, society, and emotionality, Fromm noted, she had helped him conceptualize what he called "social character." Her book was "an unusually important contribution to the progress of psychoanalytic thinking" and even therapeutic technique, Fromm insisted. Mead responded warmly and urged Fromm to attend the Culture and Personality gatherings that discussed those "configurations" integrating psyche with society. She also urged Fromm to seek out more of Geoffrey Gorer and other Culture and Personality scholars. Mead in her turn emphasized how she wished Fromm "were here to criticize and give more precise direction" to her scholarship. By 1939, Fromm and Mead were such close friends that he confided in her about his psychoanalytic colleagues and adversaries, his patients, and his growing reservations on orthodox analytic technique: "I do not think that analysis changes a personality in the sense of doing away with fundamental attributes like hatred." When Fromm congratulated Mead on her marriage to Gregory Bateson, he reflected on how important Mead and her colleagues had been to him since he arrived in New York: "If I should say what made life in New York attractive to me, the opportunity of seeing you or talking to you would be among the first things which would occur to me."[54]

In emphasizing how different cultures could produce different psychosocial "configurations," Mead, Benedict, and their colleagues participated in what would soon be called Soviet studies or "Kremlinology"—an effort to move beyond stereotypes of a monolithic Soviet political and social structure and examine the internal factions, ideologies, and machinations of Soviet elites. Running these discussions out of her New York office, Mead attracted psychoanalysts, anthropologists, and foreign policy specialists into the venture. The field blossomed after the war, centering around Harvard's Russian Institute, the State Department, and special offices in the U.S. military. Erik Erikson drew intellectual momentum from the Mead circle's Russian project, writing brilliantly about Gorky's childhood and the complex Russian society that was emerging as Gorky went off from the village of yore to the Bolshevik world of cities, factories, and heavy industry. While rubbing shoulders with those involved in Mead's project before and after the war, Fromm learned little from its efforts to fathom, in a nuanced way, the conflicts and contradictions inherent in Soviet life and governance. Indeed, although Fromm never embraced the view of a totalitarian Soviet state, neither did he ever go beyond the stock characterization of Russia as a bloated and inefficient bureaucratic managerial society.[55]

In contrast to the Russian project, Fromm was heavily influenced by the challenge that the Mead group had launched against the orthodox Freudian perspective on gender roles. Under the guise of a modernist project that underscored the efficacy of libidinal release, Mead, Benedict, and others in the group criticized the traditional interpretation for justifying patriarchy and the subordination of women. As the Mead group became intertwined with the neo-Freudian psychoanalysts, Fromm, Sullivan, Kardiner, and Sapir became more feminist than they might otherwise have been. By the time Fromm was completing *Escape*, there was accord by all members of the Mead circle on neo-Freudian gender premises: (1) the Oedipus complex was not universal but the product of monogamous patriarchal society. (2) Penis envy had nothing to do with woman's organic structure but symbolized male monopolization of power in patriarchal society. (3) With or without male support, women had to find new ways to lead productive lives without sacrificing their "biological function" of creating and sustaining life.[56]

This is not to say that Fromm was a feminist during the 1930s. It is to say that he belonged to professional and social groups that questioned the standard Freudian concepts of patriarchy and purported female shortcomings. If *Escape from Freedom* was a study of the dilemmas of humankind in an age of increasing authoritarianism, parts of it simultaneously echoed the needs of women for freedom from patriarchy. If psychoanalysis was influenced by the "modernist" concept of freeing the subjective self from untoward social constraints, Fromm felt that the field had to distance itself from patriarchy.

Katherine Dunham

Nine years younger than Fromm, Katherine Dunham was not part of the Mead circle, but she also played an important supportive role as Fromm was engaged in writing *Escape from Freedom*. Having survived a difficult and impoverished childhood in Chicago and Joliet, Illinois, she was becoming one of the first major figures to emerge in black concert dance during the early 1930s. Eventually she created her own company (primarily of student performers)—Ballet Negre. Dunham received a scholarship to the University of Chicago, where she was deeply influenced by the works of anthropologists such as Melville Herskovits and Robert Redfield, who argued for the survival of African culture and customs in African American culture. Completing her bachelor's degree in social anthropology in 1936, Dunham conducted anthropological fieldwork in the West Indies, where she detected links between the form and function of Caribbean dance and its African progenitors. Returning to Chicago in 1937, she founded the Negro Dance Group, which gave modern dance a lexicon of African and Caribbean styles of movement. She also became dance director of the Negro Unit of Chicago's Federal Theater Project. Fromm met her as she was commuting between Chicago and New York, where she also danced and choreographed. Her star rose in 1938 when she presented "L'Ag'Ya"—an exciting and expansive dance drama based on authentic African Caribbean material and costume. Her exciting production, "Tropics and Le Jazz Hot: From Haiti to Harlem" had an unexpected ten-week New York run, thrusting her into the national limelight.[57]

Fromm was blindsided by Dunham's beautiful and radiant face. She conversed with a gracious reticence about her vast knowledge of African-Caribbean cultural links. He marveled at her skill in expressing those connections in thrilling dance creations. Fromm fell for her with considerable passion, finding in her what he would soon describe as a "productive character" with creativity and a deep zest for life. He began helping to arrange for her performances in New York and hoped she could spend more time in the city. By this time, his affair with Dunham had probably begun. Because Fromm was still technically married to Frieda, he could not allow Dunham to spend nights in his Central Park West apartment. Consequently, he asked Sullivan for the personal favor of letting Dunham live in his house on East Sixty-fourth Street. Sullivan agreed, telling his friend Patrick Mullahy, a bisexual who also lived in the house, that she was exclusively Fromm's "girlfriend."[58]

The romantic part of Fromm's relationship with Dunham lasted perhaps three years—a crucial interval during the completion of *Escape from Freedom*—and probably ended in 1940 when she married John Pratt, a theatrical designer with whom she had worked in Chicago. Doubtless, Fromm's affair with Dunham contributed to his increasingly difficult rapport with Horney and their breakup. Even though Fromm seems more often than not to have been faithful to his partners, he usually began seeing other women when a long-term relationship was coming to a close, thus assuring continuing companionship. He considered the relationship with Dunham as more than a pleasurable sexual liaison.

Fromm enjoyed learning about the transmission of African dance movements to the Caribbean and into early African American dances such as juba and strut. Dunham and her associates provided his first exposure to artists and performers, and he loved it. Indeed, she helped Fromm to understand how their work was part of what has come to be called a Black Atlantic exchange of talents and ideas, which involved Paul Robeson, C. L. R. James, and Zora Neale Hurston as their work crossed the seas between Africa, the Caribbean, the United States, and Europe. From this point on, dance and musicals and their attendant ideas grew into an abiding interest of Fromm's. For the first time in his life, moreover, Fromm became sensitive to the daily constraints that even fairly prominent black women faced. Indeed, this was his first significant contact with a black person. When he thanked Sullivan for allowing Dunham to live in his house instead of Harlem (she would not live in Harlem, as it reminded her of her childhood), Fromm noted that he was coming to understand her emotional fragility: "I saw that being compelled to stay in Harlem had for her essentially a symbolic meaning and meant the breakdown of her hopes to get out of the narrow Chicago atmosphere." Dunham was struggling for a sense of autonomy and choice that could match her rich and multiple talents, and Fromm wanted to help her achieve this freedom. It is interesting to contemplate why Fromm's publications did not take more notice of African Americans in the United States at this time. Probably his European background in an interval involving Hitler's growing European atrocities helps to account for the focus in his work despite his efforts to adapt to his new country. (Later in his life, as he became more politically active, this Eurocentric focus would again be evident.) Unlike some of the other Jewish émigrés who actively endorsed A. Philip Randolph and other leaders in the early 1940s civil rights movement, Fromm did not, which makes his open participation in an interracial relationship all the more striking.[59]

As seems to have been the case with most of Fromm's lovers, Dunham and Fromm remained close friends and confidants for the remainder of their lives. Fromm celebrated when the Dunham School of Arts and Research opened in Manhattan in 1945, for example, explaining to his colleagues that she was gifting her techniques and themes to the next generation of African American dancers.[60]

In late life, when Dunham began to suffer from crippling and painful knee problems which would have dejected others her age, she reported to Fromm that she had become a civil rights activist. Above all, she was combating segregation in theaters, hotels, and restaurants. Additionally, she had become active in global networks of black scholars and intellectuals who were working to liberate people of color from the vestiges of Western colonialism. Fromm was quite attentive to all these aspects of Dunham's evolving career. For her part, Dunham kept current on Fromm's publications and told him, "I see more and more the great and positive influence you have had on my life." When she asked him to read a draft chapter from her book on Haitian dance and culture, Fromm found it brilliant, responding that the essay provided "hours of deep and total happiness. All that I have liked and admired in you comes through. There is courage, intelligent true courage . . . there is deep, basic human love."[61]

Scholars have tended to dismiss Fromm's relationship with Dunham as a minor interracial sexual fling. Yet Dunham acquainted him with the creativity, productivity, and insight of a female African American artist and the restrictions she faced. Within the world of black dance and culture, Dunham emerged for Fromm as one of the boldest and most informed students of the human condition, revealing not only basic human love, curiosity, and growth but also empathy with weakness and pain. While he and Dunham were lovers, Fromm fine tuned the focus of *Escape from Freedom*, underscoring the desirability of positive, spontaneous enjoyment of freedom—with love, autonomy, and creative productivity.

Perhaps more than Sullivan and the other women in Fromm's life at this time, Dunham awoke in him a sense of creative productivity, beauty, spontaneity, and ebullience in freedom. After all, she had deeply broadened his aesthetic sensibility and elicited a level of passion in Fromm that moved him emotionally not only beyond the rigid racial divides of "democratic" America and Nazi Germany but beyond the divide between professional specialization and popular culture. His relationship with Katherine Dunham contributed to *Escape* being a considerably richer and more empathetic account of freedom and its discontents than the theoretical essays on the topic he had crafted earlier. Through her mastery of artistic and popular culture, her understanding of the transmission of cultural rituals and attendant social psychology, and her emotional sensitivity and joyous manner, she had helped Fromm to find a deeply engaging voice that appealed to a popular as well as an intellectual audience. Holding Dunham's rich career in awe, by the early 1940s he had ceased to be the austere Frankfurt Institute researcher and was on the verge of becoming a widely admired American writer and social critic.

4

Escape from Freedom

The context for *Escape from Freedom* was exceedingly personal and complex. Although Fromm's work at the Frankfurt Institute contributed to his most important ideas, the intellectual stimulation, collegiality, and joy Fromm found with Horney, Sullivan, Thompson, and their colleagues in the Zodiac group and Culture and Personality movement was also significant. The way Katherine Dunham came to embody the richness, creative potential, and happiness inherent in freedom also played an important role in the book's creation. Fromm's preoccupation with the rescue of family members and others from a Holocaust in the making as he conceived and completed *Escape* indicates that much of his daily life was deeply embedded in the fabric of the book. Without this complex and changing context, there could not have been such a rich and historically significant text.

In March 1939, Fromm gave his friend and analysand, the Columbia sociologist Robert Lynd, a detailed outline of *Escape from Freedom*. He explained to Lynd "the theme which is nearest to my heart and which is the leitmotif of the book is the problem of freedom and anxiety or the fear of freedom or the escape from freedom." When

> the primary bonds which give security to a person are cut off, he feels basically lonely and anxious and in principle only two ways are open to him. One is to submerge his self into a higher power. . . . The other is to grasp the world and to unite with it through love and spontaneous activity (in thinking as well as in every sort of genuine productivity, including manual work).

The submersion of the self was escapism, which diminished the self and promoted conformity and authoritarianism. The counterweight to escapism was freedom through ethical behavior, which deepened as a person's sense of individual selfhood, value, self-esteem, and commitment to democratic values accelerated. In the fall of 1940, Fromm negotiated a December 1, 1940, delivery date with Holt, Rinehart, and Winston, emphasizing that owing to the urgency of the global situation, rapid publication was imperative. On December 5, 1940, Fromm wrote to his friend David Riesman that he was still revising the manuscript because "I discovered that it requires much more work than I had anticipated." Holt, Rinehart, and Winston wanted it no later than the beginning of January. Consequently, Fromm reduced his schedule for analytic patients and planned, quite uncharacteristically, to work straight through the holiday season. The deadline was met, and *Escape from Freedom* was published in 1941, as Fromm was approaching his forty-first birthday and just before Hitler began exterminating the Jews in fulfillment of his vision of a "final solution."[1]

A Thematic Statement

It was an arresting volume. Fromm's narrative line was consistently crisp and animated, and the book could be read in a few sittings. Fromm avoided the heavy footnoting and nuanced argumentation of most of his previous publications. Conveying few hints that German was his native language, he was out to communicate with a general and international, if primarily American, readership. Although he stated his differences with Freud, he presumed that the reader had no knowledge of psychoanalytic theory or social psychology and confined the elaboration of his concept of social character to an appendix essay. Fromm also announced that *Escape* was only the first of several anticipated volumes and invited his audience to read the others. He planned a subsequent book on the nature of ethics (*Man for Himself*) and another amplifying the social psychology of destructiveness (*The Anatomy of Human Destructiveness*).

For *Escape*, Fromm emphasized that he would draw largely on dated, though well-known, secondary sources such as Johan Huizinga and Jacob Burckhardt on the decline of the Middle Ages and the dawn of the Renaissance. He directly quoted from Luther and Calvin to articulate the ideologies that shaped Reformation-era Europe. Although Fromm was dependent on the works of Max Weber and R. H. Tawney, to say nothing of Marx, in explaining the connection between early Protestantism and the rise of capitalism, he did not weigh his readers down with complex and subtle lines of argumentation. Fromm openly acknowledged that he was advancing only the most cursory summary of factors prompting the Nazi rise to power and was drawing heavily from *Mein Kampf* to explain Hitler. More generally, as a free-ranging social commentator rather than a psychoanalyst, an interdisciplinary scholar, or a historian, he wrote an exciting and readily understandable volume for a large general readership, conveying his concerns about the current threats to human freedom. He was intent to convey a broad and deeply important argument and eschewed the imperatives of a specialized investigator. Although he had no plans to cease his clinical work and psychoanalytic supervision or depart from the world of scholarship, the process of completing *Escape* decidedly modified his sense of vocation and made him a generalist.

Fromm began by presenting a central thesis, which he restated many times throughout the volume:

It is the thesis of this book that modern man, freed from the bonds of pre-individualistic society, which simultaneously gave him security and limited him, has not gained freedom in the positive sense of the realization of his individual self; that is, the expression of his intellectual, emotional and sensuous potentialities. Freedom, though it has brought him independence and rationality, has made him isolated and, thereby, anxious and powerless. This isolation is unbearable and the alternatives he is confronted with are either to escape from the burden of his freedom into new dependencies and submission, or to advance to the full realization of positive freedom which is based upon the uniqueness and individuality of man.[2]

This contemporary crisis over freedom compelled Fromm to put aside a study of the "character structure of modern man." The crisis threatened "the greatest achievements of modern culture—individuality and uniqueness of personality." These achievements had been augmented through the positive use of the "freedom to," that is, the ability to act autonomously to fulfill life's purpose, including the ability to act ethically and creatively. The spread of totalitarianism, particularly the Nazi variety, subverted this positive freedom of the individual. It also subverted *negative* freedom—the "freedom from," which refers to the absence of coercions, obstacles, or restraints on the individual. Democratic societies were especially under siege and could forfeit both negative and positive freedom by conforming to the mandates of the powerful. Fromm insisted that the primary battle for the integrity of the self was not only against totalitarian states; it was also "within ourselves and our institutions." These were the book's most essential points.[3]

The struggle between freedom and conformist escapism represented an existential dilemma for humankind, Fromm insisted. Because Freud more often than not characterized the human drama in terms of the satisfaction or frustration of biologically rooted instinctual drives, Fromm argued that psychoanalytic orthodoxy fell short of addressing the problem. He did not elaborate extensively, as he had in earlier publications, on his growing departure from Freudian drive theory and its modernist agenda or on his shift toward a concept of social character, in which the instincts were given their ultimate form and function through social and economic conditions: "Human nature is neither a biologically fixed and innate sum total of drives nor is it a lifeless shadow of cultural patterns to which it adapts itself smoothly; it is the product of human evolution, but it also has certain inherent mechanisms and laws." As man evolved, he lost his instinctually based feelings of oneness or connectedness with humankind and nature. (It is interesting that Fromm did not avail himself here of Darwin's observations that man had shed much of the instinctual disposition that persisted in less evolved animals.) One became an independent, rational, self-sustaining individual, Fromm observed, but also a more isolated, lonely, and anxious person who needed desperately to feel "related to the world outside oneself." In this regard, Fromm underscored Harry Stack Sullivan's interpersonal psychology to explain the importance to modern man of regaining a feeling of relatedness to others and to the world. He emphasized Karen Horney's understanding of the paralyzing nature of the anxiety that was rooted in the individuality that characterized modern society. Fromm also found value in the writings of Margaret Mead, Ruth Benedict, John Dollard, Edward Sapir, and others within the Culture and Personality movement. Their work attested to the fact that the modern individual was a dynamic actor in a social and cultural setting.[4]

Roughly a hundred pages into *Escape*, Fromm offered the most explicit statement of his primary thesis: "Our aim will be to show that the structure of modern society affects man in two ways simultaneously: he becomes more independent, self-reliant, and critical, and he becomes more isolated, alone, and afraid." How could man utilize his newfound sense of individuality and freedom positively so that he reengaged the world and thereby curtailed his sense of fear, isolation, and loneliness? Fromm's answer was vague: the primary task for the modern self was to use one's freedom spontaneously, energetically, and uniquely through acts that would enhance his joy, his sense of viable selfhood, and his capacity to share with others. Alternatively, he could seek to cure his loneliness by subordinating himself to authority and custom through deference and conformity. How, Fromm asked, did the modern self arrive at this dilemma of apprehensiveness over newfound individuality and a crisis over whether to overcome the apprehension through positive freedom, that is, through autonomous, purposeful and ethical behavior?[5]

Escape characterized the origins of individuation as occurring on two levels: one was endemic to all newborns, and the other was the product of broader historical and cultural forces. Early in his life, the infant became an individual. Although he ceased to be fetal at birth and became independent of his mother's body with the cutting of the umbilical cord, he continued to be wholly dependent on his mother. Gradually, however, he came to regard the mother and other objects as units apart from himself. Through neurological and physical development, the infant came to grasp and master, both physically and intellectually, the diverse physical and conceptual entities external to him. He started to develop a distinction between "I" and "thou." Yet it took years before he entirely separated himself from others and fully regarded parental or any other authority as distinct from him. He grew stronger physically, emotionally, and mentally, and these elements of growth slowly emerged as an organized and integrated personality—the self. That is, as the primary ties of infancy receded in the face of individuation, "the growth of self-strength" proceeded.[6]

Whereas animals lower on the developmental scale were dominated since birth by instinctive and reflexive neurological mechanisms, the human being was the highest animal, developmentally speaking. (Again, it is curious that Fromm did not explicitly cite Darwin to advance this premise.) Man's relative freedom from instinctual determination as he grew, Fromm explained, meant that through cognitive development and learning, he gained increasing freedom in a positive sense. Man was able to determine his destiny and separate himself from nature: "Just as a child can never return to the mother's womb physically, so it can never reverse, psychically, the process of individuation." To be sure, Fromm argued, as individuation proceeded and the child gained a sense of integrated selfhood, the child also hoped to escape a disturbing sense of loneliness inherent in being an individual and thus sometimes sought to escape this sense of aloneness by submitting once again to parental and other authorities, especially if he has not developed the inner strength and productivity that would lead to solidarity with others. This submission might give the child a temporary sense of security and connectedness to others. "But unconsciously the child realizes the price it pays is giving up strength and the integrity of the self. Thus the result of submission is the very opposite of what it was to be: submission increases the child's insecurity and at the same time creates hostility and rebelliousness." Fromm concluded his narrative by reiterating that a child moved away from the primary ties of parents and nature and became an individuated self in order to gain contentment and to exercise his full freedom and independence.[7]

Though early in *Escape from Freedom* Fromm maintained that human nature was not fixed but infinitely malleable, he was describing an early developmental process that all children purportedly experienced. This universalist postulate made Ruth Benedict, Margaret Mead, and his other anthropologist friends uneasy; they noted that there were too many variations in the way children developed in different societies for there to be a single process endemic to the human condition. Fromm left their observations unanswered. Once a child became individuated, according to Fromm, he knew that he could only enhance his sense of selfhood and enjoy lasting contentment by embracing and extending his freedom and not by submitting to authority. Once more, Fromm was making a universalist assumption. His friends among the "culturists" and neo-Freudians retorted that specific societies, cultures, and historical forces affected the level of individual anxiety and loneliness, making that level quite variable. In some circumstances, the anxiety and loneliness were so intense that a child had little initial disposition to embrace freedom. Pressed on this score, Fromm only partially yielded and provided few concrete examples.

Historical Groundings

In *Escape*, Fromm held dogmatically to the universalist view that individuation and freedom were inherent parts of childhood development. Fromm insisted that before the late Middle Ages, Western society had no concept of individual freedom. Indeed, medieval man had little opportunity to move from his social class, his locality, or his vocation over the course of his life. He was frozen within a specific place in a hierarchical and stratified society irrespective of his talents or ambitions. But if he was not free, he was also not isolated or alone: "The social order was conceived as a natural order, and being a definite part of it gave a feeling of security and belonging." Moreover, within his limited social sphere, a person had considerable opportunity "to express his self in his work and his emotional life." Fromm argued that medieval society did not threaten individual freedom "because the 'individual' as a cognitive self" had not yet emerged; "man was still related to the world by primary ties." He was conscious of himself "only as a member of a race, people, party, family, or corporation—only through some general category." Man was bounded by society, but because the concept of the "individual" who could be deprived of freedom did not yet exist, bondage to society was of a fundamentally different kind than the modern deprivation of freedom. Fromm was rejecting the premise that the modern age was essentially an extension of the medieval and largely Catholic world, simply with new descriptive labels. Like Hannah Arendt and several other scholars, he saw a discontinuity. The modern age was distinctly different.[8]

Relying heavily on Jacob Burckhardt's *The Civilization of the Renaissance in Italy* (1860) rather than Max Weber to characterize this transition, Fromm described how the emergence of capitalism seriously altered this medieval order. During the late Middle Ages and spreading from Italy to Central and Western Europe, there arose a new moneyed class, which was "filled with a spirit of initiative, power, [and] ambition" but without the traditional privileges of birth and inherited status.[9]

According to Fromm, this class actively engaged in trade and industry around the Mediterranean world and into the Orient. Their success testified to the importance of self-agency and acquired wealth. During the Renaissance, they became a prosperous and powerful upper class whose economic activity and newfound prosperity promoted the view that the free individual could change his station in life—if sometimes his sense of social isolation as well. Although small artisans and the petit bourgeoisie rarely shared in this wealth and were sometimes victimized, a "growing competitive struggle for self-advancement" marked the beginning of capitalism.[10]

With it came the first signs of the birth of the modern individual, who had agency and opportunities but no durable place in the community. In a footnote but not in his primary narrative, Fromm acknowledged that his distinction between the cohesion and stratification of medieval society and the individualism, acquisitiveness, and comparative social isolation of Renaissance capitalism represented "ideal types"—abstractions that did not comport with the complex lives of the historical actors. In fact, the economic and social forces of early capitalism "had already developed within medieval society of the twelfth, thirteenth, and fourteenth centuries," and, in addition, elements of medieval society actually continued into the modern era.[11]

Fromm was so intent on presenting this larger picture of historical change that he largely dismissed the qualifications of professional historians. In a less-than-appropriate polemic, Fromm reduced professional historical research "to the gathering of countless details" shorn of interpretation. When his friend Thomas Merton, the Catholic theologian, cautioned him against an overly positive and one-dimensional picture of the Middle Ages, one shorn of qualification and nuance, Fromm gave little ground. He simply acknowledged that he may have overreacted to the very negative attitude toward the medieval era "conveyed to me in the first twenty years of my life." Fromm also felt that significant historical qualification would have weighed down a narrative that he wanted to flow vigorously and with very distinctive signposts for a general reader. The tradeoff was that professional historians have felt that *Escape from Freedom* does not comport with the demands of their craft.

Drawing conceptually from Max Weber and R. H. Tawney—without acknowledging the fullness of his debt to them—Fromm linked early capitalism to religion to explain the rise of the sense of individuality. But as a serious Marxist, he emphasized a class distinction. Early capitalism justified the competitive and acquisitive habits of individuals belonging to a new moneyed class, a class that felt sustained in its newfound individuality and economic power by the celebration of selfhood and dignity inherent in Renaissance art, music, and literature. The new wealthy also felt supported by late medieval Catholicism, which stressed human dignity and man's right to be confident of God's love within the structure of the church. The emerging sense of individuality among wealthy merchants and industrialists also promoted feelings of loneliness and isolation, but they were ameliorated by the celebration of the self and the benefits of human effort within Renaissance culture and within the late medieval church.[12]

In contrast, early Protestantism appealed to the urban middle and lower classes and to peasants who, under emerging capitalism, had lost the protections and sense of secure social structure inherent in medieval society.

This was the cost of being free and autonomous in the new capitalist marketplace. With few exceptions, they felt exploited by the new moneyed elite and trapped in an economic and social freefall. More than anyone else, Luther addressed this sense of powerlessness, anxiety, and insecurity by preaching to his constituency that man was free from the authority of the Catholic Church and its attendant institutional arrangements. However, this did not mean that these desperate people could exercise self-agency and create happier lives for themselves. Quite the opposite. For Luther, man was inherently evil and inconsequential in the larger universe. He could only find contentment and salvation if he totally relinquished any sense of selfhood and submitted entirely to the grace of God. Only when man demolished his individual will and his sense of agency could he find comfort and salvation, even though his inherently evil nature would never wholly disappear. Fromm characterized Luther's demand as very problematic and only a temporary palliative for doubt and anxiety, because, at base, man had to deploy his own agency (not God's) and forge a stable and happy rapport with society. Still, Fromm acknowledged that Luther's appeal for relief and certainty through total submission to God plus deference to constituted authority attracted a massive following. Protestantism, Fromm noted with disapprobation, essentially demanded an escape from freedom.

As he characterized Luther, Fromm referenced Hitler and other contemporary dictators who also sought the destruction of individual agency. Luther purportedly offered "a solution which had much in common with the principle of complete submission of the individual to the state and the 'leader.'" This was not the Luther portrayed by Reformation scholars. The twentieth-century counterpart to sixteenth-century Lutheranism was "the Fascist emphasis that it is the aim of life to be sacrificed for 'higher' powers, for the leader of the racial community." Clearly, Fromm was taking excessive liberties with the historical contexts not only of two very different centuries but with the substantial historical interval between them. Indeed, his suggestion of a direct road from Luther to Hitler was problematic at best. But Fromm was writing less as a historian than as a social philosopher or commentator out to advance a general argument. He used history to explain, through narrative, why he felt the world was becoming increasingly enslaved. Given Fromm's efforts to help Heinz Brandt, Sophie Engländer, and others in a family being brutalized by Hitler, there may also have been a profoundly personal dimension here.[13]

There was also Calvin of Geneva to reckon with in describing the way early Protestantism responded to the insecurities of postmedieval individuality. Fromm maintained that Calvin, like Luther, appealed to artisans, the middle classes, and to small businessmen who felt threatened and exploited by emergent capitalism. Calvin's God, even more than Luther's, was a tyrant who predestined some for grace and others for eternal damnation wholly at whim. Men were basically unequal—the saved and the damned. In a profoundly unhistorical jump to Third Reich racial hierarchy, Fromm asserted that Calvinism had "found its most vigorous revival in Nazi ideology," with its racial differentiation between Aryans and "lesser" peoples. But since only God really knew who was saved, the man who hoped to be of the elect had to put forth enormous effort in his everyday work and in being frugal—possible outer signs or forecasts of inner grace—to distinguish himself in God's eyes. That is, Calvinism promoted vigorous and relentless labor by instilling a compulsion to work and to save as virtues in themselves. For Fromm—promoting Max Weber's perspective—early capitalism found no better ally than Calvinist man because he was driven not by societal coercion but by inner compulsions to be busy, to labor, and to renounce earthly extravagance, all in the hopes of easing acute insecurity over his selection as one of God's chosen.[14]

At base, Fromm argued that in both its Lutheran and Calvinist manifestations, Protestantism served as the answer for the frightened, isolated, and uprooted of the marginal middle class and artisan class. By relinquishing their sense of viable selfhood to a tyrannical God, deferring to established power, and feeling compelled to work and be thrifty, Protestantism provided laborers with a new character structure to fit into a capitalist economic order. Under capitalism, one ceased to live "in a closed world the center of which was man." Instead, man was dominated by suprapersonal forces of capital and markets; he lost his sense of unity with his society and his sense of a place in the universe. Protestantism reinforced these feelings of insignificance. It "destroyed the confidence of man in God's unconditional love; it taught man to despise and distrust himself and others" congruent with the new competitive economic order. Together, Protestantism and capitalism forged a character structure consisting of a "compulsion to work, passion for thrift, the readiness to make one's life a tool for the purposes of an [external] personal power, asceticism, and a compulsive sense of duty." As he became a tool of capital expansion and of an arbitrary all-powerful God, man lost a sense of himself as a unique entity with agency and dignity. The Protestantism of early modern Europe became the roots of modern authoritarianism—a road from Luther and Calvin to Hitler that was oversimplified, to say the least.[15]

Fromm had not only folded Max Weber's and R. H. Tawney's interpretations of the interlocking nature of early Protestantism and early capitalism into his narrative on the emergence of the modern self. He had also been influenced by Kierkegaard's insight on the emergence of "the isolation of the individual" during the fifteenth and sixteenth centuries. Indeed, Fromm acknowledged that many probing thinkers had preceded him in his delineation of "the problem." Several reviewers expert on early Protestantism felt that Fromm had overemphasized if not outright distorted how Luther and Calvin and their followers deflated the sense of selfhood and community and encouraged conformity. In response, Fromm acknowledged that there were other dimensions to early Protestantism, but scholars generally refused to let him off the hook for his insisting on the reenactment in the twentieth century of particular historical developments of the fifteenth and sixteenth centuries. Nevertheless, Fromm's ahistorical representations of the late medieval and early modern eras engaged the present and even spoke to the general human psychological condition. Seventeen years before Erik Erikson published *Young Man Luther* (1958), Fromm merged psychology and history, though his psychology outshone his history. He explored the human psyche and the problem of freedom, past and present, in a thrilling but significantly overstated dialogue. There is little doubt why, by the 1960s, the preponderance of serious students of Clio's craft who called themselves "psychohistorians" would cite Erikson rather than Fromm as the founder of their field.[16]

To underscore the challenge to modern society, Fromm initially intended to title the manuscript *Selfishness and Self-Love*. In fact, he published an article on the topic in a 1939 issue of *Psychiatry* and subsequently turned it into one of the thematic lines of *Escape*. For centuries, "don't be selfish" had been a stock phrase, urging attentiveness to others and to other causes, the purpose of the admonition being to advance charity and philanthropy. To love others was a virtue, but to love oneself was sinful and excessive. For Fromm, quite the opposite was the case. It was essential to grasp the opportunities since the Renaissance and Reformation for newfound freedom; Fromm insisted that self-love and self-regard were imperative. One must love oneself—to affirm one's unique life, happiness, emotionality, growth, and freedom—in order to convey love and regard for others. That is, to have genuine regard for the well-being of another, one needed a sense of love and positive affirmation of oneself. One could not give to another what one did not possess. Citing Harry Stack Sullivan, Fromm insisted that one could not give genuine affection to a lover unless one had positive feelings about oneself.[17]

Contrary to Calvin and Luther, therefore, Fromm insisted that the self must never be subordinated to any cause and that subservience would disguise and weaken the true self, which would lead to greed, narcissism, and selfishness. Selfishness not only deprived a person of his freedom but also of his self-regard—indeed, his very humanity. Fromm insisted this self-depletion was the real meaning of selfishness and even narcissism:

> The person who is not fond of himself, who does not approve of himself, is in constant anxiety concerning his own existence. He has not the inner security which can exist only on the basis of genuine fondness and affirmation. He must be concerned about himself, greedy to get everything for himself, since basically his own self lacks security and satisfaction.[18]

Monopoly Capitalism and Automaton Conformity

It was through this distinction between self-love and selfishness that Fromm was able to explain the negative effects of Protestantism on man's longing for freedom and the psychological effects of the rise of monopoly capitalism during the nineteenth and twentieth centuries that spawned the problematic mass society. Although few commentators on *Escape from Freedom* have made the point, this section of Fromm's narrative anticipated many of the seminal studies offered in the decades after World War II about the self-depleting qualities of modern monopoly capitalism.

To discuss the crisis of mass society, Fromm offered only sketchy outlines of its historical development, noting that post-Reformation historical change yielded a modern individual who became "more independent, self-reliant, and critical" but also "more isolated, alone, and afraid." He argued that political restraints on the self fell by the wayside with revolutions in England, France, and America. The modern democratic state emerged based upon representative government and equal rights under law. Freedom of speech and freedom of religion arrived as the old coercive powers of church and state over the individual dissipated.[19]

However, "new enemies of a different nature have arisen; enemies which are not essentially external restraints, but internal factors blocking the full realization of the freedom of personality." Under monopoly capitalism, one became associated increasingly with large impersonal organizations and processes that demanded what Fromm called "automaton conformity." Much of what modern man "thinks and says are the things that everybody else thinks and says." Feelings and thoughts emanating from structures outside the self were falsely experienced as one's own.[20]

Fromm did not detail how the large impersonal corporations and other organizations, which were owned increasingly by elite monopoly capitalists, originated and began to demand "automaton conformity" of the worker under conditions of mass production and mass distribution of goods and services. He asserted that—but did not describe how—modern man had "been turned into a cog, sometimes small, sometimes larger, of a machinery which forces its tempo upon him, which he cannot control, and in comparison with which he is utterly insignificant." Fromm essentially abridged several centuries of history on the development of corporate organizations and attendant technologies into a discussion of the rise of "automaton conformity." Consequently, he asserted—but did not explain—how the isolated individual, reduced by the "self-compression" of early Protestantism but enhanced by the democratic political revolutions that followed, became a conformist "cog" caught in the corporate forms of monopoly capitalism.[21]

Fromm's characterization of modern man as a powerless "cog" in a large corporate organization demanding "automaton conformity" drew heavily from Weber. Although in general he was discussing "modern society," the focus was on America. Whereas the artisan and craftsman of old shaped his product as an extension of himself, the modern worker assembled a small portion of a larger product within a massive organization that cared only for profits. Estranged from the fruits of his work, the manual laborer was prized only for his physical energy on the assembly line, and the white-collar and professional workers were relevant only for their specialized knowledge. Workers generally understood that they would be "mercilessly fired" if they did not contribute to organizational profits. As the Columbia University sociologist C. Wright Mills noted a decade later in his classic *White Collar: The American Middle Classes* (1951), work under monopoly capitalism had become alienating and self-deprecating.[22]

Not only did *Escape from Freedom* anticipate Mills on the alienating nature of modern labor, but Fromm also anticipated William Whyte's seminal

The Organization Man (1956). "In the smaller enterprise of the old days," Fromm emphasized, "the worker knew his boss personally" and where he stood. But there was no such familiarity in a mammoth corporate organization. Indeed, the boss had been replaced by the anonymous power of "management" and balance-sheet considerations. The labor union was the worker's protection against "management," providing a feeling of strength against the giant impersonal organization. The problem was that the labor union, too, was growing into a mammoth organization that militated against a worker's active participation. Lacking ownership of the fruits of his labor, the modern worker felt alienated by the very nature of the modern workplace. Rather than enhance man's innate creative capacities, the workplace demanded that he fit in as a steady, predictable "organization man."[23]

In elaborating on mindless "automaton conformity," Fromm anticipated the substantial and exciting postwar literature on consumer culture. In the small independent retail store of old, the owner knew the customer personally and received him as "somebody who mattered." The proprietor was attentive to and respectful of the customer's needs and desires, and the purchasing transaction enhanced the customer's dignity and sense of importance. In contrast, a customer in a modern department store felt "small and unimportant" amid the profusion of commodities over a vast area and a large sales force that regarded the consumer as a depersonalized source of revenue. "There is nobody who is glad about his coming, nobody who is particularly concerned about his wishes." Fromm added that whereas the proprietor in the small store used "rather rational and sensible" talk to induce the customer to buy a product, modern advertising tried "to impress its objects emotionally and then make them submit intellectually." Eschewing the qualities of the merchandise, modern advertising sought to "kill the critical capacities of the customer like an opiate or downright hypnosis." Anticipating Vance Packard's important study *The Hidden Persuaders* (1957), Fromm saw that products were marketed through subtle appeals to the consumer's dreams, fears, and fantasies. Fromm also noted that a consumer movement had emerged "to restore the customer's critical ability, dignity, and sense of significance" in the face of the gigantic consumer center and the dulling barrage of advertising, but that movement had "not grown beyond modest beginnings."[24]

In sum, Fromm insisted that the "style" of modern monopoly capitalism and corporate culture was smothering the individual with a sense of smallness and inconsequentiality. One felt compelled to "fall in step like a marching soldier or a worker on the endless belt." An individual could act, "but the sense of independence, significance, has gone." Instead, Fromm charged that a pseudoself replaced the individual, who had evolved into "a reflex of other people's expectations of him." One felt "compelled to conform, to seek his identity by continuous approval and recognition of others." This was how all "feelings and thoughts can be induced from the outside and yet be subjectively experienced as one's own" while unique beliefs and emotions were repressed and ceased to be part of one's self. Fromm's insights were intended to apply not only to twentieth-century fascist regimes but to democracies such as the United States.[25]

Within a decade of the publication of *Escape from Freedom*, David Riesman published *The Lonely Crowd* (1950), perhaps the most widely heralded of all the postwar studies in social psychology. He traced the shift over the course of the nineteenth and twentieth centuries from "inner direction," where the individual sought guidance within his own unique values, memories, and experiences, to "other direction," where one sought to conform to the dominant mores of the society around him (the "crowd"). Riesman readily acknowledged that his revolutionary concept of "other direction" rested heavily upon his friend and analyst Erich Fromm's notion of the replacement of the integrated self with the "automaton conformist" and that it connected to Fromm's related concept of a "marketing personality."

There were major differences between *The Lonely Crowd* and *Escape from Freedom*. First, Riesman studied the "American national character," and his research consisted almost entirely of U.S. materials. Second, there was chronology. Published in the shadows of the Holocaust and amid the fear and scare tactics of McCarthyism and the early Cold War, *The Lonely Crowd* was an "alarmist," if cogently presented, exposé of postwar American culture. Riesman's principal claim was that the country was endangered by a threat to viable selfhood and individuality. In contrast, Fromm published his work just before Hitler instituted "the final solution" and before even the outlines of the Cold War and McCarthyism were discernable. Fromm cast his net more broadly than Riesman by examining the advent of modern individuality that engendered freedoms but also the insecurities that tempted too many Westerners to relinquish their freedoms. Finally, Fromm found "automaton conformity" to be only one of three general psychological mechanisms—the other mechanisms were "authoritarianism" and human "destructiveness"—to offer escape from the challenges and insecurities of freedom. He felt that "automaton conformity" was the primary challenge not only for the United States but for other Western democracies. As the wave of tyranny swept through Hitler's Germany, Fromm acknowledged that the other two mechanisms were just as likely in the right circumstances. Unlike *The Lonely Crowd*, *Escape from Freedom* addressed a considerably larger issue: the problem of freedom and its discontents. Prevalent in all Western societies, the democracies as well as the dictatorships, he insisted that this problem resided in the human condition.

Nazi Germany and Sadomasochism

Fascinated as Fromm was by American culture, Nazi Germany preoccupied him far more, starting with his study of authoritarian propensities in the German working class. Although *Escape from Freedom* examined the broad problem of freedom and its discontents, and even though his audience was primarily American, it was the Germany of Luther and especially of Hitler that weighed most heavily upon him.

For Fromm, "automaton conformity" was in some ways the most benign form of psychological escape. For if this conformity commingled with an "authoritarian" escape mechanism, then sadomasochism was the result. In his use of the term "sadomasochism," Fromm did not mean neurosis or perversion but instead an attitude toward authority rooted in one's social character: "He admires authority and tends to submit to it, but at the same time he wants to be an authority himself and have others submit to him." As a masochist, the authoritarian individual loved and willingly submitted to the dictates of the strong. As a sadist, he sought to dominate the weak and make them suffer. That is, the sadomasochist authoritarian felt compelled to abandon his sparse and apprehensive sense of selfhood and his fear of being a free individual both by deferring to his "betters" in their noble cause and by quashing his "inferiors." Believing "that life is determined by forces outside of man's own self," he could not comprehend the concepts of human equality or solidarity but only authoritarian notions of superior and inferior peoples. In this way, he hoped to participate in the glory and strength of a noble cause.[26]

Fromm insisted that the psychological basis of the Nazi appeal had been to this sadomasochistic authoritarian character and that *Mein Kampf* best illustrated these qualities in urging the German masses to participate in the strength and glory of the Reich and the purity of the Aryan blood line by degrading and ultimately eliminating "lesser" peoples. This was a very selective interpretation of the appeal of *Mein Kampf*. Fromm did not, for example, treat the intensity of Hitler's anti-Semitism, choosing instead to locate the Jew with the communist and the Frenchman as examples of Hitler's purportedly "lesser" groups. Nor did Fromm point to the discredited Social Darwinist premises behind the Nazi quest for Aryan purity. Like Herbert Spencer and William Graham Sumner and their perversion of Darwin's theory of evolution decades earlier, Hitler insisted that the biological purity of the "superior race" would be accomplished through the elimination of "inferior" and "contaminated" peoples. Notwithstanding these observational shortcomings, it is interesting that in his 1950 classic, *The Authoritarian Personality*, Theodor Adorno gave credence to much of Fromm's explanatory framework.[27]

Fromm believed that Nazi sadomasochism resonated psychologically far more with the lower middle class than with any other segment of German society. As such, he was not attentive to the notion of an authoritarian German national character or to the explanatory or rhetorical power of Nazi pseudoscience. Fromm's focus was overwhelmingly on social class. The strongest heirs of Lutheran and Calvinist psychological austerities, suspicions, and joylessness, Fromm argued that the lower middle class had been hit heavily by post–World War I conditions—specifically the massive inflation and economic depression—while their prestige had fallen below that of the general working class. The Nazis successfully appealed to this troubled class above all others, Fromm maintained. He got it wrong. His hypothesis about the lower middle class has not held up. The Nazis gained votes from all classes. They were popular in rural Protestant areas and garnered significant working-class and upper-middle-class votes in the cities. Indeed, the lower middle class was less supportive of Hitler than was the upper middle class. As a general rule, the higher one was in the class structure, the greater the chances that one voted for Hitler. Yet this is retrospective and was determined using research techniques that Fromm lacked. He had only his German worker study to go on, and his conclusion about the lower middle class fit his sadomasochism hypothesis.[28]

Fromm characterized "destructiveness" as an escape mechanism for authoritarians that usually blended with sadomasochism. Where sadomasochism represented a symbiotic relationship to the other (one's superiors and inferiors), destructiveness eliminated the problematic other. Citing Karen Horney, Fromm noted that destructiveness was a common reaction to anxiety, one rooted in social isolation and a sense of powerlessness—that too many circumstances were outside one's control. Those who resorted to destructiveness often led a very constricted emotional existence as they stored up multiple resentments for ultimate release: "The more the drive toward life is thwarted, the stronger is the drive toward destruction; the more life is realized, the less is the strength of destructiveness. Destructiveness is the outcome of unlived life." Predictably and problematically, Fromm characterized the lower middle class as the primary agent for the escape mechanism of destructiveness within the Third Reich. As the heirs of Calvinism and its tenet of predestination, which denied human agency, they represented the most emotionally isolated and restricted class and harbored "intense envy against those who had the means to enjoy life." If Fromm's discussion of sadomasochism was abbreviated, he admitted that his characterization of destructiveness was downright skeletal. Toward the end of his career, he would devote a substantial book, *The Anatomy of Human Destructiveness*, to the concept.[29]

Fromm therefore framed his discussion of Nazism and other authoritarian nations around the escape mechanisms of sadomasochism and destructiveness. Additionally, Fromm acknowledged that Hitler and other high-level Nazis admired the powerful and were contemptuous of the powerless. Privately, they were especially scornful of the lower middle class. They sought power within the framework of symbiotic hierarchy: to dominate another, it was necessary to submit to those above and ultimately to the Fuehrer. This conscripted, constricted, authoritarian view of selfhood became the road to glory.[30]

Optimism

Despite the threat of Nazi annihilation and the fact that Nazi Germany dominated continental Europe, with Britain alone holding out, Fromm did not advance a gloomy prognosis for the future. Indeed, he ended his book on a decidedly upbeat note. Fromm came to his conclusion with little support from empirical research or scholarly findings and even acknowledged that he was on shaky ground. Departing from his main narrative line, he asserted that there was no going back to medieval times—that the emergence of the free individual was an irreversible fact of contemporary existence. Although authoritarian, conformist, and destructive escapes from freedom might ease modern man's sense of loneliness and powerlessness, these measures offered only temporary and superficial solutions. One could not reverse life's "inherent tendency to grow, to expand, to express potentialities." For Fromm, "this respect for and cultivation of the uniqueness of the self is the most valuable achievement of human culture." Despite the pressure of "automaton conformity," there was "no higher power than this unique individual self, that man is the center and purpose of life; that the growth and realization of man's individuality is an end that can never be subordinated to purposes which are supposed to have greater dignity."[31]

Fromm closed his book with a buoyant optimism that flew in the face of his dispiriting narrative. The "automaton conformity" of Western democracies, especially America, could be successfully managed. The United States had long enjoyed Bill of Rights guarantees and representative government, Fromm pointed out. Through the New Deal, America established the new economic principle that society was responsible for all of its constituents and that none should starve or fear for their loss of livelihood. What was needed was for the New Deal to go one step further: to promote a decentralized but "planned economy" of socialism—an economic democracy that would match the existing political democracy.[32]

If Fromm's optimistic prophecy for Western democracies (especially America) jarred against his analysis of conformity pressures, an upbeat prediction for Germany was incongruous with his analysis of the roots of Nazi authoritarianism. But once the Nazis were defeated, "the authoritarian systems cannot do away with the basic conditions that make for the quest for freedom; neither can they exterminate the quest for freedom that springs from these conditions."[33]

How does one account for Fromm's prediction of the eventual spread of humanistic values, democracy, and freedom—almost as historical inevitabilities—at the close of a manuscript focusing relentlessly on the flight from freedom in the Western world? More explicitly, why had Fromm disrupted the tone of a rather hard-nosed narrative by postulating a faith in the eventual emergence of humanism? Why did he assume that people would choose lasting happiness and contentment by embracing spontaneous and creative forces inherent within themselves—that they would, in the future, be able to pursue the rational, constructive, life-enhancing choices inherent in being free individuals that they had so often rejected in the past?

Fromm's answer was a proclamation of his deep faith in humanity. Four hundred years after the Renaissance, the Reformation, and the rise of capitalism, there was no turning back to the medieval society that preceded the psychological birth of the individual. But authoritarianism and "automaton conformity" only offered temporary and self-deprecating answers for modern society's insecurity and loneliness. In time, man would learn to exercise his freedom creatively in order to enhance his life and to cure his insecurities. Fromm's problem was that he simply postulated this train of thought while the preponderance of his narrative suggested otherwise. The silver lining he provided at the end of *Escape* was an outbreak of exuberance in a volume on pathos.[34]

Fromm's upbeat prediction that man would ultimately embrace rather than continue to turn away from freedom was postulated in universalist terms. This contradicted his developing concept of social character, which he amplified in an appendix essay. To address social character, one had to examine specific conditions and values in particular social groups and to allow for significant variations between them, which Fromm had often tried to do in his main narrative. Thomas Harvey Gill spoke for many reviewers when he wrote: "one wonders if a striving for a cultural concept like justice—which changes with time and geography—can be in itself a fundamental striving." Indeed, Gill was critical of Fromm's general premise that all sorts of "spontaneous ideals" resided in the self; for Gill, the premise was vague and lacked general utility.[35]

Gill, Otto Fenichel, Victor White, and several other reviewers were distressed that Fromm's upbeat prophecy, utopian in tone, seemed tacked on—the weakest part of *Escape from Freedom*. They insisted that this prophecy was no substitute for the sound use of history, psychology, and reasoned analysis. As an émigré psychoanalyst, Fenichel was especially critical, rebuking Fromm for inadequate research and for misreading Freud. What Fenichel meant, of course, was that Fromm had almost totally broken from Freud's "modernist" agenda rooted in the centrality of libidinal drives.[36]

Even as Fromm intended for *Escape from Freedom* to reach a large general readership more than a scholarly audience, he maintained at least some element of reason and analysis and some evidential base until the end of the book. Yet it is noteworthy that Fromm was in transition here from the life of the sober, tough-minded German scholar of his years at the Frankfurt Institute. He seemed to be taking on a life more like his new friends in the Culture and Personality movement, who sometimes threw scholarly caution to the winds in the excitement of their broad-ranging interdisciplinary explorations and especially in their speculative fusions of psychoanalysis and cultural anthropology. For them, and increasingly for Fromm as he began to shift into his life after the Institute, one could sometimes become a polemical social commentator who felt that it was important to be creative and innovative, even if shortcuts in scholarship were sometimes involved.

More fundamentally, as he brought *Escape* to a conclusion, his new circle's more flexible and open "style" seemed to spark in Fromm a partial embrace of the Old Testament Jewish prophetic tradition so essential to him during his adolescence and early adulthood. His uncle, Ludwig Krause, had introduced him to the writings of Isaiah, Amos, and Hosea, with their visions of peace and harmony between nations and peoples. Rabbi Nehemia Nobel taught him the importance of committing oneself to messianic ideals—love, humility, and justice—as the building blocks for a universal humanist ethics. Fromm's significant early mentor, Salman Rabinkow, made it clear to him that the moral autonomy and free choice of the individual was the essence of Old Testament prophecy. Finally, Fromm's dissertation with Alfred Weber on Jewish law maintained that Hasidism celebrated an inner life of wholeness, joy, and sincerity—the essence of what he now invoked at the end of *Escape* as the opportunity at hand. While Hannah Arendt and Fromm rarely exchanged ideas, she examined a conflict common to Fromm and to other exponents of positive freedom. The Greeks initially emphasized *praxis* (i.e., human acts and human speech) as positive freedom, to be sure. But Arendt noted that Greek philosophy subsequently equated positive freedom with being authentic and especially with deploying reason. For the sake of maintaining a façade of consistency, Arendt speculated that exponents of positive freedom emphasized praxis and confined the alternative Greek formulation involving careful reasoning to the back burner.[37]

Even though the utopian humanist disposition central to Fromm's early life only emerged at the end of a book on man's betrayal of his own freedom and happiness, humanism would become a more conspicuous part of

Fromm's writing and thinking for the rest of his life. The Jewish prophetic tradition had perhaps been pushed into the background as Fromm mastered the imperatives of disciplined Frankfurt Institute scholarship. It burst forth, however, at the end of his first book, and this may have helped to turn it into a classic. Since publication, *Escape from Freedom* has sold over five million copies and has been translated into twenty-eight languages.

5

Clinician and Ethicist

Fromm's upbeat tone at the conclusion of *Escape from Freedom* signaled a reawakening of the Jewish prophetic tradition that had been central to his early life and persisted through the 1940s. What Fromm called "positive freedom" in *Escape*—the affirmation of man's capacity to lead a loving, reflective, productive, and psychologically extravagant, joyous, and creative life—soon came to be supplanted by references to "ethical" or "socialist" humanism. Under the heading of "humanism," Fromm elaborated a vague philosophy predicated on dialogue, hope, and human relatedness. Fromm considered his next book, *Man for Himself: An Inquiry Into the Psychology of Ethics* (1947), as "in many ways a continuation of *Escape from Freedom*," in that it outlined "the norms and values leading to the realization of man's self and his potentialities." Toward the end of *Man for Himself*, Fromm described the task of an intellectual proponent of a secular "ethical" or "socialist" humanism in words that characterized his own self-image:

> It is the task of the ethical thinker to sustain and strengthen the voice of human conscience, to recognize what is good or what is bad for man, regardless of whether it is good or bad for society at a special period of its evolution. He may be the one who "crieth in the wilderness," but only if this voice remains alive and uncompromising will the wilderness change into fertile land.[1]

For Fromm, "socialist," or "ethical," humanism and clinical work reinforced each other. During the 1940s, he distanced himself not only from orthodox Freudian psychoanalysts but from Karen Horney and other revisionist colleagues. Even at the William Alanson White Institute, where he served as the director of clinical training, he rarely discussed his ideas with his colleagues. And although liberal public intellectuals such as Arthur Schlesinger Jr., Paul Tillich, and Robert Lindner incorporated key themes from *Escape from Freedom* into their own formulations and sought meetings with Fromm, he avoided such invitations. To be sure, he continued to participate in Margaret Mead's expanding Culture and Personality movement. But he found it less compelling as time transpired. In sum, Fromm was becoming a "self-sustaining" intellectual, eschewing dialogue with and criticism from his scholarly and clinical peers. He became decidedly self-referential, drawing heavily on ideas presented in *Escape from Freedom*, much as *Escape* had drawn upon his more original and closely reasoned essays of the 1930s at the Frankfurt Institute. Fromm was essentially transitioning from participation in critical intellectual circles and becoming less resistant to recycling his ideas. He attempted to place himself within a clear philosophical tradition, especially that of Spinoza, but was less than successful. Interestingly, the same decade in which Fromm espoused the idea of productive social character was also the least productive time of his professional career. These were complicated years, with several of Fromm's "lives" in play.[2]

The Politics of Clinical Practice

In some measure, despite his increasing independence from his colleagues, Fromm's developing "socialist" or "ethical" humanism was influenced by his professional affiliations. Horney created the Association for the Advancement of Psychoanalysis (AAP) and its affiliate American Institute for Psychoanalysis (AIP) in April 1941. This had been done in reaction to the orthodox Freudian New York Psychoanalytic Society, which had disqualified Horney as both an instructor and training analyst, owing to ideological and professional differences. She welcomed Fromm as well as Harry Stack Sullivan and Clara Thompson from the old Zodiac circle into her AAP-AIP nexus, and this became the center for neo-Freudianism in America. Though technically an honorary member because he lacked a medical degree, Fromm was appointed as a training analyst and clinical supervisor with teaching privileges in AIP courses.[3]

Horney soon tried to transform the AIP into a medical organization so that it could affiliate with the New York Medical College. As negotiations proceeded, Stephen Jewett, the head of New York Medical College's department of psychiatry, insisted that only AIP analysts with medical degrees could become affiliates of his department. Jewett was willing to allow Fromm, a "mere" lay analyst, to remain on the AIP faculty, provided he was unaffiliated with the medical college. Horney, less enamored of Fromm than she was during their relationship, curtailed the flow of AIP students to him, which deprived him of his role of training analyst and clinical supervisor. Initially, he was permitted to offer AIP courses so long as they did not deal with analytic technique. But Horney pressed further, and the AIP eventually completely removed Fromm's teaching privileges. She had essentially done to Fromm what the New York Psychoanalytic Society had done to her. Regarding herself as the primary alternative to Freudian orthodoxy, Horney cut down her former lover by promoting rigid limitations on lay analysts. Fromm found these restrictions intolerable and resigned from the AAP-AIP in April 1943. Thompson, Sullivan, and several others left in sympathy.[4]

Sullivan and Thompson watched Horney humiliate Fromm, and when Fromm resigned, they were ready with an alternative: Sullivan's dream of an interdisciplinary psychiatric-psychoanalytic center under the aegis of the William Alanson White Foundation, which had long supported his research. The Washington School of Psychiatry had been little more than Sullivan's "holding company" for the Washington-Baltimore Psychoanalytic Society until the rift with Horney. Together with Frieda Janet, David Rioch, and others, Sullivan and Thompson reconfigured Sullivan's Washington School of Psychiatry by establishing New York and Washington, D.C., branches. Fromm commuted between the two cities and enjoyed working with students from a variety of backgrounds and interdisciplinary interests. The New York branch grew far more rapidly than the Washington branch during the last years of World War II. Augmented in 1946 by the G.I. Bill of Rights (which funded psychoanalytic training for physicians who had served in the military), the New York branch separated from the Washington branch and renamed itself the William Alanson White Institute of Psychiatry.[5]

In 1946, Fromm became the first director of clinical training. Despite a disinclination toward administrative tasks, he served as director until 1950. At White, moreover, Fromm was regarded as a senior training analyst with unrestricted opportunity to teach seminars in clinical psychoanalysis. He sat on important Institute committees and was privy to its inner workings. Even as the M.D. requirement was becoming increasingly mandatory in American psychoanalytic training, Fromm persuaded the faculty at White to offer full psychoanalytic training to those with doctorates in psychology and recommended training for those with doctorates in other disciplines.

He also organized research projects to study the problems of long-term psychoanalysis. Fromm reached out to social workers, nurses, educators, clergy, and other professionals in the community in order to introduce them to psychoanalytic theory and technique and invite them to Institute lectures and course offerings. Believing that anyone could benefit from psychoanalytic therapy, Fromm established a low-cost clinic at White, an innovation for the time, to serve the community. Despite these initiatives, Fromm felt increasingly marginalized at White. Many of his other policy recommendations were rejected by the faculty. He recognized that despite his seniority, Clara Thompson, who held a medical degree, had greater de facto impact on White's policies and programs. She embraced therapeutic and doctrinal diversity, while Fromm represented a more idiosyncratic approach of his own in teaching and clinical supervision, and she was willing to assume extensive management duties, but Fromm was not. Thus, even as his colleagues at White recognized Fromm as an important intellectual and usually gave him a free hand in clinical endeavors, he felt increasingly isolated and "wounded." It reached the point where he rarely sought critical comments from his colleagues on his clinical technique and theoretical writings. Characteristic of his diminishing ties to eminent and rigorous scholars, Fromm was becoming increasingly self-referential in his clinical work.[6]

Clinical Technique

What sort of a therapist and supervisor was Fromm? He greatly enjoyed conducting psychoanalytic therapy and clinical supervision, but he left little evidence of his clinical work. Nevertheless, Fromm found this work not only very satisfying but also central to his thought in other realms. Yet the analyses that he conducted invariably focused on a patient's social character, often in very concrete manifestations. This made it relatively easy to identify the specific patient in case reports and clinical publications, he pointed out, thereby breaching confidentiality. Privately, Fromm acknowledged to close colleagues like Gertrud Hunziker-Fromm and Michael

Maccoby that his writing on clinical work generally was also restricted by what he knew of unethical trysts with female patients (implying that he himself sometimes had such relationships). This misconduct was commonplace among analysts of the day, including students of both Freud and Jung. Fromm probably felt that little was gained by discussing this problematic aspect of clinical work, especially since he might well be implicated and because it might intensify his conflict with orthodox Freudians.

What was Fromm's approach to clinical practice generally and psychoanalysis in particular? The Marxist writer Harry K. Wells insightfully characterized Fromm as a "physician of the soul"—a modern-day and upbeat Ishmael seeking to draw contemporary man out of crises created by the Ahabs of the world, producing alienation, loneliness, anxiety, and despair. Rejecting the prevailing Freudian notions of cure—freeing the self from instinctual and largely sexual repressions through an objective, surgically analytic manner—Fromm resorted to dream interpretation, free associations, or whatever else might seem to eliminate gently the conformist and authoritarian self and to allow the "real" productive self to emerge. Unlike Freud and his followers, moreover, his clinical manner was warm, convivial, and, as Sandor Ferenczi put it, had "unshakable good will." In her 1950 classic, *Psychoanalysis: Evolution and Development*, Clara Thompson characterized Fromm rather specifically: he essentially sought to cultivate in the patient a respect for his "real" or "true" self instead of conforming to society. Moreover, Thompson felt that Fromm sought out patients he could respect and within whom he was able to detect a faint, if deeply repressed, glimmering of their "authentic" selves. In this respect, Thompson suggested that Fromm was an extremely judgmental clinician. The key to "Frommian" therapy was to focus on an example of "authenticity"— to encourage the "healthy" side of the patient to develop through empathy and by weaning the patient from irrational, thoughtless, conforming attitudes. To achieve this, Thompson observed, Fromm insisted that the clinician be fully in touch with his own deeper self. Otherwise, he could not love, respect, and empathize with the patient at the level required to induce change.[7]

Wells and Thompson agreed that Fromm's clinical approach was caring and compassionate. Over the course of the 1940s, Fromm described his approach to therapy in terms of his focus on social character. The psychoanalyst's task was to encourage the patient to shift out of one or several "unproductive" social character orientations. Fromm postulated but did not really demonstrate how these orientations circumscribed one's "authenticity" and one's potential to excel: (1) the "receptive orientation," where the inner self felt empty and craved replenishment from others; (2) the "exploitive orientation," which, through manipulation, captured what others had or made; (3) the "hoarding orientation," which sought to save and secure one's possessions; (4) and the "marketing orientation," which experienced the self as no more than a packaged and marketable commodity. It was by simply asserting these four "unproductive" dispositions that Fromm characterized a "productive" self—a "productive social character." In apparent contrast to the four "unproductive" orientations, the patient on the road to "productivity" became more spontaneous, happy, nurturing, responsible, rational, and loving. Simply put, Fromm regarded effective analytic therapy as the means to reduce fundamentally the patient's inner emptiness and alter an incorrect orientation toward the world, which in turn enhanced the patient's love of life.[8]

As early as 1935, when his analytic practice was small, Fromm rejected Freud's premise of therapeutic neutrality (i.e., that the psychoanalyst had to be detached and unemotional). Instead, he borrowed from Frieda Fromm-Reichmann, underscoring her empathetic and "humane" clinical manner; the analyst needed to assert his or her unconditional love and acceptance of the patient. Fromm eschewed Freud's "patricentric attitude" and "bourgeois tolerance" of accepted social practices and determined to provide the analysand full "affirmation of his right to love and happiness." It is crucial to note that Fromm's clinical approach represented part of a larger process through which he was constructing a common language and weltanschauung with other public intellectuals of his generation, who sometimes characterized themselves as cosmopolitan and "universalist." Like Fromm, they amplified the concept of a "family of man" as an alternative to the classifications of superior and inferior mankind inherent in Nazi science.[9]

As Fromm matured into an experienced therapist, he insisted that optimal therapy involved "central relatedness" between analyst and analysand. An effective therapist went "center to center" with the patient and into his "core," quickly bypassing "peripheral" social matters such as religion and occupation. Whether with neurotics or more troubled patients, effective therapy required reacting "with our human core to the human core of another person." In this "central relatedness," the clinician revealed himself not only in his words but in his voice and facial expression. Fromm later referred to this approach as "dancing," stressing the mutuality and perhaps even the artistry inherent in the therapeutic process and deep understanding of the other. "To see a person," Fromm once wrote to his friend Clara Urquhart, "means to penetrate him or her in a timeless manner and to be 'in' the person." According to patients and clinical colleagues, this was precisely Fromm's clinical manner. Gazing warmly at the patient's face with his piercing blue eyes, he seemed to help the patient come alive and embrace his or her inner core. (To be sure, Fromm's psychic penetration was so powerful, serious, and sometimes even short on empathy that the analysand sometimes grew defensive.) In experiencing the other, Fromm and his analysand simultaneously experienced themselves—the relatedness that he now called "humanism." Some years later, Fromm cogently summarized the phenomenon: "The analyst understands the patient only inasmuch as he experiences in himself all that the patient experiences."[10]

To some extent, Fromm's clinical approach of "central relatedness" resembled his captivating sessions with Salman Rabinkow. In Fromm's characterization of this teacher-student relationship, the spiritual core of each permeated and invigorated the other through a warm, nonjudgmental interchange of mind and soul. Indeed, the magic of Fromm's rapport with Rabinkow clarified a crucial component of "central relatedness." The psychoanalyst as a spiritual teacher or mentor was required to move the analysand beyond a shallow, cliché-ridden use of his mental resources and toward "penetrating" and "authentic" thought and understanding. Restoring the capacity for independent reasoning was essential in moving the patient from "lostness" to realistic contact with the world and with his own feelings. Recalling that his work with Rabinkow, Nehemia Nobel, and other Talmudic mentors, and even his friendship with Martin Buber, had focused on text, Fromm considered discussing important classics to stimulate independent thought and more genuine expression of feelings. More often, he would ask his analysand clear, concrete, detailed questions to clear up contradictions or distortions in statements and would invite the patient to join him "in rational thought about the meaning of certain things." Unlike the traditional analytic technique of free association, which Fromm also utilized, he regarded this quest for more "authentic" and rational thought and personal insight as a teaching technique with far-reaching therapeutic consequences.[11]

To establish "central relatedness" in the analytic relationship, Fromm began, as early as 1940, to abandon the analytic couch. He recalled how some of his training analysts at the Berlin Psychoanalytic Institute had owned up to napping as they sat behind the couch, listening to the analysand drone on and on. To avoid "this boredom which made the situation so unbearable," Fromm shifted his analysand to a seated position where he could establish direct eye contact and promote a more lively interpersonal relationship. "Tell me what is in your mind right NOW," he sometimes insisted, or "What comes to mind when you think of the thing you like least in yourself—the thing you are most ashamed of—most proud of?" If the patient tried to avoid such direct and urgent inquiries, Fromm redirected him with considerable emotion, and sometimes rather judgmentally. Fromm became very candid about himself at certain times, and he expected the patient to be equally frank and open.[12]

Fromm was intent on a direct relationship even if it compromised his understanding of the transference relationship (i.e., how the patient slowly and unconsciously projected powerful emotional experiences and personages onto the analyst and how the analyst countertransferred his own emotions onto the patient). His main objective in probing the patient's unconscious inner reality was to uncover whatever the patient was hiding. Indeed, contradicting Freudian clinical orthodoxy, Fromm seemed to discourage intense transferences, believing they enhanced the patient's feelings of dependency upon the therapist. Some critics have noted, however, that strong transference is unavoidable in a clinical relationship. Others, including some of Fromm's former analysands and clinical trainees, have argued otherwise. For instance, Michael Maccoby and Militiades Zaphiropoulos have noted that by failing to utilize sufficient professional insights for both the transference and the countertransference, Fromm compounded his analysands' psychological problems. In this way, he often turned them into admirers of his mannerisms, "warmth," and ideas. This often caused relationships with his patients and colleagues to be too personal and insufficiently professional and intellectual.[13]

The case of one of Fromm's closest clinical trainees and analysands is instructive. In both his personal treatment and clinical training of David Schecter at the William Alanson White Institute, Fromm failed to establish the professional limits separating the clinician/teacher from the patient/student, limits that allow the latter to exercise his autonomy rather than develop and remain in a state of dependency. As a result, Schecter, one of the most well versed of Fromm's clinical associates in the emerging field of psychopharmacology (he advised Fromm on medicating patients), did not use his own clinical and intellectual strengths to seek the psychiatric help through which he may have averted his own suicide.[14]

Fromm retorted that his active, open, and blunt approach to his patient "first arouses resistances" of all sorts that could be particularly strong and result in transference distortions. He insisted, however, that patient resistance gave him the opportunity to peel away neurotic escape mechanisms and layers of character defense, usually setting "a mental process in action." Fromm insisted that in the end even the most brittle analysand could tolerate and benefit from direct, active therapeutic inquiry into unvarnished truths. Indeed, the more the patient progressed toward self-understanding, the harder Fromm pressed to complete the task. Although Fromm was trained in Berlin to emulate Freud—to spend five days a week for up to a year with a single patient so as to ease the resistance process gradually, to determine precisely how much self-revelation the patient could tolerate at a given point in time, and to explore all aspects of transference and countertransference—he now opted against that approach.[15]

Even before the "central relatedness" between analyst and analysand was fully established, Fromm (like Freud) relied heavily on dream analysis, and he continued to do so over the course of his analytic career. Much of his clinical supervision focused on patients' dreams: "To understand a dream in a way which is satisfactory . . . gives me still probably more pleasure than any more theoretical endeavor," Fromm remarked to David Schecter, "because I love the concrete and the specific and that which one can see." Indeed, dream analysis was at the core of his 1951 study, *The Forgotten Language: The Understanding of Dreams, Fairy Tales, and Myths*. Based on lectures Fromm had delivered over the previous decade, he broke decisively with Freud on the fundamentals of dream interpretation, rejecting Freud's premise that dreams reflected entirely the "irrational and asocial nature of man." He also eschewed Jung's view that "dreams are revelations of unconscious wisdom, transcending the individual." Instead, Fromm postulated that dreams reflected "our irrational strivings as well as our reason and morality." This book addressed the issues in Freud's 1900 classic, *The Interpretation of Dreams*, and is perhaps the most aesthetically compelling exchange Fromm ever had with any of Freud's texts.[16]

For Fromm, dreams represented a symbolic language common to all humankind, and sleep freed them of the constraints of time, space, and social conditioning. A dream wove different threads of the self into a single fabric—past and present, real events and fantasies. Recall of a dream was "like a microscope through which we look at the hidden occurrences in our soul." While dreams housed the hidden desires and fantasies of the dreamer, they did not reveal how substantial ("quantitative") each thread of the dream was in the dreamer's total psyche. Fromm insisted that this "quantitative" aspect of dream interpretation had been bypassed by Freud and his followers—a decided overstatement.[17]

The preponderance of The Forgotten Language suggests how Fromm analyzed specific dreams. At the onset, Fromm insisted that the clinician had to understand the general psychology of the dreamer and to fathom the background in day-to-day life for each specific patient, even though Fromm rarely detailed the everyday existence of most of his patients. Freud postulated that the analysand had to probe beyond the manifest or surface content of the dream to elements in the repressed and sometimes frightening "latent" dream content that suggested the emotional associations of the dreamer. Just as Erik Erikson did, Fromm rejected the rigidity inherent in Freud's distinction between the manifest and latent content, focusing instead on the dream's broad symbolic language. It was crucial to detect changes in recurrent general dream patterns and how these patterns related to the primary themes and directions of the patient's life. A dream should not initially be approached for its small fragmented parts, Fromm insisted, nor for its manifest and latent qualities, but as a totality. With an understanding of the entirety of the dream, Fromm postulated that the clinician could fathom a patient's entire unconscious life and, in turn, precisely what was undermining his productiveness and happiness. "What is important is to understand the texture of the dream in which past and present, character and realistic events, are woven together into a design" revealing the basic inner motivation of the dreamer "and the aims he must set himself in his effort to achieve happiness." Paradoxically, Fromm added, it was sometimes the dreamer's apprehension of dying that renewed his faith in life and happiness.[18]

Fromm often interpreted the specific dreams of his patients in more eclectic and intuitive ways than he said they should be interpreted. In the analytic room, he regarded dreams as "many-sided," never to be forced into a "Procrustean bed" that yielded a limited kind of meaning. He debunked the sterility of "various psychoanalytic schools, each insisting that it [had] the only true understanding of symbolic language." Fromm's propensity to deemphasize theory and to be more intuitive and spontaneous in dream interpretation (even as he eschewed detail on specific patients) helps to explain why, of all his books, *The Forgotten Language* was theoretically one of the thinnest but simultaneously one of the most emotionally compelling. Fromm urged the general reader to try his hand at mastering symbolic language in order to understand his own dreams even as he cautioned against interpretive reductionism. Not uncharacteristically, he quoted from the Talmud: "Dreams which are not interpreted are like letters which have not been opened." The book's appeal did not fall into a void. Since publication, *The Forgotten Language* has sold some two million copies and has been translated into twenty-two languages.[19]

How do we assess Fromm's general effectiveness as a clinician? For the most part, his trainees, especially those at the William Alanson White Institute, remembered him as an inspiring analyst and teacher; his patients were less consistently positive. Both trainees and patients agreed that he pursued "central relatedness" with the analysand in a flexible and nondoctrinaire way. He treated the nuances of clinical technique as artificial and discarded them for a more lively exchange. With an analysand who appeared robust, physically attractive, and relatively relaxed, according to Fromm's trainees, he pressed rapidly to learn how the patient envisioned his or her "authentic" happy and creative self and what was needed to get there. According to observers, Fromm offered provocative and sometimes even offensive remarks in order to engage the patient. If some analysands became uneasy, most sensed that Fromm was seeking to "awaken" them to their choices, to enable them to become more spontaneous, joyful, exuberant, and productive. Trainees observed that he was very goal oriented and voiced confidence that his analysand would eventually master the lessons of life. Trainees and other observers recalled that Fromm's prompting involved an intellectual component—critical thought—as well as emotional and intuitive exploration. He expected results on all fronts. Although Fromm's trainees were impressed by his confidence in his therapeutic approach and trusted his clinical inclinations, they periodically feared for his more psychologically "fragile" patients.[20]

Fromm's trainees were certainly impressed by his mentoring skills. And at a time when the disciplines of psychoanalysis, psychiatry, and psychology were uneasy about women and black professionals in their ranks, Fromm reached out to both, providing an endorsement of their clinical capability. Trainees appreciated the fact that he was candid about his Jewish background and acknowledged a strong Talmudic element in his therapeutic approach. Indeed, they recalled that he often referenced the Talmud when he taught dream interpretation and sometimes would even use the Talmud to patch over his differences with Freud.[21]

Fromm worked to establish a personal rapport with trainees and patients. Where plausible, he preferred to make points through humor and interesting stories rather than with formal clinical language. As Zaphiropoulos later reflected, while humor may be a pleasant way to build interpersonal bridges, it can interfere with a professional, clinical relationship where boundary crossing is usually to be avoided. Fromm also underscored, perhaps excessively, the importance of a clinician being candid with a patient. Open to his trainees about his own likes and dislikes, he inquired about their families, their joys, and their frustrations. When he felt a bit under the weather, he jokingly prodded a physician trainee to prescribe an instant cure.[22]

There is not a great deal of information about most of Fromm's patients. Thus, it is hard to generalize concerning what they thought about his therapeutic effectiveness. Perhaps because Fromm's analysis of Karen Horney's daughter, Marianne Eckardt, produced results that she wrote about at some length and recounted to me during interviews, it is easier to comment on his clinical work with her. Before the analysis, Eckardt recounted how she had been a pleasant, conscientious, and even-tempered daughter progressing along a successful career as a psychiatrist. However, she had few close friends, was unhappy, and seemed detached from life.[23]

Because of his long affair with her mother, professional ethics mandated that Fromm refuse to take on Eckardt as his patient. To be sure, he had transgressed professional boundaries earlier with Frieda Fromm-Reichmann as well as with Robert and Helen Lynd, and he would do so again with Martha Graham, Elizabeth Taylor, and no few other patients. Perhaps because of Fromm's personal acquaintance with the Horney family, two years went by in Eckardt's analysis before she started feeling better about her life. Although Eckardt reclined on Fromm's analytic couch three times a week, she thought that she had not cultivated much of a transference relationship with him. Fromm seemed too full of himself for her to have one. In time, however, she warmed to Fromm and could tell him how traumatized she had been as a five-year-old when Horney sent her away to Switzerland, illustrating the emotional distance between mother and daughter. Eckardt felt that Fromm eventually helped her to see that a broken relationship with Karen Horney had created "a detached person who did not quite know whether she existed and did not have a sense of the other person."[24]

Bypassing the professedly neutral clinical approach with minimal show of emotion—a manner that Freud had required of his followers—Fromm felt that his more direct, blunt, and personal manner had strengthened Eckardt's fragile sense of selfhood. In 1940, he asked her to sit on a chair rather than lie on the analytic couch so as to make eye contact with him (the first time Fromm seems to have done this with a patient). "The moment we dialogued [and] he came to life for me, I came to life to myself," Eckardt recalled. She felt alive and hopeful.[25]

While Eckardt considered Fromm a kind and gifted clinician, Rollo May did not. In May 1940, Fromm agreed to take on May in a therapeutic analysis. May had established a career as a Protestant minister and Adlerian clinician and had published two books. From the start, Fromm was apprehensive that May was drifting toward an existential or "third force" school of psychology but had bypassed a basic understanding of Freud in the process. While the initial months of the analysis went well, Fromm was unable to find a spot for May on his regular appointment schedule. May prodded Fromm to meet more regularly: "I am looking forward very much to continue my work with you." Fromm then put May on a regular schedule, but the analysis proceeded with considerable coolness. The modest narcissism and quasi-prophetic temperament of both may have impeded their progress. When May contracted tuberculosis, he began missing appointments. Oddly, Fromm lacked sympathy for May and did not mention his own bout with tuberculosis, now in remission. Fromm confided to a friend that May took notes on his analytic techniques and ideas expressed in the therapy sessions, and when he discovered that May used these materials (if somewhat modified) in his books and lectures, he was furious. Fromm broke off the analysis in 1943 and sent May a final bill.[26]

Fromm and May do not seem to have met again until 1948 or 1949, when May joined the staff at the William Alanson White Institute. Their relationship improved somewhat. Fromm inquired whether May had continued with his analysis elsewhere and asked whether he might want to review his book, *The Forgotten Language*, in the *New York Times*. May responded favorably, noting that he was impressed with Fromm's general approach at staff conferences and in lectures: "here is one whose directness and depth of human communication is as refreshing as a spring in a weary land where no water is, that is, the land of [clinical] techniques and of externalistic methods and conformity." Like an ancient Hebrew prophet, May felt that Fromm now spoke "with a deep conviction of the ground of meaning in the human life." Yet May's new appreciation of Fromm did not supplant the suspicion and mistrust rooted in a very troubled and incomplete analysis. May held up Paul Tillich, not Fromm, as his mentor and Søren Kierkegaard as his spiritual guide. He judged Fromm's writing to be "superficial" and spoke privately of Fromm as "pompous" and fundamentally immature in ranting at the bureaucratic ways of a society that had nurtured him. For his part, Fromm continued to belittle May's intellectual and clinical contributions, mentioned the former analysand's "very angry mood," and found no humanism or empathy in May's "humanistic psychology."[27]

David Riesman appraised Fromm's analytic skills more highly than May had. Riesman came from a prominent Jewish family in Philadelphia. His father was known internationally for his work as a medical professor and physician at the University of Pennsylvania. His mother, Eleanor, the dominant figure in the family, graduated at the top of her college class. Elegant and cultivated, she was keenly interested in the European avant-garde, including Freud, Thomas Mann, and Oswald Spengler. Although Riesman graduated with honors in biochemistry at Harvard, attended Harvard Law School, clerked for Supreme Court Justice Louis Brandeis, practiced as a Boston trial lawyer, taught law at the University of Buffalo, and worked in the New York district attorney's office, his mother never regarded him as sufficiently creative or "first rate." He suffered from a sense of inadequacy in what appeared to be a protracted search for a satisfying vocation. In the course of her analysis with Karen Horney, Eleanor Riesman asked whether a therapeutic analysis might help David and improve the communication between mother and son. When Horney met with David briefly, she characterized him as a "very resigned" young man and recommended therapeutic analysis with Fromm.[28]

For several years during the early and mid-1940s, Riesman commuted on weekends from the University of Buffalo to Fromm's office on the Upper West Side near Columbia University for a two-hour session on Saturdays and another two hours on Sundays. Riesman insisted retrospectively that he did not really need to be analyzed but wanted "to please my mother." Not deeply motivated to wrestle with his sense of inadequacy and his unclear vocational aims, he did not characterize his work with Fromm as a full-blown "analysis": It was "really conversational—not that he didn't help me psychologically." Riesman and his parents were well aware of Fromm's credentials. For Riesman, it was very important that Fromm's education, cultivation, and eminence exceeded that of his parents. As Riesman recalled, the fact that Fromm thought well of him from the start "made an enormous difference" to him and to some extent operated as a counterbalance to Riesman's sense of inadequacy. He considered emulating Fromm by becoming an academic and a researcher.[29]

The heart of the Fromm-Riesman analytic relationship was a mutually enriching and joyous exchange of ideas that was not unlike Fromm's work with Rabinkow. Riesman had been deeply interested in the social thought of European refugee scholars and had helped establish a program to resettle them in America. Riesman was fascinated with Fromm's account as a refugee and with his account of the Frankfurt Institute studies of authoritarianism and the commodification of selfhood under modern capitalism. Above all, Riesman became enchanted with Fromm's concept of social character, especially Fromm's marketing character, and how it could be applied cogently in the study of particular cultures. As his *The Lonely Crowd* evolved into a highly acclaimed exploratory essay, Riesman's statements of indebtedness to Fromm elevated Fromm's reputation among American scholars and intellectuals. Fromm's analysis of Riesman was essentially an exuberant intellectual exchange in what was otherwise a difficult decade for both and made the two close friends and colleagues for life. Clinicians have not considered it a "depth" analytic encounter, but Riesman never belittled its influence in shaping his career and his life.[30]

An evaluation of Fromm's success with his analysands in the 1940s suggests that there was a disjuncture between his theoretical outlines for successful therapy and his concrete analytic practice. He was "uneven" as a therapist, helping to enhance the happiness and productivity of those with whom he could cultivate a mutually respectful rapport but often dismissive of others. The examples at hand show Fromm's adaptability as a clinician. His analysands had to meet the needs of their clinician, perhaps more often than was good for them.[31]

Henny Gurland

Fromm married Henny Gurland, a fellow émigré from Nazi Germany, in July 1944, soon after finalizing the divorce from Frieda and after the demise of his relationships with Karen Horney and Katherine Dunham. The marriage gave him great joy but also considerable distress. To explore it is to understand a good deal about Fromm as he became a prophet of what he called "humanism" and a clinician of "central relatedness."

Henny Gurland was born in Aachen, Germany, in 1900, shortly after Fromm was born in Frankfurt. Her mother was Catholic, jovial, and affectionate. Her father was a Jewish optician, a tobacconist, and the Aachen town poet. Educated by nuns in a Catholic high school, Henny secured secretarial training and employment in Berlin. Socialist-labor in her political orientation, she became active in youth groups affiliated with the Social Democratic Party. She also became an active Zionist. In 1922, she married Otto Rosenthal, a Jewish entrepreneur, who owned companies involved in the international trade of coal-tar chemicals. Within a year, Henny gave birth to a son, Joseph, but her marriage was troubled from the start, and she and Otto divorced in 1929. Characterizing Henny as unstable and morally unfit, Otto won custody of their son. It is unclear whether there was any substance in these charges.[32]

After the divorce, Henny became exceedingly active politically and worked as a photographer for *Vorwärts*, an organ of the German Social Democratic Party. In this capacity, she was a pioneer in the area of stark and natural black-and-white photographs with minimal retouching. As a successful SDP photojournalist and overtly anti-Nazi, her name was placed on an enemies list when Hitler came to power, and she fled to Belgium. She recrossed the German border in 1934 and took Joseph back to Belgium with her, in defiance of a divorce court's ruling. Two years later, Henny married Rafael Gurland, a Spaniard, an anti-Nazi activist, a Marxist, and a postdoctoral student at the Frankfurt Institute. Rafael had joined the diplomatic service of the Spanish Republic during the country's civil war and moved with Henny and Joseph to the Spanish embassy in Paris. Henny and Rafael soon drifted apart. He joined the French army to resist a Nazi invasion in 1939 but was captured shortly thereafter and was a German prisoner of war for two years.[33]

As the Germans advanced on Paris, with Rafael incarcerated and the marriage shaky, Henny arranged a U.S. visa for herself and Joseph. Lacking exit visas from France, however, she, Joseph, and her friend Walter Benjamin (next to Adorno, perhaps the most brilliant philosopher and social critic at the Frankfurt Institute) set out to cross the French-Spanish border on foot, illegally, in September 1940. They planned to travel across

Spain and from there go to Lisbon, from where they would board a ship to New York. Instead, they were caught by Franco's border guards as they attempted their bruising climb across the French border, which proved injurious to Henny's health. According to Henny's daughter-in-law, they were strafed by fire from hostile planes before their capture. This left Henny with metal fragments in her side, which contributed to her exceedingly painful rheumatoid arthritis, which would later make walking difficult. The Spanish guards intended to return them to the pro-Nazi Vichy regime in France for almost certain incarceration. Fearing the worst, Benjamin committed suicide. Although traumatized, Henny passed off his death as heart failure and attended to the burial. Upset over Benjamin's death, the border guards allowed Henny and Joseph to proceed through Spain to Lisbon. Henny and Joseph arrived in New York at the end of 1940.[34]

Although Henny and Rafael did not legally dissolve their marriage until 1943, it was over by the time she and seventeen-year-old Joseph took up residence in New York. Short on funds, Henny found a cheap apartment; its furnishings were donated. She was able to earn income from wealthy patrons for her innovative photoportraiture and by weaving fashionable raw wool rugs. In time Henny became close friends with Ruth Staudinger, also a skilled photographer, whose father was president of the New School for Social Research, where Fromm periodically taught. With introductions from Rafael and Walter Benjamin, Henny had also met members of the Frankfurt Institute before it relocated to Morningside Heights. Early in 1941, Ruth Staudinger threw a party for both New School and Frankfurt Institute faculty, and Fromm and Henny Gurland attended. Although they may have met in Germany, both were ready for a serious relationship when they met in New York. Fromm, for whom the intimate presence of a woman was a stabilizing influence, found Henny to fill the void left by Horney and Dunham.[35]

Erich and Henny began to see each other regularly. He was attracted by her artistic talent and her considerable intelligence. When Henny's son enrolled at the New York University College of Engineering in February 1941, Fromm generously offered to pay whatever costs Otto would not provide. By late 1941, Fromm intervened more directly by cooperating with the National Refugee Service to support Henny's application for a regular U.S. visa and ultimately American citizenship. More urgently, when Joseph was classified mistakenly as an "enemy alien," Fromm worked actively for his reclassification. He regarded the bright young man as a son. By 1943, Henny

and Erich considered marriage. Happiness had, in some measure, returned to Henny's life after two failed and dispiriting relationships and a
traumatic and injurious escape from Europe. "I am no longer homesick
[for Europe] but happy to be here," she wrote to her close friend, Izette de
Forest.[36]

At this point, the three lived together. About this time, when Erich and
Henny had become engaged, she became easily agitated, and her moods
began to change drastically. When Joseph graduated in February 1944
with a bachelor's degree in chemical engineering, for example, Henny was
elated. But soon after, when he was inducted into the U.S. Army Corps of
Engineers in a noncombat position that would enhance his research skills,
she told de Forest that her periodic struggle with anxiety and depression
had returned. Henny confided to de Forest that Rafael's departure to join
the French military in 1939 had evoked a similar downcast mood— and
that the problem had plagued her much of her life.[37]

By July 1944, Henny's depression and anxiety temporarily lifted, and
she married Erich. They rented a comfortable flat off of Central Park. Now
in their mid-forties, she baked rolls for their breakfast every morning
while he took instruction in sensory awareness training with Henny's
friend Charlotte Selver, a Holocaust émigré who led the sensory awareness
movement in New York. Her skills were legion. Selver recalled that Fromm
seemed exceedingly rushed and driven during the early years of marriage,
lecturing at the New School, the White Institute, and Bennington College
while increasing his involvement with clinical supervision and analytic
patients. He was also trying to complete *Man for Himself.* According to
Selver, his manner was so blunt and "no-nonsense" that many mutual ac-
quaintances considered him arrogant and impatient. Henny's assessment
was more charitable: "Erich wants to finish his book and he is very impatient and nervous because in New York he has not one hour for himself
[and] neither for his poor wife." Henny enjoyed her photography work, particularly a project shooting scenes of Central Park "in different 'moods,' "
but she sensed that she and Erich needed time together away from New
York. Consequently, they decided to spend long weekends in Bennington,
Vermont, where on Mondays Erich taught a course at the college. Henny
eventually stopped commuting back to the city, remaining in their Bennington apartment. Erich returned to the city on Tuesday mornings, for
jammed days of teaching, clinical work, and supervision. On Friday evenings, his suitcase filled with special baked goods and delicatessen delec-

tables to cheer Henny up, Erich returned to Bennington and seemed to make new inroads on his writing agenda. *Escape from Freedom* was a hard act to follow, but he was determined to complete its sequel by the end of 1946. Fromm's writing, if in part for financial needs, was also to bring order, control, and some stability into his life. Henny, despite bouts of depression and arthritic pain, was often happy and helped Erich with his book project, revising his manuscript to improve its readability.[38]

Almost immediately before the move to Bennington, Henny wrote a confidential letter to Izette de Forest on the state of her marriage to Erich:

> I am in love with him—and Erich likes very much the family life. His attitude toward Josi [Joseph] is wonderful—he is like a friend and a father. Those small things of daily life are so important and his harmonious way in dealing with difficulties makes me love him even more than I did before—but you know Erich and his good influence and I don't have to tell you how happy I am with him.

This was not the overly blunt, pressured, and sometimes caustic man whom many others met. Indeed, Erich seemed to have a stabilizing effect on Henny, easing her agitation and helping to blunt some of her mood shifts. He loved her deeply and was particularly taken by her intuitive qualities along with her "searching and penetrating mind which . . . so greatly contributed to my own development."[39]

Still, Erich felt that he needed professional advice about her. Sometime during this interval, he arranged, with Henny's consent, to have the prominent psychiatrist and scholar Carl Binger conduct a full assessment of Henny. Binger concluded that she was schizophrenic, even though current clinicians might classify her moods as symptomatic of a bipolar disorder. Erich had sensed by the mid-1940s that something was terribly wrong with Henny, disposing him to treat her all the more with gentle good cheer and kind sensitivity. He was gratified that she had found some support in the Bennington artistic community, but that was not enough. He financed the construction of a large house with all the comforts Henny had lacked during her difficult life, supplementing his own income with a loan from Riesman. Surrounded by two scenic and meticulously landscaped acres, the house had a soft, contemporary look, with four bedrooms, two and a half bathrooms, a formal dining room, large living room, family room, study with built-in bookcases, kitchen with all the latest appliances, and circular driveway entrance to a two-car garage. Both in their mid-forties, they did not intend to have children, and by this time Joseph lived on his own, prompting the question of why they built such a large and elegant house. It seemed at cross-purposes with their antipathy to consumerism.[40]

Fromm had a wonderful way with clinical and other older students, as his friendly and supportive relationship with Joseph suggested. Younger children held little attraction for him. On one occasion, Fromm almost let a baby he was holding slide off his lap because he was so engrossed with the story he was telling. Lewis Webster Jones, the president of Bennington College, actively solicited him to teach. He offered to pay Fromm $2,500 under an endowed professorship for teaching one day each week (the 2012 equivalent of roughly $30,000). His course, "Human Nature and Character Structure," was very popular. Fromm's lectures provided the basis for much of *Man for Himself* and at least some of *The Forgotten Language*. The class prompted Fromm to expand his reading list and to convey more of his appreciable background in social psychology and psychoanalysis to his students. No few students noted his prophetic as well as his congenial and scholarly manner. In 1948, the senior class paid Fromm an honor almost never accorded to a regular member of the faculty—the graduating students chose him for their commencement speaker. Frances Davis, a member of that senior class, who became the psychologist David Rappaport's secretary at the Austen Riggs Center, wrote to Fromm a few months after graduation: "My work with you will always have the greatest meaning for me—as it did for most of us who were in your class." The enthusiastic response of students prompted Fromm, by the end of 1948, to agree to create a second course at Bennington on the dynamics of interpersonal relations ("Education in the Art of Living"). Yet Fromm sometimes wondered whether such conviviality with his Bennington students may have had its downside. He asked President Jones whether his great popularity among them may have made them less engaged with the substantive course materials. Jones replied that this was nonsense: Fromm's students mastered far more than their required assignments. He had cultivated a love in most of them for rigorous reasoning and the life of the mind. When not teaching, Fromm spent weekends with Henny to cheer her up. Though he used these weekends to make progress on his writing, Erich spent much of his time taking care of Henny and grew increasingly vigilant as her condition deteriorated.[41]

Certainly by the summer of 1948, as Erich and Henny moved into their elegant Bennington house, she suffered from elevated blood pressure, cardiac problems, and very acute arthritic pain that seemed to exacerbate her swings into depression. Initially, doctors speculated that lead poisoning was the culprit, but eventually they understood that the acuteness of her pain derived from the injuries sustained during her escape from France. Various medications were administered to no particular effect; she preferred homeopathic treatments and eschewed most medicines. By the fall of 1948, Erich found that he was attending to Henny practically around the clock; she was usually bedridden and deeply depressed. His cousin, Gertrud Hunziker-Fromm, felt that Henny's depression was often more debilitating than her pain. Erich cancelled lectures and professional opportunities and could barely honor his teaching and clinical training obligations. There was little time to attend to correspondence, and for the first time he missed publishing deadlines. The formulator of the concept of a productive social character did not feel that he himself was being very productive.[42]

To be sure, there were short intervals where Henny seemed to rally. She felt well enough to attend Joseph's marriage to Doris Hurwitch, whom Erich and Henny adored. As a wedding gift, they gave the newlyweds a honeymoon trip to Cuba. These hopeful intervals gave Erich a sense that he might get back to serious writing and return to the lecture circuit. Indeed, during the winter of 1948–1949, he was able to deliver a series of lectures at Yale on psychoanalysis and religion. He showed the texts of each of these lectures to Henny and was delighted when she offered penetrating suggestions to help him revise them into a short book. However, in June Erich recounted to Henny's sister-in-law:

Henny has been rather ill, sometimes with severe pain, so she has not been able to sleep for many nights. For three-quarters of a year she has almost always been in bed unable to do anything, not even write letters. I have not been able to write. Apart from my [clinical] practice and other professional duties, I have been busy with Henny's illness.[43]

With uncharacteristic despondency, Erich somehow summoned the energy to teach a preponderance of his classes at Bennington and the New School, to supervise (if erratically) at the White Institute, and to maintain a reduced psychoanalytic practice. Because medical care was better in New

York than Bennington, he moved Henny back to their apartment off Central Park and commuted alone to Vermont for his Monday class. Joseph was in Boston completing graduate work in metallurgical engineering at MIT, and he and Doris helped Fromm out when they could and tried to cheer Henny up. When professional obligations took Erich to Providence and nearby Boston, he always stayed with them. David Riesman was also encouraging, ordering artistic photographs from Henny, hoping to motivate her to get back to work. Erich usually reported that she could not complete an assignment. Nevertheless, Henny made the most of her condition. She would invite her friends to join her for breakfast, and though she was in bed, they all enjoyed themselves on these occasions.[44]

By the middle of 1949, Henny's physicians recommended a trip to Mexico, specifically to the radioactive springs near Mexico City. Erich took her there twice over the next six months. The climate and warm mineral waters modestly and temporarily soothed Henny's pain while slightly easing her depression. Indeed, Mexico appeared to be Erich's last hope to restore her happiness. If Henny's dire condition could be reversed, he knew that it would ease his own burdens and remedy the joyless and comparatively unproductive aspect of his life. In *Man for Himself* (1947), Fromm had written about the essential qualities of a happy, spontaneous, and productive life, but he was well aware that he was not living it. Similar to the optimistic conclusion of *Escape from Freedom*, *Man for Himself* projected a vision of an idealized reality wholly removed from his own.

Even before he migrated to America in 1934, Fromm had been fascinated by Mexico, especially Taxco, a charming town inhabited by talented craftspeople and artists, and during the summer of 1936, he had rented a house there with Karen Horney. Fromm returned for a month with Horney the following summer. During this interval, he visited San José Purrua, near Mexico City. Both Fromm and Horney began to consider Mexico an ideal place for long-term residence. On trips to Mexico City, Fromm had cultivated a close friendship with the émigré Marxist intellectual and activist Otto Rühle, whom he had known in Germany and who now consulted with the Mexican Ministry of Education. He had spent the summer of 1940 there learning from Rühle's work on comparative fascism as he worked on completing *Escape from Freedom*.[45]

Fromm's inability to write for publication and to find time to keep up with his clinical and teaching commitments because of Henny's need for round-the-clock care and general unresponsiveness to medication made him perhaps even more eager than Henny to travel to Mexico. He picked up Spanish rapidly and continued to find Mexican art and culture to his liking. Freed of his hectic daily schedule in New York and distant from the always distasteful aspersions of orthodox American psychoanalysts, Fromm concluded that permanent residence in Mexico City proximate to the healing springs of San José Purrua might enhance both his life and Henny's.[46]

In June 1950, the couple made the move to Mexico City and spent much of their time in San José Purrua at the recommendation of her New York physicians. But Henny's health stayed precarious. The sources of the arthritic pain and the underlying depression remained mysterious to attending Mexican physicians. Fromm continued caring for her almost full time, as he had before the move, and he worried that she seemed to despair of life itself. He cancelled all appointments requiring travel to the United States, wrote little, and worried a good deal.[47]

Henny's arthritic pain did not abate, even modestly, despite visits to the mineral springs. Rather, her depression moved to a new level, even as Joseph and Doris visited with Henny's first grandchild. Fromm watched her more closely than ever at this point and was loathe to leave her alone, even for brief periods. In June 1952, he found Henny dead on the floor of their bathroom, just hours after she told him, "Now I am quite sure I shall be entirely well in a short time." Joseph publicly blamed the death on heart failure, and Doris corroborated that story after initially stating that Henny had slit her wrists to end her life. The disparate stories and Erich's constant vigilance during the last years and especially the last days of her life would indicate that suicide is the more probable explanation. "I could not help Henny," he told Henny's friend, Charlotte Selver, who was sure from context that Erich was speaking of Henny's suicide.[48]

Henny's death caused Fromm not only intense emotional distress but prompted him to consider leaving Mexico, where she was buried. Karen Horney, who regularly visited the Cuernavaca–Mexico City area, had also died in 1952, adding to Fromm's generally gloomy perspective on life. To be sure, Fromm had several short sexual encounters between the middle of 1952 and early 1953, hoping in vain that they might move him "out of that spirit of being depressed." During the last few years of Henny's life, he had corresponded regularly with Charlotte Selver, who had been apprehensive about what Henny's illness was doing to Fromm and urged him to speak about his deep sadness. Judging from the letters, she was only modestly successful. However, she proved a good friend during a difficult time, and it is almost certain from the correspondence at hand that she became one of the lovers that helped him through his depression.[49]

Man for Himself

Owing to his exceedingly busy clinical and teaching schedules and his constant attention to Henny, Erich was extremely disappointed with his literary productivity in the decade after *Escape from Freedom*. Indeed, the books he wrote, centering on ethics, religion, and symbolic language, were simply revisions of public lectures. He shifted the lectures into chapters by amplifying the logic of his own thoughts and by citing classic thinkers. Unlike the Weimar worker study and a good portion of his writing before *Escape*, these publications were not sustained by survey research or any systematically collected body of evidence, though his explication of character theory was extraordinarily significant and insightful.

Fromm also lacked a sustained focus in his writing. As he was completing *Man for Himself*, for example, he considered joining Ashley Montagu in publishing a popular volume containing selections from Freud's writings. Permission to print the selections would have to come from the executors of Freud's literary estate, however, and neither Fromm nor Montagu pursued those permissions diligently. The project never materialized. In 1948 and 1949, Fromm was invited to a few meetings concerning a UNESCO research project on the sources of political and social tensions in four countries. The project leaders wanted him to test his evolving concept of "social character" on one of those countries: Australia. Fromm considered it as a potential pilot project and a prelude to an investigation of "more complicated cultures like the United States." He proposed to conduct field work on the Australian "national character" by focusing on variables in his population sample such as "authoritarianism versus independence, suggestibility versus critical abilities, destructiveness and xenophobia versus love and affection." Ultimately, UNESCO lacked the money to support him. Fromm sought funds from Charles Dollard at the Carnegie Foundation and from Melbourne University, but he never fashioned a comprehensive proposal that might have secured their assistance.[50]

This is not to say that the books Fromm wrote during this interval were without merit. *Man for Himself: An Inquiry Into the Psychology of Ethics*

(1947) and *Psychoanalysis and Religion* (1950) amplified the lectures that he offered during the 1940s, especially at Bennington College. They were less scholarly, less precise, and less probing than the articles he had written when he worked at the Frankfurt Institute. They were assuredly less evocative than *Escape from Freedom* and less focused on the threat of authoritarianism. But they elaborated at some length on Fromm's concept of "social character" and, more peripherally, on his "humanist" credo. Indeed, the themes of these two small books overlapped, and both were situated on the borderline between ethics and religion. They were intended to advance a comprehensive philosophy of life, and both spoke in important if polemical ways to Western postwar society. Predictably, Fromm's narrative in these volumes carried a more prophetic tone than had *Escape from Freedom*.

To some extent, *Man for Himself* was a response to a 1938 classic on suicide by the eminent psychiatrist and psychoanalyst Karl Menninger. Titled *Man Against Himself*, Menninger's argument was that suicide occurred when the human capacities for life and love were overbalanced by self-destructive drives. Soon to review *Escape from Freedom* tersely for its departure from psychoanalytic orthodoxy, Menninger elaborated on Freud's dual-drive theory (the life wish versus the death wish), describing in his book the forces that moved man from a delicate balance between the two and toward suicide. Fromm had rejected Freudian drive theory entirely by this point in time and therefore opposed the very premises of Menninger's book. A person was intrinsically good, Fromm maintained, and had an abundant capacity to advocate for himself. Essentially, *Man for Himself* elaborated a saying of Rabbi Hillel that Fromm had often discussed with Rabinkow: "If I am not for myself, who will be for me?" In trusting one's own creative resources, one could develop happiness, spontaneity, and productivity in one's life. Only when ethical norms were based on external authority and revelation did they stifle the human spirit, turn a person into a joyless automaton estranged from his "true essence," and make suicide a possibility. Unlike Menninger and Freud, Fromm held himself out as an "ethical thinker" and a voice of the "human conscience" who wrote to underscore "what is good or what is bad for man."[51]

Man for Himself was therefore a conceptual alternative to orthodox Freudianism and was grounded in what Fromm regarded as universal ethics. "Ethical" man (i.e., the person who embodied Fromm's and the Jewish view of a "God" on earth) more than "psychological" man (i.e., a person who strived for productivity and personal happiness) was central to Fromm's view of leadership.

Man for Himself was completed as the Cold War unfolded, and Fromm observed competing social trends. One trend celebrated human capacity, dignity, and democracy, and the other underscored human depravity and sin and purportedly required authoritarian intervention (not unlike the Soviet incursions throughout Eastern Europe). As heirs of both negative and authoritarian Luther on the one hand and the more democratic and hopeful Jefferson on the other, Fromm asserted, quite problematically, "we consciously believe in man's power and dignity, but—often unconsciously—we also believe in man's—and particularly our own—powerlessness and badness and explain it by pointing to 'human nature.'" Whereas Freud had embraced these two opposing premises in his dual-drive theory, Fromm's "humanistic" ethics purported to assist man to draw upon his own inner resources for happiness and contentment—to advance the hopeful and caring traditions of the Renaissance and the Enlightenment. From a "humanist" perspective, Fromm insisted that the ethical imperative of the day was for man "to be himself and to be for himself." [52]

More than *Escape*, Fromm's *Man for Himself* displayed the unqualified hopefulness that would be a characteristic theme in the decades ahead. Man needed to be productive, what Aristotle characterized as "flourishing." He needed to work not simply to survive materially but to draw upon his talents to create and innovate—to liberate his spirit. Writing more from the "life" and temperament of a prophet of hope than from his "life" as a sober and cautious social critic during his Frankfurt Institute years, Fromm postulated that society needed to be organized in ways that assured its citizens of sufficient food and shelter. They must not be subjected to material scarcity so that they could instead focus on creativity. To be productive was to "give birth to one's own potentialities" without restricting the productivity of others. Where man's productivity was fundamentally blocked, he channeled his energy in ways that were destructive to him and to others. As recent history purportedly attested, both self and society were thereby endangered. [53]

Central to *Man for Himself*, Fromm postulated with minimal elaboration that one would not be productive without being rational and reflective. For self-knowledge and identity, one needed confidence in one's capacity to observe, judge, and reason. When one understood oneself, one could love and value oneself. Succinctly, with confidence in the durability of one's rational capacity, unique identity as an individual, and inner resources, a person was able to appreciate and understand these same qualities in others and to feel genuine empathy and love for the other. Reduced to its essence, the productive life was rational, spontaneous, creative, and loving, if not exuberant. This idea would form the basis for *The Art of Loving* (1956), Fromm's bestseller. "Happiness is the indication that man has found the answer to the problem of human existence: the productive realization of his potentialities and thus, simultaneously, being one with the world and preserving the integrity of his self."[54]

Fromm rightly suspected that Reinhold Niebuhr, a brilliant formulator of the Neo-Orthodox theological perspective and perhaps the most important of all of the twentieth century's theologians, would be critical of his notion to liberate the resources of the individual self. In fact, Niebuhr wrote a long and thoughtful review of *Man for Himself* in which he declared that Fromm had gone much too far in his antiauthoritarianism. Above all, Niebuhr faulted Fromm for overemphasizing self-love and the necessity of each individual to cultivate his unique productive powers. Fromm had missed the importance of duty, Niebuhr insisted, dismissing duty as no more than the "internalization" of external authority. People wanted more from life than "merely to follow their desires." They had a sense of duty to people and causes outside themselves, which enriched all of human existence. To be sure, Niebuhr acknowledged, people did not always obey this sense of duty: "its counsels are colored by the pressures and prejudices of our world. But unless we assume a perfect inner unity of personality there is something like the sense of duty." For Niebuhr, Fromm was quite wrong in invariably equating duty with authoritarianism. The sense of duty evoked a giving of the self to others in empathetic fellowship. By giving to others, adherence to duty led to an appreciation of the capacities of the self. Indeed, Niebuhr also maintained that "Christian faith regards the sense of being judged from beyond the self as a necessary part of true self-knowledge." Religious and ethical obligation was not to be equated with the internalization of authoritarianism: "an insecure and impoverished self is not made secure by the admonition [i.e., Fromm's] to be concerned for itself; for an excessive concern for its security is the cause of impoverishment." Finally, Niebuhr criticized Fromm for failing to appreciate man's need "to exceed his bounds, to obscure the contingent character of his existence." This need was served by compliance with what man perceived as divine law: "Man's sin is not disobedience to a divine fiat but the idolatry of making himself his own end."[55]

Niebuhr may have been exaggerating the limits of Fromm's ethical "humanism." After all, Fromm conceded that once man drew on his own resources, he became capable of enhancing humane values in society at large, and that in turn increased the potential for individual productivity. Nevertheless, Niebuhr's critique of Fromm's "humanistic" ethics was telling. He underscored that the prod of an external deity and of a sense of duty evoked by forces beyond the self could sometimes make man push beyond his own limitations—to come to be more productive, loving, and caring. For Niebuhr, calls to duty and cries for man to exceed his bounds (sometimes in emulation of God) could enhance the capacities of the self in a way authoritarianism could not.

Niebuhr was responding to more than an imprecision in Fromm's developing concept of a "productive social character," the "nucleus of the character structure which is shared by most members of the same culture." While individuals could still differ in character, social character shaped individual desires to act in ways consistent with social expectations. The productive character was one of several types of social character, not the behavioral entity itself. The social character was what made acting in conformity with social rules and restrictions not only gratifying but beyond conscious decision making. For example, modern industrial society had turned man "into a person who was eager to spend most of his energy for the purpose of work, who acquired discipline, particularly orderliness and punctuality." As such, to draw psychological sustenance from sources other than the self was not antithetical to individual freedom. Indeed, Fromm periodically acknowledged that the concept of a free and productive individual was in some sense an external text that people might follow even as they augmented their own productive resources. Had Fromm made this point more stridently and consistently, the strength of Niebuhr's critique might have been diluted.[56]

In some measure, *Man for Himself* clarified what Fromm meant by psychological productivity in his elaboration of the four nonproductive character types, the adjuncts to his concept of social character. Whereas the productive character type created or augmented the self and humankind, the nonproductive character took, kept, or sold resources—goods, services, even selfhood. Nonproductive man feared an empty self and tried constantly to keep it filled. He was so preoccupied with self-depletion and replenishment that joy, creativity, exuberance, and ethical propriety were beyond his grasp. He was unresponsive to both an internal and an externally rooted sense of duty and could give no thought to transcending the boundaries of the self. Therefore, while there was cogency in Niebuhr's misgivings about Fromm—the assertion that ethical propriety derived from the resources of the self exclusive of external sources—Fromm had a qualified retort. He insisted that only a productive character was capable of ethical conduct. Yet, if this qualification might have given Niebuhr pause, it could hardly eradicate the distinction between Fromm's upbeat hopefulness in human potentiality and Niebuhr's underlying skepticism.

In delineating the first three of his four nonproductive character types, Fromm drew heavily on what Freud and Karl Abraham had designated as the oral receptive, the oral sadistic, and the anal personalities. Whereas Freud and Abraham classified these as pregenital types of libido organization, Fromm regarded them as ways in which man related to the world through his concrete social situation. In Fromm's "receptive orientation" (Freud's oral receptive), a person considered the "source of all good" to be outside himself. Outside resources provided all important material things, love, knowledge, and pleasure. One needed what Karen Horney called magic helpers to furnish these resources, and one became quite anxious when the helper withdrew or recanted on what had been forthcoming. So long as a person with a receptive character had a continuous expectation of being "fed," he was optimistic and friendly. But he became anxious and distressed when the "source of supply" was threatened. He often felt "a genuine warmth and a wish to help others," but only because he assumed that by procuring their favor, he perpetuated their gifts. He was devoted and sensitive when continuously supplied but also submissive to the supplier and parasitical.[57]

Where Freud and Abraham referred to an oral sadistic stage, Fromm, consistent with his social character typology, described an "exploitive orientation." Like the receptive personality, the exploitive person felt that he could produce nothing himself. While the receptive person expected to receive what he needed as "gifts," the exploitive person took resources or ideas away from others by force or cunning: "They use and exploit anybody and anything from whom or from which they can squeeze something." The receptive person could be optimistic and confident, but an exploitive person was always suspicious and envious, desiring what he might take away from others. He regularly overrated what others had or produced and underrated his own resources. The receptive person was captivating, able to assert himself and seductive, but also egocentric.[58]

Freud's and Abraham's anal-retentive personality became Fromm's "hoarding orientation." Whereas the receptive and exploitive orientations sought to acquire from the outside world, the hoarding self had little faith in such external acquisitions. Instead, he protected all his resources, hoarding and saving as much as possible. He assumed that he had only a fixed quantity of energy, mental capacity, and possessions and was determined to order and protect them so that they would never be depleted. He did not give love but tried to acquire it by possessing the beloved. The hoarder meticulously ordered his time and resources and cherished his memories of a past golden age. He assumed things were diminished or exhausted by use—that he could not replenish them; "death and destruction have more reality than life and growth." Creating protective walls between himself and others, his sense of justice was limited to saying: "Mine is mine and yours is yours."[59]

A person who received, exploited, or hoarded had grave doubts about his capacity to produce or create. In all three cases, this person lacked faith in his own talents or powers of creation or replenishment and was plagued by a fear of inner psychological emptiness. The constant quest for the self to run as close to "full" as possible made for anxiety, dread, and joylessness. Through these three negative referents, all heavily derived from the Freudian developmental model but shorn of libidinal drives, Fromm came to equate productivity with joy, ebullience, spontaneity, creativity, and happiness. He was building a philosophy or credo of the good life by admonishing people to have faith in their capacity to lead themselves to happiness.

Fromm's marketing personality was the only character type not based on Freud and Abraham's typology. Unlike the receptive, exploitive, and hoarding orientations, which Fromm assumed had always existed, he described the marketing orientation as an adaptation to the modern capitalist marketplace, representing "the experience of oneself as a commodity and of one's value as exchange value." One's personality could be marketed or packaged to fit current fashion and demand to maximize its attractiveness in the same way products and skills were marketed. If a specific employment area specified being "cheerful," "ambitious," "reliable," or any other trait or to belong to particular churches or social clubs, a marketing-oriented person presented himself accordingly. His own attributes were experienced as commodities alienated from his self. Like Ibsen's Peer Gynt, the marketing self was made up of a number of layers with "no core to be found." Identity did not derive from his own capacities and needs but how he packaged himself so that others had a favorable opinion of him and that would enhance his marketability. The marketing personality had no inner essence. The "very changeability of attitudes is the only permanent quality of such orientation." He was willing to play any role and display whatever personality traits assured success. Mass-media advertisements and the glamorized qualities of cultural heroes helped him become attuned to current personality features that employers or purchasers sought: "Some roles would not fit in with the peculiarities of the person; therefore, we must do away with them—not with the roles but with the peculiarities. The marketing personality must be free, free of all individuality."[60]

Psychologically, Fromm held that the marketing character was not "alive" and was hardly human. He was Arthur Miller's Willie Loman, who tried to base a sales career upon his personality and, lacking inner resources, had no recourse but suicide when he became unmarketable. Fromm's marketing personality bore some resemblance to the quality of "automaton conformity" developed in *Escape from Freedom*, though by underscoring a bleak inner emptiness, it was more devastating. The marketing character also became a point of departure for William Whyte's *The Organization Man* (1956), where success in the large corporate organization attended those who molded their personalities and habits to fit corporate needs and habits. The concept of marketing character was also a forerunner of Erving Goffman's *The Presentation of Self in Everyday Life* (1959), which argued that a person changed according to how he imagined that others perceived him. The concept even anticipated what Herbert Marcuse would label "one-dimensional man." Even though Fromm advanced his "marketing character" typology without nuance or clinical support, the concept made *Man for Himself* a forerunner to the very substantial critical literature of the 1950s and 1960s on the culture and psychology of conformity.

Whereas *Escape from Freedom* ended on an upbeat note, *Man for Himself* did not. In the latter, Fromm acknowledged that everyone was a mix of productive and unproductive character structures but felt that the unproductive self was increasingly ascendant and that his humanist ethics were in retreat:

Our moral problem is man's indifference to himself. It lies in the fact that we have lost the sense of the significance and uniqueness of the individual, that we have made ourselves into instruments for purposes outside ourselves, that we experience and treat ourselves as commodities, and that our powers have become alienated from ourselves.[61]

Fromm's frequent discussions of the marketing character over the course of the 1940s had to factor into the pessimism with which he ended *Man for Himself*. Whether he thought in terms of Freud's categories of the oral receptive, the oral sadistic, and the anal personality or his first three character types (receptive, exploitative, and hoarding), he was exposing an anxious, unhappy, and unproductive self—but also a self that had the capacity for transformation. This potentiality helped Fromm to maintain his modestly upbeat, hopeful tone throughout the rest of the volume.

By 1947, as Fromm ended *Man for Himself*, one dangerous authoritarian regime—Hitler's—had been defeated—and the brutalities of Stalin's had been exposed. Yet, in America especially, the forces of the marketplace and consumer culture seemed to be expanding. The signs of psychological vacuity or emptiness that Fromm, Riesman, Whyte, and other social critics exposed or would expose were already evident. For Fromm, the danger of "automaton conformity" in the societies that opposed Hitler seemed to be easing into an even more psychologically precarious marketing character. If he remained more upbeat than most of his colleagues, Fromm was also increasingly apprehensive of the future.

Save for Niebuhr, responses to *Man for Himself* were decidedly positive. Abraham Maslow made extended marginal comments in his copy of the book. Indeed, Maslow used Fromm's volume to develop his own "humanistic psychology" based on man's purported "hierarchy of needs." Several reviewers credited Fromm for explaining that a growing disposition in American culture toward psychological interpretation of human motivation should never replace efforts to understand and facilitate human ethics. This was not an insignificant reading of *Man for Himself*, as it showed how his volume anticipated Philip Rieff's brilliant characterization of "therapeutic man"—an "order hopper" who was unbound by ethical creeds or the requirements of analytic logic and clarity.[62]

Psychoanalysis and Religion

Psychoanalysis and Religion (1950), the third book Fromm completed in this decade and which he characterized as a continuation of *Man For Himself,* was based on a modest elaboration of a series of lectures he presented at Yale during the winter of 1948–1949. Although the 1947 volume presented Fromm's psychology of ethics and *Psychoanalysis and Religion* addressed the psychology of religion, he acknowledged that the two topics were "closely interrelated and therefore there is some overlapping." Like *Man for Himself, Psychoanalysis and Religion* sold 1.5 million copies and has been translated into twenty-two languages.[63]

This acknowledgment of overlapping was an understatement. Although Fromm displayed a respectable understanding of Eastern as well as Western religions in *Psychoanalysis and Religion,* he judged them through the conceptual structure of *Man for Himself.* If "humanistic ethics" was a contradiction in terms, for Fromm it encouraged man to trust himself, cultivate his own resources, and become productive. So too, "humanistic religion," for all its ambiguity, encouraged man to cherish his own inner resources and productivity (even if not in quite the same way as humanistic ethics). Authoritarianism was the antithesis of both "humane ethics" and "humane" religious experience. If Fromm had elected to repeat the scholarly proclivities evident in his 1930s essays, he might have integrated *Psychoanalysis and Religion* into *Man for Himself* and produced a more substantive book than either alone. Instead, he transformed his reasoning process and sources for one book into the theoretical outlines of another. To be sure, Fromm's strikingly innovative contrast between productive social character and marketing character made *Man for Himself* more than a middlebrow polemic on the psychology of ethics, but *Psychoanalysis and Religion* lacked any conceptual innovation. Fromm wrote not as the hardheaded intellectual and scholar but as a prophetic commentator on the human condition, one with a doctrinal position not wholly different from that of Rollo May and far from that of the more eminent Abraham Maslow.

Fromm began *Psychoanalysis and Religion* with the same tone of despair with which he concluded *Man for Himself.* Despite man's vast scientific and technological achievement in the modern era, he has not learned to emancipate himself intellectually, emotionally, or spiritually: "Ours is a life not of brotherliness, happiness, contentment but of spiritual chaos and bewilderment dangerously close to a state of madness . . . in which the contact with inner reality is lost and thought is split from effect." In this unhappiness and spiritual impoverishment (which in some way reflected Fromm's own life at the time), man was more attracted to authoritarian religion than to humanism. Calvinism and other authoritarian religions demanded submission to a power transcending the individual. In exchange for man's abandonment of his own agency and independence, authoritarian religion soothed his sense of loneliness and his apprehensions over his limitations: "he gains the feeling of being protected by an awe-inspiring power of which, as it were, he becomes a part." Submission to external religious authority, however, promoted further unhappiness and guilt while constraining man's productive powers. The alternative—Fromm's vaguely presented delineation of a religious experience, with or without a deity— was a far better remedy for the discontented soul. By focusing on the development of man's inner resources, it promised self-realization, joy, love, and creative productivity. In contrast to authoritarian religion, this so-called humanistic religion made God "a symbol of man's own powers which he [tried] to realize in his life . . . not a symbol of force and domination, having power over man."[64]

From a psychological and philosophical standpoint, the humanist ethics of *Man for Himself* was essentially the so-called humanist religion of *Psychoanalysis and Religion*. To justify a separate book, Fromm pressed hard to draw a distinction. He insisted that there were three discernable psychological aspects of religious experience that "went beyond the purely ethical." (1) One was "the wondering, the marveling, the becoming aware of life and of one's own existence, and of the puzzling problem of one's relatedness to the world." The life process for the individual and for humanity at large became a question, not an answer. Indeed, answers in "humanistic" religious experience simply yield new questions about the nature of existence that kept one in perpetual wonderment and curiosity. (2) There was also what Paul Tillich described as an "ultimate concern" in the meaning of life and the self-realization of man (though it was strongly related to wonderment). "Ultimate concern" caused man to focus on "the welfare of the soul and the realization of the self" so that all else became secondary. "Ultimate concern" could coexist with a concept of God, but it did not have to, since the focus was on man. (3) Finally, "humanistic" religious experience prompted "an attitude of oneness not only in oneself, not only with one's fellow men, but with all life and, beyond that, with the universe." In some ways, this perspective approximated that of Ralph Waldo Emerson and even William James.[65]

Fromm sought to illustrate what was unique in humanistic religious experience by comparing it to what he regarded as successful psychoanalytic therapy. The psychoanalyst helped awaken the analysand's sense of wonder and questioning so that he could find answers of his own; so did humanistic religious experience. Unless the patient was spiritually awakened, he would simply blame others for his troubles, regardless of how the analyst characterized the source of these troubles: "If the psychoanalysis is effective it is not because the patient accepts new theories about the reasons of his unhappiness but because he acquires a capacity for being genuinely bewildered; he marvels at the discovery of a part of himself whose existence he had never suspected." In other words, the successful patient acquired an element of religious experience. The psychoanalytic process of "breaking through the confines of one's organized self—the ego—and of getting in touch with the excluded and disassociated part of oneself, the unconscious" was akin to the religious experience of "breaking down individuation and feeling one with the All." Thus the psychoanalyst was a "physician of the soul" or facilitator who helped the patient experience truth, love, freedom, and responsibility and to hear the voice of his own conscience. Like all humanistic religions, psychoanalysis therefore focused man on his soul and "his powers of love and reason." Man did the rest.[66]

More in *Psychoanalysis and Religion* than in *Man for Himself,* Fromm delineated his own version of psychoanalysis and paired it with "humanistic" religious and ethical experience. All such experience, however vaguely presented, was intended to deepen man's happiness, his freedom, and his capacity to love. The problem was that by the late 1940s psychoanalytic theory varied widely, and orthodox analysts regarded Fromm disparagingly as a neo-Freudian.

Besides comparing his vague and only partially defined concept of humanistic religion to psychoanalysis, Fromm presented several abbreviated illustrations. He found in each humanistic religion the same cultivation of the internal resources of the self that he described for humanistic ethics. For example, early Buddhism implored man to "become aware of the powers in him." As a great teacher, Buddha (the "awakened one") called upon man to live in a manner that developed his powers of reason and of love for all humanity, and in this way man would be free of irrational passion. The

Buddhist concept of Nirvana (a "fully awakened" state of mind) rejected helplessness and submission and represented "the highest powers man possesses" to know himself and humankind. In fact, Fromm was attracted to Zen Buddhism precisely because it "proposes that no knowledge is of any value unless it grows out of ourselves" rather than from external authorities. Indeed, he befriended D. T. Suzuki, one of Zen's primary practitioners.[67]

Other examples of humanistic religion came easily to Fromm. Spinoza had long been one of Fromm's favorite religious thinkers because he postulated that as God was identical to the totality of the universe, God could not change anything. To be sure, man was dependent on and could not control the totality of forces outside himself. Yet, within himself and with the blessing of God, man had vast powers of love and reason that he could count on to maximize his freedom, joy, and inner strength. For Spinoza, these represented virtue, while sadness and inner constriction signified sin. Having studied the Hasidic movement, Fromm insisted that its motto from the verse of Psalms ("Serve God in joy") was not altogether dissimilar from the teaching of Spinoza. Emphasizing feeling rather than intellect, the Hasidim elevated joy and emotional expansiveness over contrition and unhappiness. Indeed, since God promised to put an end to suffering, Hasidism insisted that man had the right to force God to fulfill that promise. For Fromm, early Christianity represented still another example of "humanistic religion, best signaled by the spirit and text of Jesus' teachings that nothing could more clearly express the humane spirituality of Jesus than his precept that 'the kingdom of God is within you.' "[68]

Although Fromm also cited many examples of authoritarian religion and authoritarian passages in both the Old and New Testament, he deliberately concentrated on manifestations of religious humanism as an offer of hope for the emergence of happiness and joy in a world where the self was being packaged, estranged, repressed, and anxious. Essentially, Buddhism, Spinoza, Hasidism, and Christ all taught that "God is not a symbol of power over man but of man's own powers." Indeed, "God is the image of man's higher self, a symbol of what man potentially is or ought to become," while authoritarian religion treated God as "the sole possessor of what was originally man's: of his reason and his love." This was straight out of Feuerbach—the notion that God was simply man's projection of himself.[69]

One concludes a reading of *Psychoanalysis and Religion* by recognizing that it was completed by a very different Fromm than the discerning and cautious scholar of the 1930s. By the late 1940s, he asserted and reiterated his ideas but rarely demonstrated them with much logic or evidence. Fromm himself had become a prophet of sorts for a productive human spirit, and, ironically, this occurred during the least productive time of his life. Though his emotionally powerful—if unqualified—assertions appealed less to scholars, he was entering a new phase of his career. Tapping into what became a vast interest of the reading public, Fromm was evolving into a bestselling author and, in some way, an icon of popular culture, especially in the United States. His humanist ideals would soon become widely known. In short order, as well, influential public officials would come to befriend him. While his American audience especially started to grow, Fromm also began to train and inspire the first generation of Mexican psychoanalysts along the lines of his humanism, both ethical and religious. The 1950s would be his decade of greatest influence as he assumed new lives.[70]

6

To Love and to Mentor

American culture in the 1950s was thoroughly captivated by at least three issues: the Cold War, McCarthyism, and the theme of love. Fromm adamantly and publicly opposed both the Cold War and McCarthyism. And as he recovered from the death of his second wife, he found the love of his life. Indeed, it was a string of amorous missives he wrote to the woman who meant the most to Fromm in his last three decades that provided the incentive and momentum to write *The Art of Loving* (1956).

This is the book most readers identify with Fromm. It was an international phenomenon, and by 1999 it had been translated into thirty-two languages and had sold more than twenty-five million copies. The book was readily available for purchase in drug stores, train depots, and airports. Through *The Art of Loving*, Fromm joined social commentators such as David Riesman and John Kenneth Galbraith as a thinker on the Left who conveyed his thoughts to a mass readership at a time when McCarthyism held currency. Indeed, he became a cult figure and icon to the Left. Students at Berkeley were more familiar with Fromm's publications in general and *The Art of Loving* in particular, according to a survey, than they were with the works of Jack Kerouac, Andre Gide, and William Whyte. If less probing and reflective than *Escape from Freedom*, the book accomplished what its predecessor could not: catapulting Fromm into an international spotlight and providing access to a mass audience.[1]

A popular leftist in a politically conservative age, Fromm's life in Mexico was hardly that of a privileged and estranged expatriate. He immersed himself in the life and culture of his new adoptive country. He founded the Sociedad Psicoanalitica Mexicana and became mentor to the first generation of locally trained Mexican psychoanalysts, who informed their practices with Fromm's constructs such as "social character" and "humanistic ethics." He would later initiate a massive, decade-long study of a small peasant village south of Mexico City to understand and help alleviate the despondency and fatalism among the villagers.

Though rooted in Mexican society, Fromm retained his American citizenship and spent several months each year teaching in the United States. Working at the White Institute and the New School and with a modest New York analytic practice, he also served as an adjunct professor at Michigan State University. All the while, he started to work for and to write on behalf of progressive political causes, defending New Deal social policies and opposing aggressive U.S. Cold War designs.

Mentor in Mexico

When Erich and Henny moved to Mexico, he felt incredibly isolated from friends and colleagues. Before Henny's death, however, Mexico City psychiatrists had begun to befriend Fromm. Several participated in a seminar on Freud's writings and clinical applications that the psychiatry professor Raul Gonzales Enriques organized at the National University of Mexico. By the time Fromm took up full-time residence in Mexico City, the seminar had evolved into a medical school course for psychiatrists in training desirous of a psychoanalytic specialty (at the time, psychoanalytic training was only available in Argentina, the United States, and what was left of post-Holocaust Europe). Jesus Zozaya, the distinguished physician and director of the University's graduate school, had profited from *Escape from Freedom* and thought that Fromm might be a very suitable instructor for the course. Zozaya discussed a possible Fromm appointment with Jose Diaz, a respected pediatrician and child psychiatrist, and Diaz recommended him highly. Zozaya then consulted three senior Mexican psychiatrists, including Raul Gonzales Enriques, and they agreed that even though Fromm was neither a physician nor a psychiatrist, he should be offered the most distinguished faculty position ever accorded a psychoanalyst at the National University: a special faculty chair at the university's medical school.[2]

Fromm would teach the current course on psychoanalysis for psychiatrists and offer periodic lectures to the general university community. The prospect of shaping psychoanalytic thought and practice in Mexico at this formative stage was compelling. He planned to offer lectures and seminars on the language of dreams and on other forms of symbolic communication that would help him amplify his concept of social character, "humanistic ethics," and other alternatives to the orthodox Freudian corpus. His students would not be "prejudiced" by mainstream American psychoanalysis. Though initially hesitant, owing to the care Henny required, Fromm accepted Zozaya's offer.[3]

At the time, there was a dormant psychoanalytic institute in Mexico City, occupied by a handful of orthodox Freudians. After Fromm established his psychoanalytic society and institute, a contingent of Freudians would emigrate from Buenos Aires to invigorate the orthodox alternative to Fromm. These rival Argentinean analysts and the Fromm-led psychoanalytic organizations entered into a period of tension that somewhat replicated the conflict between the orthodox Freudians and the neo-Freudians in the United States.[4]

Fromm's professorship on the campus of the National Autonomous University of Mexico had been largely honorary. But he quickly started training some rather eminent public officials, psychiatrists, and even medical school professors who taught at the university. When he turned to Fromm for psychoanalytic training, for example, Alfonso Millán headed the psychiatry department at the medical school. Guillermo Davila ran the national social security administration, and Ramon de la Fuente presided over several international psychiatry associations.[5]

In all, ten psychiatrists declared a psychoanalytic specialty in order to qualify as Fromm's students, and three more soon followed. All were relatively young men, idealistic and undogmatic, though they differed significantly in their life experiences. Aniceto Aramoni was a psychiatrist interested in philosophy and had a strong scholarly bent. Jorge Silva Garcia, in contrast, had been a physician in the Mexican army and had received some training at the Chicago Neuropsychiatric Institute. In fact, before returning to Mexico City he had been in contact with Franz Alexander at the Chicago Psychoanalytic Institute. All thirteen students welcomed the opportunity to move beyond the limits of traditional Mexican psychiatric training, which was based entirely on clinical apprenticeship.[6]

When Fromm began to train the first generation at the Mexican Psychoanalytic Society, he was narcissistic, stern, arrogant, driven, and irritable. Despite the coffee and pastries that he graciously provided at the start of a seminar, he had a "haughty vanity" and a readiness to put others down. This was a tightly wound and rather condescending German psychoanalyst and writer in a Third World country—not the most pleasant training for Mexico's first generation of analysts. Despite his appreciation for local art, Fromm came to Mexico with some discomfort with and even contempt for Mexican culture, which was probably not mitigated by the initial misunderstandings between teacher and students as they began their seminar. By the mid- and late 1950s, however, this attitude softened, partially thanks to Fromm's new romantic relationship and his exposure to Zen and D. T. Suzuki. The personal relationships at the Mexican Institute and his acknowledged importance likely aided in the personality shift. Jorge Silva Garcia, in the first class at the Institute, was among the first to detect the change. In contact with Fromm almost daily, Silva Garcia noticed that his face had softened and his eyes had become less foreboding, revealing "a playful roguish look." No longer puffing neurotically at a cigar, he was evolving into a "kindly, amiable, simple man" with an increased capacity to love and empathize and a new joy in living. During difficult situations, Fromm often sat down and relaxed, closing his eyes and slowing his breathing. Humor became one of his defining qualities. He cultivated a love for good jokes, often convulsing in laughter over them. Silva Garcia discovered that Fromm had a book containing six thousand Jewish jokes and had committed many of them to memory.[7]

Initially, there was something of a language barrier between students and instructor, though the students had some facility with English, and Fromm progressed rapidly in his mastery of Spanish. With his disciplined German scholarly and clinical background and given his quest to keep life orderly, Fromm was punctual, methodical, and disciplined. He started each seminar session with definite goals and lesson plans, but consistent with Mexican culture, the students had a less exacting sense of time, vague goals, and a greater disposition toward lightheartedness and fiesta. But as they spent their Wednesday evenings in Fromm's Mexico City apartment for his introductory seminar in psychoanalysis, the cultural barrier receded.[8]

The students voiced their opinions freely and frequently; Fromm replied attentively and respectfully. He passed out drafts of material that he was writing to elicit student responses. Although he had broken in part from Freud (and with extended qualifications) when it came to libido theory, dream interpretation, and the Oedipus myth, he still regarded himself as a Freudian and recommended that, after pondering his perspectives, the students arrive at their own. What mattered most, Fromm advised, was whether they were dogmatic or flexible and were willing to discuss the strengths and weaknesses of Freud's diverse texts, which were rooted in often widely varying premises. Essentially, he was drawing them into his longstanding dialogue with Freud. Fromm also introduced some of the works of Ferenczi, Alexander, Horney, and Fromm-Reichmann, theorists he liked, but also writings by Jung and Adler, which he found problematic. He explained that Aristotle, Spinoza, Marx, and Hegel added new dimensions to psychoanalytic understanding, and he freely referenced current scholarship in sociology, anthropology, and biology.[9]

The class was therefore openly interdisciplinary and rich in intellectual content, which the students appreciated. They designated themselves the Mexican Group for the Study of Psychoanalysis and were the first locally trained generation of psychoanalysts. Despite Fromm's responsibilities at the White Institute and elsewhere in the United States, his students urged him to make Mexico his principal residence for at least five years, for if he remained in the Mexico City area at least half of each year, they could complete their formal training with him and become qualified to train subsequent generations of analysts. Deeply moved by the response to the introductory seminar, Fromm agreed to stay and to offer advanced courses as well as didactic and training analyses. When the training of this first class was completed in 1956, they joined with Fromm to establish the Mexican Psychoanalytic Society. Exhibiting a certain ecumenicalism, they invited the relatively small number of Mexican colleagues trained in Argentina and America, usually along more orthodox psychoanalytic lines, to become members. Most of these returning analysts declined the invitation at the advice of the International Psychoanalytic Association and formed a separate and more orthodox society. Yet Fromm's willingness to embrace them pointed to a reticence to create a formal "school" of thought with like-minded followers, a setup that might tie him down to one place or discipline. Not only had he been bruised too badly by psychoanalytic and other hierarchically structured orthodoxies to want to emulate them, but his tendency to uproot and jump from one situation to another when so inclined made him reticent to be too firmly preoccupied with a school of his own. He was a man with several "lives" and affiliations. Viewed from the perspective of the political power struggles endemic to the psychoanalytic profession, this located him on the margins.[10]

As he trained the generation that created the Mexican Psychoanalytic Society (MPS) and helped with subsequent students, Fromm invited a steady stream of exciting intellectuals from a diversity of fields and eclectic analysts who eschewed Freudian orthodoxy to present their views and ideas. They included the theologian Paul Tillich, the psychoanalytic psychiatrist Roy Grinker, the Buddhist philosopher D. T. Suzuki, the family systems theory pioneer Nathan Ackerman, the British psychoanalytic theorist Michael Balint, and his friends from the White Institute, Clara Thompson and Edward Tauber. He even invited J. William Fulbright and Adlai Stevenson, household names in American politics who were becoming good friends. As a high-level administrator at the National University, Jesus Zozaya assured ample funding and smoothed over any potential procedural obstacles, allowing Fromm to bring in colleagues of his choice, usually as guest lecturers but sometimes simply as insightful commentators. In brief, Zozaya let him organize the training process in any way he chose. Realizing that the initial class of thirteen would be instrumental in shaping the future of much of Mexican analysis and in training subsequent generations, Fromm spent a great deal of time with each of them individually. Not only did he analyze and supervise every one of them, but he assigned each one a final graduation paper designed to provide psychoanalytic insights into specific populations, customs, or family structures in Mexican society. Fromm expected a publishable scholarly paper from each but regarded only Aniceto Aramoni's as being a finished product of that caliber. In addition to their clinical duties, Fromm prodded his students to become involved in social reform ventures in the larger community. On this count, Aramoni and most others in the first class fell short, even as they created a free mental health clinic for the poor. Subsequent trainees, considering community involvement as essential to facilitating "productive social character" in struggling local populations, did considerably more.[11]

By the mid-1950s, when the members of the first generation completed their training, they joined Fromm in teaching courses and supervising new trainees in the program, which was loosely affiliated with the National University of Mexico. One of Fromm's analysands, Roberto Fournier, was named head of the medical faculty at the university, which increased the level of support Fromm and the MPS received. Fournier required all medical students to take a course sequence taught by Fromm and his psychoanalytical trainees, and the MPS grew into a major institution in Mexican medical education. Fromm and his trainees also reorganized the university's psychology department along psychoanalytic rather than behaviorist lines. By the late 1950s, Fromm was clearly a vital presence in establishing his own psychoanalytic approach, grounded in his "social character" construct and his "ethical humanism."[12]

From the late 1950s and into the 1960s, as his original group of students assumed new responsibilities, Fromm reduced his teaching and supervisory duties in order to spend long mornings alone on his writing and research and to accept more patients and lecture invitations. When Alfonso Millán, who managed Fromm's affiliations with the University of Mexico, was named the first president of the MPS, he worked with Jorge Silva Garcia and Aniceto Aramoni to create the affiliated psychoanalytic institute that would coordinate a larger array of professional functions. Silva additionally arranged for the financing and construction of a large institute building near the university, and it opened in 1963, with counseling rooms, an outpatient clinic, a library, seminar rooms, an auditorium for public lectures, and even an apartment for institute guests.[13]

Although all the members of the first class were solid students, Fromm was especially impressed by Aramoni. By the late 1950s, he was grooming Aramoni to succeed Millán in both the Society and Institute, and as he evolved into a prolific scholar and a skilled psychoanalyst, Aramoni began modeling his career after Fromm's. He mastered all of Fromm's publications and understood—more in theory than from experience—that the concept of social character drew importance from a community setting. Aramoni and Fromm became good friends and began reviewing their respective writing projects and the affairs of the Mexican Psychoanalytic Society and Institute together.

In addition to their burgeoning professional relationship, the two developed close personal bonds. Aramoni's daughter, Rebecca, born in 1955, developed an especially strong tie with Fromm as she grew up. When Aramoni lunched at Fromm's home, he brought Rebecca because she delighted Fromm. He appreciated her energy and zest for life and was deeply respectful of her intelligence and independent spirit. As Rebecca began to decide on a vocation, Fromm advised her to follow her instincts—even to become a theatrical performer if she chose. The Aramoni family referred to Fromm as Rebecca's godfather.[14]

Fromm and Aramoni wrote to each other whenever they traveled. Aramoni openly spoke of Fromm as the man he most admired—a psychoanalytic leader who taught through his presence. As he assumed more of Fromm's duties in the Society and Institute, Aramoni perpetuated many of Fromm's practices and traditions. Indeed, Fromm once wrote to Aramoni: "I have always felt badly about the time and energy which you had to spend to continue the work I had begun and to suffer from the consequences of many mistakes I had made. Maybe I should have dissuaded you from continuing the job." Although Aramoni peppered Fromm with matters concerning which psychoanalytic candidates to admit, what new Institute courses to offer, themes for convocations, potential guest speakers, personal animosities among training analysts, unexpected expenses, potential revenues and the like, Fromm decreased his involvement over the years, hoping that Aramoni and his colleagues would make their own decisions. He recognized that he had cultivated too much dependence in his trainees and that this tendency was hard to reverse; however, he seemed unwilling to fully relinquish his central position in the group. Once, for example, he wrote to Aramoni: "It is important that the group learns to take the responsibility in my absence," even as he proceeded to offer suggestions. "But again I leave it to you," Fromm concluded his letter. "The main thing is that the group really learns to function without me and that you take your proper role." Aramoni always responded gracefully but felt pulled by his mentor in two directions—toward deference to the wishes of the "founder" on the one hand and toward independent decision making on the other. Like Fromm, he found it difficult to strike a balance. This struggle over relinquishing control of the Society and the Institute illustrated Fromm's penchant at certain times and in certain situations for "totalist" leadership.[15]

D. T. Suzuki and Zen Buddhism

One of the most exciting weeks in the history of the Mexican Psychoanalytic Society occurred in August 1957, when the prominent Japanese scholar, historian, and master of Chinese Chan (Zen) Buddhism, the eighty-six-year-old Daisetz Teitaro Suzuki, accepted Fromm's invitation to be featured in a week-long seminar on psychoanalysis and Zen. Since the 1930s, Suzuki had compellingly conveyed Zen's essential perspectives to Western philosophers, theologians, artists, psychologists, psychoanalysts, and general readers. While teaching primarily at Japanese universities, he assumed a variety of exchange professorships of Buddhist philosophy in the United States and Europe. Fluent in English and several continental European languages and having a solid understanding of Western intellectual and philosophic traditions, Suzuki effectively promoted East-West dialogue and understanding. After World War II, Suzuki was especially influential in the United States, where he helped establish Zen training centers and taught for several years at Columbia University.[16]

With a special talent in explaining to Westerners how Zen Buddhism contrasted with their tradition of dualistic and dichotomous thinking, Suzuki pointed out that Zen philosophy had been introduced to Europe and America at the same time that psychoanalysis had arrived. He suggested that like psychoanalysis, Zen sought to explicate the depths of the human psyche. The practitioner of Zen sought to penetrate deep down into the very center of his being—into a special space of "nothingness" that shared similarities with the psychoanalytic concept of an unconscious. In this space, the Zen practitioner "viewed" his own thoughts and feelings and, indeed, the spirit of everyone's essential being. Thus, "nothingness" was a space within the self filled also by all other selves and the world, representing the essential "oneness" of existence. When a person penetrated inwardly, therefore, he perceived not his separateness as a person but the edgeless space of awareness that underlay all states of mind of all animate and inanimate objects. At that point, Suzuki maintained that one's "individuality, which [he] found rigidly held together and definitely kept separate from other individual existences, becomes loosened somehow from its tightening grip and melts away into something indescribable. . . . The feeling that follows is that of complete release or a complete rest—the feeling that one has arrived finally at the destination." Once a person was able to feel this "oneness" and glimpse his true nature, he needed to stabilize the vision (i.e., to continue to see who he really was). As this realization stabilized, he moved beyond his self-image, which was not his fundamental nature, and recognized that there was nothing to achieve, nowhere to go, nothing to be. There was an imageless, still, and quiet core present in the midst of his busy life. Paradoxically, abundant energy for life's tasks emanated from this essential stillness of "oneness."[17]

Fromm became familiar with Suzuki's work on Zen in the 1940s and felt that it seemed to approximate his own humanistic revisions of psychoanalysis. After reading *Escape from Freedom* and *Man for Himself*, Suzuki agreed that he and Fromm were pursuing similar paths. A modest correspondence followed. When Erich and his third wife, Annis, were in New York in the fall of 1956, Suzuki invited them to his house for a dinner and a lengthy conversation on Zen. Fromm characterized it as "one of the most wonderful meals we ever had in our lives," with conversation that was even better. Indeed, he wrote to Suzuki that "something had clicked" that evening; he sensed that he finally understood the essence of Zen. The feeling was "quite exhilarating," and he needed to talk to Suzuki about potential applications of Zen principles to psychoanalysis. Eagerly anticipating the scheduled two weeks with Suzuki over Christmas in Mexico, Fromm asked that he consider staying "more permanently." He would organize an international conference in Cuernavaca in Suzuki's honor, hoping it would be one of the few forums to address systematically the relationship between Zen and psychoanalysis.[18]

Specifically, Fromm began to work actively with his Mexican Psychoanalytic Society colleagues and students to make the conference a historic intellectual meeting of East and West. Suzuki agreed to participate in the weeklong event, which was scheduled for August 1957, in Cuernavaca. He also promised to visit with the Fromms afterward.[19]

Fromm and the MPS issued invitations through the National University of Mexico to psychoanalysts of various perspectives and "schools" in the United States and Mexico. Jungians, orthodox Freudians, and other analysts of the already fragmented profession were invited in the hope that they might discover some common ground in their work. Fromm asked Suzuki to offer four lectures and to participate in follow-up discussions. He also planned to invite several prominent psychoanalysts to lecture on topics related to Zen. In an effort to provide cohesion to the conference, Fromm proposed to be a bridge between Suzuki's presentation of Zen and the presentations of the analysts. Ultimately, he planned to publish the conference proceedings as a book on Zen and psychoanalysis.[20]

Roughly fifty psychoanalysts from Mexico and the United States participated in the Cuernavaca conference—double the number anticipated when invitations were issued. A substantial number in the American contingent were from the White Institute. Although Suzuki's four lectures and his response to questions formed the keynote to the conference, his very presence and manner were also crucial. Fromm recalled after the event that what had begun as a traditional conference of articulate professionals, with a predictable "over-emphasis on thoughts and words," changed within two days, as "a change of mood began to be apparent. Everyone became more concentrated and more quiet." Suzuki's deep inner spirituality and the quiet introspection inherent in Zen were provoking "a visible change [that] occurred in many of the participants." To some degree,

Fromm felt, they were embracing their inner psychic depths. Suzuki's thoughts were always "firmly rooted in his being." He never belabored a point or engaged in verbal gymnastics but presented himself and Zen philosophy with kindness, with deep inner calm, and expressing a love of life. For Fromm, Suzuki's "humanity shone through the particularity of his national and cultural background." He also seemed to permeate beyond the "artificial" divisions within professional psychoanalysis. Everyone at the conference, Fromm noted, was impressed by "the light, which radiates from him."[21]

If Suzuki's presence represented the spiritual core of the conference, Fromm's paper, "Psychoanalysis and Zen Buddhism," was the signal intellectual contribution. The paper was probably his most coherent and probing reflection on the unconscious in psychoanalytic thought; Zen aided him in addressing the topic with freshness and understanding. Unlike Freud, most psychoanalysts, and many intellectuals generally, Fromm had long tempered his embrace of modernity with mystical religious traditions focusing on a place deep within the self that connected spiritually to all other selves beyond the boundaries of space or time. He had been especially fascinated by the self's sense of "oneness" with the object of its perception. Indeed, Fromm found this mystical "oneness" in the Kabala of medieval Jewry and perhaps most compellingly in Hasidism. He had also found it in Meister Eckhart, Jakob Böhme, and a few other Christian mystics, and in the mysticism found in the Sufi Islam of Rumi. And Jung, usually left unmentioned by Fromm, also influenced him. But since the late 1940s, Fromm felt that the sense of "oneness" was advanced most compellingly in Suzuki's explications of Zen, and Fromm habitually read either a passage from Meister Eckhart or a portion of a Zen text.[22]

In Suzuki's presence, Fromm opened his conference with uncharacteristic humility, acknowledging that he had yet to experience fully the *satori* (enlightenment) that was a central component of Zen: "I can talk about Zen only in a tangential way, and not as it ought to be talked about—out of the fullness of experience." Nonetheless, he felt that he had "at least an approximate idea of what constitutes Zen" which "I hope enables me to make a tentative comparison between Zen Buddhism and psychoanalysis." Fromm described the essence of Zen elaborated by Suzuki in psychological terms: "a state in which the person is completely tuned to the reality outside and inside of him; that he is fully aware of it and fully grasps it." To cultivate this "awakened" state and reach *satori*, one became "empty and ready to receive" the full reality within and without himself. In Suzuki's words, one reached "the full awakeness of the total personality to reality." Once a person arrived at this state of "awakening" and openness, Fromm asserted that life would become peaceful, joyous, and rejuvenating—indeed, ebullient. Fromm equated Zen's "awakened" state with the "productive orientation" (his psychoanalytic construct for optimal mental health). Both were antithetical to the greed and exploitation that set the self against the other—"me" against "not me." That external object or person (the "not me") ceased to be, becoming part of "me" and thereby promoting a sense of "oneness." This incorporation of the "not me" with the "me" into "oneness" eliminated any sense of alienation and produced a state of maximum energy and productivity: "I experience intensely—yet the object is left to be what it is. I bring it to life—and it brings me to life." To live in Zen was therefore "to treat yourself and the world in the most appreciative and reverential frame of mind."[23]

Perhaps because Suzuki's characterization of Zen was more a matter of one's spiritual disposition than of intellect or conceptual consistency, Fromm's portrayal of Zen Buddhism was redundant and imprecise. Of course, Fromm's knowledge of psychoanalysis far outdistanced Suzuki's, and as he compared it to Zen, his paper became clearer. Both Zen and psychoanalysis sought to achieve the same ends: insight into one's nature, freedom, happiness, love, sanity, and the liberation of thwarted energy. Both required the overcoming of greed and the coveting of possessions and notoriety, instead valuing love, compassion, and ethical conduct. Neither the Zen master nor the psychoanalyst forced one to suppress the "evil" desire of greed but expected it to "melt away and disappear under the light and warmth of enlarged consciousness." In Zen, *satori* was never achieved without humility, love, and compassion. Similarly, Fromm insisted that psychoanalysis required the evolution from an exploitive or hoarding social character into a productive character, where one grew more humble and compassionate and acquired self-understanding, an echo of what Fromm characterized in the 1940s as humanism.[24]

For Fromm, both Zen and psychoanalysis required independence from any authority external to the self. In developing psychoanalysis, Freud criticized Western religion for replacing the infantile dependence on a helping and punishing father with a dependence on God. Analysis intended to dissolve this "unfreedom." Correspondingly, Fromm noted that Zen Buddhism made no room for a powerful external God or any sort of irrational authority and sought to liberate man from all dependencies so that he might become the architect of his own fate. Although both the psychoanalyst and the Zen master initially guided the analysand or Zen student, the goal was the same: to encourage self-reliance, which could be achieved by moving beyond formal thought and rationalization and embracing one's own unique feelings and perceptions.[25]

Most importantly, Fromm equated the central psychoanalytic quest—helping the patient overcome repression by making the unconscious conscious—with Zen's primary aim of gaining enlightenment. Both psychoanalysis and Zen involved "the inner revolution of man," of becoming increasingly aware intellectually and intuitively of what one was not aware of. Indeed, Fromm noted that if one replaced the psychoanalytic terms "conscious" and "unconscious" with "greater or lesser awareness of experience in the total man," it was easier to understand that Zen and psychoanalysis shared identical goals. Both sought to overcome artificial dichotomies within the self—the distinction between subject and object, the split "within myself between the universal man and the social man," and the polarity between conscious and unconscious. Both required overcoming estrangement from others and from the wider world, abandoning the illusion of "an indestructible separate ego, which is to be preserved." Basically, Zen and psychoanalysis required one to be entirely open and responsive, internally and externally, in order to put an end to vanity and greed, "to have nothing and to be." This ultimate embrace of "oneness" was the goal of both psychoanalysis and Zen.[26]

Still, Fromm cautioned, the technique of the two differed in one respect. Psychoanalysis focused on uncovering the patient's illusions about the world on a step-by-step basis of lifting repressions so that distortions and intellectualizations diminished over time. In contrast, Zen represented a far more direct or frontal attack on alienation and distorted perception. Through the direction of the master within the monastery, Zen required of the student "the immediate, unreflected grasp of reality without affective contamination and intellectualization, the realization of the relation of self to the Universe." Zen's enlightenment resembled the child's sense of immediacy and oneness with the world. But unlike childhood, it occurred after the adult transcended both the subject-object split and the experience of estrangement.[27]

Fromm concluded his paper by insisting that since the goals of Zen and psychoanalysis were identical, the techniques, if different, were nonetheless complementary. The directness and no-nonsense bluntness of Zen technique and vision could sharpen the focus of psychoanalytic insight— "to overcome the affective contaminations and false intellectualizations" of the Western subject/object split. Similarly, the cautious penetrations of psychoanalysis into the repressed unconscious might help the Zen master guide his student against "false enlightenment" through self-induced trances, psychoses, or hysterias.[28]

At several points in his conference paper, Fromm acknowledged that his formulations were only preliminary; he had yet to enhance his knowledge of Zen Buddhism and Eastern culture. Yet this paucity of knowledge did not seem to restrain him. Just as Suzuki spent much of his life translating Eastern foundational premises into Western thinking, Fromm expressed a willingness to partake in the converse. Through Suzuki's efforts, complimented by his own, universal human experiences crossing the East/West divide could be better understood.[29]

Coming one year after the Mexican Psychoanalytic Society was recognized as an official entity, the Cuernavaca conference had a defining influence on it. Mexican psychoanalysis would pursue a broad ecumenical vision that went far beyond more orthodox Freudian and primarily Western constructs. In an attempt to "preserve" this defining week in its history, Fromm and his initial students sought to publish Suzuki's four lectures and Fromm's lengthy presentation as a book. To achieve this task, Fromm turned again to Harper, which published *Zen Buddhism and Psychoanalysis* early in 1960. Even though Fromm and Suzuki were very prominent writers—and there was a paucity of books on the topic—sales were modest. As of June 30, fewer than 4,800 copies were sold, and Fromm had come across only one book review. Still, the conceptual highlights, if not the full spirit of the conference, had been preserved in a durable form. Although initial sales were slow, the book eventually sold a million copies and was translated into sixteen languages.[30]

Until his death in 1967, Suzuki continued to travel to Mexico, where he was usually hosted by Fromm and eagerly pursued by members of the Mexican Psychoanalytic Society. Along with New York City and Kamakura (near Tokyo), Suzuki began regarding the Cuernavaca–Mexico City area as his home base. When they were not together, Fromm and Suzuki wrote long, spirited letters to each other on new writing projects, important texts each had read, and especially on new ideas. Through this correspondence, they mutually supported each other and built a solid intellectual and personal relationship. In a very real sense, Fromm trusted Suzuki, his manner, and his wisdom with an ardor comparable to his earlier mentor and friend Rabinkow.[31]

Annis Freeman and *The Art of Loving*

By December 1952, Fromm had begun to court Annis Freeman. He first met Annis and her third husband, David Freeman, a wealthy lawyer who coordinated news for American newspapers from India, at meetings held in New York in 1948 to deliberate a UNESCO project on ameliorating international political tensions. David died soon after, leaving Annis, whose two prior husbands had also passed on, childless but with considerable wealth. Like many women of her generation, she had little sense of herself without the intimate presence of a man. Annis and Fromm did not begin writing to each other until after Henny's suicide, but the correspondence quickly turned into a courtship. Two years younger than Fromm, Annis had been born into a Protestant Pittsburgh household but had grown up in Alabama and spoke with a distinctly Southern accent. During her period in India, she had developed a strong interest in Eastern spiritual traditions. She practiced astrology and had a reputation for accurate forecasts, meditated, practiced tai chi, and appreciated Fromm's deepening interest in Buddhism. A tall, sensuous, and beautiful woman, Annis adored Erich from the beginning of their courtship. Running her late husband's business in New York, she planned eventually to make a home with him in Mexico. She was extraordinarily intelligent and shared his interest in international politics and diverse cultures. He proposed to her in the fall of 1953, though he had talked of marriage only a few months into the courtship. They married in December.[32]

Because Erich lived in Mexico City and Annis in New York, their courtship involved an extensive correspondence, which underscored his deep attachment to her. He opened himself to Annis as he had never revealed himself to anybody. Love had free flow. Even after their marriage, he wrote to her several times a day, whether at home or away, declaring his affection, often citing his schedule for the day as a reason to write: "It is 10 now—I go to the office. Maybe you call me up after [the] first cup of tea. Shall be back at the latest at 2. I am all yours totally. E." In many ways, these were mundane epistles about everyday life, detailing work commitments, day-to-day problems, or thoughts, punctuated by little anecdotes or jokes—and always underscored by assurances of his love for her. He wrote to her about new books that interested him, new ideas, elegant attire he hoped she would buy, and even about his own personal introspections.[33]

If the abbreviated notes and letters to Annis seem mundane, it is well to recall the sociologist Erving Goffman's admonition that "gestures which we sometimes call empty are perhaps the fullest things of all." Indeed, epistles underscored the specific weave of the Fromm-Freeman relationship. Life without her had become unimaginable: "My beautiful love, I love you so that it hurts, but the hurt is sweet and wonderful. I wish you feel it in your sleep." Fromm punctuated every exchange with assurances of his affection. He loved her unreservedly. Indeed, the courtship of Annis most definitely set the stage for *The Art of Loving*. However, unlike the book, his short but loving notes to her were specific to their relationship, neither codified nor reified. With abundant detail, Fromm essentially told Annis that in her presence he thought less about his faults and had come to appreciate his strengths. Annis had enhanced his sense of self-worth and consequentiality.

Through these epistles, Fromm moved toward the general perspective that self-love was mandatory for a loving relationship. The point became central to *The Art of Loving* and to his subsequent books. While affirming the specific emotion-laden texture of his love for Annis, the short letters moved him toward a more theoretical message of what, at base, love was.[34]

If there was a disconnect between Fromm's articulation of love in a concrete, specific relationship and the universal love that he expounded in his text, both were rooted in the most joyous and richly contoured of his three marriages, which lasted until his death. Yet the marriage also attested to the difference between husband and wife. Unlike his first two wives, Annis was very beautiful—indeed, she was glamorous and ebullient, exuding a zest for life—qualities in women never lost on Fromm. Erich was an early riser, and Annis slept late, which he took as an opportunity to put a note by her pillow expressing his love; he only jokingly called her lazy. Annis cultivated a taste for Irish coffee, which Erich never drank, but he deferred to her and began to as well. She was no intellectual and had little taste for the books Fromm read and discussed with her, even as she regarded him as a major intellectual and a brilliant writer. It is well to note that Annis did share her husband's preoccupation with politics in the context of international affairs. Rarely did a portion of a day go by when they did not embrace and kiss. When Annis was diagnosed with breast cancer in 1958, oncologists recommended the removal of both breasts as a preventive measure. Erich strongly supported Annis's decision to have a potentially disfiguring double mastectomy. By this time, he could not conceive of life without her and privately told his cousin, Gertrud Hunziker-Fromm, that if the cancer recurred, he and Annis would die together.[35]

Fromm was obviously happy and relaxed in his marriage. This extended into how others came to see him and how he came to see himself. We have underscored, for example, how Jorge Silva and others at the Mexican Psychoanalytic Society noticed his increasing conviviality.[36]

Having loved Hasidic song and dance since he was young, Fromm listened to records of Hasidic music almost every evening and began to play the piano. He took to gourmet delicacies, serving students and visitors chocolate-covered marzipan, honey cake, and homemade pecan or orange cookies. He hired a wonderful local cook and asked her to prepare his favorite dishes. For a delectable New Year's meal—a German tradition—he spared no expense, ordering fresh salmon from Alaska. When he threw parties, he made his French champagne–heavy "Erich Fromm punch."[37]

During the mid- and late 1950s, he had a house built in Cuernavaca. Fromm underscored that this beautiful dwelling, with its music, books, and gourmet meals, would have meant little without Annis. Although she contributed to the architectural plans and the garden design and plantings, these were primarily Erich's projects. He bought several acres of land off a private road in the beautiful and isolated Rancho Cortes section of Cuernavaca, where the Tlahuica Indians had settled around AD 600. Most of the acreage lay behind the house, and the rear property line ended at a stream along a ravine, where Fromm meditated every morning. To assure isolation, Fromm bought land on the other side of the stream as well. With a landscape architect, he turned this back acreage into a vast downward sloping field of grass with intermittent flower and cactus gardens, with a variety of beautiful trees and shrubs. For what he hoped would be a long string of visits from Suzuki, he built a small and unpretentious cottage midway down toward the river, with an elegant lantern Suzuki had given him on a mound in front of it. Pink flamingos roamed the grounds.[38]

The main house was two stories tall, and the most frequented rooms faced onto the rear acreage. The bedrooms were upstairs, and an outdoor balcony overlooking the lawns was attached to the master bedroom. Facilitated by a small upstairs kitchenette with a stove and refrigerator, Erich and Annis could prepare breakfast and eat on the balcony every morning. Fromm's large downstairs study, lined with books, was his favorite room. His desk stood in front of a large window on one end of the long room, overlooking the lawns and a small swimming pool. On the other side of the study was a couch and comfortable chairs, where he worked with his analytic patients, who entered the house through a nearby front doorway. Adjacent to the study was a large open living room elegantly decorated with Mexican and Buddhist artifacts, which opened into a formal dining room that doubled as a music room.

The dining room opened into a large, state-of-the-art kitchen with considerable counter space, large high cabinets, and a sizeable refrigerator and stove. Beyond the kitchen, his secretary worked in a modest but attractive study. Save for the kitchen, all of the downstairs rooms opened onto a substantial and long roof-covered terrace framed with tables, chairs, and plants overlooking the gardens and lawn. The Fromms ate lunch and dinner on this terrace, and Erich met with students and colleagues and even staged a few professional conferences there.[39]

Fromm gave in to other pleasures that he had long deferred. He liked cars and bought a large Buick convertible, which he drove with perhaps excessive abandon. He looked forward to reading the *New York Times* each day while smoking a premier-brand Mexican cigar. In the continuing disconnect between his life and his texts, he wrote approvingly of Zen's emphasis on "having nothingness" while cultivating an appetite for caloric delicacies—he regularly visited a German bakery. Walking through Cuernavaca, he often bought a bouquet of flowers for Annis and sometimes a box of candy. Fromm was a different man from the often downcast person that his friends and family had once observed.[40]

Fromm's newfound joy in being with Annis was a backdrop to *The Art of Loving* and does much to explain why it became a global bestseller and turned him into something of a cult figure. He began to write the book while he was courting Annis and completed it in under two years. *The Art of Loving* was a very different type of book than those he had written before. To be sure, it testified to the continuing interplay between an almost mechanistically orderly persona revealed in his texts and the less stable, highly varied emotions evident in his private life. But there were few footnotes or quotations, no index, and the volume was quite short on scholarly paraphernalia. Consisting of 120 pages of highly readable text, the book could be finished in a single sitting.[41]

Fromm adamantly denied that *The Art of Loving* belonged to the popular self-help genre that had flourished in American culture from Benjamin Franklin's *Autobiography* to Dale Carnegie's *How to Win Friends and Influence People* and Norman Vincent Peale's *The Power of Positive Thinking.* When Adlai Stevenson called "Saint Paul appealing and Peale appalling," Fromm had no quarrel. Yet Fromm concluded *The Art of Loving* promoting (in the self-help tradition) a clear and sure path to self-enhancement. Throughout the volume, Fromm instructed the reader how to discover and practice love, which was not wholly unlike being a Zen apprentice. It was imperative to learn to make oneself comfortable being alone—outside the chatter and self-seeking exploitive tradition of the dominant marketplace capitalist culture. Through quietness, discipline, concentration, and patience, one should seek to listen inwardly in a close and introspective way. If the reader mastered this listening capacity properly, he would come into communication with his "true" inner core or identity, not unlike Zen meditation. When this occurred, he would discover the vast productive powers enabling him to transform his life and his society creatively. Productivity was accompanied by a state of intensity, alertness, self-love, enhanced vitality, a new self-confidence, and buoyancy. Once one had discovered how to listen to, appreciate, and indeed love oneself, it would be possible to love somebody else. And it would be possible to see the loved one rationally and objectively, to fathom the loved one's inner core as one listened to one's own core. Lively, active, heartfelt core-to-core communication between lovers would follow as a matter of course. Essentially, each was simultaneously falling genuinely in love with one's self and one's partner. When this was achieved, Fromm asserted with neither argument nor evidence, one concurrently fell in love with a larger community and even humankind—and that in some sense the capacity to love all of humankind was a prerequisite for the true love of another.[42]

Fromm prodded the reader to take this seemingly clear, direct path to love. However, at points in his narrative he warned that the path was not easy to follow because the values of contemporary society constituted a major obstacle. Differing sharply from self-help celebrants who valued material acquisition and enhanced popularity as the avenues to happiness, Fromm was a scathing critic of the status quo and the values of the marketplace. In a decade where writers on the Left were frequently blacklisted and had little influence on mass reading audiences, Fromm did not restrain his longstanding critique of managerial capitalism. To gain companionship, the worker conformed to dominant social customs. To cure his sense of inner emptiness, he spent his energies narcissistically acquiring and consuming—desperately trying to fill a psychic and spiritual void. Lacking energy, vibrancy, or productivity, such a person could neither fathom his inner core nor love another. For this victim of a dreary marketplace culture, Fromm acknowledged, sexual satisfaction might periodically be possible. But contrary to Freud's perspective and quite unlike Fromm's own life, he advised his readers that the discharge of sexual impulses was but a transient pleasure of small moment. Love transpired only when "two people experience themselves from the essence of their existence, that they are one with each other by being one with themselves, rather than by fleeing from themselves."[43]

Fromm summarized the obstacles to finding genuine love under the alienating conditions of market capitalism—not dismissing their importance but not elaborating their hazards either—as he urged his reader to pursue love. Society had to be changed, to be sure, but the reader should not await the demise of capitalist structures and values before seeking to master the art of loving. Unlike the pervasive marketing personality, which sought to exploit and acquire from others to enhance himself, Fromm urged the reader interested in experiencing love to plumb a deep reservoir of productivity within himself. Market capitalism might obscure or momentarily numb this effort, but, Fromm asserted, simply as an article of faith, that the capacity for productivity could never be obliterated. One would know when one was beginning to reach this inner productive core through a growing sense of freedom, autonomy, vibrancy, and creativity. This was a love of the self that opened an entryway to the love of another and of humankind.[44]

If productive social character was an absolute prerequisite for "the art of loving," what was the essence of love? Fromm answered on several levels. Echoing his 1939 essay "Selfishness and Self-Love," he insisted that love was the affirmation of life and growth, joy and freedom that existed within an individual, a couple, a family, a society, and humankind. Indeed, love was indivisible: "If I truly love one person I love all persons, I love the world, I love life." In contrast, "If a person loves only one other person and is indifferent to the rest of his fellow men, his love is not love but a symbiotic attachment, an enlarged egotism." Love was a faculty within the individual that at once embraced himself, another, and humankind. Despite his regard for Paul Tillich when Tillich urged him to be more precise, to distinguish love of oneself ("self-love")—a form of self-affirmation—from love of others and humankind, Fromm ignored the suggestion, insisting "love is an attitude which is the same toward all objects, including myself." Why else, he asked, would the Bible command man to love thy neighbor as thyself?[45]

Having characterized "love" as an essence that embraced the self, the other, and humankind, Fromm acknowledged that there were different kinds of love, the most important and pervasive being "brotherly love": "the sense of responsibility, care, respect, knowledge of any other human being, the wish to further his life." It was the experience of union with all humans—the sense that we are all one and fundamentally equal despite differences in talents, appearance, wealth, or knowledge: "If I perceive in another person mainly the surface, I perceive mainly the differences, that which separates us." But when one probed more deeply and penetrated the other "to the core, I perceive our identity, the fact of our brotherhood." Indeed, brotherly love was a "relatedness from center to center—instead of that from periphery to periphery." When a person was in touch with the deepest region of another, he was simultaneously in touch with his own center and identity. This elaboration of brotherly love was not entirely congruent with Fromm's argument that one could not love another unless one discovered one's own loving, productive essence. Brotherly love exhibited a relationship in which one found one's own center in fathoming that of another, and that relationship was built on cultivating reciprocity—not only with one's friends and family but also with strangers.[46]

"Motherly love" was to be distinguished from "brotherly love," but as the "unconditional affirmation of the child's life and needs," it was no less essential. Reflecting the prevailing cultural ethos of his time, Fromm asserted that a mother took absolute responsibility for the preservation of the child's life and his growth. She assured his existence. "Motherly love" also instilled in the child a love of living—the feeling that it is good to be alive. Whereas the child was once part of the mother, as he matured, the mother's love was required to ease and affirm this separation. This was the most crucial part of motherly love—sustaining and giving to the child as he became a separate self while expecting nothing in return: "The very essence of motherly love is to care for the child's growth, and that means to want the child's separation from herself." This assuredly was not true of Rosa, who until her death in 1959 viewed Fromm as an extension of herself. In contrast to motherly love, Fromm characterized fatherly love as more limited because it was conditional. In educating the child to the ways of the world, "its principle is 'I love you because you fulfill my expectations, because you do your duty, because you are like me.'" Fatherly love had to be deserved and could be lost if the child did not perform as expected. It was therefore the counterpoint to motherly love but less vital to the child's emotional nourishment. This characterization hardly fit Naphtali, whose love was often less conditional than Rosa's. Fromm's early life did not comport with his text. To some degree, Fromm seemed to be propounding Freud's notion of the "family romance"—the idealized family from which the child had to distance himself as a part of normal maturation. In his case, however, the maturation process had taken a different path.[47]

Erotic love contrasted with brotherly, motherly, and fatherly love, and for Fromm, it tended to be confused with sexual desire, which was satisfied in an orgiastic, transitory sense owing to physical union. After sexual desire was physically satisfied, the two participants felt as far apart and estranged from themselves and their society as before sexual union. In contrast, if erotic love represented "genuine" love, Fromm insisted that it arose from the essence of a person's very being and thereby experienced the essence of the other person's being. Erotic love involved more than transitory feelings and an immediate need for closeness and orgiastic release. As was true of love generally, erotic love represented an act of will, judgment, and a decision "to commit [one's] life completely to that of one other person." It was part of a universal human process of willfully affirming the self in the other since "We are all part of One." Unlike other forms of love, it was also a "completely individual attraction, unique between specific persons." In sum, "erotic love [is] exclusive, but it love[s] in the other person all of humankind, all that is alive." Fromm was, of course, departing from Freud— erotic love was more than instinctual release. But he was conflating erotic love between specific partners with love of "all of humankind." Erotic love was at once particular to partners and situations, as it had been in his life, but also mysteriously a universal phenomenon.[48]

The final form of love that Fromm delineated was the love of God, which was actually a description of developing psychological maturity. The infant loved God as part of his helpless attachment to an all-enveloping and protective mother Goddess. Eventually, the child turned to a fatherly God who demanded obedience and provided praise when his requirements were met. Many never succeeded in distinguishing the love of God from this love of one's parents and were stuck instead in a form of authoritarian obedience to a ruler, to the dictates of the marketplace, or to public opinion.

Only if one reached another level of psychological maturity, in a freer and less authoritarian society, did God cease to be an external power. At that point, "man . . . incorporated the principles of love and justice into himself, where he . . . [became] one with God." He spoke of God only in a poetic and symbolic sense. Man's love for God was essentially man's love for himself and for all human beings. This concept was a central ingredient in Fromm's ethical humanism and was not strikingly at odds with what his early Talmudic mentors emphasized as the essence of Judaism: ethical behavior toward others and society.[49]

In the context of discussing the love of God, Fromm critiqued a revival of religion in the postwar years, arguing that the love of God had essentially been subsumed by the marketplace and become an object to consume. Since formal religion was fashionable in the 1950s, especially in America, man used it to package his skills, knowledge, and even his personality to earn money and garner status. Norman Vincent Peale's contemporary bestseller, *The Power of Positive Thinking*, and similar popular self-help books (usually written by practicing Christians) emphasized the benefits of a partnership with God to business success. Rather than bringing the self into unity with God in love, justice, and truth, Fromm regarded Peale's God as a "remote General Director of the Universe Inc." who theoretically ran everything while one appropriated God's commercial endorsement to sell oneself and one's products. Fromm insisted that *The Art of Loving* was antithetical to Peale's and to similar, markedly Protestant self-help polemics. He worked to eliminate the alienating capitalist marketplace; Peale welcomed it. Notwithstanding, Fromm had written within a variant of the self-help tradition, urging the reader to embrace his own inner love and dynamism in order to enhance personal joy, happiness, and productivity.[50]

Specialists in Jewish intellectual history stand to gain by comparing *The Art of Loving* to *Peace of Mind* (1946), the enormously popular volume by Rabbi Joshua Liebman of Boston's Temple Israel. Unlike Fromm, Liebman was born in America and assumed the rabbinical calling that Fromm had decided against. Of the two, Fromm had become the more secular, eschewing celebrations that were specific to Judaism and characterizing religious affiliation as a tribalization of humankind. But there were affinities. Both were politically progressive and exceedingly articulate Jewish thinkers who wrote bestsellers that received traction from a postwar American flirtation with psychoanalysis.

Liebman contoured *Peace of Mind* to break from familiar rabbinical homilies. He harnessed depth psychology (superficially construed) to an interfaith appeal. Like Fromm in *The Art of Loving*, he briefly noted the profound post-Holocaust sadness affecting Jews and others who were now fearful of thermonuclear war. Liebman felt that despite this troubling situation and the accompanying fear and anxiety, man could find spiritual regeneration and emotional peace. For Liebman, self-acceptance would allow one to love both oneself and one's neighbor. To be sure, the rabbi recognized that humans harbored evil impulses, but he insisted that these impulses could be controlled by transforming them into "life-affirming" goals, the pursuit of which would promote love, happiness, and contentment. For Liebman, all of man's problematic dispositions could "be harnessed to the chariot of goodness" and thereby render "peace of mind." In brief, while Fromm and other secular psychoanalysts pointed toward the sublimation of untoward impulses, Liebman invoked the rabbinic sense of "sweetening" man's evil dispositions and transforming them in the service of righteousness in order to enjoy emotional tranquility.[51]

It is instructive, then, that two psychoanalytically oriented Jews wrote important and similar bestsellers that sometimes overlapped with but were never wholly congruent with Christian (primarily Protestant) self-help literature. The Jewish sense of religion being a caring, ethical conduct on behalf of community distinguished Fromm and Liebman from Carnegie and Peale. The two Jewish authors insisted that love and tranquility within the self could facilitate a loving environment and widespread personal happiness. Both *The Art of Loving* and *Peace of Mind* summoned readers away from the fears and insecurities inherent in the shadows of Auschwitz and the persistent threat of Soviet-American nuclear confrontation. Inner love and tranquility was no idle goal for either Liebman or Fromm. If Liebman and, to a considerably lesser extent, Fromm appealed to self-help individualism, the two also offered the redeeming sense of Jewish culture, with its emphasis on human relatedness. Both remembered from their early lives and training the traditional *musar* emphasis on ethics and morality, and they advocated internal exploration to render triumph over the *yetzer hara* of evil disposition.

Fromm's final chapter, "The Practice of Love," explicitly disavowed any embrace of Peale's self-help prescriptive formulas. Fromm offered "certain general requirements" to master the art of loving—or any other art—and these "requirements" characterized the formulaic "how to" appeal of

Fromm's most popular book. First, he insisted, it was essential to acquire self-imposed rational discipline in all realms of life. Currently, society was disciplined to conform to an externally prescribed and profoundly alienating work routine that disposed people, in reaction, to avoid discipline in all other aspects of their lives. As the nonworking part of their lives was rather chaotic, there could be no concerted approach to love or anything else. Without discipline, a second general requirement, concentration would be absent. Most people led a "diffused mode of life," pursuing multiple desires randomly at the same time but accomplishing little. Third, an art required patience: "If one expects quick results, one never learns an art." Unlike quick and efficient machine production, the mastery of love and any other art took a good deal of time, for it required one to pursue many unmarked paths. Finally, one had to regard mastery of an art with "supreme importance" and concern: it had to be a top priority in life.[52]

In addition to enumerating broad requirements for artistry, Fromm instructed the reader to pursue several qualities for successful loving. These were also in keeping with the "how to" tone of the book and helped explain how, during the conservative 1950s, a writer on the Left connected to a vast reading audience. For one, Fromm emphasized overcoming narcissism (i.e., the disposition to view others only as extensions of one's own inner subjectivities). In interpersonal relationships, narcissistic distortion was the rule—others tended to be viewed through the lens of one's deeply rooted inner subjectivity. Other people and things were perceived only as they were useful or dangerous. To overcome this narcissism, one had to emerge from childlike dreams of omniscience and omnipotence and gain humility—to recognize not only that there was a world outside the self but also to acquire greater objectivity about that world and the capacity to approach it with reason and soundness: "I must try to see the difference between my picture of a person and his behavior, as it is narcissistically distorted, and the person's reality as it exists regardless of my interests, needs and fears." By acquiring the capacity for humility, objectivity, and reason, one was able to view the loved one and all others as they really were. One was therefore halfway to mastering the art of loving.[53]

Fromm's prescription for treating narcissism lacked nuance. It was insufficient to urge his reader to use humility, objectivity, and reason in order to view and love others as they "really were." If most people already mired in marketplace capitalism were intensely locked in their narcissism, how did they acquire the capacity for objectivity and reason? Fromm's answer embraced the self-help tradition, with its attendant simplicities and misplaced optimism. One needed *faith* in oneself—"the confidence in one's power of thought, observation, and judgment." Faith was basically a courageous assuredness in the firmness and soundness of one's reasoned convictions—a self-confidence irrespective of what authority figures or society at large prompted one to believe. With faith in one's self came the possibility of faith in another person—a certainty "of the reliability and unchangeability of [the loved one's] fundamental attitudes, of the core of his personality, of his love." Ultimately, faith in oneself and in the loved other had "its culmination in faith in mankind"—that under the proper conditions mankind could build "a social order governed by the principles of equality, justice and love." This appealing hopefulness bypassed the problem of marketplace culture. Once again, Fromm was refusing to distinguish the particularized private love of the sort that he and Annis enjoyed from the abstract love of self, other, and humankind.[54]

Fromm concluded his instructions on learning to love by warning that it required "a constant state of awareness, alertness, activity" toward oneself and the "loved person," that more was needed than "doing something" half asleep and half awake with a sense of boredom or routine. Only if one was active and productive in all spheres of life, greeting all challenges with intensity and enhanced vitality, could these qualities enhance the art of loving.[55]

Following the formula of other classic self-help authors, Fromm focused *The Art of Loving* on individual thought and action—on cultivating and enhancing qualities within the self. Only at the end of his book did he fully and forcefully reiterate what he periodically asserted in earlier sections of his text: the severe limitations on love inherent in modern capitalist society and its focus on materialist acquisitiveness. It was difficult if not impossible to maintain a consistently loving attitude in "a production-centered, commodity-greedy society" where material enhancement of the self was the priority. "People capable of love, under the present system, are necessarily the exceptions," Fromm insisted, for capitalism marginalized love in the social structure, confining it to individual nonconformists. Thus, the social structure had to be dramatically changed from simply producing and consuming more goods and services, if man's capacity to love was to become part of his basic social existence. What was problematic about Fromm's powerful plea for revolutionary change was that it was placed toward the back of his book. Indeed, it ran at cross-purposes with his narrative line: the eminent possibility of mastering the art of loving.[56]

Not long after the book was published, Clara Thompson reported that a great many people were "very inspired by it" and that the volume seemed to resonate with American culture far more than any of his previous writings. But Thompson told Fromm she was disappointed, for he had made many of the same points in a more probing manner in his earlier books. Unlike *Escape from Freedom* or *Man for Himself, The Art of Loving* did not seem to come from the pen of a public intellectual. Earlier, millions of readers had turned to Carnegie for lessons in business success and to Peale for God's assistance in enhancing their social and economic mobility. Now, they embraced Fromm for concrete and upbeat guidelines for bringing love more amply into their lives. Fromm coupled his instructions on how the individual could garner love with the caution that it was extremely difficult to do under marketplace constraints. That warning was easy for readers to overlook amid the optimism of America's postwar economic boom. Fromm gave primacy to an upbeat message of self-enhancement in a "sunny-side up" postwar world and pushed the harsher themes of his social criticism to the periphery.[57]

Perhaps the book's massive appeal lay in Fromm's ability to draw on his personal experience; perhaps it merely resonated with an era. At a time when the majority of American youth was listening to Elvis Presley's "Love Me Tender, Love Me True" and the Four Aces' "Love Is a Many Splendored Thing," it is not surprising that a volume such as this found mass-market appeal. It is nevertheless undoubtedly true that without Annis's inspiration, the book may never have been written. The fact that Fromm was able to base his theories on his experience provided the volume with an element of authenticity it might have otherwise lacked.

Yet it must be noted, given the inspiration for *The Art of Loving*, that even here, as in many other instances, Fromm's text and lived reality were in many ways at odds. First and foremost, it is likely that Fromm's string of affairs did not stop, despite his happiness with Annis and his musings on the exclusive nature of erotic love in the book. Equally, the reflections on parental love were far removed from his own experience of possessive and anxious parents. Perhaps more importantly, though Fromm repeatedly tied the ability to love to a productive self, his attitude toward those to whom he did not attribute such a productive character, bordering often on disdain, contradicted the fundamental underpinnings of the book: that love is an attitude or readiness directed toward all humanity. Fromm's sometimes narcissistic leanings and his disregard for those he considered unproductive or physically unattractive were two instances in which his public persona seemed at odds with his personal philosophy.

Nevertheless, these deviations between author and content did not affect the book's public reception. Fromm would write other books that sold quite well, but none in the "how to" tradition and none with sales figures that even remotely approached those of this volume. By 1970, fourteen years after its publication, *The Art of Loving* had sold over 1.5 million English-language copies. Next to English-language editions, German editions sold best globally. Almost immediately after its release, the first German edition sold roughly a million copies. A German paperback edition was published in 1959, and by the early 1980s, next to the Bible, *The Art of Loving* had become the bestselling volume in the German language. In all, the book sold roughly twenty-five million copies in fifty languages. It remains in print and continues to sell well. A fiftieth-anniversary paperback was issued in 2006. On Valentine's Day in recent years, the book has been featured in the window of the Harvard Cooperative store in Cambridge, purporting to instruct those who lacked "rich, productive lives."[58]

7

Politics and Prose

The mass-market success of *The Art of Loving* stimulated sales and royalties for all of Fromm's writings, particularly in the United States. Combined with mounting lecture honoraria and his usual teaching and clinical revenues, Fromm's American income jumped from $8,850 in 1953 to $29,874 in 1959 (approximately $215,000 in 2012 dollars). Now in his late fifties, Fromm assumed a new "life," becoming a major benefactor of progressive American causes and donating to the election campaigns of Adlai Stevenson, J. William Fulbright, Phillip Hart, Eugene McCarthy, and others. Substantial checks were often followed by long personal letters, coupling praise with general and specific policy recommendations. Personal responses from these politicians often formed the basis for longstanding friendships, through which Fromm exercised important advisory roles in the higher levels of American government, including the Oval Office during the Kennedy administration.

Fromm continued to generate a constant stream of ideas on pressing public issues, and these often coalesced in his prose, especially in *The Sane Society*, which served as a theoretical guide or platform for the Committee for Sane Nuclear Policy, which Fromm helped to establish. He also worked to energize Amnesty International, the American Friends Service Committee, and the American Socialist Party. As he came increasingly to be regarded as a very important writer and thinker, roughly thirty lecture invitations from colleges and universities arrived each month. For an intellectual on the Left, this was a remarkable accomplishment. In contrast, a mid-1950s exchange with Herbert Marcuse staged in the journal *Dissent* was an event of a different order, diminishing his reputation among American academics, although it had minimal impact on his wider readership. When Tom Hayden, a leader of the New Left, fashioned his Port Huron statement in 1962 to launch Students for a Democratic Society, he drew heavily from Fromm's writings, especially *The Sane Society*. Forty-eight years later, Hayden underscored to me that his Port Huron statement owed much to Fromm's plea to recover man's humanism and sanity in a world heading for nuclear war. In brief, Fromm, his money, his political activism, and his ideas helped form planks in the bridge of change from the conformity of McCarthyism and the early years of the Cold War to the more protean and rebellious 1960s.

The Sane Society

There was a certain continuity between *Escape from Freedom* (1941) and *The Sane Society* (1955). Whereas *Escape* addressed the nature of authoritarianism during the years when Hitler and Stalin ravaged much of the world, *The Sane Society* spoke to Cold War culture, consumerism, and a deteriorating democracy. Essentially, Fromm pursued "sane" alternatives to the pressures of postwar consumerism and conformity in the West and to a nuclear arms race that had run amok. He regarded the book as a blueprint for the "good society," and it guided participants in all phases of the American peace movement. Fromm summarized his essential message succinctly: "The normal drive for survival has been put out of action by present propaganda. We must . . . try to bring the voice of sanity to the people."[1]

Sales figures for *The Sane Society* were substantial—roughly three million copies sold worldwide during its first fifty years. The book was widely excerpted. Negative reviews came from the orthodox psychoanalytic establishment in America. In other quarters, the volume received glowing praise. Not long after publication, the book placed fifth on the *New York Times* bestseller list and was the top selection for the *Pastoral Psychology* Book Club. It commanded considerable attention from influential figures such as Paul Tillich, Robert Merton, and Joseph Wood Krutch. *Perspectives*, a popular journal that addressed public issues, became the first of many publications to ask Fromm for an article that summarized *The Sane Society*. Harvard faculty members, who sometimes joked that *The Art of Loving* was either a sex manual or a self-help book, thought differently about *The Sane Society* and invited Fromm to discuss it as the Distinguished George W. Gay Lecturer. Hundreds of invitations to present in other venues followed. If there was any doubt about Fromm's status as a major writer and thinker, especially in the United States, the book overwhelmed the skeptics.[2]

Indeed, Fromm positioned *The Sane Society* alongside *Escape from Freedom*; he felt that both books focused on why alienated man feared freedom and voted for authoritarianism. But *Escape* had not focused on the "automaton conformity" underscored in *The Sane Society*, which Fromm saw dominating the United States and other Western postwar democracies. This conformity was a "socially patterned defect" through which an estranged population adjusted to an unhealthy society. The combination of "automaton conformity" and the façade of democratic governance yielded a disheartening result.

Fromm began writing *The Sane Society* early in the spring of 1953. He identified a "pathology of conformity" as the central problem; David Riesman, William Whyte, Richard Hofstadter, and others also regarded this as the downside of postwar democracies, though they were somewhat more hopeful than Fromm. Early in the volume, Fromm set forth his contempt for clinicians in democratic nations who promoted "insanity" in their clients by encouraging them to conform to dominant social customs instead of helping them discover their own unique passions and needs. "Automaton conformity" robbed democratic societies of their individuality and spontaneity. Indeed, Fromm embraced the pervasive myth in social science circles that prosperous and peaceful postwar democracies exhibited the highest rates of suicide, alcoholism, and other manifestations of severe mental disturbance. Those who did not suffer from mental illness were plagued, nevertheless, by general boredom and depression. If the material needs of the developed world had been satisfied, their spiritual and emotional requirements had not. Much as he had in *Escape*, the Fromm of *The Sane Society* acted as a severe critic of contemporary society. Unlike *Escape*, however, Fromm also played the part of a prophet of a quasi-utopian "humanistic" society.[3]

To make his case, Fromm enumerated essential needs for "sane" living. In a tone both less cautious and more prophetic, Fromm expanded on the theme that he had suggested for years. First, a person needed to unite with others—to share with them his passions and ideals without relinquishing the characteristics that made him unique. He required a balance of individuation and symbiosis, the only effective counterpoint to individual narcissism and social conformity. This was hardly a new formulation in personality theory, but what was unique was Fromm's insistence that love was the only passion that held the two needs in balance:

Love is union with somebody, or something outside oneself, under the condition of retaining the separateness and integrity of one's own self. It is an experience of sharing, of communion which permits the full unfolding of one's own inner activity. . . . Indeed, out of the very polarity between separateness and union, love is born and reborn.[4]

Second, Fromm postulated that man needed to produce and create—that is, to transcend his passive circumstances. When man's need to create could not be satisfied, he turned destructive and hateful. "To create," Fromm wrote, "presupposes activity and care. It presupposes love for that which one creates." There was no compromise: "if I cannot create life, I can destroy it. To destroy life makes me also transcend it." Fromm was elaborating Freud's dual-instinct theory—the life wish versus the death wish—but in his own lexicon, which tied the love of life to a nebulous notion that he came increasingly to call "humanism."

Third, Fromm emphasized man's need for a sense of rootedness: the purported security that a mother conferred to the newborn. Fromm insisted that humankind had always found its deepest sense of connectedness and unconditional embrace through motherly love—a firm rootedness in the deepest emotional sense of place—even as motherly love retarded the development of reason and individuality by perpetuating childlike dependencies. Fromm cited Bachofen's description of a prehistoric matriarchy, which had been supplanted by a patriarchal society that promoted reason, conscience, discipline, individuality, hierarchy, and inequality. Notwithstanding this displacement, man continued to find rootedness and a sense of place in the motherly embrace. This was more than a twist on Freud's preoccupation with patriarchy. Fromm spoke to the primacy of motherly love.

Fourth, Fromm postulated man's basic need of a sense of his own unique identity, to depend upon himself as the active center of his powers and experiences rather than to find it by conforming to others. In acquiring this unique identity, man required a frame of orientation that encompassed not only thought and reason but emotion and intuition. Fromm's formulation was compatible with Erik Erikson's concept of "psychosocial identity," although he never acknowledged this.[5]

In essence, Fromm was arguing that a sane society consisted of citizens who were self-directed. They depended upon their own capacities to love and to create, to think and to reason, to feel connected to themselves and to others. In contrast, insane societies forced the individual to conform to pervasive beliefs and practices—to forfeit his uniqueness. Consistent with *Escape from Freedom* and *Man for Himself*, Fromm argued that alienation was the primary impediment to sanity. Alienation made it impossible for man to experience himself as an active bearer of his own powers; it required him to depend on powers outside himself. Just as mass alienation had facilitated the Nazi movement in the 1930s, Fromm insisted that it had also become a symptom of the capitalist marketplace of postwar democracies.

"Man in Capitalistic Society" was the most compelling chapter in *The Sane Society*, enumerating as it did the reasons why twentieth-century marketplace society produced this sense of estrangement. The mythology of capitalism maintained that when a person pursued his own material profit, he contributed to the happiness of all. However, the reality was that the laws of the marketplace bypassed human needs. The capitalist expanded his enterprise not because he wanted to; rather, the laws of the marketplace socialized him to pursue expansion in the interest of greater profits. Indeed, "as a business grows, one has to continue making it bigger, whether one wants to or not." Man eventually marketed himself as well as his products in return for the income that allowed him to consume.[6]

Marx had furnished Fromm with the theoretical foundation for "Man in Capitalist Society." Since the early 1920s, when he studied with Salman Rabinkow, Fromm informed his social analyses with orthodox Marxist formulations. But by the late 1920s, as his psychoanalytic training deepened, Fromm found that orthodoxy to be insufficiently psychological. In the mid-1930s, he and others at the Frankfurt Institute came across the work of a younger and more psychologically compelling Marx. Though written in 1844, Marx's *Economic and Philosophical Manuscripts* (also called *The Paris Manuscripts*) had not been published until 1932. It is unclear why Fromm did not draw from the 1844 Marx in his work at the Frankfurt Institute. As he wrote *The Sane Society*, however, Fromm drew from the *Manuscripts* abundantly. Like the Marx of 1844, Fromm spoke to the estrangement that capitalism inflicted upon the human psyche, thus clarifying for readers in the conservative consumer culture of the 1950s how capitalism abstracted and distorted the qualities that made them human. The capitalist way mandated market manipulation, acquisition, and consumption, substituting monetary values for human ones of love and community. Paraphrasing the 1844 Marx, Fromm stated the matter succinctly: "We consume, as we produce, without any concrete relatedness to the objects with which we deal; we live in a world of things, and our only connection with them is that we know how to manipulate or to consume them."[7]

Fromm went beyond this social critique by underscoring Marx's utopian alternative, where man could cease to feel estranged from himself and could live in a classless society of justice, brotherliness, and reason. For Marx, such a transformation signaled the end of a "pre-history" of alienation and the beginning of a more creative human history. For Fromm, it was the transition from the estrangement and discontent inherent in marketplace society to a postcapitalist sane society.[8]

Hoping to mix utopian visions with practical steps to create a sane society, Fromm (like Marx before him) focused on the workplace. Workers felt no joyous and creative connectedness to their labor. They shared "a vague feeling that life is useless." The solution was to create labor communities where workers assumed a degree of ownership in a company and participated in making vital decisions.[9]

Fromm also advocated a political transformation that would give weight to voters' choices. In discussing elections, the news media and the politicians relied on polemical, entertaining, and fanciful clichés rather than "a concrete, meaningful picture of the world." This notion would return in the historian Daniel Boorstin's description of a world of "pseudo-events," discussed in his important study *The Image* (1961). Political parties and bureaucracies packaged opportunistic messages for electoral consumption. For Fromm, in contrast, localism was vital if democracy was to become meaningful, and he emphasized a restoration of the New England town meeting tradition, where citizens discussed issues face to face. It is instructive here that Hannah Arendt had also made the case for local participatory politics as a means to a revitalized polis. The two were not far apart in their goals.[10]

Another path to sanity was cultural transformation. Here, too, the decisive factor was decentralization— "concrete face-to-face groups, active responsible participation"—as a means of reversing man's feelings of estrangement and atomization and to restore his sense of community. The essential task was to enhance man's contributions to a community's shared culture. Fromm referred to this shared culture as "collective art," which elevated man above the culture of the marketplace and consumerism. Fromm was discomfortingly vague, here. Was he describing an individual who needed to be cooperative and emotionally grounded in order to produce collective art? Or did the "humanistic community" and its aesthetic sensibilities create the integrated and psychologically stable individual?[11]

Fromm's final path toward a sane society involved transforming both education and religion. Schools in Western democracies taught life's practical tasks rather than the humanistic ideals of Western civilization, thereby cultivating marketable conformist personalities. Fromm proposed to eliminate "the harmful separation between theoretical and practical knowledge." Coupled with education, Fromm valued "humanistic" religion as culturally transformative: it eschewed idolatry and notions of an all-powerful God and elevated the needs of man—dignity, brotherly love, reason, and "the supremacy of spiritual over material values." A humanistic religion championed the precepts of love and justice and represented the ethical core of a sane society.[12]

Fromm's discussion of education and religion was too abbreviated to add much to his case for political and cultural transformation. For example, although he insisted that a decentralized community where people communicated face to face was central to "sanity," he bypassed problems inherent in reestablishing localism in a world where urbanization, industrialization, and corporate development were agencies for even greater centralization. Resting too heavily on visions of a lost world of medieval villages and New England town meetings as his models for a vaguely stated humanism in a sane society, Fromm was involved in a politics of prophecy.

The Sane Society was a weaker book than *Escape from Freedom* in part because the two books spoke to different times. *Escape* addressed a world endangered by dictatorships and world war. *The Sane Society* addressed an America that he saw immersed in consumerism and conformity. *The Sane Society* was the more political book, offering measures to restore democracy; *Escape* was the more psychological volume, elaborating on the alienation and sadomasochism central to an authoritarian personality. Finally, *Escape* was more tightly argued and intellectually probing, rooted as it was in Fromm's articles at the Frankfurt Institute. *The Sane Society* was easier to read, arranged by a sequential presentation of artificially separated categories, while its lines of reasoning were less rigorously backed up.

The *Dissent* Debate

Although the 1950s in many ways contained the high points in Fromm's career as a social commentator, his 1955–1956 debate with Herbert Marcuse in the journal *Dissent* represented a significant defeat. The charges that Marcuse issued against Fromm were not new: they replicated the case Adorno and Horkheimer had built against Fromm in the late 1930s to justify his dismissal from the Frankfurt Institute. The two had underscored Freud's basic premise that instinctual life and inner subjectivity precluded harmony between the self and the society. Instincts sought release, while society, in the interest of its survival, had to foreclose that option or modestly reduce those constraints. Fromm had not been entirely ready, at that time, to dismiss the import of instinctual life. But he had begun to advance what was to become his concept of social character, in which external social structures did much to shape the inner self. More than Horkheimer, Adorno warned his Frankfurt colleagues of Fromm's readiness to downgrade the import of instinctual life and subjectivity as an essential element in character formation. Adorno also voiced suspicion that Fromm's emphasis on social structures carried the corollary of potential harmony between self and society, and that potential might become a rationale for control by external agencies over the freedom of the self. When Marcuse attacked Fromm in the pages of *Dissent*, he invoked Horkheimer's and especially Adorno's earlier briefs against Fromm.

Unlike Fromm, Marcuse was primarily a philosopher and a political theorist who had worked for American intelligence agencies during the 1940s. Yet he remained affiliated with the Frankfurt Institute after Fromm left. His book *Reason and Revolution: Hegel and the Rise of Social Theory* (1941) did not mention Freud or psychoanalysis but was a major rehabilitation of Hegel, locating him at the core of a German idealist tradition with strong affinities to Marx. *Reason and Revolution* also examined elements of what had come to be called "critical theory." Invoking Hegel, Marcuse defended continental radicalism against the empiricism and positivism that he felt were inherent in liberalism. At base, *Reason and Revolution* posited that it was not possible to be critical of the existing social order or to promote greater egalitarianism without first understanding the connections between human reason, freedom, and happiness.[13]

Marcuse's next book, *Eros and Civilization* (1955), represented his first serious exploration of psychoanalysis. Beginning in 1952, when he accepted a professorship at Columbia University, Marcuse became a familiar figure in the academy. He befriended the so-called New York intellectuals of the anti-Stalinist Left—social critics such as Lionel Trilling and Alfred Kazin, who frequented the offices of *Partisan Review*. Marcuse also spent time at Harvard, Brandeis, and the San Diego campus of the University of California. Unlike Fromm, Marcuse took advantage of comprehensive university libraries and a community of scholars. In *Eros and Civilization*, however, Marcuse paid little attention to the large corpus of Freud's clinical writing, focusing instead on Freud's metapsychology. More specifically, Marcuse addressed Freud's philosophical critique of civilization as an agency that constrained libidinal drives. He included an explosive essay in the epilogue of *Eros and Civilization*—a critique of "neo-Freudian revisionism"—which attacked Fromm and *The Sane Society*. Marcuse submitted this essay in slightly modified form to *Dissent* a short time before *Eros and Civilization* was published.

Launched on a small budget in the winter of 1954 by Irving Howe and Lewis Coser, *Dissent* was one of the few serious American publications that coupled unwavering opposition to McCarthyism and Stalinism with commitments to democratic socialism, civil liberties, and racial equality. Indeed, *Dissent* represented a thoughtful counterpoint to the ready compromises of many Democratic Party liberals and their Cold War orthodoxies. *Dissent* also opposed the romanticized view of the Soviet Union as a worker's paradise, a view advanced, for example, by the American Communist Party leader Herbert Aptheker and by the *Monthly Review* editors Paul Sweezy and Leo Huberman. Close colleagues of the "New York intellectuals," Howe and Coser were suspicious of abstract "programs" for remaking the world but, unlike Cold War liberals, they hoped to maintain a reflective commitment to democratic socialism. They included Fromm on their editorial board owing to his prominence, his critique of mass culture, and the widely acknowledged importance of *Escape from Freedom* in the scholarly community. But Howe and Coser soon regretted their selection, finding Fromm arrogant and difficult to work with, often uncompromising, sometimes naïve in his politics, and wedded to utopian visions of a democratic socialist society. In time, the two *Dissent* editors lost any sense of affinity with Fromm and thus had no compunction about offending him by publishing Marcuse's essay "The Social Implications of Freudian 'Revisionism.'"[14]

Dissent had been short on articles relevant to psychoanalysis, and the essay appeared to be a good fit. Having accepted Marcuse's piece, Howe and Coser offered Fromm the option to respond. In the summer of 1955, *Dissent* introduced Marcuse's essay as a "controversial article" and announced that Fromm would reply in the next issue. Marcuse then replied to Fromm's reply, to which Fromm offered a counterrebuttal; the exchange extended into 1956. This caustic and uncivil debate grew into one of the most intriguing exchanges in postwar intellectual history.

Marcuse attacked neo-Freudians in general and Fromm in particular for bypassing Freud's vital constructs: libidinal theory, the concept of a death instinct, the primal horde of patricides, and the concept of an Oedipus complex. Strategically, Marcuse duplicated the line of attack against the neo-Freudians that the leftist American social critic Paul Goodman had advanced in a 1945 issue of *Politics*; if Fromm knew of the article, he did not think to reference it. By underplaying the role of instinctual drives at the expense of social forces, Goodman pointed out that the "free personality" postulated by the neo-Freudians had "sprung from nowhere . . . without a past . . . without an unconscious and transparent through and through." The self, therefore, had no referent other than society—no inner psychological depth or psychic struggles and therefore no capacity for independent social critique.[15]

Consistent with Adorno, Horkheimer, and Goodman, Marcuse noted that by deemphasizing drives in their largely sexual manifestations, Fromm and other neo-Freudians failed to explore much beyond the repressive nature of society. By deemphasizing sexuality, early childhood experiences, and the unconscious, they removed any vantage point from which man could resist the values of society. As Marcuse put it:

> the playing-down of the biological level, the mutilation of the instinct theory, makes the personality definable in terms of objective cultural values divorced from the repressive ground which denies their realization. In order to present these values as freedom and fulfillment, they have to be expurgated from the material of which they are made.

Fromm was guilty of this, Marcuse insisted, for espousing "idealistic ethics"—human productivity, love, and sanity in a society that was alienated and market driven. Only after the problem of instinctual repressions had been navigated could man struggle against unproductive and unloving practices in social relations. Therefore, Marcuse insisted, there needed to be a "fundamental change in the instinctual as well as the cultural structures."[16]

Orthodox Freudians on the Left, especially Marcuse's friends among the "New York intellectuals," praised his critique of neo-Freudianism, but so did leftist intellectuals generally. Freudian modernism, so called, with its focus on inner subjectivities and the importance of libidinal drives in character formation, was popular at the time among a good many academics and social critics. To a large extent, this marginalized Fromm's concept of social character, since it gave primacy to social structures and institutions external to the self.

Fromm's reply to Marcuse appeared in the next issue of *Dissent*, and it was astute. For one, he noted that it was problematic for Marcuse to label him a neo-Freudian, as by doing so Marcuse ignored basic differences between himself, Horney, and Sullivan: "This lumping together has the unfortunate result that Marcuse substantiates his brief against me by quoting Horney or Sullivan whenever there is no passage from my writings which would serve the purpose." Second, while the Freudian metapsychology that Marcuse embraced was concerned with problems inherent in civilization at large, Fromm found that it bypassed the difficulties intrinsic to capitalism. The indignities of the capitalist marketplace explained why both he and Marcuse had embraced Marx. For Fromm, Marcuse was recanting on their common effort to fuse Marx and Freud. Third, Fromm held that Marcuse wrongly assumed that man was primarily a biological being who required instinctual (largely sexual) gratification. Man was also a self-conscious social and moral person who needed to relate to others and to possess a frame or orientation within the context of his society. Indeed, the human, unlike other species, had transcended the natural world of impulse and restraint: "He is life aware of itself." Fromm was clearly no Freudian modernist focused on inner psychic tensions, often to the exclusion of outer social structures. In the context of the *Dissent* debate, Marcuse was.[17]

Fourth, Fromm insisted that Marcuse's advocacy of instinctual release through greater sexual satisfaction was congruent with twentieth-century capitalism's tenet of mass consumption. Modern capitalism promoted a "greed for things and the inability to postpone the satisfaction of wishes." Whether one consumed by acquiring sexual partners and satisfying sexual passions or by accumulating other goods and services, one participated in a malfunctioning marketplace society. Finally, Fromm accused Marcuse of pessimism to the point of nihilism by assuming that only when repression of the instinctual had dehumanized and alienated man would he be spurred to revolution. Worse was better. Marcuse found no potential, Fromm insisted, for any creative productivity, happiness, or genuine love under capitalism. As such, Marcuse ignored the Marxist dialectic—that within capitalism, there were limited potentialities for self-transformation and happiness. However, these potentialities could "migrate" into "socialist humanism."[18]

Although a debate such as this typically ended with the rebuttal from the "aggrieved" party, Marcuse's exchange with Fromm seemed to carry a momentum of its own. Moreover, over the course of the debate, *Dissent* subscribers and others in the intellectual Left had interchanges of their own. Indeed, the debate enlarged *Dissent*'s modest readership. Consequently, when Marcuse asked Howe and Coser if he could rebut Fromm's rebuttal, they consented, without asking Fromm. The deck was stacked.

Marcuse argued that Fromm's rebuttal misinterpreted Freud on many counts. Freud had not advocated emancipation through unrestrained sexual release; indeed, he had underscored how the inhibition and sublimation of sexual instinct promoted artistic and cultural accomplishments. Freud also held that as restraints on instinctual life promoted discontent, a tradeoff was always involved, and those restraints sometimes had to be eased. Freud had offered a radical social critique, Marcuse concluded. In contrast, Fromm's "road to sanity" represented palliatives for "a smoother functioning of the established society." For Marcuse, Fromm's emphasis on worker participation in management and decision making stood for nothing save "more and better industrial psychology and scientific management." The essential problem, for Marcuse, was that as the years went by, Fromm moved further and further away from the instinctual basis of human personality. He had instead embraced "positive thinking which leaves the negative where it is—predominant over the human existence." What Fromm decried as modern "alienation" Marcuse characterized as widespread resistance to a repressive, if well-managed, status quo. "Alienation" was actually the refusal of workers to settle for Fromm's palliatives.[19]

In this last issue of the *Dissent* exchange, after Marcuse had attacked Fromm a second time, Fromm penned a short counterrebuttal. He was distraught, realizing that Howe and Coser essentially agreed with Marcuse.

More important, he knew that Marcuse had made his concept of social character problematic and, more generally, had damaged his very standing as a social critic. Fromm simply asserted that Marcuse's retort did "not add much to his original article." Rather than protect *The Sane Society* against Marcuse's savage critique, Fromm pushed the discussion to a more precise level of discourse. He sparred with Marcuse on two issues: whether Freud had postulated "that happiness is satisfaction of the sexual instinct" and whether Freud felt that "man has an inherent wish for unlimited sexual satisfaction." For Fromm, "Freud's point is not to doubt that genital satisfaction is the source of happiness." But Freud had also noted that man would "never be completely happy because any kind of civilization forces him to frustrate the full satisfaction of his genital desires." Fromm's problem here (and Marcuse's too) was that given the vast corpus of Freud's writings over many decades, Freud's various references to sexual impulses yielded to a diversity of reasonable interpretations. Having studied Freud longer and more systematically than had Marcuse, Fromm did underscore the range of Freud's remarks on sexual impulses. But he did not avail himself of the opportunity to outdo Marcuse on the issue of who had a greater command of the breadth of Freud's writings. Had he done so, he might have turned the direction of the debate back his way. Instead, Fromm's fallback position at the end of the debate was simply to note that Freud acknowledged qualities beyond man's instinctive life that contributed to one's humanity. Marcuse had been able to assert categorically (as Freud did not always do) that instinctive expressions and the minimization of repressions were the essentials for a free and happy society.[20]

The *Dissent* exchange damaged Fromm's quest for academic and scholarly respectability and seemed to cast him in a marginalized role. In some ways, this was comparable to what he felt as a child in his parents' home and what he had experienced when he had been dismissed from the Frankfurt Institute. The pervasive view among social commentators, scholars, and psychoanalysts was precisely what Fromm had expected: that Marcuse had bested him. This appraisal of who had won and who had lost the *Dissent* exchange is difficult to sustain from the specific texts that Marcuse and Fromm had written, but at the time this was of little consequence. For decades after the encounter, leading scholars and social critics, including H. Stuart Hughes, Paul Robinson, Christopher Lasch, and Russell Jacoby, reiterated Marcuse's line of attack against Fromm. They also presumed, flaunting the laws of chronology, that given that Marcuse had "bested"

Fromm in 1955–1956, Fromm could not have played a pivotal role twenty-five years earlier, during the founding years of the Frankfurt Institute. They read history backward. The sociologist Neil McLaughlin called this specious conclusion the "origins myth," which essentially rewrote history to deprive Fromm of his formidable role in the development of a prestigious and scholarly institution. The *Dissent* exchange thus doubly damaged his reputation and did much to make him what McLaughlin characterizes as a "forgotten intellectual."[21]

Fromm never forgave Marcuse for his aggressive posture in the *Dissent* exchange or Howe and Coser for facilitating the debate. Up till then, he had not been apprehensive over discussions and dialogues with scholars and social critics. But after the perceived drubbing Marcuse had given him, Fromm determined never to put himself in a similar situation again. He became especially cautious in Marcuse's presence. When Marcuse and Fromm wound up traveling on the same train a few years later, Fromm ignored him. Marcuse tried to mend the breach by asking Fromm to review his book, *One-Dimensional Man*, in the *New York Times Book Review*. Pleading a heavy workload, Fromm refused, commenting to a friend, the Trotskyite scholar Raya Dunayevskaya, that "our rightwing enemies" would benefit if he publicly attacked Marcuse as Marcuse had attacked him—a strange contention. Though he had only partially read *Eros and Civilization* at the time of the *Dissent* exchange, Fromm subsequently studied it, and he did carefully examine Marcuse's *One-Dimensional Man*. He was "really shocked," Fromm wrote Dunayevskaya, about Marcuse's "incompetent treatment of Freud" in both books and about how Marcuse revealed "an alienation and despair masquerading as radicalism." In another letter, Fromm mentioned to his Swedish friend Margit Norell that Marcuse focused on Freud's abstract and theoretical metapsychology but knew nothing about "the whole clinical empirical part of Freud's discoveries"—particularly dream interpretation, resistance, and unconscious processes generally. Worse yet, Marcuse's "statement that [he tried] to reduce the conflict between the individual and capitalist society is just plain dishonest." The problem was that Marcuse's charge against Fromm of acquiescence in the status quo had "been taken over by people who apparently do not even bother to read most of [Freud's] books."[22]

It is ironic that although the Marcuse attack damaged Fromm's reputation within important intellectual circles, his general influence expanded in the 1950s, underscoring a gap between academic and popular discourse.

His books sold in the millions globally (especially in the Americas and Germany), he influenced major American political figures, he was in demand as a lecturer, and he was a leading presence in Mexican psycho-analysis. Far more than Marcuse, Adorno, or Horkheimer, Fromm's repu-tation was international and extended beyond intellectual and scholarly circles.

The implications of the *Dissent* debate can be stated more explicitly. Fromm used sections of *The Sane Society* to delineate organizational forms and procedures that would enable a society's transition into democratic socialism. Having devalued liberal and social democratic traditions, Mar-cuse did not concern himself with the specific vulnerabilities of market-place culture and or with the possible paths leading to democratic reform. Rather, he postulated that when "surplus repression" (i.e., beyond what was needed for society to function) was dissolved, a "new man" would emerge in a humane social order. Marcuse's utopian vision was to gain currency among left-leaning student activists of the 1960s, to be sure. But scholars and former New Left activists such as Todd Gitlin and Maurice Isserman, who have studied these issues with a scholar's eye, have con-cluded that Marcuse's arguments do not nullify the position laid out by Fromm.

Even if the Fromm-Marcuse debate did not extend beyond academic and intellectual circles, it made Fromm less receptive to peer criticism. Whereas *Escape from Freedom* had grown out of a decade of dialogue with tough-minded Frankfurt Institute colleagues, the perceptive circle around Margaret Mead, and Horney and Sullivan, Fromm's subsequent volumes (beginning with *Man for Himself* in 1947) were not sharpened by such criti-cal dialogues. Indeed, he remained in Mexico for nearly a quarter-century even as he acknowledged that his students and colleagues there (with ex-ceptions) offered neither telling nor persistent critiques of his ideas. In brief, Fromm became decidedly more self-referential after the *Dissent* ex-change, and it was this, more than the debate, that may have diminished his intellectual acumen in the years that followed.

Political Activism

Reflecting the royalties from *The Art of Loving*, *The Sane Society*, prior pub-lications, lucrative lecture invitations, obligations at the White Institute, an occasional course at Michigan State University, fees from his private patients, and funds from Mexico, Fromm's taxable income more than tripled over the course of the 1950s. Money ceased to be a matter of personal concern.

At the beginning of that politically conservative decade, Fromm was preoccupied with Henny's illness, his move to Mexico, and mentoring and training, and he did not participate in the initial struggle against McCarthyism. But he was not victimized by it either. To be sure, the Federal Bureau of Investigation had compiled a large file on Fromm. Fortunately, FBI agents were able to distinguish his commitment to Marxism and democratic socialism from an allegiance to the American Communist Party. Relatively immune from Red Scare intimidations and uninterested in hoarding his substantial royalties, Fromm gave abundantly to progressive social causes. There is no evidence that his philanthropy was a guise either to lower his tax liabilities or to enhance his reputation. Rather, his program of patronage complimented his increasing political activism. Fromm explained that he was embracing Jewish ethics (not Jewish institutional forms) through donations and political action: it was not enough ethically to offer trenchant commentaries concerning public affairs. One must act politically for one's beliefs, and dispensing funds was one of several forms of political action. Indeed, Fromm regarded his role as a major patron to progressive causes less as a form of philanthropy than as a component of his program for political action. He offered money and advice, often behind the scenes, to important power brokers who had little time for his prophetic jeremiads. But they occasionally found value in data he had come across on specific public issues about which he had expert knowledge.[23]

Prompted by deepening American-Soviet hostilities and the fear of a nuclear weapons exchange, Fromm sought to initiate conversations with likeminded American public intellectuals who were estranged from both American Cold War liberalism and the heavy-handed Stalinist machinations in the Soviet Union. In early 1955, he coauthored with Daniel Bell, Lewis Mumford, and Max Lerner a "statement of conscience" critical of American policy toward China and put up most of the money required to publish it as a half-page advertisement in the New York Times. The advertisement was addressed to President Eisenhower and advocated U.S. recognition of communist China, cessation of American support for Chiang Kai-shek's dictatorial regime in Formosa, and a conference of the major powers to diffuse Far Eastern tensions. Next, Fromm cofounded and bankrolled SANE (the National

Committee for a Sane Nuclear Policy), and he urged his activist colleagues to oppose the Soviet-American nuclear arms race. He gave generously to the American Friends Service Committee and promoted its peace policies. As a friend of Norman Thomas, the head of the American Socialist Party, Fromm became one of its major financial supporters. In 1960, he wrote the party's manifesto of principles, which advocated international coexistence and an end to the Cold War. Bertrand Russell, perhaps the most respected social commentator turned peace activist in the West, regarded Fromm as a friend who gave meaning to the term "philanthropy."[24]

It is less known that Fromm influenced two of the three presidential campaigns of Adlai Stevenson as well as the policies of J. William Fulbright, the most highly regarded foreign policy specialist in the U.S. Senate. Additionally, Fromm played an advisory role to various congressional liberals, and some within the Kennedy administration periodically took Fromm's foreign policy perspectives seriously. Early in the 1960s, Fromm guided Amnesty International and its coordination with high-level American and European government officials in a brilliantly orchestrated diplomatic effort to rescue a close relative, Heinz Brandt, from almost certain death in an East German labor camp. Later in that decade, he financially supported and sometimes advised the presidential hopeful Senator Eugene McCarthy. Occasionally, U.S. State Department officials asked for Fromm's assessment of the politics of postwar Germany. There was a kind of contradiction here. While Fromm was very public about being a democratic socialist and peace activist, behind the scenes he sometimes influenced officials who shaped the problematic American foreign policy during the most difficult years of the Cold War. Usually, these two forms of political action—in and out of public view—required different patterns of conduct. Yet there were moments when Fromm was unmindful of the distinctions.

Political Activism: Adlai Stevenson

Fromm's connection to Adlai Stevenson illustrated his tendency to personalize his professional and intellectual relationships. He took no part in the Illinois governor's bid for the presidency in 1952, although he wrote many checks to the campaign. Though inattentive to Stevenson's less-than-stellar record on issues of civil rights and poverty, Fromm was impressed that

Stevenson addressed global issues in the months before the election and was informed on most of the issues. Ten days after the Republican candidate, General Dwight Eisenhower, won the presidential election by a substantial margin, Fromm began a correspondence with Stevenson, admiring that Stevenson had challenged the "irrational sentimental approach of mass manipulation" dominating politics. Indeed, Stevenson showed how "the potential of reason and decency in man can be touched by a political leader." His campaign was "contributing to the process of clarification and catharsis in the American people." The governor had faith in man's ability to discover his productive potential and to defy authoritarian manipulations that subverted American democracy. Fromm sent him an inscribed copy of *Escape from Freedom*. He recommended that Stevenson run again in 1956 and promised to work hard and to donate abundantly.[25]

Stevenson promptly replied to Fromm's verbose letter, underscoring how important it was to him: "It recharges my depleted battery." He was pleased that Fromm characterized his campaign as a beacon of light for humanistic values; he would "always feel nourished by your belief that it is worthwhile." The governor reported that he was reading *Escape from Freedom* and noted that Fromm's portrayal of demagogy applied not only to European fascism but to McCarthyism in America. Indeed, Stevenson sensed "the undercurrents of authoritarianism" in the United States, agreeing with Fromm that these troubling symptoms required "diagnosis and public disclosure—over and over—I suspect." The governor suggested that if he decided to run a second time, he was counting on Fromm to assist him. For Fromm, the potential for a cooperative effort seemed to be in place. For Stevenson, it may have been more a matter of being polite and respectful.[26]

Distracted by Henny's death and then by courting Annis, Fromm took a long time to reply to Stevenson. In March 1954, he mailed a five-page, single-spaced letter—apparently, Fromm considered such a daunting missive the right length for an active national political figure who had, at best, only a few minutes to peruse it. The governor needed to know, Fromm cautioned, that he was a democratic socialist in a McCarthyite climate. It could be "embarrassing to you politically, to have any such connections." If this did not matter to Stevenson (as it didn't), Fromm was willing to brief the governor on his special policy interests, particularly as they pertained to European politics and culture. Reflecting an elevated sense of self-importance verging on narcissism, Fromm invited Stevenson to Mexico to begin these policy discussions and to lecture at the National University during the visit.[27]

This was but the start of the letter. Fromm provided Stevenson, at considerable length, with a historical perspective on why Western civilization was in crisis. He restated the historical narrative line of *Escape from Freedom*, even though Stevenson had told him that he was already familiar with the book. Fromm recommended that Stevenson try to reignite the basic ideals of Western humanism through a spiritual message emphasizing the dignity of the free individual with love and solidarity and reason.[28]

Like Norman Mailer, Arthur Schlesinger Jr., and other social commentators enchanted by the political process early in the Cold War, Fromm hoped to assist the governor, but his letter was far too long and lacked tact. He concluded the letter by underscoring the nature of Stevenson's leadership role in the Democratic Party. The governor would become "the spearhead and rallying point" for "the renaissance and development of the humanistic heritage of the Western world." Unlike President Eisenhower, who had more pressing tasks than to take up the culture of the marketplace, Fromm predicted that Stevenson would lead a "crusade for human solidarity" and would "reconvert a population which has been drowned in materialism, to the spirit of humanism." Eisenhower and the Republicans had gained political traction, Fromm simplistically asserted, by campaigning against New Deal programs and denouncing government activism. In contrast, Fromm would have Stevenson and the Democrats "speak in the name of the American ideal of individual initiative, decentralization, and the vision that men should begin to think by themselves, and cease to be robots." He proposed, as he had in a draft of *The Sane Society*, that Stevenson call for small town meetings in the colonial New England tradition. Issues discussed at these meetings could become the agenda of government agencies and elected officials. Heavy on abstraction, written in a portentously prophetic tone, and inordinately long, the letter demonstrated that Fromm had little sense that Stevenson had more pressing concerns to address and was simply being convivial.[29]

But there was another dimension to the relationship. Fromm had drafted a program for a second run for the White House premised on "a better life in human terms." There is no record of Stevenson explicitly responding to Fromm's electoral plan, but the evidence suggests that he was not dismissive. Indeed, before his presidential run in 1956, Stevenson conferred privately with Fromm and the more politically adept David Riesman to discuss foreign policy issues. They focused on the arms race and the hydrogen bomb. But discussion was most intense when they got to the status of Berlin as the primary point of tension between East and West. In this face-to-face exchange, Stevenson was impressed by Fromm's understanding of European politics and especially by Fromm's capacity to garner and to analyze key German documents not always available to American policy makers. He promised to draw on Fromm's nuanced understanding of East German and Soviet motivations as they affected Berlin. Fromm insisted that to reduce tensions between the superpowers and avert a nuclear catastrophe, the United States had to reach an accord with the Soviets that encompassed more than the Berlin problem. Agreement on arms control was even more important, Fromm argued. Stevenson took extensive notes during the meeting and enthusiastically promised to stay in contact with Fromm. This time, in a dialogue with a specific agenda, Stevenson was being more than polite. He was learning from Fromm.[30]

Fromm's role in the 1956 Stevenson presidential campaign was unremarkable. The two corresponded, especially about European issues. Seeing himself not as a political advisor but as more of a policy consultant, Fromm sent Stevenson more reading material than a candidate in the thick of a presidential race could possibly absorb. The two wrote and conversed on a first-name basis at this point, and Stevenson valued Fromm as one of his few contacts on the campaign trail who was an intellectual and a scholar. When John F. Kennedy won the White House in 1960 and installed Stevenson as the U.S. ambassador to the United Nations, Fromm hoped that "Adlai" would call on him more frequently. When tensions with the Soviets were particularly acute and the new president seemed excessively belligerent, Fromm asked Stevenson to give Kennedy a lesson in Russian politics—that Khrushchev was practicing "conservative state capitalism" while professing socialism. Indeed, Khrushchev was "frozen into a very rigid ritualistic thinking" and presided over "a centralized, managerial state capitalism" averse to nuclear brinksmanship. Fromm had astutely assessed the situation and asked Stevenson to explain to Kennedy that the United States could negotiate successfully with the Soviets.[31]

Although Fromm and Stevenson got together from time to time, letters remained their primary mode of communication. After Stevenson read one of Fromm's letters to the *New York Times* recommending far-reaching disarmament agreements with the Soviets, he let Fromm know that he was skeptical, especially of Soviet willingness to sign and live by a disarmament treaty with effective inspection of the weapons that were to be reduced or eventually eliminated. Stevenson reported that at President Kennedy's urging he and several others in the administration were trying to conclude a test ban treaty with the Soviets containing mechanisms to verify potential atomic tests but that the Soviet military was opposed: "They have their Pentagon too!" To amplify the point, Ambassador Stevenson sent Fromm a copy of a highly classified document—a comprehensive disarmament treaty with the verification measures that Kennedy proposed to the Soviets. Stevenson and his friend "Erich" needed to "have a talk about these things." Fromm responded that U.S. anti-Soviet hysteria could be eased if Kennedy publicized all of the disarmament proposals the Soviets had offered to America. Additionally, Fromm recommended that the United States "soften" its presence in Berlin—a major contributor to Soviet-American tensions. Largely through symbolic troop reductions and less bellicose rhetoric, the Berlin situation could be ameliorated. In a subsequent letter, Fromm told Stevenson about his recent trip on behalf of SANE to an international peace conference hosted by the Soviets in Moscow. He was more convinced than ever, after this meeting, that long-term peace with Russia could occur if the post–World War II territorial lines were recognized. Fromm knew that Stevenson would pass the suggestion on to the president.[32]

The friendship that developed with Stevenson created a modest niche for Fromm in foreign policy debates. In some measure, Fromm had to be listened to because friends in West Germany regularly sent him documents that the State Department lacked and needed. These documents revealed much not only about West German politics but about secret negotiations between East Germany and the Soviets. More generally, Fromm was able to discuss nuances in the relationship of German politics to American-Soviet relationships, which U.S. foreign policy specialists valued. But he never stopped using his Stevenson connection and frequently urged the U.N. ambassador to counter the hawks in the Kennedy administration. Fromm did not realize that Stevenson was secondary to Dean Rusk, McGeorge Bundy, and others on the hawkish side that had the president's ear. Nor could he understand why Stevenson was unwilling to assume a gadfly role in high-level foreign policy discussions. Of course, Stevenson understood what Fromm did not: his role in the administration would be weakened beyond what it already was if he became a gadfly. In sum, Fromm's contact with Stevenson did not, in itself, give him a great deal of influence. But it is striking that a very vocal peace activist on the Left, unschooled in the ways of insider politics, could be involved in private communications with officials at the highest level of the government.

Political Activism: David Riesman

Fromm's contact with Stevenson signaled his initial interest in political activism. David Riesman took Fromm to the next level. With Riesman, Fromm became more active and better able to navigate the complexities of American political life. This was hardly surprising, for their social perspectives had always been similar. Riesman acknowledged that his concept of "Other Direction" derived markedly from Fromm's concept of a social character structure pegged to marketing and consumption. If Riesman and Fromm were apprehensive of trends in contemporary culture, they shared upbeat, often nearly prophetic visions of the good society. Fromm's notion of a productive character type capable of drawing on his inner resources and finding happiness and creativity resembled Riesman's vision of an autonomous man who could lead himself to freedom.

If Fromm's rapport with Stevenson had enhanced his confidence in the political realm, his friendship with Riesman helped him feel much more at ease and proficient on a variety of political stages. Indeed, from time to time the three met together not only to discuss global tensions but to ponder American electoral politics. Whereas Riesman may have been a bit more sympathetic to the American foreign policy establishment than Fromm, they both worked to reverse the U.S.-Soviet nuclear arms race and to mitigate global tensions. Correspondence between Fromm and Riesman discussing the dangers of the Cold War was profuse. The two trusted each other, and almost every letter was personally supportive of the other. Riesman was troubled about Fromm's deteriorating health and tried to arrange social visits involving their wives to relax his friend. He was congratulatory whenever Fromm published a book and found it "extraordinary that you can work so hard." Fromm was also keenly supportive of Riesman's research projects. Fromm named Riesman beneficiary of one of his life insurance policies and confided to him what he never told to others: that he simply could not get along with I. F. Stone, Sidney Hook, and Erik Erikson.[33]

Fromm was reassured that Riesman could guide him through the nuances of American politics. Indeed, Riesman was usually more comfortable than Fromm in the public realm, having had extensive and wide-ranging legal experience. In 1947, Riesman prodded Fromm to join with other American Jews to provide a non-Zionist alternative in the Middle East—namely to lobby for the creation of a multinational Jewish-Arab state in Palestine. The two joined the editorial board of the *Jewish Newsletter* to help publicize this cause. Fromm gathered support for that project from transplanted Israeli intellectuals such as his old friend Martin Buber as well as the Reform rabbi Judah Magnes. With Fromm's help, Riesman published an article in *Commentary* about how difficult it was for American Jews to deal with the slaughter of six million European Jews and that this genocide explained the newfound interest in Zionism. With the state of Israel less than conciliatory toward its Arab neighbors, Fromm and Riesman opposed Jewish-American groups lobbying American government officials to take a decidedly pro-Israel orientation. Riesman and Fromm pursued, instead, a "realistic" balance between the interests of Israel and its Arab neighbors. They also spoke out against Israel's "Sampson [sic] complex"—an overly rigid negotiating policy toward those who came to be called the "Palestinians" under the guise of averting a second Holocaust.[34]

By the mid-1950s, even as the *Dissent* debate was raging and *The Art of Loving* was transforming Fromm into an international celebrity, Riesman led him into a good many political ventures. Based upon years of investigation, Fromm became a formidable analyst of ways in which conflicts between the occupying powers in postwar Berlin jeopardized American-Soviet relationships. Riesman insisted that because this was one of Fromm's areas of expertise, he was obligated to persuade America's foreign policy makers to embrace a less aggressive attitude toward the Soviets in their shared governance of Berlin. Indeed, Riesman scheduled regular visits for Fromm with two influential senators, J. William Fulbright and Philip Hart, to discuss the matter. Riesman also put Fromm in contact with leaders of the American Friends Service Committee, who had been working for a modus vivendi between the Soviets and the Americans over nuclear weapons. In time, Fromm became one of the most important advocates and funders of the AFSC and took an increasing interest in Amnesty International. Although Fromm had written to A. J. Muste and supported his pacifist Fellowship of Reconciliation, Riesman cemented their friendship. When Cold War tensions escalated, Fromm campaigned with Riesman for a nuclear test ban, for a ban on the hydrogen bomb, and to eliminate the Polaris missile–carrying submarine. Indeed, some of Fromm's books and articles published between the mid-1950s and the early 1970s were rooted in foreign policy discussions with important politicians as well as with peace activists. In brief, the Riesman connection differed from the Stevenson bond in that with Stevenson Fromm was required to work confidentially among powerful political insiders. With Riesman, there was a better balance between vocal work in the peace movement for all to see, on the one hand, and the more pragmatic insider politics on the other.[35]

Political Activism: J. William Fulbright

Among Fromm's political relationships, one of the longest and most convivial was with Senator J. William Fulbright, who Riesman introduced to Fromm in the mid-1950s. Each was attracted by the erudition of the other and by the other's determination to reduce Cold War hostilities. Fulbright was taken with Fromm's detailed grasp of German politics. He was even more impressed that Fromm, as a Jew and a major social commentator, was able to maintain a critical attitude toward Israel and to understand that a comprehensive settlement in the Middle East required recognition that Arabs and Palestinians, too, shared important political, economic, and territorial interests. Indeed, Fulbright confided to Fromm how his congressional colleagues "find their relations with the Jewish community in this country so politically beneficial that they have no real interest in seeking a comprehensive settlement that would remove this issue [support for Israel] from their political armory." He was attracted to Fromm's standard and rather polemical case against Zionism, detailing why he felt that Israel was evolving into a militaristic and not a humanistic democratic society, which development was defying Judaism's historic "humanist" tradition of ethical conduct toward others. Fulbright found considerable value in Fromm's observations on the motivations and attitudes of the Israelis and asked him to outline suggestions to persuade "the American Jewish community that the long-term security of Israel is dependent upon a political solution rather than military might." Fulbright urged Fromm to write opinion columns and letters in this regard to the *New York Times*, *Newsweek*, the *New*

Yorker, and *Time.* By doing so, Fulbright explained, others would have the benefit of Fromm's understanding of the Middle East and his sympathy with the Arabs. More generally, Fromm would help him to pressure Congress and the president to reexamine their Middle East perspectives.[36]

Fromm's relationship with Fulbright deepened over time. He came to regard Fromm as an important intellectual who was quite knowledgeable about foreign affairs. Fulbright even read Fromm's exchange with Marcuse in *Dissent* and could not understand why scholars were convinced that Marcuse had emerged the victor. Had it taken place in the Senate chamber, Fulbright joked, Fromm would have won hands down. Fromm sought to help Fulbright politically, realizing how difficult it was for a politician from an ultraconservative, doggedly segregationist state, running on a platform of progressive foreign policy, to retain his Senate seat, and he made substantial financial contributions to Fulbright's reelection campaigns. Fromm suggested campaign themes that might appeal to Arkansas voters—"concepts of individualism, the importance of values to live what one professes as against being subject to the manipulation of the big machine." Fulbright took these suggestions seriously. As chairman of the Senate Foreign Relations Committee, Fulbright invited Fromm to testify on hot topics such as allied access to Berlin and Soviet global intentions. Fromm praised his friend for essentially using committee hearings to promote Soviet-American détente. Though averse to travel, Fromm went to Washington to testify before Congressional committees when Fulbright felt it was essential: "I do not feel entitled to neglect anything in which I could be helpful." Fulbright's commitment to the public realm and to matters of public policy was also Fromm's.[37]

Fulbright and Fromm developed a good many common positions. Both favored a comprehensive Middle East peace settlement, the reduction of Cold War tensions, and ridding the world of nuclear weapons. They exchanged publications and speeches and had dinner together whenever they were in the same city. "We did enjoy so much seeing you and Annis. You stimulate our tired & empty brains," Fulbright jested after one of the dinners. Once Fulbright (in a misreading of *Democracy in America*) asked Fromm if Tocqueville had been right to question American democracy—"they say the Lord looks out for the U.S. along with babies and idiots." When Fulbright faced a formidable reelection campaign in 1974 owing to the pro-Zionist financial contributions to his opponent, who campaigned demagogically for the votes of lower-class whites, Fromm tried to help

Fulbright financially and was among the first to console Fulbright when he was defeated: "you are so much a man resting in himself that it will not do you any harm." He counseled Fulbright to write a weekly newspaper column as a voice of "sanity, humanity, and reason."[38]

Political Activism: John F. Kennedy

Fromm's role as a major funder for and political advocate of antiwar politics in America during the increasingly heated exchanges with the Soviets took two forms. One was a politics of prophecy, where Fromm energized the likeminded—be it within SANE, within the American Socialist Party, or, more generally, with progressive political activists. A good many of his writings and lectures were intended to diminish the tensions of the Cold War. This was no small achievement in the conservative political climate of the 1950s. But Fromm's other form of political activity was less well known: his willingness to work continuously with members of the political establishment. This led to contact with a young and charismatic president of the United States.

Solid friendships with the ambassador to the United Nations and the chairman of the Senate Foreign Relations Committee contributed to Fromm's connection to Kennedy. The two acquainted the president with Fromm's foreign policy perspectives, especially on Germany and European politics generally, and his anxiety over nuclear weapons. There was some receptivity. Kennedy had read *Escape from Freedom*. He had also read Fromm's proposal in the special fall 1960 issue of *Daedalus* for a cautious, reasoned, and reversible sequence of steps in a program that Fromm mislabeled "unilateral disarmament." Running for the presidency, Kennedy found the proposal interesting.[39]

Kennedy was also familiar with some of Fromm's guest columns and letters to the editor appearing in the *New York Times*. Fulbright briefed him on Fromm's testimony before his Senate Foreign Relations Committee. Periodically, one of Fromm's unpublished position papers found its way to the Oval Office.

Most important, Fromm's perspectives reached the president through the "Harvard connection": the central figures being McGeorge Bundy and David Riesman. When Bundy had been dean of Harvard College, Michael Maccoby was his special assistant, and the two developed a strong working relationship. Maccoby had studied briefly with Riesman at the University of Chicago and was all praise. In 1958, Bundy brought Riesman to Harvard. At the time, Carl Kaysen was a professor of economics at Harvard and consulted on projects with both Bundy and Riesman. When Kennedy named Bundy his national security advisor, others in the "Harvard Connection" automatically enjoyed greater influence. Bundy hired Kaysen as his special assistant and initially considered bringing Maccoby in as another assistant. Kaysen admired *Escape from Freedom* and thought well of Fromm; Riesman and Maccoby talked with Fromm several times a week. It is no surprise, therefore, that the three brought Fromm to Bundy's attention. From the beginning of the Kennedy administration, Bundy determined to give the president a wide spectrum of perspectives on important foreign policy issues. He considered Fromm when he sought a dove perspective.[40]

During the Berlin Crisis of 1961 and the Cuban Missile Crisis of 1962, Maccoby and Reisman were determined that Bundy have access to Fromm's ideas, particularly those based on important information and documents on the Germany situation that Fromm had but that were unavailable to the State Department. Fromm therefore sometimes came up in Bundy's briefings of Kennedy. There is no way of telling how seriously Kennedy took Fromm's perspectives. He enjoyed contact with intellectuals and scholars but often tended to dismiss doves as unrealistic. It is clear, though, that Bundy briefed Kennedy on some of Fromm's positions on international affairs, and the president never sought to eliminate them from his briefings.[41]

There is interesting but hardly conclusive evidence to the effect that, at least once between the resolution of the Cuban Missile Crisis in late October 1962 and the president's watershed June 1963 American University commencement address, Kennedy personally contacted Fromm. Both Kaysen and Riesman attested to Kennedy's initiative here. Maccoby had not heard Fromm mention it but thought it could well have happened. Perhaps under normal circumstances privately discounting recommendations from dove intellectuals, the president knew too well that the world had nearly been destroyed and that new perspectives were essential. If Kennedy sought Fromm out after the Cuban Missile Crisis, discussion may have involved the logic behind Fromm's ideas in the *Daedalus* article and elsewhere of gradually escalating U.S. steps toward nuclear disarmament, so long as the Soviets reciprocated after each step.[42]

The address Kennedy gave at American University six months before he was assassinated was probably the most important of his presidency. It called for a reversal of the Cold War policies of the Truman and Eisenhower administrations. Kennedy advocated détente with the Soviets, open discussions on arms control measures, a ban on nuclear testing, and ultimately the elimination of all nuclear weapons. Many close advisors contributed to Kennedy's address, and Theodore Sorensen probably wrote a first draft. Anticipating widespread objections to his proposal on the ground that the Soviets could not be trusted, Kennedy offered an important rebuttal, insisting that U.S. initiatives be introduced in "stages," where each step by the U.S. had to be matched by an equivalent Soviet step. This course of action involved "far fewer risks than an unabated, uncontrolled, unpredictable arms race" that would culminate in nuclear annihilation. Kennedy's well-chosen words and the logic behind his plan broadly approximated the strategy Fromm offered in his *Daedalus* article.[43]

FIGURE 1 *(left)* Erich Fromm as a child. Rosa, his mother, maintained him in long hair and girl's attire well past the age when German boys switched to more masculine clothing and shorter hair.

FIGURE 2 Erich Fromm as a very young child, posing on a rocking horse. His mother took him regularly to Samson & Company, a Frankfurt photographic studio catering to Jewish families.

FIGURE 3 *(top, facing page)* Frieda Reichmann was eleven years older than Fromm. He fell in love with her in the early 1920s. They married in 1926 while she was his analyst—a professional breach. It was a troubled and childless marriage. Yet she watched over and funded Fromm's training as a psychoanalyst and was heavily responsible for his development as a clinician.

FIGURE 4 *(bottom, facing page)* Georg Groddeck directed the Marienhohe sanitarium in Baden Baden. It featured a fusion of psychoanalytic therapy with psychosomatic medicine. Frieda Reichmann brought Fromm there in the hopes of improving their marriage. The facility was also a center for intellectual exchanges, drawing major figures from the psychoanalytic movement, including Sandor Ferenczi, Karen Horney, and Freud himself. In some measure, Groddeck encouraged eclectic, nondoctrinaire clinical theories and approaches within an increasingly orthodox profession.

FIGURE 5 *(above)* Alfred Weber was Fromm's mentor at the Heidelberg University in the early 1920s. A sociologist and the brother of Max Weber, he supervised Fromm's dissertation and allowed him to follow his interests in studying early Jewish history, particularly the Hasidic movement, through social psychology. Heavily through Weber, Fromm became an interdisciplinary and eclectic scholar. Fromm found him courageous as a German gentile who vocally opposed Hitler.

FIGURE 6 *(above)* Max Horkheimer (left) with Theodor Adorno. They were central figures in the Frankfurt Institute for Social Research. Fromm spent the 1930s as a Frankfurt Institute researcher, where he conducted an exceedingly important survey research study of the authoritarian propensities of German workers. He also wrote a string of articles that were the deepest and most scholarly of his career, paving the way for his classic *Escape from Freedom* (1941).

FIGURE 7 *(top, facing page)* Karen Horney was a very astute psychoanalytic pioneer with a unique perspective on neurosis and a more favorable perspective than Freud on the psychology of women. Although fifteen years older than Fromm, they lived together through much of the 1930s. She schooled him in the politics of psychoanalytic societies.

FIGURE 8 *(bottom, facing page)* Katharine Dunham, the prominent African American dancer, founded an all-black dance company and did much to establish the scholarly study of African dance. She had a romance with Fromm in the early 1940s and a lifelong friendship thereafter. They dated openly at a time when interracial romance was still a taboo in American society. Dunham became an important civil rights activist.

FIGURE 9 *(top)* Henny Gurland was a journalist and photographer friendly with Frankfurt Institute scholars. In resistance to the Vichy regime in France, she was wounded severely, and it may have contributed to her bad case of rheumatoid arthritis. She was bedridden through the 1940s, and Fromm attended to her closely, moving with her to Mexico in 1950 in hopes that the mineral springs near Mexico City might relieve her condition. They afforded no relief, and she committed suicide within a year.

FIGURE 10 Erich Fromm did much to bring psychoanalysis to Mexico in the early 1950s. Alfonso Millán (foreground) and Aniceto Aramoni (background) were among the first of his analysands, and they helped Fromm establish the Mexican Psychoanalytic Institute and Society.

FIGURE 11 Erich Fromm and Annis Freeman in Mexico shortly after they were married in 1953. They were deeply in love, doubtless contributing to *The Art of Loving* (1956).

FIGURE 12 *(above, left)* David Riesman, the prominent sociologist, was one of Fromm's best friends since the mid-1940s. Whereas Riesman drew heavily on Fromm's signature concept of social character in his scholarship, Fromm followed Riesman in the late 1950s and all of the 1960s into the world of American national politics and the global peace movement.

FIGURE 13 *(above, right)* Michael Maccoby was Fromm's analysand and colleague in Mexico during the 1960s. They studied the social psychology of poverty in a small Mexican village. Like Riesman, Maccoby accelerated Fromm's political activism and became his lifelong confidant.

FIGURE 14 *(top, facing page)* Fromm and Annis Freeman at the World Council of Peace in Moscow in 1962. Fromm criticized the bellicosity of Nikita Kruschchev and other high Soviet leaders (who were in attendance) much as he had chastised American leaders for their celebration of warrior virtues.

FIGURE 15 Fromm and Annis Freeman still very much in love in their old age.

FIGURE 16 Oswaldo Sagastegui, the prominent Mexican caricaturist, made a remarkable sketch after Fromm died in 1980. It caught many of Fromm's essential qualities. We see a vibrant man with big head and a puny body, seeking a balance in his life between books, held in one arm, and the flowers of the lover of life and people in the other, as he walks the valentine-marked path of Love's Prophet.

PART III

GLOBAL CITIZENSHIP

By the mid- to late 1950s, Fromm joined several other public intellectuals who had soured on the Cold War hostilities. An "insane" and bellicose bipolar world, he argued, could end with nuclear war and the elimination of humankind. In this desperate situation, the initiatives of several nonaligned "Third Way" nations seemed to offer alternatives, especially by shoring up democracy and promoting "socialist humanism" in a world without war. Turns of events during the 1960s in Poland, Yugoslavia, and Czechoslovakia were especially promising. More generally, a number of Central and Eastern European reformers were veering not only from Soviet military hegemony and bloated state bureaucracies but also balking at undue influence from American corporate capitalism. By positioning themselves between the Soviets and the Americans, Fromm hoped this movement for a "Third Way" might steer the world away from a nuclear nightmare.

By the early 1970s, however, as the American military debacle in Vietnam persisted with no immediate end in sight, and as the Soviet Union ruthlessly suppressed insurgent movements in the countries along its borders, Fromm became discouraged. Indeed, he saw the nation-state itself as a major source of world instability, a bellicose mouthpiece for necrophilia: the love of death and destruction. The road to humanism, he and close associates insisted, was through "biophilia": the love of life and the joy one derived from creative labor. Now prominent globally, Fromm spent his last years less as a peace activist and even more as a global crusader against the "Having," or consuming aspect of selfhood, in a world where the nation-state promoted consumption to fuel economic growth. Fromm favored instead a "Being" existence, where love, labor, and benevolence bounded the inner self.

8

Prophecies for a Troubled World

Erich Fromm's 1962 volume, *Beyond the Chains of Illusion: My Encounter with Marx and Freud*, was the closest he came to writing an autobiography. The opening essay addressed aspects of his early life and was an invaluable personal testimony; the final chapter expounded on the three broadly prophetic goals synthesized in his book. Fromm acknowledged a primary debt to Marx more than Freud, although throughout his discussion, Freud's thinking was more central. The volume sold roughly 1.5 million copies and was translated into eighteen languages.[1]

Fromm's first goal addressed his belief that society needed to embrace life, love, growth, and joy. These were the aspects of a "productive social character" that he came increasingly to equate with humanism, and they were part of what he called his "credo." Without these virtues, society opted for spiritual death—ossification, dull repetitive labor, and unhappiness. Within months of writing *Beyond the Chains*, Fromm described these choices as forming a binary: biophilia versus necrophilia.

The former stood for a heightened sense of aliveness through which humankind confirmed his powers and his sense of self. But if man "will not choose life and does not grow, he will by necessity become destructive, a living corpse." Which of the two one would choose would be strongly influenced by one's surrounding family and society. At first glance, biophilia and necrophilia seem to be restatements of Freud's instinct-based binaries of eros and thanatos. To some degree, of course, they are. Yet for Fromm the instinctual forces that Freud saw as fundamental in themselves were reconstructed and altered by the historically changing customs of society.[2]

Fromm proceeded to his second goal: once man elected life and growth, he would "arrive at the experience of universality." He would drop the "archaic ties of blood and soil" and come to see himself as "a citizen of the world whose loyalty is to the human race and to life, rather than to any exclusive part of it." He would love humankind and cease to be bound by destructive tribal and crudely nationalist loyalties.[3]

In human history over the past four thousand years, Fromm postulated, man had emancipated himself from the blind power of natural forces and assumed increasing control over his surroundings. He had mastered new organizational forms and developed technologies giving him great powers to produce goods and services. The problem was that these promising new organizations had evolved into heavy-handed bureaucracies whose primary task was to create or manufacture the blind need to consume. For Fromm, it did not matter whether these bureaucracies represented Western capitalism or Soviet or Chinese variations of communism. Consequently, his third visionary goal was to supplant bureaucracies with participatory democracies through which people could shape their resources and surroundings.[4]

Fromm's final goal was a call for man to reinstate his ability to reason—"the capacity to recognize the unreality of most of the ideas that man holds, and to penetrate the reality veiled behind . . . deception and ideologies." Indeed, twentieth-century man had the capacity, through reason, to renew hope and faith in his inherent dignity and talents. Above all, modern man, with his vast powers of reason, had to dispel the Cold War illusions of triumph through national military might, for these illusions were pushing the world toward the brink of nuclear war.[5]

Fromm had been working to actualize his prophetic goals long before he set them forth in *Beyond the Chains of Illusion*, and he continued to elaborate on them until his death eighteen years later. But by the 1960s—the high years of the Cold War—he felt that if those goals were not realized in short order, countries would annihilate each other. This decade, to Fromm, represented a more dangerous time than under the dictatorships of the 1930s and 1940s. With the superpowers now brandishing nuclear weapons far more powerful than the atomic bomb that had obliterated Hiroshima, human extinction was more than a possibility. Fromm had made the case for a series of steps through which America would take the initiative and pressure the Soviets for a matching response so as to rid the world of nuclear weapons. As opposed to an endless arms race, this was a more rational and life-affirming option, he insisted, and therefore more consistent with his goals.

Between 1959 and 1965, Fromm published five books, edited an internationally prepared volume on humanism, penned a manifesto for the American Socialist Party, and wrote many articles. His life as a writer had never been so prolific. He also reestablished contact with eclectic but reform-oriented European psychoanalysts averse to the Cold War and created the International Federation of Psychoanalytic Societies. Fromm continued to be a dominating presence in the Mexican Psychoanalytic Society and in the supervision of the early generations of Mexican psychoanalysts. He taught and supervised at the William Alanson White Institute in New York and periodically ran a few undergraduate courses at Michigan State University. All the while, he retained a clinical practice that required him to see his analysands with some regularity. Fromm also received roughly one invitation a day to lecture at an American university, and he was summoned regularly to testify before U.S. Congressional committees on foreign policy issues. He remained active in the National Committee for a Sane Nuclear Policy and joined David Riesman as a central presence in and donor to the Committee on Correspondence (a collectivity of scholars that publicized the dangers of nuclear war). Finally, he worked to build a global coalition of democratic socialists—a "third way" embracing neither American corporate capitalism nor Soviet state socialism. Fromm recruited intellectuals and scholars in America, Canada, and Western Europe for this coalition but focused on the Soviet "satellites" of Poland, Yugoslavia, Czechoslovakia, and Hungary.

These were the most active—almost frenzied—years of Fromm's existence. His pace staggers the imagination, for he seemed to have been living many of his "lives" at the same time. Why did he shoulder so many tasks during this six-year interval? Why did he not lighten his burden? He certainly understood that it was impossible to write so many books with much depth in so short a time. Assuredly, he could have delegated his duties in the Mexican Psychoanalytic Society and at the White Institute. There were other capable activists to assume some of his tasks in the peace movement and the American Socialist Party.

Several factors contributed to this relentless pace. At base, Fromm was trying to perform three tasks that would help to reorganize his goals in a more serviceable direction. One was personal. He was using a manic-like pace to define his own talents and capacities—and their limits. Second, he was presenting his own activist political mission and his mission for the world: to avoid nuclear war, keep the peace, and transform America and the planet into a sane society where humanism defined the nature of life. Third, he was formulating a credo lined with prophecies and was testing the means to achieve it—how, in terms of ideas and tactics, could peace, sanity, and humanism be implemented? In brief, Fromm felt he and the planet carried a great burden—and had a remarkable opportunity—within a short window of time. At least in part, his many publications during this period must be read with a view to appreciating this integrative task.

Fromm's great burst of energy began in 1959, shortly after the death of his mother. Rosa had always sought to control her only son, and he had found it difficult to free himself from that emotional cage. Life with Annis in Cuernavaca in the years immediately after his marriage to her was joyous, to be sure, and her dislike of Rosa seemed to help Fromm establish greater emotional distance from his mother. But Rosa grew deeply depressed living alone in her New York apartment with her son thousands of miles away. By 1957, Fromm felt compelled to visit her more frequently. Rosa complained of all she had lost in fleeing the Third Reich, especially her prized boxes of expensive silverware. Fromm hired a New York attorney with special experience in restitution law, and after extensive proceedings and much involvement on Fromm's part, Rosa received a paltry 1,500 marks from the German authorities for the silverware. Fromm found the claim process difficult and demeaning, and it seemed to underscore his mother's power over him. When she died at the age of eighty-two, Fromm did not grieve deeply. Rather, he experienced relief and newfound productivity.[6]

There was another personal but very different source of this new vitality. Fromm's growing list of health problems suggested to him that his life would be short. After years of suffering from tuberculosis during the late 1920s and most of the 1930s, he had been relatively healthy until the mid-1950s, when at various times he suffered from chronic intestinal polyps, diverticulitis, "eye tension" that retarded reading, throat infections, bronchial inflammations, frequent bouts of cold and flu, viral grippe, and periods of exhaustion. What is striking in his letters to friends from the late 1950s through the mid-1960s was that he rarely allowed these illnesses, however severe, to interfere with his peace activities, his lecturing schedule, and his publication commitments. More concerned with Annis's illnesses than his own, Fromm viewed his infirmities not as cause to slacken his pace but as reason to accelerate it. Time was short, he was on a mission, and he had to find the means to achieve it in a very dangerous world.[7]

Psychoanalytic Politics

Unusually energized from the late 1950s until at least the mid-1960s by the nuclear arms race, Fromm wanted his psychoanalytic profession to become more involved in the peace movement; specifically, psychoanalysts needed to be more attentive to the role of social and political circumstances and to become political activists in the face of the indifference of most orthodox Freudian psychoanalytic societies. In this context, Fromm pointed out that Freud was not always a "Freudian" on public issues: he often but not always despaired of ever overcoming man's warrior capacities.

Fromm's displeasure with the apolitical aspect of many leaders of the psychoanalytic community was augmented by a sense of personal marginalization. With the migration of most European analysts to America after the rise of Hitler, the American Psychoanalytic Association (APA) had come to dominate the International Psychoanalytic Association (IPA). Until 1936, Fromm had paid dues to the German Psychoanalytic Society (DPG), an affiliate of the IPA. At that point, he protested the increasing Aryanization of the DPG through the expulsion of its Jewish members and was among the first to resign formally and publicly. Two years later, the IPA forged an agreement with the APA to the effect that non–medically trained analysts would be deprived of membership in full standing with no right to participate in the affairs of the IPA. After the war, the DPG was reconstituted as a formal affiliate of the IPA. Fromm thought that he should be fully included in the new DPG-IPA affiliation. But he garnered only the token position as an IPA member-at-large.

In 1953, Fromm discovered that he no longer even appeared on the IPA membership list. He wrote to Ruth Eissler, the IPA executive secretary in New York, asking her to account for the omission. Eissler replied that since 1946, IPA membership had depended on membership in a component society. Because Fromm had resigned from the old DPG and had no desire to rejoin the not fully de-Nazified DPG, he had ceased to be a member of any IPA-affiliated society. Although Eissler noted that Fromm also belonged to the Washington Psychoanalytic Society, it was not a recognized "component society" of the IPA. As a lay analyst, he would therefore have to present his credentials to apply for IPA reinstatement before a joint IPA-APA screening committee (to which Eissler belonged). Fromm replied that even if he sent his credentials to the joint committee, he would be denied reinstatement because "my psychoanalytic views do not correspond to those of the majority." Eissler retorted that she could not understand why anyone would be interested in IPA membership unless he or she stood for the "basic principles of psychoanalysis." Fromm replied that he sought to "remain" an IPA member and not to become one; he should not have been dropped from membership in the first place. After Eissler failed to respond, Fromm realized that she was not the only high IPA figure intent on keeping him out of the organization. Heinz Hartmann and Ernst Kris, among others, operating behind the scenes objected to his explicit theoretical departure from Freud's metapsychology and were leery of Marxist-Freudian fusions.[8]

Exclusion from the major international psychoanalytic organization hurt Fromm deeply. He considered one of his more important "lives" to be that of a psychoanalyst, and he regarded his formulations on personality structure to be at least periodically in dialogue with Freud's. The exclusion was followed by troubles with the Washington Psychoanalytic Society, caused by Fromm's status as a lay analyst and his unorthodox analytic training practices in Mexico. At this point, Fromm found it too painful and unproductive to seek affiliation with any relatively orthodox psychoanalytic organization. This problem echoed his exclusion from the Frankfurt Institute and from some American intellectual circles following the *Dissent* debate. Indeed, the sense of estrangement reached back to his feelings as a child in his parents' home. Instead of being derailed by this state of affairs or compromising on his ethical stance, he began traveling regularly to Europe, especially to Germany and Austria, to meet with a new circle of colleagues including philosophers, theologians, and (less often) psychoanalysts. Several among them, including Adam Schaff and Raya Dunayevskaya, shared his Marxist sympathies and favored social activism. In a September 1961 presentation in Dusseldorf, Fromm outlined a common basis for theoretical and organizational affiliation of unorthodox societies and postulated an eclectic Freudianism that emphasized social and clinical data and humanistic values rather than Freud's metapsychological premises. In 1962, unorthodox German and Austrian groups banded with the William Alanson White Institute and with Fromm's Mexican Psychoanalytic Society to form the International Federation of Psychoanalytic Societies (IFPS). In the years that followed, the IFPS emerged as a viable alternative to the IPA. Fromm was regarded as one of the founders of this new organization.[9]

Helping to forge a global organizational alternative to psychoanalytic orthodoxy, Fromm staked out his position in a slim 1959 volume, *Sigmund*

Freud's Mission: An Analysis of His Personality and Influence, and character-ized it as a rebuttal to Ernest Jones's monumental three-volume *Life and Work of Sigmund Freud* (1953–1957). Fromm also wanted to state his case against psychoanalytic orthodoxy. He insisted that Jones had exalted Freud as a flawless pioneer while unfairly castigating Sándor Ferenczi and others who had sometimes creatively modified Freud's often-changing approach. Fromm also pointed out the pettiness of Freud's closest associates, an in-ner circle that included Fromm's former analyst, Hanns Sachs. Indeed, Fromm contested the proprietorship claims of orthodox psychoanalysts at large. David Riesman wrote that Fromm had written "a beautiful, clear and vivid and moving book." The volume constituted the first of several of Fromm's efforts to invoke Marx somewhat erratically as a "remedy" for Freud's "shortcomings" and, in the mix, as essentially yielding to his con-cept of social character.[10]

Fromm argued that Freud was "the last great representative of rational-ism," whose life ended amid the irrationalism of Hitler, Stalin, and the emerging "shadows of the Holocaust." Freud's rationalism led to his dis-covery of the unconscious and how it operated within dreams, neurotic behavior, character traits, myths, religion, and especially early childhood experiences. Simultaneously, Freud struck a blow at rationalism by show-ing that conscious thought controlled only a small measure of human behavior—that man was dominated by an "underworld" of powerful irra-tional forces. By underscoring both the rational and irrational in the hu-man condition, Fromm insisted that Freud had culminated "the most im-portant trend in Western thought since the seventeenth century: the attempt to rid man of the illusions which veil and distort reality." In this essential task, Freud was congruent with Marx.[11]

Fromm noted that Freud suffered from an acute sense of insecurity, and this deficit caused him to "seek to control others who depend on him, so that he can depend on them." That is, Freud's insecure craving for rec-ognition and fame caused him to seek a loyal following that embraced his every thought and position: "Freud's pursuit of a blind following made for the long-term intellectual sterility of his movement . . . dogma, ritual and idolization of the leader replaced creativity and spontaneity." Dissenters such as Adler, Rank, and Jung were ostracized.[12]

Fromm devoted much of *Freud's Mission* to four "inherent errors and limitations" in the development of the psychoanalytic movement. First, it suffered from "the very defect it aims at curing: repression." Freud and his followers repressed their ambition "to conquer the world with a messianic ideal of salvation," and this repression produced many "ambiguities and dishonesties." Second, because Freud had spawned an authoritarian movement run by an entrenched bureaucracy, there was nobody to elaborate and modify creatively the gaps in his theory of human motivation. Third, Freud's greatest discovery—the human unconscious—tended to be limited to an explication of libidinal strivings and their repressions. Freud often made little of the wider social and political aspects of human existence. Fourth, neither Freud nor his followers were able to transcend their "liberal middle class attitude toward society." They remained prisoners of this limited worldview and could never offer penetrating criticism of the dominant values of the society in which they lived. For Fromm, this detachment and capacity for solid social criticism was what Marx added to Freudian drive theory.[13]

Freud's Mission was more an extended philippic than a closely reasoned or well-researched manuscript. Conclusions were postulated without much evidence or reasoning. In fact, Fromm acknowledged that he had not covered the topic adequately and planned an extended multivolume study, but this was never written. Nevertheless, it represented his most explicit reckoning with Freud. In a sense, it had the quality of two prophets locked in intense conversation.

Marx's Concept of Man

Marx's Concept of Man (1961) was largely a sequel to *Freud's Mission* and included the first English translation of the young Marx's 1844 *Economic and Philosophical Manuscripts*. Fromm's friend T. B. Bottomore of the London School of Economics had translated the manuscripts from German. Active in the British Labour Party and longtime secretary of the International Sociological Association, Bottomore was an eminent Marxist scholar and a democratic socialist. Fromm found the translation excellent and was gratified when Bottomore critiqued his extended eighty-six-page introduction to the manuscripts, which represented Fromm's first extended discussion of Marx since his Frankfurt Institute days. His essay, coupled with Bottomore's English translation, provided American audiences a "new" and exciting look at the young Marx. Fromm's premise, left undemonstrated in his introduction, was that Marx's later and more systematized writings revealed considerably less about the human condition.

Fromm used *Marx's Concept of Man* to argue that the young Marx of the *Economic and Philosophical Manuscripts* filled Freud's conceptual gaps by offering a thoroughgoing critique of the capitalist society and values that orthodox Freudians had uncritically accepted. Fromm found Marx deeply sensitive to inner, and often unconscious, psychological motivation. Indeed, Fromm's Marx was essentially a socialist humanist and a formulator of what he called "productive social character." Purportedly, Marx had been far more than an economic determinist and materialist aiming to abolish private property and funnel wealth from the capitalist to the worker. Soviet leaders and scholars had "misused" the essential Marx to justify what Fromm characterized as their conservative state bureaucratic capitalism. But the greatest ignorance and distortion of Marx the humanist occurred in the United States. If Marx was to be rescued from both Cold War antagonists and used to guide the world to a saner "third way" alternative, Fromm insisted, he needed to be presented free of Soviet and American distortions.[14]

In characterizing the 1844 Marx, Fromm was essentially expounding his own prophetically tinged credo for the 1960s. Marx's essential concept was to transform man from an alienated laborer who detested his routine work and consumed to fill a sense of inner emptiness. Estranged man worked simply *to have* goods and services, not *to be* a vibrant, loving, creative, and productive entity. For Marx, "true" socialism represented "the emancipation from alienation, the return of man to himself, his self-realization." Only through humanistic socialism would man cease to be miserable, cease being an estranged cog in the process to enhance productivity and profits for the few; he would transcend the chronic "antagonism between man and nature, and between man and man."[15]

Fromm concluded his introduction to Marx's *Economic and Philosophical Manuscripts* with discussions of the personal and private Marx. Dismissing the pervasive characterization of Marx as lonely, arrogant, and authoritarian, Fromm postulated that Marx enjoyed a long and happy marriage. He was also a wonderful father "free from any taint of domination," and his relationship to his children was "as full of productive love as that to his wife." Purportedly, Marx's relationship with his colleague, Frederich Engels, was almost frictionless. In sum, Marx exemplified Fromm's concept of a loving, creative, productive character. He was on very shaky ground with these assertions, for his biographical knowledge of Marx was skeletal. One is pressed to find any evidential base for Fromm's characterization of Marx as "the productive, non-alienated man whom his writings visualized as the man of a new society." In fact, Fromm refused to consider what some scholars had concluded—that Marx felt a sense of estrangement from society. But what may have mattered more was that Fromm was trying to counter the demonization of Marx in America and the West as a result of the residues of McCarthyism and the heightened tensions with the Soviet Union.[16]

Unlike Marcuse's and Dunayevskaya's earlier and more ponderous scholarship on the 1844 manuscripts, *Marx's Concept of Man* decidedly influenced the American reading public, stimulating a broad-ranging and less stereotypical discussion of the early Marx not only among U.S. scholars and social commentators but also in *Newsweek* and other mass-media outlets. What this underscored was that Fromm was becoming less a scholar and more a publicist, educating a vast readership on profound ideas and classic books that they might otherwise have missed. His clear and accessible prose helped make this possible. So did his capacity to connect to the culture and values of society at large. This was an important venture he was engaged in and represented one of his most essential "lives."

Marx and Freud

Beyond the Chains of Illusion (1962) was Fromm's fullest effort to present his thoughts on Freud and Marx between two covers. Even more than in *Sigmund Freud's Mission* and *Marx's Concept of Man*, however, Fromm made the elaboration of their thoughts secondary to the development and explication of his own prophesies. Here he presented his approach to psychoanalysis as a social-psychological one, fusing his clinical and philosophical ideas. If man was to invoke his powers of reason to cultivate a happy, creative, productive life, Fromm insisted, he must eliminate illusions that obscured reality. Freud and Marx became Fromm's modalities for transcending illusions and addressing life's basic issues.

Although Fromm was disenchanted with orthodox Freudians, he credited Freud more generously than he had in *Freud's Mission* for promoting a new level of understanding of the human condition. Indeed, Fromm never began a book or article before first determining Freud's position on the topic. Freud had "postulated that man can become aware of the very forces which act behind his back—and that in becoming aware of them he enlarges the realm of freedom and is able to transform himself from a helpless puppet moved by unconscious forces to a self-aware and free man who determines his own destiny."[17]

In *Beyond the Chains of Illusion*, Fromm went beyond *Freud's Mission* in one important particular, insisting that though Freud had focused on the individual unconscious, he was also concerned with the social unconscious. Indeed, Fromm credited Freud with establishing that human character was dynamic and social. Character consisted of an interactive system of underlying strivings inherent in both the self and the society. In effect, Freud had given Fromm the basis for his concept of social character. For Fromm, Freud had shown how "man acts and thinks according to his character," which was represented in the active, changing structure of the energy system within him. Fromm's concept of social character consisted of the instinctual energy within the self that Freud had emphasized, but that energy was then shaped and reshaped by external social structures to the point where instinct and social structure were inseparable. Fromm and Freud diverged here as Fromm underscored an interesting conceptual interplay, and, most important, he modified but did not eliminate the centrality of instinctive life. Many who have written on Fromm have missed this point.[18]

Praising Freud in *Beyond the Chains of Illusion* as "the founder of a truly scientific psychology," Fromm continued to characterize Marx as a thinker with "much greater depth and scope than Freud." Whereas Freud's talking cure could induce profound individual change by exposing the tangled internal webs of a person's libidinal organization and by enhancing ego strength, Marx found reality in the total socioeconomic structure of society. Whereas Freud had been "a liberal reformer" defending the individual's "natural drives against the forces of social convention," Marx issued a revolutionary prescription for society's ills. Unlike Freud, Marx delineated the psychologically crippling effect of class exploitation inherent in capitalism and "thus could have a vision of the un-crippled man and the possibilities for his development, once society had become entirely human." The more man worked at tasks that had no bearing on his unique human qualities while enhancing the profits of the "propertied classes," the more man lost a sense of himself and became alienated from life generally and from others. The estrangement from the workplace extended to an estrangement from society and from life itself. Whereas Freud helped Fromm the clinician working with a patient to ease libidinal repression, Marx helped Fromm, the democratic socialist, propound an alternative to a repressive class-based society.[19]

What was needed to restore humanity to man? Freud's path (i.e., helping the individual come to grips with his inner repressions), while exceedingly useful, was insufficient. Fromm construed Marx's prescription of communism as essentially strong support for socialist humanism. Marx recognized that man "is only complete as a man, if he is related to his fellow men and to nature." Only that free and open relationship (not sustained by class distinctions or the exploitations inherent in the capitalist marketplace) would make man happy, and this could transpire when the economic base of society was transformed (i.e., when socialism was achieved). Drawing on aspects of Zen Buddhism as well as Marx, Fromm posited that man would then be free to cultivate all of his potentialities in relation to others and to nature. As he summarized to his friend, Father Thomas Louis Merton, Marx was propounding "a non-theistic mysticism like Zen Buddhism" that would overcome "the subject-object split" and thereby facilitate a deep "union between man and man, and man and nature." Not entirely a restatement of Marx, this constituted one of Fromm's prophetic visions.[20]

Nonetheless, Fromm refused to distinguish himself conceptually from Marx and acknowledged to Merton that this was by design. Fromm was essentially quoting Marx at length and equated this material with his standard if vague conceptualizations of the good society: humanism, productive social character, and the art of loving. Put succinctly, in *Beyond the Chains of Illusion* Fromm fused his own social psychology with what he considered to be the core of Marx's. Fromm augmented this position with the most valuable aspects of the Freudian corpus: the concept of the unconscious, the dynamic quality of human character, and the broad efficacy of psychoanalytic clinical techniques. Not entirely blending Marx and Freud, Fromm extracted elements from both, concluding the book with his distinctive credo. He was a Marxist and still fully a Freudian, but above all, he had become a "Frommian," drawing on his own preexisting prophetic formulations.[21]

A Socialist Party Manifesto

Over the course of the 1960s, as his political activities increased, Fromm as a committed social humanist applied his prophetic disposition to international affairs. "The last few years have made me feel increasingly strongly that I have come back to where I started" in his student days, Fromm told his friend Karl Polanyi in 1960, "although of course, as I had hoped, on a somewhat different and deepened level." He heralded socialist humanism as an alternative to the dangerous Cold War clash between American marketplace society and what he characterized as a bureaucratized Soviet state capitalism. The primary Cold War rivals and their allies were so attentive to augmented military power that they were directing the world toward a nuclear war that could exterminate most of humankind.[22]

Fromm underscored this perspective in a 1960 pamphlet drafted for the American Socialist Party: *Let Man Prevail: A Socialist Manifesto*. Since his years in Weimar Germany, he had regarded himself as a democratic socialist. But he had not been active in socialist politics until 1958, when he joined the American Socialist Party. Although Fromm was impressed by Norman Thomas, the Socialist Party's longstanding leader, the organization had not regained the vibrancy and influence it had enjoyed earlier in the century. Prompted by Thomas's quest for organizational revitalization, Fromm was assigned to prepare a position paper in pamphlet form so that party members and socialists generally could gain a clearer sense of their goals. While drafting and amplifying the *Manifesto*, Fromm tested the message on college student audiences and wrote to Karl Polanyi of "the very favorable response" of 1,200 at Yale and over two thousand at the University of Chicago. The students were swayed by his humanist socialist vision over the bleak alternatives of "Western capitalism and communist Khrushchevism," for it promised to save humankind from its most destructive dispositions.[23]

Fromm's *Manifesto* was a polemic for what he referred to as "a third solution"; the pamphlet asserted but did not demonstrate its essential arguments. He rejected both the "managerial free enterprise system" of America and the West generally and the "managerial communist system" of the Soviets and their allies; both deprived man of his spiritual essence as they drove the world toward nuclear extinction. Insisting that both Western market capitalism and Soviet state-managed capitalism negated man's creativity and happiness and bypassed "the spiritual tradition of humanism," Fromm considered the "free enterprise system" of the West as the less degrading of the two because it allowed more civil liberties and greater political rights.[24]

For Fromm, the biggest problem with managed free enterprise and "a vulgarized distorted socialism" was that they were both entirely materialistic, placing economic gain above reverence for human life. Moreover, both had paralyzed human rationality to the point where the pride in a common humanity had subsided and a nuclear war destroying millions had become a probability. "It is clear," Fromm warned, "that atomic armament is likely to lead to universal destruction and, even if atomic war could be prevented, that it will lead to a climate of fear, suspicion, regimentation, which is exactly the climate in which freedom and democracy cannot live." In both systems, thinking was so divorced from human feeling that "people tolerate the threat of an atomic war hovering over all mankind."[25]

Fromm concluded his *Manifesto* by underscoring the benefits of socialist humanism and its potential to lead humankind away from the precipice of nuclear obliteration. Socialist humanism sought peace between nations and worked to outlaw nuclear war under any conditions. It valued "greater freedom and human growth" over greater economic production: "all production must be directed by the principle of its social usefulness, and not by that of its material profit for some individuals or corporations."[26]

Fromm's *Manifesto* was more than a proclamation of broad humanist goals. It also offered lists of reforms for the party to consider, such as racial and gender equality, guarantees for religious freedom, fuller separation of church and state, "measures in the direction of socialized medicine," and the expansion of general government assistance for the unemployed, the infirm, and the elderly. Fromm also wanted the Socialist Party to promote government support for the arts and for services in all areas where private sector initiatives were lacking. This was a strong and vibrant domestic agenda for realistic reform within existing institutional arrangements, but it fell far short of being revolutionary.[27]

Fromm's most compelling recommendations for a Socialist Party platform were in the area of peacekeeping. Embracing an ideological and prophetic stance, he called for the abolition of "any kind of armed forces" and a "commonwealth of nations" more powerful than the United Nations to gradually replace national sovereignty. This was a far more radical position than he had adopted with respect to his domestic agenda. In the interim,

Fromm sought continuous disarmament negotiations, for the only "way to avoid total destruction lies in total disarmament." The Socialist Party was to stand for negotiations between the United States and the Soviets, following a basic formula: that "the two power blocs accept their present economic and political positions and renounce every attempt to change them by force."[28]

Fromm's *Manifesto* had problematic aspects, for the specific measures he proposed were pegged first to the United States and then only toward the other more prosperous industrial societies. He insisted that the American Socialist Party be a decentralized democratic body with free and open participation in decision making by all members. Yet he advanced a general philosophy for the party and positions on specific issues that were beyond challenge or debate and were to be accepted as a matter of course. Fromm the democrat clashed with Fromm the all-controlling prophet. In addition, he failed in the *Manifesto* to draw on the past history, workings, and considerable accomplishments of the American Socialist Party, as if it had no past. Rather than describing the concrete texture of the party's daily operations, Fromm articulated his own vague and utopian vision of the general nature of humanist socialism. The process of drafting the document made clear that Fromm had difficulty working politically with others within the structures of an organization. Although the party's national chairman offered copies of Fromm's platform to the membership, it was never adopted as the formal party position, not least because he did not consult with party leaders as he drafted it.[29]

May Man Prevail?

Even if Socialist Party leaders had endorsed his *Manifesto*, Fromm knew that it alone would have been insufficient to mobilize American and global opinion against the dangers of the increasing Cold War animosities. Indeed, the party had minimal impact on political discourse in Cold War America. As he completed the *Manifesto*, Fromm began writing *May Man Prevail?* which he completed in less than a year. His frenzied writing pace continued amid his many other responsibilities. This was his first book explicitly directed to the crisis of international relations and the misdirection of American foreign policy. A great deal of speed and energy was required for Fromm to discuss much of what he knew on a vast topic in so little time. Under these constraints, prophecies sometimes tended to supplant the reasoned presentation of data. The book was published in 1961, was translated into seven languages, and sold roughly half a million copies. Although he regarded this as a decent sales record, Fromm especially wanted the book to influence members of the U.S. Congress. Still somewhat removed from the realities of the political process, he sent each member of Congress, the White House, and the State Department a mimeographed copy several months before publication, at his own expense, assuming that they all would read it. Time continued to be at a premium for Fromm during these years, and there was much to do.[30]

Fromm, acutely fearful of the possibility of nuclear war, had read C. Wright Mills's prediction in *The Causes of World War Three* (1958) that thermonuclear conflict between the superpowers was an "insane" likelihood. By mid-1961, Fromm predicted that man *might not* prevail. An acute crisis over the control of Berlin occurred in the middle of the year as preparations were made to build a wall separating the eastern and western zones of the city. Soviet Premier Khrushchev threatened to sign a treaty with the East German government ending American, British, and French access to West Berlin. In response, President Kennedy ordered an increase in American troop strength and a domestic bomb shelter program. For Fromm, Kennedy's response to Khrushchev's provocation exemplified a misguided American deterrence theory. Fromm's book was intended to emphasize its folly.

The premise behind American policy, Fromm noted, was that there was a relatively homogeneous communist camp (the USSR and China) "out to conquer the world by force or subversion." The threat of a crippling response would be a deterrent, or so the logic went. Fromm asserted that America's deterrence policy threatened a nuclear exchange. What he did not consider was that the shapers of American policy were considering other possibilities if deterrence failed. That is, he did not factor in that several of them had pondered the same risky state of affairs that he had.[31]

To demonstrate the folly of American deterrence policy, Fromm devoted much of *May Man Prevail?* to an interesting if sometimes problematic interpretation of the evolution of the Soviet Union, building his case on a good deal of Russian history and translations of policy documents of the Soviet leadership that had made their way to the West and often published in the *New York Times*. With these limited sources, Fromm fashioned himself a reporter to the West on the way the Soviet elite operated. With firmer academic ties, he might have gained a foothold in the emerging field of

Soviet studies, with colleagues to acquaint him with more restricted documents, scholarly articles, and in-house analyses, therefore giving him a more nuanced understanding. But Fromm's distance from the academy had always posed such a limitation. From his circumscribed knowledge base, Fromm postulated that the Soviet Union had evolved into a conservative centralized managerial society not wholly unlike Western capitalist nations. Soviet leaders were far more interested in internal economic growth than in exporting socialist revolution or contesting the West militarily. This was Fromm's appraisal of the Soviet state, and he stuck doggedly to it, with minimal exploration of other interpretive possibilities. The chain of events that fashioned this managerial society began, Fromm claimed, when Stalin assumed power in the late 1920s and followed his basic aim to establish a highly industrialized, centralized Russian nation through totalitarian state planning, so that Russia could quickly become the dominant industrial power in Europe. After the death of Lenin, Stalin organized a reign of terror to eliminate Trotsky and the old Bolsheviks who opposed "his transformation of the socialist goal into one of reactionary state managerialism." It took Stalin thirty years to transform Russia from an economically backward nation into an economic power. But the costs were horrendous, Fromm concluded: slave labor camps, arbitrary arrests of dissenters, and a police state.[32]

Fromm acknowledged that he had been "a rather fanatical anti-Communist" during Stalin's reign "because of my deep indignation about the inhumanity which, to me, was the same in Stalin's system as in Hitler's." The Soviet state had evolved into "a Conservative industrial bureaucracy, which I dislike for its conservatism and its stuffiness, but against which I have no feelings of emotional indignation." The Soviet elite severely limited political freedom, to be sure, and they ran a "reactionary welfare state." But Fromm assumed that the more it satisfied the material needs of its population, the more it might shed police-state tactics. Run by an overlapping industrial, political, and military bureaucracy, the Soviets had completed a "managerial revolution" but not a socialist one.[33]

American Cold War deterrence theory assumed that the Soviet Union was an aggressive expansionist power seeking world domination through military and economic adventurism and that this must be countered by a Western display of resistance. If the Soviet threat was sufficiently forceful, America and its Western allies would threaten to deploy nuclear weapons. The problem, Fromm argued, was that this posture was blind to the disparity between the professed communist revolutionary ideology of the Soviets under Khrushchev and the reality of "conservative state managerialism." Because the Soviet ruling elite was preoccupied with internal concerns—recovering from the devastation of World War II, developing the country's natural resources, averting economic crises and unemployment, and satisfying consumer demands—they were uninterested in a humanist socialist system and sought only to enhance the management of material resources. They had no interest in exporting revolution abroad or in procuring global domination. Khrushchev's preference was to reduce or eliminate the Cold War arms race so as to free up resources for his domestic economy: "What he needs is peace, a reduction in the armaments burden, and unquestioned control over his own system," especially given America's superior military power.[34]

Fromm found confirmation for his portrayal of Khrushchev's Russia from a document that the Soviet Communist Party released in mid-1961 and that the *New York Times* translated, published, and characterized as "a new declaration of war against the free world," owing to its alarmist Marxist-Leninist proclamation for communist victory over the West. More circumspect, Fromm examined the context and crucial language within the document and pointed out that in the specific text the party program was not calling for world revolution. In fact, the document contained a mixture of oversimplified Marxist and Leninist thought, welfare-state ideals mixed with the values of the capitalist marketplace, rigid Victorian morality, and a Calvinist work ethic. The Soviets had, in fact, asserted that "socialism" would win not by war but by "the example of a more perfect social organization" that yielded "economic superiority." Most importantly, the party program suggested that global peace and coexistence were required for the realization of its economic and social goals. As Fromm summarized, the party required peaceful coexistence to assure the better "organization of a centrally directed state economy, and [to increase] the material satisfaction for its inhabitants." Far from advocating global destruction, Fromm insisted that the Soviet text revealed encouraging signs of commitment to world peace.[35]

May Man Prevail? addressed another concern for American policy makers: China. If Russia under Khrushchev was a modestly prosperous status quo power, Fromm saw China congruent with the nations of Asia, Africa, and Latin America emerging from colonialism, embracing nationalism, and pushing hard for industrialization. A peasant society short on material resources and financial capital, China had turned to human capital "by centrally organizing and directing the physical energy, the passions and the thoughts of its inhabitants." To discipline the work force through communitarian production and minimal consumption, the Chinese leadership turned to what Robert Jay Lifton later characterized as "thought reform," which was quite distinct from the Stalinist liquidation of dissidents. All values of individualism and free thought were scorned as the "evil" within man, Fromm explained.[36]

For Mao Tse-tung, Fromm explained, the pace of industrialization had to be accelerated. Hence, foodstuffs necessary to feed the growing population were often exported to help pay for plants and machinery. Mao was determined to transform China into a powerful industrial state and a world power regardless of the human cost. As such, China encouraged "revolutionary" groups in the Third World to throw off ruling elites. With this and other aspects of the Chinese experience in mind, Fromm underscored the problematic nature of equating Russia with China in the making of a "Communist bloc." Instead, he recognized a schism between the two countries before many other commentators had. Above all, Chinese leaders assumed that nuclear war was a possible if undesirable option and that such a war would be less destructive to their vast and decentralized population of seven hundred million (even if half were killed) than it would be to either the Russians or the Americans.[37]

Based on very limited sources of information, Fromm dismissed the possibility that China had embraced a policy of large-scale military aggression despite periodic rhetoric about surviving a nuclear exchange. Its leaders had been circumspect in their dealings with South and Southeast Asian nations. America should recognize the Peking government, work to seat it in the United Nations, and support China's economic needs. A more benevolent Western attitude toward the Peking regime would encourage China to feel more secure about concentrating on its own domestic development while pursuing peace. Essentially, his recommended policy for China was not fundamentally different from the one he advocated toward Russia: conciliation, generosity, and negotiations.[38]

Actually, Fromm was more worried about Germany than about China. He felt that German postwar rearmament could provoke nuclear confrontations, especially between the United States and Russia. At the onset of the Kennedy presidency, Germany, with its quest to rearm, seemed to be doing just that. Fromm's colleagues in the German peace movement supplied him with internal German government documents to that effect, documents that the secretary of state lacked, and Fulbright and other U.S. Senate doves drew on his expertise on German affairs. In *May Man Prevail?* he asked whether Russia was justifiably apprehensive of a rearmed West German Federal Republic and argued that it was. Indeed, he insisted that there was not much point in pursuing Soviet-American peaceful coexistence without a demilitarized West Germany. The faulty premise here was that Fromm assumed that West and East Germany decidedly shaped Soviet and U.S. policies rather than the other way around.[39]

There was no reason for the Soviets to assume that West Germany lacked aggressive intentions, Fromm argued, though his position seemed more descriptive of the German past than of the postwar period. Since the late nineteenth century, he maintained, German industrialists had pursued raw materials and new markets through military expansion and territorial appropriation. Indeed, the old Junker military class maintained a coalition with these industrialists, and it had been the driving force behind World War I and crucial to Hitler's expansion in the 1930s and early 1940s.[40]

The United States and its allies wrongly assumed that the German desire for military expansion had ceased with Hitler's defeat in 1945, Fromm argued. With de-Nazification and postwar West German political leadership launching an "economic miracle" and establishing a democratic state, American foreign policy elites and their allies hoped that a rearmed West Germany might counterbalance potential Soviet expansion. But the old military-industrial alliance was alive in the Adenauer government, Fromm argued. Generals from West Germany's *Bundeswehr* were demanding atomic weapons and an enlarged navy, negotiating for military bases in Spain, and hoping to restore lost territories. Given the readiness of Germany to attack Russia only a few decades earlier, it was hardly surprising that the Soviets should feel threatened by the powerful country to its west. Why did Britain and the United States fail to see, Fromm asked, that "a new powerful Germany . . . could turn against the West just as well as against the East"? Fromm's focus on Germany more than the Soviets or even China as the major military concern for the United States in the postwar world was problematic at best.[41]

May Man Prevail? contained an explicit program that Fromm hoped would form the basis of a new American foreign policy devoted to preventing a nuclear war: "the very situation of two powers prepared to destroy each other if and when necessary, creates a considerable probability for the decision to start a war by either side, even though both would prefer to avoid it." Accidents, miscalculations, military escalations, or actions by desperate third nations would eventually provoke military leaders on either side to launch a nuclear attack. To avert this disaster, Fromm insisted, in a prophetic tone, that America must take steps to dismember its nuclear arsenal with the expectation of Soviet reciprocity. Like C. Wright Mills three years earlier, Fromm insisted that such a bold American initiative was nowhere as risky as the continuation of the arms race: "to believe that a strategy of mutual threats with ever-more destructive weapons can, in the long run, prevent a nuclear war, and that a society following this road could preserve its democratic character, is a great deal more unrealistic." Fromm's argument was logical, to be sure, but it excluded other possibilities. As it happened, care, self-restraint, curtailed, provocations, and a continuous dialogue between the major powers avoided a nuclear war even as Fromm had assumed otherwise. In addition, as Charles O. Lerche Jr. and other specialists on the Cold War have suggested, by the early 1960s both the Soviets and the Americans were moving haltingly toward an implicit understanding. Since neither had any hope of success in a first strike against the other, both countries realized that there was no point in deploying nuclear weapons. There are serious flaws in these retorts to Fromm, to be sure. Neither the Soviets nor the Americans could dissuade China, halt the proliferation of nuclear weapons, or guarantee against miscalculations. It was problematic to assume that rationality would always reign. In both the Berlin Crisis and the Cuban Missile Crisis, the major powers very nearly went to war. Perhaps by sheer luck and some common sense in the higher ranks of leadership, peace was maintained.[42]

Fromm recognized that his proposal for continuous and mutual arms reduction called for measures to improve the general relationship between the two powers. The most effective plan was through "the mutual recognition of the status quo, the mutual agreement not to change the existing political balance of power between the two blocs." America and its allies needed to abandon their challenges to Soviet hegemony over its Eastern European "satellite" countries and interests, and the Soviets had to accept U.S. spheres of influence in Western Europe and the Americas. If the greatest point of Soviet-American tension was over Germany and especially Berlin, Fromm maintained, Western acknowledgement of Soviet control over the East could alleviate Russian fears of a reunited and fully rearmed German nation.[43]

Despite his undue emphasis on the German threat, Fromm's focus through much of his book was accurate. With the Soviets and the Americans in productive negotiations, it would be less difficult for the superpowers to respect the nonaligned status of countries in Africa, Latin America, the Middle East, and even Europe. India, Egypt, and Yugoslavia underscored this point; they were pursuing a humanistic democratic socialism that was neither like American capitalism nor Soviet state managerialism nor Chinese "anti-individualistic communism." These nonaligned countries required massive aid without strings attached from the major powers in order to jumpstart their economies. When that transpired, Fromm believed, these countries would be free to pursue their nonaligned "third force" agendas congruent with their conditions and traditions. This would further dissipate Soviet-American tension.[44]

Fromm was exceedingly hopeful of the "third way" or "third force" experiment in democratic socialism and saw its potential in so-called underdeveloped countries. Unlike the West, the Soviets, or the Chinese, ventures in humanistic democratic socialism appealed to "the sense of self-respect, individual initiative, social responsibility, and the pride of the individual." It simultaneously promised economic growth comparable to Russia's rigidly centralized bureaucratic system. Yugoslavia, for example, had already reached an annual industrial growth rate equivalent to Russia's. Moreover, the success of democratic socialism in parts of the "underdeveloped" world purportedly undermined the Russian and Chinese claims that their systems were ideal models. Like several other parts his book, researched and written in less than a year, Fromm had precious little evidence behind these points.[45]

In sum, *May Man Prevail?* advanced two contrasting lines of argument. The first was a rather pragmatic program to move the world from the brink of nuclear war through reciprocal disarmament between the United States and the Soviets. Each had to accept the other's spheres of influence. Second, however, Fromm insisted nearly as a prophecy on the right of peoples in "underdeveloped" countries to cultivate democratic socialism. Under this logic, Russia could continue to dominate and stifle East Germany or Hungary because they were both within its sphere of influence but could not control Egypt or India, both unaligned and veering toward democratic socialism. How could Fromm, love's prophet, reconcile these disparate fates for nations—all of which wanted freedom and autonomy? He did not try, save to imply that emerging unaligned democratic socialist nations might somehow mediate the conflict between the Cold War antagonists. Despite Fromm's prophetic disposition, he was unpersuasive in justifying arrested development and thwarted democracy for countries in a major power's sphere of influence but assurances of freedom for the others.

This comported with the uneven logic of *May Man Prevail?* It offered a respectable examination of modern Russian society, history, and foreign policy but a far more sketchy discussion of China. He knew much about Germany but overused it to explain the Soviet- American conflict. The information he provided concerning specific "third force" countries including Yugoslavia and India was very sparse, despite their important place in his argument. In addition, Fromm's major points tended to be repeated, as if to compensate for problems of evidence and logic. The stylistic elegance and skillful interchange between evidence and argument that characterized *Escape from Freedom* and even *The Sane Society* were wanting in this 1961 study of the Cold War world. What was clear was that Fromm was a prophetic writer on a mission, writing at a frenzied pace, hoping to avert a nuclear war, which seemed quite possible in a very troubled world.

9

A Third Way

Fromm was deeply committed to a democratic socialist alternative to Western capitalism and what he labeled Soviet "managerialism." He equated democratic socialism with "humanism": the freedom of each individual, when sustained by society, to pursue a life of creative labor and happiness. Fromm thought that nonaligned "third force" countries had the greatest potential to travel down this path.

Fromm was swayed by a plan proposed in 1960 by Karl Polanyi for enlisting the support of a coalition of politically concerned intellectuals who would reinforce one another's resources and ideas. A maverick Eastern European economic historian, in his 1944 classic, *The Great Transformation*, Polanyi propounded "humanistic socialism," a system where economic conduct was subsumed by social relations of care and reciprocity. Polanyi contrasted his humanistic socialism with the capitalist marketplace, where economic profit was valued more than community. Realizing that his perspectives overlapped decidedly with Fromm's, Polanyi confided "that our friendship of twenty years' standing should bear fruit for others." They should contact several likeminded socialist thinkers in London, Budapest, Milan, New York, and other locations who had resisted the "sticky plastic" of Stalinism, fascism, and marketplace capitalism. Polanyi's intent was to organize these colleagues, pool their knowledge, and pursue effective political action globally.[1]

Fromm volunteered to be the primary facilitator of such an effort. In 1963, he wrote excitedly to Angelica Balabanoff, a friend and active Italian socialist, of his attendance at a philosophy congress in Yugoslavia where several Czech, Polish, and Yugoslav delegates, in open disagreement with delegates from Russia, East Germany, and Hungary, campaigned for an environment of freedom and dignity as a viable alternative to state socialism. Fromm characterized these delegates as young intellectuals "who have a real and deep faith in man and in socialism, and who are not afraid to voice their criticism of the Soviet concepts." With this group in mind, Fromm contacted a good friend in London, Clara Urquhart, who introduced him to her associate Albert Schweitzer. In addition, she agreed with Fromm that a new international journal, *Humanist Studies*, might help attract colleagues. They planned to publish the journal quarterly and feature critical essays from scholars who believed that "the alternative between Western capitalism and Communist Khrushchevism is humanist socialism." The two invited Schweitzer and Robert Oppenheimer to join the editorial board, which they hoped would also include their mutual friend Norman Thomas.

Fromm also made a point of contacting two British humanist socialist scholars: his friend T. B. Bottomore and Richard Titmuss. Titmuss taught at the University of London, had served in the cabinet of several Labour governments, and wrote prodigiously to promote egalitarian social policies. Both were enthusiastic when Fromm proposed an international arrangement to unite socialist humanist thinkers.[2]

Fromm also turned to a Polish philosopher, Adam Schaff, who interpreted Marx along Fromm's humanist lines. Schaff was particularly interested in what the Soviet Marxists avoided—the problem of alienation. Fromm was especially intent on recruiting Catholic thinkers such as the Austrian Jesuit Karl Rahner. Fromm characterized Rahner to Schaff as a man "in the forefront of the liberal movement of the church" with a "sense of tolerance" and creative energy. Other clergymen included the Brazilian archbishop Dom Helder Camara and the Trappist monk Thomas Merton. The unifying agent here was adherence to Fromm's "Credo"—to social arrangements and values that celebrated human life, growth, joy, and creativity. In *Escape from Freedom*, Fromm fancied medieval Catholicism as a springboard for Western humanism and found in Catholic public intellectuals such as Rahner, Camara, and Merton a take on Catholicism at one with their democratic socialist beliefs.[3]

Fromm emphasized that the *Humanist Studies* collectivity and other ventures to unite humanist socialists must go beyond a shared ideological position to recruit fellow activists for "what they represent as human beings." Personality and ethical conduct were no less important than doctrines. Rahner and Jean Danielou (a historian of early Christianity and pastor to the poor) represented liberal Catholicism; Schweitzer and Paul Tillich stood in for socially conscious Protestantism. If Bertrand Russell represented philosophy and Robert Oppenheimer represented science, both were primarily dedicated to all of humankind. In the end, Fromm's effort to establish *Humanist Studies* never came to fruition. Nonetheless, he stood at the hub of a global network of socially activist humanists.[4]

Over time, the network included the former Mexican president Lazaro Cardenas, whom Fromm characterized as a leader of great "moral stature"; A. J. Muste, a leading American pacifist; Lucien Goldmann, a Marxist professor of the sociology of literature in Paris and Brussels who had worked with Jean Piaget in Geneva; and the brilliant Brazilian educational thinker and champion of universal literacy in Latin America, Paulo Freire. He also recruited Raya Dunayevskaya, who had been Trotsky's secretary and was an informed critic of Soviet bureaucratic structures. As Fromm's informal organization grew, Bottomore explained to him that the most essential similarities among the participants were their devotion to decentralized, nonauthoritarian socialist practices and that he had been especially impressed by the Yugoslav system of worker self-management.[5]

Fromm regarded Yugoslavia, Poland, and Czechoslovakia as the countries most ready for change. "I have a lovely correspondence with a number of Yugoslav, Polish and Czechoslovak philosophers and intellectuals," Fromm wrote in 1964 to Angelica Balabanoff, and "my books are being translated in all these countries." He expressed confidence "that in these small countries a truly socialist movement will continue to develop, in spite of the ups and downs of the political situation." If these nations could continue to establish their independence from Soviet controls while resisting consumerism and "the purely materialist interest in money," he wrote Dunayevskaya, they would build viable humanist socialist societies. When Balabanoff cautioned against excessive optimism, Fromm discounted her advice.[6]

Fromm was particularly enthusiastic about the Praxis school of Marxist humanists (primarily philosophers and sociologists) originating in Zagreb and Belgrade who were attracted to "authentic" Marxism. He studied the school's journal (*Praxis*), first released in 1964, and quickly befriended key participants: Gajo Petrović, Ljuba Stojic, Svetozar Stojanović, Rudi Supek, Predrag Vranicki, and especially Mihailo Marković. Indeed, in his preface to Marković's *From Affluence to Praxis* (1974), Fromm asserted that the group sought "to return to the real Marx as against the Marx equally distorted by right wing social democrats and Stalinists." He was particularly keen on Marković's exposition of Marx on alienation, Petrović on the essentially creative and practical nature of human beings, and Milan Kangrga on man's creativity and productive capacity. Fromm was also pleased that these Praxis thinkers had translated several of his books and articles into Serbo-Croatian and that they were inspired by the writings of Karl Korsch, György Lukács, Antonio Gramsci, and his friends Lucien Goldmann and Ernst Bloch.[7]

The Praxis group demonstrated considerable courage in opposing Yugoslav President Tito's modified Marxist-Leninist policies. Though Fromm characterized Yugoslavia as a "Third Way" country, he was insufficiently attentive to Tito's subtle censorship techniques despite the fact that Praxis scholars were insisting that Tito hardly advanced a "Third Force" position and was no civil libertarian. In turn, Tito and his supporters characterized Praxis intellectuals as "professional anticommunists" and "enemies of self-managing socialism." Periodically, *Praxis*, the group's journal, was banned. Although most of the Praxis scholars held firm against pressures of this sort, a few reembraced the Tito state.[8]

If Marković and the other Praxis philosophers were key adherents of Fromm's initiative in Yugoslavia, Adam Schaff became his main man in Poland. Indeed, with the possible exception of Bottomore in London, Schaff evolved into Fromm's principal associate in developing a global network of humanist socialists. Thirteen years Fromm's junior, Schaff had studied law and economics in Paris and philosophy in Poland. In 1945, Schaff completed his doctorate in philosophy at the Soviet Academy of Sciences and returned to Nazi-occupied Poland with the Red Army. He was appointed to a chair in Marxist philosophy at Warsaw University. While closely following Stalinist Soviet doctrinal interpretation and specializing in epistemology, Schaff became an official of the Polish Communist Party and took a leading role in its attacks on non-Marxist philosophic currents. But when Wladyslaw Gomulka returned to power in Poland in 1956—the year of Khrushchev's revelation of Stalinist atrocities—Schaff became less doctrinaire. Indeed, Schaff was influenced decidedly by Lester Kolakowski, a leading Polish anti-Stalinist who warned the Gomulka government not to summon Soviet troops to quash political liberalization, as the Soviets had in Hungary late in 1956. Schaff discovered that Kolakowski admired Marx's 1844 manuscripts and coupled it with the works of Lukács and Gramsci in emphasizing that Stalinist interpretations corrupted Marx's humanist goals. Amplifying Kolakowski's work, Schaff became a central figure in Polish Marxist humanism, although his elevated position in the

Polish Communist Party suggests remnants of Stalinism in his weltanschauung. He embraced existentialism and phenomenology and argued
for an interpretation of Marx that emphasized human freedom.[9]

Fromm's friendship with Schaff was cemented after Schaff reviewed
Marx's Concept of Man for a Polish philosophy journal. He wrote to Fromm,
lauding the way the book characterized Marx as a humanist with astute
psychological insights. Fromm was overjoyed when Schaff's letter arrived,
replying that very day to state how excited he was about "the increasing
renaissance of Marxist humanism" globally. He promised to send Schaff
copies of many of his other books, describing himself as "a socialist since
my student days" but actively so only in recent years. Fromm invited Schaff
to a world peace conference in London and asked him to contribute to an
international symposium on humanist socialism.[10]

Fromm and Schaff maintained a lively correspondence during the mid-
1960s and met on a few occasions. Fromm especially admired Schaff's energetic and vigorous life and his kindness, authenticity, and courage in trying to expose to people in the Soviet orbit the poverty of a reductionist state
socialism. By March 1964, Fromm noted how he and Schaff were of one
"essence" and held similar beliefs. When Schaff sought to couple Marxism
with psychoanalysis despite the "official" Polish perspective that they were
antithetical, Fromm was delighted.[11]

By the mid- and late 1960s, Schaff became the primary disseminator of
Fromm's writings in Poland, translating Fromm's works into Polish, supervising their sale and distribution, and ensuring that they were reviewed in important Polish newspapers and periodicals. Schaff was especially pleased that *The Art of Loving* sold over fifty thousand copies within
a few days on the Polish market. Coupled with other books translated into
Polish, Schaff happily reported that Fromm had become a "very popular"
and esteemed author in his country and had established a fine reputation
among Polish social scientists. Fromm, in turn, procured the English
translation of Schaff's *Marxism and the Human Individual* (1965) and
worked to have it published by McGraw-Hill in paperback for a large American audience, explaining that it represented a breath of fresh air from Soviet Marxism. McGraw-Hill issued Schaff a contract; Fromm shepherded
it through a difficult publication process and had Norman Thomas endorse
the volume. Fromm also wrote a glowing introduction to the U.S. edition,
characterizing it as a major publishing event. Schaff would introduce
Americans to the renaissance of Marxist humanism within Soviet-bloc

socialist countries, and this was purportedly part of a more general rebirth of humanism throughout the world, a rebirth that, Fromm claimed, was being led by Albert Schweitzer, Bertrand Russell, Albert Einstein, and Pope John XXIII. For Fromm, Schaff and other humanists—extolling values of human dignity, creativity, and joy—represented man's best hope against the threat of nuclear extinction.[12]

With Schaff in his growing international network of humanist socialists, Fromm sought to publish a volume illustrating "the scope and aliveness of humanist-socialist thought today" in order to demonstrate that this movement was "no longer the concern of a few dispersed intellectuals but was flourishing throughout the world, developing independently in different countries." Even as Fromm's effort to launch *Humanist Studies* was unsuccessful, he pursued an alternative: a multiauthored volume exhibiting the thoughts and talents of his network. With his reputation for publishing profitable bestsellers and his name on the cover as editor, Fromm knew that he would have no difficulty lining up a large U.S. commercial publishing house. Titling the edited volume *Socialist Humanism: An International Symposium*, he rapidly procured a contract from Doubleday for a substantially sized hardcover first printing and a subsequent paperback from Doubleday's Anchor Books division. Fromm insisted that the project be "a volume of an international nature which could be published in several languages, to indicate that the increasing renaissance of Marxist humanism is a world-wide phenomenon." Published in 1965, the book soon appeared in nine languages and sold half a million copies, modest sales compared to most other Fromm publications.[13]

When Doubleday offered Fromm a five-thousand-dollar advance for *Socialist Humanism*, Fromm pledged to divide the money equally among the contributors. He would contribute an introduction of about twenty pages and a substantive essay connecting humanist psychoanalysis to Marxist thought. Fromm directed other contributors to write six-thousand-word essays on topics of their choosing that pertained to humanism, to socialism, and more broadly to the nature of man and his needs. Although contributors would write for a general global market, Fromm directed them to appeal to intellectuals, students, and artists. In this instruction, Fromm seemed to be influenced by the concept of an "intelligentsia," which Kolakowski and other Eastern European socialist dissidents had emphasized since the mid-1950s. Initially, Fromm planned on fifteen contributors; he ended up with thirty-five. There were no contributors from Russia, China, or Latin America, and only Leopold Senghor, the poet and president of Senegal, represented Africa. About one-third were from Yugoslavia, Poland, and Czechoslovakia; most of the others were from the United States, Britain, Italy, Germany, and France. In a letter to Schaff, Fromm suggested explaining the geographic limitation to the English-speaking readership of the first edition: "the closeness of thought with regard to humanist Marxism which exists in Poland, Czechoslovakia and Yugoslavia, and at the same time shared by a number of Western writers." Essentially, Fromm's priority was to connect writings by Eastern European dissidents to those of humanists in the United States and Western Europe.[14]

Guided by Schaff in Poland and Bottomore in Britain, Fromm solicited several contributors who were not part of his network. Because they stood for the "third force" of democratic socialism, each contributor also had to be relatively "free of any cold war tinge." In brief, each author had to have the reputation as well as the intellectual posture for "the independent and free man who is fully alive." But Fromm sometimes allowed other factors to intrude. He rejected Roger Garaudy, a member of the French Communist Party who tried to reconcile Catholicism and Marxism, because Bottomore disliked him intensely. On the other hand, Fromm solicited and accepted what he characterized as a "confused" article from Herbert Marcuse exemplifying "a pseudo-radicalism in a peculiarly veiled language" because otherwise "everybody would believe that I rejected his paper because I did not like his views." Clearly, Fromm had not recovered from his drubbing at the hands of Marcuse a decade earlier.[15]

Fromm found that it took far more time and effort than anticipated to complete *Socialist Humanism*. Correspondence with authors was often prolonged and exhausting. Some essays arrived in such poor English translations that Doubleday required Fromm to have them retranslated. Other contributors substantially exceeded the word limit. When Fromm recommended cuts, contributors sometimes disputed his advice. Fromm worried that Eastern European writers risked retribution from Stalinist regimes for appearing in *Socialist Humanism* alongside Western anti-Stalinists. To mitigate the risk, he insisted that all contributors excise references blatantly adverse to "Soviet practice and ideology." "Communism" was not to be singled out as an enemy, and all expressions "which are aggressive and could possibly smack of cold war language" had to be deleted. Several contributors balked at such limitations, and this required time-consuming negotiations. But Fromm almost always got his way.[16]

Indeed, Fromm worked assiduously to turn *Socialist Humanism* into a coherent thirty-five-author volume that convinced the public of "the vitality of humanist socialism" globally as against the rigidities, hierarchies, and "objective" laws of the Stalinist state. A consistent theme of his work characterized man as a subjective and social being who sought creative expression and happiness. He had an ethical grounding, to be sure, and could be inspired toward socialist revolution. Above all, man sought a sense of wholeness and identity in a world of other sociable and supportive beings. When man enabled others to gain identity, happiness, and dignity, he helped himself. Human bonding and caring was far more central to these contributors than the Stalinist interpretation of Marx. Indeed, they defined themselves in opposition to Stalin's *Dialectical and Historical Materialism* (1938), in which the agent of history was not the human being but the hard "objective" material factors in the "means of production." Almost all contributors cited the young, flexible, and humanistic Marx of the 1844 *Economic and Philosophical Manuscripts* and championed a realization of the "essence of man" and his "passionate strivings," full "consciousness," and "independence." These were alternatives not only to the "alienation" and "crippling" qualities of the Stalinist state, they insisted, but also to the Western marketplace and attendant capitalist exploitation.[17]

It was quite an achievement for Fromm to have established these points of thematic unity among sophisticated intellectuals of widely disparate backgrounds and from decidedly different countries and experiences. Within the pages of *Socialist Humanism*, Eastern Europeans seemed to share a kindred spirit with Western Europeans and Americans. Even Leopold Senghor and Nirmal Bose, Gandhi's secretary and an anthropologist, wrote essays that were compatible with most of the other contributors. The publishing venture fortified Fromm and his colleagues in the belief that humanist socialism constituted a vibrant movement and a viable, "third force" alternative to both Western capitalism and Soviet managerialism. Indeed, they considered themselves heirs to Max Shachtman and others who had called for a "third camp" of democratic socialists in a dangerous bipolar world. *Socialist Humanism* was perhaps the most cited and celebrated collective global expression of 1960s third-way socialism, providing an international context to the increasing number of works by members of Fromm's expanding circle of colleagues.

Heinz Brandt

As the *Socialist Humanism* book was being formulated, Fromm considered dedicating it to his second cousin, Heinz Brandt. Fromm had been working to free Brandt from an East German prison, where he had been incarcerated as a political prisoner by Walter Ulbricht's hard-line regime. In the end, Fromm dismissed the idea of the dedication, fearing it might endanger contributors to the volume living in the Soviet sphere of influence. But the temptation was understandable, for between mid-1961 and mid-1964, a campaign to free Brandt was one of the primary activities not only of democratic socialists globally but of civil libertarians and peace activists who were navigating the borders between liberalism and socialism. By orchestrating this international effort, Fromm not only demonstrated his commitment to political activism but also his capacity to bypass ideology and play the part of a shrewd tactician.[18-]

Decades earlier, during his eleven years of Nazi incarceration, Brandt had been partially sustained by support networks of communists in the German prison system. At the end of the war, he became a paid Communist Party functionary in the GDR (East Germany), where he worked for democratic socialism and social justice. But Brandt quickly grew disillusioned with the dictatorial and bureaucratic dispositions of the GDR and spoke out against the regime. Fearing arrest in 1958, he fled with his wife Annelie and their three young children to Frankfurt, in the Federal Republic. There, he found a job as an editor of *Metall*, the newspaper of the local Metalworkers' Trade Union. Through this mouthpiece, Brandt opposed both GDR Stalinism and Federal Republic rearmament. In June 1961, he represented *Metall* at a trade union congress in West Berlin, where he was kidnapped by the GDR State Security Service and incarcerated in East Berlin as an enemy of the state.[19]

From the time of Brandt's kidnapping by the GDR until his release from prison several years later, Fromm worked relentlessly to free his cousin. Between mid-June 1961 and early May 1962, the GDR kept Brandt in almost total isolation, making it difficult for Fromm to learn where he was and what he had been accused of doing. Fromm discovered that a secret trial for espionage had begun on May 2 (a month before the kidnapping), an event that contradicted the GDR's assurances of open proceedings. The East Berlin district attorney promised to drop his charges if Brandt stated publicly that he had voluntarily returned to live in the GDR. When Brandt refused the deal, he was convicted of sedition and sentenced to thirteen years of hard prison labor. As Brandt had already survived Auschwitz, Fromm worried about his cousin's health. The GDR refused Fromm's requests for leniency and instead publicized Brandt's purported immoralities—alcoholism, distribution of pornography, and womanizing. Brandt's health deteriorated under these dire conditions. In order to secure Brandt's release, Fromm demonstrated remarkable sophistication in complex international negotiations.[20]

Fromm secured Brandt's freedom three years later by working closely with his wife, Annelie, the one person with whom the GDR allowed Brandt to correspond. Writing to Clara Urquhart, Fromm detailed how impressed he was with Annelie, who continued to reside in Frankfurt. She came from a poorly educated East German working-class family, had rarely traveled, and had little contact with the West. But Fromm admired her intelligence and insight. Like Brandt, she had initially joined the East German Communist Party, believing it to be the path to peace and socialism. She lost faith in the party when she learned of its Stalinist bent. Annelie worked tirelessly to gain information and to network with figures in the peace movement, the democratic socialist movement, and the Metalworkers' Union. She made a point of updating Fromm on her husband's condition and on the nuances of German politics. Fromm rarely wrote a letter on the case without her input and approval.[21]

Fromm and Annelie forged a mutually supportive relationship during their efforts to help Heinz. Fromm saw to her financial needs and arranged for her travel schedule as she solicited support for her husband. The rapport and trust between Fromm and Annelie was remarkable, given their very different backgrounds. Each helped the other navigate an extremely complex set of circumstances. When Fromm considered writing to a Ukrainian member of the Central Committee of the Soviet Communist Party with whom he had developed a rapport, for example, he checked with Annelie on the details. She felt it was important to pressure Ulbricht with a steady stream of international protests against her husband's incarceration. But Fromm cautioned that outraged protests could rigidify the GDR. Several supporters recommended that Fromm write a book or pamphlet on Brandt to publicize his decency as a voice for peace and disarmament in Germany. He talked it over with Annelie and they concluded that a protest document might prod Ulbricht to issue a pardon.[22]

The substantial global resources and moral influence of the London-based Amnesty International also proved decisive. When Clara Urquhart introduced Fromm to Amnesty's president, Peter Benenson, they became instant friends. Benenson shared what he had learned from his many rescue experiences, provided financial resources and publicity, and urged Amnesty affiliates to help with the Brandt case. And he suggested that Fromm use select German contacts to sell the Federal Republic on a prisoner exchange involving Brandt with the GDR. The problem, Fromm explained, was that because Brandt had been critical of West German rearmament, the Federal Republic would find little advantage in bringing him home. Prodded by Fromm, Benenson named Brandt the Amnesty International "Prisoner of the Year" for 1963, which placed significant pressure on Ulbricht to resolve the case. Yet Fromm and Benenson feared that Ulbricht would remain intransigent, for the GDR dictator did not want to give the appearance of yielding to Western pressure. Something more was needed to persuade the GDR, and Benenson suggested that Bertrand Russell could help.[23]

At the time, Russell enjoyed a stellar reputation in both East and West as a champion of peaceful coexistence and freedom of thought. Renowned as a philosopher and mathematician, he was a Nobel laureate and wielded substantial moral authority. A democratic socialist critical of the Stalinist state and a supporter of Amnesty International, he was also a friend of Khrushchev and was highly regarded in the USSR and the GDR. In fact, the East German government had awarded Russell a special medal of honor. Having admired *Escape from Freedom*, he welcomed direct communication with Fromm on the Brandt case. In May 1962, Fromm sent Russell an epistle that systematically reviewed the case and proposed a meeting with Russell to plot strategy.[24]

Russell's response to Fromm was encouraging: "I shall do anything you advise with respect to Brandt." He agreed to see Fromm in London before the 1962 Moscow Conference on Disarmament and was drafting a letter to the president of the conference, which included a plea for Brandt. Russell confided to Fromm that Khrushchev had recently written one of his characteristically friendly letters to him, and, with Fromm's guidance, he would incorporate a plea for Brandt in his reply to the Soviet leader.[25]

Fromm had a fruitful meeting with Russell in London. Subsequently, they met in Wales, where Fromm asked Russell to write a foreword to the proposed pamphlet defending Brandt. After informing Khrushchev of the need to free Brandt, Russell calculated that the Soviet leader would communicate with Ulbricht. Under Fromm's guidance, Russell next wrote a private letter to Ulbricht asking for amnesty to be extended to Brandt as "a particular favor." Russell told Ulbricht that his own "efforts in the West to oppose dangerous and uncompromising militarism are hindered by things such as the imprisonment of Heinz Brandt." Ulbricht seemed to soften on the issue of amnesty but insisted that Brandt remain in East Germany; if Brandt returned to Frankfurt, the image of the GDR as a civil and freedom-loving nation would suffer. After Russell explained Ulbricht's new posture, Fromm conferred with Annelie, who in turn outlined a response that Fromm asked Russell to communicate to Ulbricht: that for "compelling reasons" Brandt's family could not move to East Germany. Instead, Swedish authorities would allow him to relocate there (leaving ambiguous whether his family would join him in Sweden). The crucial issue in the negotiation, Annelie pointed out, was for her husband to be able to leave the GDR, and that would provide him de facto freedom. The proposed relocation in Sweden might give Ulbricht a face-saving vehicle if he released Brandt. Russell agreed with this logic—that once Brandt was freed and permitted to leave the GDR for Sweden, he could then rejoin his family in Frankfurt.[26]

Ulbricht continued to balk, and Russell grew impatient, even threatening to return his GDR Medal of Honor—a blow to East German prestige. Fromm counseled Russell to delay the return of the medal—that the threat itself might prod Ulbricht into a declaration of amnesty. Russell disregarded Fromm's sound advice and returned the medal, and he publicized plans to prepare an article criticizing the GDR's treatment of Brandt for a West German publication. Fromm recognized that Russell's rash actions had closed the door to direct private negotiations with the GDR, leaving few viable options, though he felt there was a remote chance that Russell's conduct could provoke the Russians "to suggest to the East Germans that they do something." When Benenson commented on the seemingly hopeless situation, Fromm replied that "the only thing to do is to go on showing [the GDR] that we have not forgotten the case." Often brash and dismissive, Fromm demonstrated uncharacteristic pertinacity and calm in these difficult circumstances. He appeared to be engaging the "life" of an extraordinarily skillful diplomat and strategist throughout the course of the case.[27]

Fromm never learned precisely why the GDR released Brandt in May 1964 and allowed him to return directly to Frankfurt. In his foreword to Brandt's autobiographical *The Search for a Third Way* Fromm wrote that "The miracle was wrought when Bertrand Russell gave the campaign its greatest impetus by returning a medal awarded him by the East German Communists." Privately, Fromm advanced two other and in some ways more persuasive explanations for his cousin's release. First, he confided to Annelie his suspicion that owing to an international wave of sympathy for Amnesty's "Prisoner of the Year" and Russell's friendship with Khrushchev, the Russians had ordered the GDR to release Heinz. Had Annelie not insisted to Fromm and he to Russell that as a precondition of any such release from prison Heinz had to be allowed to leave the GDR, Fromm was sure that Heinz would have spent the rest of his life in East Germany. In a letter to Clara Urquhart, Fromm advanced a second perspective on the Brandt release, crediting Urquhart with persuading Russell's trusted assistant, Charles Ellis, to prod Russell to approach Khrushchev.[28]

Shortly after Heinz returned to his family in Frankfurt, Fromm and Annis hosted the Brandts at their home in Cuernavaca, where he and Heinz spent much time talking through Heinz's traumatic experiences. "Eleven years in Nazi prisons and three years in a Communist prison leave traces which are very difficult to erase," Fromm observed. The Brandts and the Fromms took increasing pleasure in each other's company. At Fromm's urging, Heinz began his autobiographical *The Search for a Third Way*. His "third way" was the socialist humanism Fromm had spent the past half decade elaborating. Though Fromm had grown increasingly distant from his extended family since World War II, the two cousins grew closer as Brandt, the longtime activist, became something of a scholar and writer.[29]

A Breathtaking Pace

Happy in his marriage, Fromm found increasing joy and contentment as a social commentator and political activist, with supportive third-way colleagues. Without them, it would have been inconceivable for Fromm to have carried on the complex and trying negotiations in the Brandt campaign with such calm, balance, and subtlety. As he approached old age,

Fromm had become an adroit diplomat in certain situations and had been able to rein in some of the more impatient and prophetic aspects of his personality. There were important shifts and revisions among the array of "lives" he was living.

There were tradeoffs. In addition to his display of diplomatic acumen, Fromm was writing more books and articles than ever before, but they lacked the profundity of *Escape from Freedom* (1941) or even *Man for Himself* (1947). Volumes such as *May Man Prevail?* (1961), *Marx's Concept of Man* (1961), and *Beyond the Chains of Illusion* (1962) linked Marx to Freud in exciting ways and addressed problems in the most dangerous Cold War years with reasoned solutions. But these more recent books borrowed heavily from conceptual structures and historical perspectives that Fromm had developed in the 1930s and early 1940s, culminating with the publication of *Escape from Freedom*. He became an increasingly self-referential writer, often drawing on the premises of his early publications. In brief, Fromm had not taken adequate advantage of the tough but significant criticisms of discerning colleagues in quite some time. Although Urquhart, Schaff, and even Bottomore were eager to read and discuss Fromm's drafts, they did not offer hard criticisms and voiced no displeasure in the redundancy that had become a staple of his writing. Most definitely, they were not like his colleagues at the Frankfurt Institute.

To be sure, David Riesman continued to be a thorough critic who spoke his mind. But Riesman had a talent for mixing tough commentary with optimal conviviality and good cheer. The speed with which Fromm published was matched by heightened activity in the peace movement. In view of his new activism, the thoroughness and the scholarly aspects of his writing had to give, Fromm acknowledged to Riesman. By late April 1966, he told Riesman that he was scheduled to deliver twenty lectures in as many days—"a hectic time." Riesman marveled at his energy even as he privately fretted that Fromm's pace was excessive and even troublesome. The frenzied, sometimes even hypomanic, behavior since early in the decade had not dissipated.[30]

Oswaldo, the prominent Mexican caricaturist, completed a sketch of Fromm (see centerfold) that was based on his salient memories at this point in Fromm's life. In true caricaturist form, Fromm's large head rested on a small and frail body that seemed barely to support the weight and pressure, perhaps unintentionally reflecting the immense responsibilities bearing down on his aging self. Meticulous dress—a tie, a well-pressed white shirt, and a dark jacket—only modestly fortified the infirm body. A large pair of glasses framed Fromm's bright, determined eyes and powerful jaw. The discernable mind-body imbalance that Oswaldo captured seemed to be compounded by a heavy stack of books under Fromm's right arm and a much lighter bouquet of flowers in his left hand. Oswaldo pictured Fromm walking off at perhaps too vigorous a clip, leaving behind pairs of fragile little hearts as footprints. Despite the dangers of the Cold War and a variety of obligations weighing heavily on him, the caricature depicted the Fromm who had impressed the world as Love's Prophet.

10

"Life Is Extravagance": Almost

etween June 1961 and August 1962, Soviet-American tensions over Berlin escalated. Germany in general and Berlin in particular were focal points for an intensification of the Cold War. The city had been divided into American, French, British, and Soviet administrative zones, but Khrushchev sought to cut off the Soviet sector from the three Western powers. Confrontations between the Soviets and the Allies followed. The underlying problem for the GDR was that millions of East Germans were defecting to West Germany through Berlin. Khrushchev and Ulbricht of the GDR built the Berlin Wall to cut off the migrations west. It was a point of demarcation between east and west that, if breached, could bring on nuclear war.

In October 1962, after the Berlin situation had cooled, the Cuban Missile Crisis erupted. Khrushchev had been building a secret nuclear missile installation in Cuba. Kennedy declared a "quarantine" against Cuba and demanded that the missile sites be dismantled. This was another Soviet-American confrontation, each side threatening to use nuclear weapons against the other. At the last minute, a deal was struck. Khrushchev agreed to dismantle the missile sites; Kennedy's pledged not to attack Cuba and to remove nuclear missiles from Turkey.

As tensions mounted in Germany and the Cuban Missile Crisis transpired, Fromm was actively writing letters to the editor, preparing articles, and speaking publicly, relying on all the information he could muster. He characterized the willingness of the superpowers to risk extinguishing life on Earth as the spirit of "necrophilia," which was antithetical to "biophilia." Fromm had begun to examine necrophilia, noting that it drew meaning from what the Greeks called *nekros* (death, decay, and corpselike qualities). Whereas the sadist and the sadomasochist found pleasure in making others suffer, the necrophiliac craved the disintegration of living forms. The Holocaust and the bombings of civilian populations in Dresden, Hiroshima, and Nagasaki showed how lethal the guns of war could be. For Fromm, necrophilia was the most significant threat of modern times.

There was a personal component to Fromm's new interest. For years, Fromm and his London friend Clara Urquhart had discussed his health problems and dietary habits. Despite Fromm's concerns about his health, he continued to relish his cigars, liquor, pastries, breads, and cheeses; exercise was a low priority. In one of his loving epistles to Annis, he seemed to say it all: "Life Is Extravagance." One should take up all the pleasures life has to offer, including some that might not enhance one's health. "Extravagance" was the essence of biophilia, much as bellicosity, war, and the destruction of life were core elements in necrophilia. Freud would have invoked his terms eros and thanatos, but Fromm considered the biophilia/necrophilia binary as less a product of instincts and more a product of social experiences.

In July 1962, Fromm, accompanied by Annis, Freeman, Riesman, and Norman Thomas, left for the Soviet Union to attend the World Congress for General Disarmament and Peace, which was being held in the Kremlin (see centerfold). Jean-Paul Sartre and Bertrand Russell were among the two thousand delegates from one hundred countries in attendance. Many peace organizations in the West boycotted the event, doubting that Khrushchev would allow candid discussions. However, perspectives critical of the Soviets were allowed. After Khrushchev's long diatribe denying blame for the Cold War, other delegates spoke, including Fromm, who drew applause for castigating high-altitude U.S. nuclear tests and then criticizing the Soviets for testing a fifty-seven-megaton bomb. Khrushchev offered no retort. That was a high moment for Fromm. But there were low moments as well. Writing to Urquhart in September 1962, for example, Fromm confided his despair "that there is hardly any chance that atomic war will be avoided" because "the reason why people are so passive toward the dangers of war lie in the fact that the majority just does not love life." Therefore, Fromm decided to focus his public presentations on the importance of embracing life, emphasizing the love of life over the destruction of war. This change in emphasis represented a major strategic shift in his thinking. By underscoring the necessity of joyous living—biophilia—Fromm came to assume, perhaps naively, that he might gain more traction when he rammed up against foreign policy hawks such as Herman Kahn, who held out the possibility of limited nuclear war (a proxy for necrophilia).[1]

Fromm's distress deepened in the last months of 1962. Recovering from his perennial late fall flu and bouts with bronchitis, he felt compelled to issue a forewarning of sorts on the devastating consequences of necrophilia. Indeed, he pondered preparing a book-length study of the struggle between biophilia and necrophilia, tentatively titled *The Heart of Man*. In some respects, it would serve as a counterpart to *The Art of Loving*.

Early in 1963, Fromm drafted a chapter, "On the Psychological Causes of War," centered on necrophilia and biophilia. He cited Hitler and Stalin to exemplify necrophilia, as both dictators were enamored with force, destruction, and a willingness to kill. A "necrophilic" orientation involved an attraction to death—a quest to transform the organic into the inorganic. A "necrophilious" person was cool and distant, committed to "law and order" and fearful of life because it seemed disorderly and uncontrollable. He tended to be "cold, his skin looks dead, and often he has an expression on his face as though he were smelling a bad odor." For such a person, "not life but death is loved; not growth, but destruction." In contrast, Fromm connected biophilia to his concept of productive character orientation—attraction to the process of life, to creating and building rather than retaining and consuming. Such a person prized life's adventures and opportunities, not predictable certainties, and sought to influence others through love and reason rather than force or bureaucratic mandate.[2]

Fromm did not consider biophilia and necrophilia as synonyms for Freud's eros (the life instinct) and thanatos (the death instinct) and skirted the issue of his terms' ontological status. As far back as Augustine, philosophers and theologians asked whether human "evil" was distinctive or whether it was the absence of "good." Fromm simply postulated that biophilia was inherent in human nature and that necrophilia prevailed when a society seemed intent on destroying itself. Society moved along a continuum between biophilia and necrophilia, but survival mandated that society embrace biophilia, a quality that emerged in a society that facilitated material security, justice, freedom, and creative work. Here his plea for a humanistic democratic socialist social order was implicit.[3]

Fromm concluded his draft chapter by emphasizing that his dichotomy between necrophilia and biophilia was responsive to the most vital question of the day: why was there no overwhelming public protest against the preparations for nuclear war? If the Americans and the Soviets launched their nuclear weapons, half of each country's population would be incinerated, and the survivors would envy the dead. How, then, could parents with children and grandchildren, who had so much to live for, acquiesce in the nuclear arms race by submitting to leaders willing to incite a nuclear war?

Fromm's answer was familiar: "intellectualization, quantification, abstraction, bureaucratization, and reification—the very characteristics of modern industrial society—are applied to people rather than to things." Living under such circumstances necessitated "becoming more distant to life and more attracted to death." Thus, when prominent nuclear strategists advised Americans that they could survive a nuclear exchange with the Soviets even at a cost of millions of deaths, many were lulled into acquiescence in this "insanity." "They were already far gone in the direction of necrophilia." Fromm ended his jeremiad with the telling admission that his dichotomy between necrophilia and biophilia related heavily to his personal determination to live life "extravagantly" and joyously before death intruded. The nuclear threat was central to those binaries, but so were personal concerns. This admission foreshadowed a problematic quality in the conceptualization of biophilia and necrophilia. Fromm invoked universal opposites on the one hand, but he was almost entirely concerned with the contemporary threat of nuclear war and his personal agenda on the other.[4]

Fromm's draft chapter of *The Heart of Man* underscored his longstanding disposition toward prophetic declarations. Given that nuclear war had almost erupted over Soviet missiles in Cuba a few months earlier, he felt compelled to disseminate his warning about necrophilia quickly and in compelling language. At the same time, he recognized that as he had only very recently begun thinking explicitly about necrophilia as the antithesis of biophilia, he stood to benefit from the evaluation of astute social critics. Consequently, he availed himself of an offer by the Peace Education Division of the American Friends Service Committee for its "Beyond Deterrence" forum series. The division would procure critiques of his draft chapter from six formidable intellectuals, allow Fromm to respond, and then disseminate the dialogue in pamphlet form. Fromm stood to benefit from this procedure as he enlarged the draft chapter into a full-scale book.

All but one of the critics (the Topeka-based psychiatrist Roy Menninger) were probing and cogent. Thomas Merton, the prominent Trappist monk, poet, and social activist, suggested that Fromm needed to clarify his central conceptualization. For Merton, Fromm was essentially arguing for humankind to "preserve intact a life-giving central integrity" in its spiritual existence, in the face of depersonalized organizations "which are outside us and alien to us." Because materialism and bureaucracy corrupted this "spiritual center," Merton noted, the forces of death and destruction became appealing. Fromm agreed that this was his central point; indeed, he considered Merton's words in this general area more compelling than his own. The eminent Protestant theologian and existentialist philosopher Paul Tillich and the leading foreign policy specialist of the "realist" camp, Hans Morgenthau both insisted that war was caused by a political and social process within nations and not by a psychological necrophilia resident within individuals. Both took issue with Fromm's chapter title, "The Psychological Causes of War." Fromm agreed that his title was misleading and changed it to "War Within Man." He also concurred that necrophilia was only one of several factors contributing to a decision to wage war and as such he was making a reductionist argument. The eminent sociologist and social theorist Pitirim Sorokin and the leading psychiatrist and critic of psychotherapeutic methods Jerome Frank pointed out that Fromm's construct could not account for a multiplicity of factors that explained why some went to war and killed while others did not. They also questioned Fromm's assertion that necrophilia was less prominent in preindustrial societies. Fromm agreed that necrophilia was hardly exclusive to the twentieth century even though the modern era had witnessed unprecedented atrocities. Necrophilia could overlap with altruism, Fromm maintained by way of qualification, and it was only "one of the different kinds of psychic motivations resulting in destructive acts." Ultimately, Tillich, Morgenthau, Frank, and Sorokin responded that Fromm's concept of necrophilia was polemical and required considerable refinement and qualification. Somewhat uncharacteristically, Fromm for the most part agreed.[5]

Yet despite his acknowledgment of the validity of most of the criticisms, Fromm altered nothing significant beyond the title, leaving the biophilia/necrophilia binary unrevised, and it constituted the conceptual core of *The Heart of Man: Its Genius for Good and Evil.* One is hard put to explain why Fromm made no changes, but there is an interesting speculation. When engaged in his characteristic prophetic disposition, Fromm tended to write books quickly, polemically, and without taking astute critics very seriously. This was characteristic of most of the books he wrote in the 1960s. After the AFSC forum, the prophet won out over the serious and cogent critics who had evaluated his work. But this came at a cost: Fromm's biophilia/necrophilia binary lacked the precision and persuasive power it might have had.[6]

Published in 1964, *The Heart of Man* sold roughly two million copies and was translated into eighteen languages. It was one of his most popular books of the decade. While expounding upon his biophilia/necrophilia binary, Fromm hastily addressed narcissism. Together, he noted, these three components formed a theoretical and psychoanalytically informed understanding of the human capacity for destruction—and for love.[7]

In the book, as in the initial draft chapter, Fromm defined necrophilia as a "syndrome of decay" and a hardening of the heart that was augmented by anal, narcissistic, and incestuous regressions. On the other hand, biophilia was a "syndrome of growth," creativity, and joy, amplified by freedom and independence. This biophilia/necrophilia binary, if not entirely persuasive in the abstract, could have found better grounding and concreteness had Fromm borrowed from Hannah Arendt's earlier discussion of "radical evil" in *The Origins of Totalitarianism* (1950). "Radical evil" was the political process of rendering of individuals and groups "superfluous" and "mere life." In this vein, Fromm might have argued for a politics of life—and of death—and that biophilia and necrophilia drew meaning from the concrete politics of families and communities.[8]

Fromm settled on *The Heart of Man* as his final title, and this was telling. Even after the Cuban Missile Crisis and several scary confrontations over Berlin, he felt there was potential within the human heart for "goodness" and life. The heart would not harden so long as a person retained "the capacity to be moved by the distress of another human being, by the friendly gaze of another person, by the song of a bird, by the greenness of grass." Fromm wrote metaphorically of the human heart as the door to unconscious spirituality and, quite literally, as the organ that perpetuated life in the human body. He was rallying the life forces within himself and within society.[9]

You Shall Be as Gods

The Heart of Man represented Fromm as an ethical prophet for humankind. In discussing biophilia, he referenced a soft, empathetic spirituality in the human condition, a spirituality that had been a stabilizing force in Fromm's own life. In the years following the completion of *The Heart of Man*, he limited his usual work schedule and immersed himself in the study of the Hebrew Bible. He did this not so much because it was a lifelong passion but because he seemed intent on rebalancing his own life by becoming more spiritual. As he told Ernst Simon, a friend since adolescence: "If you say I have turned away from the life of a practicing Jew which I led until the end of my twenties, you are of course perfectly right, but my interest in and love for the Jewish tradition has never died and nobody can talk to me for any length of time who will not hear a Talmudic or Hasidic story."[10]

Fromm explained to Angelica Balabanoff that this did not mean that he had "returned to the Jewish religion." Rather, the Hebrew Bible was "a truly revolutionary book" that addressed man's deepest spiritual needs and the human quest for freedom and creativity. The Hebrew Bible illustrated man's capacity, with God's blessing, to live a happy and vibrant life in the face of great adversity. Fromm told the distinguished sociologist Robert Merton that together with the Talmud, the Hebrew Bible remained his spiritual and ethical anchor even as he had long ceased formal "participation in Jewish religion or any other form of Jewish life."[11]

Fromm turned to his next book, *You Shall Be as Gods*, in the spring of 1964 and completed it in 1966. As he worked on the volume, he wrote letters about its progress to friends. The project was a joyous and energizing undertaking, he reported, balancing out the gravity of his apprehensions of a nuclear holocaust. By July 1964, he told Balabanoff that he had settled on a theme—the Hebrew Bible's account of the stateless Jewish people who refused to worship a secular authority. Instead, they assumed a rebellious spirit to the point of demanding that God "remain true to his own principles." This direct, nonhierarchical relationship between man and God was inherent in "Abraham's plea with God to spare Sodom and Gomorrah"—not to destroy those cities in retribution for wickedness within Sodom. Fromm also wrote excitedly to Clara Urquhart of the old Jewish concept of the Messiah, who, "as a representative of man has to be consulted by God." The emphasis of the Talmud was on "the glory and strength of man" rather than the submission to God evident in Christian doctrine. By early 1965, Fromm told Adam Schaff that the more he worked on his project, the more convinced he was that the Hebrew Bible was a revolutionary text advocating liberation from social oppression. Marx's works carried the same message, Fromm noted, if couched in secular terms. As *You Shall Be as Gods* was nearing completion, Fromm mentioned to Urquhart that unlike Catholicism (which viewed Christ's initial arrival as the first act of salvation), Judaism had long held that the arrival of the Messiah coincided with universal peace and brotherhood rendered through human efforts. In brief, Fromm planned to use biblical text to elaborate a Jewish tradition that reaffirmed ancient faith in human capacity. The Jewish Bible could serve as a guide for modern man in his quest for freedom, self-fulfillment, and discovery of his true inner spirituality. For Fromm, his book was transforming into a Judaic *midrash* blending ancient wisdom with contemporary concerns and ethical teaching (i.e., *muscar*) with an invocation of criticism and reproof (i.e., *tockachot*). The project helped him revive his own inner spirituality in the face of personal and global adversities.[12]

You Shall Be as Gods ultimately sold about two million copies in fifteen languages. After completing the book, Fromm acknowledged that he was emphasizing the progressive, humanistic, and historically dominant traditions of Jewish life at the expense of the "nationalistic, xenophobic, and reactionary elements" that were especially evident in the aggressive posture of the modern Israeli state. His purposes were polemical and political as well as philosophic and personal: he reported that the universal humanism of the Old Testament prophets, steeped in justice toward all, was being undermined by the aggressive policies of modern Israel against its Arab neighbors.[13]

Indeed, since April 1948, Fromm had preferred polemical assertion over nuanced discussion of the emerging Jewish state. In a public letter for the *New York Times* endorsed by Martin Buber, Leo Baeck, Albert Einstein, and other Jewish leaders, Fromm warned of the need to curb violent exchanges between Jews and Arabs in Palestine. This violence contradicted "the basic principles of civilization to which Jews have contributed: devotion to the rule of justice and moral law, respect for the individual, affirmation of life." By 1960, Fromm publicly attacked the Israeli government for illegally kidnapping the formidable Nazi Adolf Eichmann from Argentina and trying him under a questionable Israeli law, in the name of world Jewry: "The State of Israel has failed to conquer the Nazi spirit by not rising to a higher moral attitude than that of lawless revenge." A higher morality was at the heart of Jewish law and custom; for Israel to violate it was to return to "the spirit of the conquerors of Canaan." By 1962, Fromm remained very distressed over Israel's apparent propensity to live by the sword while appropriating Arab land: "prophetic Messianism has always been for me one of the most beautiful ideas, and I feel that the State of Israel has just prostituted this idea for its own political purposes." During the spring of

1966, Fromm confided to Schaff that a principal motive for publishing *You Shall Be as Gods* was to reawaken in Jews a realization that universal humanism, not the belligerent Israeli nation-state, resided at the heart of their tradition. Jews needed to be reacquainted with the message of the Old Testament prophets.[14]

You Shall Be as Gods was Fromm's most spiritual volume. It was also his first effort in many years at close textual commentary. He acknowledged that the work was inspired by the nineteenth-century neo-Kantian Marburg philosopher Herman Cohen and his posthumous classic *The Religion of Reason out of the Sources of Judaism* (1919). Two of Fromm's most important teachers, Nobel and Rabinkow (who was heavily influenced by Cohen) had acquainted him with Cohen's classic. *The Religion of Reason* combined systematic commentaries on text in the Hebrew Bible with discussions of other vital sources of Jewish tradition to yield a "religion of reason." For Cohen, Judaism was predicated on universal ethics and a commitment to social justice. Because the teachings of Old Testament prophets were based on universality, Cohen held that this precluded loyalty to a state, even a Jewish state. If the concept of an external God was helpful to spur man to act ethically, ethical behavior was superior to faith (i.e., what Cohen elaborated as "ethical monotheism"). Fromm was positioning himself in the tradition of German Jewish Talmudic scholarship and in the spirituality of his student days, a time in his life of hope, inspiration, and even innocence—a time prior to World War I, the rise of Nazism, and the risk of nuclear annihilation.[15]

Fromm announced the book's theme succinctly. Although the Hebrew Bible was "a book of many colors, written, edited, and re-edited by many writers in the course of a millennium," it depicted "the evolution of a small, primitive nation headed by spiritual leaders insisting on the existence of one God and on the nonexistence of idols. This monotheism expanded into a religion "with faith in a nameless God, in the final unification of all men, in the complete freedom of each individual." Fromm argued that this essential message had resided at the center of Jewish thought for centuries. As the Jewish people had lacked a country for most of their history, "prophetic teachings and not Solomon's splendor, became the dominant, lasting influence on Jewish thought." Those teachings underscored "the prophetic vision of a united, peaceful mankind, of justice for the poor and helpless." From their wandering, countryless existence, Jews had been "able to develop and uphold a tradition of humanism."[16]

Early in *You Shall Be as Gods*, Fromm explained that the Jewish tradition of a "belief in God" did not mean that God had specific attributes or the authority to impose dogma on society. To know God was to love God, which was essentially to embrace life and to conduct oneself ethically. By embracing God as a living totality, Fromm insisted, man accepted the wholeness of his own life and his own totality. The Old Testament and the Talmud expounded ethical law—the principles governing man's conduct in the business of life. To be sure, man could never be God, but if he allowed his personality to unfold and "be holy," man would walk with (not beneath) God. Unfortunately, man often got sidetracked by worshipping idols—the state, the leader, the king, wealth, or technology—in the mistaken belief that these were emanations of God. To welcome God was to negate idols; man must never transfer his and God's passions to an idol, for this idol worship led to dire psychological consequences. To embrace an idol was to elevate an estranged, alienated, and therefore decaying aspect of one's self. It was to embrace necrophilia.[17]

The God of the Hebrew Bible was the embodiment of vibrant human life. For Fromm, the Hebrew God also embraced a "religious" human experience that was beyond conceptualization. Fromm referred to this as the "X experience," which he felt was most clearly expressed in Zen Buddhism and in mystical realms of Jewish, Muslim, and Christian thought. It was akin to "the finger that points to the moon"—the human reality behind our words. The "X experience" entailed letting go of all forms of personal narcissism—of one's ego, one's greed, and one's fears—making "oneself empty in order to be able to fill oneself with the world, to respond to it, to become one with it, to love it." This was the essence of the biblical reference that man was made in the image of God. Man was becoming "as God" by carrying within himself "all of humanity."[18]

Fromm's discussion of the Book of Psalms was important; it seemed to register the shifting moods of his own life, extending back to his troubled childhood with a depressed mother and a somewhat manic father. He maintained that the Book of Psalms was the most popular prayer book within the Jewish community—the most evocative expression of "man's hopes and fears, his joys and his sorrows." Psychologically, the psalms registered the emotions within the self that were inherent in religious experience but not alluded to in formal doctrine. Fromm noted that there were single-mood psalms, but he focused on the more complex and dynamic psalms; the latter reflected a change of mood within the poet and registered the onset of the "X experience." The poet began in a low mood—sadness, despair, fear, sometimes profound depression. But over the course of composing the psalm, the poet's mood noticeably changed; he became confident and enjoyed a glimmer of hope and faith, even exuberance. The poet then shifted back into a much deeper despair. Only by experiencing this full depth of despair, Fromm explained, could the poet liberate himself from anxiety in order to embrace hope, faith, aliveness, and openness to the world.[19]

Fromm demonstrated this pattern of mood changes in several of the forty-seven dynamic psalms, and as he wrote he seemed to be examining whether he was sufficiently embracing life, joy, and hopefulness, despite his ill health and his preoccupation with necrophilia and nuclear war. He emphasized that the movement of the dynamic psalms over the past two thousand years had found their "most distinct and beautiful expression" in a great number of Hasidic songs. Fromm remembered feeling great joy when he and Rabinkow sang them together, the teacher and apprentice embracing the whole spirit of "radical humanism." Although he meditated with scripture much of his life, chanting (especially after dinner) seemed to allow him to maintain contact with the ebb and flow of his emotions. Studying the psalms helped him better understand how sorrow and happiness, despair and hope were part of a life process that prevented the heart from hardening and decaying. In a sense, Fromm acted as his own clinician as well as a prophet for humankind.[20]

The two years Fromm spent writing his book about the Hebrew Bible contributed profoundly to his spirituality and with that his sense of stability. While remaining a nontheist and a nonpractitioner, Fromm acknowledged (as he had not since he was a young man) that Sabbath observation was life affirming, representing a day free of the mundane practical concerns of materialist society and thus a day especially suited to contemplate and to fortify one's sense of joyous living. Indeed, Fromm recommended that Sabbath observation be embraced by everyone.[21]

Identifying much of his life with Hosea, Isaiah, and Amos and their vision of the "end of days" when nations "will beat their swords into plowshares," Fromm's tone was decidedly autobiographical. Though he did not call himself a prophet, his characterization of the prophet's role was uncannily similar to his own activism and writing. The prophet was a revealer of truth. But a prophet's realm was never purely spiritual; it was always "of this world" and therefore profoundly political. Drawing heavily upon Albert Camus' *The Rebel* (1951), Fromm described the prophet's duty as "rebel" quite clearly. He was to warn people against problematic and dangerous if often popular ideas of social justice. He was to push against the current, expecting rebuff, and (consistent with Hegel) he had no expectations of achieving utopia until the end of history. However, Camus cautioned that the rebel might, at times, become so distressed with the status quo that he might bypass the role of outside critic and become a "revolutionary". This was hazardous, Camus had warned, for the revolutionary and his quest for utopia could promote tyrannical and "totalistic" solutions, including wars of extermination. Fromm's fusion of a prophetic disposition with the role of rebel carried with it a risk (if perhaps a limited one). Under certain circumstances, the prophet could garner so much energy and fervor that he might become Camus' revolutionary. He might embrace the totalistic solutions of the revolutionary and could find that it was not easy to return to being a rebel.[22]

Madison Square Garden

While he completed *You Shall Be as Gods* in the late fall and early winter of 1966, Fromm became more active in the peace movement. He wrote a public letter to Pope Paul VI requesting that the Vatican convene a global conference to discuss imminent risks to human survival, combat in Vietnam being among these dangers. Since its founding, Fromm had been a central figure in the National Committee for a Sane Nuclear Policy (SANE) as well as a very early opponent of the war in Vietnam. He hoped that President Kennedy would withdraw troops from the area and had represented SANE in discussions with a few Kennedy administration advisors, though from a characteristically ideological stance that was less than persuasive. When Kennedy was murdered, Fromm feared that Lyndon Johnson would not be able to contain pressure from the Defense Department and the generals for extended military "adventurism" in Southeast Asia.

Fromm and his colleagues in SANE had cause to be apprehensive. Early in 1965, Johnson launched a massive troop callup for the Vietnam war, which continued into 1966 and hardly disposed the administration to initiate a serious plan for withdrawal. Under these circumstances, SANE selected Fromm as the keynote speaker at a major anti–Vietnam War rally to be held at Madison Square Garden on December 8, 1966. The hope among

SANE leaders was that Fromm could hold the organization together, as SANE had split between those who sought a dialogue with the Johnson administration in order to press for serious negotiation to end the war and those who repudiated the administration, demanding unilateral American withdrawal. Fromm favored discussing measures with Johnson's advisors that might lead to a negotiated settlement with the North Vietnamese and Viet Cong. However, he had never been averse to blunt public castigations of heads of state, even as this limited his access to those who formulated foreign policy.[23]

Normally, Fromm traveled from Mexico City to New York City in a comfortable Pullman railroad car, for he disliked air travel, but he felt pressed for time because of his increased writing and speaking obligations and realized that a flight would save him several days of travel time. When he arrived at his New York apartment on Riverside Drive to rest and prepare for the rally, Fromm felt that he was coming down with the flu. Always reticent to cancel a scheduled obligation owing to ill health, especially when the sponsor was an organization very dear to him, he took a taxi to Madison Square Garden.

As Fromm stepped onto the stage, to loud applause, and walked toward the podium to deliver his address, he seemed temporarily to regain his strength. The Garden was packed. Here was an internationally prominent figure, short and modestly plump, wearing his characteristic conservative dark suit. Despite his advanced years, his hair remained dark and thick and was combed straight back. Rimless bifocals emphasized his bushy eyebrows and called attention to his large ears, but the intensity and energy of the sixty-six-year-old speaker showed plainly in his face—rather square with creases along the brow and cheeks. Speaking elegant and flawless English with only traces of a German accent, his voice was rich and strong. The presentation was concise and spirited: he insisted that the killing in Vietnam must stop. The war exemplified "the indifference to life and the brutalization of man which has been increasing year by year since the First World War." The Nazi Holocaust and the World War II Allied bombings of Dresden, Hiroshima, and Nagasaki illustrated society's bent for brutality and destruction. Since 1914, man's heart and sensibility had been brutalized. Unlike most previous wars, where the aim had been to capture enemy territory, "success" in Vietnam was measured by "the number of enemies killed in a hunt." Fromm insisted that civilized society was based on "the love of life and all that is living," yet society was being undermined by "that most terrible perversion that man is capable of: the attraction to decay and death." If humankind had any hope of stemming "the tide of death and dehumanization" epitomized by Adolph Eichmann, the skillful supervisor of the Nazi extermination "machine," society had to say "stop killing. Stop it now" in Vietnam and in all other theaters of combat.[24]

Fromm's speech met with a loud, standing, and continuous ovation. He retained his erect posture even as he felt the energy draining from his body. Fromm left the Garden, walked into a very chilly winter night, returned by taxi to his apartment, and realized that his flu had gotten worse. But there were several important appointments in New York that required his attention in the days ahead. One evening not long after his speech at the Garden, as he waited outside in the extreme cold and icy rain to summon a taxi, he felt a sharp pain in his chest and gasped for air; he was having a massive heart attack. Fromm was confined to bed for ten weeks under Annis's care and was required to curtail his work for the better part of a year.[25]

Two months after the heart attack, he wrote to Aniceto Aramoni that he was not returning to his home in Cuernavaca any time soon. His New York cardiologist had recommended complete rest for three or four months. Fromm downplayed the seriousness of his cardiac condition, telling Adam Schaff he hoped to return to work soon. For rest and to speed his recovery, he and Annis decided in mid-February, after stopovers in Baden-Baden and Freiburg, to journey to the Hotel Muralto in the small town of Locarno, located on the northern tip of Lake Maggiore near the Swiss Alps and the Italian border. Erich and Annis had visited Locarno before, and they now headed back both for the beauty and tranquility of the area and because it was not far from a renowned cardiology and massage therapy center in Freiburg. Recuperation in Locarno went well, and by early April 1967 Fromm wrote to Schaff that he felt considerably better: "I am glad that I read a good deal and have many fresh thoughts." Later that spring, he and Annis began to take short trips from Locarno, visiting his favorite cousin Gertrud and her artist husband, Max, in Zurich and enjoying the warmer climate of Croatia. In May, Fromm attended his first public event since the Madison Square Garden rally—a peace conference in Geneva. Convalescence in Europe enabled him to separate himself from the internal politics of the Mexican Psychoanalytic Society and Institute. But he was less successful the year after his heart attack at distancing himself from American politics. After all, he had come to be regarded as an important critic of U.S. foreign policy. As the Vietnam War accelerated, Senate Foreign Relations Committee Chair William Fulbright convened a joint executive session with the Senate Armed Services Committee to discuss the conflict. Fromm's name came up for "expert" testimony. But Fulbright reported to the group that his friend was still recovering from serious illness; Fromm remained in Locarno. The visit there helped reconnect him emotionally with his European roots. It was not until the fall of 1967 that he and Annis returned to New York and from there to Mexico. They anticipated returning to the delightful little town in the Swiss Alps.[26]

The heart attack convinced Fromm that he was nearing the end of his life. He confided to Schaff that additional and potentially fatal coronary attacks could occur and that it was necessary for him to be very careful. His father had died in 1933 at only sixty-four, very possibly of a sudden heart attack. Friends who knew Fromm well recalled that he was now very concerned about his health, staying informed about medications, vitamins, and special diets and carefully measuring the limits of his physical endurance. The heart attack at sixty-six augmented Fromm's preoccupation with illness. Annis, too, might not have much longer to live, given that her cancer could recur.[27]

A few months before his Madison Square Garden appearance, Fromm had published an article on the psychology of old age for the *Journal of Rehabilitation*, arguing that once a person reached his mid-sixties and found financial security, he was often disposed to simply consume, "kill time," and focus on sickness and death. In the alternative, Fromm prophesied old age as a time "to make living [one's] main business," as there was now time to confront the spiritual and religious issues inherent in being human. Man could finally "live according to his true character," rather than expediently. He had the opportunity to become "more alive than he has ever been rather than feeling less alive." By embracing life and becoming "truly and generally interested in the world," a person facing old age could live a happier and more vibrant existence, reversing the gloom inherent in bodily decay. This, Fromm had told Annis, was living joyously and with "extravagance." Having confronted his own mortality, Fromm turned that experience into a prophecy.[28]

11

Hope and Stasis

Amid a long recuperation period in Locarno after his severe heart attack, Fromm defied his doctors and attended the May 1967 *Pacem in Terris* conference in Geneva. He talked with some of the other delegates but gave no presentation and did not stay long. He told his friend Michael Maccoby that one could believe all illness was psychosomatic until one reached one's sixties; then illness seemed to strike with a vengeance. Maccoby discerned that after his brush with death, Fromm "became gentler, more sympathetic. He became more interested in individual spiritual development, more in tune with the Buddhist vision of transcendence, of becoming one with nature." Although spirituality had been a stabilizer in his life ever since he studied with Salman Rabinkow, he now pursued it avidly, resuming his reading of Meister Eckhart and other mystics and meditating at a set time and place each day. As Fromm's spirituality deepened while he rebounded from the heart attack, Maccoby remembered watching him lie on the floor to practice dying.[1]

Nevertheless, contemplation of his own mortality and his emotional embrace of inner spirituality never extinguished his activity on behalf of nuclear disarmament and world peace. Fromm was deeply disturbed by the accelerating body count in Vietnam—all done purportedly in the effort to turn back "global communism."

By the end of 1967, Eugene McCarthy, the junior senator from Minnesota, was speaking out vociferously against the war. Indeed, that became the essential plank in his uphill challenge to incumbent President Lyndon Johnson for the 1968 Democratic Party nomination. Fromm found that McCarthy's life's paralleled his own in interesting ways. McCarthy had grown up in the intellectual Catholic world of the 1930s among the Benedictine monks at St. John's Abbey (Minnesota), where he had sought to pursue the priesthood. Fromm had studied with Talmudic scholars and considered becoming a rabbi, and his mentor Rabinkow had done much to dispose him toward a radical vision of social justice and an appreciation of socialism. Similarly, McCarthy's mentor at St. John's had urged his student to distance himself from the sinful world of the bourgeoisie, which had been corrupted by the internal contradictions of capitalism. McCarthy ultimately decided against the priesthood, just as Fromm decided against the rabbinate. After McCarthy tried unsuccessfully to establish a Catholic anticapitalist commune in rural Minnesota, he ended up teaching sociology at a small Catholic college in St. Paul. In several of his publications, Fromm had sketched out (more as a heuristic device than a historical reality) a Catholic Middle Ages with a strong sense of community, where spirituality and humane, caring relationships predominated over marketplace considerations.[2]

In 1948, Minnesota's left-leaning Democratic-Farmer-Labor Party recruited McCarthy to run for Congress. A decade later, he won a seat in the U.S. Senate, where, with John F. Kennedy, he represented Cold War liberalism, coupling domestic reform with resistance to Soviet expansionism. That was not Fromm's path. McCarthy first came to his attention at the 1960 Democratic Party convention, where McCarthy nominated Adlai Stevenson: "Do not leave this prophet without honor in his own party." Fromm was impressed by the spiritual thrust of McCarthy's speech. By the mid-1960s, McCarthy had repudiated the Johnson administration's intervention in Vietnam. Pope John XXIII's antiwar encyclical *Pacem in Terris* proclaiming that "We must obey God rather than men" became McCarthy's springboard for attacking American involvement in Vietnam on ethical grounds. Fromm, who regarded John XXIII as a spiritual ally in the struggle against nuclear weapons and warfare, was encouraged by McCarthy's spirited new opposition to the war.[3]

By 1967, McCarthy's critique of the war blended with that of Fulbright and other Senate doves. He demanded the cessation of American bombing in North Vietnam, negotiations, a coalition government in Saigon, and U.S. troop withdrawals. A few Senate doves and peace activists encouraged McCarthy to challenge Johnson for the Democratic nomination. Although they had no hope of McCarthy winning the nomination, they sought to frighten Johnson into altering his Vietnam policy.

After McCarthy declared himself a candidate, significant money flowed into the campaign. Fromm was among the largest initial donors to this "man of peace" who loved poetry and philosophy. The first primary election

took place in New Hampshire on March 12, after which newspapers reported that McCarthy had "defeated" Johnson. In fact, he finished a strong
second. Exit polls suggested that many New Hampshire voters did not
know precisely what McCarthy stood for but had marked their ballots as a
protest against the incumbent administration. Robert Kennedy, a formidable challenger, declared his candidacy in mid-March. In response, Johnson halted the bombing of North Vietnam, announced that he now favored
a negotiated settlement, and—to the shock of many Americans—dropped
out of the race for the nomination two weeks later. Fromm trusted neither
Johnson's claim of withdrawal from reelection nor the sincerity of his plan
to end the war. He feared that Johnson's announcement would ultimately
sway a "critical mass" of voters: "he snatched victory out of defeat" and put
himself out as a "selfless, humble father of the people, doing precisely
what his opponents proposed to do."4

Despite Fromm's poor health and perhaps because he deeply admired
McCarthy, he decided that the McCarthy campaign needed his ideas, plus
more of his financial assistance. The day Kennedy entered the race, Fromm
completed a long "Memo on Political Alternatives" that he hoped to expand into a book that would become the basis of the McCarthy campaign.
The memorandum emphasized a dangerous "new society" of "totally bureaucratized industrialism" that was taking hold in the West (especially in
the United States). This society programmed man "by the principles of
maximum production, maximum consumption and minimal friction" so
that he became an unfeeling and smoothly functioning part of a "mega-
machine"—passive and emotionless, living in a state of low-grade depression. It was time for man to pursue "humanistic industrialism" through
organizational decentralization, local worker management, and other structural changes dedicated to "the optimum value for man's development."
Fromm did not go so far as to mandate the socialization of private property, but the democratic institutional structure of his proposed society
would promote basic "human needs." Fromm had essentially propounded
this program since *The Sane Society* (1955). In brief, Fromm advocated a
democratic grassroots movement globally but especially in the United
States, to assure a humanistic alternative to "worship of the mechanical
and death."5

From this point on, Fromm was in demand on college campuses. His
campaign memorandum was usually the text he presented, advocating socialist humanism, participatory democracy, and an end to the war in Viet-

nam. His position was compatible with much of the New Left political program. This accounted for some of his popularity, even though he was only minimally interested in student protest culture (of course, he promoted the idea of small groups of citizens gathering to establish a humanist approach for society at large). These groups were expected eventually to coalesce and become agencies for fundamental humanist transformation. Fromm's memorandum and most of his speeches at rallies concluded with this vague outline of a movement for change. He hoped McCarthy and his staff would find utility in a book that would expand on the themes of the memorandum and give conceptual coherence to the campaign.[6]

On April 13, before Vice President Hubert Humphrey entered the race as a stand-in for Johnson, Fromm wrote a long letter to McCarthy offering his services. It resembled his first letter to Stevenson sixteen years earlier; this one was likewise peppered by a substantial amount of narcissism. "If I could be of any use for your campaign by writing memoranda which could be used for campaign speeches, or personal discussion" Fromm noted, "I would be most happy to arrange my time accordingly." He also pointed out that McCarthy's effort was "creating hope among millions of people choked by the sense of political and human impotence" and that this was why he had decided to transform his "Memo" into a short book.[7]

Fromm's long letter, a philosophic disquisition on the need for new alternatives, was, like his letter to Stevenson, inappropriate for a busy presidential candidate. Fromm the prophet was on center stage here, representing one of his "lives," and outdistancing Fromm the pragmatic tactician of the Brandt rescue. His epistle described a society "in which all men become a vast machine." Life was increasingly bureaucratic and production oriented and required man to live "without being alive." Deprived of "all that is human—love, interest, joy, freedom—his energies turn into destructiveness." Necrophilia was in ascendance.[8]

Fromm concluded by acknowledging that his letter was far too long, though there is some evidence that McCarthy appreciated the letter. He encouraged Fromm to join his campaign effort, to help shape his campaign message, and to complete the proposed book promptly. Fromm consented on all counts, with marked enthusiasm. He put aside other writing projects so that Harper and Row could publish the volume (wisely renamed *The Revolution of Hope*) in early August 1968. Whereas Fromm would gloomily confide to close friends that nuclear war was a real possibility, in *The Revolution of Hope* he seemed to rally his own spirits as well as those of his readers. By 1997, roughly 2.5 million copies had reached readers in twenty different languages.[9]

As the campaign proceeded, the country was rocked by the train of events of 1968: the Tet offensive, Martin Luther King's assassination, Robert Kennedy's assassination, global student unrest, and the Soviet invasion of Czechoslovakia to put down protests. Fromm had by then become exceedingly active in the McCarthy campaign, donating $20,000 (roughly $135,000 in 2012 dollars) at this point and paying his own expenses when he traveled to speak at McCarthy rallies. After an intense week-long campaign swing in California, he found himself exhausted but wrote excitedly to his cousin Gertrud Hunziker-Fromm that he could not let up and had promised to finish *The Revolution of Hope* with dispatch. Fromm also conveyed a sense of urgency in a public interview with Frederick Roevekamp, insisting that McCarthy was "neither a hero, a Savior or a demagogue" but a new type of political leader championing democracy through a grassroots volunteer campaign. Fromm and McCarthy met a few times in the months before the Democratic nominating convention, and on each occasion, Fromm felt energized. He developed a deep trust in the personal character of the senator. At the same time, Fromm confided to Schaff about his "ups and downs" on the campaign trail, "sometimes working too much and then having to pay for it by some exhaustion which forces me to rest for several days or to go very slowly for a while." He told Schaff that the campaign was not only a protest against the U.S. fiasco in Vietnam—among its other foreign policy blunders—but a campaign for participatory democracy. Fromm also mentioned that he was enjoying the opportunity to work with McCarthy supporters who were neither scholars nor professionals and therefore represented a significant share of the audience for his books of the 1960s.[10]

As the Democratic convention in Chicago approached in late August, the McCarthy campaign made use of Fromm's name and talents, and several campaign staffers studied Fromm's books for usable ideas and language. "California Citizens for McCarthy" bought space in the *Los Angeles Times* for Fromm's "Why I Am for McCarthy" essay, which presented Fromm's portrait of the senator's productive, life-affirming character and his vision of a humane society. Fromm also asserted that McCarthy appealed to a substantial number of Americans who feared that their lives were slipping away in a materialist society dominated by the prospect of nuclear war. With Michael Maccoby, a social psychologist Fromm had hired to help him complete a concurrent project in Mexico, Fromm also conducted a poll for publication in the *Los Angeles Times*. In the poll, 160 from widely different economic and social backgrounds living near Santa Cruz agreed to answer a series of questions on their candidate preferences. The questions were designed to measure the potential voter's "love of life" (biophilia) as opposed to his or her attraction to death and the inanimate and mechanical (necrophilia). In this methodologically flawed survey, the results seemed to be clear. Far outdistancing the other candidates, 77 percent of those who favored McCarthy were "life loving." A month before the convention, McCarthy invited Fromm to Chicago for several scheduled appearances intended to influence Democratic delegates. Four days before convention proceedings began, Fromm, Lewis Mumford, Dwight MacDonald, and other left-leaning social critics published a letter in the *New York Review of Books*. Penned by Fromm, the letter claimed that of those who had survived the primary elections, McCarthy was "the people's choice." To hand the nomination to Humphrey would undermine the democratic process. In contrast to Fromm's public letter, McCarthy recognized, as the convention neared, that Humphrey was the choice of rank-and-file Democrats, not simply of the party bosses. The vice president would go on to win the nomination with ease.[11]

Although Fromm's *The Revolution of Hope* (a campaign document for a now defunct campaign) was completed in early August, it did not appear in print until September, after Humphrey's nomination. Still, publication at this late date comported with McCarthy's proclamation that new ideas were more important than whether he personally won or lost. If the junior senator from Minnesota sometimes let political maneuvering dilute this proposition, his "high-riding" if exhausted supporter did not. Fromm was feeling increasingly drained as the months wore on, but only after he finished *The Revolution of Hope* did he yield to his doctor's insistence that he rest. The book addressed grave planetary crises amid its upbeat exhortations. Unlike the wholly upbeat *The Art of Loving*, Fromm's all-time bestseller, *The Revolution of Hope* balanced the negative against the positive in assessing the fate of humankind.[12]

The Revolution of Hope, characterized as "a response to America's situation in the year 1968," included only a few direct references to McCarthy and his campaign in its plea for "new directions, for a renewal of values . . . for a new psycho-spiritual orientation." Fromm's overwhelming focus was on the "crossroad" that presented itself to humankind at this precise moment: "one road leads to a completely mechanized society with man as a helpless cog in the machine—if not to destruction by thermonuclear war; the other to a renaissance of humanism and hope—to a society that puts technique in the service of man's well being." This humanist crusade predated McCarthy's candidacy, and despite a discouraging Humphrey-Nixon race for the White House, Fromm insisted that the crusade continue past the 1968 election. In the back of the book, one found a tear-out questionnaire, to be mailed to Fromm, that "enrolled" readers of the book in the movement. The questionnaire allowed readers to select forty or fifty eminent citizens to serve on a National Council. Citizens-at-large could also join a twenty-five-member face-to-face group who would dispatch ideas and concerns to the National Council.[13]

The questionnaire was ineffective. Only three thousand readers completed it and mailed it to Fromm, and of those only a very small minority offered to help support Fromm's proposed movement. Several nominated Fromm and McCarthy for the National Council, but few other nominees were suggested. This was hardly grassroots democracy. Acknowledging that the questionnaire venture had not worked, Fromm sought to meet with McCarthy to launch a postconvention campaign outside the auspices of the Democratic Party. "For reasons of health," Fromm forewarned McCarthy, his part in this effort had to be limited. McCarthy agreed to meet with Fromm to discuss the possibility, but the meeting was low on the senator's priorities and never occurred. Fromm's proposal in *The Revolution of Hope* for a postelection continuation of the McCarthy campaign had few takers after the senator took a pass. Dejected and despondent after the election, McCarthy began to distance himself from the peace movement. As on other occasions in his life, Fromm could be impressed by the seeming authenticity and strength of character of a new friend or colleague to the extent of overlooking their negative qualities, ending up disappointed.[14]

The Revolution of Hope was more than a campaign document. It was a significant polemic in its own right and another illustration of Fromm's remarkable capacity to connect to the concerns of whole societies and cultures. The book especially appealed to those who considered their lives to be at a turning point and yearned to be more hopeful about the future. The hopeful person sought "to transcend the narrow prison of his ego, his greed, his selfishness, his separation from his fellow man, and hence his basic loneliness." He hoped to be open and vulnerable to the world while retaining a firm sense of his own identity and purpose. In a word,

Fromm's lesson was that man had to be an energetic participant in the life process.[15]

Fromm acknowledged that it was difficult to characterize "hope" and easier to discuss what it was not. For the first time in any of his books, he instructed the reader to "mobilize his own experiences" as he read the text. Perusing Fromm's observations about the nature of hope, the reader was assigned to fashion his own specific thoughts and feelings on what it meant to be hopeful. He needed to kindle within himself "an inner readiness." Consistent with his own clinical approach, Fromm prompted the reader to summon an active "being" mode—to discover and to invigorate the hopefulness within himself. A personally active and introspective engagement with Fromm's text could prompt a "revolution of hope," or so Fromm hoped.[16]

To enhance hopefulness and the love of life, Fromm explicated what his friend Lewis Mumford called the "mega-machine," which purportedly eradicated the small, convivial, and productive (and doubtless somewhat mythical) community of old. Community had been replaced by a "totally organized and homogenized social system in which society as such functions like a machine and men like its parts." Maximized efficiency came through uniform bureaucratic rules. Individual idiosyncrasies became obstacles. As production increased, people needed to consume the products. Toward that end, people learned to view themselves as consumers rather than workers or creators, even as this realization resulted in a sense of spiritual emptiness and unimportance.[17]

Fromm concluded *The Revolution of Hope* by pleading directly to the reader to mobilize against the "mega-machine" and for its antithesis. Society must elaborate the vision of *The Sane Society* and struggle to establish it. Man had to elevate himself and his unique human needs and perspectives so that they would be primary—"the basis for humane planning reform." The definition of man and the qualities essential to his happiness had to "become the ultimate source of values."[18]

For Fromm, the first task in the process of replacing the "mega-machine" with a thoroughly sane and "humanistic" society was to involve man in the planning process. He had to shed his customary passivity—his sense of "impotence" and inconsequentiality. To restore man's confidence in his own capacities, power could no longer flow from the top down. A two-way dialogue needed to be established between decision makers and those affected by their decisions. An equitable dialogue would shift the focus from issues of power and authority to creating a good and durable product or service that enhanced man's existence. Whatever facilitated participation in the production and distribution of goods and services was what mattered.[19]

Reverting to his prophetic persona, Fromm echoed a familiar line: the best way to facilitate such dialogue on all levels was through face-to-face groups that exchanged information, debated, and made decisions for each unit of a particular enterprise. Arguing much as he had thirteen years earlier in *The Sane Society*, Fromm maintained that in America, organizing such groups was the equivalent of restoring and enlarging the old town meeting tradition of grassroots democracy, which technocracy had purportedly subverted. He elevated the ideal of the early American town meeting, which in reality was nothing like Fromm had envisioned.[20]

Predictably, the book ended on a positive note. Although humankind stood at a dangerous crossroads, Fromm proclaimed that fresh new ideas were afloat, ideas shorn of clichés and bureaucratic jargon. A growing number of scientists, artists, businesspeople, and a new breed of politicians were proposing reforms to humanize technology while enhancing man's creative potential. The appeal of *The Revolution of Hope* did not lie in its concepts or arguments, however, most of which Fromm had already presented in earlier writings. Rather, the appeal was in his mode of presentation—a brisk, compelling narrative that advanced intellectual content at a deeply emotional level. In effect, to read the book was like attending a therapeutic session. Fromm's traditionally powerful prophetic exhortations about current dangers and solutions merged seamlessly with a soft spirituality, a sense of inner calm, and a profound hopefulness. Recognizing that his readers were standing at the edge of the abyss created by the mega-machine and the prospect of nuclear war, Fromm's narrative promoted confidence that a whole new and deeply attractive existence was a realistic possibility. On these terms, rather than for its potent intellectual content, *The Revolution of Hope* was a very successful book.

Social Character in a Mexican Village

The McCarthy campaign and *The Revolution of Hope* represented Fromm's last serious engagement with American politics. For much of 1968, he was so absorbed by the political process that he ignored his health problems and set aside some of his writing obligations. He was convinced that Mc-Carthy's defeat, Richard Nixon's victory in the 1968 presidential election, and the continuation of the Vietnam War all frustrated any reason for hope in America's future. Riesman explained to him that U.S. political culture was deeply conservative and that hopes for progressive reform ran against the grain—Humphrey's electoral defeat in 1968 had been altogether pre-dictable, and McCarthy's would have been even more so. Fromm reflected on Riesman's perspectives as he did on few others, especially as he watched McCarthy embrace quirky postelection postures that included the en-dorsement of some right-wing Republicans. But Fromm was exhausted. He was also probably somewhat depressed. A disposition toward depres-sion had been with him since childhood and had been hard for him to shake after defeats like this.

After the campaign, Fromm and Annis spent more time outside the United States, alternating between winters in Cuernavaca and summers in Locarno. He also had a project with his colleague and former analysand Michael Maccoby to complete: a close study of a small and impoverished Mexican village. Fromm also wanted to complete a three-volume work on the nature of psychoanalysis. He felt strongly that these two substantial projects, which had been interrupted by his work on the McCarthy cam-paign, could restore his flagging reputation as a serious thinker. And he was in a rush to complete both projects before his health declined further.[21]

For decades, Fromm valued a consistent publication schedule and al-ways sought to bring a new project to a rapid conclusion before starting a new one. He wrote almost every morning—the routine made him feel productive and acted as a stabilizer, particularly in the face of occasional, sometimes serious, personal distress. He then meditated for an hour after writing, which had also helped to calm and structure his life.

In 1957, Fromm had begun to study Chiconcuac, a small village with rich soil, a temperate climate, and a long growing season, fifty miles south of Mexico City. For generations, many Chiconcuac villagers had lived in haciendas and served under semifeudal proprietors. Ignorant, docile, and depressed peon field laborers, these families cultivated sugar cane and rice and were perpetually indebted to the hacienda proprietors. After the Mexi-can Revolution and the abolition of the hacienda system, each laborer was provided with a small plot of land that he could farm but could neither rent nor sell. Nevertheless, he remained downcast, dependent, and without ambition, living much as he had under the hacienda. In addition to labor-ers, earlier in its history Chiconcuac had attracted a modest number of free peasants who owned small plots of land that the erstwhile hacienda propri-etors had continually threatened to appropriate. The free peasants, more assertive and productive than the laborers, were intent on preserving and maintaining their ownership of the land. Though they were far better off than the laborers, Fromm insisted, they nevertheless had no knowledge of advanced agricultural methods and lacked the skills for successful em-ployment in urban areas. Despite their economic and social differences, both the laborers and free peasants, together with an increasing number of poor landless migrants who had moved to the village, lived in "a cultural and spiritual desert." Precapitalist customs of the fiesta, neighborly con-versation and assistance, and song and collective recreation had lost their sway over most villagers. But the values of a modern industrial society had not filled that void, and the villagers felt marginalized. Television and li-quor replaced any sense of community and productivity.[22]

As a Jew who often resided in a dominant Gentile culture, an aca-demic on the outskirts of academe, and a psychoanalyst free of Freudian orthodoxies, Fromm always empathized with marginalized segments of society. Indeed, he often considered himself to be on the outside looking in. Coupled with a sense of estrangement, Fromm shared with the villag-ers a reliance on tradition. Indeed, he had long embraced the cohesion of a mythical Catholic past in his quest to bypass capitalism and its bureaucra-tization and to move toward a humanist future. The village seemed to res-onate with the vision of a medieval world that likely never existed but whose conceptualization sometimes anchored Fromm intellectually.

Situated not far from his Cuernavaca home, Fromm visited Chiconcuac on several occasions. With a population of only eight hundred, he calcu-lated that it would be possible to observe each villager closely in the context of the community. It presented an ideal setting for Fromm to conduct em-pirical research that might shore up his concept of social character. The Mexican Ministry of Health had established a Center of Rural Welfare in the village, and Fromm's friend Jose Zozaya relied on the center to procure additional government funds. Zozaya gave Fromm the money for the startup costs on his social character project. Several of Fromm's trainees in the Mexican Psychoanalytic Society offered to help Fromm with the project. Yale's Foundations Fund for Research in Psychiatry provided grant money for Fromm to hire a full-time associate to administer the details of the project. Finally, the National Autonomous University of Mexico promised to send student and faculty volunteers to provide the villagers medical and social services. This combination of resources made the Chiconcuac project very promising.[23]

In part, Fromm regarded the village project as a means of demonstrating the utility of the questionnaire protocol he had designed and compiled at the Frankfurt Institute three decades earlier. At the time, it had been regarded as a very innovative research instrument, one capable of accessing and assessing a person's deep or underlying character structure. The assumption was that the same protocol could be used across cultures and time periods.

The Frankfurt Institute never published the analysis and conclusions of the German worker project based on the tabulations of responses to the questionnaires. But despite the passage of time, Fromm continued to feel that the protocol had been an excellent attitudinal assessment vehicle and felt that the study that came of it had been his major accomplishment as a researcher. He was determined to use the protocol as part of his study of Chiconcuac. The specific and idiosyncratic wording of the respondents' answers to the questionnaire would reveal their character structures. At Chiconcuac, the questions would be designed to elicit a full range of information on each respondent's social character, including parental and family relations, the capacity to love and to create, tendencies to hoard and to share, attitudes of personal independence or docile submissiveness, and much more.[24]

Revised extensively and administered to villagers of all backgrounds, the purpose of the questionnaire became more precise: to explore connections between villagers' work lives, family relations, economic conditions, and underlying character structures. Unlike the Weimar project, moreover, the interpretation of each villager's answers would be supplemented by standard projective psychological tests (the Rorschach or Thematic Perception Test), dream interpretation and storytelling, a great deal of data on the place of the respondent in the economic and social structures of Chiconcuac, and even general staff observations of village life. By redesigning the questionnaire to profile a villager on a deep and comprehensive level and by supplementing interpretation of the responses with additional information, Fromm hoped that his Mexican village project would demonstrate that, beyond his popular writings, he was still a serious social researcher.

By early 1959, Fromm had articulated his principal aim for the Chicon-cuac project. Primarily through the heavily revised questionnaire (administered to all adults over age sixteen and half of the children) but supplemented by interviews, staff observations, and all sorts of data on the community, he would discern which factors inhibited and which increased creativity and productivity among the villagers. Economic surveys, statistical analyses, anthropological field observations, and other methodologies would also be used. He intended to learn how to remedy the dire legacy of the hacienda system—lethargy, alcoholism, and indifference to life. He sought to introduce happiness, a zest for life, and creative work into this peasant village, which had long suffered from cultural drabness, poverty, and fatalism. "I have been convinced for a long time," Fromm wrote to the psychologist Charles Wrigley, "that the Mexican village can emerge from its lethargy, and especially from the evil of alcoholism only if the creative impulses of the peasant are awakened." There were studies of Mexican towns and villages before Fromm's, but the Chiconcuac project was emerging as a more ambitious undertaking than many of them. The agenda that was falling into place was essentially to understand an impoverished Third World village through quantitative survey data combined with a psychodynamic perspective and a picture of village life that merged social, economic, and historical perspectives into a synthetic narrative. Added to all of this was a reform agenda: the goal was ultimately to enhance the quality of life of the villagers.[25]

For the first three years of the project, Fromm worked closely with two American anthropologists, Theodore and Lola Schwartz, a married couple recommended by Margaret Mead. They were fluent in Spanish and had studied segments of the rural Mexican population. Theodore had assisted Mead herself during some of her anthropological field work. Lola, his wife, was completing her dissertation in anthropology and sought to use the village as a research site for her manuscript. Like Mead, both deployed an ethnographic approach, seeking out the broad patterns of a culture. The couple moved to Chiconcuac when Fromm hired them for the project. Through the Schwartzes' friendships with the villagers and their abundant observations and interviews, Fromm secured intimate details that supplemented the findings from his questionnaire.[26]

But after the first fifty villagers were assisted in completing the questionnaire, trouble erupted. Fromm candidly acknowledged to the Schwartzes and to others that he had little capacity to apply quantitative methods to tabulate the results of the overwhelmingly qualitative questionnaire material. Therefore he could not himself create a statistical profile of the social character types among the villagers. He would have to depend on staff for this work. Theodore had the statistical background to take charge in this area, but, according to Fromm, he lacked a refined understanding of the concept of social character, perhaps because he was unacquainted with the psychoanalytic perspective and lacking in social science training. Fromm reported to Mead that Theodore "showed his antagonism to my methods in no uncertain terms." He seemed not to respect the general direction of the project based on the questionnaires. Theodore also seemed dismissive of the promise of confidentiality that Fromm had given the villagers, and this was a very important issue, perhaps endangering what support Fromm had from the Mexican government. Because of controversies over other local research projects in small Mexican communities, particularly the classic ethnographic study by Oscar Lewis, *The Children of Sanchez*, Fromm feared that carelessness about confidentiality could hurt his reputation as a serious research scholar. Lewis's project had developed a "culture of poverty" thesis as the broad social pattern he was examining, using a specific community as a case study. He argued that in adapting to extreme and persistent poverty, the lives of the poor were, of necessity, entirely oriented to the present. They had no concept of long-term planning or the imperatives of civil society. Very little beyond the family was germane. After the study was published, Lewis's subjects were easy to identify, and to their distress, they were hounded by the media.[27]

Fearing a similar scandal, Fromm (who had sometimes compromised the identity of his clinical patients) was particularly insistent at Chiconcuac on the complete confidentiality of the informants and even the name of the village. What was commonplace and acceptable among anthropologists engaged in ethnographic investigation was a serious ethics violation in the practice of psychoanalysis and kindred clinical approaches. Of course, it was far easier for the clinician to guarantee privacy in the confines of his office than it was for anthropologists engaged in their field research. Based on what Mead had taught them, the Schwartzes assumed that there would be no problem describing and essentially identifying the village and the villagers. With trouble afoot, Theodore charged that Fromm had no idea what ethnographic research entailed: he and his wife were concerned not with specific individuals or their identities but with the broad patterns of a culture. He asked Mead to intervene in their conflict with Fromm and to resolve the dispute. Fromm was infuriated that Theodore had drawn Mead, his longtime friend, into the matter, even though he knew that she understood the ethics of both fields and might be helpful. For his part, Fromm called on Riesman to mediate, knowing that the Schwartzes respected him for his understanding of ethnography, and Riesman also appreciated the ethics of psychoanalytic practice. In the end, Mead and Riesman both worked hard to resolve the dispute, often cooperatively, but they did not succeed.[28]

Although Lola Schwartz was not formally a staff member of the village project, she was completing a dissertation on Chiconcuac villagers and, like Theodore, did not conceal the identities of her subjects in her manuscript. In addition to conflicting sets of ethics, Fromm accused the couple of helping some of the villagers migrate illegally to the United States, an indictment that could influence the government to close down the project. Although Fromm praised the Schwartzes very modestly in *Social Character in a Mexican Village* for gathering data on the lives of the villagers, he felt they were insufficiently deferential to his intentions. Just as he had some difficulty in relinquishing control over the protocols of the Mexican Psychoanalytic Society, Fromm expected to exercise considerable control over his Chiconcuac project and insisted that Theodore recognize "that he was employed to help in a study the aims of which were set" by him. However, when it became clear that neither Theodore nor Lola would subordinate their ethnographic research agendas to Fromm's exploration of his concept of social character, among other items, Fromm was intent on firing them. Coupled with their violation of confidentiality, he noted gross disparities between the field observations of the Schwartzes and the preliminary responses to his questionnaires. When he took measures to replace them, Theodore fought back, writing to Mead, Riesman, and others that Fromm himself was the source of problems in the study. According to Schwartz, Fromm "felt uncomfortable surrounded by the village people . . . overwhelmed by their needs" and hardly ever drove down from his home in Cuernavaca to be with them. Writing to Riesman in early January 1967, Theodore accused Fromm (perhaps excessively) of being dictatorial: "In spite of the fact that he set his life against authoritarianism, I found him often authoritarian though he strove against this tendency in himself when he recognized it. His self-knowledge seemed to me far less complete than he believed."[29]

Before the conflict with the Schwartzes became unmanageable, Riesman put Fromm in contact with Michael Maccoby, who was finishing a doctorate in social psychology while assisting McGeorge Bundy, the dean of Harvard College. Riesman wielded great influence with the Harvard faculty, had mentored Maccoby, and was favorably disposed toward Fromm's Chiconcuac project as a means of grounding the concept of social character. Indeed, Riesman reiterated to Bundy, Maccoby, and others that Fromm's acquainting him with that concept in the 1940s provided the basis for the distinction between "inner" and "other" direction in his 1950 classic *The Lonely Crowd*. Coincidentally, like Fromm, Maccoby had been attracted to rabbinical and Talmudic studies. He was not only conversant with most of Fromm's books but admired Fromm's political activism for nuclear disarmament and his socialist humanism. Fromm in turn was impressed by Maccoby's general understanding of social and political theory, his mastery of statistical techniques, and his skill with projective psychological testing. Maccoby had studied briefly with Robert Redfield, who had written about the nearby village of Tepotzlan and had emphasized the value of the comparative study of peasant culture. Fromm asked whether Maccoby might want to join his staff (which still included the Schwartzes) as a researcher. Maccoby was interested but hardly sold on the idea of working with Fromm on the Chiconcuac project.[30]

By 1960, Fromm's problems with the Schwartzes had become so acute that he asked Riesman to help him persuade Maccoby to work for him so he could replace the couple. Riesman recommended that Fromm invite Maccoby to Cuernavaca for a visit. Maccoby arrived, and an instant and life-long bond of trust and camaraderie sealed their friendship. Maccoby understood that in addition to Fromm's strong desire to improve conditions in the village, he was determined to demonstrate his concept of social character not only empirically but statistically, through his revised and more psychoanalytically organized questionnaire. Maccoby's extensive training in quantitative techniques and institutional research exceeded Theodore Schwartz's. Moreover, he had far more sympathy with Fromm's rather idiosyncratic fusion of Freud and Marx and how it was basic to the concept of social character. Fromm intended the Schwartzes to introduce Maccoby to the villagers and wanted Maccoby immediately to become his major understudy. Sensing Fromm's eagerness to include him on the project and aware that Fromm had analyzed Riesman, Maccoby requested that when the institutional arrangements for his work were in place, Fromm give him a personal analysis followed by a training analysis in clinical technique. Fromm agreed, and Maccoby joined the project.[31]

Maccoby moved to Cuernavaca with his family in 1960, and he and Fromm quickly became solid colleagues on the Chiconcuac study. As Fromm promised, Maccoby became his analysand. Since his departure from the Frankfurt Institute, Fromm knew that save for Riesman, he lacked a steady long-term critic of his research and writing who accepted him on his own terms. To be sure, Fromm always considered Maccoby his "junior" as a scholar and student of social character and never saw him as the sort of hardnosed critic of his work that Horkheimer or Lowenthal had been. But Fromm appreciated that he and Maccoby usually thought alike and that, unlike the Schwartzes, Maccoby had Fromm's interests at heart. They exchanged jokes, read one another's drafts, and greatly enjoyed the work involved in research and writing. Before he moved to Cuernavaca, Maccoby considered himself a humanist socialist. During his work with Fromm, he began to consider himself more a social commentator who might address broad social issues. Recognizing Fromm's minimal grasp of statistics and his intention to be regarded as a social scientist, Maccoby treaded lightly. His discussions with Fromm focused on descriptive and theoretical narrative relating to the villagers. Despite his deficiencies in statistical research, Fromm insisted that it was essential to tabulate the interpretive responses to the questionnaires numerically and to report the psychological testing results statistically. He also wanted to use factor analysis, which involves processing a large number of variables, to demonstrate that similar peasant behaviors could sometimes be the result of different character types.[32]

Like Theodore, Maccoby noted Fromm's disinclination to visit the village. He also told Fromm that his presence in Chiconcuac was unnecessary. Fromm found this comforting, for he was troubled and often sleepless over the level of defeatism, cynicism, alcoholism, and even violence that permeated village life. Indeed, when Fromm discovered that a number of mothers had placed their children in a special village orphanage so the children could receive free social services, he was angry and indignant and assigned Maccoby to stop the practice and address the underlying problem. In sum, Maccoby made almost the perfect project partner for Fromm, and the Schwartzes left in 1961. Maccoby assumed much of the research and methodological concerns, dutifully discussing his findings with Fromm and following the older man's lead in arriving at preliminary conclusions. By 1963, Fromm was comfortable with Maccoby's hard-working, take-charge attitude and found that it complimented his own theoretical background and general supervisory role. A monumental case study of the Chiconcuac peasantry could finally be accomplished. Indeed, Fromm was so confident that Maccoby was moving the project along the right track and was properly attending to the daily work with questionnaires, projective tests, factor analyses, and write-ups of preliminary results that he permitted other projects to consume much of his time, returned to his regular writing schedule, and was happier and more in his element as a result.[33]

Fromm's first heart attack kept him away from Mexico and the Chiconcuac project through much of 1967. That year, Theodore wrote to Fromm from Hawaii that he and Lola wanted to publish their firsthand observations of the villagers even though their accounts of specific individuals violated Fromm's requirement of the strictest confidentiality. The letter arrived during the most critical months of Fromm's recuperation. He fired back a long letter to Theodore informing him that he needed rest rather than attend to this new distraction. Fromm reminded Theodore that the project required that the staff adhere precisely to "psychoanalytic social psychology by the very nature of which there is no description of any one single individual." Fromm would allow the Schwartzes to publish their village material only if it adhered to this requirement. Lola's dissertation clearly did not, Fromm noted, for it was possible to identify the villagers in her narrative. The Schwartzes countered that at the time Lola showed her finished dissertation to Fromm to look over, he had not provided any feedback about it. She therefore assumed Fromm had no objections. She then submitted the completed dissertation to her doctoral committee, and the committee formally approved it. Learning of this, Fromm reprimanded the committee for doing so and asked that it reconsider. The committee refused, posing an important ethical wrinkle. What gave Fromm authority to interfere, as an outsider, with the work of a legitimate faculty committee performing its designated function? Was Fromm in breach of university autonomy in matters such as this? Conversely, what right did Lola have to compromise the guidelines that she had cause to know governed the village project? Should an ethical breach in the workplace preclude use of the accumulated data within a project in academe?[34]

Beyond the dissertation conundrum, Theodore argued that Fromm was impeding the general process of anthropological study and hindering their efforts to publish findings based on two years of fieldwork. To conclude matters, Fromm pleaded with Theodore to move beyond "the atmosphere of annoyance and recriminations" and that "my physical condition makes it inadvisable" to go on fighting. Riesman, also aware of Fromm's fragile health, once more played the role of intermediary and tried to mollify the Schwartzes. The problem resolved itself when Theodore received a professorial appointment at UCLA and became preoccupied with other matters, freeing Fromm and Maccoby to wrap up *Social Character in a Mexican Village* without his interference. In her evaluation of the entire dispute, Mead got it right. What Fromm considered an ethical breach from the perspective of a psychoanalyst, she maintained, was no breach at that time in the professional training of anthropologists. Ethics here did not cross disciplines, and there was no universal standard for ethical inquiry.[35]

By the time his book was almost completed, Fromm seemed somewhat more robust. He wrote a portion of the first chapter on theory and methodology and the eleventh, concluding chapter. Maccoby assumed responsibility for the rest. He sent each chapter draft to Fromm for critique. Often the two met to discuss potential revisions, and then Maccoby would finalize a chapter. A chapter might be rewritten and revised several times before it met with Fromm's approval. In late April 1968, Fromm wrote to Mead that there was a rapidly evolving "manuscript between Maccoby and myself which we are constantly revising." The manuscript would soon be ready for publication.[36]

Unlike Fromm's other books, *Social Character in a Mexican Village* did not make for quick, arresting reading, weighed down as it was by the methodological discussions, tables, and statistics that Fromm wanted Maccoby to include. Maccoby, who did most of the writing, lacked Fromm's gift for eloquent prose, rich metaphors, and choice phrasings. He elaborated the concept of social character very well, however, and he explained the distinction between productive and nonproductive character quite clearly (with perhaps a greater rigidity than Fromm). All of these elements may help in part to explain why it was Fromm's weakest-selling book, but other factors contributed to poor sales as well. The study was a product of the interdisciplinary Culture and Personality movement. This had flourished in the 1930s but was out of fashion by 1970. In addition, influential scholars of the 1960s and 1970s, such as the anthropologist Robert Levine, felt that market economies were the keys to change in locations such as Chiconcuac; Fromm and Maccoby assumed otherwise. Psychoanalysts and social psychologists generally ignored the book because it did not seem pertinent to their own work. Fromm was also distressed when Prentice-Hall "failed completely in giving any publicity to the book." Indeed, Prentice-Hall relinquished publication rights after only seven years. By 1997, no more than 150,000 copies had sold worldwide (which was rather minimal for a Fromm publication), and there were only three translations from the English text—Spanish, Swedish, and German. As might be expected, the most impressive sales for *Social Character in a Mexican Village* came from Mexico. The Spanish edition was reprinted seven times and was used in several university courses. The underlying problem was that the general targeting of the readership for *Social Character in a Mexican Village* was off. It appealed neither to a scholarly nor a popular audience.[37]

Yet even though the narrative line was weighed down by statistics and other details, the book told an arresting story that began with the founding of Chiconcuac. By the 1950s, the town had grown into a poor peasant society consisting of a small group of landowners and a large group of landless peasants and migrants who barely subsisted on their meager wages. The peasants and migrants felt that their lives were constricted by poverty, boredom, and sparse opportunities. Most of the peasant majority lacked productive entrepreneurial skills or the capacity to save what they acquired. According to Fromm and Maccoby, there was a constant "conflict between cynicism and hopelessness on the one hand and faith, often a childlike faith, on the other." Interestingly, this was the same conflict that the Dutch historian Johan Huizinga had portrayed among late medieval European peasants in his classic study *The Waning of the Middle Ages* (1919). Chiconcuac seemed like a throwback in time.

A good deal of Fromm's and Maccoby's narrative concerned Chiconcuac's culture of poverty and despair, where neither literacy nor education was prized. Many chose the less risky (and less profitable) practice of producing sugar cane rather than the more profitable choice of growing rice and vegetables. Cane production required less work and enabled workers to join a government-run cooperative providing medical care and life insurance. Very few planted a combination of more lucrative crops along with a minimal cane crop, which would be a way to garner profits yet remain eligible for the government cooperative. The choice to mix the crops grown was therefore a strong predictor of a villager's social character.[38]

Amid the unstable marriages and high rates of alcoholism that characterized the peasant culture in Chiconcuac, the quality of village life deteriorated. Nevertheless, a privileged elite emerged who worked hard and cultivated profitable rice and vegetable crops. They also prized the modern work skills that were more evident in Mexico City. Unlike most peasants, they trusted their powers of reasoning and understanding and felt confident that they could shape their own lives. Fromm and Maccoby described them as the "new entrepreneurs" who were dominating village government, and they also noted a deepening gap between a minority who felt hopeful and prosperous and the overwhelming majority who were poor and dejected. This was the present and the future of Chiconcuac unless reforms were instituted.[39]

Fromm and Maccoby underscored three institutional resources for reform that stood to enhance life not only in Chiconcuac but in other impoverished peasant villages, their ultimate goal being to find vehicles for mitigating poverty in Third World countries generally. First, the national government's CONASUPO program (Compania Nacional de Subsidios Populares) merited support. It offered to buy (at decent prices and beyond what private buyers would pay) the crops the peasants harvested in their villages. Peasants selected by Chiconcuac and other villages would attend CONASUPO schools for training in weighing and evaluating the quality of their neighbors' crops and providing a legally binding receipt before the crop was deposited in a community silo for wider government distribution. Fromm and Maccoby thought the CONASUPO project would work in Chiconcuac. It protected peasants from the potential price exploitation of private crop speculators and, by showing that the program could be trusted, it helped address the distrustful aspect of peasant life. It was a promising beginning.[40]

The second reformist institution was a large orphanage, Nuestros Pequenos Hermanos (Our Little Siblings), started by Father William Wasson in Cuernavaca. He also accepted a good many orphans and abandoned children from Chiconcuac and surrounding villages. Some of the adolescents had prison records; most of the younger children had lived in violent neighborhoods. Within this devoutly Catholic institution, Wasson promised a secure and "nourishing" space where the children could mature, even though experts predicted he would end up with simply another failed juvenile correctional facility. Almost all of the youngsters proved to be cooperative and responsible, which Fromm and Maccoby attributed to Wasson's refusal to allow his orphanage to become a rule-bound correctional facility. In fact, Wasson regarded the orphanage as a loving family. He minimized bureaucracy and encouraged client self-management. Fromm concluded that Wasson cultivated an atmosphere of trust, productivity, and life affirmation within the community, an atmosphere based on "unconditional love," respect for the rights of others, emphasis on community obligations, and the treatment of each child as a distinct and important individual.[41]

The third example was the Chiconcuac's Boys' Club, which had originated through a cooperative venture between Fromm's small Chiconcuac project research staff and volunteers from the American Friends Service Committee who lived in the village. These two groups organized a group of twenty adolescent boys. Initially, Theodore Schwartz supervised the venture. Maccoby took over in 1961 and used the AFSC volunteers to supervise the boys' activities, which included new methods of farming and animal husbandry. Half of the club's profit from crop sales was reinvested; the other half was distributed to each boy who participated. A small business soon emerged, with regular crops, valuable milk-bearing cows and goats, and hundreds of egg-laying chickens. For a downcast peasant village, this was a major achievement. As the older boys began to guide the younger ones, Maccoby and other project staff consciously assumed more peripheral roles. Several of the boys went on to successful careers, bypassing the general pessimism of the village.[42]

Fromm and Maccoby agreed that the CONASUPO program, Wasson's orphanage, and the Boys' Club had made discernable inroads against traditional defeatist village behavior. Did this suggest a general approach to Third World poverty, they asked, as they compared the successes in Chiconcuac to community work in Sicily conducted by Fromm's friend Danilo Dolci and work in Brazil by another friend, Paolo Freire. In the end, they postulated that reform was possible in all peasant communities, but they rejected the premise of most social researchers of the late 1960s and early 1970s that the answer was in expanding market forces. Programs held the greatest promise when they emphasized productive work through cooperation, education, mutual respect, and love. For Fromm, a "life affirming community" trumped one based on the marketplace. From a lifelong socialist humanist, this was a predictable perspective.[43]

Fromm and Maccoby concluded their study with an unsettling qualifier. The changes they had observed in the village were promising starts, but they were only starts in a long and difficult process. Socioeconomic conditions existing over centuries formed the social character structures within a society, and once these were in place, they resisted change mightily. Human beings took a good long while—often generations—to adapt to fundamental changes in their very character and being. The gloom and despair of most of the Chiconcuac villagers had not lifted, even as life became more hopeful for others who benefited directly from the initial reforms. Despite the enormity of the task ahead, Fromm and Maccoby hoped the exciting changes they had studied would be a spur to other reformist changes and for those to connect to a chain of still others, so that over the generations the pervasive lethargy and despair of most Chiconcauc villagers would recede.[44]

Though Maccoby conducted a disproportionate share of the research and the writing of the book, he emphasized that Fromm had shaped not only the research methods and the conclusions but every other important aspect of the volume, especially the animating narrative line. It was probably Fromm's most evidence-driven publication since the German worker project at the Frankfurt Institute. In brief, it was a solid and important work of scholarship. Fromm's prophetic hope for the village was there, but it tended to be subsumed by layers of data and observations on the despondent and sometimes nearly hopeless quality of much of peasant life. The characteristically buoyant Fromm seemed chastened by the alcoholism, violence, and poverty in the village and by the pervading sense of despair. Published two years after *The Revolution of Hope*, Fromm found *Social Character in a Mexican Village* a much more difficult book to complete, and its storyline was more sober.[45]

Fromm's serious coronary condition may have contributed to his cautionary assessment of Chiconcuac. Maccoby spotted his skepticism and dejection in their regular work sessions on the manuscript. Aniceto Aramoni felt that Fromm's downcast mood was unmistakable whenever they discussed the village project, especially after the heart attack. Indeed, while Fromm made the trip from Cuernavaca to Chiconcuac fairly regularly before his heart attack, there is no record of his traveling there afterward.[46]

The village was not the only project of Fromm's where skepticism and despair were evident. The very limited achievements of the 1968 McCarthy campaign and its aftermath (the election of Richard Nixon) made Fromm apprehensive about the fruits of political activism. Escalating Vietnam War casualties and the danger of global nuclear annihilation also contributed to his deflated spirits. Even the American landing of a man on the moon in July 1969 evoked cynicism. Glowing reports of the moon landing on television were "fraudulent, inhuman, insensitive," Fromm confided to Maccoby, and outer space would soon just become a new battleground for nuclear war. Clearly, the specter of death both personal and global was weighing heavily on Fromm, whose last major book would explore human destructiveness.[47]

12

Love and Death

E ven before 1970, when *Social Character in a Mexican Village* was published, Mexico was wearing a bit thin on Erich and Annis. He had retired from the National Autonomous University in 1965 and also curtailed his responsibilities in the Mexican Psychoanalytic Institute in order to spend more time with her and on his writing projects. Yet the couple thought increasingly of residing again in the United States. Erich's cardiologist in New York had cautioned him against the high altitudes of the Mexican capital. Frequent bouts of shortness of breath made the risk apparent. Moreover, his professional obligations had worn him down. Despite retirement from its faculty, the National Autonomous University continued to call on Fromm for teaching and advisory functions, as did colleagues from the Mexican Psychoanalytic Society and Institute.[1]

It is significant that although Fromm enjoyed Mexican life and culture, he remained involved with customs and developments in the United States. Skilled in learning languages, he had mastered Spanish with ease but preferred to speak in English or German. He enjoyed all but the spiciest Mexican foods and liked a number of the dishes, but more often he ate the foods that he had when he lived in New York. Indeed, an ideal meal consisted of lamb or pasta with steamed vegetables, mashed potatoes, and a tray of fresh fruit, followed by gourmet coffee diluted significantly with cream and a pastry or two. He savored good French wines, and every now and then enjoyed top-of-the-line bourbon. Fromm read Mexican newspapers and magazines and closely followed local and national news. But he kept up with European and American publications and bought the most recent copy of the *New York Times* as soon as it arrived. Fromm liked visits from North American and European friends, intellectuals, clinicians, and artists even as he maintained considerable contact with Mexican psychoanalysts, scholars, and cultural figures. But there was one aspect of Mexican culture to which he refused to accommodate—the sense of time. He was never able to shed the German habit of punctuality. He set off for meetings and appointments with a stiff marching soldierly gait, arriving precisely at the designated hour, and was always dismayed and distressed that his Mexican colleagues were almost invariably tardy.[2]

The most pressing reason for leaving Mexico was hardly the culture and not even the high altitude but Fromm's unease with the increasing factionalism among key figures in the Mexican Psychoanalytic Institute. He did not know how to handle the problem. The more he withdrew from Institute activities, the worse the infighting became. Initially, the disagreement centered on a struggle between three potential successors. Fromm had groomed Alfonso Millán to be the first president of the Mexican Psychoanalytic Society because he was oldest of the three and enjoyed a stellar reputation as a clinician. But Jorge Silva Garcia and Aniceto Aramoni would not accept Fromm's choice. A former soldier and physician, Silva Garcia prized organization and discipline (as Fromm did). He sought a chain of command with himself at the top, which became apparent as he planned the new building to house the Mexican Psychoanalytic Institute. On the other hand, Aramoni was an unusually productive scholar who held Silva Garcia in low regard. Millán aligned with Silva at various times and with Aramoni at others, complicating the leadership struggle. This was exacerbated by a challenge to their hegemony in Mexico after the arrival of several eminent Freudian psychoanalysts from Buenos Aires who turned the longstanding if lackluster and orthodox Mexican society into a significant rival to Fromm's Mexican Psychoanalytic Society and Institute.[3]

Yet Fromm contributed to this troubling state of affairs by favoring Aramoni to succeed him in all of his duties, in hardly subtle and sometimes tasteless ways. He regarded Aramoni not only as a proficient scholar and intellectual but as a talented psychiatrist and psychoanalyst, and he said as much. For Aramoni's daughter, Rebeca, Fromm was a second father. She counted on him for guidance and direction. Aramoni himself never ceased to regard Fromm as his mentor and the permanent leader of the Mexican Institute and considered himself only as a stand-in. Unknown to Silva Garcia, Fromm often briefed Aramoni on Institute organizational and personnel developments and offered his prize student a steady stream of advice. When Aramoni mentioned to Fromm that several Institute students were being considered for admission and others might be expelled, for example, Fromm gave specific recommendations while complaining that Aramoni and other senior analysts had "to take the responsibility in my absence." Part of the difficulty, therefore, was not only that Fromm overtly favored Aramoni but that he was unwilling to separate himself from the politics that he found so distressing and draining.[4]

Since early 1967, when they first visited Locarno, near the Switzerland-Italy border, as part of Erich's recovery from his massive heart attack, the couple had been delighted by the town: it was at a lower altitude and had a milder climate in spring and summer, with pleasant winters. Locarno was also attractive because it revived Fromm's sense of being not only a citizen of the world but also a European. It was not far from Germany and was also a short train ride away from Zurich and his closest living relative—his bright and delightful psychoanalyst cousin, Gertrud Hunziker-Fromm. She and Joseph Gurland, Henny's son, were the only relatives he still regarded as family. Fromm also found that he could write more efficiently during short stays in Locarno than he had been able to in Mexico. There were also tax benefits to living in Switzerland. As well, he and Annis liked exploring the small villages and their surrounding pine forests. They often spent warm days enjoying the Black Forest spas in Hinterzarten and Baden Baden. Fromm wrote to Clara Urquhart that he enjoyed "my secluded life in Locarno and work with great pleasure."[5]

The friends Fromm made during his summers in Locarno were evolving into a circle of convivial colleagues, reminiscent of the close and often emotionally grounding or stabilizing intellectual circles he had been a part of since the 1930s. The group now included Max Kreutzberger, a German Jew and retired director of the Leo Baeck Institute; Boris Luban-Plozza, an ambitious doctor from Ascona; and Ivan Illich, his former neighbor from Cuernavaca. Kreutzberger had lived in Palestine for twenty years, where he had opposed the formation of the Jewish state, and, like Fromm, he was displeased with the Israeli discrimination against Arabs. He and Fromm often sat at a table piled high with books and joyously examined passages together, much like Talmudic scholars. Luban-Plozza was active in the psychoanalyst Michael Balint's movement to enhance doctor-patient communication. Fromm recommended that he become a clinician and trained him in therapeutic technique. Fromm was also attracted by the integrity, kindness, and profound ethical commitments of Luban-Plozza's wife, Wilma. She was remarkably bright, if usually silent, in the circle's discussions, but Fromm found that what she did say was always very profound. Gertrud and Max Hunziker-Fromm often joined them from Zurich. Fromm loved to cook with Max, sometimes for the entire circle of colleagues. Periodically, the two could be found in their stockings sliding down the hall of a hotel. Illich now spent much of his time in France and Germany, and Fromm delighted in his wry sense of humor and his intellect. A longstanding critic of medical, educational, and other established institutions, Illich was a European celebrity and was especially admired by the French Left. As a Roman Catholic priest, he had run afoul of both the Vatican and the CIA. Through Kreutzberger, Fromm had also been introduced to Nyanaponika Mahathera. Born a Jew and Kreutzberger's school companion in Germany, he fled the Nazis and ended up in an internment camp. After Kreutzberger moved to Locarno, Nyanaponika often visited him. By that time, he had become a charismatic Sri Lankan Buddhist spiritual leader even as he continued to study Western classics. Since the death of Suzuki, Fromm had been searching for a spiritual mentor. He had always sensed a conflict (despite Suzuki's eclecticism) between Zen Buddhism's deeply antirational approach and his own priorities of love and reason. An exponent of Theravada Buddhism, Nyanaponika's *The Heart of Buddhist Meditation* embraced reasoned "mindfulness" far more than Suzuki had, and he persuaded Fromm to resume meditation exercises as a method of integrating Buddhism with the values of Western Enlightenment. Fromm spent hours listening to him describe his celebration of joyous living shorn of greed or hatred. The fellowship of colleagues such as these merged well with the other benefits of Locarno.[6]

In September 1973, when Erich and Annis decided to settle in Locarno year round, he finally made a full break from the Mexican Psychoanalytic Institute, despite the fact that Aramoni and other trainees tried to lure him back. By the fall of 1974, he told Aramoni that there was no turning back; he was "so completely immersed in my [writing] work . . . and enjoy so much going ahead with it" that he would no longer involve himself with the Institute: "If I were in Mexico I would just get involved with many divergent interests and be used by each group in their fight against the others. I am at this point just too old to indulge in this." Aramoni, Silva, and other senior Institute analysts continued trying to woo Fromm back in the years that followed, but to no effect. In February 1976, he wrote to Aramoni that he was putting his Cuernavaca house on the market: "As long as I can write I probably shall not want to lose energy and time" traveling between Cuernavaca and Locarno. Fromm asked his Institute colleagues to

mail him all his books and correspondence files. Fromm had finally decided to spend his last few years, "if I should live that long," in Europe.[7]

During his decades in Mexico, Fromm employed personal secretaries
who typed his manuscripts from handwritten drafts, which he then edited
and they retyped. They also took dictation for his voluminous personal
and professional correspondence. Since the mid-1950s, Beatrice ("Trixie")
Meyer had been especially important to Fromm. When he constructed the
Cuernavaca house, he assigned Meyer a special study off the long porch
that overlooked the lawn and gardens. Save for Fromm's own study, this
was the optimal place for writing and reflection. Suspecting a romantic liaison with her husband, Annis disliked Meyer. Nevertheless, Fromm kept
her on in Mexico well into the 1970s. For Annis, the move to Locarno resolved this problem; Meyer's Locarno successor, Joan Hughes, whom Annis liked, was a very reserved and plain-looking British woman with a dry
wit, a frumpy wardrobe, and apparently minimal sexual appeal. Hughes
had boundless energy and a schoolmarm's proficiency. She meticulously
checked over Fromm's manuscript drafts and made sure that his publishing deadlines were met. Hughes typed without error and kept Fromm
abreast of his daily correspondence. Unlike "Trixie," Fromm always called
her "Mrs. Hughes," keeping the relationship distant and professional.[8]

Substantially downsizing, Erich and Annis bought a modest apartment
in the Casa La Monda complex in Moralto (a district of Locarno) and furnished it very simply. They enjoyed a breathtaking fifth-floor view of Lake
Maggiore and the peak of Mount Gambarogno on the opposite shore.
Fromm drafted his remaining works at a desk looking out upon that view.
Adjacent shelves were stuffed with source materials; manuscript drafts
were piled high on his desk. It became necessary for him to rent a first-floor
room to contain the overflow of books and other materials sent from Mexico. Fromm vowed to spend his remaining days writing and publishing.[9]

Quest for Scholarship

Fromm rarely practiced psychoanalysis in Locarno. Indeed, he had taken
on very few analysands during his last years in Mexico. Yet what amounted
to an analysis through years of correspondence with Chaim Kaplan, a
young postal worker turned sometime Talmudic scholar, heavily affected
Fromm in his last years. Their exchange mixed personal troubles (primar-

ily Kaplan's but to a lesser extent Fromm's) with major scholarly concerns and Kaplan's writing projects. Kaplan's presence seemed to prompt Fromm to systematize and deepen his research for *The Anatomy of Human Destructiveness*, his last major scholarly undertaking, and to complete the book after what, for him, was an inordinate number of years. In turn, Kaplan, who may have been schizophrenic, was helped in very significant ways through his contact with Fromm.

Fromm encouraged Kaplan to pursue his Talmudic studies, guiding his study of Talmudic texts and of classic commentaries on those texts. Some of his letters addressed Kaplan's delays in finishing an anthology, critiqued Kaplan's other projects, and advised the young man on his professional and family life. When Kaplan graduated from Yeshiva College, Fromm recommended that he pursue the rabbinate. The underlying problem, from Fromm's perspective, was that Kaplan could not summon "the courage and the confidence to be yourself."[10]

In turn, Kaplan's work plus the Mexican village project rekindled Fromm's commitment to scholarly investigation. The preponderance of Fromm's books had strayed from serious scholarship until he teamed up with Michael Maccoby. Although Maccoby publicly gave Fromm credit for the essentials of the book, the fact was that Maccoby did most of the research and wrote the first drafts of most of the chapters. The question now was whether Fromm would be up to a sequel—another work of serious scholarship—but this time entirely on his own. In the course of his exchanges with Kaplan and a false start or two, Fromm determined that *The Anatomy of Human Destructiveness* would be that sequel. Kaplan agreed, sensing that despite his advanced years Fromm was up to it.[11]

However, before he took on the *Anatomy* project, Fromm had intended to finish a massive work: four volumes on what he called "humanistic" psychoanalysis. Given his substantial income from royalties, it is curious that he sought funding from the Lillia Hyde Foundation. The volumes would represent a thoroughgoing extension of Freud's theoretical framework beyond its focus on the instincts and would embrace a humanistic existentialist alternative. Drawing substantially on his clinical work, the project would be framed around his core concept of social character. Once again, he would be grappling with integrating Freud's "modernist" agenda, focused on instinctual life, particularly the libido, with his alternative formulation—that external social structures shaped instinctual life. Fromm planned to finish the project in two years. Because he was proposing not much more than a detailed and nuanced version of many earlier writings, and given the amazing speed with which he completed books, he probably expected that two years was sufficient. But he was overlooking one essential: that scholarly work took a good deal more time and effort. Moreover, he had never before undertaken such a large project. In addition, he was apprehensive that the clinical materials he planned to use for the project might violate the confidentiality of his patients. And finally, his heart attack in December 1966 and his substantial recovery period delayed the launching of the project and could continue to do so.

Early in 1970, Fromm published a rather insubstantial book. Initially, it was intended to be the first of the four volumes. Titled *The Crisis of Psychoanalysis*, it sold eight hundred thousand copies in sixteen languages. At this point in his career, Fromm's name alone seemed to assure substantial sales, at least for the preponderance of his publications. The book consisted of Fromm's essays written between 1932 and 1969 on the interrelationship between psychoanalytic and sociological perspectives. The one new essay in the collection, "The Crisis of Psychoanalysis," argued that psychoanalysis had initially been a radical and penetrating theory on the repression of sexuality that flew in the face of middle-class respectability. But Freud's followers bureaucratized the psychoanalytic movement, buried the radical critique, and acquiesced in pressures for social conformity. For Fromm, this bureaucratization explained why contemporary psychoanalysis was in crisis and fast becoming irrelevant. Of course, this assertion underscored the fact that Freud's libidinal focus was at odds with Fromm's concept of social character. Was his social character construct therefore part of the contemporary crisis? Here Fromm might simply have stated that initially he was an adherent of Freud's "modernist" agenda but had gradually built his social character construct as an improvement on it.[12]

Fromm had harbored his misgivings about the bureaucratization of psychoanalytic orthodoxy since the late 1940s, so in essence he was not staking out new territory. But there was something unexpected in *The Crisis of Psychoanalysis*: a succinct but telling three-page epilogue. It underscored what an apprehensive social commentator Fromm had become, believing as he did that war was a function of the aggressions built into the nation-state. By some point in the next half-century, he predicted, life on Earth would cease to exist, owing to nuclear, chemical, and biological warfare between nations. Paul Goodman, the social critic, and the biologist Paul Ehrlich issued similar warnings. Invoking *The Heart of Man*, Fromm attributed this horrifying outcome to necrophilia, claiming that the love of death had become a pathological perversion among global leaders, even as they appealed to honor, order, property, and a mythic golden age while promising a free and glorious future. He then pointed out the heroic biologists, economists, theologians, and philosophers protesting against the politics of necrophilia. But psychoanalysts, freed of their conformist perspectives, were especially capable of exposing the dangerous attitudes of the politicians. Indeed, they were equipped to help all of humanity, as they could better spot those leaders who promoted aggression and death behind their lofty ideologies—"to see them for what they are, and not for what they say."[13]

More concisely than *The Heart of Man*, these concluding pages in *The Crisis of Psychoanalysis* made the case for the urgency of the human situation. Fromm's discussion was polemical, amorphous, often illogical, and wholly lacking in evidence. Instead, he offered the world the words of a prophet determined somehow to move a threatened world away from the precipice. More specifically, what might he do to maximize his effectiveness? Fromm was less disposed in late life to speak at peace rallies, sign petitions, and dash off opinion columns, as they represented the various faces of polemic discourse that, for the most part, had not persuaded policy makers of the potential destruction at hand. The threat of nuclear extinction seemed no less real in the late 1960s and early 1970s than earlier, Fromm claimed. Despite his contacts with high-level American political figures like William Fulbright and, more recently, Edward Kennedy, he was apparently unfamiliar with the array of safety procedures and understandings the Americans and the Soviets had put into place to avert a repeat of the Cuban Missile Crisis.[14]

Putting aside many of his protest tools of the past, Fromm sought an effective way to persuade scholars, policy makers, and power brokers of the looming conflagration. Perhaps he might write something new, different, and scholarly concerning the human condition, something that might have the influence that his polemics seemed to lack. Kaplan was telling him, loud and clear, what he had often told Kaplan: dispassionate scholarship and rigorous analysis just might have a real effect on the world.

Fromm decided that the last pages of *The Crisis of Psychoanalysis* were hardly enough. He would put aside the next three volumes in the project and focus on a long single volume titled *The Anatomy of Human Destructiveness*. In this effort, he was determined to learn from and be respectful

of research scholars in a variety of disciplines, especially the neurosciences, in which most psychoanalysts were terribly deficient. He would
seek out the formidable critics he had generally bypassed since *Escape from
Freedom*. Maccoby had tactfully suggested that Fromm stop relying on
old and often superseded data to support his conceptual dispositions. So
Fromm plunged into research, reading scholarly literature on a variety of
new topics and at an exhaustive pace. His bookshelves in Locarno soon
filled up with the publications of formidable scholars and researchers in
various disciplines. Kaplan, strongly interested in the sciences, mailed
Fromm several books. Fromm hired Jerome Brams, a clinical psychologist
by training who he happened to like, even though Brams was unfamiliar
with neuroscience, physical anthropology, or other areas of inquiry. Nor
was Brams experienced in finding pertinent, state-of-the-art publications
in research libraries. Scarcely more equipped than Brams for such an undertaking, Fromm understood at almost an intuitive level that this was his
last opportunity to inform his writings with close scholarship and textual
exploration. As such, he proceeded along a time-consuming path without
a proficient research assistant. It was a path that few social commentators
had been willing to walk during their final years. Fromm acknowledged to
Annis that he needed to live three more decades to complete *The Anatomy
of Human Destructiveness* and then continue on to other scholarly projects
on his agenda.[15]

Lorenz and Skinner

In addition to his desire to produce a thoroughly researched scholarly
work, Fromm was motivated by the publication and distressing reception
of Konrad Lorenz's influential, if strongly polemical, *On Aggression* in
German in 1963 and in English translation three years later. Fromm initially read *On Aggression* with considerable distaste, but he considered the
argument so flawed that he assumed it would not be taken seriously.
Fromm found otherwise when he met his good friend Senator Fulbright
in Geneva and found that he was enormously impressed with Lorenz's
book. And Fromm acknowledged that other popular polemics published at
roughly the same time—among them Robert Ardrey's *African Genesis*
(1961) and *The Territorial Imperative* (1967) and Desmond Morris's *The
Naked Ape* (1967), which explored the same theme on innate human

aggressiveness—helped give Lorenz's book very wide currency and attendant celebrity status.[16]

An Austrian-born founder of ethnology but also a paleontologist and physician, Lorenz had embraced the chauvinistic concept of German "racial strength"—the biologically pure and racially superior Aryan uncontaminated by lesser peoples—which was perhaps the core premise of the Nazi vision of the good society. In the early 1940s, Lorenz served on the medical staff of the German army. Anticipated by his earlier writings, *On Aggression* postulated that man, like other animals, was a passive creature governed by his genetic inheritance. Fromm found this position repulsive. Lorenz also insisted that aggressive impulses were innate, had a genetic component, and were intended for species preservation. Man was hostage to these inborn impulses; he resorted to aggression to gain territory and other goods that assured "the survival of the group." For Lorenz, aggression limited the distribution of a species in a propitious way, assuring the survival of the strongest and the protection of its offspring. Fromm determined to focus his research on human aggression and offer an alternative explanation.[17]

Fromm's outrage at Lorenz's thesis was predictable. As early as 1949, in his essay "Psychoanalytic Characterology and Its Application to the Understanding of Culture," Fromm questioned whether aggressive impulses were innate, insisting that the premise had never been validated by systematic research. He began *The Anatomy of Human Destructiveness* by reiterating this point. But his initial tone in taking on Lorenz was polemical, and he never entirely shed that tone as his book progressed. Even as it is understandable that a Jewish émigré from Hitler's Germany would harbor strong hostilities toward an ex-Nazi who had never convincingly recanted, Fromm's tone ran at cross purposes with his quest to present an extended interdisciplinary study through meticulous scholarship.

Fromm charged that Lorenz's assertions were offensive and dangerous, denying the very choices and responsibilities that characterized a human being. Lorenz also rationalized the violence and brutality of the modern state as a normal manifestation of human aggression. And most disturbing, Lorenz discounted the human capacity to avert the most dangerous form of aggression—nuclear war. In sum, Fromm charged that Lorenz explained away all forms of human aggression in his "insane" premise that they were "due to biological factors beyond human control." Beyond this public rebuttal, Fromm wrote to Riesman that he could pin down concretely the dangers of Lorenz's perspective. As it happened, Fromm had chanced across an obscure 1940 paper in which Lorenz defended Nazi laws for the elimination of "inferior types" to help realize the "biological necessities" of the alleged German race. It is unclear why Fromm made no mention of this paper in *Anatomy*. Writing to Ernst Simon, Fromm insisted that Lorenz had always been a "reactionary nationalist" and a Social Darwinist who defied abundant anthropological, social, and psychological evidence to assert that "aggression is innate in man" and could not be averted. He would write at least the first part of *Anatomy* to refute Lorenz's harmful premises: to demonstrate that there was nothing innately biological or socially inevitable about human aggression. Man could forestall destructive aggressiveness, including violence and war, through his own volition. He had the capacity to shape his own social, economic, and political circumstances to assure peace and tranquility.[18]

Fundamentally, Lorenz's assertion of biological determinism was troublesome for Fromm for the same reasons that Freud's formulation seemed incomplete. Perhaps hoping somehow to solidify his distance from Lorenz, Fromm did not acknowledge that his biophilia/necrophilia dialectic was both an extension and a modification of Freud's eros and thanatos binary. Fromm underscored a significant difference: Freud's dialectic was rooted in biological instincts and not in the specific social circumstances he had emphasized. Fromm was essentially electing not to engage the fact that eros (like biophilia) represented life, love, hope, and contact with other living organisms so that they could thrive. In contrast, thanatos (like necrophilia) represented the quest for the inorganic at some level, even a return to the painlessness of the womb. As Fromm sought to shift the duality from one that involved instincts to one that was socially grounded, he made his case largely through assertion rather than nuanced argument accompanied by evidence. Had he acknowledged that, differences aside (and assuredly significant differences), he was essentially amplifying and putting a special twist on Freud's eros/thanatos duality, Fromm would have been able to use Freud to good advantage in building his case against Lorenz.

Fromm had spent years critiquing Freud's hydraulic theory of the instincts: the premise that there were pent-up energy sources that sought release. In *Beyond the Pleasure Principle* (1920), Freud altered his depiction of a clash between sexual instincts and the ego, characterizing instead a clash between eros and thanatos. Freud postulated that thanatos, the death

instinct, was the most invidious form of aggression and that it was countered by a strong life instinct (eros). Lorenz found no such counterpoint in
his characterization of the instinct of aggressiveness that simply assaulted
or destroyed other living forms. Here, too, Fromm could have used Freud
to better advantage.

Fromm pointed out how Lorenz embraced a "romantic, nationalist pa-
ganism" that assigned to man the same innate and instinctive aggressiveness as is discerned in certain birds or fish or other animal species—it
simply could not be contained in the interests of "civilization" or any other
human goal. Lorenz failed to realize what Darwin had explained and
Freud and Fromm had understood: unlike these species, man had evolved
to the point where he developed a capacity for reason, logic, and empathy.
There was abundant evidence, Fromm postulated, as Freud recognized
before him, that man could transcend the destructive aggressiveness of
less evolved animals. Moreover, Fromm envisioned far more than the man-
ageable unhappiness required for social cohesion for which Freud was
willing to settle. But he insisted that Freud's posture was far more thoughtful and modestly more hopeful than Lorenz's.[19]

The starkness of Lorenz's argument provoked an almost equally stark
retort from Fromm. Perhaps because of their intellectual differences, each
adapted the portion of Darwin's outline of the evolutionary process that fit
his perspective. Lorenz focused on the revengeful and aggressive qualities
of animals necessary for primates and man in order to survive. Fromm
expounded on the Darwin who described man's qualities of self-conscious-
ness, reasoning, and even aesthetic sensibilities as man distanced himself
from less evolved species.

To be sure, Fromm read very widely not only to contest Lorenz but also
to lay the groundwork for the rest of *Anatomy*, and he attempted to become
conversant with scholarship in genetics, physical and comparative anthropology, animal behavior, cognitive psychology, linguistics, the neurosciences, and other fields on both sides of the science/humanities divide.
However, the assignment was huge, and corners had to be cut, and he
necessarily had to treat most of the available research in cursory fashion.
Even though he might partially have compensated for his lack of expertise
by evaluating the internal logic of the research materials he studied,
Fromm took a reasonable course. He confided to Fulbright that it would
have taken far more than the half-dozen years he put into *Anatomy*. The
book was "even now only a rough outline of what should be a work of three

or four volumes if I had the time to write them." Like most of his writing after he left the Frankfurt Institute, it was a volume that might "suggest further studies" based on more substantial research.[20]

If Fromm considered Lorenz's view of inherent human destructiveness wrongheaded, B. F. Skinner's position on behavioral conditioning struck him as equally so. The doctrine of behaviorism, originated by John B. Watson early in the twentieth century, argued against the value of human passions in trying to understand human behavior. Rather, what was relevant was to detect and modify "scientifically" the precise external reinforcements that shaped human behavior. Skinner's popular extension of Watson ("neobehaviorism") focused on "operant" conditioning—the systematic application of positive reinforcements to alter the behaviors of animals and humans along "socially desired" lines. Skinner found relevance in man's genetic endowment, but that aside, both animal and human behavior were wholly determined by externally applied reinforcement. Man was essentially malleable, and nothing in his nature was above alteration for socially desired ends. Hatred, aggression, and other forms of untoward conduct could be obliterated with appropriate external manipulation. Whereas Lorenz postulated that aggression was innate and could not be curtailed, Skinner held the opposite: deleterious aggressive behaviors could readily be modified through social conditioning. Fromm held firm to his position between the two.[21]

Much like his ideologically driven dismissal of Lorenz, Fromm dismissed Skinner's perspective with minimal resort to the close, reasoned scholarship he admired in Kaplan. For Fromm, Skinner was simply wrong in asserting that aggression could be contained or eliminated by managing the environment. Skinner's fallacy was to ignore man's internal emotional world and, indeed, human complexity. What the Skinnerian behavioral tradition failed to recognize was that man was a totality—a complex whole with a personality, a social character, interior motives, and intense passions all working in tandem. In brief, Skinner was overlooking man's active, responsible, and reflective role in society. As Skinner justified an emerging technocratic or cybernetic society that manipulated man's labor, consumption, and thought so that he became "adjusted" to dominant institutions and ideologies, he overlooked the fate of man and how man grew alienated from himself. Indeed, Skinner's vision threatened man's very being, replacing it with a meek, alienated self: "Skinner recommends the hell of the isolated, manipulated man of the cybernetic age as the heaven of progress. He dulls our fears of where we are going" while insisting that modern industrialism and its myriad controls can produce a utopia— a peaceful social order without aggression and based on "scientific humanism."[22]

Fromm cited a good deal of scholarship critical of Skinner. With important exceptions, however, he did not engage the logic, consistency, or evidence behind a scholar's conclusion. For example, he cited a Carl Rogers exchange with Skinner but did not critique the rather straightforward and problematic argument that Rogers advanced. More importantly, he lauded Noam Chomsky's acclaimed 1959 review of Skinner's *Verbal Behavior* and Chomsky's subsequent critique of the linguistic position of behaviorism. Chomsky theorized that mankind shared innate linguistic capacities—the inherent ability to generate words and sentences—which was an argument antithetical to Skinner's view of language as an array of conditioned responses. Fromm tended to agree with Chomsky, though he disagreed with Chomsky's consistent essentialism. Bypassing the opportunity to reconcile his differences with Chomsky, Fromm took the easy path: Chomsky presented his case against Skinner "so thoroughly" and "brilliantly" that he did not need to address Chomsky's biological determinism. Fromm embraced Kenneth MacCorquodale's important 1970 critique of Skinner's premises and Hasan Ozbekhan's much-cited and even more critical 1966 paper, "The Triumph of Technology," but he failed to evaluate the logic behind either essay.[23]

The Human Disposition

Finding nothing in either Lorenz or Skinner to explain man's aggressive and destructive nature, Freud's drive theory was therefore suspect; Fromm directed much of *Anatomy of Human Destructiveness* to his own answer to the question. Before it became part of his book, Fromm sketched out his answer in an August 1971 letter to Urquhart: "Human destructiveness is not caused by animal inheritance but by the existential condition of man, which under certain conditions results in destructiveness and cruelty much greater than that of any animal on the basis of instincts." But the main potential for aggression is mobilized by external social circumstances "which in themselves can be changed." This was congruent with Fromm's humanist frame of reference, where potential for good and evil in modern man rested on an inner disposition molded by outward social structures.[24]

Fromm synthesized J. P. Scott's research on animal aggression, which supported his own views that animal aggression was externally, not internally, initiated. He also cited research on primate behavior, proposing that the lack of territorialism in primates indicated that competition for territory was not the basis for human aggressiveness. Thus, it followed that destructive aggression was a human problem, but the problem did not begin with the earliest human societies. There was disequilibrium in early humans between their instincts and their cerebral development, Fromm explained, but this disequilibrium did not result in destructive aggression. For support, Fromm relied not only on anthropological studies but also geological, ethnological, and social research concerning primitive hunters and food gatherers that contradicted the popular stereotype of early man as a "killer." His point was that malignant aggression was neither instinctive nor otherwise inherent in the human condition. This posture was also congruent with the Culture and Personality movement in which Fromm had been a participant. It stressed the significance of cultures and societies rather than inborn characteristics as the major influence on individual thoughts and behaviors.[25]

Fromm stuck closely to mainstream scholarship in arguing that man's animal heritage did not demonstrate that he was inherently aggressive. But his adherence to established research literature began to weaken in his coverage of the beginnings of organized food-producing societies that prioritized consumption, territoriality, exploitation, and sometimes cruelty—the beginnings of man's destructive propensities. Here Fromm drew heavily on the speculations of Marx, Engels, and Bachofen. But he was dismissive of scholarship that pointed to inborn patterns of destructiveness. Indeed, he would not give any credence to the contention that destructiveness was "part of human nature." If man, beyond his most primitive food-gathering existence, had sometimes become "the only primate who can feel intense pleasure in killing and torturing," it was essential that this trait never be characterized as a core quality in "human nature." Finding pleasure in aggression and slaughter was an existential choice of some men under certain conditions. However, if aggression and destructiveness were caused by human agency, Fromm insisted that they could also be averted by human agency.[26]

Malignant Aggression

In the remainder of *Anatomy*, Fromm explicated the different types of human aggressiveness and destructiveness that occurred after the key historic disjunction—the point at which some men were willing to torture and kill. Here Fromm distinguished "benign" from "malignant" aggression. "Benign" aggression included accidents, playful contests that were not intended to hurt, many acts of self-assertion, a mindless determination to achieve a goal, and the defense of a perceived vital interest. Pressures to conform socially sometimes prompted benign aggression. But it was "malignant aggression" (the joy in killing) that became Fromm's focus.[27]

Whereas Fromm had discussed the struggle between biophilia and necrophilia in *The Heart of Man* (1964), he honed in on that binary in *The Anatomy of Human Destructiveness*, where his focus was on the propensity for "malignant aggression" in complex societies. Why was man in "civilized" societies so biologically maladaptive? Fromm largely bypassed Freud's response to this question in *Civilization and Its Discontents* (1930)— that suppression of the libido became essential for a cohesive "civilized" society. Having strayed from Freud's focus on instincts as he built his concept of social character, Fromm asked a different set of questions. Since man was not wholly dominated by instincts, why had he, at least in certain situations, shown himself to be "a killer and destroyer of his own species without any rational gain?" Why did he sometimes lust to control, harm, and destroy others? What was there in minimal instinctive determination and maximal brain development that led some down this path?[28]

Consistent with Fromm's disposition for opposites, which afforded him "answers" in fields of great complexity, Fromm divided malignant destructiveness into two forms. There was spontaneous destructiveness, which rose to the surface owing to extraordinary external circumstances. Wars, religious or political conflicts, struggles over scarce resources, and even a sense of individual insignificance contributed to this malignant behavior. It was action born of frenzy uncontrolled by conventional inhibitory forces. The violent outbreak between Muslims and Hindus during the partition of India, which contributed to hundreds of thousands of deaths, was one example. The anticommunist purge in Indonesia in 1965, where perhaps a million alleged communists and many Chinese were slaughtered, was another. Real or imagined atrocities brought on by real or imagined events could prompt violent revenge.[29]

Although spontaneous aggression signaled a terrible "malignancy," what worried Fromm more was the second form, where aggression was rooted in man's character structure—in that part of his already socialized self that was influenced by society. His concept of social character housed the answer. Fromm argued that the sadistic aspect of the authoritarian character type and the necrophilic character type operated in tandem, forming a partnership between the two most evil potentialities of the human condition. To illustrate the interplay between sadism and necrophilia, Fromm moved into the most interesting and consequential part of *Anatomy*. Indeed, it had the essentials of a book in itself, focusing first on Heinrich Himmler, the erstwhile head of the SS, and then Adolf Hitler. The two of them were responsible for the deaths of millions of people, left Europe in ruins, and attested to the depravity of man. Though research in several parts of *Anatomy* had been thin, Fromm was on firmer footing in modern German history, where he was conversant with much of the scholarship on these two men.

Fromm referred to Himmler as one of the most brutal sadists and exemplars of necrophilia in modern times. To characterize Himmler, Fromm borrowed from his explanation of the sadomasochist core of the authoritarian personality in *Escape from Freedom*. Himmler showed that sadism could emerge from a life devoid of love, creative productivity, or joy and lead to a life of apparent omnipotence. The latter quality provoked a seeming capacity to control other human beings completely while turning them into detested objects and inflicting pain on them. In addition to borrowing from *Escape*, Fromm almost certainly drew on Hannah Arendt's works, especially *Origins of Totalitarianism* (1950) and *Eichmann in Jerusalem* (1963). Though he did not cite either book in *Anatomy*, his description of Himmler at once differed from and resembled Arendt's treatment of Eichmann. While Fromm examined Himmler's sadism, Arendt characterized both Nazis as skilled and efficient managers/administrators of agony and mass extermination. Fromm, too, acknowledged certain qualities of bureaucratic efficiency in Himmler and, moreover, referred explicitly to Himmler's "banality," an aspect that Arendt emphasized in her book on Eichmann—the "banality of evil." While Arendt's Eichmann was "thoughtless" and strikingly ordinary, Fromm's Himmler was "lifeless," duplicitous, and devoid of genuine concern for anyone but himself. Like Arendt's Eichmann, Fromm's Himmler was quite orderly, compulsive, ambitious, and definitely devoted to Hitler. Unlike Arendt's Eichmann, however, sadism was at the core of Fromm's description of Himmler. Arendt's emphasis in both *Origins of Totalitarianism* and *Eichmann* on the systematic efficiencies of Nazi extermination efforts has proven more congruent with the historiography of recent decades. But the clear, if limited, overlap between Fromm's discussion of Himmler and many of Arendt's points in *Eichmann* is compelling.[30]

Fromm relied heavily on Bradley F. Smith's solidly researched 1971 biography of Himmler and Josef Ackerman's biography of the prior year. Fromm also paid attention to Himmler's diaries, letters, and other sources that were cited extensively in both books. Based on these sources, he sketched out his own interpretive narrative of Himmler's life, a life continually marked by attention to small details. It was "a textbook illustration for the anal (hoarding) sadomasochistic character, in which we have over-orderliness and marked pedantry as outstanding traits." From the age of fifteen, Fromm noted, Himmler kept meticulous records of himself—when he woke up, ate, bathed, and other particulars. He began keeping index-card records of every object he gave to or received from others. Additionally, Himmler sought to overcome his own feelings of inadequacy by exercising control over others, often through cruelty.[31]

Largely relying on Smith and Ackerman, Fromm narrated Himmler's evolution from an insecure and overly meticulous young man with a poor self-image to a high-ranking Nazi. After several rejected applications to serve in the German army in World War I as an officer and not a "lowly" soldier, he was accepted for officer training but was fearful of seeing combat at the front lines. When it was clear that the war was almost over, Himmler hoped for very modest exposure on the front lines in order to become a professional army officer. He was not given this assignment, reinforcing his already negative self-image.[32]

Following the war, Himmler pursued his studies in Munich, where he read anti-Semitic literature, joined the Nazi party, and through useful career connections plus duplicities and lies, worked his way up in the party structure. A career break occurred in the mid-1920s, when Gregor Strasser, the leader of Bavaria's Nazi Party, took Himmler on as his assistant. He ingratiated himself with Strasser and became his deputy.[33]

Himmler the sadist sought total control over others and enjoyed inflicting misery. Fromm cited a family situation that arose in 1923–1924 as an

illustration. Jealous of his brother's marital engagement, Himmler convinced his Roman Catholic parents that the fiancée was "indiscreet." After
the marriage was called off, Himmler pressed further to destroy the woman's reputation. For Fromm, the episode revealed how Himmler essentially took control of the members of his family—a prelude to the all-controlling sadist that he was to become.[34]

Himmler's career and power rose meteorically, and Fromm traced it
with considerable nuance, describing Himmler joining the SS in 1925, being appointed SS Reichsführer in 1929, and by 1933 becoming responsible
only to Hitler. When World War II broke out, he was the country's top security officer (by this time head of all police and nonpolitical detective
forces) and designed the detention, forced labor, and concentration-camp
systems. Next, he set in motion plans to kill millions of unarmed and powerless Jews, Poles, Russians, and other prisoners. Unlike Hitler, Himmler
persistently investigated new and more expedient ways to kill, settling on
the gas chamber. With abundant detail, Fromm also described Himmler's
program for the systematic breeding of Germans in order to create an
Aryan master race. In describing Himmler's meticulous control of situations and people, Fromm found his thematic line. Sadism coupled with
managerial innovations and ruthless political maneuvering all served to
launch Himmler's career and to ameliorate his self-doubt. To be sure,
Himmler was not the only broker of death whom Fromm wrote about, but
the portion of *The Anatomy of Human Destructiveness* devoted to Himmler
was the most compelling part of the entire book, underscoring rather precisely what Fromm meant by malignant aggression. Fromm provided concrete details here for some of the generalizations about the authoritarian
personality that he had simply outlined in *Escape from Freedom*. It was
Fromm at his peak as an intellectual and scholar in his last decade.

Fromm emphasized sadism as Himmler's defining quality. He was
writing as a psychoanalyst, a clinician, and an ethicist who was qualified
to discuss individual and social psychology but not to explicate organizational behaviors and systems. Beginning with *Escape*, he had used sadomasochism to chart twentieth-century catastrophes. If Fromm had emphasized managerial, technological, and systemic aspects of the Nazi
killing machine rather than the social character of Nazi leaders, he would
have been closer to a paradigm that was emerging among scholars of the
Holocaust. Without routine access to the publications and bibliographical

guides of academics, however, Fromm was only vaguely familiar with this recent turn in the specialty literature.[35]

Fromm concluded his discussion of Himmler by circling back to Himmler's early life and family circumstances. The task here was to explain that Himmler was defined through a "dry, banal, pedantic, dishonest, unalive" family in which "there were no values except the insincere profession of patriotism and honesty, there was no hope except that of managing to hold on to their precarious position on the social ladder." In brief, there were few spiritual or intellectual resources conducive to a happy and creative family life. In its bleakness, Himmler's situation, though more dire, may have approximated some of the circumstances of Fromm's boyhood home.[36]

More than any other personality in *Anatomy*, Fromm asked the "question within a question" about Hitler: why was he perhaps the most destructive person in history? Why did he exemplify the most extreme form of malignant aggression? Fromm's treatment of Hitler was considerably more expansive, if far more repetitive, than his analysis of Himmler. Fromm had been collecting material on Hitler since the late 1920s for the German workers project at the Frankfurt Institute, but he provided his most extended discussion of the Fuehrer as he elaborated the necrophilic character type.

Though Fromm never cited Arendt's *Origins of Totalitarianism*, his treatment of Hitler and characterization of necrophilia very closely approximated her concept of "absolute evil." There were numerous examples in *Anatomy* that described how Hitler hated life and wanted to destroy it—how, perhaps more than any other twentieth-century dictator, he epitomized necrophilia. Fromm had cited examples of Hitler's antipathy to life in several of his earlier books and articles, and he referenced a good many more in *Anatomy*. Most conspicuously, Fromm noted that Hitler often disregarded military and diplomatic advice in his killing sprees. In fact, he ordered the killing of millions of Jews, Poles, Russians, and other "undesirables" more from whim than strategy. Hitler displayed little of the meticulous, bureaucratic efficiencies of Himmler or Eichmann. Toward the end of World War II, he even issued orders that would assure the destruction of many Germans, their dwellings, and their cities. This, Fromm noted, was a clear example that Hitler hated all of humankind. When Hitler was shown a newsreel of the bombing of Warsaw and its residents,

Fromm noted that he expressed great glee, joking about "corpse tea." Hitler's facial expressions were unusual—he always looked as if he were smelling decomposing substances or horrible odors. He could never muster a free, spontaneous laugh; that expression always resembled a smirk. Hitler readily rationalized this human destruction, including the elimination of the food supply and other provisions, for the growth and splendor of Germany. Whatever person or group he classified as an "enemy" was ordered murdered because all "enemies" aimed to destroy Germany. "Defective" people, including homosexuals, were particularly appropriate candidates for death, Fromm observed. Regularly ordering murders and executions, Hitler sometimes tried to hide his joy over this destruction of lives by being absent when the killing occurred. He risked the lives of his troops and eventually the lives of all Germans, even himself. People were never quite real to him but rather instruments that could be eradicated in no few circumstances. Fromm held, through perhaps a somewhat overdrawn characterization, that Hitler not only ordered death and destruction impulsively (like a child throwing a tantrum) but that he was entirely without empathy and passion. All such "suffering caused him no pain or remorse" but was tolerable and often pleasurable. Hitler displayed strong elements of Himmler's sadism, much as Himmler displayed some measure of necrophilia. But for Fromm, Hitler was more "advanced" in his quest for human destructiveness.[37]

If Hitler was fascinated by ruin and death, this hardly meant that he (or others who embraced necrophilia) could simply be dismissed as crazy, sick, paranoid, or psychotic. It seems that Fromm was influenced significantly in this assertion by the clinician Walter Langer's secret wartime report to American military authorities (later published as *The Mind of Adolf Hitler*). Fromm pointed out, as Langer had earlier, that Hitler had multiple dimensions. To call him a man of evil and mentally ill was to identify only part of the man. The most difficult task in understanding Hitler, Fromm noted, was to appreciate his rational and calculating side. He was even able to persuade others to like him. Indeed, he was politically quite adept and manufactured a "veneer" to provide the appearance of normalcy. For Fromm, Hitler was "an excellent actor"—a showman or salesman who enjoyed playing the role of being friendly, kind, and considerate. He was able to deceive others and especially himself. Fromm insisted that Hitler "had two faces: the friendly one, and the horrifying one—and both were genuine." Lacking an empathetic core or any principles, values, or convictions congruent with human needs, Hitler "could 'play' the kindly gentleman and not be aware himself at that moment that it was a role." He could "show a front of kindliness; courtesy; love of family, of children; of animals; he will speak of his ideals and good intentions." Fromm emphasized that Hitler could not have become chancellor of Germany or have been aided in committing such atrocities had he not been such an eminently rational and adept salesman. A demagogue to be sure, Hitler was "a politician of outstanding skill." When Germany was defeated in World War I and then humiliated by the provisions of the Treaty of Versailles, Fromm detailed how Hitler built a career by persuading demoralized army officers and other political groups of the correctness of his plea for nationalism, anticommunism, and militarism. Through exceptional political skills, he enlisted financial support from bankers, industrialists, and other conservative and rightist elements to the point that he soon held the reins of power.[38]

Bypassing a number of classic historical studies on aspects of the Third Reich, Fromm revealed in *Anatomy* (as he had in *Escape from Freedom*) his distance from historical scholarship—a quality not uncommon among social critics writing to large reading publics. His treatment of Hitler serves as a case in point. Fromm tended to repeat his appraisal of the Fuehrer as both a skilled politician and salesman mixed with a heavy dose of necrophilia. He did so only to reiterate the various personal qualities of perhaps the most savage leader in modern history. His larger point was that brutal leaders such as Hitler were difficult to understand because they wore deceptive garb. They often played the part of actors or salesmen, using these roles as a cover for their detestation of life until they were in a position to inflict horrible damage. Fromm underscored how the fate of civilization rested on the capacity of those who were life affirming to expose and oppose the salesmen of death wherever they appeared. In this regard, Fromm seemed to be embracing a prophetic posture on behalf of humankind.[39]

Meeting Speer

As he constructed his appraisal of Himmler and Hitler, Fromm realized that this material would be the most powerful and intriguing segment of *Anatomy*. He decided to meet with Albert Speer to help enhance this segment and flesh out the full meaning of malignant aggression. As Hitler's chief architect and then the Third Reich minister of armaments and war production, Speer was involved in the prosecution of Jews. At the Nuremberg trials (and later in published memoirs), Speer claimed to accept responsibility for his role in the crimes of the Nazi regime with seeming sincerity and directness, and his expression of remorse probably saved him from the executioner. He spent twenty years in Spandau Prison in West Berlin and published acclaimed works on the Third Reich, including his prison diaries. Released in 1966, he reiterated how wrong and deluded he had been and that he would spend the balance of his life exposing the brutal crimes of the Nazi regime. Speer's account of his life and associates in the Third Reich was long and detailed. Yet exemplary scholars including Dan van der Vat and Gitta Sereny maintain quite convincingly in their books and articles that much of Speer's apology after his release was self-serving. While it is unclear whether Speer fabricated his story, told the truth, or deluded himself into thinking he was telling the truth, the issue at hand is to determine why Fromm believed without qualification Speer's postprison writings and the truth of his life story.

In the fall of 1972, as Fromm was working on the Himmler and Hitler sections of *Anatomy*, he wrote to a Frankfurt scholar and friend, Robert Kempner, asking him to arrange a meeting with Speer. Fromm was impressed by Speer's *Inside the Third Reich* (1970), especially by the characterization of Hitler. The study "offers by far the richest material on [Hitler's] personality I have come across." Fromm openly acknowledged that his interest in Hitler was psychological rather than historical, and he hoped Speer would consent to meet with him. Speer agreed, and they met in October in Heidelberg for half a day. Fromm found the meeting exceedingly helpful and wrote to Maccoby that Speer provided details fully compatible with his views of sadism and necrophilia as components of malignant aggression. Now Fromm felt confident that he was closer to completing the last section his book. Fromm also mentioned to Maccoby that after meeting Speer, he believed that the man had "genuinely repented his participation" in the Nazi regime. He also reported that Speer was well read and intelligent and "quite a human being." This was hardly an atypical perception. Former Nazis who were scholarly, gentle, and cultured had sometimes been invited to present at prominent American universities, including Yale and Harvard, and at other scholarly forums. Erudition and polish appeared to combine in a credible way with Nazi professions of contrition, and American academics sometimes suspended critical judgment.[40]

Fromm was pleased with Speer for appearing to confirm, from firsthand observation, his view that Hitler embraced necrophilia but displayed strong political skills. Because Speer claimed to agree with Fromm's character- ization of the Fuehrer, Fromm was less reticent to accept Speer's other perspectives on the Third Reich, even as he balked at systematic study of the interpretations of eminent historians specializing in the topic. It is obvious that Fromm admired and respected Speer. A warm correspon- dence and a few more visits followed. Fromm flooded Speer with ques- tions about the nature of Hitler's necrophilia and asked whether Hitler's interest in architecture was "the only aspect of life" he could ever em- brace. Speer read over Fromm's description of Hitler and suggested a number of changes in both fact and interpretation. Fromm, impressed and trusting, made the changes with gratitude, and reported to Speer that *Anatomy* was about to go to press. He reiterated the warmth and trust he felt for Speer, and added on a personal note that he wholly disbelieved the attacks that were being made against Hitler's architect. Indeed, Fromm asked Speer whether he could emphasize in *Anatomy* how deeply he trusted not only Speer's scholarly commitment but his repentance.[41]

The Fromm-Speer correspondence continued for several years. He cau- tioned Speer to be wary when a journalist offered to write Speer's biogra- phy, mixing the question with his own aversion to a biography of himself. Fromm warned the ex-Nazi that it was hard for a biographer to understand "that Hitler was essentially a necrophilic person and that you are truly a biophilic person." When Speer asked Fromm for advice on whether to pub- lish an account of his dreams pertaining to his Nazi past, Fromm re- sponded that it was a high-risk venture—that even psychoanalysts might arrive at "superficial and distorted conclusions." He advised Speer to pub- lish accounts of only a very limited number of his dreams and volunteered to review the accounts as a cautionary measure. Yet he wanted people to understand how "extraordinary" Speer was. The two found comfort in talking about Goethe, Schiller, and the intellectual and cultural mentors each regarded as important. Fromm counted on regular correspondence from Speer. When there was a gap, as occurred in the fall of 1974, Fromm was upset, fearing that this did not "fit the picture I had of [Speer] and the friendship we had cultivated." The lull in letters was apparently due to a mix-up in correspondence, and Fromm was relieved when Speer contin- ued writing to him.[42]

It is noteworthy that Fromm, the Jewish émigré, glossed over Speer's Nazi affiliations as he completed *Anatomy*, much as he did earlier in the book in his treatment of Lorenz. Both men had shifted the discourse away from their Nazi pasts, if in different ways. Lorenz destroyed evidence, issued denials, lied, and evaded questions. In contrast, Speer probably believed the story he constructed (whether or not it was true), and that belief likely saved his life. Moreover, he found that he could repeat the story with perfect ease. Fromm believed Speer's story and never questioned any of its less-than-plausible particulars. What mattered was that he did not focus on either man's past, concentrating instead on their current writing and their ideas.

Clearly, Speer was very important to Fromm in bringing *Anatomy* to a close with confidence in his understanding of Hitler. In some measure, Speer also supported Fromm's hope in the human capacity to embrace life, even if one was weighed down by a Nazi past. While it seems likely that Speer was lying or that he at least tricked himself into believing in the veracity of his fabrications, trust and hope had long been essential to Fromm, especially in seemingly convivial relationships. There was, for example, cause to believe that his close friend, Adam Schaff, the Polish "third way" intellectual, had never entirely shed, much less formally repudiated, his Stalinist history. Moreover, Fromm's record as a clinician suggests that if he could easily relate to a patient, he was sometimes hoodwinked by those of his patients who seemed to be doing well. Whether sincere, duplicitous, or a mix of the two, Fromm trusted Speer as a man of good character who assured him that he had completed the most difficult but important part of *Anatomy*. With this assurance, Fromm felt that he had successfully concluded the most scholarly and ambitious of his books.

Reviews were mixed. Lewis Mumford and Ashley Montagu, among others, characterized it as a groundbreaking study. The Mexican psychoanalysts that Fromm had trained spoke of it as his most important book. But *Anatomy* created little stir among American psychoanalysts, especially the more orthodox, and negative reviews came primarily from that quarter. Professional historians, even those identifying with the new subfield of psychohistory, were generally inattentive. Because *Anatomy* was the longest of Fromm's books and engaged specialized scholarly literatures, Henry Holt and Company, the publisher, had not expected large sales. But after a feature story on it appeared in the *New York Times*, sales picked up. Indeed, most of Fromm's books commanded large readerships at this point in his career. Roughly three million copies of *Anatomy* were sold in the quarter-century after publication, and it was translated into seventeen languages.[43]

To Have or to Be?

During the mid-1970s, Fromm spent quite a bit of time worrying about troublesome world events. His "life" as a political commentator resurfaced, if quite modestly. He was especially attentive to the Israeli relationships with its Arab neighbors. Fromm's conviction that tolerance and respect were due everyone contributed, he maintained, to his critique of the Israeli state and its policies. While the Nazi experience made the tragic consequence of zealous nationalism blatantly transparent, the underlying problem with Israel, Fromm explained to his more sympathetic friends, was that it was an outgrowth of Zionism. For a few years he had been a Zionist himself and had participated in the Zionist youth movement in Germany, but he quit at the age of twenty-two, proclaiming to Zionist colleagues: "I cannot stand your nationalism." Salman Rabinkow explained to him at the time that Zionism was in conflict with a Jewish humanism that celebrated all of humankind. When Fromm made the firm decision to quit the Zionist movement, he felt relieved. Nationalism in all forms, including Zionism, hardened the human heart. It was clear to Fromm, based on Israel's brief history, that "political Zionism is one of the false Messiahs" because it elevated displays of crude power over the real "spirit of Judaism." He confided to his Italian friend Angelica Balabanoff that unlike Zionism, "prophetic Messianism has always been for me one of the most beautiful ideas, and . . . the State of Israel has just prostituted this idea for its own political purposes." Consequently, Fromm refused to visit Israel and even declined to visit with any relative who was a "fanatical partisan of [Israeli] policies."[44]

In addition, Fromm corresponded with Maccoby, Riesman, and Fulbright about Yugoslav affairs and the right-wing Pinochet coup in Chile. He was also disturbed (wrongly, it turned out) by what he regarded as signs of strong and recurrent fascist values in Germany. Most of all, he worried during the 1970s, as he had in the 1960s, about America's problematic foreign policy and the persistent danger of the U.S.-Soviet rivalry ending in nuclear war. In 1974, Fromm presented a formal statement, "Remarks on the Policy of Détente," to the Senate Foreign Relations Committee, and he wrote a follow up article for the *New York Times* ("Paranoia and Policy"). Fromm's contention in both pieces echoed his 1960 article for *Daedalus* that President Kennedy had taken seriously. Unless the Americans and the Soviets put aside their paranoid fears, established mutual trust, and halted a "suicidal" arms race, a nuclear nightmare threatened the world. Recognizing his disposition under these circumstances to be downbeat, if not downright depressed, Fromm sought equanimity in various ways. He told Aramoni that one must not "utilize the general misery as a rationalization for one's own depression." Instead, Fromm discovered "great pleasure" from reading cogent philosophers. Indeed, as long as he could find people who valued truth, compassion, and hope, "life is livable." Fromm told Mumford that he was pursuing pleasant diversions, one of which was humming a vital phrase in an old Hasidic song: "And in spite of it all, and in spite of it all . . . " To some extent, while continuing to be current on international developments, he seemed to be withdrawing from his formidable role in the public realm.[45]

In the meantime, Fromm's health was growing increasingly precarious. He saw specialists regularly, had a few surgeries, and took many medications. Reflecting in a letter to Karl Darmstadter, who found himself on the verge of moving to a nursing home, Fromm felt that moving to such a facility—something he himself might have to contemplate in the not-too-distant future—might have an advantage: possessions undermined the ability to be. Fromm reinforced this point in a second letter: "After all, shouldn't we try to give up the need to have something, even a home and lifelong customs, in order to be able to fully be?" (Since Fromm was not defending homelessness, he probably meant relinquishing a "house" or a "residence.") He recommended that Darmstadter reread the passage in Goethe's *Faust* underscoring how "the less we have the more we are, the stronger we are." What was important was rich experience and happiness: "To enjoy every moment is the most important thing there is; the smile in the face of others, a thought, the sight of a tree."[46]

Here Fromm was summarizing the theme of what would essentially become his last book—a synthesis of his most important ethical and psychological observations over the decades. Initially, it was to have been two books—a short popular polemic like *The Art of Loving* that he hoped to complete in two or three months and then a fuller, more theoretical work. The longer, more developed book on having and being would be anchored in a nuanced and lengthy discussion of Marx, Meister Eckhart, and Zen Buddhism, which all shared much the same perspectives on the have/be binary. Mixing several short and more accessible mass-market books with a longer volume containing some research, nuance, and extended commentary was consistent with Fromm's publishing pattern. But Fromm soon realized that that sort of mix was no longer possible: by the mid-1970s, he lacked the energy and argumentative cogency to conduct the extensive research necessary for a long and complex theoretical book. He would ultimately write only the shorter volume but include within it the insights of Marx, Freud, Meister Eckhart, Bachofen, Freud, Rabinkow, D. T. Suzuki, Mumford, and others who had provided guidance to him over the years. When asked by his friend Tristram Coffin for a sense of this book, Fromm responded that it concerned the ascendance of "naked greed and complete alienation," which left people "unhappy, confused, lonely and bitter." Further, this greed was part of a "having" orientation based on egotism, maximum profit, minimal social solidarity, and scant love. Man was desperate and hopeless, lacking a vision of life beyond acquiring and greed. If he did not find a new orientation soon, a dictatorial "man on the white horse" would appear to offer false visions of order and meaning—somebody like Hitler. As a counterpoint, Fromm proposed a "being" modality, where man could mobilize a new faith, new aspirations, and new visions.[47]

Fromm clearly knew what he intended to say in *To Have or to Be?* and cast his message within the contrasting binaries that always helped him frame his arguments. The book contained less a new message than a synthesis of his writings against authoritarianism, necrophilia, consumerism, and the depleted sense of self. All exemplified the "having mode." What he now called the "being mode" connected decidedly to his concepts of productive social character and biophilia—drawing upon and enjoying the creative and spiritual resources of the self who was in turn sustained by a supportive society. Restricting himself to these binaries, Fromm did not consider the potential overlap between the having and being modalities, nor whether either required "doing."

Fromm felt his dichotomy between having and being, which had previously been invoked by several thinkers he knew or had read, had been especially strong in Marx. He turned to the Russian scholar Raya Dunayevskaya for assistance on this subject, as he often felt ill and had considerable trouble locating appropriate passages from Marx among his thousands of incomplete notecards. She had read all of Fromm's books, had assisted him a great deal with *Marx's Concept of Man*, and they corresponded regularly for many years. Fromm had been extremely impressed with her book *Marxism and Freedom*, which drew on the early humanist Marx, and felt she had provided one of the most profound essays in his 1965 anthology, *Socialist Humanism*. Indeed, Fromm found it remarkable that a Russian had been able to elaborate what was essentially a variant of Western rather than Soviet Marxism. He also felt that her distaste for patriarchal institutions was even stronger than his own and that she was able to illuminate the intellectual contributions of Rosa Luxemburg and the chauvinism shown toward Luxemburg by Lenin and Trotsky. Without finding Fromm abundant and pertinent quotes for *To Have or to Be?*, his discussion of Marx's juxtaposition of the having and being modalities would have been thin. Indeed, she may have provided more on Marx than he had counted on: Dunayevskaya sketched out the intellectual precedents for Marx's dichotomy between having and being and the evolution of Marx's formulation of the having/being contrast chronologically through his publications (including his footnotes). Fromm was gratified that Dunayevskaya did far more for him than he requested. Indeed, she was reminding Fromm of the thoroughness with which a conscientious scholar worked. He almost certainly realized that *To Have or to Be?*, even at this early stage, would not measure up to her standards or his own. He knew that he was not performing as a scholar should and was much surprised when sales boomed.[48]

If Fromm was indebted to Dunayevskaya for helping him with Marx, he was also indebted to Rainer Funk, a young theology student and priest in training, for assisting him as he developed the book. Funk was studying at the University of Tubingen with Alfons Auer, a professor of Catholic ethics. Though Funk had no training in the social sciences or social psychology, he had more experience than Brams conducting research in large university libraries. Auer told Funk that Fromm's view of ethics without a higher god might be especially helpful to Funk.

Funk was impressed with Fromm's manner and his writing, and the two got on well from the start. Fromm understood that Funk had been trained in Catholic theology and did not pressure him to change. Indeed, Fromm had been impressed by the Catholic Middle Ages, which he idealistically portrayed as a precapitalist community and therefore a caring one. He was not asking Funk to become a "humanist" who disavowed a conventional God, though Funk was particularly impressed with the passages

Fromm showed him from Meister Eckhart suggesting that "man created himself." Having read all of Fromm's books, Funk was swayed by Fromm's psychological orientation, even though he did not have as keen an understanding as Maccoby about the sociological and economic aspects in Fromm's concept of social character. He hastily completed his dissertation at Tubingen, replete with the new ideas that Fromm inspired. Fromm was pleased. He admired Funk's energy and thoroughness in presenting sources on theology and ethics. By 1974, Fromm acknowledged that he was too frail even occasionally to visit libraries and archives, locate books and articles, and take notes systematically. After his assistant Brams left, Fromm invited Funk to become his new research assistant, to help him complete *To Have or to Be?*

Fromm felt the job would be demanding; Funk would have to commute frequently-between Locarno and Tubingen. Funk did more than locate the sources Fromm needed. He often provided Fromm with more precise data than he had and was especially attentive to the nature of the texts by Meister Eckhart and Karl Marx that Fromm studied. Intelligent but hardly as profound a theoretician as Fromm, Funk was good with details. He discovered, for example, that the English edition of Eckhart's writings, with which Fromm worked, contained sermons that were not actually Eckhart's. Funk also worked on specific issues in Greek hedonism and Plotinus's concept of the *Hen* (the One), to be sure Fromm used these materials correctly. He critiqued specific details in the evolving manuscript and corroborated every one of Fromm's quotations. Fromm urged Funk to raise questions about anything he had written, to reorganize paragraphs, and to recommend more systematic presentation of whole chapters. Funk was an asset as Fromm's research assistant. *To Have Or To Be?* would have lacked appropriate sources and consistent accuracy of detail had it not been for Funk. For his part, Funk became a "Frommian," having acquired a new mentor who inspired him profoundly, providing his essential philosophic and social orientation.[49]

It is easy to understand why Funk and others were so crucial to Fromm's book's success. His long list of chronic illnesses, sometimes attended by short bouts of depression, had slowed him down. A fall that broke his arm and three attacks of gallstones (two accompanied by jaundice) also set him back several months. When Aramoni learned that Fromm's book was proceeding at only a modest pace, he offered to provide funds for Fromm to hire more assistants so that he could complete it more rapidly. Predictably,

Fromm pushed ahead as quickly as his health permitted, despite Annis's warning that he was overtaxing himself. The decision to write a relatively brief volume was fortuitous, for he was barely able to do even that. Harper and Row, his publisher, insisted that the complete manuscript be ready to go through its final editorial process by late May 1976. Realizing that even with Funk's help Fromm would not make that deadline, his editor at Harper traveled to Locarno early in May to help him complete what was to be the last book wholly under his control, assuring that *To Have or to Be?* would be published later in the year.[50]

Because Fromm had essentially summarized the theme for *To Have or to Be?* in letters to friends and in parts of earlier books and articles, he had entered this project with some momentum and now had Funk by his side. He began by arguing that the industrial revolution led to material abundance and unlimited consumption, the substitution of human labor by machine-driven labor, the replacement of human thought by computers, and the rise of new bureaucratic imperatives that led not to happiness but to mass discontent. The dream of becoming "independent masters of our lives" had not materialized. Moreover, technical progress created environmental hazards and nuclear weapons with the capacity to destroy humankind. Fromm characterized the creation of "a society of notoriously unhappy people; lonely, anxious, depressed, destructive." The new "question within a question" that Fromm asked was: "What is good for Man?" The answer could not be endless production and never-ending consumption. It could not be what the psychologist Philip Cushman, a "Frommian" of sorts, called the "empty self," a self that was temporarily soothed by "filling up" on consumer products and other possessions, only to feel depleted again in short order.[51]

For Fromm, the spread of this having mode—the society and its inhabitants who existed on a diet of property and greed—was evident in our language. In recent centuries, nouns had been replacing verbs. Verbs designated a state of inner activity—a being mode—while nouns stood for things and possessions. We possess a house, an idea, and even love itself. One did not love but became a man with love; it had become something external to man, which he consumed. People had ceased to speak of "the experience of love" as contributing to internal joy and excitement. Fromm noted that it had become "deceptively simple" to express "to have." "Being" or "to be" had become more difficult to explicate. In Spanish, the word *ser* (a form of "to be" used to express identity or nature) had been replaced by the verb *estar* (a changing condition or location). People rarely spoke in the "being" mode about their "true nature" or their feelings. Instead, they were more preoccupied with how they "appear" to others—the external world. This was hardly a new conceptualization of modern society. In fact, it closely approximated the social psychologist Erving Goffman's notion in *The Presentation of Self in Everyday Life* (1959) that people are how they think others see them. This idea was also close to the concept of "other direction" that Riesman underscored in *The Lonely Crowd* (1950). Yet Fromm worded the phenomenon a bit differently: people had nearly lost the capacity to speak of processes within themselves and instead spoke of externalities.[52]

Fromm's presentation was circular, doubling back on itself and reiterating the same theme with different phenomena rather than offering a sequential unfolding of his thematic structure or even a dialectical unfolding. Within a few pages, for example, he contrasted the two modes in terms of remembering, conversing, and reading. Remembering in the being mode required one to be vitally interested in the subject, to make connections among items actively, and to recall words or ideas by productive acts of thinking and feeling. By encouraging "free associations as Freud characterized, one encouraged active, productive memory work." Dreams and memories would be recalled by activating parts of ourselves. In contrast, the having mode of remembering was to summon external objects— a photograph, a set of notes, a recording—and thereby to reconstruct thoughts that could be consumed. The information is at one's fingertips, but it has not come from within. Similarly, a conversation in the having mode was prepared for in advance to benefit the self. One sought to control the discourse by having and manipulating information. Conversation in the being mode, on the other hand, was spontaneous and sharing and bypassed external gains or other external advantages. It was a free-flowing process, and discussion was like a dance of joy for all parties with no particular outcome in sight. Fromm also used the dance metaphor to refer to his clinical approach—the free and open exchanges between analyst and patient. The dance had long been Fromm's concept of helping a troubled patient shift in the direction of becoming a productive person who took joy in the creativity of his work (a "productive social character"). With regard to reading, Fromm insisted that it was not much different than conversing. A reader in the having mode read to appropriate information from an author—to consume the data or themes the author intended to convey—the kind of consumption of information typical of school work. In the being mode, however, reading was an active process within the self where one created one's unique moods, insights, and emotions. One carried on a dialogue not only with the author but with oneself. One learned to hear not only the author's voice but to respond internally in a rich and imaginative exchange.[53]

Authority, faith, and love were also concepts Fromm analyzed in terms of the having/being dichotomy. Once again, he explicated the concepts as opposites within a binary. Having authority was based on power, exploitation, titles, force, tradition, and other factors. External insignia and official designations substituted for genuine and empathetic governance. Cruelty and callousness were permitted if the ruler wore the garb of tradition and a title of authority. This type of leader displayed the apparel and appearance of authority in order to dominate society. In contrast, a being authority exuded knowledge from one's inherent competence and from a vibrant and engaging personality. The being as an authority figure did not need to issue orders, to bribe, or to threaten. Such a leader exemplified the happy, proficient, and productive self—a master of living. In the having mode, faith was the consumption of answers external to the self without rational proof. Authorities claiming infallible knowledge and spouting desired dogma created the answers that one accepted on faith as acts of submission. These answers were consumed as articles of faith, much as Fromm described the response to dictators in *Escape from Freedom*. In the being mode, however, faith was an inner attitude or orientation. Here, one did not have faith but *was* faith. One did not submit to a God but experienced divine qualities within oneself. One was swayed not by an external authority but by compelling subjective and empirical evidence processed within the self, hopefully in a rational way. Thus, religious experience in the being mode was essentially a faith within the self that promoted a faith in others and in humankind. Fromm had long referred to this state as humanism and claimed that its faint beginnings were found in the late Middle Ages and in the Renaissance. Interestingly, he did not point out that this humanism also closely resembled the Quaker notion of "the inner light of God" residing in each person and connecting him to all other people, creating an egalitarian unity of humanity. Drawing from *The Art of Loving*, Fromm insisted that meaningful love was behavior: there was only the *act* of loving. Such behavior cultivated in the self and in the other an aliveness and a self-renewal. In contrast, the love experience in the having mode was not love at all. Rather, it had the effect of confining or restricting the other.[54]

Reduced to its essence, *To Have or to Be?* presented a contrast between the having and the being modalities across a wide range of human experiences. Each experience was treated briefly. Fromm sometimes postulated or asserted instead of reasoning through his points, so his descriptions of having and being were static concepts. He never really explained how action was involved in both modalities until he turned to Eckhart. Without action, having and being could not account for the consequences of either. Finally, the binary of having and being precluded treating both concepts along a continuum. That is, some forms of having were closer to being than others.

Even though Fromm planned to focus the preponderance of *To Have or to Be?* on Eckhart and Marx, the two became subsidiaries of sorts to Fromm's binaries. He introduced Eckhart as a German Dominican priest from the late thirteenth and early fourteenth centuries, having vast influence on Catholics of this period. Fromm focused on and richly explicated Eckhart's classic sermon on poverty, "Blessed are the poor in spirit . . . " insisting that Eckhart was not referring to external needs and things but to their absence. "Poverty" was a freeing of the self from possessions—a spiritual cleansing. As in Buddhist thought, Fromm noted, Eckhart preached that the essential task was to free the self from cravings and acquisitions—to distance oneself from the urge to acquire things. For Eckhart, to seek or even to do God's will was a craving. Only if one had no material desires could one cease to engage all but an inner spiritual self. This state reflected the being mode.[55]

Continuing to address the text of Eckhart's sermon, Fromm explained that when Eckhart asserted that "a man ought to be empty of his knowledge," he was essentially arguing that one should not seek knowledge as a possession. One must not be "filled" with knowledge and try to hang onto it. To invoke the being mode, one needed to rid oneself of the fetters of being ego-bounded or egocentric—elements of the having mode. Further, the ego should not be allowed to destroy one's freedom simply to be—to pursue true self-realization. One's life should not be determined and structured by others; it should flourish by being one's "own creation." But what, for Eckhart, did it mean to be? According to Fromm, Eckhart had two overlapping meanings. On one level, to be meant not to focus on one's tasks, not to concern oneself with the nature or number of the tasks.

Rather, what was relevant was how the task connected to the inner spirit that energized one's behavior. It was this dynamic core within oneself that truly mattered. Indeed, being was "the state of productive inner activity" designed to overcome all "ego-boundedness." In describing Eckhart well into the book, Fromm had finally and explicitly taken up the matter of action and movement, describing the productive being as active and alive.[56]

Although Marx wrote centuries after Eckhart, Fromm found his message on the essential alternatives in human existence equally in line with Eckhart and with his own. To be sure, Marx spoke in terms of secular economic categories and often characterized utopian socialism, while Eckhart talked more of religious aspects of the self and addressed a holy spiritual community. For Marx, capitalism was based on characteristics similar to those of Fromm's having mode, which eradicated the human spirit and drained its creative potential. Having and acquiring things blinded man to his inner self. The harder one slaved for money and wealth, the sooner one's humanity was lost. Fromm underlined a vital sentence in Marx's critique: "The less you are and the less you express your life—the more you have and the greater is your alienated life." To seek out material goods as one's primary goal was to alienate the self—to fail to "express [one's] life." According to Fromm, Marx's "sense of having" was very much akin to Eckhart's "ego-boundedness"—the self constructed through acquisition. Although Marx used different terms to describe entering into the process of being, they were also similar to Eckhart's. The process both described and involved the sharing of aspects of one's inner core with others. In this way, one facilitated a deep inner connectedness to a universal reality shared by humanity and promoting reciprocity between individuals. Love in the being mode meant evoking love from the inner core of another; trust begot another's trust. The genuine opening of aspects of one's being to the corresponding aspect in others encouraged others to do the same and promoted a humane community. While Eckhart compared being to "a vessel that grows . . . and will never be full," Marx described it as the production of an aspect of the self that evoked an identical animating quality of another.[57]

While Eckhart did not comprehend that his humanism exceeded his theism, and although Marx did not recognize that what he propounded was a religiosity, Fromm felt that both were committed to the same goal. Both prized the being modality—selfhood and the simultaneous emergence of joyous, productive social character in others. Fromm suggested that the world would realize the advent of a humane society—one in transition from having to being—when a number of social qualities permeated society's current bureaucratic, greedy, materialistic, and unhappy existence. Once these qualities became discernable, man would cease to hoard and exploit and could escape the chains of his material possessions. Then he would seek to give and share. When he began to show confidence in what he was becoming, man would experience a need for relatedness, love, and solidarity with the world around him. He would understand that there was no need for greed, hate, or the deception of others. He would recognize life's alternatives: growth or decay, life or death. In brief, the being society closely approximated what Fromm had called the "sane society." Indeed, he said as much.[58]

It was not difficult to discern the message of *To Have or to Be?* When the book was published in 1976, it was exceedingly popular among European students and professionals, Germans and Italians in particular, who spoke out at the time for new, less materialist and consumer-driven lifestyles. In fact, like America in the 1960s, much of Europe was experiencing a "counterculture" movement during the mid-1970s and the early 1980s.

Quickly and unintentionally, under these circumstances, Fromm reached guru status. It surprised him. His book supported protests against material consumption, against nuclear weapons, against the American presence in Vietnam, and for environmental protection. A cartoon in a German newspaper showed a young man with long hair and poorly groomed beard telling a bookstore proprietor that he would not sleep if he could not read a copy of Fromm's new volume. Pope John Paul II, who appreciated Fromm's propensity to find community in late medieval Catholicism, spoke of *To Have or to Be?* as a great spiritual book with humane values— not the problematic values of consumption and the marketplace. When his health permitted, Fromm gave newspaper, magazine, radio, and television interviews in Germany and Italy; radio interviews were particularly frequent. With regularity, the media characterized his ideas as no less important than Freud's. Initial sales were modest in the United States, where other Fromm books, including *The Art of Loving*, remained popular. But in Europe, *To Have or to Be?* became an extremely popular volume that some commentators characterized as a European counterpoint to problematic American values. Though global sales never surpassed *The Art of Loving*, the book enjoyed tremendous success in Germany, where, within a few weeks of publication, 140,000 hardback copies had been sold; it reached bestseller status in subsequent paperback sales. By the mid-1990s, 1,080,000 copies had been sold in Germany and ten million copies world wide. Translated into twenty-six languages, its themes permeated the cultural mainstream. The book was even summarized in a simplistic one-liner on the internationally acclaimed television drama *CSI*. *To Have or to Be?* also caused a resurgence in the sales of *The Art of Loving* in German-speaking countries. By 1981, *The Art of Loving* had sold five million copies in Germany alone. Both books continued to be in demand well after Fromm's death in 1980. Sales remained substantial not only in Europe but in Mexico, Japan, and Korea.[59]

Legacy in the Making

Late in 1975, the Deutsche Verlags-Anstalt, a respected German publishing house that had done well with *The Anatomy of Human Destructiveness*, made Fromm an interesting offer. The house would publish a twelve volume German edition of Fromm's collected works (*Erich Fromm Gesamtausgabe*) that would include virtually everything Fromm had published, including roughly 220 articles and even several unpublished manuscripts. Not up for the task of compiling and editing this massive collection himself, Fromm turned to Funk, who was then helping him to ready *To Have or to Be?* for publication. He asked Funk to become editor and to take charge of the whole *Gesamtausgabe* project. There was no realistic alternative, and Funk had earned Fromm's trust. German was Funk's native tongue, but his English would pass, and he had become familiar with almost all of Fromm's publications over a period of only a few years. Moreover, Fromm felt that Funk had the dedication and the energy to carry the project through to completion. Funk did not have to be persuaded to take on the project. He jumped at the opportunity. By this point, he had become deeply dedicated to Fromm and to assuring Fromm's intellectual legacy. Volumes 1 and 4 were published in February 1980—a month before Fromm died. The remaining volumes were published by late 1981. The publisher expected that libraries in German-speaking countries would buy the set. Sales exceeded Fromm's, Funk's, and the publisher's expectations: German, Swiss, and Italian scholars and families bought the set for their home libraries. Initially, the *Gesamtausgabe* sold over six thousand copies. A paperback edition followed and sold another ten thousand copies.

With such high sales for a large and costly reference collection, it was clear that by the time of his death, Fromm had become more than a celebrity in German-speaking Europe. He was an exceedingly well-regarded public intellectual and social commentator.[60]

The publication of Fromm's *Gesamtausgabe* assured that he would be remembered for a long time to come. Much to Fromm's delight, Wolfgang Bonss, a young German scholar and sociologist with a keen interest in history and a graduate degree from Frankfurt University, added to Fromm's legacy. In 1977, Bonss visited Fromm in Locarno. He was intrigued by Critical Theory, the ideas of Max Horkheimer, and the early history of the Frankfurt Institute. He had also been attentive to empirical sociology and its manifestations in survey research and knew about Fromm's work directing the Institute's 1929–1932 survey of the attitudes of the late Weimar German working class. Like most of his colleagues, he had no idea what had become of the data or the precise conclusions of that study.

Bonss and Fromm got on well, and Fromm gave him access to a special room on the bottom floor of his Locarno apartment building where books and other materials were stored. As luck would have it, Bonss came across a box with fragments of the unpublished Weimar worker study, including complete and incomplete questionnaires and preliminary tabulations of the survey results, which suggested that many more workers displayed authoritarian propensities than the project researchers or leaders of the Institute had expected. From the materials at hand, Bonss also derived a strong sense of early twentieth-century social science methodologies. He understood the pioneering aspect of Fromm's and his colleagues' efforts to access subjective perceptions in relationship to social and political realities. The book that Bonss assembled from the box of fragments in Fromm's storeroom approximated what Fromm had expected Horkheimer to publish forty-three years earlier. To be sure, Fromm acknowledged that his initial survey project had lost some of its import after Hitler came to power. By 1980, when Bonss brought out *The Working Class in Weimar Germany*, it became one of many primary sources that German historians and social scientists could ponder. But it won Fromm recognition for a study conducted early in his career that few scholars knew about, even though it had been a crucial precedent for Adorno's 1950 classic, *The Authoritarian Personality*. Though Bonss's publication, listing Fromm as author, was published a few months after Fromm's death, the knowledge that his project would finally be out for all to see was tremendously significant for Fromm. What he had regarded for decades as one of the major contributions of his scholarly career now had a future in research libraries for decades to come.[61]

The Final Years

Having been in poor health since he was diagnosed with tuberculosis in 1931, numerous illnesses complicated Fromm's last years. He consulted regularly with physicians and took a good many drugs, some of which combined in dangerous interactions. He suffered from increasingly severe glaucoma, which was treated unsuccessfully with a variety of eye drops. Cataracts impeded his vision, and no consistently reliable surgical remedy existed at the time. Fromm began wearing special, exceedingly strong reading glasses to accomplish any writing. Annis had health setbacks, too. In 1978, her breast cancer returned, and she had surgery to excise a small malignant tumor. This was not her last struggle with the cancer. As Annis's health took a turn for the worse, Erich's deteriorated rapidly. He suffered a second heart attack in 1977 that slowed him down considerably. A year later, Fromm suffered a massive heart attack that was by far the worst of the three. His heart stopped, and he was considered clinically dead for several minutes before a nearby physician managed to stimulate the heart to resume its beat. Some brain damage and proximate memory loss no doubt resulted. In addition to his heart problems, he may have experienced mild strokes after the 1978 attack. He also had a discernable hearing loss, depression intruded periodically, had little appetite, and lost weight. Every now and then, he was able to read for an hour and to have short interviews concerning *To Have or to Be?*, but the downturn continued. In September 1979, Annis candidly reported to Aramoni that her husband had been able to accomplish very little over the past two years. She read letters from his closest friends to him. On good days, he dictated brief responses to some of them.[62]

Fromm became increasingly dependent on Funk. Late in 1977, he asked Funk to be his literary executor, effective upon his death. Funk warmed to the challenge, which stood to put him in charge of all of Fromm's unpublished and published writings and Fromm's vast correspondence. He came to see in the executorship a global authority over all of Fromm's correspondence and other literary materials, regardless of where they were

housed. A claim of this magnitude suggested heavy emotional identification with Fromm. Even before Fromm died, Funk began to stand in for
him on several public occasions. Funk's decision to establish a good-sized
Fromm archive in his own home in Tubingen suggested that Fromm had
become central to his professional life.[63]

As early as 1956, Fromm described the nature of a book on Freud he
intended to write in a letter to his friend Izette de Forest. He assumed,
quite problematically, that as a psychoanalyst who had spent a lifetime
distinguishing his contributions from Freud's, he was a credible evaluator
of Freud's ideas. He would outline what "the decisive, fruitful ideas of
Freud were," critiquing those ideas that he found problematic while praising others that stood the test of time. In late 1976 and early 1977, before his
second heart attack, he wrote a very rough draft of the first 155 pages of
Greatness and Limitations of Freud's Thought, essentially summarizing
the thoughts on Freud that he had repeated many times before. But he
lacked the energy, the short-term memory, and the capacity to concentrate
after the second attack and especially after his massive third attack. Clearly,
Fromm was in no condition to complete the volume on his own and often
permitted himself to be guided by Funk. For example, Fromm accepted
Funk's recommendation to fill out Greatness and Limitations by including a
selection on dream interpretation from The Forgotten Language. Funk also
recommended that much of the epilogue of Anatomy of Human Destructiveness be presented as Fromm's critique of Freud's theory of instinctual
life. He edited Fromm's 155-page typescript and penned a conclusion.
Privately, Funk claimed that "I prepared the book," while acknowledging
that "it was really not a new book with new . . . ideas" but summaries of
previous materials that Fromm had published. Indeed, it was a volume of
recapitulation—and that was precisely the point. "Since my critique of
Freud has its own continuity," Fromm began the work, "I cannot avoid referring back to earlier statements I have made on the subject." In this, his
last evaluation of Freud, Fromm underscored the continuing significance
of Freud's thoughts on his own, accepting some of them, rejecting others, and responding to quite a few of Freud's ideas with mixed and changing emotions. Unfortunately, illness precluded a clearer and fuller explanation of how he had stood in his last years on Freud's focus on libidinal
drives as they compared to his concept of social character. Had this been
possible, Greatness and Limitations would have been an exceedingly important final publication.[64]

Fromm's Sri Lankan Buddhist friend, Nyanaponika Mahathera, a periodic participant in Fromm's Locarno circle, now urged him to maintain an "inner freedom" as the body deteriorated: "If your body is ill, your mind should not be ill." Fromm responded to Nyanaponika that he was wholly in accord—that "periods of illness or physical incapacity have never been 'lost' time." These were occasions for "deepening experiences and spiritual recuperation." While in hospitals and at home in bed, Fromm learned, as he told Mumford, "to meditate and analyze myself" much of the day. Fromm was making "good use" of this "very wholesome opportunity." He was doing "quite a bit of thinking even though this was not 'working' in the proper sense." Similarly, Fromm informed Ernst Simon that being confined to bed rest was a blessing in the sense that it facilitated "quiet thinking." He explained to Chaim Kaplan that though reading and writing were very difficult in old age, he still enjoyed reflecting on classic Jewish texts. Three weeks before his death, Fromm described how he was placing himself more fully in the being mode—quietly thinking and being introspective and limiting himself to life's essentials.[65]

After the massive 1978 heart attack, Fromm did not expect to live very much longer. Late in 1978, Gérard Khoury, one of Fromm's former analysands, proposed conducting and tape recording an extended interview in which Fromm might tell his life story, including those who had been very important to him, such as Rabinkow, Horkheimer, and Riesman. Originally from a wealthy family in Lebanon, Khoury took up permanent residence in France, where he became a successful businessman, translator, and historian, translating Fromm's *Revolution of Hope* into French. Traveling to Lebanon often to visit with family and friends, he kept himself well informed about Middle East conflicts and kept Fromm current on Al Fatah and other Arab organizations that were, in various ways, battling with the state of Israel. He prepared briefing papers and complimented them with detailed discussions with Fromm, who found the data exceedingly helpful. Their friendship and trust deepened. Fromm recognized that the interview would reverse their former clinical relationship, with Khoury now asking the questions about the life and feelings of his analyst. But Fromm waived this consideration and consented to the interview, which probably represented the last extended appraisal of his life, thought, and values. Like his books, the transcript of the interviews would serve as a document for posterity. With Annis present and watchful, Khoury ended up conducting two interviews—one in December 1978, not long after the last of his three heart attacks—and the other in February 1979, a year before Fromm's death. Fromm told Annis that despite his illnesses, he wanted to be "totally present" and alert in the interviews and to articulate his thoughts with his characteristic enthusiasm and cogency. He was quite successful on all counts.[66]

Khoury prepared extensively for the interviews, which were later transcribed and finally published. Although Fromm sometimes tended to stray from Khoury's questions, perhaps owing to his short-term memory loss, he usually responded coherently. When Khoury asked him to review his early years, Fromm replied at length, providing an invaluable source of knowledge about his childhood. His parents' difficult relationship made him feel estranged and marginalized. The Talmudic scholars and rabbis who compensated for the stability he lacked at home served as role models, showing Fromm how to live a life rooted in ethics, scholarship, and a commitment to community. Curiously, Fromm did not reveal much about Rabinkow, Nobel, or other mentors. Instead, he stressed their collective importance in drawing him from the "crucible" at home and toward a more productive life.

It is especially striking that Fromm included little information about his years at the Frankfurt Institute. Perhaps his bitterness over the way Horkheimer and Adorno terminated him had never subsided. Fromm had much to say about his encounters with psychoanalysis and discussed the topic with clarity and often subtlety. For many years, Fromm had intended to prepare a detailed, multivolume study of the evolution of diverse psychoanalytic techniques but ended up giving higher priority to other writing projects. In his interview with Khoury, Fromm seemed to be discussing aspects of what that long study might have been, reiterating that Freud's discovery of the unconscious was always fundamental to his thought. Indeed, he turned to Freud for a theoretical foundation, including an engagement with Freud's modernist agenda, before beginning any project. He felt that his clinical approach resembled that of two unorthodox analysts— Georg Groddeck and Sandor Ferenczi—whom he met in Baden Baden in the late 1920s and early 1930s. Their approach, and his as well, was to observe and listen intently and sympathetically to all aspects of the patient's life, the goal being to fathom a feeling within himself that approximated the patient's story and that resonated with aspects of his own psyche.

In the last hour of his sessions with Khoury, Fromm offered comments that paralleled his critique of contemporary psychoanalysts, and he emphasized the need for social transformation from a having to a being mode of existence. The having modality was implanted so deeply in society that conversion to the being mode was exceedingly difficult. Nonetheless, the strong response to the book that promoted him to guru status in much of Europe suggested that there was still hope—that many people sought greater integration with an inner spirituality and self-knowledge but simply did not know how to accomplish that state. Then Fromm speculated on a point that he had not emphasized in *To Have or to Be?*—whether early matriarchal societies such as Bachofen described might have been predicated more on the being than the having disposition. Could the being modality be promoted, Fromm wondered, by women's capacity to create and sustain life? He offered this idea as a ray of hope for what he considered a very troubled world dominated by the having modality. Fromm concluded the interviews expressing a faith that if the human race did not destroy itself through nuclear war, it would experience "tremendous development" in insight and ethics in the years ahead.

Reflecting on the hours of interviews, Khoury felt that even as Fromm's writing days were over, he remained a social critic to be reckoned with and still able to articulate the essentials of humanism. He gave Khoury a somewhat uneven and rambling view of his life and experiences. But he was quite cogent, sometimes even nuanced, in his lengthy discussions of psychoanalytic thought and technique. Freud was more on his mind than Marx, as perhaps Freud always was. His closing remarks appropriately focused on humanity's present and future and were at once probing, distressing, and inspirational to those who still had faith in the possibility of a humanist society. A few years after Fromm's death, Annis asked Khoury for a copy of tape-recorded version of the interviews so that she could hear his voice and perhaps imagine him speaking in his very inspiring way.

Death and Ceremonials

Fromm was quite ill and sometimes unpredictable in the months before his death. He could barely read and no longer write. He would often wake up at night and, perhaps not entirely conscious of where he was, speak of global tensions and criticize the problematic actions of heads of state. He listened constantly to his Bach records, as he found them soothing. In mid-February 1980, aware of Fromm's very delicate condition, Boris Luban-Plozza and Ivan Illich threw an eightieth birthday party for him in Locarno. Always one for joyous celebrations, Fromm was delighted, perhaps a bit exuberant, and rallied to the occasion, smiling as Luban-Plozza and Illich summarized his achievements with great warmth and affection. In response, Fromm, speaking with clarity and a smile, told jokes and anecdotes quite appropriate for the occasion. The dignity and presence Fromm had displayed during the interviews with Khoury were still evident in the weeks before his death. It may be that in his own way Fromm was rallying in the face of the death that he knew was near.[67]

On the morning of March 18, 1980, five days before his eightieth birthday, Annis heard her husband breathing with difficulty on the living room couch. This was his fourth heart attack, and he died within a few minutes. Annis called Gertrud Hunziker-Fromm, who quickly took a train to Locarno. The two, both in shock, summoned Ivan Illich for guidance. Formerly a priest and experienced in ceremonials after death, he took charge. Fromm had requested a small and understated event. Illich, with the help of Annis and Hunziker-Fromm, prepared a guest list limited to thirteen friends and colleagues for the funeral. Fromm's close friends in the vicinity, Boris Luban-Plozza and Hans Jürgen Schultz, were invited. So was Ruth Liepman, Fromm's longtime literary agent. Funk was an obvious selection. So was Joan Hughes, his proficient and caring secretary. Save for Gertrud Hunziker-Fromm, no family members were invited. Illich organized the funeral to take place on the grounds of a nearby crematorium in Bellinzona, close to a Jewish neighborhood and graveyard. Though cremation ran against Jewish tradition, Fromm had not been a practicing Jew for much of his life, and he had requested that his ashes be scattered in Lake Maggiore. Illich complied on both counts and presided over the service. Adhering to Swiss tradition, four uniformed pallbearers carried the flower-covered casket into the crematorium. Illich and Luban-Plozza escorted Annis, and when they noticed her distress stayed with her for the rest of the funeral service. Illich and Schultz addressed the group, Illich briefly and Schultz in a somewhat longer presentation. They both referred to Fromm's most spiritual book, *You Shall Be as Gods*, and also tried to explain how Fromm's humanism weaved in and out of different religious and philosophical traditions and had been perhaps his guiding orientation. Luban-Plozza petitioned city officials to rename a park or a street or some other public site after Fromm but was unsuccessful. Owing to

Fromm's low profile in the community, all that could be secured was a small metal plaque affixed to the front of Fromm's apartment building.[68]

Annis had a hard time without Erich. They had been happily married for twenty-seven years, focusing their lives on each other's needs. Fromm's passion for Annis inspired *The Art of Loving*, his most popular book. She received many letters of condolence, both personal and professional. Nya-naponika Mahathera admitted the "deeply felt impact" of his death and urged Annis to "bear this loss serenely and preserve good health." In contrast, James Luther Adams, a professor at the Harvard Divinity School, wrote to Annis to state how important it was that her husband's *Gesamtausgabe* was to be available in German and how articles about his books were appearing in important reference sources. Steven Schwarzschild, who taught philosophy and Jewish Studies at Washington University in St. Louis and whose father had known Fromm from childhood in the Frankfurt Jewish community, wrote that Fromm had been "a fatherly friend to me."

But these and other letters did not seem to cheer her up. Always disposed to a cigarette or two, she became a chain smoker after Erich passed away. She tried to keep up with friends in Europe and America and to have Funk, whom she disliked, removed as literary executor. But she did not succeed on either count. Speaking neither German nor Italian in the southern part of Switzerland and with friendships dwindling, Annis decided to return to Montgomery, Alabama, where her sister still resided. She was put on medication, perhaps an antidepressant, by a New York physician friend, in whom she confided that "the death of Erich has shaken me seriously." With her unabated grief over Erich's death, heavy smoking, and a history of cancer, Annis died of colon cancer in 1983.[69]

Obituaries, memorial statements, and other notices of Fromm's death appeared in large number in *Le Monde* and *Le Figaro* (Paris), *Uno Más* and *Exelsior* (Mexico City), the *New York Times*, the *Washington Post*, the *Times* (London), the *Frankfurter Neue Presse*, *Il Sabato* (Rome), *Trouw* (Holland), *Hufvudstadsbladet* (Helsinki), *Nin* (Serbia), *Tiroler Tageszeitung* (Innsbruck), and many other papers around the world. Despite Fromm's persistent criticism of Israel, a favorable and lengthy obituary even appeared in *Israel-Nachrichten* (Tel Aviv). By the time of his death, Fromm had been regarded for some years as a figure of global importance. He had not considered himself German, American, Mexican, or Swiss but connected to humanity everywhere. Most public notices summarily reviewed one or two of his "lives" and a few of his books. Some discussed his passion for sincerity and principle. Others observed that unlike Freud, who viewed the human being primarily in terms of the individual self, Fromm viewed the human being as inseparable from his social and economic conditions. A few obituaries commented that Fromm attempted conceptually to link Freud with Marx. Several others mentioned his limitless energy and his celebration of a humane society. Most touched on the fact that he publicly championed humanitarian values, and several quoted his salient observation that "love is the only satisfactory solution to the problems of human existence." Some underscored his opposition to militarism, his attack on consumer culture, and his reservations about technological solutions to human problems. Only a few mentioned that he was a democratic socialist. Several discussed his opposition to all forms of authoritarianism and cited *Escape from Freedom* as a profound reckoning with the phenomenon. Unfortunately, few sought to present a holistic view of Fromm, one that integrated his life and presence with his writings. The psychologist David Elkind stood out among those who tried, maintaining that Fromm was basically concerned with our special qualities as humans and with the "ethics of friendship." According to Elkind, Fromm sought not only in his writings but in his very being to promote a world in which people were in close touch with one another, helped and supported one another, and listened closely to one another's perspectives. If he questioned others' perspectives, he did so warmly, gently, and supportively. For Elkind, Fromm's humanism was like an "ethical touching" where each person carried within himself a profound and loving connection to all of humanity.[70]

Perhaps the most striking recollection came from Rose Spiegel, who trained with Fromm at the William Alanson White Institute. She emphasized how Fromm had contributed profoundly to her intellectual and emotional development. His continued influence on her was evident in a dream she had a few days after his death, in which somebody told her that Fromm "was quite well and was writing another book."[71]

A Bibliographical Note

This was the most difficult of my books to complete, largely because Erich Fromm's wife destroyed many of his personal letters after he died. Rainer Funk protected much that was not destroyed, and his Fromm Archive in Tubingen is the principal source for this volume. I have studied almost every file in that facility, which took nearly a decade. A few items that fill gaps in the Fromm Archive may be found in the Fromm Papers at the New York Public Library. But there are other important collections. The David Riesman Papers in the Harvard University Archive houses dozens of letters between Fromm and Riesman. The correspondence tells much about both men, their colleagues, and their very important friendship over the decades. There is a small but important correspondence in the Max Horkheimer Collection at Frankfurt University. It is revealing about Fromm's important role in the Frankfurt School. Charlotte Selver played an important role in the lives of Fromm and his second wife, Henny Gurland, and a good portion of her papers are located in the archive of the University of California at Santa Barbara. I never cease to be surprised by materials that pop up in the Archive of the History of American Psychology at the University of Akron. This time, I found interesting Fromm materials in its Abraham Maslow Papers. Fromm's cousin, Gertrud Hunziker-Fromm, was very close to him since childhood. She invited me to her home in Zurich every year over much of a decade. Together we reviewed and discussed a very large and deeply informative correspondence she had with Fromm, much addressing family and personal life. The Margaret Mead Papers in the Library of Congress represents one of the best sources concerning Fromm's activities in the Culture and Personality movement and his rapport with quite a few of his colleagues. Over the years, Mead's daughter Mary Catherine Bateson reviewed this material with me and helped me to understand the very important relationship between Fromm and Mead.

With many private papers destroyed, interviews for this project became crucial. What turned out to be the most helpful was one with Marian Rothbacher in Vienna. It led me to the remarkable letters of Sophie Engländer from Berlin that Rothbacher preserved. The letters had circulated through the Fromm family in exile in diverse parts of the world during the Nazi period. They were like a glue that held the family together. The Fromm Archive now houses copies of all the letters that Rothbacher showed me during a two-day interview, and the family file is a treasure trove for all who study the Hitler years. Fromm's closest colleagues in later life, Michael Maccoby and Rainer Funk, plied me with informative stories over many years, at first through formal interviews and then through direct conversations, e-mails, and telephone calls. I interviewed Karen Horney's daughter, Marianne Eckardt, four or five times over the years. Dozens of personal recollections came of it. Doris Gurland, the wife of Fromm's stepson, recounted many talks she had with Fromm, usually of a personal nature. So did Moshe Budmore, the general executor of Fromm's estate. Mitiades Zaphiropoulos, Fromm's colleague at the White Institute, had much to say about Fromm the clinician. My interviews in Mexico City included Jorge Silva-Garcia and Aniceto Aramoni, Fromm's closest colleagues there. Meeting at Silva's home to discuss Fromm, I discovered that Silva had worked with my father during the Spanish Civil War and that both had been gun runners for the Abraham Lincoln Brigade. Salvador and Sonya Millán were of the generation of clinicians that followed. They told me everything they knew about Fromm in Mexico and gave me copies of every document concerning Fromm that they had. Over the years, I had many e-mail exchanges with Salvador, mixed with some telephone conversations, and these were always helpful. Gerard Khoury, Fromm's analysand, told me much about Fromm. Khoury also gave me a transcribed copy of one of the most important sources for this biography: many hours of interviews of Fromm in his final years, where he reflected on the entire course of his life. I interviewed others who knew Fromm in different contexts, usually colleagues but also people with whom he had financial transactions, secretaries, cooks, and others who took care of his needs over the years.

Scholars have written much on and related to Fromm that have essentially been based on reading his books and articles but unfortunately not on archival investigations. The problem was compounded by the fact that not very many of these scholarly studies drew on *Erich Fromm Gesamtausgabe* (Funk's twelve-volume collection in German of Fromm's published works). The quality of scholarship on Fromm varies, and I shall note only a few books: Don Hausdorff's *Erich Fromm* (1972) was the first in a string of intellectual biographies. Hausdorff was one of Fromm's colleagues during his short teaching stints at Michigan State University. The volume was thin on data and analysis but represented a commendable effort, to be fair. John Schaar wrote *Escape from Authority* (1961), a tough but important critique of Fromm's writing (especially *Escape from Freedom*) when Fromm was at the height of his fame as a social commentator. But Schaar quite properly refused to give Fromm a "free pass." Harry Wells's *The Failure of Psychoanalysis* (1963) was even more critical of Fromm at this time, if from a rather rigid Marxist perspective. It lacked Schaar's eye for nuance. Daniel Burston's *The Legacy of Erich Fromm* (1991) was the strongest of the comprehensive intellectual biographies. I learned a good deal from it, supplemented by conversations with Burston over many years. Michael Maccoby's anthology with Mauricio Cortina, *A Prophetic Analyst: Erich Fromm's Contribution to Psychoanalysis* (1996) housed several strong scholarly essays on Fromm's thought, the most important being Maccoby's "The Two Voices of Erich Fromm." Lawrence Wilde, *Erich Fromm and the Quest for Solidarity* (2004), brought out Fromm's political and philosophic legacy thoughtfully and concisely. Svante Lundgren's *Fight Against Idols* (1998) focused on Fromm's writings on religion. It was stronger than John S. Glenn, *Fromm: A Protestant Critique* (1966). G. P. Knapp, *The Art of Living* (1989), illustrated the hazards of trying to integrate Fromm's life with his texts without consulting archival collections or the *Erich Fromm Gesamtausgabe*. Neil McLaughlin wrote a wonderful series of probing articles that added up to a book on why Fromm lost currency among scholars. See, e.g., "How to Become a Forgotten Intellectual," *Sociology Forum* 13, no. 2 (1998): 214–246. Kevin Anderson and Richard Quinney, *Erich Fromm and Critical Criminology* (2000), presented some important essays by Fromm on social deviancy and contextualized them commendably. Douglass Kellner wrote many interesting, informed, and astute on-line essays concerning Fromm. There is also Kellner's admirable book *Herbert Marcuse and the Crisis of Marxism* (1984), which sheds light on Fromm. Stephen Bronner's treatment of Fromm in a chapter in his book, *Of Critical Theory and Its Theorists* (1994), was exciting and profound.

A crucial interval in Fromm's emergence as a scholar of note was at the Frankfurt Institute during the 1930s. There have been three excellent and comprehensive histories of the Institute that explained much about Fromm. One was Martin Jay's brilliant *The Dialectical Imagination* (1973), followed by Rolf Wiggershaus's treasure trove of information, *The Frankfurt School* (1986), and Thomas Wheatland's important *The Frankfurt School in Exile* (2009). One can also learn much from two books by Fromm's longtime friend and colleague Leo Lowenthal. The most helpful is his *Critical Theory and Frankfurt Theorists* (1989), but *An Unmastered Past* (1987) is also useful. Henry Pachter's *Weimar Studies* (1982) affords an extremely sensitive portrayal of Weimar culture and politics from the perspective of a participant observer. I profited from Detlev Claussen's *Theodor W. Adorno* (2003, 2008); it clarified and contextualized the emergence of Critical Theory and the conflict-ridden aspect of the Fromm-Adorno relationship at the Institute. Seyla Benhabid's *Critique, Norm, and Utopia* (1986) is also well worth consulting on the intellectual foundations of Critical Theory.

In this life-and-times biography, the psychoanalytic world that surrounded Fromm was exceedingly important. In this area, I became indebted to the late Paul Roazen, who wrote *Freud and His Followers* (1976) and a string of other books and articles that did much to contextualize Fromm. Roazen's work connects nicely with Eli Zaretsky, *Secrets of the Soul* (2004), on the culture of the psychoanalytic movement. There continues to be much profit in rereading two books by Philip Rieff: *Freud* (1959) and *The Triumph of the Therapeutic* (1966). Mark Edmundson is an exceedingly interesting intellectual historian and cultural critic, and I found his *The Death of Sigmund Freud* (2007) very helpful in understanding how, during his last years, Freud had interesting intellectual affinities with Fromm. One gets a sense of Fromm's frustrations dealing with the petty politics of the more orthodox American psychoanalytic institutes from Douglas Kirshner, *Unfree Associations* (2002). But I could hardly have done without Peter Gay's remarkable *Freud: A Life for Our Time* (1988). Nor could I have dispensed with Nathan G. Hale's pair of books that contextualized the history of U.S. psychoanalysis: *Freud and the Americans* (1971) and its follow up, *The Rise and Crisis of Psychoanalysis in the United States* (1995).

Biographies of figures close to Fromm abound, and only a few can be referenced here. The sole biography of Frieda Fromm-Reichmann was written by Gail Hornstein, *To Redeem One Person Is to Redeem the World* (2000). Ann-Louise Silver's anthology, *Psychoanalysis and Psychosis* (1989), housed a good deal of interesting material on Fromm-Reichmann as clinician and was put together by an unusually sensitive Fromm-Reichmann scholar. Knud Andresen has published the only biography of Heinz Brandt and a good one at that: *Widerspruch als Lebensprinzip* (2007). Bernard Paris's remarkable biography, simply titled *Karen Horney* (1994), was especially good on the Fromm-Horney relationship. Susan Quinn, *A Mind of Her Own* (1987), was a strong and somewhat more general biography of Horney. The only full biography of Harry Stack Sullivan has been Helen Perry's *Psychiatrist of America* (1982). Patrick Mullahy was also a Sullivan scholar, and there remains profit in consulting his *The Contribution of Harry Stack Sullivan* (1995). Although Fromm's good friend J. William Fulbright was a politician and not a clinician, one can see from Randall Woods, *Fulbright: A Biography* (1995), why Fromm was so taken by the senator. He was perhaps even more taken, if only in the short term, by Eugene McCarthy. The best account of the man and his 1968 presidential campaign is Dominic Sandbrook, *Eugene McCarthy and the Rise and Fall of Postwar American Liberalism* (2005).

There have been dozens of books and articles broadly contextualizing the intellectual climate of World War II and the postwar years when Fromm and his generation of public intellectuals were most active. Paul Gorman's *Left Intellectuals and Popular Culture in Twentieth-Century America* (1996); Wilfred McClay's *The Masterless* (1994); and Russell Jacoby's *The Last Intellectuals* (1987) were particularly helpful. A series of articles by David Hollinger on the cosmopolitan qualities of Fromm's generation and Hollinger's book *Post-Ethnic America* (1995) helped to "frame" the general topic. Three other works, all quite remarkable, were especially important to me in more ways than I can delineate here: Alan Nadel's *Containment Culture* (1995), Richard King's *Race, Culture, and the Intellectuals* (2004), and Ellen Herman's *The Romance of American Psychology* (1995).

There are also some very useful books on the cultural and political climate of the 1950s and 1960s, when Fromm was most active and important. Nothing was better on the global peace movement of the period than Lawrence Wittner, *Resisting the Bomb* (1997). Alan Petigny's *The Permissive Society* (2009) and Stephen Whitfield's *The Culture of the Cold War* (1991) broadly covered the 1950s, and with much insight. Daniel Horowitz's *Vance Packard and American Social Criticism* (1994) and Daniel Geary's study of C. Wright Mills, *Radical Ambition* (2009), were excellent biographies of two important social critics of the 1950s and into the 1960s. Like Fromm, they were strong opponents of the American socioeconomic status quo. Todd Gitlin's *The Sixties* (1987) called back the context of the decade when the two of us worked on SDS. projects. The year 1968 was exceedingly important for Fromm: he participated in Eugene McCarthy's campaign for the presidency and wrote its campaign manifesto. For good coverage of the McCarthy bid and many related developments of the time, see Jules Witcover, *The Year the Dream Died* (1997). Bruce Schulman's remarkable book *The Seventies* (2001) dipped back into the 1960s and helped me to understand American political culture during Fromm's final years.

During the last few years when I was preparing this biography, I treated myself to Michael Sherry, *In the Shadow of War* (1995). It was a deft portrayal of the militarization of American culture, which Fromm adamantly resisted. In contrast, Yuri Slezkine's *The Jewish Century* (2004) was a brilliant analysis of twentieth-century Judaism globally—the world in which Fromm was raised. Slezkine built a convincing case for the proposition that Jews of the period, as entrepreneurial minorities, made remarkable social and intellectual adaptations to modernity and, in some sense, became modernity's symbolic representations. John Cuddihy's classic, *The Ordeal of Civility* (1974), fit well with *The Jewish Century*. Cuddihy delineated how twentieth-century Jewish intellectuals critiqued the dominant Gentile culture that limited innovation and opportunity for the Jewish professional class, the working class generally, and the colonized peoples of the world. Repeatedly, Fromm's life and thought came to mind as I studied the Slezkine and Cuddihy volumes.

Notes

PI = Personal interview; TI = Telephone interview; TRI = Tape-recorded interview; LJF = Lawrence J. Friedman

1. The Unsteady Apprentice

1. "I felt quite at home": "Autobiographical Sidelights by Erich Fromm," *International Forum on Psychoanalysis* 9 (2000): 251. Fromm on "a medieval atmosphere": Gérard Khoury, interviews with Erich Fromm, Locarno, 1978–1979, transcript in Fromm Archive. On Seligmann Bamberger, see Leo Jung, ed., *Jewish Leaders, 1750-1940 (New York: Bloch 1953,1964)*, 179–195; and Leo Jung, *The Bamberger Family: The Descendants of Rabbi Seligman Bär Bamberger*, 2nd ed. (Jerusalem, 1979), ix, x, xi. Admitting to his "idealized" portrayal of Bamberger: Erich Fromm to Ernst Simon, Oct. 9, 1973. On Bamberger's centrality to Fromm: Gertrud Hunziker-Fromm, TRI by LJF, Zurich, May 9, 2004.

2. Jung, ed., *Jewish Leaders*, 183–195; Hunziker-Fromm, TRI by LJF, May 10, 2004.

3. Gertrud Hunziker-Fromm, TRI by LJF, Zurich, May 9, 2004, detailing the early generations of the Bamberger and Fromm family.

4. See Miriam Rothbacher, TRI by LJF, Vienna, May 18, 2004; and Gertrud Hunziker-Fromm, TRI by LJF, Zurich, May 10, 2004, for details of the family history.

5. Erich Fromm, TRI by Gérard Khoury, 1978–1979, especially on defending Rosa against Naphtali. Family photographs in the Fromm Archive in Tubingen assisted me greatly in understanding Erich's relationship with both parents, as did the Rothbacher and Hunziker-Fromm interviews. The Fromm archivist did not allow the author to publish the childhood photographs. Finally, it is extremely important to study Erich's autobiographical essay, "Some Personal Antecedents," in *Beyond the Chains of Illusion* (New York: Continuum, 1962, 1990); and Rainer Funk, *Erich Fromm: His Life and Ideas* (New York: Continuum, 2000), chap. 1.

6. Erich Fromm, TRI by Gérard Khoury, 1978–1979. The 1978–1979 interview Fromm gave to Gérard Khoury houses his retrospective remarks on his father and rich detail on the evolving father-son relationship. Dorothy Gurland, PI by LJF,

Providence, RI, August 23, 2009 on Fromm's memory of his father as "a sick man" and "a very odd man" and likely mentally ill.

7. On his "suffering" childhood: Erich Fromm to Annelie Brandt, Sept. 10, 1963. On being an "unbearable, neurotic child": Fromm, *Beyond the Chains of Illusion*, 5. On Erich in relation to Gertrud's father, Emmanuel: Gertrud Hunziker-Fromm, TRI by LJF, Zurich, May 9–10, 2004.

8. The most detail I have received on Ludwig Krause was from Miriam Rothbacher, TRI by LJF, Vienna, May 18, 19, 2004. The interview is supplemented nicely by portions of Fromm, "Some Personal Antecedents"; and Funk, *Erich Fromm*, esp. 14.

9. The abundant photograph collection in the Fromm Archive is telling on family dynamics. Erich Fromm to Annelie Brandt, Sept. 10, 1963, Fromm Archive.

10. On Sussman: Funk, *Erich Fromm*, 20, 32. On the suicide of the young woman: Fromm, *Beyond the Chains of Illusion*, 4.

11. On the suspension of humanistic values in the German gymnasium, such as the Woehlerschule he attended: Fromm, *Beyond the Chains of Illusion*, 7–9; Fromm to Lewis Mumford, April 29, 1975, Fromm Archive; Fromm to Albert Speer, Feb. 13, 1974, Fromm Archive.

12. On "partisanship and objectivity": Fromm, *Beyond the Chains of Illusion*, 6–7; and Fromm to Clara Urquhart, July 10, 1967, Fromm Archive. On "a deeply troubled": Fromm, *Beyond the Chains of Illusion*, 9.

13. Rainer Funk, "The Jewish Roots of Erich Fromm's Humanistic Thinking," 1988, unpublished mss., Fromm Archive, 2–4; Funk, *Erich Fromm*, 37–43; Daniel Burston, *The Legacy of Erich Fromm* (Cambridge, Mass.: Harvard University Press, 1991), 12–13.

14. Funk, "Jewish Roots," 3–5; Funk, *Erich Fromm*, 37–39.

15. Funk, *Erich Fromm*, 40–43; Burston, *The Legacy of Erich Fromm*, 12.

16. Funk, *Erich Fromm*, 40–41.

17. Ibid. Funk, *Erich Fromm*, 38–42, is particularly helpful on the Nobel circle. Fromm's obituary for Nobel is found in the Frankfurt *Neue Jüdische Presse* (February 2, 1922).

18. Copies of Fromm's transcripts at the University of Heidelberg are available in the Fromm Archive. Funk, *Erich Fromm*, 44, 50–52, is very helpful on the decision to study in Heidelberg.

19. Erich Fromm to Alfred Weber, Dec. 23, 1975, Fromm Archive, with his retrospective feelings on Weber. Burston, *The Legacy of Erich Fromm*, 100–101, places Alfred Weber's social thought in perspective.

20. Erich Fromm, *Das Jüdische Gesetz: Ein Beitrag Zur Soziologie des Diaspora-Judentums* (Ph.D. dissertation, University of Heidelberg, 1922). First published under this title posthumously in 1989 by the Munich publishing house of Wilhelm Heyne and edited by Rainer Funk. It is noteworthy that Jorge Silva, Fromm's student at the Mexican Psychoanalytic Society and Institute, will soon be bringing out a Spanish edition of Fromm's dissertation.

21. Ibid. (1989 ed.), 70–92, 134–156. See also Rainer Funk, *Erich Fromm's Kleine Lebensschule* (Freiburg: Herder, 2007), 60–62.

22. Ibid. (1989 ed.), 157–187. Funk, *Erich Fromm's Kleine Lebensschule*, 62–64.

23. Recalling Naphtali's fear he would commit suicide at his dissertation defense: Frieda Fromm-Reichmann, "Reminiscences of Europe," in *Psychoanalysis and Psychosis*, ed. Ann-Louise Silver (Madison, Conn.: International Universities Press, 1989), 480–481; and Erich Fromm, TRI by Gérard Khoury, 1978–1979, in Fromm Archive. On Weber suggesting an academic career: Erich Fromm to Alfred Weber, Dec. 23, 1975, Fromm Archive. See also Funk, *Erich Fromm*, 52–53.

24. One of the best sources on Rabinkow is J. J. Schacter, ed., "Reminiscences of Shlomo Barukh Rabinkow," in *Sages and Saints*, ed. Leo Jung (Hoboken, N.J.: Ktav Publishing House, 1987). In it, Fromm has a short essay (99–105) underscoring Rabinkow's centrality to his life and reviewing those qualities that impressed him most. Fromm, "Memories of Rav Zalman Baruch Rabinkow" (ca. 1964); and Fromm, "Memories of Rabbi Salman Baruch Rabinkow" (1971), both in the Fromm Archive, have even more detailed comments. "Rabinkow influenced my life": Fromm to Frau T. E. Rabinkow-Rothbard, July 9, 1964, Fromm Archive. An almost identical remark on Rabinkow as his principal influence appears in Fromm's reminiscence in Schacter, "Reminiscences," 103. See also Fromm to Ernst Simon, Oct. 9, 1973, Fromm Archive, recalling their time together with Rabinkow. Finally, see Fromm to Leo Jung, June 10, 1970, Fromm Archive, citing discussion of Rabinkow in *The Autobiography of Nahum Goldmann* (New York: Holt, Rinehard, and Winston, 1969), 45–47, as very much the mentor Fromm remembered.

25. Fromm, "Memories of Rav Zalman Baruch Rabinkow"; and Fromm, "Reminiscences of Rabinkow," in Jung, *Sages and Saints*, 99–105, detailing his study with Rabinkow. In *Sages and Saints*, 98–99, Abraham Frankel described how Rabinkow used the Lithuanian rather than the Hungarian method of Talmudic study.

26. Ibid., plus Funk, *Erich Fromm's Kleine Lebensschule*, 61–63.

27. Ibid. In all three of his reminiscences on Rabinkow, Fromm often implicitly and explicitly compares his qualities with Rabinkow's. On Rabinkow's hands, cleanliness, and other personal qualities: Fromm to Rose Cohn-Wiener, May 10, 1973, Fromm Archive. Fromm to Lewis Mumford, Apr. 29, 1975, Fromm Archive, compares himself to Rabinkow as both became disenchanted with Zionism.

28. The best attempt to connect Fromm's 1922 dissertation with Rabinkow's 1929 article is Rainer Funk, "Humanism in the Life and Work of Erich Fromm: A Commemorative Address on the Occasion of His Ninetieth Birthday," 1990, Fromm Archive. Funk astutely underscores how Fromm corrected a draft of an essay on Rabinkow so that it spoke more to the mentor-student relationship than how they were always "studying together" (6).

29. S. B. Rabinkow, "Individuum und Gemeinschaft im Judentum," in *Die Biologie der Person*, ed. T. Brugsch and F. H. Levy (Berlin: Urgan & Schwarzenberg, 1929), 799–824.

30. Rainer Funk has written two very thoughtful and richly documented papers that, in part, underscore how central Rabinkow's humanistic Judaism was to

Fromm even as Fromm turned from Judaism and became a secular humanist. See his "The Jewish Roots of Erich Fromm's Humanistic Thinking" (1988) and "Humanism in the Life and Work of Erich Fromm" (1990), both in Fromm Archive. Although I see Fromm's 1922 dissertation reflecting differences as well as similarities with Rabinkow and his 1929 article—suggestive of a fruitful early 1920s tension between them—Funk sees this difference emerging later, when Fromm distanced himself from Judaism (without Rabinkow's disapproval). However, Funk is also attentive to a collegial quality in their relationship.

31. "Frieda Fromm-Reichmann Autobiographical Tapes" (1956). Transcript in Fromm Archive.

32. Fromm-Reichmann, "Reminiscences in Europe," 469–481; "Frieda Fromm-Reichmann Autobiographical Tapes" (1956); Klaus Hoffmann, "Notes on Frieda Fromm-Reichmann's Biography," *Fromm Forum* 2 (1998): 24–25, is especially good on Reichmann's early professional background.

33. Ibid. The rape and the romance with Fromm is treated in Gail Hornstein, *To Redeem One Person Is to Redeem the World: The Life of Frieda Fromm-Reichmann* (New York: The Free Press, 2000). Hornstein claims (61–62) that Fromm seduced Reichmann during the analysis and that he was then a "ladies' man." Hornstein's shortage of primary evidence on Fromm on these matters makes somewhat problematic her characterization of his sexual life as a young man.

34. "Frieda Fromm-Reichmann Autobiographical Tapes" (1956) provides much detail on the origins and activities of the therapeuticum and her secret affair with Erich. See also Fromm-Reichmann, "Reminiscences of Europe," 479–480.

35. All of the Reichmann quotations: "Frieda Fromm-Reichmann Autobiographical Tapes" (1956). See also Hornstein, *To Redeem One Person*, 61–62; and Ann-Louise Silver, "Introduction to Fromm-Reichmann's 'Female Psychosexuality' and 'Jewish Food Rituals,'" *Journal of the American Academy of Psychoanalysis* 23, no. 1 (1995): 4.

36. Frieda Fromm-Reichmann, "Das Jüdische Speiseritual," *Imago* 13 (1927): 235–246; Erich Fromm, "Der Sabbath," *Imago* 13 (1927): 234. "We announced": Fromm-Reichmann, "Reminiscences of Europe," 481. See also Silver, "Introduction," 5.

37. On Frieda's memory of Erich having told her "Having a child is nothing": Hornstein, *To Redeem One Person*, 69. On Fromm confiding to Silva that Frieda could not have children: Jorge Silva García, TRI by LJF, Mexico City, March 21, 2004. Ann-Louise Silver, "Frieda Fromm-Reichmann and Erich Fromm," *International Forum on Psychoanalysis* 8, no. 1 (April 1999): 22, cogently argues that Frieda deeply wanted a child, while Erich wanted enhanced professional productivity instead. On the stillbirth or myoma and her reaction to its physical dimensions: Frieda Fromm-Reichmann to Georg Groddeck, July 31, August 16, 1932 (Fromm Archive). Hornstein, *To Redeem One Person*, 69, citing only the Fromm-Reichmann letter of July 31, 1932, to Groddeck, discounts the possibility of a stillbirth and claims it was entirely a myoma. On her closeness to Groddeck amid the troubled marriage: see also Fromm-Reichmann to Groddeck, August 23, 1933, Fromm Archive. On the import of Fromm being an only child in his decision to avoid having a child: Gertrud Hunziker-Fromm, TRI by LJF, Zurich, July 30, 2003, and May 10,

2004. Mauricio Cortina, PI by LJF, Washington, D.C., Feb. 1, 2003, recalls Fromm telling him that having children attached one to the current culture and values. On Fromm breaking up emotionally when asked if he regretted having no children: Rainer Funk, PI by LJF, Tubingen, July 25, 2003.

38. An excellent account of Groddeck's life and thought, particularly his relation to Freud, is provided by Martin Grotjahn, "George Groddeck: The Untamed Analyst," in *Psychoanalytic Pioneers*, ed. Franz Alexander (New York: Basic Books, 1966), 308–320. See also Romano Biancoli, "Georg Groddeck, the Psychoanalyst of Symbols," *International Forum of Psychoanalysis* 6 (1997): 117–125. An insightful discussion of the relationship between Groddeck on the "it" and Freud on the "id" is provided in Jaap Bos, David Park, and Petteri Pietikainen, "Strategic Self-Marginalization: The Case of Psychoanalysis," *Journal of the History of the Behavioral Sciences* 41, no. 3 (Summer 2005): 212–213.

39. Funk, *Erich Fromm*, 62–63; Fromm to Sylvia Grossman, Nov. 12, 1957, Fromm Archive; Fromm to Jack L. Rubins, Sept. 26, 1972, Fromm Archive.

40. Fromm to Groddeck, Aug. 15, 1934, Fromm Archive; Fromm to Grossman, Nov. 12, 1957, Fromm Archive.

41. On the formation of the Southwest German Psychoanalytic Study Group and its key participants: Erich Fromm to Jack L. Rubins, Sept. 26, 1922, Fromm Archive. See also Thomas Plankers and Hans-Joachim Rothe, "'You Know That Our Old Institute Was Entirely Destroyed . . . ': On the History of the Frankfurt Psychoanalytical Institute 1929–1933," *Psychoanalysis and History* 1, no. 1 (1998), esp. 103–109.

42. Romano Biancoli, "Mother Fixation and the Myth of Demeter," *International Forum of Psychoanalysis* 6, no. 1 (April 1998): 28–29; Burston, *The Legacy of Erich Fromm*, 15–16; Hendrik M. Ruitenbeek, ed., *Heirs to Freud* (New York: Grove Press, 1966), 7, 87–94.

43. Erich Fromm, "Psychoanalyse und Soziologie," in *Zeitschift für Psychoanalytische Pädagogik* 3 (1929): 268–270.

44. Hornstein, *To Redeem One Person*, 67; Gertrud Hunziker-Fromm, TRI by LJF, Zurich, May 10, 2004; Silver, "Fromm-Reichmann and Fromm," 21–22. Rainer Funk to Bernard Paris, July 19, 1990, Fromm Archive, is particularly instructive, noting what Fromm told him about Groddeck's interpretation of his tuberculosis in 1931.

2. Frankfurt Scholar

1. Rolf Wiggershaus, *The Frankfurt School: Its History, Theories, and Political Significance* (Cambridge, Mass.: The MIT Press, 1995), chaps. 1 and 2, represent a very thorough coverage of the origins of the Institute for Social Research. For further analysis, see Martin Jay's *The Dialectical Imagination: A History of the Frankfurt Institute of Social Research* (Boston: Little & Brown, 1973).

2. Ibid., plus Thomas Plankers and Hans-Joachim Rothe, "'You Know That Our Old Institute Was Entirely Destroyed . . . ': On the History of the Frankfurt

Psychoanalytic Institute 1929–1933," *Psychoanalysis and History* 1, no.1 (1998): 101–114, on the overlap between the Institute for Social Research and the Frankfurt Psychoanalytic Institute during Fromm's early years in both.

3. Erich Fromm, "Psychoanalyse und Soziologie," *Zeitschrift für Psychoanalytische Pädagogik* 3 (1928–1929): 268–270.

4. Erich Fromm, "Memorandum for Dr. Kurt Rosenfeld" [1939], Fromm Archive, Tubingen. Rainer Funk, *Erich Fromm: His Life and Ideas* (New York: Continuum, 2000), 72–73.

5. Erich Fromm, *The Dogma of Christ, and Other Essays on Religion, Psychology, and Culture* (London: Routledge & Kegan Paul, 1963), includes the English translation of the 1930 essay.

6. Horkheimer to Sigmund Freud, Mar. 18, 1932, Fromm Archive and also Fromm Collection, New York Public Library.

7. These two Fromm essays on criminology are presented in English translation in Kevin Anderson and Richard Quinney, eds., *Erich Fromm and Critical Criminology: Beyond the Punitive Society* (Urbana: University of Illinois Press, 2000). 123–156.

8. Ibid., plus Wiggershaus, *The Frankfurt School*, 118–120.

9. Ibid. For a helpful critique of Frromm's posture here, see Richard Quinney, "Socialist Humanism and the Problem of Crime: Thinking About Erich Fromm in the Development of Critical Criminology," *Crime, Law, and Social Change* 23, no. 2 (1995): 147–156.

10. Ibid. There is also profit in noting Martin Jay, *Permanent Exiles: Essays on the Intellectual Migration from Germany to America* (New York: Columbia University Press, 1986), 23–24, 109.

11. Erich Fromm, "Politik und Psychoanalyse," *Psychoanalytische Bewegung* 3, no. 5 (September–October 1931): 440–447.

12. Erich Fromm, "The Method and Function of an Analytic Social Psychology: Notes on Psychoanalysis and Historical Materialism," *Zeitschrift für Sozialforschung* 1 (1932): esp. 39–40, 53.

13. Erich Fromm, "Psychoanalytic Characterology and Its Relevance for Social Psychology," is found in English translation in Fromm's *The Crisis of Psychoanalysis* (New York: Holt, Rinehart and Winston, 1970), 163–187; and in German in *Zeitschrift für Sozialforschung* (Hirschfeld-Leipzig, 1932). I used the article as it appeared in the Fromm Papers of the New York Public Library.

14. Ibid., 177–187.

15. Ibid., esp. 183–184 and n. 21.

16. Ibid., and focused on 185–187.

17. Ibid., esp. n. 30 and n. 37.

18. For a most cogent summary of the essence of early Critical Theory, see Wilfred M. McClay, *The Masterless: Self and Society in Modern America* (Chapel Hill: University of North Carolina Press, 1994), 205–206.

19. Wolfgang Bonss, ed., *The Working Class in Weimar Germany: A Psychological and Sociological Study* (Warwickshire: Berg, 1984), does an excellent job of introducing the principal actors in the study, contextualizing it, and, most importantly,

publishing the study for the first time. Bonss's introduction (1–33) is especially helpful.

20. Ibid., 13–14.

21. Ibid., 24–26; Wiggershaus, *Frankfurt School*, 170–172. See also recollections of the German worker study in Erich Fromm to Martin Jay, May 14, 1971, Fromm Archives; and Erich Fromm and Michael Maccoby, *Social Character in a Mexican Village: A Sociopsychoanalytic Study* (Englewood Cliffs, N.J.: Prentice-Hall, 1970), 23–26.

22. Ibid., plus Wiggershaus, *Frankfurt School*, 171.

23. Ibid. See also David Smith, "The Ambivalent Worker: Max Weber, Critical Theory, and the Antinomies of Authority," *Social Thought and Research* 21, no. 1–2 (1998): 64–67, for especially cogent commentary on Fromm's unrepresentative sampling.

24. Wolfgang Bonss, editor of the 1980 published version of the German worker project, was able to construct his text from Fromm's surviving materials. Bonss maintains (*The Working Class*, 8) that 584 of the 1,100 completed questionnaires survived the institute's move to New York in 1934. Since Bonss was able to inspect the materials physically, this seems to be a credible finding. However, in Erich Fromm to Martin Jay, May 14, 1971, Fromm Archive, Fromm denied that any of the questionnaires were lost and that his staff analyzed seven hundred (not 584) of them. In all likelihood, either Fromm's memory was playing tricks on him concerning the loss of materials or he meant to refer to the 1,100 questionnaires that were initially returned in Germany.

25. Bonss, *The Working Class*, esp. 28, 228–230; Wiggershaus, *Frankfurt School*, 173; Fromm to Charles A. Pearce, June 22, 1938, Fromm Archive.

26. Bonss, 228–230; Fromm to Michael Maccoby, April 11, 1974, Maccoby private papers, reflects in detail on the German workers project and the different estimates of surviving questionnaires.

27. Wilhelm Reich to Erich Fromm, June 5, 1932, Fromm Archive; Funk, *Erich Fromm*, 74. In the third edition of *The Mass Psychology of Fascism* (New York: Farrar, Straus & Giroux, 1970), 219, it is noteworthy that Reich discussed Fromm and chastised him for disregarding how sexual repression of the masses augmented their craving for authority. Perhaps rooted in a clash between two large egos, neither Fromm nor Reich acknowledged intellectual kinship with the other. Only a few of Fromm's articles cited Reich on fascism and authoritarianism, even after he published *Mass Psychology*. Conversely, although Reich knew of Fromm's German worker investigation in its preliminary stages, he did not refer to it in his book. To be sure, *Mass Psychology* rooted working-class authoritarianism in a patriarchal family structure that promoted sexual repression, economic exploitation, and a fear of freedom. Fromm critiqued *Mass Psychology* in a 1936 report on his German workers study and praised it as a pioneering work. He noted (as few other critics had) that the Reich volume had overemphasized the importance of genital sexuality.

28. Max Horkheimer to Charles P. Muller, Nov. 12, 1938; Friederich Pollock to Fromm, Oct. 10, 1932, both in Fromm Archive. The most comprehensive study of the move to Columbia, which established Fromm's central role in the relocation, is

Thomas Wheatland, "Critical Theory on Morningside Heights: From Frankfurt Mandarins to Columbia Sociologists," *German Politics and Society* 22, no. 4 (Winter 2004): 1–85. See also Wiggershaus, *Frankfurt School*, 143–148; Funk, *Erich Fromm*, 74–77; and Fromm to Horkheimer, Nov. 4, 1938, Horkheimer Archive, Frankfurt.

29. Fromm, "The Theory of Mother Right and Its Relevance for Social Psychology" (1934), in *Love, Sexuality, and Matriarchy* (New York: International Publishing Corporation, 1997), 21–37.

30. Ibid., 38–45.

31. Fromm, "On the Theory of Mother Right and Its Relevance for Social Psychology" (1934), "The Male Creation" (1934), and "Robert Briffault's Book on Mother Right" (1933), plus some subsequent Fromm papers on Bachofen in *Love, Sexuality, and Matriarchy*, 19–84 but esp. 30–45.

32. Fromm, *Love, Sexuality, and Matriarchy*, 38–45; Funk, *Erich Fromm*, 75. Fromm, "The Social Psychological Significance of the Theory of Matriarchy," *Zeitschrift für Sozialforschung* 3 (1934): 215.

33. Fromm, "Robert Briffault's Book on Mother Right" (1933), in *Love, Sexuality, and Matriarchy*, 76–84.

34. Erich Fromm to Tom Bottomore, Mar. 26, 1974, Fromm Archive; Wiggershaus, *Frankfurt School*, chap. 3; Wheatland, "Critical Theory on Morningside Heights," 1–3.

35. Fromm, "Sozialpsychologischer Teil," in *Studien über Autorität und Familie, Forschungsberichte aus dem Institut für Sozialforschung* (Paris: Felix Alcán, 1936), 78–134. Wiggershaus, *Frankfurt School*, 151.

36. Fromm, "Sozialpsychologischer Teil," 95, 123.

37. Ibid., 109–116.

38. Ibid., 109, 113–116.

39. Ibid., 111, 120–125.

40. Ibid., 125.

41. Ibid., 128–134.

42. Ibid., 114 n. 30.

43. Ibid., 131–135. See also Wiggershaus, *Frankfurt School*, 270.

44. The most detailed account of Fromm's travel to seek recovery from illness during the 1930s is in Funk, *Erich Fromm*, 74–88.

45. On his four-hundred-dollar monthly salary: Erich Fromm to Whom It May Concern, Dec. 31, 1936. On contract conditions, salary, and expenses: Frederick Pollock to American Consul General, Berlin, Jan. 6, 1939, Société Internationale de Recherches Sociales; and Erich Fromm, Agreement, June 1937, Fromm Archive. In the Fromm Archive, one finds expense statements Fromm submitted to the Institute during the late 1930s. See the Horkheimer-Fromm correspondence in the Horkheimer Archive, Frankfurt, esp. Horkheimer to Fromm, Dec. 10, 1935; and Fromm to Horkheimer, Nov. 4, 1938. Fromm memorandum to Kurt Rosenfeld, Nov. 16, 1939, Fromm Archive.

46. Fromm to Kurt Rosenfeld, Nov. 19, 1939; and Fromm to Friederich Pollock, Nov. 7, 1939, Fromm Archive. Horkheimer to Fromm, Nov. 7, 11, 1939, in

Horkheimer Archive. Wiggershaus, *Frankfurt School*, 271; Martin Jay, *Dialectical Imagination*, 167–168.

47. Ibid.

48. Fromm to Rosenfeld, Nov. 16, 1939, Fromm Archive; Wiggershaus, *Frankfurt School*, 271–272; Fromm to Harcourt, Brace, and Company, Apr. 27, 1937, Fromm Archive.

49. Wiggershaus, *Frankfurt School*, 265–271; Fromm to Martin Jay, May 14, 1971, Fromm Archive. "The manner of a girlfriend": Adorno to Horkheimer, Nov. 2, 1934, Horkheimer Archive.

50. Adorno to Horkheimer, Sept. Nov. 2, 1934, Horkheimer Archive; Fromm to Jay, May 14, 1971, Fromm Archive; Wiggershaus, *Frankfurt School*, 270–271; Jay, *Dialectical Imagination*, 116–117.

51. Erich Fromm to Karl A. Wittfogel, Dec. 18, 1936, Fromm Archive; Fromm to Max Horkheimer, Sept. 10, 1937, Horkheimer Archive.

52. Erich Fromm, "A Contribution to the Method and Purpose of Analytical Social Psychology" (1937), Fromm Papers, New York Public Library, and Fromm Archive, 2–9. This essay was published for the first time in the *Yearbook of the International Erich Fromm Society* 6 (1995): 189–236, but I am quoting from the original 1937 draft that Fromm translated into English.

53. Ibid., 23, 33, 42 (mentioning Marx), 44.

54. Wiggershaus, *Frankfurt School*, 265–267; Adorno to Horkheimer, Mar. 21, 1936, Horkheimer Archive; Fromm to Raya Dunayevskaya, Oct. 2, 1976, Fromm Archive, recalling how he described Adorno as "a puffed up phrase-maker." Richard H. King, *Race, Culture, and the Intellectuals* (Washington, D.C.: Woodrow Wilson Center Press, 2004), 75.

55. Wiggershaus, *Frankfurt School*, 268; Martin Jay, "The Frankfurt School's Critique of Marxist Humanism," *Social Research* 39 (1972): 301.

56. Jay, "Frankfurt School's Critique," 294–305, brilliantly discusses this difference between Fromm on the one hand and Adorno and Horkheimer on the other. Wiggershaus, *Frankfurt School*, 268. Adorno to Fromm, Nov. 16, 1937, Fromm Papers, New York Public Library, seems to defer to Fromm in the Institute hierarchy but already indicates a marked difference between the two in their perspectives on social psychology. "On account of grave scientific differences . . .": Theodor Adorno, *Letters to His Parents, 1939–1951* (Cambridge: Polity Press, 2006), 62–63 (July 23, 1940, letter).

3. The Americanization of a European Intellectual

1. Wilhelm Reich to Erich Fromm, March 9, June 5, July 12, August 3, Sept. 3, 5, Oct. 31, 1932, Fromm Archive, Tubingen. Louise Hoffman, "Psychoanalytic Interpretations of Adolf Hitler and Nazism, 1933–1945: A Prelude to Psychohistory," *Psychohistory Review* 11, no. 1 (Fall 1982): 76–77, linking Reich's *Mass Psychology* to Fromm's *Escape from Freedom*. Fromm recounting early worries of the Nazi menace: Gerard

Khoury, TRI by LJF, Aix-en-Provence, Oct. 24, 2005. See also Martin Jay, *The Dialectic Imagination: A History of the Frankfurt School and the Institute of Social Research, 1923–1950* (Boston: Little, Brown, 1973), 94–97.

2. Fromm to Margaret Mead, Dec. 26, 1936, Fromm Archive; Fromm to Gustav Bally, Oct. 10, 19, 1936, Jan. 4, Mar. 4, 1937, May 24, 1938, Fromm Archive. See also Fromm to Karl Wittfogel, Dec. 18, 1936, Fromm Archive.

3. Fromm to Otto Rühle, Dec. 29, 1937; and Fromm to Horkheimer, Feb. 1938, Fromm Archive. Fromm to Horkheimer, Nov. 7, 1938, Max Horkheimer Archive, Frankfurt.

4. Gertrud Hunziker-Fromm, TRI by LJF, Zurich, May 9, 2004, on the import of giving the canary the option of freedom. Fromm to Robert Lynd, Mar. 1, 1939, Fromm Archive. Alexis de Tocqueville, *Democracy in America* (New York: Vintage, 1945), 2:347. See also Charles Pearce to Fromm, Mar. 17, 1937; and Fromm to Charles Pearce, June 22, 1938, Fromm Archive. On "finally" being cured of tuberculosis: Rainer Funk, *Erich Fromm: His Life and Ideas* (New York: Continuum, 2000), 87. Lynd's efforts are acknowledged in Fromm to Lynd, Mar. 1, 1939, Fromm Papers, microfilm reel, New York Public Library. See also Thomas Wheatland, "Critical Theory on Morningside Heights: From Frankfurt Mandarins to Columbia Sociologists," *German Politics and Society* 22, no. 4 (Winter 2004): 1–87.

5. Fromm to Carl Müller-Braunschweig, Mar. 11, 1936, Archive of the British Psychoanalytic Society, and reprinted in Funk, *Erich Fromm*, 128. On the 1938 Davos meeting where she and Erich discussed the threat to their relatives: Gertrud Hunziker-Fromm, TRI by LJF, Zurich, May 10, 2004.

6. Funk, *Erich Fromm*, 77; Erich Fromm, "Declaration of Intention," Nov. 21, 1934, and "Petition, for Naturalization," Jan. 5, 1940, Certificate #4768531. Copies of both were ordered from the U.S. Citizenship and Immigration Services. Rainer Funk commented that Fromm's library contained very few volumes from his time in Germany.

7. Funk, *Erich Fromm*, 48; Rosa Fromm to Erich Fromm, Apr. 2, 1935, Fromm Archive; Erich Fromm to Harold Lasswell, Nov. 21, 1936, Fromm Archive.

8. U.S. individual income tax returns filed by Fromm for 1937, 1938, and 1939, Fromm Archive. Fromm to Frankfurter Sparkasse, June 26, 1936; and Fromm to Charles Somlo & Co., Jan. 7, June 22, Dec. 14, 1937, Fromm Archive. Miscellaneous receipts for money orders sent to Rosa Fromm, Fromm Archive. The exact 2008 equivalents of the 1936 amounts are $77,670.63 to $93,204.76 (the Frankfurt Institute salary), $31,068.25 from the psychoanalytic practice, and $3,184.50 in monthly payments to Fromm's mother. These amounts represent the purchasing-power equivalents and were calculated with the help of www.measuringworth.com. I had to make rough estimates without the existence of a revised formula for Fromm's income in 2012 dollars, but these cannot be far off the mark.

9. Funk, *Erich Fromm*, 48–49; Fromm to Max Horkheimer, Dec. 1, 1938; and Horkheimer to Fromm, Dec. 1, 1938 (cable), Horkheimer Archive; Bella Fromm to Erich Fromm, Apr. 27, 1939, Fromm Archive. Bella was from the National Coordinating Committee.

10. Affidavit of Support for Heinz Brandt (by Fromm), New York County Clerk, Mar. 5, 1941; Fromm Papers, New York Public Library, promising Ludwig Krause to help his grandchildren.

11. Knud Andresen to LJF (e-mail), Dec. 13, 14, 2005; and especially Andresen, *Widerspruch als Lebensprinzip: Der Undogmatische Sozialist Heinz Brandt, 1909–1986* (Bonn: Dietz, 2007), 82–139, detailing (as Heinz Brandt's biographer) his sundry imprisonments and deportations. See also Fromm, "Heinz Brandt as a Man of Faith" (1963); Fromm to Clara Urquhart, Feb. 27, 1964; EF memo about Mr. Gotsche's letter, Jan. 2, 1964; all in Fromm Archive. Miriam Rothbacher, TRI by LJF, Vienna, May 19, 2004.

12. Knud Andresen to LJF, Dec. 13, 14, 2005 (e-mail); Miriam Rothbacher, TRI by LJF, Vienna, May 19, 2005.

13. Charles Somlo to Fromm, Nov. 17, 1936, Jan. 6, 1937; Fromm to Max Horkheimer, Dec. 22, 1938, Horkheimer Archive, Frankfurt; Hermia Neild to Fromm, Apr. 5, 1939; and Fromm to Neild, n.d. (1939); Madame Favez to Fromm, Feb. 17, 1939; all in Fromm Archive. Miriam Rothbacher, TRI by LJF, Vienna, May 19, 2004. Knud Andresen, e-mail to LJF, Dec. 13, 2005.

14. Madame Favez to Fromm, Jan. 26, Feb. 28, 1940; Fromm to Favez, Apr. 25, 1940; all in Fromm Archive. Fromm to Ernest Levy, June 19, 1940 (Fromm Archive) asking for Shanghai money from him and William Reichart in Boston at Gertrud Brandt's request. Fromm's affidavits of support (Fromm Archive) are dated Jan. 1939, Dec. 19, 1940, and March 5, 1941. The 1941 affidavit contains Fromm's "Since this young man has lost his father" remark. See also Knud Andresen to LJF, Dec. 13, 14, 2005.

15. Fromm, "Heinz Brandt as a Man of Faith" (1963), and Fromm to Clara Urquhart, Feb. 27, 1964, both in Fromm Archive. Miriam Rothbacher, TRI by LJF, Vienna, May 19, 20, 2004. Correspondence between Gertrud Brandt and Lisa Jacob, largely covering the year 1941, was held for decades by Lili Brandt but eventually made its way to Miriam Rothbacher, who allowed me to make copies. Another set of copies are in the Fromm Archive. Knud Andresen, e-mail to LJF, Dec. 13, 14, 2005. Andresen quotes Brandt's "luck, luck, and luck again" remark. See also Andresen, *Widerspruch als Lebensprinzip*, 127–158.

16. Ibid., plus Knud Andresen, e-mail to LJF, June 16, 2004, Dec. 14, 2005 (detailing Fromm's correspondence with and support for Brandt from 1945 on).

17. I deposited copies of all of Sophie Krause Engländer's letters to Eva Engländer Krakauer between 1939 and 1942 in the Fromm Archive. Archivist Rainer Funk provides a wonderful contextual introduction to the larger Krause family and reproduces some of Sophie's letters in "Erleben von Ohnmacht im Dritten Reich," *Fromm Forum* 9 (2005): 35–79.

18. Miriam Rothbacher, TRI by LJF, Vienna, May 19, 2004. Sophie Engländer to "Meine Kinder" (Eva and Bernhard Krakauer), May 1, 1939; David Engländer to "Meine Kinder," June 18, 1939.

19. Rothbacher, TRI by LJF, Vienna, May 18, 19, 2004.

20. Sophie Krause Engländer to Eva Krakauer, Jan. 1, 1940 (on no "rich" American relative); Aug. 8, 1939 (hoping "Erich would chip in"); Aug. 12, 1940; and June 20,

1941 (on Fromm helping Heinz Brandt and implying that he should also help her more). Miriam Rothbacher, TRI by LJF, Vienna, May 18, 19, 2004, recalling that her mother, Eva Krakauer, felt that the childless Fromm lacked a sense of family responsibility and preferred the politically active Heinz Brandt over Sophie and David.

21. Sophie Engländer to Eva Krakauer and family, Apr. 18, May 1, May 6, May 10, June 6, June 28, 1939. Although Sophie's letters to Eva reveal details on these family migrations, the most comprehensive account is provided in Miriam Rothbacher, TRI by LJF, Vienna, Mar. 18, 2004.

22. See, e.g., Sophie Krause Engländer to Eva Engländer Krakauer, Mar. 30, 1939, June 5, 1939, Nov. 16, 1941. Miriam Rothbacher, TRI by LJF, Vienna, May 19, 2004. Erich Fromm "Affidavit of Support" (for Martin and Johanna Krause), May 1941, Fromm Archive.

23. Sophie Krause Engländer to Eva Engländer Krakauer, July 13, Aug. 29, 1942; Sept. 30, 1939; Nov. 2, 1940.

24. Sophie Krause Engländer to Eva Engländer Krakauer, May 5, July 11, Oct. 10, Oct. 17, Nov. 10, 1939; Mar. 9, Aug. 12, 1940; June 20, 1941. Miriam Rothbacher, TRI by LJF, Vienna, May 18, 19, 2004.

25. Sophie Krause Engländer to Eva Engländer Krakauer, Oct. 10, 1939; Jan. 11, Oct. 20, 1940; Nov. 11, 16, 1941.

26. For Fromm's efforts in the Peter Glück case, see Fromm to Glück, Feb. 5, 1940; Fromm Affidavit of Support for Glück, Aug. 1940; Fromm to Sheba Stronski, Dec. 5, 1940; Fromm to John Norman, June 3, 1943; Eva Wiegelmesser to Erich Fromm, Dec. 12, 1940; Catherine Fitzgibbon to Erich Fromm, Aug. 10, 1940. All of this correspondence on Fromm's role in specific emigration cases is found in the Fromm Archive.

27. Fromm to Joe Stone, Oct. 1, 1936; and John Dollard to Fromm, Feb. 8, 1938, both in Fromm Archive; Rainer Funk to LJF, Nov. 23, 2005. On Fromm's enthusiastic acquisition of English: Funk, PI by LJF, Tubingen, Jan. 1, 2004.

28. Joanne Meyerowitz, "'How Common Culture Shapes the Separate Lives': Sexuality, Race, and Mid-Twentieth-Century Social Constructionist Thought," *Journal of American History* 96, no. 4 (2010): 1057–1084.

29. Ibid. For one of the stronger presentations on the "modernist" and heavily Freudian turn in early and mid-twentieth-century thought and values, see Dorothy Ross, *After Freud Left: New Reflections on a Century of Psychoanalysis in America* (Chicago: University of Chicago Press, 2011).

30. Funk, *Erich Fromm*, 104; Marianne Horney Eckardt, "Karen Horney: A Portrait," unpublished paper (1950), 5; Eckardt, PI by LJF, Laguna Woods, Calif., Dec. 17, 2005.

31. Renate Horney, PI by LJF, Laguna Woods, Calif., June 26, 2004, recalls Fromm visiting the Horney house in Berlin almost as a family member. For the beginnings of the break from psychoanalytic orthodoxy in Berlin, see Funk, *Erich Fromm*, 104; Bernard J. Paris, *Karen Horney: A Psychoanalyst's Search for Self-Understanding* (New Haven, Conn.: Yale University Press, 1994), 144; Janet Sayers, *Mothers of Psychoanalysis: Helene Deutsch, Karen Horney, Anna Freud, Melanie Klein* (New York: W. W. Norton, 1991), 88–102.

32. Sayers, *Mothers*, 102–111; Funk, *Erich Fromm*, 76–77.

33. Erich Fromm to Paul Roazen, Sept. 5, 1973, Fromm Papers, recalling his admiration of Horney as "a rather courageous person" and her bold critique of psychoanalytic orthodoxy. Sayers, *Mothers*, 105; While Paris, *Horney*, chap. 21, treats Horney's sex life in some detail, especially the particulars of her relationship with Fromm, one learns no little amount from Marianne Horney Eckardt, PI by LJF, Laguna Hills, Calif., Sept. 9, 2006, Feb. 3, 2007; Daniel Burston, *The Legacy of Erich Fromm* (Cambridge, Mass.: Harvard University Press, 1991), 23.

34. Karen Horney, *The Neurotic Personality of Our Time* (New York: Norton, 1937), esp. 290; Sayers, *Mothers*, 113.

35. Karen Horney, *New Ways in Psychoanalysis* (New York: Norton, 1939); Karen Horney, *Self-Analysis* (New York: Norton, 1942). See also Sayers, *Mothers*, 122–126, 130–133.

36. On insisting he was not a formal member of the Zodiac circle but recalling these early friendships: Funk, *Erich Fromm*, 105; Fromm to Jack L. Rubins, Sept. 26, 1972, Fromm Archive. On Fromm explicating to the Zodiac circle the psychological basis of the Nazi appeal: Helen S. Perry, *Psychiatrist of America: The Life of Harry Stack Sullivan* (Cambridge, Mass.: Harvard University Press, 1982), 354–355.

37. Horney, *Self-Analysis*, 205–238; Paris, *Horney*, 145–147. Sayers, *Mothers*, 130–133.

38. For a very cogent discussion of building distance in the Fromm-Horney relationship, see Paris, *Horney*, 145–148.

39. Marianne Horney Eckardt, PI by LJF, Laguna Woods, Calif., July 4, 2003, Dec. 17, 2005; and Eckardt, TI by LJF, June 17, 2004, for her analysis with Fromm and its considerable impact on her relationship with her mother.

40. Paris, *Horney*, 144–147. On recalling seeing firsthand the presence of Dunham as Fromm's "girl friend": Patrick Mullahy to Helen Swick Perry, Aug. 8, 1965, Perry private collection.

41. Paris, *Horney*, 147–155; Fromm to Jack L. Rubins, Sept. 26. 1972, Fromm Archive; Marianne Horney Eckardt, PI by LJF, Laguna Woods, Calif., Dec. 17, 2005. See also Douglas Noble and Donald L. Burnham, "A History of the Washington Psychoanalytic Institute and Society," in *Psychoanalysis and Psychosis*, ed. Ann-Louise Silver (Madison, Conn.: International Universities Press, 1989), chap. 26.

42. In his rich biography of Horney, Paris clearly recognizes (146–150) that the course of the Horney-Fromm relationship both helped shape and was shaped by *Escape from Freedom*. As Fromm's biographer, my emphasis on this connection naturally differs somewhat from his.

43. Fromm, *Escape from Freedom* (New York: Henry Holt, 1941, 1965); Fromm to Harry Stack Sullivan, Nov. 29, 1939, Fromm Archive. For the eight reviews of *Escape from Freedom*, see *Psychiatry* 5 (1942): 109–134.

44. Perry, *Psychiatrist of America*, remains the most thorough and sensitive work on Sullivan's life, even though his relationship with Fromm could have been expanded. Chapter 23 covers his work with schizophrenics at Sheppard-Pratt.

45. Sullivan initially sketched out his theoretical position in 1932–1933, and it is available in his *Personal Psychopathology* (New York: Norton, 1972). See also Sullivan's *Schizophrenia as a Human Process* (New York: Norton, 1962), which contains selected Sullivan papers published between 1924 and 1935. Clara Thompson, "Sullivan and Fromm," *Contemporary Psychoanalysis* 15, no. 9 (1979): 195–200, brilliantly elaborates Sullivan's interpersonal psychoanalysis and shows how it overlaps decidedly with Fromm's perspectives. See also Stephen A. Mitchell and Margaret J. Black, *Freud and Beyond: A History of Modern Psychoanalytic Thought* (New York: Basic Books, 1995), chap. 3. Fromm summarized Sullivan's essential theory in "Harry Stack Sullivan's *Conceptions of Modern Psychiatry*" (1940), Fromm Archive.

46. Indications of Fromm's early response to Sullivan's thought are suggested in Funk, *Erich Fromm*, 108, 112–114; Fromm, "Harry Stack Sullivan's *Conceptions of Modern Psychiatry*" (1940), Fromm Archive; and Thompson, "Sullivan and Fromm," 195–197, 199. See also Patrick Mullahy to Helen Swick Perry, Aug. 7, 1965, Perry private papers. Direct Fromm-Sullivan correspondence is not in evidence before 1936.

47. Thompson, "Sullivan and Fromm." 195–197; Fromm, "Sullivan's Conceptions," Fromm Archive.

48. Perry, *Sullivan*, 380–388, shows Sullivan's support for Fromm at a consistent level.

49. Harry Stack Sullivan to Erich Fromm, Oct. 21, 1939; and Fromm to Sullivan, Oct. 27, 1936, Fromm Archive. Funk, *Erich Fromm*, 105–108.

50. Sullivan to Fromm, June 21, 1936; Fromm to Sullivan, June 26, 1936, Fromm Archive, on the nomination to the *Biographical Directory*. On praising the journal *Psychiatry* "covering the field": Fromm to Victor Gollancz, Nov. 3, 1942. On love as "readinesses" and illustrating how Sullivan helped Fromm frame theoretical issues: Fromm to Sullivan, Nov. 29, 1939, Fromm Archive. In gratitude, Fromm sent him Alsatian wine. See also Fromm to Sullivan, Apr. 31, 1936; and Sullivan to Fromm, Oct. 28, 1940, both in Fromm Archive.

51. Perry, *Sullivan*, 201–212.

52. Thompson's "Freud and Sullivan" essay came to be framed in the 1930s as she brought them together, but it was not completed until 1956. It appeared in M. R. Green, ed., *Interpersonal Psychoanalysis: The Selected Papers of Clara Thompson* (New York: Basic Books, 1964), and was reprinted in *Contemporary Psychoanalysis* 15, no. 9 (1979): 195–200.

53. Ibid.

54. Fromm to Margaret Mead, July 28, 1935, Jan. 18, 1939, May 20, 1946, Margaret Mead Papers, Library of Congress. Mead to Fromm, Jan., 1936, Feb. 2, 1936, Fromm Archive.

55. David Engerman, *Know Your Enemy: The Rise and Fall of America's Soviet Experts* (New York: Oxford University Press, 2009), is perhaps the top recent study of the emergence and progression of the field of Soviet studies and includes the Mead group as one of the constituencies. Mead wrote interesting letters to Erikson on the background of her group's Russian project and encouraged his involvement (Feb. 1, 8, Aug. 19, Mead Papers, B4, Library of Congress).

56. Mari Jo Buhle, *Feminism and Its Discontents: A Century of Struggle with Psychoanalysis* (Cambridge, Mass.: Harvard University Press, 1998), esp. 99–124, is one of the few studies to flesh out the feminist link between the neo-Freudians and Mead's cultural anthropologists. Clara Thompson summarized the three gender premises of the neo-Freudians in her book *Psychoanalysis: Evolution and Development* (New York: Thomas Nelson & Sons, 1950), which summarized the evolution of their thought. See also Thompson's *On Women*, ed. Maurice Green (New York: Mentor, 1971); it is noteworthy that Fromm wrote the foreword to the book.

57. A good deal of information on Dunham's early career is provided in Jennifer Dunning, "A Katherine Dunham Celebration," *New York Times* (January 14, 1979), D14; and Sally Sommer, "Katherine Dunham,"www.pbs.org/wnet/freetodance/biographies/dunham.html.

58. Fromm to Katherine Dunham, Feb. 20, 1937; and Dunham to Fromm (telegram), Feb. 24, 1937, both in Fromm Archive, on Fromm helping with her New York performances. Fromm to Dunham, June 25, 1940 (telegraph) shows Fromm wiring her money. On recalling the events leading to Sullivan taking Dunham into his house: Fromm to Sullivan, Oct. 6, 1939, Fromm Archive. See also Patrick Mullahy to Helen Swick Perry, Aug. 7, 1965, Perry private papers, recalling as a student residing in Sullivan's house how Fromm had persuaded Sullivan to let Dunham live there.

59. Fromm to Dunham, Feb. 20, 1937; and Fromm to Sullivan, Oct. 6, 1939, both in Fromm Archive.

60. There is a wonderful correspondence file in the Fromm Archive covering the Fromm-Dunham relationship after their affair ceased. Letter exchanges actually picked up in the 1960s, and these letters recounted earlier years.

61. "I see more and more": Dunham to Fromm, Dec. 9, 1966; "I thank you": Fromm to Dunham, Jan. 1, 1967, in Fromm Archive. On recollections of her relationship with Fromm and the evolution of her health and career: Dunham to Fromm, Nov. 30, Dec. 2, Dec. 21, 1966, Jan. 20, 1967. See also Fromm to Dunham, Dec. 16, 1966, on his heart troubles, advising her against using LSD, and offering to send her a safe antidepressant medication. All of these letters are in the Fromm Archive.

4. Escape from Freedom

1. Fromm to Robert Lynd, Mar. 1, 1939; Fromm to Stanley Rinehart Jr., Nov. 12, 1940; Fromm to David Riesman, Dec. 5, 1940, all in Fromm Archive, Tubingen.

2. Erich Fromm, *Escape from Freedom* (New York: Owl Books edition of Henry Holt and Co., 1994), ix–xi. The pagination of this paperback edition is identical to the original 1941 Holt, Rinehart, and Winston edition. For the best discussion of positive and negative freedom, see Isaiah Berlin, "Two Concepts of Liberty" in *Four Essays on Liberty* (London, 1969).

3. Ibid.

4. Ibid., 8 n. 3, 10, 12, 12 n. 6, 17, 20.

5. "Our aim is to show": Ibid., 104.

6. Ibid., 25–32.

7. Ibid.

8. Ibid., 39–43.

9. Ibid., 39–45, esp. 39–40 n.1 on periodization and 46–47 n. 5 deploying Burck-hart to understand early capitalism with the "growing competitive struggle for self-advancement." Fromm to Thomas Lewis Merton, Dec. 8, 1954, Fromm Archive.

10. Ibid.

11. Ibid.

12. Fromm, *Escape*, 46–48, 73–74.

13. Ibid., 78, 81, 83.

14. Ibid., 85, 87–91, 93.

15. "Destroyed the confidence": ibid., 97–98, 100–101. "Compulsion to work": 101–102. "In a closed world": 62.

16. For a sampling of the many reviews taking issue with *Escape from Freedom* on early Protestantism, see those by Anton Boisen, Patrick Mullahy, and M. F. Ashley Montagu in Harry Stack Sullivan's journal *Psychiatry* 5 (1942). Fromm acknowledged several of the failings of *Escape* in his remarkable letter to Thomas Merton, Dec. 8, 1954, Fromm Archive.

17. Fromm, "Selfishness and Self-Love," *Psychiatry* 2 (1939): 507–514, 523; Fromm, *Escape*, 110–117 (114 n. 2 on Sullivan).

18. Fromm, *Escape*, 116; and Fromm, "Selfishness and Self-Love," 521, both present the "the person who is not fond of himself" remark. For other remarks on how the absence of self-regard creates a depleted and greedy, always acquisitive personality, see Fromm's "Selfishness and Self Love," 518–523; and *Escape*, 119–121. It is instructive that much the same appraisal of the depleted self is presented half a century later in Philip Cushman's seminal article "Why the Self Is Empty: Toward a Historically Situated Psychology," *American Psychologist* 45, no. 5 (1990), esp. 600.

19. Fromm, *Escape*, 104–105, 107, 123–125.

20. Ibid.

21. Ibid.

22. Ibid., 118–119, 125.

23. Ibid., 125–126.

24. Ibid., 126–128.

25. "Style," "powerful though smooth," "fall in": ibid., 131. "A reflex," "compelled to conform": 203. See 183–204 for Fromm's fullest discussion of "automaton conformity."

26. Ibid., 149–156, 162–169, delineating sadomasochism. "He admires": 162. "That life is determined": 169.

27. Ibid., 220–235, analyzing *Mein Kampf* as the major source for the Nazi sado-masochist appeal. Fromm to Dr. Hartshorne, Jan. 8, 1940, Fromm Archive, acknowledging that "the theme of the Jews is so complex that it really requires a longer discussion" than he provided in *Escape*.

28. Fromm, *Escape*, 207–219. Timothy S. Brown, *Weimar Radicals: Nazis and Communists Between Authenticity and Performance* (Oxford: Berghahn Books, 2009), argues cogently that communist and Nazi extremisms in the Weimar Republic overlapped a great deal in its appeal, undermining Fromm's claim of working-class hostility toward the Nazi regime and ideology. Richard F. Hamilton, *Who Voted for Hitler* (Princeton, N.J.: Princeton University Press, 1982), takes on the lower-middle-class hypothesis and demonstrates through massive electoral statistical and other data that it does not hold up.

29. Fromm, *Escape*, 177–183. 179 n. 11, citing Horney. "The more the drive," "an intense envy": 182.

30. Ibid., 228–236.

31. Ibid., 236. "This respect for," "there is no higher power": 262–263.

32. Ibid., 270–274.

33. Ibid., p. 238 on "the authoritarian systems." For amplification of how Germany would ultimately throw off the Nazis: Fromm to Dr. Hartshorne, Jan. 8, 1941, Fromm Archive.

34. Fromm, *Escape*, 236–237.

35. Thomas Harvey Gill's review of *Escape*, in *Psychiatry* 5 (1942): 111.

36. Ibid.; Otto Fenichel, "Psychoanalytic Remarks on Fromm's Book *Escape from Freedom*," *Psychoanalytic Review* 31 (1944): 147–149, 152; Victor White, review of *Escape from Freedom* in *The Dublin Review* 212 (January 1943): 69. Russell Jacoby, *The Repression of Psychoanalysis: Otto Fenichel and the Political Freudians* (New York: Basic Books, 1983), provides the context for Fenichel's critique of Fromm.

37. Martin Jay's *The Dialectical Imagination: A History of the Frankfurt Institute of Social Research* (Boston: Little & Brown, 1973), 65, brilliantly presents Arendt's critique not only of Fromm but of most participants in the Frankfurt Institute.

5. Clinician and Ethicist

1. Erich Fromm, *Man for Himself: An Inquiry Into the Psychology of Ethics* (repr.; New York: Owl Books edition of Henry Holt, 1990), vii, 244. See also Fromm to Clara Urquhart, Dec. 20, 1971, Fromm Archive, Tubingen, for a clear continuation of his 1940s orientation. For a very cogent explication of "ethical" or "socialist" humanism, see Martin Halliwell and Andy Mousley, *Critical Humanism: Humanist/ Antihumanist Dialogues* (Edinburgh: Edinburgh University Press, 2003), chap. 3.

2. K. A. Cuordileone, *Manhood and American Political Culture in the Cold War* (New York: Routledge, 2005), 6–9, 99–100, argues compellingly that through *Escape from Freedom*, Fromm profoundly influenced the immediate postwar generation of liberal public intellectuals, including Schlesinger Jr., Lindner, and Tillich. Correspondence in the Fromm Archive, however, indicates that during the decade after *Escape*, he engaged in somewhat more limited exchanges with such figures.

3. Marianne Horney Eckardt, "Organizational Schisms in American Psychoanalysis," in *American Psychoanalysis: Origins and Development*, ed. Jacques Quen and Eric Carlson (New York: Brunner/Mazel, 1978), 144–149. Clara Thompson,

"History of the White Institute," *William Alanson White Newsletter* 8, no. 1 (Fall 1973): 3–5.

4. Ibid., plus Eckardt, TRI by LJF, Laguna Hills, Calif., July 4, 2003.

5. Helen Swick Perry, *Psychiatrist of America: The Life of Harry Stack Sullivan* (Cambridge, Mass.: Belknap Press of Harvard University Press, 1982), 385–391; Thompson, "History of the White Institute." Marianne Eckardt, TI by LJF, June 17, 2004, reviewing the origins of the White Institute.

6. Thompson, "History of the White Institute." Recalling Fromm as director of clinical training in the late 1940s: Robert M. Crowley, "Tribute to Erich Fromm," *Contemporary Psychoanalysis* 17, no. 4 (1981): 441–443. On Fromm's de facto marginalization at the White Institute: Marianne Eckardt, TI by LJF, June 17, 2004. Erich Fromm, "Foreword" (1964), Fromm Papers, New York Public Library (an introduction to the Clara Thompson papers), acknowledges that Thompson essentially ran White in its early years and did it well. For his reflections on the White Institute's first decade, see also Fromm to Clara Thompson, Apr. 12, 1956, Fromm Archive.

7. Harry K. Wells, *The Failure of Psychoanalysis: From Freud to Fromm* (New York: International Publishers, 1963), 191–196; Clara Thompson, *Psychoanalysis* (1950; repr. New Brunswick, N.J.: Transaction, 2003), 209–210. Fromm's paper, "Die gesellschaftliche Bedingtheit der Psychoanalytischen Therapie," in *Zeitschrift für Sozialforschung* (1935), is the first and perhaps the most comprehensive articulation of his clinical approach. This paper was published in English under the title "The Social Determinants of Psychoanalytic Theory," *International Forum of Psychoanalysis* 9, no. 3–4 (October 2000): 149–165.

8. Edward S. Tauber, "Erich Fromm: Clinician and Social Philosopher," *Contemporary Psychoanalysis* 15 (1970): 202–205, excellently summarizes the productive and unproductive orientations delineated in Fromm's *Man for Himself* (1947).

9. Erich Fromm, "The Social Order and Its Relation to Psycho-Analytic Therapy," *Zeitschrift für Sozialforschung* 4, no. 3 (1935): 365–397.

10. Fromm address at Memorial Meeting for Harry Stack Sullivan, White Institute, May 17, 1949, 5, Fromm Archive, distinguishing the "core" from the "periphery" and reacting "with our human core" even with psychotic patients. Fromm to Clara Urquhart, June 29, 1964, Fromm Archive. For witnesses to and elaborations of Fromm's "center to center" approach, see Leonard Feldstein, "The Face of Erich Fromm," *William Alanson White Newsletter* 15, no. 1 (Winter 1981): 5; Enzo Lio, "Erich Fromm: Psychoanalyst and Supervisor," *Fromm Forum* 2 (1998): 31–34; David E. Schecter, "Contributions of Erich Fromm," *Contemporary Psychoanalysis* 17, no. 4 (1981): 475; Marianne Horney Eckardt, "The Core Theme of Erich Fromm's Writings and Its Implication for Therapy," *Journal of the American Academy of Psychoanalysis* 11 (1983): 397–398. On center-to-center relatedness and "So that's you. And that's me too": Erich Fromm, "The Aim of the Psychoanalytic Process," *Fromm Forum* 2 (1998): 17–18 (reprint of presentation to William Alanson White Institute). Marco Bacciagaluppi, "Erich Fromm's Views on Psychoanalytic 'Technique,'" *Contemporary Psychoanalysis* 25, no. 2 (April 1989): 233, quoting Fromm's

"The analyst understands the patient only. . . . " See also Gérard Khoury, interview of Fromm, *Fromm Forum* 12 (2008): 35.

11. Fromm to Gertrud Hunziker-Fromm, Mar. 29, 1964, Hunziker-Fromm private papers, Zurich, reviewing the evolution of his technique for restoring "authentic thinking" in the patient. "In rational thought": Erich Fromm, "Remarks on the Problem of Free Association," *Psychiatric Research Reports* 2 (December 1955): 3.

12. Erich Fromm, *Greatness and Limitations of Freud's Thought* (New York: Harper & Row, 1980), 40, recalling his Berlin training with the couch and "this boredom," which he changed by "face to face" analysis. For comments on the timing of Fromm's transition to the chair, see Marianne Horney Eckardt, "From Couch to Chair," in *The Clinical Erich Fromm: Personal Accounts and Papers on Therapeutic Technique*, ed. Rainer Funk (Amsterdam: Editions Rodopi, 2009), 71–72. On Fromm's frequent questions for his analysands: Fromm, "Remarks on the Problem of Free Association," 4–5. For Fromm's pressing sense of urgency in his clinical work, see Bacciagaluppi, "Erich Fromm's Views on Psychoanalytic 'Technique,'" 234–235.

13. Fromm's students and colleagues differ on the import of his downplaying the transference issue. Michael Maccoby argues that it limited his clinical effectiveness in his essay "The Two Voices of Erich Fromm," in *A Prophetic Analyst*, ed. Michael Maccoby and Mauricio Cortina (New York: Aronson, 1996), chap. 2. Salvador Millan differs, arguing that Fromm was sufficiently attentive to transference ("The Social Dimension of Transference," in *A Prophetic Analyst*, chap. 9). Militiades Zaphiropoulos, TI by LJF, Nov. 14, 2005, substantially agrees with Maccoby. Interestingly, Ruth Lesser points out in her essay, "There Is Nothing Polite in Anyone's Unconscious," in *The Clinical Erich Fromm*, 91–99, that Fromm discouraged a focus on the broad analytic relationship, that is, transference and countertransference.

14. There is a file in the Fromm Archive of correspondence between Schecter and Fromm that points to Schecter's dependency and inability to foster his own autonomy (see, e.g., Fromm to Schecter, March 28, 1974). But the file affords only a few clues on why he committed suicide after Fromm's death. Some of Schecter's articles on Fromm indicate that he could not separate his conceptual and clinical work from Fromm's. See, e.g., Schecter's "Contributions of Erich Fromm," *Contemporary Psychoanalysis* 17, no. 4 (1981): 468–480; Schecter, "Awakening the Patient," in *The Clinical Fromm*, 73–83; and esp. Schecter, "On Human Bonds and Bondage," *Contemporary Psychoanalysis* 11, no. 4 (October 1975): 435–455 (which focuses on dependency and autonomy in a tribute to Fromm).

15. For Fromm on direct intervention versus potential transference distortions, see Erich Fromm, *Psychiatric Research Reports* 2 (December 1955): 3–6; Schecter, "Contributions of Erich Fromm," 475–478; Bacciagaluppi, "Erich Fromm's Views on Psychoanalytic 'Technique,'" 234–236; and especially Michael Maccoby, TRI by LJF, Washington, D.C., Feb. 2, 2003. Greta Bibring had warned Maccoby before his own analysis with Fromm that Fromm was reticent to analyze patient transference.

16. Fromm to David Schecter, Mar. 28, 1974, Fromm Archive. Erich Fromm, *The Forgotten Language: An Introduction to the Understanding of Dreams, Fairy Tales,*

and Myths (1951; repr. New York: Grove, 1957), 47, 109, defining his view of what a dream reveals as against Freud's and Jung's views. See 167–168 on the dream "like a microscope" but with no "quantitative" dimension. See also Biancoli, "The Humanism of Erich Fromm," *Contemporary Psychoanalysis* 28, no. 4 (1992): 720–721, for a cogent comment on Fromm's approach to dream interpretation.

17. Fromm, *The Forgotten Language*, 47, 109–110, 167–174.

18. Ibid., esp. 185, 192, 157 ("What is important"), 263 (apprehensions of death). On Fromm's approach to dream interpretation, see also Jay Kwawer, "A Case Seminar with Erich Fromm," *Contemporary Psychoanalysis* 11, no. 4 (October 1975): 454.

19. Fromm, *The Forgotten Language*, 9–10. On going into detail on Fromm's eclectic approach to dream interpretation: Gertrud Hunziker-Fromm, TRI by LJF, Zurich, May 10, 2004. See also Gérard Khoury's interview of Fromm published in *Fromm Forum* 12 (2008): esp. 35. Sales figures come from 1997 estimates by Rainer Funk, Fromm's literary executor.

20. Miltiades Zaphiropoulos, TI by LJF, Nov. 14, 2005; Tauber, "Erich Fromm," 206–207; Schecter, "Contributions of Erich Fromm," 470–473; Rose Spiegel, "Tribute to Erich Fromm," *Contemporary Psychoanalysis* 17, no. 4 (1981): 438–439; Ralph M. Crowley, "Tribute to Erich Fromm," *Contemporary Psychoanalysis* 17, no. 4 (1981): 443–444; Edward Tauber and Bernard Landis, "On Erich Fromm," *Contemporary Psychoanalysis* 11, no. 4 (October 1975): 414–417.

21. Ibid., especially the comments of Zaphiropoulos, Spiegel, and Tauber.

22. Ibid., particularly comments in my interview with Zaphiropoulos.

23. Helen Lynd interview by Mrs. Walter Gelhorn, 1973, transcript, 27–28, Columbia Oral History Project, Butler Library. Marianne Horney Eckardt, "Reflections on 'What Helps a Patient?'" unpublished 1980 lecture to Nassau County Psychoanalytic Group, esp. 4–9 on her analysis with Fromm. That analysis was also covered in some detail in Eckardt, TRI by LJF, Laguna Hills, Calif., July 4, 2003; and Eckardt, TI by LJF, June 17, 2004.

24. Eckardt, TRI, July 4, 2003.

25. Eckardt, TRI, July 4, 2003; and Eckardt, TI, June 17, 2004.

26. Rollo May to Fromm, Oct. 16, 1940, June 15, 1942, and Nov. 6, 1942, all in Fromm Archive in and the Fromm Papers. I have also drawn heavily on Robert Abzug's excellent biography in process on May and on his thoughts on Fromm's analysis of May. On May cribbing material from Fromm's analytic sessions: Daniel Burston, *The Legacy of Erich Fromm* (Cambridge, Mass.: Harvard University Press, 1991), 164–165. May's book, *Man's Search for Himself* (1954) lends some credence to Burston's charge of cribbing. See also May, *Power and Innocence: A Search for the Sources of Violence* (New York: Delta, 1972), 227.

27. Fromm to May, Sept. 28, 1951, May Papers, University of California at Santa Barbara, expressing warmth toward May. See May on Fromm at the White Institute, and favorable to Fromm's approach, in *Pastoral Psychology* 6, no. 56 (September 1955): 10. May to Fromm, Oct. 9, 1965, holding up Tillich and on Fromm's "superficial writing"; Fromm to May, Oct. 18, 1965, on "angry mood," both in May Papers.

28. Two outstanding sources on Riesman's early life and his analysis with Fromm are David Barboza, "An Interview with David Riesman," *Partisan Review* (1994): 574–585; and Wilfred M. McClay, *The Masterless: Self and Society in Modern America* (Chapel Hill: University of North Carolina Press, 1994), 238–255, 336 n. 30. See also Steven Weiland's very stimulating article "Social Science Toward Social Criticism: Some Vocations of David Riesman," *Antioch Review* 44 (Fall 1986): esp. 446–454. Although I have reviewed the extensive Fromm–Riesman correspondence in the Fromm Archive, it offers only suggestive glimmerings into the analysis.

29. Barboza, "An Interview with Riesman," 575–576, 582–584; McClay, *Masterless*, 336 n. 30.

30. Barboza, "An Interview with Riesman," 575–577; McClay, *Masterless*, 253–255. Robert J. Lifton, TI by LJF, Aug. 13, 2008, recounts in some detail what Riesman told him about being analyzed by Fromm. Erich Fromm, "Individual and Social Origins of Neurosis," in *Personality in Nature, Society, and Culture*, ed. Clyde Kluckhohn and Henry A. Murray (New York: Knopf, 1949), esp. 11. See also parts of Riesman to Rainer Funk, Oct. 10, 1980, Fromm Archive. Although the evidence on Robert Lynd's wife, Helen, is fragmentary for her analysis with Fromm, it had an intellectual quality, like Riesman's (i.e., he "cured" her writing block). See Mrs. Walter Gellhorn, interview of Helen Lynd, 1973, transcript, 27–28, Columbia Oral History Project.

31. Mauricio Cortina, PI by LJF, Washington D.C., July 30, 2009.

32. Joseph Gurland, "The Story of My Mother: Henny (Meyer) Gurland, 1900–1952," 3–5, Fromm Archive.

33. Ibid., 5–9.

34. Ibid., 13–16; plus Joseph Gurland to Rainer Funk, Dec. 28, 1992; and Gurland to Rolf Tiedemann, June 25, 1981, both in Fromm Archive. On the metal in Henny's side: Doris Gurland, PI by LJF, Providence, R.I., Aug. 23, 2009.

35. Joseph Gurland, "The Story of My Mother," 17–18; Rainer Funk, *Erich Fromm: His Life and Ideas* (New York: Continuum, 2000), 122.

36. Joseph Gurland, "The Story of My Mother," 18; J. H. Coler to Erich Fromm, Nov. 13, 1941, Fromm Archive (Fromm helping Henny through the National Refugee Service). "I am no longer homesick": Henny Gurland to Izette de Forest, Nov. 26, 1943, Fromm Archive. Burston, *The Legacy of Erich Fromm*, 25, emphasizes the rapidity of the development of the Fromm–Henny Gurland relationship and Fromm's early offer to fund Joseph's education.

37. Henny Gurland to Izette de Forest, Feb. 20, 1944. Joseph Gurland, "Application for Federal Employment," n.d. (1946), Fromm Archive, details his wartime duties with the army.

38. On her photography work, the pending move to Bennington, and how "Erich wants to finish his book": Henny Gurland to Izette de Forest, June 5, 1946, Fromm Archive. On Selver's impression of Fromm, his busy schedule in New York, and the move to Bennington: Funk, *Erich Fromm*, 122–126.

39. Henny Gurland to Izette de Forest, June 5, 1946, Fromm Archive. On Henny's "searching and penetrating mind": Erich Fromm, *Psychoanalysis and Religion* (New Haven, Conn.: Yale University Press, 1950), v.

40. On Binger telling him of Henny as schizophrenic: Michael Maccoby, PI by LJF, Cambridge, Mass., May 6, 2005. Detail on the new Bennington home (the address at the time was 228 Murphy Road) is provided in a residential listing form when it was put up for sale (Fromm Archive). Fromm mentions the loan from Riesman in a letter dated Sept. 10, 1976.

41. Lewis Webster Jones to Erich Fromm, June 17, July 8, 1942 and Fromm to Jones, July 10, 1942, all in the Fromm Archive and covering many aspects of his teaching at Bennington, including his self-doubts which he expressed to Jones. A long obituary appearing in the Bennington *Quadrille* (March 1980), described Fromm's teaching there and his selection as commencement speaker. On Fromm's almost letting the baby slide off his lap: Doris Gurland, PI by LJF, Providence, R.I., Aug. 23, 2009. The exact 2008 equivalent of $2,500 1946 dollars is $27,546.44, based on purchasing-power equivalents, and was calculated using www.measuringworth.com. Fromm to Frances Davis, Aug. 18, 1948; and Davis to Fromm, Sept. 3, 1948, Fromm Archive. On preparing to teach a second Bennington course on interpersonal relations: Fromm to Ernest Oppenheimer, Dec. 3, 1948, Fromm Archive. Fromm was also very much in demand at the New School. When he decided not to teach there in 1949, the New School's president, Bryn Hovde, strongly urged him to reconsider.

42. Funk, *Erich Fromm*, 126–127; Joseph Gurland, "Henny Gurland," 19 (underscoring Henny's elevated blood pressure problem, which others have omitted). For evidence of Erich Fromm attending to Henny night and day while rejecting invitations and opportunities, see, e.g., Fromm to M. F. Ashley Montagu, Dec. 31, 1947; and Fromm to Lucien Hanks, Oct. 14, 1948, both in Fromm Archive. Doris Gurland, PI by LJF, Providence, R.I., Aug. 23, 2009, on Henny's treatment. Gertrud Hunziker-Fromm, PI by LJF, Zurich, July 30, 2003, on Henny's depression being more debilitating than her pain.

43. On Gurland's 1948 marriage and the honeymoon gift: Rainer Funk, "Joseph Gurland" (obituary), *Fromm Forum* 9 (2005): 49. On the trip to the ocean: Fromm to William Gutman, Mar. 29, 1949, Fromm Archive. Fromm to Henry Pachter, Dec. 5, 1949, hopeful of a get-together; and Fromm to Djane Herz, Dec. 23, 1949, declining a concert invitation (both letters in Fromm Archive). The foreword of Fromm's published Yale lectures (*Psychoanalysis and Religion*) thanked Henny for her suggestions. Funk, *Fromm*, 126, quoting Fromm's June 3, 1949, letter to his sister-in-law.

44. Funk, *Erich Fromm*, 127; On Joseph and Dorothy Gurland living in Boston and Fromm staying with them: Fromm to Clyde Kluckhohn, March 22, 1949. On Henny being unable to complete the photograph order: Fromm to David Riesman, Nov. 29, 1949. All letters are found in the Fromm Archive. Doris Gurland, PI by LJF, Providence, R.I., Aug. 23, 2009.

45. Jorge Silva Garcia, TRI by LJF, Mexico City, March 21, 2004; and Renate Horney, PI by LJF, Laguna Hills, Calif., June 26, 2004. Fromm to Mr. Spratling, March 17, 1937; Fromm to Otto Rühle, Nov. 16, 1937, May 3, 1940; Fromm to Mrs. Durieux, May 14, 1937; Fromm to Señor Guadalupe, May 14, 1937; all in Fromm Archives.

46. Silva Garcia, TRI by LJF, Mexico City, March 21, 2004; Gertrud Hunziker-Fromm, PI by LJF, Zurich, July 30, 2003; Rainer Funk, PI by LJF, Tubingen, March 16, 2003; Fromm to Djane Lavois Herz, Dec. 23, 1949, Fromm Archive.

47. Rainer Funk, PI by LJF, Tubingen, March 16, 2003; Funk, *Erich Fromm*, 127. The Fromm-Selver correspondence of the early 1950s after the move to Mexico is in the Selver Papers, Special Collections, University of California, Santa Barbara. See especially Fromm to Selver, Sept. 29, Oct. 2, Oct. 7, Oct. 28, Nov. 2, Nov. 12, 1952; Selver to Fromm, Oct. 16, 1952.

48. Funk, *Erich Fromm*, 127, on Henny's health and the trips and ultimate move to Mexico City. On his "hope that Mexico will help to bring about her recovery": Fromm to Djane Herz, Dec. 23, 1949. On the birth of his first child and its effect on Erich: Joseph Gurland, "Henny Gurland," 19. Here Joseph attributed Henny's death to "heart failure" though he almost certainly knew otherwise. Funk, PI by LJF, Tubingen, March 16, 2003, presenting his account and private archival data indicating that death came when Henny slit her wrists. Doris Gurland confirmed this to Funk. For a reference to Erich Fromm's discovery of Henny after her suicide, see also Rainer Funk, "Meet Erich Fromm," in Erich Fromm, *The Art of Loving* (New York: Harper Perennial, 2006), 16. For an additional reference to Fromm's discovery of Henny and the quote "Now I am quite sure," see Fromm to Izette de Forest, July 22, 1952. For Charlotte Selver's recollection and contextualization of Fromm's statement that he could not help Henny, see Charlotte Selver, PI by Rainer Funk, St. Ulrich, Aug. 10, 1997, Fromm Archive. Translated from the German original ("Ich konnte Henny nicht helfen") by Anke Schreiber.

49. On Henny's final years and death and their effect on Fromm: Funk, *Erich Fromm*, 136; and Funk, PI by LJF, Tubingen, March 18, 2003. Acknowledging the affairs after Henny's death: Fromm to Annis Freeman, March 25, 1953. Robert Coles sensitively recounts helping Horney when he was a medical student at Columbia-Presbyterian Medical Center in New York as she was dying of cancer; see Coles's *The Secular Mind* (Princeton, N.J.: Princeton University Press, 1999), 83–85. Fromm to Charlotte Selver, Feb. 26, 1953; Selver to Fromm, Oct. 16, 1953, Selver Papers, University of California, Santa Barbara. For strong suggestions of an affair between Fromm and Charlotte Selver, see Fromm to Selver, Dec. 6, 19, 1952, Feb. 15, 1953, Fromm Archive.

50. Erich Fromm to Ashley Montagu, May 7, Dec. 31, 1947, Fromm Papers, on a book concerning Freud's publications. The UNESCO project and Fromm's potential role in it are covered in Fromm to Pendleton Herring and Herbert Abraham, Jan. 1, 1949; Fromm to O. A. Oesar, May 20, 1949 ("more complicated"); Fromm to Charles Dollard, March 4, 1949 (on Carnegie Foundation funding and "authoritarianism versus independence"). All letters in Fromm Archive.

51. Fromm, *Man for Himself*, 213–214, 244. Menninger's negative review in K. Menninger, "Loneliness in the Modern World," *The Nation* (March 14, 1942): 154.

52. Fromm, *Man for Himself*, 206, 210–213.

53. Ibid., 187–191, 206, 216.

54. Ibid.

55. Ibid., *Man for Himself,* 212 n. 67, suspecting criticism from Niebuhr. Reinhold Niebuhr, review of *Man for Himself* in *Christianity and Society* 13, no. 2 (Spring 1948): 26–28.

56. Erich Fromm, "Psychoanalytic Characterology and Its Application to the Understanding of Culture," in *Culture and Personality,* ed. S. Stansfeld Sargent and Marian W. Smith (New York: Viking, 1949), 1–12.

57. Fromm, *Man for Himself,* 62–63, 114.

58. Ibid., 64–65, 115.

59. Ibid., 65–67, 115.

60. Ibid., 67–78.

61. Ibid., 248.

62. Maslow's fully annotated copy of *Man for Himself* is in the Archives of the History of American Psychology, University of Akron. For astute reviews showing how *Man for Himself* anticipated Rieff's *The Triumph of the Therapeutic: Uses of Faith After Freud* (1966) and Rieff's earlier book, *Freud: The Mind of the Moralist* (1959), see, e.g., Asher Brynes, "End of Psychological Man Proclaimed," *Saturday Review* 31 (July 2, 1948): 25–26; and Milton Singer essay's on *Man for Himself* in *Ethics* 58 (1947–1948): 220–222.

63. Fromm, *Psychoanalysis and Religion,* v. Sales figures come from 1997 estimations by Rainer Funk, Fromm's literary executor.

64. Ibid., 1–2, 35–37.

65. Ibid., 94–95.

66. Ibid., 96–99, 91–92.

67. Ibid., 38–41 (especially 41 n. 4 on Suzuki).

68. Ibid., 41–42, 47–48.

69. Ibid., 49–50. Like Feuerbach, Fromm had a strong affinity to a younger and more flexible Marx than appeared in *Das Kapital.* In some ways, however, the young Marx was more determined to render historical change than Fromm and assuredly more so than Feuerbach.

70. Ibid., 84. Perhaps an indicator of Fromm's increasing popularity, *Psychoanalysis and Religion* was reviewed favorably by three popular psychology ("how to") reviewers—H. A. Overstreet in the *New York Times Book Review* 29, no. 10 (1950): 5–6; Andrea Nobile in *Filosofia Torino* 17 (1966): 124–126; and M. H. Maskin in *The New Republic* 124 (1951): 21–22.

6. To Love and to Mentor

1. David Riesman to Fromm, Nov. 2, 1960 (Riesman Papers, Harvard University), on an unpublished study conducted at UC Berkeley in 1959 by Hilde Himmelweig of the London School of Economics, asking whether students were vaguely familiar with the works of a number of leading "names." Students were more familiar with Freud, Faulkner, and Berlin than Fromm, but less with Jack Kerouac, Gide, William Whyte, and Riesman.

2. Jorge Silva Garcia, "Fromm in Mexico: 1950–1973," *Contemporary Psychoanalysis* 25, no. 2 (April 1989): 246–249; John Reichert, TRI of Alfonso Millán, circa 1985, transcript in Fromm Archives, Tubingen.

3. Ibid., plus Aniceto Aramoni, TRI by LJF, Mexico City, March 17, 2004; and Michael Maccoby to LJF, Sept. 29, 2011 (e-mail).

4. Maccoby to LJF, Sept, 28, 29, 2011 (e-mails). See also Marie Langer, *From Vienna to Managua: Journey of a Psychoanalyst* (London: Free Association Books, 1989), 131–133.

5. Maccoby to LJF, Sept. 29, 2011 (e-mail); and Maccoby, PI by LJF, Cambridge, April 13, 2012.

6. Ibid., plus Silva Garcia, TRI by LJF, Mexico City, March 21, 2004.

7. Silva Garcia, "Fromm in Mexico," 245; Silva Garcia, TRI by LJF, Mexico City, March 21, 2004. See also Michael Maccoby, TRI by LJF, Washington, D.C., Feb. 2, 2003.

8. Alfonso Millán, TRI by John Reichert, Mexico City, circa 1985, transcript in Fromm Archive; Salvador Millán, PI by LJF, Mexico City, March 16, 2004; Silva Garcia, "Fromm in Mexico," 248–250; Silva Garcia, TRI by LJF, Mexico City, March 21, 2004. Salvador Millán, "Mexican Time: Erich Fromm in Mexico—A Point of View," initially appeared in the *Jahrbuch der Internationalen Erich Fromm Gesellschaft* (1995) and has been modestly revised. It brilliantly discusses the contrast between Fromm's precise German sense of time, punctuality, and exactitude and the more joyous, less disciplined qualities in the culture that his Mexican students knew.

9. Alfonso Millán, TRI by Reichert, circa 1985, Fromm Archive; Salvador and Sonja Millán, PI by LJF, Mexico City, March 17, 2004; Silva Garcia, "Fromm in Mexico," 251; Silva Garcia, TRI by Reichert, circa 1985, Fromm Archive.

10. Ibid.

11. Alfonso Millán, TRI by Reichert, circa 1985; Aniceto Aramoni, TRI by LJF, Mexico City, March 17, 2004; Rebecca Aramoni Serrano, PI by LJF, Mexico City, March 21, 2004.

12. Alfonso Millán, TRI by Reichert, circa 1985, Fromm Archive.

13. Rainer Funk, *Erich Fromm: His Life and Ideas* (New York: Continuum, 2000), 131–132.

14. Aniceto Aramoni, TRI by LJF, Mexico City, March 17, 2004; Rebecca Aramoni Serrano, PI by LJF, Mexico City, March 21, 2004.

15. Fromm to Aniceto Aramoni, Oct. 8, 1973 ("I have always felt badly"); Feb. 7, 1967 ("It is important that the group learns . . . The main thing is that the group really learns to function without me"); Aramoni to Fromm, July 2, 1973, Sept. 26, 1973, Jan. 25, 1976, Nov. 5, 1975, July 9, 1979; all in Fromm Archive. There are many more letters in the Aramoni files in the Fromm Archive that underscore the problems inherent in this dependency relationship. See also Aramoni, TRI by LJF, March 17, 2004.

16. A. Irwin Switzer, *D. T. Suzuki: A Biography* (London: The Buddhist Society, 1985), provides a very comprehensive account of Suzuki's life and thought.

17. D. T. Suzuki, *Zen Buddhism: Selected Writings of D.T. Suzuki* (New York: Anchor, 1956), 103–108. See also D. T. Suzuki, *An Introduction to Zen Buddhism* (1934), republished with a foreword by C. G. Jung (London: Rider & Co, 1948); D. T. Suzuki, *The Training of the Zen Buddhist Monk* (repr. New York: University Books, 1959); D. T. Suzuki, *Zen and Japanese Culture* (New York: Pantheon, 1959).

18. Fromm to D. T. Suzuki, Oct. 18, 1956, Fromm Archive, on the dinner in New York, the December trip to Cuernavaca, and an offer of a permanent residence for Suzuki at Fromm's expense. See also Suzuki to Fromm, Sept. 9, 1955, May 7, 1956, Fromm Papers, New York Public Library.

19. Suzuki to Fromm, n.d. (Nov. 1956); Fromm to Suzuki, Nov. 15, 18, 1956, all in Fromm Papers, NYPL.

20. Suzuki to Fromm, Feb. 14, March 13, 1957; Fromm to Suzuki, Jan. 29, Feb. 25, March 3, 1957, all in Fromm Papers, NYPL.

21. Fromm, "Memories of Dr. D. T. Suzuki," 1–3, Fromm Archive.

22. Funk, *Erich Fromm*, 134, underscores the importance of spiritual religion in Fromm's life.

23. Fromm, "Psychoanalysis and Zen Buddhism" (the 1959 revised edition of Fromm's 1957 conference paper), 3–8, Fromm Papers, NYPL.

24. Ibid., 9–10.

25. Ibid., 10–11.

26. Ibid., 14–19.

27. Ibid., 17–20.

28. Ibid., 21.

29. Ibid., 3, 8, 11, 21.

30. Fromm to Maurice Green, Dec. 13, 1958; Fromm to Suzuki, Nov. 19, 1960, on sales and royalties. Both letters are in the Fromm Archive. See also Fromm to Suzuki, July 3, 1958, June 15, 1960 (listing Suzuki as senior author), Fromm Papers. Sales figures are 1997 estimations by Rainer Funk, Fromm's literary executor.

31. On the increasingly personal support each gave to the other since the 1957 conference: Fromm, "Memories of Dr. D. T. Suzuki." On Suzuki's gifts of trees and seeds: Fromm to Suzuki, July 3, 1958. On his hearing loss and need to focus on writing: Suzuki to Fromm, July 21, 1959. On how "irksome" it was to accomplish tasks in old age: Suzuki to Fromm, April 27, 1966. All in Fromm Archive. On traveling to New York for advice on Annis's potential breast cancer: Fromm to Suzuki, Aug. 2, 1958, Fromm Archive.

32. Funk, *Erich Fromm*, 136–138; Gertrud Hunziker-Fromm, TRI by LJF, Zurich, May 9, 10, 2004; Funk, PI by LJF, Tubingen, March 18, 200.

33. In Funk, *Erich Fromm*, 138, the Fromm archivist Rainer Funk published one of many notes of deep affection Fromm wrote to Annis Freeman. It typifies the epistles Fromm wrote to Annis not only while they were engaged to be married but for the next several decades.

34. Ibid.

35. Gertrud Hunziker-Fromm, TRI by LJF, May 9, 2004 (including reference to the suicide pledge after Annis was operated on for cancer); Hunziker-Fromm, PI

by LJF, Zurich, July 30, 2003; Maccoby, TRI by LJF, Feb. 2, 2003; Dec. 18, 19, 2008. Funk, PI by LJF, Locarno, May 8, 2004, Hernando Ibarra, TRI by LJF, Cuernavaca, March 19, 2004, corroborating the cancer surgery and describing differences between Annis and Erich that seemed to endear them to each other. Sandy Lee Maccoby, TRI by LJF, Washington, D.C., Feb. 2, 2003, recalling as next-door neighbors in Cuernavaca how Annis was glamorous, worshipped Erich, and taught the principles of astrology. Fromm to Selver, Dec. 2, 1952, on initial contact with Annis, Fromm Archive.

36. Jorge Silva Garcia, "Fromm in Mexico," 245; Silva Garcia, TRI by LJF, Mexico City, March 21, 2004. See also Michael Maccoby, TRI by LJF, Washington, D.C., Feb. 2, 2003.

37. The best source on Fromm's food and drink and cigar favorites in Mexico is one of Alicia Garcia's son's, Hernando Ibarra. See Ibarra, TRI by LJF, Cuernavaca, March 19, 2004. On Fromm's love for Hassidic music and the piano: Silva Garcia TRI by LJF, Mexico City, March 21, 2004; and Silva Garcia to John Reichert, June 1, 1985. On Fromm's Buick, cigars, and Hassidic music: Michael Maccoby, TRI by LJF, Washington, D.C., Feb. 2, 2003. On New Year's Day Alaskan salmon: Rainer Funk, PI by LJF, Tubingen, May 15, 2004. On "Erich Fromm punch" and the love of baked goods: Salvador Millán, PI by LJF, Mexico City, March 21, 2004.

38. Carmen Delachica owned the Fromm's Cuernavaca house from 1976 until her death in 2005, and she let me walk through it and the grounds leisurely in March 2004 and answered a great many of my questions about the estate. See also Delachica, TRI by LJF, Cuernavaca, March 19, 2004.

39. Ibid., plus Hernando Ibarra, TRI by LJF, Cuernavaca, March 19, 2004.

40. These particulars of Fromm's joyous everyday life in Cuernavaca are reported in Michael Maccoby, TRI by LJF, Washington D.C., Feb. 2, 2003; and especially Maccoby, PI by LJF, Cambridge, April 14, 2012. Salvador Millán, PI by LJF, Mexico City, March 20, 21, 2004. Jorge Silva Garcia TRI by LJF, Mexico City, March 21, 2004.

41. Rainer Funk, "Titles by Erich Fromm," Fromm Archive, lists the sales figures and translations of all of Fromm's books by 1997 (at which time, *The Art of Loving* had been translated into thirty-three languages). In Funk, *Erich Fromm*, 139, Funk writes that the book had been translated into fifty languages. *The Art of Loving* was by far the best seller and the most frequently translated volume.

42. Fromm, *The Art of Loving* (repr. New York: Continuum Centennial Edition, 2000), 97–120.

43. Ibid., chap. 3, addressed why love was so difficult to fathom in modern Western capitalist society. Fromm took issue with Freud on 83; see 93 on love only occurring when "two people experience themselves from the essence of their existence." Maslow made extensive notes between 1957 and 1968 on Fromm's writings, especially *Man for Himself* but also *The Art of Loving*, as evident in the Maslow collection in the History of American Psychology Archive at the University of Akron.

44. Fromm, *The Art of Loving*, 24.

45. Ibid., 42, 52 n. 13, responding to Tillich. John N. Schaar, *Escape from Authority: The Perspectives of Erich Fromm* (New York: Basic Books, 1961), 134–136, makes

a very cogent case against Fromm's conflation of self-love, love of another, and love of humankind. Love, Schaar insists, is not an embrace of all of humanity but of particular human beings with unique characteristics in specific contexts.

46. Fromm, *The Art of Loving*, 42–44.

47. Ibid., 36–41, 44–47.

48. Ibid., 48–52.

49. Ibid., 57–74, esp. 63, 73–74. Fromm's secularism and his cultural Judaism from this point on in his life were well characterized in Moshe Budmor, TI by LJF, April 22, 2008; and Rainer Funk, PI by LJF, Tubingen, July 15, 2003.

50. Fromm, *The Art of Loving*, 95–96.

51. Joshua Loth Liebman, *Peace of Mind* (New York: Simon & Schuster, 1946). For perhaps the most penetrating of all discussions of Liebman and his book, see Andrew R. Heinze, *Jews and the American Soul: Human Nature in the Twentieth Century* (Princeton, N.J.: Princeton University Press, 2004), 217–239.

52. Fromm, *The Art of Loving*, 97–100.

53. Ibid., 107–109.

54. Ibid., 111–115.

55. Ibid., 115–116.

56. Ibid., 117–120.

57. Clara Thompson to Erich Fromm, Nov. 24, 1956, Fromm Archive.

58. For sales figures on *The Art of Loving*, the most comprehensive data comes from the Fromm Archive. Various editions of the book advertise sales figures on the book jackets. Rainer Funk synthesized much of the sales data in a May 6, 2008, letter to me; other figures are available in Funk, *Erich Fromm*, 139. I personally saw the volume in the window of the Harvard Cooperative on Valentine's Day 2008 and in all subsequent years. Indeed, a month before February 14, 2012, the Coop had stocked dozens of copies, anticipatory of Valentine's Day purchases.

7. Politics and Prose

1. Lawrence S. Wittner, *Resisting the Bomb: A History of the World Nuclear Disarmament Movement, 1954–1970* (Stanford, Calif.: Stanford University Press, 1997), 52; and Rainer Funk, *Erich Fromm: His Life and Ideas* (New York: Continuum, 2000), 141, on Fromm's role in the founding of SANE.

2. Long-term sales figures for *The Sane Society* are noted in Rainer Funk, "Titles by Erich Fromm," Fromm Archive, Tubingen. On the growing number of lectures he was asked to give after *The Sane Society*: Fromm to Richard Schifter, July 29, 1960, Fromm Archive. Fromm's summary of the book ("The Present Human Condition") appeared in *Perspectives* 16 (Summer 1956): 71–77. On the Gay lecture: *New York Times* (April 26, 1957). On *The Sane Society* and the widespread currency of the arguments Fromm made in it: Fromm to Thomas L. Merton, April 13, 1955; Merton to Fromm, Sept. 12, 1955, Fromm Archive.

3. Erich Fromm, *The Sane Society* (New York: Rinehart and Winston, 1955; repr. Owl Books, 1990), vii–viii, 3–21.

4. Ibid., 30–36. "Love is": 31.

5. "To create" and "if I cannot create life": ibid., 37. On matriarchy, patriarchy, and brotherly love: 44–45. "An inalienable right": 57. On identity: 60–62. On a frame of orientation with "an object of devotion": 63–65.

6. "As a business grows": Fromm, *Sane Society*, 86, 94–99. Quoting Stevenson and asserting "We do not submit": 102.

7. Ibid., 131–134, citing and deploying the 1844 Marx.

8. On Marx's utopianism: ibid., 236. On the current embrace of humanist activities: 207. Delineating the qualities of a sane society: 276.

9. Ibid., 295–336, esp. 295, 331, 335–336; Fromm, "The Present Human Condition," *The American Scholar* 25 (Winter 1955–1956): esp. 35.

10. Fromm, *Sane Society*, 339–343.

11. "Here again": ibid., 350. "Act out" and the meaning of "collective art": 347–348.

12. On education: ibid., 344–346. On humanistic religion: 349–352.

13. Although there is a good deal of scholarship on the young Marcuse, perhaps the most penetrating remains Richard King, *The Party of Eros: Radical Social Thought and the Realm of Freedom* (Chapel Hill: University of North Carolina Press, 1972), chap. 4.

14. For excellent discussions on *Dissent*'s early years and positions, and especially the perspectives of Howe and Coser on Fromm and related matters, see Maurice Isserman, *If I Had a Hammer: The Death of the Old Left and the Birth of the New Left* (Urbana: University of Illinois Press, 1993), 89–108; and Joanne Barkan, "Cold War Liberals and the Birth of Dissent," *Dissent* (Summer 2006): 95–102.

15. Herbert Marcuse, "The Social Implications of Freudian 'Revisionism,'" *Dissent* 2, no. 3 (Summer 1955): 221–240; Paul Goodman, "The Political Meaning of Some Recent Revisions of Freud," *Politics* 2, no. 7 (July 1945): 198–202.

16. Marcuse, "The Social Implications of Freudian 'Revisionism,'" 231–234, 238–239.

17. Erich Fromm, "The Human Implications of Instinctive 'Radicalism,'" *Dissent* 2, no. 4 (Autumn 1955): 342–349.

18. Ibid.

19. Herbert Marcuse, "A Reply to Erich Fromm," *Dissent* 3, no. 1 (Winter 1956): 79–81.

20. Erich Fromm, "A Counter-Rebuttal," *Dissent* 3, no. 1 (Winter 1956): 81–83.

21. For prominent intellectuals who largely reiterated Marcuse's critique of Fromm, see, e.g., H. Stuart Hughes, *The Sea Change: 1930–1965* (New York: Harper & Row, 1975); Paul Robinson, *The Freudian Left* (New York: Harper & Row, 1969); Russell Jacoby, *Social Amnesia: Conformist Psychology from Adler to Laing* (Boston: Beacon Press, 1975); Christopher Lasch, *The Culture of Narcissism* (New York: Basic Books, 1979). Neil McLaughlin's remark is from his article "Origin Myths in the Social Sciences: Fromm, the Frankfurt School, and the Emergence of Critical Theory," *Canadian Journal of Sociology* 24, no. 1 (1999): 109–139.

22. On Fromm's recall of the train incident with Marcuse: Gertrud Hunziker-Fromm, TRI by LJF, Zurich, May 10, 2004. On Marcuse asking for a review of

One-Dimensional Man and Fromm politely refusing: Marcuse to Fromm, Dec. 8, 1963; Fromm to Marcuse, January 8, 1964, Fromm Archive. Fromm to Raya Dunayevskaya, July 31, 1968; Fromm to Margit Norell, June 28, 1971, Fromm Papers, New York Public Library. In a letter to Fromm, Nov. 30, 1976, Fromm Archive, Dunayevskaya suggested that the fact that Fromm had been far more critical of Israel during the 1950s than Marcuse may have been an unstated factor in his attack on Fromm.

23. Fromm detailed his income and some of his donations during the 1950s and early 1960s in letters to his attorney Richard Schifter, April 17, 1959; July 29, 1960; June 3, 1960, Fromm Archive. Schifter put much of this data together in a memorandum: "In the Matter of Erich Fromm—Memorandum of Law and Fact" (1960), Fromm Archive.

24. A copy of Fromm's full FBI file (where his name is misspelled "Erick") was procured under the U.S. Freedom of Information Act and can be found in the Fromm Archive. Fromm to Norman Thomas, John Bennett, Lewis Mumford, Clarence Pickett, Max Lerner, Daniel Bell, Stephen Siteman, April 22, 1955, Fromm Archive, fashioning the public letter to the president on America's China policy. David Riesman to Rainer Funk, Oct. 10, 1980, Fromm Archive, outlining in considerable detail his work with Fromm and Fromm's funding for AFSC and the Committee on Correspondence. See also Fromm to Adam Schaff, May 8, 1962; Fromm to Thomas Merton, Nov. 3, 1960; Karl Polanyi, June 22, 1960; and Fromm to Polanyi, Nov. 21, 1960; Fromm to Bertrand Russell, Nov. 6, 1962; and Russell to Fromm, July 22, 1966, all in Fromm Archive.

25. Erich Fromm to Adlai Stevenson, Nov. 15, 1952, Fromm Archive. Fromm to Charlotte Selver, Nov. 15, 1952, Fromm Archive, indicates he had donated to the 1952 Stevenson campaign.

26. Adlai Stevenson to Erich Fromm, Nov. 26, 1952, Fromm Archive.

27. Fromm to Stevenson, March 24, 1954, Fromm Archive.

28. Ibid.

29. Ibid.

30. David Riesman to Rainer Funk, Oct. 10, 1980, Fromm Archive, notes the details of his and Fromm's 1956 meeting with Stevenson.

31. Stevenson to Fromm, Oct. 23, 1961; Fromm to Stevenson, January 20, 1961, Fromm Archive.

32. Stevenson to Fromm, May 1, 1962; Fromm to Stevenson, May 31, 1962, Sept. 15, 1962, Fromm Archive. Emphasizing how Fromm got documents on Germany unavailable to high U.S. officials and how he used this material to explain the Soviet relationship to the United States: Riesman to Funk, Oct. 10, 1980, Fromm Archive.

33. For a few illustrations of the strong personal dimension in the Riesman-Fromm political activist correspondence, see Riesman to Fromm, June 18, 1973, March 20, 1974; Fromm to Riesman, Oct. 9, 1947, April 19, 1955 (on life insurance), Feb. 1, March 6, 1975, Feb. 12, 1976. All letters are in the Fromm Archive.

34. On Riesman's background in law and the public sphere: Wilfred M. McClay, *The Masterless: Self and Society in Modern America* (Chapel Hill: University of

North Carolina Press, 1994), 236. On his and Fromm's early efforts in countering Zionism and pushing for a binational state in Palestine: Riesman to Rainer Funk, Oct. 10, 1980. On the *Commentary* article: Riesman to Fromm, Oct. 19, 1947. Recalling their work to secure a change in U.S. policy toward Israel: Riesman to Fromm, Dec. 17. 1973. On Israel's "Sampson [*sic*] complex": Riesman to Fromm, January 13, 1975. All letters are in the Fromm Archive.

35. Riesman to Funk, Oct. 10, 1980, Fromm Archive, provides the most detailed information available on how Riesman guided Fromm into a diversity of political activist ventures over the course of the 1950s and early 1960s, especially the Committee on Correspondence. See also Riesman to Brian R. Betz, Aug. 15, 1972, Fromm Archive.

36. On how Congressmen "find their relations with the Jewish community": J. William Fulbright to Erich Fromm, Nov. 25, 1975. "Your observations" and how to "be persuasive with the American Jewish community": Dec. 22, 1973. Urging Fromm to write to the *New York Times*: n.d. (1973). Urging Fromm to publish in a variety of national publications: Fulbright to Fromm, Aug. 21, 1975. All letters between Fulbright and Fromm are in both the Fulbright Papers at the University of Arkansas and in the Fromm Archive.

37. Fulbright to Fromm, May 7, 1968, and April 1, 1974, acknowledges Fromm's substantial contributions to the Fulbright reelection campaigns. Offering advice on campaign themes: Fromm to Fulbright, n.d. (Spring 1968). On testifying before Senate Foreign Relations Committee hearings: Fulbright to Fromm, April 11, 1972; Fromm to Fulbright, June 10, 1974. On the centrality of Fromm to Fulbright's intellectual stimulation: Fulbright's biographer, Randall Wood, to LJF, Dec. 17, 2008. See, pertinent to this point, Tristram Coffin to David Riesman, Oct. 10, 1966; Coffin to Fromm, Nov. 6, 1966, both in Fromm Archive.

38. "We did enjoy so much seeing you and Annis": Fulbright to Fromm, April 25, 1968. On health issues and surgeries for their wives and the zest for life evident in Erich and Annis: Fulbright to Fromm, Nov. 24, 1975. "Tocqueville was right": Fulbright to Fromm, n.d. (1973). On Fromm's finding an "inner questioning" in America: Fulbright to Fromm, Oct. 31, 1967. "You are so much a man resting in himself": Fromm to Fulbright, June 10, 1974. On Fromm contributing to the campaign and on sources for the Fulbright defeat: Tristram Coffin to David Riesman, March 30, June 23, May 18, 1974. All in Fromm Archive. On donating to the campaign: Fromm to Michael Maccoby, April 11, 1974 (Maccoby private papers).

39. Erich Fromm, "The Case for Unilateral Disarmament," *Daedalus* (Fall 1960), reprinted in *Arms Control, Disarmament, and National Security*, ed. Donald G. Brennan (New York: George Braziller, 1961), 187–197. Much of the exchange between Kennedy and *Daedalus*'s editor Gerald Holton is available in the archival holdings of the American Academy in Cambridge and supplemented by several discussions I had with Holton in June 2009 and May 2012. Discussions with Michael Maccoby in April 2011 focused on what Kennedy had read of Fromm's, the 1960 *Daedalus* article, and Fulbright and Stevenson acquainting Kennedy with Fromm's foreign policy perspectives.

40. Michael Maccoby elaborates the "Harvard connection" quite cogently in Maccoby, TRI by LJF, Washington, D.C., Feb. 2, 2003; Maccoby, TI by LJF, Jan. 16, 2007; Maccoby, PI by LJF, Apr. 14, 2012.

41. On Maccoby's thoughts on Kennedy's contact with Fromm: Maccoby, TI by LJF, Jan. 16, 2007; Maccoby, PI by LJF, Cambridge, April 14, 2012.

42. On several occasions in the 1990s, both Riesman and Kaysen told me that Kennedy contacted Fromm soon after the Cuban Missile Crisis. Riesman showed me his notes to that effect and was known for his accuracy and his memory. Kaysen's account of the Kennedy contact comported in all essentials with Riesman's. While Fromm never recounted to Maccoby the direct Kennedy contact with him, Maccoby felt it was entirely possible. Maccoby, PI by LJF, Apr. 14, 2012. Also see Riesman to Funk, Oct. 10, 1980, Fromm Archive.

43. Robert Dallek, *An Unfinished Life: John F. Kennedy, 1917–1963* (Boston: Little, Brown, 2003), 613–623; "far more security and far fewer risks": 620. I am especially indebted to Professor Dallek for helping me to understand how Bundy saw to it that the president knew of all perspectives (including Fromm's) on international relations concerns.

8. Prophecies for a Troubled World

1. Sales figures are 1997 estimates by Rainer Funk, Fromm's literary executor.

2. Erich Fromm, "Credo," in *Beyond the Chains of Illusion: My Encounter with Marx and Freud* (New York: Simon & Schuster, 1962; repr. New York: Continuum, 2001), 175–177.

3. Ibid., 178.

4. Ibid., 179–181.

5. Ibid., 180–182.

6. Rainer Funk, *Erich Fromm: His Life and Ideas* (New York: Continuum, 2000), 136, reproduces Fromm's 1953 wedding dinner photograph. It and other photographs of Fromm with his mother are found in abundance in the Fromm Archive, Tubingen. On bringing Rosa to his Cuernavaca home owing to her depression: Fromm to Izette de Forest, Oct. 31, 1957, Fromm Archive. The Hessisches Hauptstaatsarchiv in Wiesbaden has extensive records of Fromm's restitution actions (register no. W 54353) through Paul Simon on Rosa's behalf beginning in 1958 and extending to 1965, several years after her death. Beyond official documents, it houses several very revealing letters written by Simon to German authorities explaining the course of the legal actions and underscoring Fromm's distress with the process. On Fromm's sense of relief and energy with Rosa's death in 1959, confirming my own sense of the sparse documentary record: Rainer Funk, e-mails to LJF, Oct. 12, 13, 2006.

7. Rainer Funk, "Krankheiten": an incomplete list of Fromm's bouts of illness from 1932 to 1978, based on letters in the Fromm Archive. Fromm's correspondence with Adam Schaff, Angelica Balabanoff, and Clara Urquhart reveals considerably more illnesses, hospitalizations, and general periods of convalescence during

the 1960s than Funk's long list indicates. Funk, *Erich Fromm*, 150, reports Annis's bout with breast cancer, and it is alluded to in several of Fromm's letters to friends. Salvador Millán, PI by LJF, Mar. 17, 2004, Mexico City, discusses Annis's breast cancer in some detail and her limited diet, which Fromm shared for a year as a token of support.

8. Paul Roazen, "The Exclusion of Erich Fromm from the IPA," *Contemporary Psychoanalysis* 37, no. 1 (2001): 5–42, is the most detailed account. It is based heavily on Fromm–Eissler correspondence in the Fromm Archive. The most important letters in this correspondence are Fromm to Eissler, May 28, 1953; Eissler to Fromm, Jun. 11, 1953; Fromm to Eissler, Jun. 29, 1953 ("my psychoanalytic views do not correspond"); Eissler to Fromm, Jul. 27, 1953; Fromm to Eissler, Aug. 26, 1953.

9. For Fromm's growing difficulties with the Washington Psychoanalytic Society, see, e.g., Stanley Olinick to Fromm, May 20, 1955; Fromm to Olinick, May 31, 1955; Fromm to Sidney Berman, March 5, 1959; and Berman to Fromm, Mar. 30, 1959, all in Fromm Archive. For Fromm's efforts in establishing the International Federation of Psychoanalytic Societies, see Funk, *Erich Fromm*, 134–135; Roazen, "Exclusion of Fromm," 37.

10. The evolution of Fromm's critique of the three-volume Jones biography of Freud is clearly indicated in Fromm to Izette de Forest, Oct. 31, Nov. 14, Dec. 10, 1957, Jun. 14, 1958; de Forest to Fromm, Feb. 18, Oct. 22, Nov. 6, Dec. 17, 1957, May 25, 1958, all in Fromm Archive. On praising *Sigmund Freud's Mission*: David Riesman to Fromm, Feb 10, 1959, Riesman papers, Harvard Archives.

11. Erich Fromm, *Sigmund Freud's Mission: An Analysis of His Personality and Influence* (New York: Harper and Row, 1959), 115–117.

12. Ibid., 117–119, 106–108.

13. Ibid., 107–111, summarizes his critique of Freud and his movement, especially the four essential problem areas discussed earlier in the manuscript.

14. Erich Fromm, *Marx's Concept of Man* (New York: Frederick Ungar, 1961), 1 n. 1, 43.

15. Ibid., 33–39, 41–43, 69.

16. Ibid., 80–83. Some of the strongest scholarship on Marx is available in Theodor von Laue's books and articles, which are more comprehensive than Fromm's characterization.

17. Fromm, *Beyond the Chains of Illusion*, 88–89, 100–101.

18. Ibid., 71–78.

19. Ibid., 12, 26, 43–44 n. 1, 45–47, 49.

20. Ibid., 67–70. Fromm to Thomas Louis Merton, Oct. 6, 1961, Fromm Archive.

21. "Comes so close to my own feeling": Fromm to Merton, Oct. 9, 1961, Fromm Archive.

22. Fromm to Karl Polanyi, Apr. 14, 1960, Fromm Archive.

23. Fromm to Robert J. Alexander, Aug. 29, 1958, Fromm Archive, accepting membership on the Socialist Party-Social Democratic Federation National Committee and agreeing to write *What Is Socialism?* Fromm to Karl Polanyi, Apr. 14, May 4, Nov. 21, 1960, Fromm Archive, recalling his decision to join the Socialist

Party and concerning his lectures to students based on early drafts of the manifesto. See also Fromm to Werner Thonnessen, Jan. 23, 1960, Fromm Archive, sending a draft of the manifesto for translation and publication in Germany.

24. Erich Fromm, *Let Man Prevail: A Socialist Manifesto and Program* (New York: The Call Association, 1960), 10–11, 18–19.

25. Ibid., 12, 14.

26. Ibid., 21–23.

27. Ibid., 25–28, 33.

28. Ibid., 26, 32.

29. Ibid., esp. 3. See Fromm to Miss Larry Gulotta, Aug. 22, 1969, Fromm Archive, on how he was "puzzled" that his manifesto "has been bought by so many people, and yet the number of people within the Socialist Party who would stand for its ideas, is so small."

30. Rainer Funk, "Titles from Erich Fromm" (1997), Fromm Archive, on sales figures and translations for *May Man Prevail?* On taking "a year off from my regular writing to work on this book" and pegging it to Congress through advanced mimeographed copies: Fromm to J. William Fulbright, Sept. 7, 1974, Fromm Archive.

31. Erich Fromm, *May Man Prevail? An Inquiry Into the Facts and Fictions of Foreign Policy* (Garden City, N.Y.: Doubleday-Anchor, 1961), ix, xi.

32. Ibid., 42–46. In Fromm to Angelica Balabanoff, Oct. 14, 1961, Fromm Archive, he acknowledges that Lenin too practiced centralized terrorism but aimed for a socialist society rather than Stalin's "reactionary state capitalism."

33. Fromm to Tristram Coffin, Nov. 16, 1966, Fromm Archive; Fromm, *May Man Prevail?* 47, 81, 84–85.

34. Fromm, *May Man Prevail?* 111, 135–138. See also Fromm, "Khrushchev and the Cold War" (unpublished 1961 paper, Fromm Archive).

35. Erich Fromm, "The New Communist Program" (1961), Fromm Archive.

36. Fromm, *May Man Prevail?* 142–145, 150–151. It is interesting that Fromm drew heavily on Robert J. Lifton, *Thought Reform and the Psychology of Totalism* (New York: W. W. Norton, 1961), for his crucial discussion of the Chinese approach to thought reform.

37. Fromm, *May Man Prevail?* 147, 150–152, 157–158. Fromm considerably enlarges upon these comments on China in "Memo on Foreign Policy" (unpublished ms., 1965), Fromm Archive.

38. Fromm, *May Man Prevail?* 162–164; Fromm, "Memo on Foreign Policy" (1965).

39. Fromm, *May Man Prevail?* 167–168.

40. Ibid., 169–172.

41. Ibid., 172–173, 211.

42. Ibid., 185, 195–199, 207; Erich Fromm, "The Case for Unilateral Disarmament," *Daedalus* 89, no. 4 (Fall 1960): 1015–1028. The parallel to C. Wright Mills's *The Causes of World War Three* (1958) becomes especially striking in Daniel Geary, "Becoming International Again: C. Wright Mills and the Emergence of the Global New Left, 1956–1962," *Journal of American History* 95, no. 3 (December 2008): 723–725. Charles O. Lerche Jr., *The Cold War and After* (New York: Prentice-Hall,

1965), on the early 1960s accord on no first use between the United States and the Soviets.

43. Fromm, *May Man Prevail?* 217–221. Fromm to Bertrand Russell, Nov. 16, 1962, Fromm Archive, elaborates considerably on his solution to Berlin as a solution to the entire German "problem."

44. Fromm, *May Man Prevail?* 157–161, 226–230. See also Fromm, "Remarks on a Realistic Foreign Policy" (1961), Fromm Archive, written in conjunction with *May Man Prevail?*

45. Fromm, *May Man Prevail?* 230–239; on Yugoslavian growth with freedom: 230 n. 48; "they will act as a dam": 239.

9. A Third Way

1. Karl Polanyi to Fromm, March 18,1960, January 13, 1961, Fromm Archive, Tubingen.

2. Fromm to Angelica Balabanoff, Aug. 27, 1963. Fromm to Clara Urquhart, Apr. 18, Oct. 1, 1963. All of these letters are in the Fromm Archive.

3. Fromm to Urquhart, Apr. 18, Oct. 1, 1963, Fromm Archive. Fromm's first mention of the *Humanist Studies* venture can be found in a letter dated Jan. 23, 1960, to Thönnessen, where Fromm mentions sending one hundred letters, receiving five positive answers. In a letter to Karl Polanyi dated Apr. 14, 1960, Fromm notes "the alternative between Western capitalism." On Rahner and others like him: Fromm to Adam Schaff, Oct. 5, 1963, Fromm Archive.

4. On "what they represent as human beings" and the "spirit" of democratic socialism: Fromm to Adam Schaff, Nov. 8, 1963, Fromm Archive. On the board of editors Fromm selected in 1963 for *Humanist Studies* and the failure of the venture: Rainer Funk, *Erich Fromm: His Life and Ideas* (New York: Continuum, 2000), 148. On the mailing of one hundred letters with only four replies: Fromm to Polanyi, Apr. 19, 1960. Repeated references to the strains on Fromm's financial resources can be found in the Fromm-Riesman correspondence about the Committee of Correspondence. For several examples, see Riesman to Fromm, Jun. 12, 1962 ("In every way you are much the most generous among us . . . it won't surprise you to know that those who can least afford it on the whole (not including me) give the most"); Fromm to Riesman, Feb. 19, 1963 ("I am at the moment somewhat short of funds"); Riesman to Fromm, Mar. 4, 1964, ("it is heroic what you have managed to do in the light of all the other demands on your resources.") All three letters in Riesman papers, Harvard Archive.

5. On Cardenas: Fromm to Urquhart, Jan. 5, 1962. Fromm to A. J. Muste, Aug. 20, 1963; Fromm to Paulo Freire, Oct. 14, 1966, Mar. 22, 1968; Fromm to Raya Dunayevskaya, Oct. 29, 1966. Bottomore to Fromm, Dec. 7, 1973; Bottomore to Brian Betz, Jul. 17, 1972. All in Fromm Archive.

6. Fromm to Angelica Balabanoff, Jul. 16, 1964; Fromm to Raya Dunayevskaya, Oct. 29, 1966, warning of the danger of consumerism and "materialist interest in money." Balabanoff to Fromm, n.d. All three letters in Fromm Archive.

7. Funk, *Erich Fromm*, 147; Mihailo Marković to Fromm, Oct. 15, 1971, Fromm Archive; Mihailo Marković and Robert S. Cohen, *Yugoslavia: The Rise and Fall of Socialist Humanism: A History of the Praxis Group* (Nottingham: Spokesman Books, 1975).

8. On protesting to Tito and other Yugoslavian officials: Fromm to Gajo Petrović, Feb. 10, 1975. Fromm to Dragoslav Marković (president of Serbia), Nov. 15, 1974; Fromm to Toma Granfil (Yugoslav ambassador to the United States), Nov. 15, 1974, Mar. 15 and Oct. 1, 1975, all in Fromm Archive.

9. For information on Schaff, I draw heavily on his correspondence with Fromm in the Fromm Archive and from Erich Fromm, ed., *Socialist Humanism: An International Symposium* (Garden City, N.Y.: Doubleday, 1966), 141.

10. Fromm to Schaff, May 8, 1962, Fromm Archive, and referencing Schaff's Mar. 21 letter to him, which is not in the archive.

11. On their common "essence" and "my respect": Fromm to Schaff, Mar. 9, 1964. Approving of Schaff's interests in linking Marxism to psychoanalysis: Fromm to Schaff, Aug. 30, 1966. Admiring him as a person: Fromm to Schaff, Oct. 4, 1966. All letters in Fromm Archive.

12. On promoting Fromm's books in Poland and the success of *The Art of Loving*: Schaff to Fromm, May 23, 1973. Fromm to Norman Thomas, Aug. 19, 1966. Fromm to Richard B. Fisher, Apr. 6, 1965; and to Thomas Kelley, Mar. 9, 1969, pushing Schaff's book with McGraw-Hill. Fromm reports to Schaff on his contacts with McGraw-Hill in Fromm to Schaff, Mar. 9, 1969: all in Fromm Archive. Adam Schaff, *Marxism and the Human Individual* (New York: McGraw-Hill, 1970), ix–xii, representing Fromm's laudatory introduction to this American edition.

13. On "the scope and aliveness": Fromm's introduction to Schaff, *Marxism and the Human Individual*, xi n. 1. "No longer a concern of a few dispersed intellectuals": Fromm, *Socialist Humanism*, x. "A volume of an international nature": Fromm to Schaff, May 8, 1962. Rainer Funk, "Titles by Erich Fromm," 1997, Fromm Archive, listing the global sales figures and translations for *Socialist Humanism*.

14. Fromm to contributors to *Socialist Humanism*, Apr. 21, 1963 (Fromm Archive) establishing the financial arrangements, the guidelines for the articles, and the focus on intellectuals and students. Fromm to D. T. Suzuki, Apr. 29, 1964, and Fromm to Schaff, Mar. 9, 1964, both in Fromm Archive.

15. On the importance of what a contributor stood for as a human being and on the decision to exclude Garaudy: Fromm to Norman Thomas, Aug. 18, 1962; Fromm to Schaff, Nov. 8, 1963. On excluding Garaudy: Fromm to Schaff, Feb. 8, 1964. On including Marcuse's contribution: Fromm to Schaff, Mar. 9, 1964. All in Fromm Archive.

16. Fromm to Herbert Marcuse, Jan. 8, 1964; Fromm to Raya Dunayevskaya, Apr. 15, 1964; Fromm to Adam Schaff, Mar. 9 and Aug. 5, 1964. All in Fromm Archive.

17. The clearest and richest elaboration of these themes defining humanist socialism in *Socialist Humanism* are by Danilo Pejović (199–210), Adam Schaff (141–150), and Milan Prucha (151–161).

18. Considering dedicating *Socialist Humanism* to Brandt: Fromm to Adam Schaff, Mar. 9, 1964, Fromm Archive.

19. Erich Fromm's foreword to Heinz Brandt, *The Search for a Third Way: My Path Between East and West* (Garden City, N.Y.: Doubleday, 1970), xi–xvi; Fromm to Peter Benenson, Nov. 22, 1963, including his short essay on Brandt as a "Man of Faith." Brandt to Schaff, Mar. 9, 1964. Fromm memo re. letter from Mr. Gotsche, Jan. 2, 1964. All in Fromm Archive. Knud Andersen, *Widerspruch als Lebensprinzip: Der undogmatische Sozialist Heinz Brandt (1909–1986)* (Bonn: Dietz, 2007), chap. 5, is especially helpful on the Brandt conflict with the GDR in the early 1960s.

20. On Brandt's damaged hand: Fromm to Clara Urquhart, Feb. 27, 1964. On Brandt's purported immoralities: Fromm memo re. letter from Mr. Gotsche, Jan. 2, 1964. On the letters to world leaders he has written: Fromm to Annelie Brandt, Dec. 27, 1961. On paying for the Canon Collins trip: Fromm to Annelie Brandt, Oct. 16, 1962. On the Collins trip and contact with the Peace Union in West Germany: Fromm to Peter Benenson, Aug. 17, 1962, Fromm Archive.

21. Fromm to Clara Urquhart, Oct. 20, 1963, providing a detailed description of Annelie Brandt. The Fromm–Annelie Brandt correspondence in the Fromm Archive is extremely helpful.

22. On attending to her financial needs: Fromm to Annelie Brandt, Jan. 2, 1963. On the member of the Soviet Communist Party Central Committee: Fromm to Annelie Brandt, Dec. 6, 1961. On avoiding making the Ulbricht government "more rigid": Fromm to Annelie Brandt, May 30, 1962. On the pamphlet or book: Fromm to Annelie Brandt, Jan. 5, Sept. 29, 1962. See also Annelie Brandt to Fromm, Aug. 1, 1962. All in Fromm Archive.

23. Fromm to Peter Benenson, Aug. 17, Sept. 21, Oct. 3, 1962; Mar. 15, May 31, 1963; Jan. 20, 1964. Benenson to Fromm, Sept. 3, Oct. 15, 1962; Feb. 20, May 16, 1963. On the importance of the Amnesty "prisoner of the year" announcement and on his work with Benenson: see also Fromm to Urquhart, Oct. 20, 1963. On the importance of the Russell connection: Fromm to Urquhart, Jan. 2, 1964.

24. Fromm to Bertrand Russell, May 30, 1962.

25. Bertrand Russell to Fromm, Jul. 1, 1962; Russell to President of the Moscow Conference on Disarmament, Jul. 4, 1962, both in Fromm Archive. See also Fromm to Michael Maccoby, Jul. 21, 1962, Fromm Archive.

26. Fromm reported on his strategic meetings and discussions with Russell in Fromm to Annelie Brandt, Aug. 28, 1963; and Fromm to Clara Urquhart, Jan. 2, 1964. A copy of Russell's letter to Ulbricht, Jan. 26, 1963, is in the Fromm Archive. On meeting with Annelie and suggesting that Russell urge Ulbricht to allow Heinz Brandt to go to Sweden: Fromm to Russell, Dec. 14, 1963 (cable copy). On her crucial role in shaping these negotiations, particularly Russell's response to Ulbricht, see Fromm to Annelie Brandt, Jun. 15, 1964.

27. The particulars of Russell returning the medal of honor and agreeing to write the article are reported in Fromm to Urquhart, Jan. 14, 1964. In this letter, Fromm also remarks on how Russell's action made him "quite sad" but hoping that the Russians now might prod the GDR. On how Russell's action closed off "discreet private appeals": Charles Ellis to Urquhart, Jan. 31, 1964 (copy in Fromm Archive). "The only thing to do": Fromm to Benenson, Jan. 20, 1964. Erich Fromm, "Prophets and Priests," in *Bertrand Russell, Philosopher of the Century: Essays in His*

Honor, ed. Ralph Schoenman (London: Allen & Unwin, 1967), 6–7, portrays Russell with some balance but also as Fromm would have liked to have seen himself.

28. Fromm, in Brandt, *Search for a Third Way,* xiv. Fromm to Annelie Brandt, Jun. 15, 1964; Fromm to Urquhart, Jan. 14, 1964 (misdated; actually Jan. 14, 1965). Both in Fromm Archive.

29. Fromm to Annelie Brandt, Jun. 15, 1964, instructing her on Heinz's care, a vacation, and a visit with him. On the Brandts' visit to Cuernavaca: Fromm to Urquhart, Jan. 14, 1964 (misdated; actually 1965); see also Benenson to Fromm, Dec. 14, 1964. All in Fromm Archive.

30. Fromm to Riesman, April 26, 1966, Riesman Papers, Harvard.

10. "Life Is Extravagance": Almost

1. Fromm to Clara Urquhart, Sept. 29, 1962, Fromm Archive, Tubingen.

2. Erich Fromm, "War Within Man: A Psychological Inquiry into the Roots of Destructiveness" (Philadelphia: American Friends Service Committee, 1963), 4–8. This manuscript was initially titled "On the Psychological Causes of War," which can be found in both the Fromm Papers, New York Public Library, and the Fromm Archive.

3. Ibid., 9–11.

4. Ibid., 14–16.

5. For Merton and Fromm: ibid., 28, 33. For Tillich, Morgenthau, and Fromm: 20–21, 31. For Frank, Sorokin, and Fromm: 19, 25–26, 32.

6. Erich Fromm, *The Heart of Man: Its Genius for Good and Evil* (New York: Harper & Row, 1964, 1968), esp. 37–61, 108–114, 148–150.

7. Sales figures are a 1997 estimation by Rainer Funk, Fromm's literary executor.

8. Fromm, *The Heart of Man,* esp. 37–61, 108–114, 148–150.

9. Ibid., 150.

10. Ibid., 20. Fromm to Ernst Simon, Jan. 7, 1977, Fromm Archive.

11. Fromm to Angelica Balabanoff, Jul. 16, 1964; Fromm to Thomas Merton, Feb. 7, 1966, both in Fromm Archive.

12. Fromm to Balabanoff, Jul. 16, 1964; Fromm to Clara Urquhart, Jul. 16, 1964; Fromm to Adam Schaff, Jan. 13, 1965; Fromm to Urquhart, Jan. 10, 1966. All in Fromm Archive.

13. Sales figures come from 1997 estimations by Rainer Funk, Fromm's literary executor.

14. Erich Fromm, "For a Cooperation Between Jews and Arabs," *New York Times* (April 18, 1948). Drafts of this Fromm-written public statement are in the Fromm Archive. On the Eichmann trial: Fromm letter to the editor, *New York Times* (June 17, 1960); Fromm to Balabanoff, Oct. 29, 1962, Fromm Archive. "Prophetic Messianism has always been": Fromm to Schaff, Mar. 21, 1966. On "my deep roots in the humanistic tradition of Judaism, which, as I see it, the Israelis are thoroughly destroying by a reversal of all values": see also Fromm to Mumford, Apr. 29, 1975, Fromm Archive.

15. Erich Fromm, *You Shall Be as Gods: A Radical Interpretation of the Old Testament and Its Tradition* (New York: Holt, Rinehart and Winston, 1966), 13.

16. Ibid., 6–9, 15.

17. Ibid., 31, 40, 42–44. For a very helpful discussion of this chain of Fromm's thought, see Svante Lundgren's *Fight Against Idols: Erich Fromm on Religion, Judaism, and the Bible* (Frankfurt: Peter Lang, 1998).

18. Fromm, *You Shall Be as Gods*, 57–62, 81, 226–227.

19. Ibid., 202–203, 207–208, 220.

20. Ibid., 220–221. For a brilliant comment on Fromm's chapter on the psalms, see Marianne Horney Eckardt, "The Theme of Hope in Erich Fromm's Writing," *Contemporary Psychoanalysis* 18, no. 1 (1982): esp. 145–46. See also Rainer Funk, *Erich Fromm: His Life and Ideas* (New York: Continuum, 2000), 53–54, on Rabinkow's lifelong importance to Fromm.

21. Fromm, *You Shall Be as Gods*, 197–99. Also see Erich Fromm, "Meaning of the Sabbath," in *Jewish Heritage Reader*, ed. Lily Edelman (New York: Taplinger, 1965), 138–141.

22. Fromm, *You Shall Be as Gods*, 117–118. In addition to Camus' *The Rebel* (1951), I am underscoring a persisting theme in Robert J. Lifton's writing: the revolutionary "totalist" who felt compelled to do more than bump against societal ills.

23. For cogent discussions of SANE during the years of the Vietnam War and Fromm's role in the organization, see Milton S. Katz, *Ban the Bomb: A History of SANE* (New York: Greenwood Press, 1986); and Lawrence Wittner, *Resisting the Bomb: A History of the World Nuclear Disarmament Movement, 1954–1970* (Stanford, Calif.: Stanford University Press, 1997). Wittner to LJF (e-mail), April 27, 28, 2011, was exceedingly helpful in understanding schisms within SANE at the time and other internal issues. So was Swarthmore College Peace Collection Curator Wendy Chmielewski, TI, April 29, 2011.

24. Erich Fromm, "The War in Viet Nam and the Brutalization of Man," delivered at SANE Madison Square Garden Rally, Dec. 8, 1966, Fromm Papers. The address may also be found in the Fromm Archive.

25. Michael Maccoby, telephone interview by LJF, Jan. 16, 2007, recalling the details of the Madison Square Garden rally and the subsequent heart attack. See also Funk, *Erich Fromm*, 153.

26. Fromm to Aniceto Aramoni, Feb. 7, 1967; Fromm to Adam Schaff, Apr. 10, 1967, both in Fromm Archive. Fromm to Schaff, Apr. 26, June 24, 1967, Fromm Archive, on his short trips from Locarno. See also Funk, *Erich Fromm*, 153; and Salvador Millán, "Tangible Memories" (2008). 1967 Executive Sessions of the Senate Foreign Relations Committee were made public in 2007, and the session where Fromm was discussed is to be found in vol. 19 of the proceedings of the 1st session of the 90th Congress.

27. On cardiac "repetitions": Fromm to Adam Schaff, Aug. 29, 1967, Fromm Archive. Much of the data on Fromm's health problems and concerns and those of his wives have been reviewed in earlier chapters. Two of his close friends viewed the 1966 heart attack heavily in this larger health context. See, e.g., Marianne Horney

Eckardt, PI by LJF, Laguna Hills, Calif., Feb. 3, 2007; and Gertrud Hunziker-Fromm, TRI by LJF, Zurich, May 9, 2004.

28. Erich Fromm, "The Psychological Problem of Aging," *Journal of Rehabilitation* (October 1966), reprinted in Erich Fromm, *On Disobedience and Other Essays* (London: Routledge & Kegan Paul, 1984), 117–132. The article may also be found in the Fromm Papers.

11. Hope and Stasis

1. Michael Maccoby, "Fromm Didn't Want to Be a Frommian," in *The Clinical Erich Fromm*, ed. Rainer Funk (Amsterdam: Rodopi, 2009), 141–143, which closely approximates Maccoby, TI by LJF, Jan. 16, 2007, on Fromm's deeper embrace of spirituality after the heart attack. Gerald Holton, PI by LJF, June 5, 2009; and Nina Holton, PI by LJF, May 6, 2012, both recall their friend, Erich Fromm, recounting that the actress Elizabeth Taylor was one of his patients in Cuernevaca and how she would lie down and pretend she was dead while having sexual intercourse. It is, of course, unclear whether this connected to the part of Fromm's meditation ritual where he would lie on the floor to practice dying. What is clear is that Fromm was violating patient confidentiality.

2. There is a modest file in the Fromm Archive indicating Fromm's growing interest in the junior senator from Minnesota and on Fromm's role in the 1968 campaign. The best study of the Senator's life and the 1968 campaign is Dominic Sandbrook, *Eugene McCarthy and the Rise and Fall of Postwar American Liberalism* (New York: Random House, 2005). For the campaign and the broader context of U.S. developments in 1968, see Jules Witcover, *The Year the Dream Died: Revisiting 1968* (New York: Warner Brothers, 1977). There is also value in consulting Eugene McCarthy and Christopher Hitchens, *1968: War and Democracy* (Red Wing, Minn.: Lone Oak Press, 2000). See Riesman to Stewart Meacham, Mar. 21, 1968, Riesman Papers, Harvard Archive, on Fromm's early interest in McCarthy.

3. Ibid., plus Fromm to Eugene McCarthy, April 13,15, 1968, Fromm Archive.

4. Sandbrook, *Eugene McCarthy*, chap. 9, represents the most cogent coverage of the 1968 New Hampshire primary where Johnson was "defeated." Fromm to Eugene McCarthy, Apr. 15, 1968, Fromm Archive, contains Fromm's response to Johnson's speech withdrawing his candidacy.

5. Erich Fromm, "Memo on Political Alternatives," Mar. 16, 1968, 1–6, Fromm Archive.

6. Ibid., 6–8.

7. Fromm to Eugene McCarthy, Apr. 13, 1968, Fromm Archive.

8. Fromm to McCarthy, Apr. 15, 1968, Fromm Archive.

9. Erich Fromm, "Preface to the French Edition, *The Revolution of Hope*" (March 1970), first draft, Gerard Khoury private papers, Aix-en-Provence, reflecting on how the book broke from "academic fashion" and was profoundly "appealing to the love for life." Fromm's private reservations are best captured in his letter

to Stewart Meacham of Feb. 3, 1968, Riesman Papers, Harvard Archive. The sales figures come from 1997 estimates by Rainer Funk, Fromm's literary executor.

10. Fromm to Schaff, July 24, 1968; and Fromm to Gertrud Hunziker-Fromm, July 5, 1968; both in the Fromm Archive. The interview of Fromm by Frederick Rovekamp in May 1968 was published in *Fromm Forum* 9 (2005): 31–40.

11. Erich Fromm, "Why I Am for McCarthy," *Los Angeles Times* (May 29, 1968; California Citizens for McCarthy advertisement). *New York Times* (July 14, 1968) covers the Fromm-Maccoby poll of Santa Cruz voters. McCarthy to Fromm, July 1968, inviting him to help acquire delegates, Fromm Archive. "The People's Choice," *New York Review of Books* 11, no. 3 (August 22, 1968) contains the appeal to convention delegates. It is signed by Fromm and others but is clearly in Fromm's writing style. Humphrey received 1,761 delegate votes to 601 for McCarthy in the Democratic Party nominating convention.

12. Fromm to Gertrud Hunziker-Fromm, July 5, 1968; Fromm to Adam Schaff, July 24, 1968; both in Fromm Archive. Michael Maccoby, TI by LJF, Jan. 16, 2007, presented an excellent review of Fromm's role in the McCarthy campaign, including financial contributions and meetings with the senator.

13. On the book being "a response" to the 1968 situation, which saw America and the world "at the crossroad": Erich Fromm, *The Revolution of Hope: Toward a Humanized Technology* (New York: Harper & Row, 1968), xvii–xviii; on the McCarthy campaign representing "a longing": 145; explaining the Council, Clubs, and Groups structure preceding the questionnaire: 151–162.

14. On the three thousand responses and his health problems: Fromm to Sarah-Sue Wittes, Apr. 9, 1970, Fromm Archive. On the minimal response to the questionnaires and on Fromm's bitterness over McCarthy failing to meet with him after the convention: Michael Maccoby, TI by LJF, Jan. 16, 2007. Jeremy Larner, *Nobody Knows: Reflections on the McCarthy Campaign* (New York, 1969), appraises McCarthy as drifting and uninspiring during and especially after the campaign from the perspective of one of his speechwriters. Book sales and translations of *The Revolution of Hope* are reported in Rainer Funk, "Titles by Erich Fromm," Fromm Archive.

15. Fromm, *The Revolution of Hope*, 13, 21, 135–137.

16. Ibid., 11–12. Mumford's (and Fromm's) mythic organic community of old is cogently discussed in Richard Chase, "The Armed Obscurantist," *Partisan Review* (Summer 1944): 346–348.

17. Fromm, *The Revolution of Hope*, 30, 32–38. It is interesting that Fromm's characterization of a consumption-centered "technological society" with people who feel constantly depleted was a predecessor statement of the psychologist Philip Cushman's classic article, "Why the Self Is Empty: Toward a Historically Situated Psychology," *American Psychologist* 45, no. 5 (May 1990): 599–611.

18. Fromm, *The Revolution of Hope*, 96–97.

19. Ibid., 100–105.

20. Ibid., 107–111.

21. Fromm, "Preface to the French Edition, *The Revolution of Hope*," reflecting retrospectively on the 1968 campaign and book.

22. Erich Fromm and Michael Maccoby, *Social Character in a Mexican Village* (Englewood Cliffs, N.J.: Prentice-Hall, 1970), 31–40, 134.

23. Fromm and Maccoby, *Mexican Village*, ix–xiii; Fromm to Harold Anderson, Mar. 4, 1957; Fromm to Charles F. Wrigley, Mar. 19, 1959, Fromm Archive. Aniceto Aramoni, TRI by LJF, Mexico City, Mar. 17, 2004.

24. Fromm and Maccoby, *Mexican Village*, 24–30, demonstrates quite conclusively how he regarded the Weimar study, particularly the interpretive questionnaires, as the major forerunner to the Chiconcuac project and a central motive for pursuing it. See also Fromm to Charles Wrigley, Mar. 17, 1959, Fromm Archive; and Michael Maccoby, TRI by LJF, Washington, D.C., Feb. 2, 2003.

25. Fromm to Charles Wrigley, Mar. 17, 1959, Fromm Archive.

26. Fromm and Maccoby, *Mexican Village*, x–xi; Theodore Schwartz to David Riesman, Jan. 26, 1967, copy in Fromm Archive. Michael Maccoby, PI by LJF, Cambridge, Mass., May 6, 2005.

27. Fromm and Maccoby, *Mexican Village*, x–xi. Michael Maccoby, TRI by LJF, Washington, D.C., Feb. 2, 2003. Fromm to Margaret Mead, Apr. 20, 1968 (Schwartz "showed his antagonism"); Fromm to David Riesman, Jan. 19, 1967; Theodore Schwartz to David Riesman, Jan. 18, 26, 1967, all in Fromm Archive.

28. Ibid., plus Oscar Lewis, *The Children of Sanchez: Autobiography of a Mexican Family* (New York: Penguin, 1961); Maccoby, TI by LJF, Dec. 18, 19, 2008. Riesman to Margaret Mead, Feb. 1, 1968; and to T. Schwartz, Jan. 23, 1967, Riesman Papers, Harvard Archives, connecting the "scandal" Oscar Lewis created in *Children of Sanchez* to one that Theodore and Lola Schwartz might have created with the Chiconcuac project. Fromm to Riesman, Mar. 19, 1968, Riesman Papers, reveals Fromm's and Maccoby's close attentiveness to the Lewis book and the untoward "sensationalism" it created. Together with my December 2008 interview of Maccoby, Fromm's March 1968 letter indicates how the two (to a certain extent at least) shared Lewis's hardnosed conclusions that made little of reformist "amelioration."

29. Ibid., plus Fromm to Riesman, Jan. 4, 19, Aug. 19, 1967; Theodore Schwartz to Fromm, Feb. 4, 1968; Schwartz to Riesman, Jan. 10, 1967; Fromm to Schwartz, Mar. 19, 1968; Lola Schwartz to Fromm, Jan. 31, 1968; all in Riesman Papers, Harvard Archive. Especially telling is Fromm to Riesman, Feb. 22, 1968, on Theodore: "that he was employed to help . . . "

30. Maccoby, "Fromm Didn't Want to Be a Frommian," 141–143. See also Maccoby's introduction to the 1996 edition: Erich Fromm and Michael Maccoby, *Social Character in a Mexican Village* (New Brunswick, N.J.: Transaction, 1996), esp. xxi.

31. Maccoby, TRI by LJF, Washington, D.C., Feb. 2, 2003. Maccoby, "Fromm Didn't Want to Be a Frommian," 141–143.

32. Maccoby, TRI by LJF, Washington, D.C., Feb. 2, 2003; PI, Cambridge, May 6, 2005; TI, Jan. 16, 2007.

33. Ibid., plus Maccoby's introduction to the 1996 Transaction edition of *Mexican Village*, xxi–xxii. On the orphanage issue that distressed Fromm: Salvador and Sonia Millán, "His Deeply Inspirational Presence and Thoughtfulness," in *The Clinical Erich Fromm*, ed. Rainer Funk (2009), 157–158. Rainer Funk, PI by LJF,

Tubingen, July 15, 2003, agreeing with Maccoby that Fromm was often absent from the village project research. Funk also points out that Maccoby's hegemony in the process of formulating the book is evident in his rather rigid dichotomization between productive and nonproductive social character. See also David Riesman to Fromm, Dec. 7, 1966, Jan. 17, 1967, Fromm Archive.

34. Fromm to Theodore Schwartz, Feb. 11, 1967; Riesman to Fromm, Dec. 7, 1966, Jan. 17, 23, 1967; Schwartz to Riesman, Jan. 18, 1967; Fromm to Margaret Mead, Apr. 20, 1968. Copies of all of this correspondence are in the Fromm Archive. See also Maccoby, TRI by LJF, Washington, D.C., Feb. 2, 2003. In Riesman's Feb. 1, 1968, letter to Fromm (Riesman Papers, Harvard Archive), he reported on Mead's defense of the Schwartzes. Nina Holton, PI by LJF, Cambridge, Mass., Mar. 4, May 5, 2009, recounts the occasional breaches of client confidentiality.

35. Fromm to Schwartz, Feb. 11, 1967, and Schwartz to Riesman, Jan.18, 1967, both in Fromm Archive. Riesman to Fromm, Feb. 1, 1968, Riesman Papers, Harvard Archive. Maccoby, TRI by LJF, Washington, D.C., Feb. 2, 2003.

36. Fromm to Mead, Apr. 20, 1968, Fromm Archive; Maccoby, TI by LJF, Jan. 16, 2007; Fromm to V. I. Dobrenkov, Apr. 11, 1970, Fromm Archive. In his introduction to the 1996 Transaction edition of *Mexican Village*, xxi, Maccoby detailed the process of working with Fromm on the book, what he (Maccoby) wrote and revised, and what Fromm wrote.

37. Sales figures and translations of *Social Character in a Mexican Village* are reported in Rainer Funk, "Titles by Erich Fromm" (1997), Fromm Archive. See also Fromm and Maccoby, *Mexican Village*, 32–33, 39; and Maccoby's introduction to the 1996 Transaction edition of *Mexican Village*, xiv–xvii (with Fromm's letter complaining about Prentice-Hall); and Daniel Burston, *The Legacy of Erich Fromm* (Cambridge, Mass.: Harvard University Press, 1991), 129. The recollection that Fromm aspired to produce a work similar to that of Oscar Lewis comes from Michael Maccoby, PI by LJF, Jan. 16, 2007.

38. Fromm and Maccoby, *Mexican Village*, 130–135.

39. Ibid., 99–100, 130–31, 200–203.

40. Ibid., 210–213.

41. Ibid., 213, 217, Millán, "His Deeply Inspirational Presence and Thoughtfulness," 6. Maccoby's and Fromm's recollections of Wasson are provided in "Obituary: Father William B. Wasson," *International Erich Fromm Society* 11 (2007): 78, with Maccoby emphasizing his religious faith and Fromm how he showed "that one can organize and be efficient."

42. Fromm and Maccoby, *Mexican Village*, 217–224.

43. Ibid., 224–225, 231.

44. Ibid., 235–236; Maccoby, TI by LJF, Jan. 16, 2007.

45. Fromm and Maccoby, *Mexican Village*, 134.

46. Maccoby, TI by LJF, January 16, 2007; Aramoni, TRI by LJF, March 17, 2004.

47. Fromm to Maccoby, July 22, 1969, on the moon landing (original letter with Maccoby).

12. Love and Death

1. Aniceto Aramoni, TRI by LJF, Mexico City, Mar. 17, 2004; Salvador Millán, PI by LJF, Mexico City, Mar. 21, 2004; Aniceto Aramoni to Fromm, Feb. 1, 1967, Fromm Archive, Tubingen.

2. Aramoni, TRI by LJF, Mexico City, Mar. 17, 2007; Salvador Millán, PI by LJF, Mexico City, Mar. 20, 21, 2004; Rebecca Aramoni Serrano, PI by LJF, Mexico City, Mar. 21, 2004; Michael and Sandy Lee Maccoby, TRI by LJF, Washington, D.C., Feb. 2, 2003; Hernando Ibarra, TRI by LJF, Cuernavaca, Mar. 19, 2004.

3. Aniceto Aramoni, TRI by LJF, Mexico City, Mar. 17, 2007; Jorge Silva, TRI by LJF, Mexico City, Mar. 22, 2004; Salvador Millán, PI by LJF, Mexico City, Mar. 17, 18, 2004; Rebeca Aramoni Serrano, PI by LJF, Mexico City, Mar. 21, 2004. For the arrival of the Buenos Aires contingent of orthodox psychoanalysts, see Marie Langer, *From Vienna to Managua: Journal of a Psychoanalyst* (London: Free Association Books, 1989), 132–133. A cogent discussion of the Argentine psychoanalytic context at the time is provided in Jorge Balan, *Cuentame tu Vida: Una Biografía Colectiva del Psicoanalysis Argentino* (Buenos Aires: Planeta Argentina, 1991), 228–236.

4. Aramoni to Fromm, Feb. 1, 1967; Fromm to Aramoni, Feb. 7, 1967, both in Fromm Archive. See also Rebeca Aramoni Serrano, PI by LJF, Mar. 21, 2004; and Salvador Millán, PI by LJF, March 19, 20, 21, 2004.

5. Rainer Funk, PI by LJF, Tubingen, Mar. 16, 2003; Michael Maccoby, TRI by LJF, Washington, D.C., Feb. 2, 2003; Fromm to Aniceto Aramoni, Sept. 1, 1973, Fromm Archive; Moshe Budmore, TI by LJF, Apr. 22, 2008; Fromm to Clara Urquhart, Aug. 4, 1969, Fromm Archive. On the Swiss tax benefits as one of several motives for the move: Fromm to Gail Bashein, May 15, 1975, Fromm Archive.

6. Rainer Funk to LJF, June 24, 2008; Rainer Funk, *Erich Fromm: His Life and Ideas* (New York: Continuum, 2000), 162–163. Gertrud Hunziker-Fromm, TRI by LJF, Zurich, May 9, 2004. On Kreutzberger's backgound: Fromm to Karl Darmstadter, Feb. 13, 1974, Fromm Archive. On the Fromm-Illich relationship, see Brian Betz to Ivan Illich, June 29, 1972, Fromm Archive; and Illich's reply on the same letter. For data on Nyanaponika Mahathera in the Fromm Archive, see Max Kreutzberger to Fromm, Jan. 11, 1972; Fromm to Nyanaponika, Dec. 4, 1972, Sept. 4, 1973, May 2, Dec. 1, 1975; and Nyanaponika to Fromm, Aug. 28, Oct. 13, Dec. 31, 1972, Mar. 21, Oct. 31, 1973, Apr. 6, Nov. 13, 1975.

7. Aramoni to Fromm, Feb. 1, 1967, Aug. 26, 1973, Mar. 3, Aug. 27, 1974, all exemplifying how Aramoni acknowledged that his generation needed to run the Mexican Psychoanalytic Institute's affairs while somehow keeping Fromm involved in those affairs. On being away from institute affairs: Fromm to Aramoni, Feb. 7, 1967. On the benefits of writing in the Swiss Alps: Fromm to Aramoni, Sept. 1, 1973. "So completely immersed in my work": Fromm to Aramoni, Sept. 27, 1974. On putting his Cuernavaca house up for sale: Fromm to Aramoni, Feb. 11, 1976. All correspondence in the Fromm Archive. On the transporting of books and correspondence to Locarno: Moshe Budmore, TI by LJF, Apr. 22, 2008.

8. Funk, PI by LJF, Tubingen, Mar. 16, 2003. On his relationship to Beatrice Mayer: Fromm to de Forest, July 21, 1958, Tavis de Forest private collection. Fromm to Aramoni, Feb. 11, 1976, Fromm Archive; Rebecca Aramoni Serrano, PI by LJF, Mexico City, Mar. 21, 2004; Annis Freeman to Clara Urquhart, Mar. 24, 1970, Fromm Archive.

9. In 2006, I visited the Locarno-Muralto area and, from the fifth floor of Casa La Mondo, mixed joy with envy as I witnessed the arresting view that Fromm saw daily. Relevant to this Muralto apartment is Rainer Funk's "Erich Fromm's Kleine Lebensschule," (Freiburg: Herder, 2007), 7–27.

10. Fromm to Kaplan, Feb. 14, Apr. 11, 1972, Fromm Archive.

11. See, e.g., Fromm to Kaplan, Feb. 17, 1973, on Kaplan's inspiration in the completion of *Anatomy of Human Destructiveness*.

12. Erich Fromm, *The Crisis of Psychoanalysis: Essays on Freud, Marx, and Social Psychology* (New York: Henry Holt, 1970), chap. 1. It is instructive to note that in the *Dissent* exchange of 1955, Marcuse had accused Fromm, Sullivan, and Horney of betraying Freud through promotion of social conformity.

13. See the brilliantly succinct three-page epilogue in Fromm's *Crisis of Psychoanalysis*. For Fromm's 1966 critique of Horney and Sullivan, see Richard Evans, ed., *Dialogue with Erich Fromm* (New York: Harper & Row, 1966), 59.

14. Charles O. Lerche's brilliant volume *The Cold War and After* (1965) argued this point of first strike becoming a nonoption of the American and the Soviet leadership after 1963. The preponderance of scholarship since has, with important qualifications, sustained his argument.

15. Annis Freeman to Clara Urquhart, Mar. 24, 1970, Fromm Archive, reporting how her husband "sighed yesterday and said he needed another 30 years to write all the things that he hasn't written yet." On Brams and Fromm moving into wholly new areas of research: Maccoby, e-mail to LJF, June 15, 2011.

16. Fromm to J. William Fulbright, Mar. 19, 1974, Fromm Archive, recounting Fulbright's initial and very favorable response to Lorenz. Erich Fromm, *The Anatomy of Human Destructiveness* (New York: Holt McDougal, 1973), 23, notes how the arguments in the Ardrey and Morris books approximated Lorenz's argument.

17. Konrad Lorenz, *On Aggression* (New York: Harcourt Brace, Jovanovich, 1966), which closely parallels Konrad Lorenz, *Evolution and Modification of Behavior* (Chicago: University of Chicago Press, 1965), in its essential argumentative structure.

18. Fromm to David Riesman, Nov. 2, 1973; Fromm to Ernst Simon, Apr. 12, 1975 (both in Fromm Archive). Fromm, *Anatomy*, 38–39.

19. Fromm, *Anatomy*, 38–54, 499–501, 515–517.

20. Fromm to Fulbright, Mar. 19, 1974, Fromm Archive.

21. B. F. Skinner most fully amplified his neobehaviorism in *Science and Human Behavior* (New York: Macmillan, 1953) and *Beyond Freedom and Dignity* (New York: Knopf, 1971).

22. Fromm, *Anatomy*, 56–68, esp. 63–65.

23. Fromm presents these anti-Skinner sources in his case against Skinner in footnotes in *Anatomy*, esp. 56–68. It is interesting to note that Chomsky was given

the annual Erich Fromm Award of the International Fromm Society in March 2010, in Stuttgart, for his intellectual affinity with Fromm.

24. Fromm to Clara Urquhart, Aug. 3, 1971, Fromm Archive.

25. Fromm, *Anatomy*, 133–142.

26. Ibid., 204–205, 208.

27. Ibid., 213–245.

28. Ibid., 246, 252.

29. Ibid., 302–313.

30. Fromm to Clara Urquhart, Sept. 18, 1963, Fromm Archive, discussing Arendt's *New Yorker* articles that preceded *Eichmann in Jerusalem*. Fromm, *Anatomy*, 334–335. Arendt and Fromm maintained a modest correspondence, which one can find in the Fromm Archive.

31. Fromm, *Anatomy*, 336–344; Bradley F. Smith, *Heinrich Himmler: A Nazi in the Making, 1900–1916* (Stanford, Calif.: Hoover Institute, 1971); Josef Ackermann, *Heinrich Himmler als Ideologe* (Göttingen: Musterschmidt, 1970); Bradley Smith, "Diaries of Heinrich Himmler's Early Years," *Journal of Modern History* 31, no. 3 (1959): 206–224. Peter Loewenberg, "The Unsuccessful Adolescence of Heinrich Himmler," *American Historical Review* 76, no. 3 (June 1971): 612–641. Fromm probably did not recognize the partial similarity between young Himmler's situation at home and Fromm's own parents: a mother who treated the son as younger than he was and a less-than-respectable and weak father.

32. Fromm, *Anatomy*, 345–346.

33. Ibid., 350–351.

34. Ibid., 353–355.

35. Ibid., 358–359.

36. Ibid., 360–361.

37. Ibid., 446–450, 476, 479. The propensity of Hitler and others in the Nazi command to regard homosexuals as "defective" people is covered well in Richard Plant, *The Pink Triangle: The Nazi War Against Homosexuals* (New York: Henry Holt, 1986).

38. Fromm, *Anatomy*, 470–471, 474–475, 479–480.

39. Ibid., 482–485.

40. Fromm to Robert M. W. Kempner, Sept. 15, 1972, Fromm Archive; Fromm to Maccoby, Oct. 11, 1972 (sent to me courtesy of Maccoby).

41. Fromm to Speer, June 1, 23, 1973, Fromm Archive.

42. Fromm to Speer, Oct. 11, 20, 1972; Nov. 3, 28, 1973; Sept. 20, Oct. 7, 1974; August 7, 1975, all in Fromm Archive.

43. "Sales Figures and Translations of Fromm's Books" (estimates to 1997) and "Book Titles by Erich Fromm and their Translations" (on translations to 2011), both in Fromm Archive. These and other materials in the Archive pinpoint sales figures for *The Anatomy of Human Destructiveness* rather precisely. A global array of reviews of the book, including those referenced here, are available in archival files for *Anatomy*.

44. Fromm to Karl Darmstädter, Jan. 27, 1975; Fromm to Lewis Mumford, Apr. 29, 1975; Fromm to Fulbright, Feb. 11, 1976; Fromm to Ernst Simon, Jan. 7, 1977;

Fromm to Angelica Balabanoff, Oct. 29, 1962; Fromm to Hans Krause, May 27, 1971, all in Fromm Archive.

45. Fromm to Michael Maccoby, June 22, Sept. 27, 1973; David Riesman to Michael Maccoby, Dec. 20, 1973; all reflecting Fromm's continued interest and concern over international affairs, including Yugoslavia and Chile, Michael Maccoby collection. Fromm to Aniceto Aramoni, Feb. 13, 1974; Fromm to Lewis Mumford, Oct. 16, 1973, both in Fromm Archive. The 1974 paper for the Senate Foreign Relations Committee, "Remarks on the Policy of Détente," appeared in the *New York Times* (December 11, 1975) as "Paranoia and Policy."

46. Fromm to Karl Darmstädter, Jan. 27, Nov. 3, 1975, Fromm Archive.

47. Fromm to Tristram Coffin, Oct. 25, 1974, Fromm Archive.

48. See, e.g., Fromm to Raya Dunayevskaya, Feb. 12, 1974; and (summarizing the collaboration) Dunayevskaya to Fromm, Mar. 13, 1974; and Fromm to Dunayevskaya, Feb. 18, 1976, all in Fromm Archives. The research she did for him is very well exemplified by Dunayevskaya to Fromm, Mar. 13, 1974; and Fromm to Dunayevskaya, July 8, 1975, Fromm Archive. See also Kevin Anderson, "On the 100th Anniversary of His Birth: Erich Fromm's Marxism Dimension," *Theory and Practice Newsletter* (August–September 2000): 3–4.

49. Fromm to Rainer Funk, June 27, 1973, July 3, 1974, Nov. 7, 1975, April 24, 1976. I learned the most about the evolving Fromm-Funk relationship through conversations with Funk over many years and particularly in two long e-mail letters he wrote to me (Jan. 21, 2007; May 31, 2008).

50. Fromm to Funk, Nov. 7, 1975; Fromm to Clara Urquhart, Mar. 18, 1975; Fromm to Dunayasakya, Feb. 18, 1976; Joan Hughes to Funk, Apr. 24, 1976; Aramoni to Fromm, Jan. 25, 1976, Fromm Archive.

51. Erich Fromm, *To Have or to Be?* (New York: Harper & Row, 1976), 1–11. Philip Cushman, "Why the Self Is Empty: Toward a Historically Situated Psychology," *American Psychologist* 45, no. 5 (May 1990): 559–611.

52. Fromm, *To Have or to Be?* 20–25. For the difference between *ser* and *estar*, see http://www.wordreference.com/es/en/translation.asp?spen=ser.

53. Fromm, *To Have or to Be?* 29–34.

54. Ibid., 34–44.

55. Ibid., 56.

56. Ibid., 55–61.

57. Ibid., 144–146.

58. Ibid., 157–159.

59. Abundant sales figures for *To Have or to Be?* over a long period of time are found in the Fromm Archive. Supplementary sales data was reported in e-mails from Fromm archivist Rainer Funk in May 2008 and November 2009. See also reports on sales from Michael Maccoby to LJF, Dec. 19, 2008. For a few examples of Fromm's guru status, see *Roth-Hilpoltsteiner Volkszeitung* (March 2, 1977) and *Deutsches Allgemeines Sonntagsblatt* (March 20, 1983).

60. Funk to LJF (e-mail), Jan. 31, 1977; Funk, PI by LJF, Tubingen, Mar. 22, 2009; plus Funk's compilation of all of Fromm's book sales to 1999.

61. Erich Fromm, *The Working Class in Weimar Germany: A Psychological and Sociological Study* (Cambridge, Mass.: Harvard University Press, 1984), came out a few years after the German edition. The Bonss background is noted in his introduction to the volume. Additionally, the Fromm Archive now houses information on Bonss and all of the elements that Bonss assembled to form the book.

62. Rainer Funk, *Erich Fromm: His Life and Ideas* (New York: Continuum, 2000), 164; Fromm to Fulbright, June 2, 1976, Fulbright Papers, University of Arkansas. Fromm to Annelie and Heinz Brandt, Apr. 28, 1978; Joan Hughes to David Riesman, July 31, 1975; to Funk, June 22, 1978; to Paul Roazen, July 31, 1978; and to Helen Hatchett, Mar. 11, 1980; Fromm to Aniceto Aramoni, June 28, 1979, all in Fromm Archive. Funk, PI by LJF, Tubingen, Mar. 18, 2003. Annis Fromm to Aniceto Aramoni, Sept. 26. 1979, Fromm Archive, reporting on Erich being able to do very little since the 1978 heart attack.

63. Fromm to Funk, Nov. 16, 1977, asking Funk to take charge of his writings and be his literary executor; Funk to Erich and Annis Fromm, Feb. 10, 1978, typifying Funk's extensive work on Fromm's manuscripts; Annis Fromm to Gérard Khoury, Nov. 28, 1979, on Funk standing in for Fromm in public occasions, all in Fromm Archive. Funk, PI by LJF, Tubingen, Mar. 18, 2003, Oct. 10, 2009, reviewing all of his activities with Fromm in Fromm's final years and underscoring Funk's broad construction of his duties as literary executor. Funk's e-mails to LJF, Dec. 15, 2011, January 6, 11, 22, 23, 2012, underscore a global vision of the executor function and a deep commitment to the acquisition of Fromm materials.

64. Fromm to Izette de Forest, Nov. 26, 1956, Taves de Forest private collection, outlining what eventually became *Greatness and Limitations*. Funk e-mail to LJF, May 31, 2008, acknowledging that "I prepared the book" and discussing how he had. Funk to Fromm, Oct. 2, 1978, Fromm Archive, discussing what he had done to complete the book and to bring it toward publication. Funk, e-mail to LJF, June 13, 2010, reviewing his considerable role in "not really a new book." The statement regarding the continuity and repetitious quality of Fromm's critique of Freud can be found in the preface (xi) of the 1980 Harper & Row edition.

65. Nyanaponika Mahathera to Fromm, Dec. 4, 1977; Fromm to Nyanaponika Mahathera, June 1, 1978; Fromm to Lewis Mumford, Nov. 7, 1975, Dec. 14, 1977; Fromm to Ernst Simon, Oct. 24, 1977; Fromm to Funk, Nov. 7, 1975; Fromm to Chaim Kaplan, Jan. 24, 1980, all in Fromm Archive.

66. A full audio copy and transcript of Khoury's interview of Fromm has been deposited in the Fromm Archive. See also Khoury, PI by LJF, Oct. 24, 2005, Oct. 7, 2009, on the nature and conditions of the 1978–1979 interviews. Helpful too is Gérard Khoury, "A Crucial Encounter," in *The Clinical Erich Fromm*, ed. Rainer Funk (Amsterdam: Rodopi, 2009), 161–168; and interviews in France that I conducted with Khoury in 2005 and 2009.

67. Annis Freeman to Aniceto Aramoni, Sept. 26, 1979, Fromm Archive, describing much of her husband's condition before the death. *Locarno Giornale del Popolo* (February 18, 1980) provides a comprehensive description of Fromm's birthday party.

68. Gertrud Hunziker-Fromm, TRI by LJF, May 10, 2004, provided an extensive and touching discussion of Fromm's death and the memorial service. See also Funk, *Erich Fromm*, 164; *Fromm Forum* 7 (2003): 60. The only photographs of the ceremony from unidentified Swiss newspapers are in the Fromm Archive.

69. Annis's health history before Erich's death is recounted in Fromm to Funk, June 22, 1978; and Fromm to Aramoni, Aug. 29, 1977, both in Fromm Archive. The examples of letters of condolence are Nyanaponika Mahathera to Annis Freeman, Mar. 24, 1980; and James Luther Adams to Annis Freeman, July 18, 1980, Fromm Archive. On her medication and how Erich's death continued to disturb her: Annis Freeman to Isadore Rosenfeld, Mar. 16, 1984.

70. A list of newspaper and other notices of Fromm shortly after his death is to be found in the Fromm Archive. See David Elkind, "Erich Fromm," *American Psychologist* 36, no. 5 (May 1981): 521–522, for the complete text; a shorter version appeared in the *Newsletter of the William Alanson White Institute* 15 (Winter 1980–1981). See also Elkind's obituary for Fromm in the *New York Times* (March 19, 1980).

71. Rose Spiegel, "Reminiscence of Erich Fromm," *Contemporary Psychoanalysis* 17, no. 4 (October 1981): 436–441.

Index